T0320323

Introduction to Machine Learning with Applications in Information Security

Introduction to Machine Learning with Applications in Information Security,
Second Edition provides a classroom-tested introduction to a wide variety of
machine learning and deep learning algorithms and techniques, reinforced via
realistic applications. The book is accessible and doesn't prove theorems, or dwell
on mathematical theory. The goal is to present topics at an intuitive level, with
just enough detail to clarify the underlying concepts.

The book covers core classic machine learning topics in depth, including Hidden
Markov Models (HMM), Support Vector Machines (SVM), and clustering. Additional
machine learning topics include k-Nearest Neighbor (k-NN), boosting, Random
Forests, and Linear Discriminant Analysis (LDA). The fundamental deep learn-
ing topics of backpropagation, Convolutional Neural Networks (CNN), Multilayer
Perceptrons (MLP), and Recurrent Neural Networks (RNN) are covered in depth.
A broad range of advanced deep learning architectures are also presented, includ-
ing Long Short-Term Memory (LSTM), Generative Adversarial Networks (GAN),
Extreme Learning Machines (ELM), Residual Networks (ResNet), Deep Belief
Networks (DBN), Bidirectional Encoder Representations from Transformers (BERT),
and Word2Vec. Finally, several cutting-edge deep learning topics are discussed,
including dropout regularization, attention, explainability, and adversarial attacks.

Most of the examples in the book are drawn from the field of information security,
with many of the machine learning and deep learning applications focused on mal-
ware. The applications presented serve to demystify the topics by illustrating the use
of various learning techniques in straightforward scenarios. Some of the exercises in
this book require programming, and elementary computing concepts are assumed
in a few of the application sections. However, anyone with a modest amount of computing experience should have no trouble with this aspect of the book.

Instructor resources, including PowerPoint slides, lecture videos, and other
relevant material are provided on an accompanying website: http://www.cs.sjsu.
edu/~stamp/ML/.

Chapman & Hall/CRC Machine Learning & Pattern Recognition

A First Course in Machine Learning
Simon Rogers, Mark Girolami

Statistical Reinforcement Learning: Modern Machine Learning Approaches
Masashi Sugiyama

Sparse Modeling: Theory, Algorithms, and Applications
Irina Rish, Genady Grabarnik

Computational Trust Models and Machine Learning
Xin Liu, Anwitaman Datta, Ee-Peng Lim

Regularization, Optimization, Kernels, and Support Vector Machines
Johan A.K. Suykens, Marco Signoretto, Andreas Argyriou

Machine Learning: An Algorithmic Perspective, Second Edition
Stephen Marsland

Bayesian Programming
Pierre Bessiere, Emmanuel Mazer, Juan Manuel Ahuactzin, Kamel Mekhnacha

Multilinear Subspace Learning: Dimensionality Reduction of Multidimensional Data
Haiping Lu, Konstantinos N. Plataniotis, Anastasios Venetsanopoulos

Data Science and Machine Learning: Mathematical and Statistical Methods
Dirk P. Kroese, Zdravko Botev, Thomas Taimre, Radislav Vaisman

Deep Learning and Linguistic Representation
Shalom Lappin

Artificial Intelligence and Causal Inference
Momiao Xiong

Introduction to Machine Learning with Applications in Information Security, Second Edition
Mark Stamp

Entropy Randomization in Machine Learning
Yuri S. Popkov, Alexey Yu. Popkov, Yuri A. Dubno

For more information on this series please visit: https://www.routledge.com/Chapman--HallCRC-Machine-Learning--Pattern-Recognition/book-series/CRCMACLEAPAT

Introduction to Machine Learning with Applications in Information Security

Second Edition

Mark Stamp

CRC Press
Taylor & Francis Group
Boca Raton London New York

CRC Press is an imprint of the
Taylor & Francis Group, an **informa** business

A CHAPMAN & HALL BOOK

Second edition published 2023
by CRC Press
6000 Broken Sound Parkway NW, Suite 300, Boca Raton, FL 33487-2742

and by CRC Press
4 Park Square, Milton Park, Abingdon, Oxon, OX14 4RN

CRC Press is an imprint of Taylor & Francis Group, LLC

© 2023 Mark Stamp

First edition published by CRC Press 2017

ISBN: 978-1-032-20492-5 (hbk)
ISBN: 978-1-032-20717-9 (pbk)
ISBN: 978-1-003-26487-3 (ebk)

DOI: 10.1201/9781003264873

Typeset in Latin Modern font
by KnowledgeWorks Global Ltd.

Publisher's note: This book has been prepared from camera-ready copy provided by the authors.

Access the Support Material: http://www.cs.sjsu.edu/~stamp/ML/

Contents

Preface

Since the start of The R Series of Chapman & Hall/CRC in 2011, numerous books have been published on the statistical analysis and modelling of data using **R**. To date, no book has been published in this series on how these data can best be collected. From my point of view this was an omission, as scientific research often starts with data collection. If the data collection is part of the project, it might be a good idea to start thinking right at project start instead of after the data have been collected, to make a well-founded decision on how many data are needed, and on the type of sampling design.

My experience as a statistical consultant is that many researchers pay insufficient attention to the method for data collection. Too many researchers start thinking when the data are there. Often, I had to conclude that the way the data were collected by fellow researchers was suboptimal, or even unsuitable for their aim. I hope that this new book may help researchers, practitioners, and students to implement proper sampling designs, tailored to their problems at hand, so that valuable data are collected that can be used to answer the research questions.

Over the past decades, numerous wall-to-wall data sets have been collected by remote sensing devices such as satellites and drones. These remote sensing images are valuable sources of information on the natural environment and resources. The question may arise about how useful it still can be in this big data era to collect data in the field at a restricted number of sampling locations. Do we really need these data to estimate a population mean or total, for instance of the aboveground biomass or carbon stocks in the soil, or to map these study variables? In many cases the answer is that it is indeed still useful to collect sample data on the study variable, because the remote sensing images provide only proxies of the study variable. The variables derived from the remote sensing images can be related to the study variable, but we still need groundtruth data of the study variable to model this relation. By combining the wall-to-wall data of covariates and the sample data of the groundtruth, we can increase the accuracy of the survey result compared to using only one of these data sources.

The handbook *Sampling for Natural Resource Monitoring* (SNRM) (de Gruijter et al., 2006) presents an overview of sampling strategies for the survey of natural resources at a given point in time, as well as for how these resources can be monitored through repeated surveys. The book presented here can be seen as a follow-up on SNRM. In SNRM, spatial sampling designs for survey and space-time designs for monitoring are described and illustrated with notional and real-world examples. Estimators for global and local quantities in space and in space-time, and for the variance of these estimators are presented. However, neither the computer code for how a sample with a given design can be selected, nor the code for how the estimates can be computed is presented in SNRM. The publication at hand fills this gap.

This book describes and illustrates classical, basic sampling designs for a spatial survey, as well as more recently developed, advanced sampling designs and estimators. Part I of the book is about random sampling designs for estimating a mean, total, or proportion of a population or of several subpopulations. Part II focuses on sampling designs for mapping.

The computer code is written in the popular programming language **R** (R Core Team, 2021). There are several good reasons for choosing **R** as a language. First, it is open-source, giving users the right to view the source code and modify it to their needs. Second, as a result of this open-source, numerous add-on packages have been developed, and this number is still increasing. Happily enough, also quite a few add-on packages have been published for sampling design and analysis. All these add-on packages make the writing of computer code much more simple. Even very advanced statistical methods for sampling design and statistical analysis are now within the reach of many scientists: only a few lines of **R** code are needed to do the work. A risk is that the appliers of the packages may not fully understand the implemented statistical method. This understanding is not needed to obtain a result. For this reason, I decided not to jump to the add-on packages right after the theory, but to follow a more gradual approach. First, I show in the simplest possible **R** code how a sample can be selected with a given sampling design, and how the population parameters can be estimated. After this, I point out how the same result can be obtained with an add-on package.

The target group of this book is researchers and practitioners of sample surveys, as well as students in environmental, ecological, agricultural science or any other science in which knowledge about a population of interest is collected through spatial sampling. I have added exercises to most chapters, making this book suitable as a textbook for students. The answers to the exercises can be found in the appendix of this book. Large parts of the book are self-contained, requiring no prior knowledge of statistics. For the chapters in Part I on more advanced sampling designs, such as balanced sampling, and advanced estimators of population parameters (model-assisted estimators), knowledge of matrix algebra and regression analysis is required. For the final chapters of Part II, basic knowledge of geostatistics is required. This knowledge is also needed for some chapters in Part I. For this reason, I have added a chapter introducing the basics of geostatistics (Chapter 21).

An online version of this book is available at https://dickbrus.github.io/ SpatialSamplingwithR/. You can also find the book updates there. Additionally, the SpatialSamplingwithR[1] GitHub repository contains the **R** scripts of the exercises. This is also the place where you can report errata and comment on text and **R** code.

Information about the version of **R** and the versions of the **R** packages used to compile this book can be found in the file SessionInfo.rds on github. My intention is to update the book as soon as a new version of an **R** package is available on CRAN which requires an update of the **R** code.

Acknowledgments

In 2006 our handbook *Sampling for Natural Resource Monitoring* (SNRM) was published (de Gruijter et al., 2006). Soon after this milestone, Jaap de Gruijter retired from Wageningen University and Research (WUR). I am now in the final stage of my career at WUR. For a couple of years I had been thinking of a revision of our handbook, to repair errors and to include new developments in sampling design. Then I realised that to increase the impact of SNRM, it might be a better idea to write a new book, showing by means of computer code how the sampling designs can be implemented, and how the sample data can be used in statistical inference.

A nice result of the publication of SNRM was that I was asked to give sampling courses at many places in the world: China, Ethiopia, Uzbekistan, Australia, and various countries in the European Union. I have very pleasant memories of these courses, and they made my life as a scientist very joyful. For these courses I wrote numerous scripts with computer code, using the popular programming language **R** (R Core Team, 2021). My naïve idea was that all I had to do was bundle these **R** scripts into an Rmarkdown document (Xie et al., 2020), and add some text explaining the theory and the **R** code. As usual, it proved to be much more work than expected, but I am very happy that I was able to finish the job just before my retirement.

I could not have written this book without the help of many fellow researchers. First, I am very grateful for the support I received from the authors of various packages used in this book: Thomas Lumley for his support with package **survey**, Yves Tillé and Alina Gabriela Matei with package **sampling**, Anton Grafström with package **BalancedSampling**, Giulio Barcaroli and Marco Ballin with package **SamplingStrata**, Andreas Hill and Alex Massey with

---

[1] https://github.com/DickBrus/SpatialSamplingwithR/tree/master

package **forestinventory**, and Martins Liberts with package **surveyplanning**. I am ultimately responsible for all shortcomings of the **R** code.

Second, I would like to thank the following researchers for their valuable comments on parts of the book: Gerard Heuvelink (Wageningen University and ISRIC World Soil Information, the Netherlands), Yuha Heikkinen (Luke, Natural Resources Institute, Finland), David Rossiter (Cornell University, USA, and ISRIC World Soil Information, the Netherlands), Steve Stehman (SUNY College of Environmental Science and Forestry, USA), Anton Grafström (Swedish University of Agricultural Sciences), Dennis Walvoort (Wageningen University and Research, the Netherlands), and Ben Marchant (British Geological Survey, United Kingdom). Dennis Walvoort also was very supportive with the building of the **R** package **sswr** containing the data sets and some functions used in this book and improving the **R** code chunks.

Third, I would like to thank Alexandre Wadoux (University of Sydney) for preparing the data set of aboveground biomass and numerous environmental and climatological covariates of Eastern Amazonia, Brazil; Coen Bussink (United Nations Office on Drugs and Crime) for giving permission to use data on the occurrence of opium poppy fields in Kandahar, Afghanistan; Akmal Akramkhanov for providing the data set with measurements of the salinity of soil at a farm which is part of a regional Cotton Research Station in Khorezm, Uzbekistan, collected in the ZEF/UNESCO Landscape Restructuring project in the Khorezm province, with financial support by the German Ministry for Education and Research (BMBF; project number 0339970A); Lin Yang (Nanjing University) and A-Xing Zhu (Nanjing Normal University) for giving permission to use the data on soil organic matter concentration in Xuancheng, Anhui province, China, collected in a project supported by the National Natural Science Foundation of China (project numbers 41471178, 41971054, 41431177); the Ethiopian Agricultural Transformation Agency (my contact was Hailu Shiferaw) for allowing me to use the soil organic matter data of the western part of the Amhara region in Ethiopia which I used for training; Siegfried Hofman (Flemish Institute for Technological Research) for giving permission to use the nitrate-N data of several agricultural fields in Flanders, Belgium; and Budiman Minasny (University of Sydney) for giving permission to use the raster maps with terrain attributes in Hunter Valley, Australia.

Last but not least, I would like to thank my sister-in-law, Marijke Compaijen, who carefully read the entire manuscript. She identified and corrected all kinds of errors and made several helpful suggestions. I am very grateful for her extremely precise work.

1

Introduction

This book is about sampling for spatial *surveys*. A survey is an inventory of an object of study about which statistical statements will be made based on data collected from that object. The object of study is referred to as the population of interest or target population. Examples are a survey of the organic carbon stored in the soil of a country, the water quality of a lake, the wood volume in a forest, the yield of rice in a country, etc. In these examples, soil organic carbon, water quality, wood volume, and rice yield are the study variables, i.e., the variables of which we want to estimate the population mean or some other parameter, or which we want to map. So, this book is about *observational research*, not about experiments. In experiments, observations are done under controlled circumstances; think of an experiment on crop yields as a function of application rates of fertiliser. Several levels of fertiliser application rate are chosen and randomly assigned to experimental plots. In observational research, factors that influence the study variable are not controlled. This implies that in observational research no conclusions can be drawn on causal relations.

If the whole population is observed, this is referred to as a *census*. In general, we cannot afford such a census. Only some parts of the population are selected and the study variable is observed (measured) for these selected parts (the population units in the sample) only. Such a survey is referred to as a *sample survey*. The observations are subsequently used to derive characteristics of the whole population. For instance, to estimate the wood volume in a forest, we cannot afford to measure the wood volume of every tree in the forest. Instead, some trees are selected, the wood volume of these trees is measured, and based on these measurements the total wood volume in the forest is estimated.

1.1 Basic sampling concepts

In this book the populations of interest have a spatial dimension. In selecting parts of such populations for observation, we may account for the spatial coordinates of the parts, but this is not strictly needed. Examples of spatial sampling designs are designs selecting sampling units that are spread throughout the

1

study area, often leading to more precise estimates of the population mean or total as compared to sampling designs resulting in spatial clusters of units.

Two types of populations can be distinguished: discrete and continuous populations. *Discrete populations* consist of discrete natural objects, think of trees, agricultural fields, lakes, etc. These objects are referred to as *population units*. The total number of population units in a discrete population is finite. A finite spatial population of discrete units can be denoted by $\mathcal{U} = \{u(\mathbf{s}_1), u(\mathbf{s}_2), \ldots, u(\mathbf{s}_N)\}$, with $u(\mathbf{s}_k)$ the unit located at $\mathbf{s}_k$, where $\mathbf{s}$ is a vector with spatial coordinates. The population units naturally serve as the *elementary sampling units*. In this book the spatial populations are two-dimensional, so a vector $\mathbf{s}$ has two coordinates, Easting and Northing.

Other populations may, for the purpose of sampling, be considered as a physical continuum, e.g., the soil in a region, the water in a lake, the crop on a field.

 If interest lies in crop properties per areal unit of the field, the population is continuous. However, if interest lies in properties per plant, the population is discrete and finite.

Such continuous spatial populations can be denoted by $\mathcal{U} = \{u(\mathbf{s}), \mathbf{s} \in \mathcal{A}\}$, with $\mathcal{A}$ the study area. Discrete objects that can serve as elementary sampling units do not exist in *continuous populations*. Therefore, we must define the elementary sampling units. The elementary sampling units can be areal units, e.g., 10 m squares; or circular plots, e.g., with a radius of 5 m; or "points", i.e., units of such a small area, compared to the area of the population, that the area of the units can be ignored.

In this book a population unit and an elementary sampling unit can be an individual object of a discrete population as well as an areal sampling unit or a point of a continuous population.

The size and geometry of the elementary units used in sampling a continuous population is referred to as the sample support. The total number of elementary sampling units in a continuous population can be finite, e.g., all 25 m × 25 m (disjoint) raster cells in an area (raster cells in Figure 1.1), or infinite, e.g., all points in an area, or all squares or circular plots with a given radius that are allowed to overlap in an area (circles in Figure 1.1).

Ideally, with areal elementary sampling units, the selected elementary units are exhaustively observed, so that a measurement of the total or mean of the study variable within an areal unit is obtained, think for instance of the total aboveground biomass. In some cases this is not feasible, think for instance of measuring the mean of some soil property in 25 m squares. In this case, a sample of points is selected from each selected square, and the measurement is done at the selected points. These measurements at points are used to estimate the mean of the squares. Stehman et al. (2018) introduced the concept of a response design as "the protocol used to determine the reference condition of an

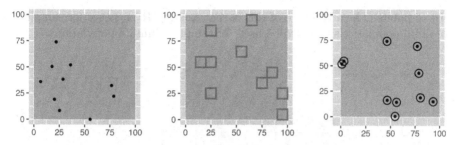

FIGURE 1.1: Three sample supports: points, squares, and circles. With disjoint squares, the population is finite. With points, and squares or circles that are allowed to overlap, the population is infinite.

element of the population". So, in the case just mentioned the response design is the sampling design and the estimator for the mean of the soil property of the 25 m squares.

Ideally, the sample support is constant, but in some situations a varying sample support cannot be avoided. Think, for instance, of square sampling units in an irregularly shaped study area. Near the border of the study area, there are squares that cross the border. The part of a square that falls outside the study area is not observed. So, the support of the observations of squares crossing the border is smaller than that of the observations of squares in the interior of the study area. See also Section 3.4.

To sample a finite spatial population, the population units are listed in a data frame. This data frame contains the spatial coordinates of the population units and other information needed for selecting sampling units according to a specific design. Think, for instance, of the labels of more or less homogeneous subpopulations (used as strata in stratified random sampling, see Chapter 4) and the labels of clusters of population units, for instance, all units in a polygon of a map (used in cluster random sampling, see Chapter 6). Besides, if we have information about covariates possibly related to the study variable, which we would like to use in selecting the population units, these covariates are added to the list. The list used for selecting sampling units is referred to as the *sampling frame*.

If the elementary sampling units are disjoint square grid cells (sample support is a square), the population is finite and the grid cells can be selected through selection of their centres (or any other point that uniquely identifies a grid cell) listed in the sampling frame.

In this book also continuous populations are sampled using a list as a sampling frame. The infinite population is discretised by the cells of a fine discretisation grid. The grid cells are listed in the sampling frame by the spatial coordinates of the *centres* of the grid cells. So, the infinite population is represented by a finite list of points. The advantage of this is that existing **R** packages for sampling of finite populations can also be used for sampling infinite populations.

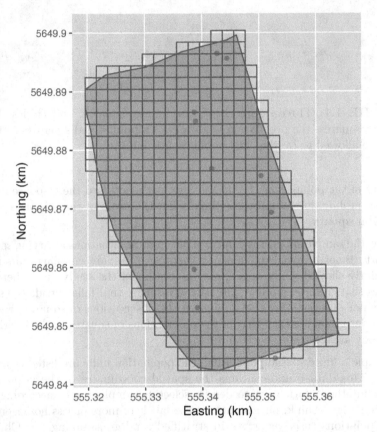

FIGURE 1.2: Sampling of points from discretised infinite population. The grid cells are randomly selected with replacement. Each time a grid cell is selected, a point is randomly selected from that grid cell.

If the elementary sampling units are points (sample support is a point), the population is infinite. In this case, sampling of points can be implemented by a two-step approach. In the first step, cells of the discretisation grid are selected with or without replacement, and in the second step one or more points are selected within the selected grid cells. Figure 1.2 is an illustration of this two-step approach for simple random sampling of points from a discretised infinite population. Ten grid cells are selected by simple random sampling with replacement. Every time a grid cell is selected, one point is randomly selected from that grid cell. Note that a grid cell can be selected more than once, so that more than one point will be selected from that grid cell. Note also that we may select a point that falls outside the boundary of the study area. This is actually the case with one grid cell in Figure 1.2. The points outside the study area are discarded and replaced by a randomly selected new point inside the study area. Finally, note that near the boundary there are small areas not covered by a grid cell, so that no points can be selected in these areas. It is important that the discretisation grid is fine enough to keep the discretisation error so small that it can be ignored. The alternative is to extend the discretisation grid beyond the boundaries of the study area so that the full study area is covered by grid cells.

1.1.1 Population parameters

The sample data are used to estimate characteristics of the whole population, e.g., the population mean or total; some quantile, e.g., the median or the 90th percentile; or even the entire cumulative frequency distribution.

A finite population total is defined as

$$t(z) = \sum_{k \in \mathcal{U}} z_k = \sum_{k=1}^{N} z_k \;, \tag{1.1}$$

with N the number of population units and z_k the study variable for population unit k. A finite population mean is defined as a finite population total divided by N.

An infinite population total is defined as an integral of the study variable over the study area:

$$t(z) = \int_{\mathbf{s} \in \mathcal{A}} z(\mathbf{s}) \, \mathrm{d}\mathbf{s} \;. \tag{1.2}$$

An infinite population mean is defined as a finite population total divided by the area, A, covered by the population.

A finite population proportion is defined as the population mean of an 0/1 indicator y with value 1 if the condition is satisfied, and 0 otherwise:

$$p = \frac{\sum_{k=1}^{N} y_k}{N} \;. \tag{1.3}$$

A cumulative distribution function (CDF) is defined as

$$F(z) = \sum_{z' \leq z} p(z') \;, \tag{1.4}$$

with $p(z')$ the proportion of population units whose value for the study variable equals z'.

A population quantile, for instance the population median or the population 90th percentile, is defined as

$$q_p = F^{-1}(p) \,, \tag{1.5}$$

where p is a number between 0 and 1 (e.g., 0.5 for the median, 0.9 for the 90th percentile), and $F^{-1}(p)$ is the smallest value of the study variable z satisfying $F(z) \geq p$.

In surveys of spatial populations, the aim can also be to make a map of the population.

> The parameters defined in this subsection are parameters of spatial populations, i.e., populations observed in a relatively short period of time related to the dynamics of the study variable. We assume that the study variable does not change during the survey period. In Chapter 15 parameters are defined for space-time populations.

1.1.2   Descriptive statistics vs. inference about a population

When we observe only a (small) part of the population, we are uncertain about the population parameter estimates and the map of the population. By using statistical methods, we can quantify how uncertain we are about these results. In decision making it can be important to take this uncertainty into account. An example is a survey of water quality. In Europe the concentration levels of nutrients are regulated in the European Water Framework Directive. To test whether the mean concentration of a nutrient complies with its standard, it is important to account for the uncertainty in the estimated mean. When the estimated mean is just below the standard, there is still a large probability that the population mean exceeds the standard. This example shows that it is important to distinguish computing descriptive statistics from characterising the population using the sample data. For instance, we can compute the sample mean (average of the sample data) without error, but if we use this sample mean as an *estimate* of the population mean, there is certainly an error in this estimate.

1.1.3   Random sampling vs. probability sampling

Many sampling methods are available. At the highest level, one may distinguish random from non-random sampling methods. In random sampling, a subset of population units is randomly selected from the population, using a (pseudo) random number generator. In non-random sampling, no such random number generator is used. Examples of non-random sampling are (i) convenience sampling, i.e., sampling at places that are easy to access, e.g., along roads; (ii) arbitrary sampling, i.e., sampling without a specific purpose in mind; and (iii) targeted sampling, e.g., at sites suspected of soil pollution.

In the literature, the term *random sampling* is often used for arbitrary sampling, i.e., sampling without a specific purpose in mind. To avoid confusion the term *probability sampling* is used for random sampling using a (pseudo) random number generator, so that for any unit in the population the probability of selecting that unit is known. More precisely, a probability sample is a sample from a population such that every unit of the population has a positive probability of being included in the sample. Besides, these *inclusion probabilities* must be known, at least for the selected units, as they are needed in estimation. This is explained in following chapters.

1.2 Design-based vs. model-based approach

The choice between probability or non-probability sampling is closely connected with the choice between the design-based or the model-based approach for sampling and statistical inference (estimation, hypothesis testing). The difference between these two approaches is a rather technical subject, so, not to discourage you already in this very first chapter, I will keep it short. In Chapter 26 I elaborate on the fundamental difference of these two approaches and a third approach, the model-assisted approach, which can be seen as a compromise of the design-based and the model-based approach.

In the design-based approach, units are selected by probability sampling (Table 1.1). Estimates are based on the inclusion probabilities of the sampling units as determined by the sampling design (design-based inference). No model is used in estimation. On the contrary, in the model-based approach a statistical model is used in prediction, i.e., a model with a random error term, for

TABLE 1.1: Statistical approaches for sampling and inference.

Approach	Sampling	Inference
Design-based	Probability sampling required	Based on sampling distribution (no model used)
Model-based	Probability sampling not required	Based on statistical model

instance a regression model. As the model already contains a random error term, probability sampling is not required in this approach.

Which statistical approach is best largely depends on the aim of the survey, see Brus and de Gruijter (1997) and de Gruijter et al. (2006). Broadly speaking, the following aims can be distinguished:

1. estimating parameters for the population;
2. estimating parameters for several subpopulations; and
3. mapping the study variable.

A map of the study variable is obtained by predicting the study variable at the points of a very fine grid that discretises the study area, or by predicting the means of the study variable for fine grid cells. Many mapping methods are available. In this book a statistical model is applied to predict the study variable, for instance a linear regression model, or a spatial linear mixed model as used in kriging.

When the aim is to map the study variable, a model-based approach is the most natural option. This implies that for this aim probability sampling is not necessarily required. In principle, both approaches are suitable for estimating (sub)population parameters. The more subpopulations are distinguished, the more attractive a model-based approach becomes. Model-based estimates of the subpopulation means or totals are potentially more accurate (depending on how good the model is) than model-free design-based estimates. On the other hand, an advantage of design-based estimation is that an objective assessment of the uncertainty of the estimated mean or total is warranted, and that the coverage of confidence intervals is (almost) correct.

A probability sample can also be used in model-based inference. This flexibility can be attractive when we have a dual aim, mapping as well as estimation of parameters of (sub)populations. When units are not selected by probability sampling, model-free design-based estimation is impossible, and model-based prediction is the only option.

1.3 Populations used in sampling experiments

In this book various data sets are used to illustrate the sampling designs. Four data sets, Voorst, Kandahar, Eastern Amazonia, and the Iberian Peninsula (Spain and Portugal), are exhaustive, i.e., for all population units, data of the study variable and ancillary data are available. The first two exhaustive data sets are obtained through simulation, i.e., by drawing numbers from a probability distribution. Sample data from these two study areas are used to calibrate a statistical model. This model is subsequently used to simulate values of the study variable for all population units. Voorst actually is an infinite population of points. However, this study area is discretised by the cells of a fine grid, and the study variable, the soil organic matter (SOM) concentration, is simulated for all centres of the grid cells. Kandahar is a finite population consisting of 965 squares of size 5 km × 5 km. The study variable is the area cultivated with poppy. Eastern Amazonia is a map in raster format, with a resolution of 1 km × 1 km. The study variable is the aboveground biomass as derived from remote sensing images. The aboveground biomass value of a raster cell is treated as the average biomass of that raster cell. The data set Iberian Peninsula is a time series of four maps in raster format with a resolution of 30 arc sec. The study variable is the annual mean air temperature at two metres above the earth surface in °C.

The exhaustive data sets are used in the first part of this book on probability sampling for estimating population parameters. By taking the population as the reality, we know the population parameters. Also, for any randomly selected sample from this population, the study variable values for the selected sampling units are known, so that we can *estimate* the population parameters from this sample. An estimated population parameter can then be compared with the population parameter. The difference between these two is the *sampling error* in the estimated population parameter. This opens up the possibility of repeating the random selection of samples with a given sampling design a large number of times, estimating the population parameter for every sample, so that a frequency distribution of the estimated population parameter is obtained. Ideally, the mean of this frequency distribution, referred to as the *sampling distribution*, is equal to the population parameter (mean sampling error equals zero), and the variance of the estimated population parameters is small. Another advantage is that sampling designs can be compared on the basis of the sampling distribution, for instance the sampling distributions of the estimator of the population mean with stratified random sampling and simple random sampling, to evaluate whether the stratification leads to more accurate estimates of the population mean.

Furthermore, various data sets are used with data for a sample of population units only. These data sets are described at places where they are first used.

All data sets are available by installing the **R** package **sswr**. This package can be installed from github with function install_github of package **remotes** (Csárdi et al., 2021).

```
library(remotes)
install_github("DickBrus/sswr")
```

The package can then be loaded. You can see the contents of the package and of the data files by typing a question mark, followed by the name of the package or a data file.

```
library(sswr)
?sswr
?grdVoorst
```

1.3.1   Soil organic matter in Voorst, the Netherlands

The study area of Voorst is located in the eastern part of the Netherlands. The size of the study area is 6 km × 1 km. At 132 points, samples of the topsoil were collected by graduate students of Wageningen University, which were then analysed for SOM concentrations (in g kg^{-1} dry soil) in a laboratory. The map is created by conditional geostatistical simulation of natural logs of the SOM concentration on a 25 m × 25 m grid, followed by backtransformation, using a linear mixed model with spatially correlated residuals and combinations of soil type and land use as a qualitative predictor (factor). Figure 1.3 shows the simulated map of the SOM concentration.

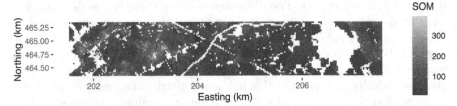

FIGURE 1.3: Simulated map of the SOM concentration (g kg^{-1}) in Voorst.

The frequency distribution of the simulated values at all 7,528 grid cells shows that the SOM concentration is skewed to the right (Figure 1.4).

Summary statistics are:

```
 Min. 1st Qu.  Median    Mean 3rd Qu.    Max.
10.75   49.45   68.15   81.13  100.63  394.45
```

The ancillary information consists of a map of soil classes and a land use map, which are combined to five soil-land use combinations (Figure 1.5). The first letter in the labels for the combinations stands for the soil type: B for *beekeerdgrond* (sandy wetland soil with gleyic properties), E for *enkeerdgrond* (sandy soil with thick anthropogenic humic topsoil), P for podzols (sandy soil with eluviated horizon below the topsoil), R for river clay soil, and X for other sandy soils. The second letter is for land use: A for agriculture (grassland, arable land) and F for forest.

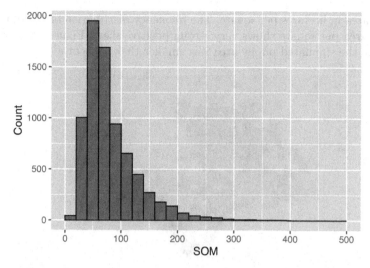

FIGURE 1.4: Frequency distribution of the simulated SOM concentration (g kg⁻¹) in Voorst.

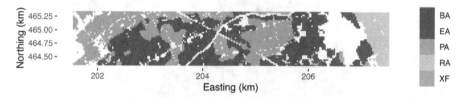

FIGURE 1.5: Soil-land use combinations in Voorst.

1.3.2 Poppy fields in Kandahar, Afghanistan

Cultivation of poppy for opium production is a serious problem in Afghanistan. The United Nations Office on Drugs and Crime (UNODC) monitors the area cultivated with poppy through detailed analysis of aerial photographs and satellite images. This is laborious, and therefore the analysis is restricted to a probability sample of 5 km squares. These sample data are then used to estimate the total poppy area (Anonymous, 2014).

In 2014 the poppy area within 83 randomly selected squares in the province of Kandahar was determined, as well as the agricultural area within all 965 squares in this province. These data were used to simulate a map of poppy area per 5 km square. The map is simulated with an ordinary kriging model for the logit transform of the proportion of the agricultural area cultivated with poppy within 5 km squares. For privacy reasons, the field was simulated *unconditionally* on these sample data. Figure 1.6 shows the map with the agricultural area in hectares per 5 km square, and the map with the simulated

poppy area in hectares per square. The frequency distribution of the simulated
poppy area per square shows very strong positive skew (Figure 1.7). For 375
squares, the simulated poppy area was smaller than 1 hectare (ha).

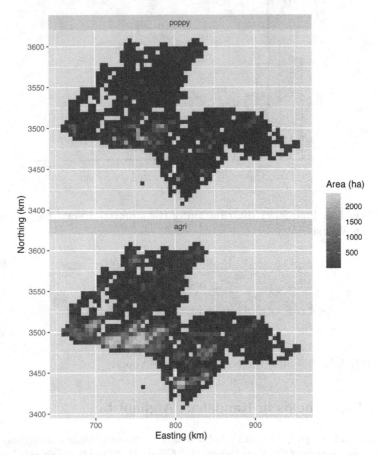

FIGURE 1.6: Agricultural area and simulated poppy area, in ha per 5 km
square, in Kandahar.

1.3.3   Aboveground biomass in Eastern Amazonia, Brazil

This data set consists of data on the live woody aboveground biomass (AGB)
in megatons per ha (Baccini et al., 2012). A rectangular area of 1,642 km × 928
km in Eastern Amazonia, Brazil, was selected from this data set. The data were
aggregated to a map with a resolution of 1 km × 1 km. Besides, a stack of five
ecologically relevant covariates of the same spatial extent was prepared, being
long term mean of MODIS short-wave infrared radiation (SWIR2), primary
production in kg C per m^2 (Terra_PP), average precipitation in driest month

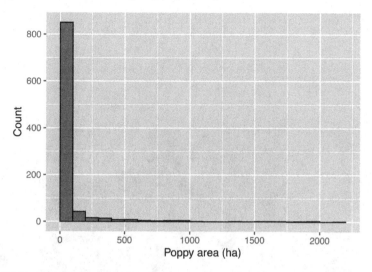

FIGURE 1.7: Frequency distribution of simulated poppy area in ha per 5 km square, in Kandahar.

in mm (Prec_dm), elevation in m, and clay content in g kg[-1] soil. All covariates were either resampled by bilinear interpolation or aggregated to conform with the grid of the aboveground biomass map. Figure 1.8 shows a map of AGB and SWIR2.

Figure 1.9 shows a matrix of two-dimensional density plots of aboveground biomass and the five covariates, made with function ggpairs of **R** package **GGally** (Schloerke et al., 2021). The covariate with the strongest correlation with AGB is SWIR2. The Pearson correlation coefficient with AGB is -0.80. The relation does not look linear. The correlation of AGB with the covariates Terra_PP and Prec_dm is weakly positive. All correlations are significant, but this is not meaningful because of the very large number of data used in computing the correlation coefficients.

1.3.4 Annual mean air temperature in Iberia

The space-time designs of Chapter 15 are illustrated with the annual mean air temperature at two metres above the earth surface (TAS) in °C, in Iberia (Spain and Portugal, islands excluded) for 2004, 2009, 2014, and 2019 (Figure 1.10). These data are part of the data set CHELSA[1] (Karger et al., 2017). The raster files are latitude-longitude grids with a resolution of 30 arc sec. The data are projected using the Lambert azimuthal equal area (laea) projection. The resolution of the resulting laea raster file is about 780 m × 780 m.

---

[1] https://chelsa-climate.org/wp-admin/download-page/CHELSA_tech_specification_V2.pdf

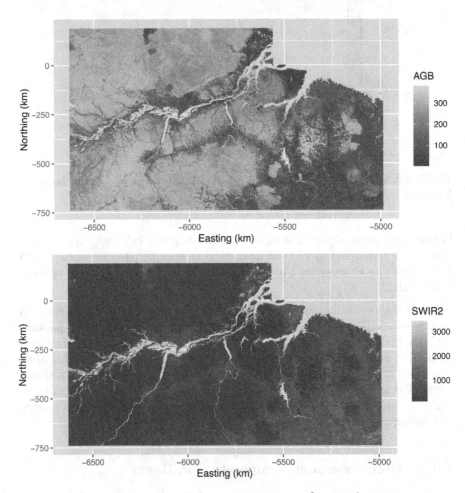

FIGURE 1.8: Aboveground biomass (AGB) in 10^9 kg ha^{-1} and short-wave infrared radiation (SWIR2) of Eastern Amazonia.

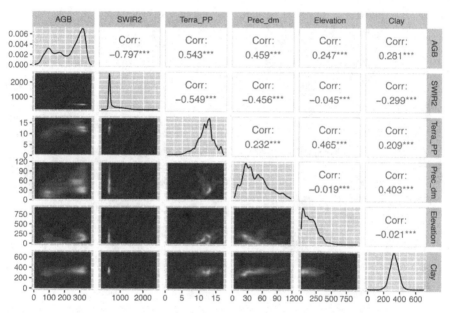

FIGURE 1.9: Matrix of two-dimensional density plots of AGB and five covariates of Eastern Amazonia. Terra_PP values are divided by 1000.

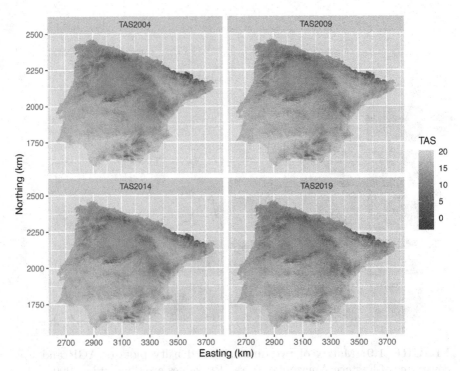

FIGURE 1.10: Annual mean air temperature in Iberia for 2004, 2009, 2014, and 2019.

Part I

Probability sampling for estimating population parameters

2

Introduction to probability sampling

To estimate population parameters like the mean or the total, *probability sampling* is most appropriate. Probability sampling is random sampling using a random number generator such that all population units have a probability larger than zero of being selected, and these probabilities are known for at least the selected units.

The probability that a unit is included in the sample, in short the inclusion probability of that unit, can be calculated as the sum of the selection probabilities over all samples that can be selected with a given sampling design and that contain this unit. In formula:

$$\pi_k = \sum_{\mathcal{S} \ni k} p(\mathcal{S}) , \tag{2.1}$$

where $\mathcal{S} \ni k$ indicates that the sum is over all samples that contain unit k, and $p(\mathcal{S})$ is the selection probability of sample $\mathcal{S}$. $p(\cdot)$ is called the *sampling design*. It is a function that assigns a probability to every possible sample (subset of population units) that can be selected with a given sample selection scheme (sampling algorithm). For instance, consider the following sample selection scheme from a finite population of N units:

1. Select with equal probability $1/N$ a first unit.

2. Select with equal probability $1/(N-1)$ a second unit from the remaining $N-1$ units.

3. Repeat this until an nth unit is selected with equal probability from the $N-(n-1)$ units.

This is a selection scheme for simple random sampling without replacement. With this scheme the selection probability of any sample of n units is $1/\binom{N}{n}$ (there are $\binom{N}{n}$ samples of size n, and each sample has an equal selection probability), and zero for all other samples. There are $\binom{N-1}{n-1}$ samples of size n in which unit k is included. The inclusion probability of each unit k therefore is $\binom{N-1}{n-1}/\binom{N}{n} = \frac{n}{N}$. The sampling design plays a key role in the design-based approach as it determines the sampling distribution of random quantities

computed from a sample such as the estimator of the population mean, see
Section 2.1. The number of selected population units is referred to as the
sample size.

 In sampling with replacement, each unit can be selected more than once. In
this case, the sample size refers to the number of draws, not to the number
of unique population units in the sample.

A common misunderstanding is that with probability sampling the inclusion
probabilities must be equal. Sampling with unequal inclusion probabilities can
be more efficient than with equal probabilities. Unequal probability sampling
is no problem as long as the inclusion probabilities are known and proper
formulas are used for estimation, see Section 2.1.

There are many schemes for selecting a probability sample. The following
sampling designs are described and illustrated in this book:

1. simple random sampling;
2. stratified random sampling;
3. systematic random sampling;
4. cluster random sampling;
5. two-stage cluster random sampling;
6. sampling with probabilities proportional to size;
7. balanced and well-spread sampling; and
8. two-phase random sampling.

The first five sampling designs are basic sampling designs. Implementation of
these designs is rather straightforward, as well as the associated estimation
of the population mean, total, or proportion, and their sampling variance.
The final three sampling designs are more advanced. Appropriate use of these
designs requires more knowledge of sampling theory and statistics, such as
linear regression.

Arbitrary (haphazard) sampling vs. probability sampling

In publications it is commonly stated that the sampling units were selected
at random (within strata), without further specification of how the sampling
units were precisely selected. In statistical inference, the sampling units are
subsequently treated as if they were selected by (stratified) simple random
sampling. With probability sampling, all units in the population have a positive
probability of being selected, and the inclusion probabilities are known for

all units. It is highly questionable whether this also holds for arbitrary and haphazard sampling. In arbitrary and haphazard sampling, the sampling units are not selected by a probability mechanism. So, the selection probabilities of the sampling units and of combinations of sampling units are unknown. Design-based estimation is therefore impossible, because it requires the inclusion probabilities of the population units as determined by the sampling design. The only option for statistical analysis using arbitrarily or haphazardly selected samples is model-based inference, i.e., a model of the spatial variation must be assumed.

Exercises

1. Suppose a researcher selects a sample of points from a study area by throwing darts on a map depicting the study area. Is the resulting sample a probability sample? If not, why?

2.1 Horvitz-Thompson estimator

For any probability sampling design, the population total can be estimated as a weighted sum of the observations (measurements) of the study variable on the selected population units:

$$\hat{t}_\pi(z) = \sum_{k \in \mathcal{S}} w_k z_k \,, \tag{2.2}$$

with $\mathcal{S}$ the sample, z_k the observed study variable for unit k, and w_k the *design weight* attached to unit k:

$$w_k = \frac{1}{\pi_k} , \tag{2.3}$$

with π_k the inclusion probability of unit k. The estimator of Equation (2.2) is referred to as the Horvitz-Thompson estimator or π estimator. The z_k/π_k-values are referred to as the π-expanded values. The z-value of unit k in the sample is multiplied by the reciprocal of the inclusion probability of that unit, and the sample sum of these π-expanded values is used as an estimator of the population total. The inclusion probabilities are determined by the type of sampling design and the sample size.

> An *estimator* is not the same as an *estimate*. Whereas an estimate is a particular value calculated from the sample data, an estimator is a formula for estimating a parameter. An estimator is a *random variable* and therefore has a probability distribution. For this reason, it is not correct, although very common, to say 'the variance (standard error) of the estimated population mean equals ...'. It is correct to say 'the variance (standard error) of the estimator of the population mean equals ...'.

Also for infinite populations, think of points in a continuous population, the above estimator for the population total can be used, but special attention must then be paid to the inclusion probabilities. Suppose the infinite population is discretised by N cells of a fine grid, and a simple random sample of n cells is selected. The inclusion probabilities of the grid cells is then n/N. However, constraining the sampling points to the centres of the cells of the discretisation grid is not needed and even undesirable. To account for the infinite number of points in the population we may adopt a two-step approach, see Figure 1.2. In the first step, n cells of the discretisation grid are selected by simple random sampling *with replacement*. In the second step, one point is selected fully randomly from the selected grid cells. If a grid cell is selected more than once, more points are selected in that grid cell. With this selection procedure the inclusion probability density is n/A, with A the area of the study area. This inclusion probability density equals the expected number of sampling points per unit area, e.g., the expected number of points per ha or per m^2. The inclusion probability density can be interpreted as the global sampling intensity. Note that the local sampling intensity may strongly vary; think for instance of cluster random sampling.

The π estimator for the *mean* of a finite population, $\bar{z}$, is simply the π estimator for the total, divided by the total number of units in the population, N:

$$\hat{\bar{z}}_\pi = \frac{1}{N} \sum_{k \in \mathcal{S}} \frac{1}{\pi_k} z_k . \tag{2.4}$$

For infinite populations discretised by a finite set of points, the same estimator can be used.

For infinite populations, the population total can be estimated by multiplying the estimated population mean by the area of the population A:

$$\hat{t}_\pi(z) = A\hat{\bar{z}}_\pi \ . \tag{2.5}$$

The π estimator can be worked out for the different types of sampling design listed above by inserting the inclusion probabilities as determined by the sampling design. For simple random sampling, this leads to the unweighted sample mean (see Chapter 3), and for stratified simple random sampling the π estimator is equal to the weighted sum of the sample means per stratum, with weights equal to the relative size of the strata (see Chapter 4).

2.2 Hansen-Hurwitz estimator

In sampling finite populations, units can be selected with or without replacement. In sampling with replacement after each draw the selected unit is replaced. As a consequence, a unit can be selected more than once. Sampling with replacement is less efficient than sampling without replacement. If a population unit is selected in a given draw, there is no additional information in this unit if it is selected again. One reason that sampling with replacement is still used is that it is easier to implement.

The most common estimator used for sampling with replacement is the Hansen-Hurwitz estimator, referred to as the p-expanded with replacement (pwr) estimator by Särndal et al. (1992). With direct unit sampling, i.e., sampling of individual population units, the pwr estimator is

$$\hat{t}_{\mathrm{pwr}}(z) = \frac{1}{n} \sum_{k \in \mathcal{S}} \frac{z_k}{p_k} \ , \tag{2.6}$$

with p_k the *draw-by-draw selection probability* of population unit k. For instance, in simple random sampling with replacement the draw-by-draw selection probability p of each unit is $1/N$. If we select only one unit k, the population total can be estimated by the observation of that unit divided by p, $\hat{t}(z) = z_k/p_k = Nz_k$. If we repeat this n times, this results in n estimated population totals. The pwr estimator is the average of these n elementary estimates. If a unit occurs multiple times in the sample $\mathcal{S}$, this unit provides multiple elementary estimates of the population total.

A sample obtained by sampling with replacement is referred to as an *ordered sample* (Särndal et al., 1992). Selecting the distinct units from this ordered sample results in the *set-sample*. Instead of using the ordered sample in the pwr estimator, we may use the set-sample in the π estimator. This requires computation of the inclusion probabilities for sampling with replacement. For instance, for simple random sampling with replacement, the inclusion probability of each unit equals $1 - \left(1 - \frac{1}{N}\right)^n$, with n the number of draws. This probability is smaller than n/N, the inclusion probability for simple random sampling without replacement. There is no general rule on which estimator is most accurate (Särndal et al., 1992). In this book I only use the pwr estimator for sampling with replacement.

Sampling with replacement can also be applied at the level of clusters of population units as in cluster random sampling and two-stage cluster random sampling. If the clusters are selected with probabilities proportional to their size and with replacement, estimation of a population parameter is rather simple. This is a second reason why sampling with replacement can be attractive. With cluster sampling, the Hansen-Hurwitz estimator is

$$\hat{t}_{\mathrm{pwr}}(z) = \frac{1}{n} \sum_{j \in \mathcal{S}} \frac{t_j(z)}{p_j} , \tag{2.7}$$

with $t_j(z)$ the total of the cluster selected in the jth draw. If not all population units of a selected cluster are observed, but only a sample of population units from a cluster, as in two-stage cluster random sampling, the cluster totals $t_j(z)$ are replaced by the estimated cluster totals $\hat{t}_j(z)$.

Exercises

2. Consider a population of four units ($N = 4$). What is the inclusion probability of each population unit for simple random sampling without replacement and simple random sampling with replacement of two units ($n = 2$)?

2.3　Using models in design-based approach

Design-based estimates of population parameters such as the mean, total, or proportion (areal fraction) are model-free: no use is made of a model for the spatial variation of the study variable. However, such a model can be used to optimise the probability sampling design. In Chapter 13 I describe how a model can be used to compare alternative sampling designs at equal costs or equal precision to evaluate which sampling design performs best, to optimise the sample size given a requirement on the precision of the estimated population parameter, or to optimise the spatial strata for stratified random sampling.

A model of the spatial variation can also be used at a later stage, after the data have been collected, in estimating the population parameter of interest. If one or more ancillary variables that are related to the study variable are available, these variables can be used in estimation to increase the accuracy. This leads to alternative estimators, such as the regression estimator, the ratio estimator, and the poststratified estimator (Chapter 10). These estimators together are referred to as model-assisted estimators. In model-assisted estimation the inclusion probabilities, as determined by the random sampling design, play a key role, but besides, modelling assumptions about how the population might have been generated are used to work out an efficient estimator. The role of a model in the model-assisted approach is fundamentally different from its role in the model-based approach. This is explained in Chapter 26.

For novices in geostatistics, Chapters 10 and 13 can be quite challenging, and I recommend skipping these chapters and only return to them after having read the introductory chapter on geostatistics (Chapter 21).

3

Simple random sampling

Simple random sampling is the most basic form of probability sampling. There are two subtypes:

1. simple random sampling with replacement; and
2. simple random sampling without replacement.

This distinction is irrelevant for infinite populations. In sampling with replacement a population unit may be selected more than once.

In **R** a simple random sample can be selected with or without replacement by function `sample` from the **base** package. For instance, a simple random sample without replacement of 10 units from a population of 100 units labelled as $1, 2, \ldots, 100$, can be selected by

```
sample(100, size = 10, replace = FALSE)
```

```
[1]  21   7   5  16  58  76  44 100  71  84
```

The number of units in the sample is referred to as the sample size ($n = 10$ in the code chunk above). Use argument `replace = TRUE` to select a simple random sample with replacement.

When the spatial population is continuous and infinite, as in sampling points from an area, the infinite population is discretised by a very fine grid. Discretisation is not strictly needed (we could also select points directly), but it is used in this book for reasons explained in Chapter 1. The centres of the grid cells are then listed in a data frame, which serves as the sampling frame (Chapter 1). In the next code chunk, a simple random sample without replacement of size 40 is selected from Voorst. The infinite population is represented by the centres of square grid cells with a side length of 25 m. These centres are listed in tibble[1] `grdVoorst`.

---

[1] A tibble is a data frame of class `tbl_df` of package **tibble** (Müller and Wickham, 2021). Hereafter, I will use the terms tibble and data frame interchangeably. A traditional data frame is referred to as a `data.frame`.

```
n <- 40
N <- nrow(grdVoorst)
set.seed(314)
units <- sample(N, size = n, replace = FALSE)
mysample <- grdVoorst[units, ]
mysample
```

```
# A tibble: 40 x 4
        s1      s2      z stratum
     <dbl>   <dbl> <dbl> <chr>
 1 206992 464506.  23.5 EA
 2 202567 464606. 321.  XF
 3 205092 464530. 124.  XF
 4 203367 464556.  53.6 EA
 5 205592 465180.  38.4 PA
 6 201842 464956. 159.  XF
 7 201667 464930. 139.  XF
 8 204317 465306.  59.4 PA
 9 203042 464406.  90.5 BA
10 204567 464530.  48.1 PA
# ... with 30 more rows
```

The result of function `sample` is a vector with the centres of the selected cells of the discretisation grid, referred to as discretisation points. The order of the elements of the vector is the order in which these are selected. Restricting the sampling points to the discretisation points can be avoided as follows. A simple random sample of points is selected in two stages. First, n times a grid cell is selected by simple random sampling *with replacement*. Second, every time a grid cell is selected, one point is selected fully randomly from that grid cell. This selection procedure accounts for the infinite number of points in the population. In the code chunk below, the second step of this selection procedure is implemented with function `jitter`. It adds random noise to the spatial coordinates of the centres of the selected grid cells, by drawing from a continuous uniform distribution unif$(-c, c)$, with c half the side length of the square grid cells. With this selection procedure we respect that the population actually is infinite.

```
set.seed(314)
units <- sample(N, size = n, replace = TRUE)
mysample <- grdVoorst[units, ]
cellsize <- 25
mysample$s1 <- jitter(mysample$s1, amount = cellsize / 2)
mysample$s2 <- jitter(mysample$s2, amount = cellsize / 2)
mysample
```

```
# A tibble: 40 x 4
        s1       s2      z stratum
     <dbl>    <dbl>  <dbl> <chr>
 1 206986. 464493.   23.5 EA
 2 202574. 464609.  321.  XF
 3 205095. 464527.  124.  XF
 4 203369. 464556.   53.6 EA
 5 205598. 465181.   38.4 PA
 6 201836. 464965.  159.  XF
 7 201665. 464941.  139.  XF
 8 204319. 465310.   59.4 PA
 9 203052. 464402.   90.5 BA
10 204564. 464529.   48.1 PA
# ... with 30 more rows
```

Variable stratum is not used in this chapter but in the next chapter. The selected sample is shown in Figure 3.1.

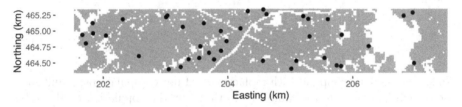

FIGURE 3.1: Simple random sample of size 40 from Voorst.

Dropouts

In practice, it may happen that inspection in the field shows that a selected sampling unit does not belong to the target population or cannot be observed for whatever reason (e.g., no permission). For instance, in a soil survey the sampling unit may happen to fall on a road or in a built-up area. What to do with these dropouts? Shifting this unit to a nearby unit may lead to a biased estimator of the population mean, i.e., a systematic error in the estimated population mean. Besides, knowledge of the inclusion probabilities is lost. This can be avoided by discarding these units and replacing them by sampling units from a back-up list, selected in the same way, i.e., by the same type of sampling design. The order of sampling units in this list must be the order in which they are selected. In summary, do not replace a deleted sampling unit by the nearest sampling unit from the back-up list, but by the first unit, not yet selected, from the back-up list.

3.1   Estimation of population parameters

In simple random sampling without replacement of a finite population, every possible sample of n units has an equal probability of being selected. There are $\binom{N}{n}$ samples of size n and $\binom{N-1}{n-1}$ samples that contain unit k. From this it follows that the probability that unit k is included in the sample is $\binom{N-1}{n-1}/\binom{N}{n} = \frac{n}{N}$ (Lohr, 1999). Substituting this in the general π estimator for the total (Equation (2.2)) gives for simple random sampling without replacement (from finite populations)

$$\hat{t}(z) = \frac{N}{n} \sum_{k \in \mathcal{S}} z_k = N\bar{z}_{\mathcal{S}} \,, \tag{3.1}$$

with $\bar{z}_{\mathcal{S}}$ the unweighted *sample mean*. So, for simple random sampling without replacement the π estimator of the population mean is the *unweighted* sample mean:

$$\hat{\bar{z}} = \bar{z}_{\mathcal{S}} = \frac{1}{n} \sum_{k \in \mathcal{S}} z_k \,. \tag{3.2}$$

In simple random sampling with replacement of finite populations, a unit may occur multiple times in the sample $\mathcal{S}$. In this case, the population total can be estimated by the pwr estimator (Särndal et al., 1992)

$$\hat{t}(z) = \frac{1}{n} \sum_{k \in \mathcal{S}} \frac{z_k}{p_k} \,, \tag{3.3}$$

where n is the number of draws (sample size) and p_k is the draw-by-draw selection probability of unit k. With simple random sampling $p_k = 1/N, k = 1, \dots, N$. Inserting this in the pwr estimator yields

$$\hat{t}(z) = \frac{N}{n} \sum_{k \in \mathcal{S}} z_k \,, \tag{3.4}$$

which is equal to the π estimator of the population total for simple random sampling *without replacement*.

Alternatively, the population total can be estimated by the π estimator. With simple random sampling with replacement the inclusion probability of each unit k equals $1 - \left(1 - \frac{1}{N}\right)^n$, which is smaller than the inclusion probability with simple random sampling without replacement of size n (Särndal et al., 1992). Inserting these inclusion probabilities in the general π estimator of the population total (Equation (2.2)), where the sample $\mathcal{S}$ is reduced to the unique units in the sample, yields the π estimator of the total for simple random sampling with replacement.

With simple random sampling of *infinite* populations, the π estimator of the population mean equals the sample mean. Multiplying this estimator with the area of the region of interest A yields the π estimator of the population total:

$$\hat{t}(z) = \frac{A}{n} \sum_{k \in \mathcal{S}} z_k \ . \tag{3.5}$$

As explained above, selected sampling units that do not belong to the target population must be replaced by a unit from a back-up list if we want to observe the intended number of units. The question then is how to estimate the population total and mean. We cannot use the π estimator of Equation (3.1) to estimate the population total, because we do not know the population size N. The population size can be estimated by

$$\widehat{N} = \frac{n - d}{n} N^* \ , \tag{3.6}$$

with d the number of dropouts and N^* the supposed population size, i.e., the number of units in the sampling frame used to select the sample. This yields the inclusion probability

$$\pi_k = \frac{n}{\widehat{N}} = \frac{n^2}{(n - d)N^*} \ . \tag{3.7}$$

Inserting this in the π estimator of the population total yields

$$\hat{t}(z) = \frac{(n - d)N^*}{n^2} \sum_{k \in \mathcal{S}} z_k = \frac{(n - d)N^*}{n} \bar{z}_{\mathcal{S}} = \widehat{N} \bar{z}_{\mathcal{S}} \ . \tag{3.8}$$

A natural estimator of the population mean is

$$\hat{\bar{z}} = \frac{\hat{t}(z)}{\widehat{N}} = \bar{z}_{\mathcal{S}} \ . \tag{3.9}$$

This estimator is a so-called ratio estimator: both the numerator and denominator are estimators of totals. See Section 10.2 for more information about this estimator.

The simple random sample of size 40 selected above is used to estimate the total mass of soil organic matter (SOM) in the population. First, the population mean is estimated.

```
mz <- mean(mysample$z)
```

The estimated mean SOM concentration is 93.3 g kg^{-1}. Simply multiplying the estimated mean by the area A to obtain an estimate of the population total is not very useful, as the dimension of the total then is in g kg^{-1} m^2. To estimate the total mass of SOM in the soil layer $0 - 30$ cm, first the soil volume in m^3 is computed by the total number of grid cells, N, multiplied by the size of the grid cells and by the thickness of the soil layer. The total is then estimated by the product of this volume, the bulk density of soil (1,500 kg m^{-3}), and the estimated population mean (g kg^{-1}). This is multiplied by 10^{-6} to obtain the total mass of SOM in Mg (1 Mg is 1,000 kg).

```
vol_soil <- N * 25^2 * 0.3
bd <- 1500
tz <- vol_soil * bd * mz * 10^-6
```

The estimated total is 197,545 Mg (420 Mg ha^{-1}).

Note that a constant bulk density is used. Ideally, this bulk density is also measured at the sampling points, by collecting soil aliquots of a constant volume. The measured SOM concentration and bulk density can then be used to compute the volumetric SOM concentration in kg m^{-3} at the sampling points. The estimated population mean of this volumetric SOM concentration can then be multiplied by the total volume of soil in the study area, to get an estimate of the total mass of SOM in the study area.

The simulated population is now sampled 10,000 times to see how sampling affects the estimates. For each sample, the population mean is estimated by the sample mean. Figure 3.2 shows the approximated sampling distribution of the π estimator of the mean SOM concentration. Note that the sampling distribution is nearly symmetric, whereas the frequency distribution of the SOM concentrations in the population is far from symmetric, see Figure 1.4. The increased symmetry is due to the averaging of 40 numbers.

If we would repeat the sampling an infinite number of times and make the width of the bins in the histogram infinitely small, then we obtain, after scaling so that the sum of the area under the curve equals 1, the *sampling distribution* of the estimator of the population mean. Important summary statistics of this sampling distribution are the expectation (mean) and the variance.

When the expectation equals the population mean, there is no systematic error. The estimator is then said to be *design-unbiased*. In Chapter 21 another type of unbiasedness is introduced, model-unbiasedness. The difference between design-unbiasedness and model-unbiasedness is explained in Chapter 26. In

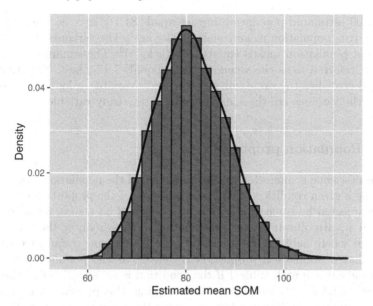

FIGURE 3.2: Approximated sampling distribution of the π estimator of the mean SOM concentration (g kg^{-1}) in Voorst for simple random sampling of size 40.

following chapters of Part I unbiased means design-unbiased. Actually, it is not the estimator which is unbiased, but the combination of a sampling design and an estimator. For instance, with an equal probability sampling design, the sample mean is an unbiased estimator of the population mean, whereas it is a biased estimator in combination with an unequal probability sampling design.

The variance, referred to as the sampling variance, is a measure of the random error. Ideally, this variance is as small as possible, so that there is a large probability that for an individual estimate the estimation error is small. The variance is a measure of the *precision* of an estimator. An estimator with a small variance but a strong bias is not a good estimator. To assess the quality of an estimator, we should look at both. The variance and the bias are often combined in the *mean squared error* (MSE), which is the sum of the variance and the *squared* bias. An estimator with a small MSE is an *accurate* estimator. So, contrary to precision, accuracy also accounts for the bias.

Do not confuse the *population* variance and the *sampling* variance. The population variance, or spatial variance, is a *population characteristic*, whereas the sampling variance is a *characteristic of a sampling strategy*, i.e., a combination of a sampling design and an estimator. The sampling variance quantifies our *uncertainty* about the population mean. The sampling variance can be manipulated by changing the sample size n, the type of sampling design, and the estimator. This has no effect on the population variance. The average of the 10,000 estimated population means equals 81.1 g kg⁻¹, so the difference with the true population mean equals -0.03 g kg⁻¹. The variance of the 10,000 estimated population means equals 55.8 (g kg⁻¹)². The square root of this variance, referred to as the *standard error*, equals 7.47 g kg⁻¹. Note that the standard error has the same units as the study variable, g kg⁻¹, whereas the units of the variance are the squared units of the study variable.

3.1.1 Population proportion

In some cases one is interested in the proportion of the population (study area) satisfying a given condition. Think, for instance, of the proportion of trees in a forest infected by some disease, the proportion of an area or areal fraction, in which a soil pollutant exceeds some critical threshold, or the proportion of an area where habitat conditions are suitable for some endangered species. Recall that a population proportion is defined as the population mean of an 0/1 indicator y with value 1 if the condition is satisfied, and 0 otherwise (Subsection 1.1.1). For simple random sampling, this population proportion can be estimated by the same formula as for the mean (Equation (3.2)):

$$\hat{p} = \frac{1}{n} \sum_{k \in \mathcal{S}} y_k \ . \tag{3.10}$$

3.1.2 Cumulative distribution function and quantiles

The population cumulative distribution function (CDF) is defined in Equation (1.4). A population CDF can be estimated by repeated application of the indicator technique described in the previous subsection on estimating a population proportion. A series of threshold values is chosen. Each threshold results in n indicator values having value 1 if the observed study variable z of unit k is smaller than or equal to the threshold, and 0 otherwise. These indicator values are then used to estimate the proportion of the population with a z-value smaller than or equal to that threshold. For simple random sampling, these proportions can be estimated with Equation (3.10). Commonly, the unique z-values in the sample are used as threshold values, leading to as many estimated population proportions as there are unique values in the sample.

Figure 3.3 shows the estimated CDF, estimated from the simple random sample of 40 units from Voorst. The steps are at the unique values of SOM in the sample.

```
ggplot(mysample, mapping = aes(z)) +
  stat_ecdf(geom = "step") +
```

```
scale_x_continuous(name = "SOM") +
scale_y_continuous(name = "F")
```

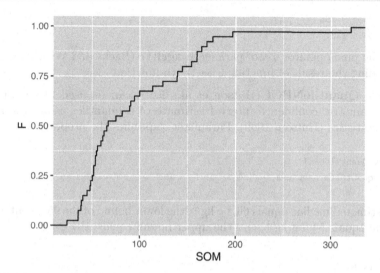

FIGURE 3.3: Cumulative distribution function of the SOM concentration (g kg^{-1}) in Voorst, estimated from the simple random sample of 40 units.

The estimated population proportions can be used to estimate a population quantile for any population proportion (cumulative frequency, probability), for instance the median, first quartile, and third quartile, corresponding to a population proportion of 0.5, 0.25, and 0.75, respectively. A simple estimator is the smallest kth order statistic with an estimated proportion larger than or equal to the desired cumulative frequency (Hyndman and Fan, 1996).

The estimated CDF shows jumps of size $1/n$, so that the estimated population proportion can be larger than the desired proportion. The estimated population proportions therefore are often interpolated, for instance linearly. Function quantile of the **stats** package can be used to estimate a quantile. With argument type = 4 linear interpolation is used to estimate the quantiles.

Function quantile actually computes sample quantiles, i.e., it assumes that the population units are selected with equal inclusion probabilities (as in simple random sampling), so that the estimators of the population proportions obtained with Equation (3.10) are unbiased. With unequal inclusion probabilities these probabilities must be accounted for in estimating the population proportions, see following chapters.

```
quantile(mysample$z, probs = c(0.25, 0.5, 0.75), type = 4) %>%
  round(1)
```

```
 25%   50%   75%
50.4  65.6 138.7
```

Note the pipe operator `%>%` of package **magrittr** (Bache and Wickham, 2020) forwarding the result of function `quantile` to function `round`.

Package **QuantileNPCI** (Hutson et al., 2019) can be used to compute a non-parametric confidence interval estimate of a quantile, using fractional order statistics (Hutson, 1999). Parameter `q` specifies the proportion.

```
library(QuantileNPCI)
res <- quantCI(mysample$z, q = 0.5, alpha = 0.05, method = "exact")
```

The estimated median equals 66.2 g kg^{-1}, the lower bound of the 95% confidence interval equals 54.0 g kg^{-1}, and the upper bound equals 98.1 g kg^{-1}.

Exercises

1. Compare the approximated sampling distribution of the π estimator of the mean SOM concentration of Voorst (Figure 3.2) with the histogram of the 7,528 simulated SOM values (Figure 1.4). Explain the differences.

2. What happens with the spread in the approximated sampling distribution (variance of estimated population means) when the sample size n is increased?

3. Suppose we would repeat the sampling 10^{12} number of times, what would happen with the difference between the average of the estimated population means and the true population mean?

3.2 Sampling variance of estimator of population parameters

For simple random sampling of an infinite population and simple random sampling with replacement of a finite population, the sampling variance of the estimator of the population mean equals

$$V(\hat{\bar{z}}) = \frac{S^2(z)}{n} \,, \tag{3.11}$$

with $S^2(z)$ the *population* variance, also referred to as the spatial variance. For finite populations, this population variance is defined as (Lohr, 1999)

$$S^2(z) = \frac{1}{N-1} \sum_{k=1}^{N} (z_k - \bar{z})^2 \,, \tag{3.12}$$

and for infinite populations as

$$S^2(z) = \frac{1}{A} \int_{\mathbf{s}\in\mathcal{A}} (z(\mathbf{s}) - \bar{z})^2 \, d\mathbf{s} \,, \tag{3.13}$$

with $z(\mathbf{s})$ the value of the study variable z at a point with two-dimensional coordinates $\mathbf{s} = (s_1, s_2)$, A the area of the study area, and $\mathcal{A}$ the study area. In practice, we select only one sample, i.e., we do not repeat the sampling many times. Still it is possible to *estimate* the variance of the estimator of the population mean if we would repeat the sampling. In other words, we can estimate the sampling variance of the estimator of the population mean from a single sample. We do so by estimating the population variance from the sample, and this estimate can then be used to estimate the *sampling* variance of the estimator of the population mean. For simple random sampling *with replacement* from finite populations, the sampling variance of the estimator of the population mean can be estimated by

$$\hat{V}(\hat{\bar{z}}) = \frac{\widehat{S^2}(z)}{n} = \frac{1}{n(n-1)} \sum_{k\in\mathcal{S}} (z_k - \bar{z}_\mathcal{S})^2 \,, \tag{3.14}$$

with $\widehat{S^2}(z)$ the *estimated* population variance. With simple random sampling, the *sample* variance, i.e., the variance of the sample data, is an unbiased estimator of the population variance. The variance estimator of Equation (3.14) can also be used for *infinite* populations. For simple random sampling *without replacement* from finite populations, the sampling variance of the estimator of the population mean can be estimated by

$$\hat{V}(\hat{\bar{z}}) = \left(1 - \frac{n}{N}\right) \frac{\widehat{S^2}(z)}{n} \,. \tag{3.15}$$

The term $1 - \frac{n}{N}$ is referred to as the finite population correction (fpc).

In the sampling experiment described above, the average of the 10,000 *estimated* sampling variances equals 55.7 (g kg^{-1})^2. The true sampling variance equals 55.4 (g kg^{-1})^2. So, the difference is very small, indicating that the estimator of the sampling variance, Equation (3.15), is design-unbiased.

The sampling variance of the estimator of the total of a finite population can be estimated by multiplying the estimated variance of the estimator of the population mean by N^2. For simple random sampling without replacement this estimator thus equals

$$\hat{V}(\hat{t}(z)) = N^2 \left(1 - \frac{n}{N}\right) \frac{\widehat{S^2}(z)}{n} . \tag{3.16}$$

For simple random sampling of infinite populations, the sampling variance of the estimator of the total can be estimated by

$$\hat{V}(\hat{t}(z)) = A^2 \frac{\widehat{S^2}(z)}{n} . \tag{3.17}$$

The sampling variance of the estimator of a proportion $\hat{p}$ for simple random sampling without replacement of a finite population can be estimated by

$$\hat{V}(\hat{p}) = \left(1 - \frac{n}{N}\right) \frac{\hat{p}(1 - \hat{p})}{n - 1} . \tag{3.18}$$

The numerator in this estimator is an estimate of the population variance of the indicator. Note that this estimated population variance is divided by $n - 1$, and not by n as in the estimator of the population mean (Lohr, 1999).

Estimation of the standard error of the estimated population mean in **R** is very straightforward. To estimate the standard error of the estimated total in Mg, the standard error of the estimated population mean must be multiplied by a constant equal to the product of the soil volume, the bulk density, and 10^{-6}; see second code chunk in Section 3.1.

```
se_mz <- sqrt(var(mysample$z) / n)
se_tz <- se_mz * vol_soil * bd * 10^-6
```

The estimated standard error of the estimated total equals 20,334 Mg. This standard error does not account for spatial variation of bulk density.

Although there is no advantage in using package **survey** (Lumley, 2021) to compute the π estimator and its standard error for this simple sampling design, I illustrate how this works. For more complex designs and alternative estimators, estimation of the population mean and its standard error with functions defined in this package is very convenient, as will be shown in the following chapters.

First, the sampling design that is used to select the sampling units is specified with function svydesign. The first argument specifies the sampling units. In this case, the centres of the discretisation grid cells are used as sampling units, which is indicated by the formula id = ~ 1. In Chapter 6 clusters of population units are used as sampling units, and in Chapter 7 both clusters and individual units are used as sampling units. Argument probs specifies the inclusion probabilities of the sampling units. Alternatively, we may specify the weights with argument weights, which are in this case equal to the inverse of the inclusion probabilities. Variable pi is a column in tibble mysample, which is indicated with the tilde in probs = ~ pi.

The population mean is then estimated with function svymean. The first argument is a formula specifying the study variable. Argument design specifies the sampling design.

```
library(survey)
mysample$pi <- n / N
design_si <- svydesign(id = ~ 1, probs = ~ pi, data = mysample)
svymean(~ z, design = design_si)
```

```
       mean    SE
z 93.303 9.6041
```

For simple random sampling of finite populations without replacement, argument fpc is used to correct the standard error.

```
mysample$N <- N
design_si <- svydesign(id = ~ 1, probs = ~ pi, fpc = ~ N, data = mysample)
svymean(~ z, design_si)
```

```
       mean    SE
z 93.303 9.5786
```

The estimated standard error is smaller now due to the finite population correction, see Equation (3.15).

Population totals can be estimated with function svytotal, quantiles with function svyquantile, and ratios of population totals with svyratio, to mention a few functions that will be used in following chapters.

```
svyquantile(~ z, design_si, quantile = c(0.5, 0.9))
```

```
$z
      quantile    ci.2.5    ci.97.5        se
0.5  65.56675  53.67764   99.93484  11.43457
0.9 164.36975 153.86258  320.74887  41.25353
```

```
attr(,"hasci")
[1] TRUE
attr(,"class")
[1] "newsvyquantile"
```

Exercises

4. Is the sampling variance for simple random sampling without replacement larger or smaller than for simple random sampling with replacement, given the sample size n? Explain your answer.

5. What is the effect of the population size N on this difference?

6. In Section 3.2 the true sampling variance is reported, i.e., the variance of the estimator of the population mean if we would repeat the sampling an infinite number of times. How can this true sampling variance be computed?

7. In reality, we cannot compute the true sampling variance. Why not?

3.3   Confidence interval estimate

A second way of expressing our uncertainty about the estimated total, mean, or proportion is to present not merely a single number, but an interval. The wider the interval, the more uncertain we are about the estimate, and vice versa, the narrower the interval, the more confident we are. To learn how to compute a confidence interval, I return to the sampling distribution of the estimator of the mean SOM concentration. Suppose we would like to compute the bounds of an interval $[a, b]$ such that 5% of the estimated population means is smaller than a, and 5% is larger than b. To compute the lower bound a and the upper bound b of this 90% interval, we must specify the distribution function. When the distribution of the study variable z is normal and we know the variance of z in the population, then the sampling distribution of the estimator of the population mean is also normal, regardless of the sample size. The larger the sample size, the smaller the effect of the distribution of z on the sampling distribution of the estimator of the population mean. For instance, even when the distribution of z is far from symmetric, then still the sampling distribution of the estimator of the population mean is approximately normal if the sample size is large, say $n > 100$. This is the essence of the central limit theorem. Above, we already noticed that the sampling distribution is much less asymmetric than the frequency distribution of the simulated values, and looks much more like a normal distribution. Assuming a normal distribution, the bounds of the 90% interval are given by

$$\hat{\bar{z}} \pm u_{(0.10/2)} \cdot \sqrt{V(\hat{\bar{z}})} \,, \tag{3.19}$$

where $u_{(0.10/2)}$ is the 0.95 quantile of the standard normal distribution, i.e., the value of u having a tail area of 0.05 to its right. Note that in this equation the sampling variance of the estimator of the population mean $V(\hat{\bar{z}})$ is used. In practice, this variance is unknown, because the population variance is unknown, and must be estimated from the sample (Equations (3.14) and (3.15)). To account for the unknown sampling variance, the standard normal distribution is replaced by Student's t distribution (hereafter shortly referred to as the t distribution), which has thicker tails than the standard normal distribution. This leads to the following bounds of the $100(1 - \alpha)\%$ confidence interval estimate of the mean:

$$\hat{\bar{z}} \pm t_{\alpha/2}^{(n-1)} \cdot \sqrt{\hat{V}(\hat{\bar{z}})} \,, \tag{3.20}$$

where $t_{\alpha/2}^{(n-1)}$ is the $(1 - \alpha/2)$ quantile of the t distribution with $(n-1)$ degrees of freedom. The quantity $(1 - \alpha)$ is referred to as the confidence level. The larger the number of degrees of freedom $(n-1)$, the closer the t distribution is to the standard normal distribution. The quantity $t_{1-\alpha/2}^{(n-1)} \cdot \sqrt{\hat{V}(\hat{\bar{z}})}$ is referred to as the margin of error.

Function qt computes a quantile of a t distribution, given the degrees of freedom and the cumulative probability. The bounds of the confidence interval can then be computed as follows.

```
alpha <- 0.05
margin <- qt(1 - alpha / 2, n - 1, lower.tail = TRUE) * se_mz
lower <- mz - margin
upper <- mz + margin
```

More easily, we can use method confint of package **survey** to compute the confidence interval.

```
confint(svymean(~ z, design_si), df = degf(design_si), level = 0.95)
```

```
       2.5 %   97.5 %
z 73.92817 112.6771
```

The interpretation of a confidence interval is not straightforward. A common misinterpretation is that if the 0.90 confidence interval estimate of the population mean equals $[a, b]$, then the probability that the population mean is in this interval equals 0.90. In classical sampling theory, this cannot be a correct interpretation, because the population mean is not a random variable, and consequently the probability that the population mean is in an interval does not exist. However, the estimated bounds of the confidence interval are random variables, because the estimated population mean and also the estimated sampling variance vary among samples drawn with a probability sampling design. Therefore, it does make sense to attach a probability to this interval.

Figure 3.4 shows the 90% confidence interval estimates of the mean SOM concentration for the first 100 simple random samples drawn above. Note that both the location and the length of the intervals differ between samples. For each sample, I determined whether this interval covers the population mean.

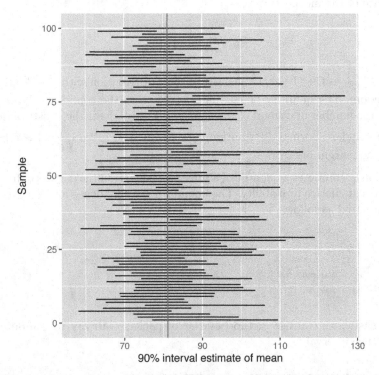

FIGURE 3.4: Estimated confidence intervals of the mean SOM concentration (g kg^{-1}) in Voorst, estimated from 100 simple random samples of size 40. The vertical red line is at the true population mean (81.1 g kg^{-1}).

Out of the 10,000 samples, 1,132 samples do not cover the population mean, i.e., close to the specified 10%. So, a 90% confidence interval is a random interval that contains in the long run the population mean 90% of the time.

3.3.1 Confidence interval for a proportion

Ideally, a confidence interval for a population proportion is based on the binomial distribution of the number of sampling units satisfying a condition (the number of successes). The binomial distribution is a discrete distribution. There are various methods for computing coverage probabilities of confidence intervals for a binomial proportion, see Brown et al. (2001) for a discussion. A common method for computing the confidence interval of a proportion is the Clopper-Pearson method. Function BinomCI of package **DescTools** can be used to compute confidence intervals for proportions (Signorell, 2021).

```
library(DescTools)
n <- 50
k <- 5
print(p.est <- BinomCI(k, n, conf.level = 0.95, method = "clopper-pearson"))
```

```
       est      lwr.ci     upr.ci
[1,] 0.1 0.03327509 0.2181354
```

The confidence interval is not symmetric around the estimated proportion of 0.1. As can be seen below, the upper bound is the proportion at which the probability of 5 or fewer successes is 0.025,

```
pbinom(q = k, size = n, prob = p.est[3])
```

```
[1] 0.025
```

and the lower bound of the confidence interval is the proportion at which the probability of 5 or more successes is also equal to 0.025. Note that to compute the upper tail probability, we must assign $k - 1 = 4$ to argument q, because with argument lower.tail = FALSE function pbinom computes the probability of $X > x$, not of $X \geq x$.

```
pbinom(q = k - 1, size = n, prob = p.est[2], lower.tail = FALSE)
```

```
[1] 0.025
```

For large sample sizes and for proportions close to 0.5, the confidence interval can be computed with a normal distribution as an approximation to the binomial distribution, using Equation (3.18) for the variance estimator of the estimator of a proportion:

$$\hat{p} \pm u_{\alpha/2}\sqrt{\frac{\hat{p}(1-\hat{p})}{n-1}} . \tag{3.21}$$

This interval is referred to as the Wald interval. It is a fact that unless n is very large, the actual coverage probability of the Wald interval is poor for p near 0 or 1. A rule of thumb is that the Wald interval should be used only when $n \cdot min\{p, (1-p)\}$ is at least 5 or 10. For small n, Brown et al. (2001) recommend the Wilson interval and for larger n the Agresti-Coull interval. These intervals can be computed with function BinomCI of package **DescTools**.

3.4 Simple random sampling of circular plots

In forest inventory, vegetation surveys, and agricultural surveys, circular sampling plots are quite common. Using circular plots as sampling units is not entirely straightforward, because the study area cannot be partitioned into a finite number of circles that fully cover the study area. The use of circular plots as sampling units can be implemented in two ways (De Vries, 1986):

1. sampling from a finite set of fixed circles; and
2. sampling from an infinite set of floating circles.

3.4.1 Sampling from a finite set of fixed circles

Sampling from a finite set of fixed circles is simple, but as we will see this requires an assumption about the distribution of the study variable in the population. In this implementation, the sampling units consist of a finite set of slightly overlapping or non-overlapping fixed circular plots (Figure 3.5). The circles can be constructed as follows. A grid with squares is superimposed on the study area, so that it fully covers the study area. These squares are then substituted by circles with an area equal to the area of the squares, or by non-overlapping tangent circles inscribed in the squares. The radius of the partly overlapping circles equals $\sqrt{a/\pi}$, with a the area of the squares, the radius of the non-overlapping circles equals $\sqrt{a}/2$. In both implementations, the infinite population is replaced by a finite population of circles that does not fully tessellate the study area. When using the partly overlapping circles as sampling units we may avoid overlap by selecting a systematic sample (Chapter 5) of circular plots. The population total can then be estimated by Equation (3.1), substituting A/a for N, and where z_k is the total of the kth circle (sum of observations of all population units in kth circle). However, no unbiased estimator of the sampling variance of the estimator of the population total or mean is available for this sampling design, see Chapter 5.

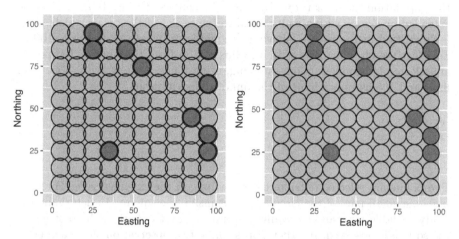

FIGURE 3.5: Simple random sample of ten circular plots from a square discretised by a finite set of partly overlapping or non-overlapping circular plots.

With simple random sampling without replacement of non-overlapping circular plots, the finite population total can be estimated by Equation (3.1) and its sampling variance by Equation (3.16). However, the circular plots do not cover the full study area, and as a consequence the total of the infinite population is underestimated. A corrected estimate can be obtained by estimating the mean of the finite population and multiplying this estimated population mean by A/a (De Vries, 1986):

$$\hat{t}(z) = \frac{A}{a}\hat{\bar{z}},$$ (3.22)

with $\hat{\bar{z}}$ the estimated mean of the finite population. The variance can be estimated by the variance of the estimator of the mean of the finite population, multiplied by the square of A/a. However, we still need to assume that the mean of the finite population is equal to the mean of the infinite population. This assumption can be avoided by sampling from an infinite set of floating circles.

3.4.2 Sampling from an infinite set of floating circles

A simple random sample of floating circular plots can be selected by simple random sampling of the centres of the plots. The circular plots overlap if two selected points are separated by a distance smaller than the diameter of the circular plots. Besides, when a plot is selected near the border of the study area, a part of the plot is outside the study area. This part is ignored in estimating the population mean or total. To select the centres, the study area must be extended by a zone with a width equal to the radius of the circular plots. This is illustrated in Figure 3.6, showing a square study area of 100 m × 100 m. To select ten circular plots with a radius of 5 m from this square, ten points are selected by simple random sampling, using function runif, with -5 as lower limit and 105 as upper limit of the uniform distribution.

```
set.seed(129)
s1 <- runif(10, min = -5, max = 105)
s2 <- runif(10, min = -5, max = 105)
```

Two points are selected outside the study area, in the extended zone. For both points, a small part of the circular plot is inside the square. To determine the study variable for these two sampling units, only the part of the plot inside the square is observed. In other words, these two observations have a smaller support than the observations of the other eight plots, see Chapter 1.

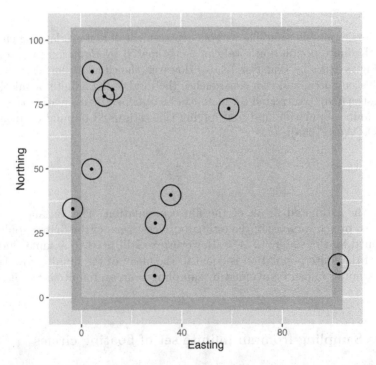

FIGURE 3.6: Simple random sample of ten floating circular plots from a square.

In the upper left corner, two sampling units are selected that largely overlap. The intersection of the two circular plots is used twice, to determine the study variable of both sampling units.

Given the observations of the selected circular plots, the population total can be estimated by (De Vries, 1986)

$$\hat{t}(z) = \frac{A}{a}\frac{1}{n}\sum_{k \in \mathcal{S}} z_k , \qquad (3.23)$$

with a the area of the circle and z_k the observed total of sampling unit k (circle). The same estimate of the total is obtained if we divide the observations by a to obtain a mean per sampling unit:

$$\hat{t}(z) = A\frac{1}{n}\sum_{k \in \mathcal{S}} \frac{z_k}{a} . \qquad (3.24)$$

The sampling variance of the estimator of the total can be estimated by

$$\hat{V}(\hat{t}(z)) = \left(\frac{A}{a}\right)^2 \frac{\widehat{S^2}(z)}{n} , \qquad (3.25)$$

with $\widehat{S^2}(z)$ the estimated population variance of the totals per population unit (circle).

Exercises

8. Write an **R** script to select a simple random sample of size 40 from Voorst.
   - Use the selected sample to estimate the population mean of the SOM concentration (z in the data frame) and its standard error.
   - Compute the lower and the upper bound of the 90% confidence interval using the t distribution, and check whether the population mean is covered by the interval.
   - Compare the length of the 90% confidence interval with the length of the 95% interval. Explain the difference in width.
   - Use the selected sample to estimate the total mass of SOM in Mg in the topsoil ($0 - 30$ cm) of Voorst. Use as a bulk density 1,500 kg m^{-3}. The size of the grid cells is 25 m × 25 m.
   - Estimate the standard error of the estimated total.
   - Do you think this standard error is a realistic estimate of the uncertainty about the estimated total?

4

Stratified simple random sampling

In stratified random sampling the population is divided into subpopulations, for instance, soil mapping units, areas with the same land use or land cover, administrative units, etc. The subareas are mutually exclusive, i.e., they do not overlap, and are jointly exhaustive, i.e., their union equals the entire population (study area). Within each subpopulation, referred to as a stratum, a probability sample is selected by some sampling design. If these probability samples are selected by simple random sampling, as described in the previous chapter, the design is stratified *simple* random sampling, the topic of this chapter. If sampling units are selected by cluster random sampling, then the design is stratified *cluster* random sampling.

Stratified simple random sampling is illustrated with Voorst (Figure 4.1). Tibble grdVoorst with simulated data contains variable stratum. The strata are combinations of soil class and land use, obtained by overlaying a soil map and a land use map. To select a stratified simple random sample, we set the total sample size n. The sampling units must be apportioned to the strata. I chose to apportion the units proportionally to the size (area, number of grid cells) of the strata (for details, see Section 4.3). The larger a stratum, the more units are selected from this stratum. The sizes of the strata, i.e., the total number of grid cells, are computed with function tapply.

```
N_h <- tapply(grdVoorst$stratum, INDEX = grdVoorst$stratum, FUN = length)
w_h <- N_h / sum(N_h)
n <- 40
print(n_h <- round(n * w_h))
```

```
BA EA PA RA XF
13  8  9  4  7
```

The sum of the stratum sample sizes is 41; we want 40, so we reduce the largest stratum sample size by 1.

```
n_h[1] <- n_h[1] - 1
```

The stratified simple random sample is selected with function strata of package **sampling** (Tillé and Matei, 2021). Argument size specifies the stratum sample sizes.

The stratum sample sizes must be in the order the strata are encountered in tibble grdVoorst, which is determined first with function unique.

Within the strata, the grid cells are selected by simple random sampling *with replacement* (method = "srswr"), so that in principle more than one point can be selected within a grid cell, see Chapter 3 for a motivation of this. Function getdata extracts the observations of the selected units from the sampling frame, as well as the spatial coordinates and the stratum of these units. The coordinates of the centres of the selected grid cells are jittered by an amount equal to half the side of the grid cells. In the next code chunk, this is done with function mutate of package **dplyr** (Wickham et al., 2021) which is part of package **tidyverse** (Wickham et al., 2019). We have seen the pipe operator %>% of package **magrittr** (Bache and Wickham, 2020) before in Subsection 3.1.2. If you are not familiar with **tidyverse** I recommend reading the excellent book *R for Data Science* (Wickham and Grolemund, 2017).

```
library(sampling)
ord <- unique(grdVoorst$stratum)
set.seed(314)
units <- sampling::strata(
  grdVoorst, stratanames = "stratum", size = n_h[ord], method = "srswr")
mysample <- getdata(grdVoorst, units) %>%
  mutate(s1 = s1 %>% jitter(amount = 25 / 2),
         s2 = s2 %>% jitter(amount = 25 / 2))
```

 The name of the package is added to function strata (sampling::strata), as strata is also a function of another package. Not adding the name of the package may result in an error message.

Figure 4.1 shows the selected sample.

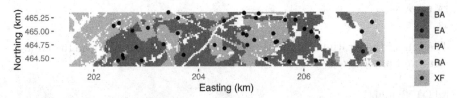

FIGURE 4.1: Stratified simple random sample of size 40 from Voorst. Strata are combinations of soil class and land use.

4.1 Estimation of population parameters

With simple random sampling within strata, the estimator of the population mean for simple random sampling (Equation (3.2)) is applied at the level of the strata. The estimated stratum means are then averaged, using the relative sizes or areas of the strata as weights:

$$\hat{\bar{z}} = \sum_{h=1}^{H} w_h \, \hat{\bar{z}}_h \, , \qquad (4.1)$$

where H is the number of strata, w_h is the relative size (area) of stratum h (stratum weight): $w_h = N_h/N$, and $\hat{\bar{z}}_h$ is the estimated mean of stratum h, estimated by the sample mean for stratum h:

$$\hat{\bar{z}}_h = \frac{1}{n_h} \sum_{k \in \mathcal{S}_h} z_k \, , \qquad (4.2)$$

with $\mathcal{S}_h$ the sample selected from stratum h.

The same estimator is found when the π estimator is worked out for stratified simple random sampling. With stratified simple random sampling without replacement and different sampling fractions for the strata, the inclusion probabilities differ among the strata and equal $\pi_k = n_h/N_h$ for all k in stratum h, with n_h the sample size of stratum h and N_h the size of stratum h. Inserting this in the π estimator of the population mean (Equation (2.4)) gives

$$\hat{\bar{z}} = \frac{1}{N} \sum_{h=1}^{H} \sum_{k \in \mathcal{S}_h} \frac{z_k}{\pi_k} = \frac{1}{N} \sum_{h=1}^{H} \frac{N_h}{n_h} \sum_{k \in \mathcal{S}_h} z_k = \sum_{h=1}^{H} w_h \, \hat{\bar{z}}_h \, . \qquad (4.3)$$

The sampling fractions are usually slightly different, even with proportional allocation (Section 4.3), because n_h/N_h cannot be made exactly equal for all strata. Sample sizes necessarily are integers, so n_h/N_h must be rounded to integers.

The sampling variance of the estimator of the population mean is estimated by first estimating the sampling variances of the estimated stratum means, followed by computing the weighted average of the estimated sampling variances of the estimated stratum means. Note that we must square the stratum weights:

$$\hat{V}(\hat{\bar{z}}) = \sum_{h=1}^{H} w_h^2 \, \hat{V}(\hat{\bar{z}}_h) \, , \qquad (4.4)$$

TABLE 4.1: Size (Nh), sample size (nh), estimated mean (Mean), estimated variance (Variance), and estimated standard error of estimator of mean (se) of the five strata in Voorst.

Stratum	Nh	nh	Mean	Variance	se
BA	2,371	12	91.1	946.3	8.9
EA	1,442	8	58.3	555.5	8.3
PA	1,710	9	59.4	214.7	4.9
RA	659	4	103.2	2,528.8	25.1
XF	1,346	7	133.9	3,807.3	23.3

where $\hat{V}\!\left(\hat{\bar{z}}_h\right)$ is the estimated sampling variance of $\hat{\bar{z}}_h$:

$$\hat{V}\!\left(\hat{\bar{z}}_h\right) = (1 - \frac{n_h}{N_h})\frac{\widehat{S^2}_h(z)}{n_h} \, , \tag{4.5}$$

with $\widehat{S^2}_h(z)$ the estimated variance of z within stratum h:

$$\widehat{S^2}_h(z) = \frac{1}{n_h - 1} \sum_{k \in \mathcal{S}_h} \left(z_k - \hat{\bar{z}}_h\right)^2 . \tag{4.6}$$

For stratified simple random sampling with replacement of finite populations and stratified simple random sampling of infinite populations the fpcs $1 - (n_h/N_h)$ can be dropped.

```
mz_h <- tapply(mysample$z, INDEX = mysample$stratum, FUN = mean)
mz <- sum(w_h * mz_h)
S2z_h <- tapply(mysample$z, INDEX = mysample$stratum, FUN = var)
v_mz_h <- S2z_h / n_h
se_mz <- sqrt(sum(w_h^2 * v_mz_h))
```

Table 4.1 shows per stratum the estimated mean, variance, and sampling variance of the estimated mean of the SOM concentration. We can see large differences in the within-stratum variances. For the stratified sample of Figure 4.1, the estimated population mean equals 86.3 g kg^{-1}, and the estimated standard error of this estimator equals 5.8 g kg^{-1}.

The population mean can also be estimated directly using the basic π estimator (Equation (2.4)). The inclusion probabilities are included in data.frame mysample, obtained with function getdata (see code chunk above), as variable Prob.

```
head(mysample)
```

	s1	s2	z	stratum	ID_unit	Prob	Stratum
1135	202554.8	464556.7	186.99296	XF	1135	0.005189017	1
2159	204305.5	464738.9	75.04809	XF	2159	0.005189017	1
4205	203038.3	465057.0	138.14617	XF	4205	0.005189017	1
4503	202381.1	465096.7	69.43803	XF	4503	0.005189017	1
5336	203610.4	465237.8	78.02003	XF	5336	0.005189017	1
5853	205147.1	465315.5	164.55224	XF	5853	0.005189017	1

The population total is estimated first, and by dividing this estimated total by the total number of population units N an estimate of the population mean is obtained.

```
tz <- sum(mysample$z / mysample$Prob)
print(mz <- tz / sum(N_h))
```

```
[1] 86.53333
```

The two estimates of the population mean are not exactly equal. This is due to rounding errors in the inclusion probabilities. This can be shown by computing the sum of the inclusion probabilities over all population units. This sum should be equal to the sample size $n = 40$, but as we can see below, this sum is slightly smaller.

```
pi_h <- tapply(mysample$Prob, INDEX = mysample$stratum, FUN = unique)
print(sum(pi_h * N_h))
```

```
[1] 39.90711
```

Now suppose we ignore that the sample data come from a stratified sampling design and we use the (unweighted) sample mean as an estimate of the population mean.

```
print(mean(mysample$z))
```

```
[1] 86.11247
```

The sample mean slightly differs from the proper estimate of the population mean (7.238). The sample mean is a *biased* estimator, but the bias is small. The bias is only small because the stratum sample sizes are about proportional to the sizes of the strata, so that the inclusion probabilities (sampling intensities) are about equal for all strata: 0.0050494, 0.0055344, 0.0052509, 0.006056, 0.005189. The probabilities are not exactly equal because the stratum sample sizes are necessarily rounded to integers and because we reduced the largest sample size by one unit. The bias would have been substantially larger if an equal number of units would have been selected from each stratum, leading to much larger differences in the inclusion probabilities among the strata. Sampling intensity in stratum BA, for instance, then would be much smaller compared to the other strata, and so would be the inclusion probabilities of the units in this stratum as compared to the other strata. Stratum BA then would be underrepresented in the sample. This is not a problem as long as we account for the difference in inclusion probabilities of the units in the estimation of the population mean. The estimated mean of stratum BA then gets the largest weight, equal to the inverse of the inclusion probability. If we do not account for these differences in inclusion probabilities, the estimator of the mean will be seriously biased.

The next code chunk shows how the population mean and its standard error can be estimated with package **survey** (Lumley, 2021). Note that the stratum weights N_h/n_h must be passed to function svydesign using argument weight. These are first attached to data.frame mysample by creating a look-up table lut, which is then merged with function merge to data.frame mysample.

```
library(survey)
labels <- sort(unique(mysample$stratum))
lut <- data.frame(stratum = labels, weight = N_h / n_h)
mysample <- merge(x = mysample, y = lut)
design_stsi <- svydesign(
    id = ~ 1, strata = ~ stratum, weight = ~ weight, data = mysample)
svymean(~ z, design_stsi)
```

```
      mean      SE
z 86.334 5.8167
```

4.1.1 Population proportion, cumulative distribution function, and quantiles

The proportion of a population satisfying some condition can be estimated by Equations (4.1) and (4.2), substituting for the study variable z_k an 0/1 indicator y_k with value 1 if for unit k the condition is satisfied, and 0 otherwise (Subsection 3.1.1). In general, with stratified simple random sampling the inclusion probabilities are not exactly equal, so that the estimated population proportion is not equal to the sample proportion.

These unequal inclusion probabilities must also be accounted for when estimating the cumulative distribution function (CDF) and quantiles (Subsection 3.1.2), as shown in the next code chunk for the CDF.

```
thresholds <- sort(unique(mysample$z))
cumfreq <- numeric(length = length(thresholds))
for (i in seq_len(length(thresholds))) {
  ind <- mysample$z <= thresholds[i]
```

```
  mh_ind <- tapply(ind, INDEX = mysample$stratum, FUN = mean)
  cumfreq[i] <- sum(w_h * mh_ind)
}
df <- data.frame(x = thresholds, y = cumfreq)
```

Figure 4.2 shows the estimated CDF, estimated from the stratified simple random sample of 40 units from Voorst (Figure 4.1).

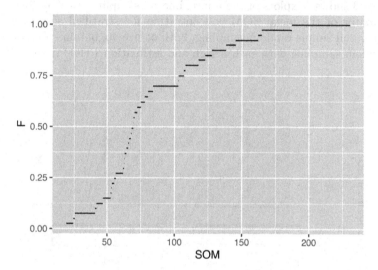

FIGURE 4.2: Estimated cumulative distribution function of the SOM concentration (g kg^{-1}) in Voorst, estimated from the stratified simple random sample of 40 units.

The estimated proportions, or cumulative frequencies, are used to estimate a quantile. These estimates are easily obtained with function svyquantile of package **survey**.

```
svyquantile(~ z, design_stsi, quantile = c(0.5, 0.8))

$z
      quantile    ci.2.5   ci.97.5        se
0.5   69.56081  65.70434  84.03993  4.515916
0.8  117.73877 102.75359 161.88611 14.563887

attr(,"hasci")
[1] TRUE
attr(,"class")
[1] "newsvyquantile"
```

4.1.2   Why should we stratify?

There can be two reasons for stratifying the population:

1. we are interested in the mean or total per stratum; or
2. we want to increase the precision of the estimated mean or total for the entire population.

Figure 4.3 shows boxplots of the approximated sampling distributions of the π estimator of the mean SOM concentration for stratified simple random sampling and simple random sampling, both of size 40, obtained by repeating the random sampling with each design and estimation 10,000 times.

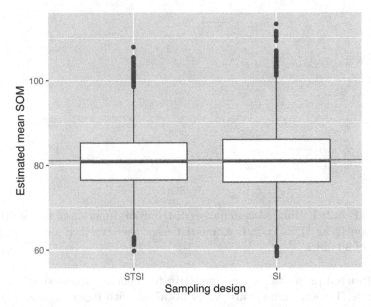

FIGURE 4.3: Approximated sampling distribution of the π estimator of the mean SOM concentration (g kg^{-1}) in Voorst for stratified simple random sampling (STSI) and simple random sampling (SI) of size 40.

The approximated sampling distributions of the estimators of the population mean with the two designs are not very different. With stratified random sampling, the spread of the estimated means is somewhat smaller. The horizontal red line is the population mean (81.1 g kg^{-1}). The gain in precision due to the stratification, referred to as the stratification effect, can be quantified by the ratio of the variance with simple random sampling and the variance with stratified simple random sampling. So, when this variance ratio is larger than 1, stratified simple random sampling is more precise than simple random sampling. For Voorst the stratification effect with proportional allocation (Section 4.3) equals 1.310. This means that with simple random sampling we need 1.310

more sampling units than with stratified simple random sampling to obtain an estimate of the same precision.

The stratification effect can be computed from the population variance $S^2(z)$ (Equation (3.12)) and the variances within the strata $S_h^2(z)$. In the sampling experiment, these variances are known without error because we know the z-values for all units in the population. In practice, we only know the z-values for the sampled units. However, a design-unbiased estimator of the population variance is (de Gruijter et al., 2006)

$$\widehat{S^2}(z) = \widehat{\bar{z^2}} - \left(\hat{\bar{z}}\right)^2 + \hat{V}\left(\hat{\bar{z}}\right) , \tag{4.7}$$

where $\widehat{\bar{z^2}}$ denotes the estimated population mean of the study variable squared (z^2), obtained in the same way as $\hat{\bar{z}}$ (Equation (4.1)), but using squared values, and $\hat{V}\left(\hat{\bar{z}}\right)$ denotes the estimated variance of the estimator of the population mean (Equation (4.4)).

The estimated population variance is then divided by the sum of the stratum sample sizes to get an estimate of the sampling variance of the estimator of the mean with simple random sampling of an equal number of units:

$$\hat{V}(\hat{\bar{z}}_{\mathrm{SI}}) = \frac{\widehat{S^2}(z)}{\sum_{h=1}^{H} n_h} . \tag{4.8}$$

The population variance can be estimated with function s2 of package **survey-planning** (Breidaks et al., 2020). However, this function is an implementation of an alternative, consistent estimator of the population variance (Särndal et al., 1992):

$$\widehat{S^2}(z) = \frac{N-1}{N} \frac{n}{n-1} \frac{1}{N-1} \sum_{k \in \mathcal{S}} \frac{(z_k - \hat{\bar{z}}_\pi)^2}{\pi_k} . \tag{4.9}$$

An estimator is consistent if it converges in probability to the true value of the parameter as the sample size tends to infinity (Särndal et al., 1992).

```
library(surveyplanning)
S2z <- s2(mysample$z, w = mysample$weight)
```

The design effect is defined as the variance of an estimator of the population mean with the sampling design under study divided by the variance of the π estimator of the mean with simple random sampling of an equal number of units (Section 12.4). So, the design effect of stratified random sampling is the reciprocal of the stratification effect. For the stratified simple random sample of Figure 4.1, the design effect can then be estimated as follows. Function SE extracts the estimated standard error of the estimator of the mean from the output of function svymean. The extracted standard error is then squared to obtain an estimate of the sampling variance of the estimator of the population with stratified simple random sampling. Finally, this variance is divided by the variance with simple random sampling of an equal number of units.

```
v_mz_SI <- S2z / n
res <- svymean(~ z, design_stsi)
SE(res)^2 / v_mz_SI
```

```
           z
z 0.6903965
```

The same value is obtained with argument deff of function svymean.

```
design_stsi <- svydesign(
    id = ~ 1, strata = ~ stratum, weight = ~ weight, data = mysample)
svymean(~ z, design_stsi, deff = "replace")
```

```
      mean      SE   DEff
z 86.3340  5.8167 0.6904
```

So, when using package **survey**, estimation of the population variance is not needed to estimate the design effect. I only added this to make clear how the design effect is computed with functions in package **survey**. In following chapters I will skip the estimation of the population variance.

The estimated design effect as estimated from the stratified sample is smaller than 1, showing that stratified simple random sampling is more efficient than simple random sampling. The reciprocal of the estimated design effect (1.448) is somewhat larger than the stratification effect as computed in the sampling experiment, but this is an estimate of the design effect from one stratified sample only. The estimated population variance varies among stratified samples, and so does the estimated design effect.

Stratified simple random sampling with proportional allocation (Section 4.3) is more precise than simple random sampling when the sum of squares of the stratum means is larger than the sum of squares within strata (Lohr, 1999):

$$SSB > SSW, \tag{4.10}$$

with SSB the weighted sum-of-squares between the stratum means:

$$SSB = \sum_{h=1}^{H} N_h (\bar{z}_h - \bar{z})^2, \tag{4.11}$$

and SSW the sum over the strata of the weighted variances within strata (weights equal to $1 - N_h/N$):

$$SSW = \sum_{h=1}^{H} (1 - \frac{N_h}{N}) S_h^2 \ . \tag{4.12}$$

In other words, the smaller the differences in the stratum means and the larger the variances within the strata, the smaller the stratification effect will be. Figure 4.4 shows a boxplot of the SOM concentration per stratum (soil-land use combination). The stratum means are equal to 83.0, 49.0, 68.8, 92.7, 122.3 g kg^{-1}. The stratum variances are 1799.2, 238.4, 1652.9, 1905.4, 2942.8 (g kg^{-1})^2. The large stratum variances explain the modest gain in precision realised by stratified simple random sampling compared to simple random sampling in this case.

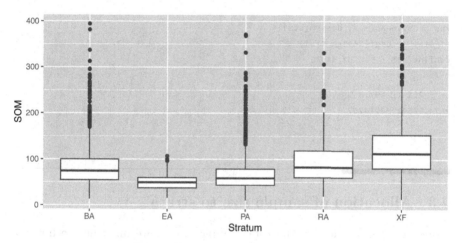

FIGURE 4.4: Boxplots of the SOM concentration (g kg^{-1}) for the five strata (soil-land use combinations) in Voorst.

4.2 Confidence interval estimate

The $100(1 - \alpha)\%$ confidence interval for $\bar{z}$ is given by

$$\hat{\bar{z}} \pm t_{\alpha/2, df} \cdot \sqrt{\hat{V}\left(\hat{\bar{z}}\right)} \ , \tag{4.13}$$

where $t_{\alpha/2, df}$ is the $(1 - \alpha/2)$ quantile of a t distribution with df degrees of freedom. The degrees of freedom df can be approximated by $n - H$, as proposed by Lohr (1999). This is the number of the degrees of freedom if the variances within the strata are equal. With unequal variances within strata, df can be approximated by Sattherwaite's method (Nanthakumar and Selvavel, 2004):

$$df \approx \frac{\left(\sum_{h=1}^{H} w_h^2 \frac{\widehat{S^2}_h(z)}{n_h} \right)^2}{\sum_{h=1}^{H} w_h^4 \left(\frac{\widehat{S^2}_h(z)}{n_h} \right)^2 \frac{1}{n_h - 1}} \,. \tag{4.14}$$

A confidence interval estimate of the population mean can be extracted with method confint of package **survey**. It uses $n - H$ degrees of freedom.

```
res <- svymean(~ z, design_stsi)
df_stsi <- degf(design_stsi)
confint(res, df = df_stsi, level = 0.95)
```

```
        2.5 %    97.5 %
z 74.52542 98.14252
```

4.3   Allocation of sample size to strata

After we have decided on the total sample size n, we must decide how to apportion the units to the strata. It is reasonable to allocate more sampling units to large strata and fewer to small strata. The simplest way to achieve this is proportional allocation:

$$n_h = n \cdot \frac{N_h}{\sum N_h} \,, \tag{4.15}$$

with N_h the total number of population units (size) of stratum h. With infinite populations N_h is replaced by the area A_h. The sample sizes computed with this equation are rounded to the nearest integers.

If we have prior information on the variance of the study variable within the strata, then it makes sense to account for differences in variance. Heterogeneous strata should receive more sampling units than homogeneous strata, leading to Neyman allocation:

$$n_h = n \cdot \frac{N_h \, S_h(z)}{\sum\limits_{h=1}^{H} N_h \, S_h(z)} \; , \tag{4.16}$$

with $S_h(z)$ the standard deviation (square root of variance) of the study variable z in stratum h.

Finally, the costs of sampling may differ among the strata. It can be relatively expensive to sample nearly inaccessible strata, and we do not want to sample many units there. This leads to optimal allocation:

$$n_h = n \cdot \frac{\dfrac{N_h \, S_h(z)}{\sqrt{c_h}}}{\sum\limits_{h=1}^{H} \dfrac{N_h \, S_h(z)}{\sqrt{c_h}}} \; , \tag{4.17}$$

with c_h the costs per sampling unit in stratum h. Optimal means that given the total costs this allocation type leads to minimum sampling variance, assuming a linear costs model:

$$C = c_0 + \sum_{h=1}^{H} n_h c_h \; , \tag{4.18}$$

with c_0 overhead costs. So, the more variable a stratum and the lower the costs, the more units will be selected from this stratum.

```
S2z_h <- tapply(X = grdVoorst$z, INDEX = grdVoorst$stratum, FUN = var)
n_h_Neyman <- round(n * N_h * sqrt(S2z_h) / sum(N_h * sqrt(S2z_h)))
```

These optimal sample sizes can be computed with function `optsize` of package **surveyplanning**.

```
labels <- sort(unique(mysample$stratum))
res <- optsize(labels, n, N_h, S2z_h)
round(res$nh, 0)
```

```
[1] 14  3  9  4 10
```

Table 4.2 shows the proportional and optimal sample sizes for the five strata of the study area Voorst, for a total sample size of 40. Stratum XF is the one-but-smallest stratum and therefore receives only seven sampling units. However, the standard deviation in this stratum is the largest, and as a consequence with optimal allocation the sample size in this stratum is increased by three points, at the cost of stratum EA which is relatively homogeneous.

TABLE 4.2: Proportional and Neyman sample sizes in stratified simple random sampling of Voorst with a total sample size of 40.

Stratum	Nh	Sh	nhprop	nhNeyman
BA	2,371	42.4	12	14
EA	1,442	15.4	8	3
PA	1,710	40.7	9	9
RA	659	43.7	4	4
XF	1,346	54.2	7	10

Nh: stratum size; Sh: stratum standard deviation.

Figure 4.5 shows the standard error of the π estimator of the mean SOM concentration as a function of the total sample size, for simple random sampling and for stratified simple random sampling with proportional and Neyman allocation. A small extra gain in precision can be achieved using Neyman allocation instead of proportional allocation. However, in practice often Neyman allocation is not achievable, because we do not know the standard deviations of the study variable within the strata. If a quantitative covariate x is used for stratification (see Sections 4.4 and 13.2), the standard deviations $S_h(z)$ are approximated by $S_h(x)$, resulting in approximately optimal stratum sample sizes. The gain in precision compared to proportional allocation is then partly or entirely lost.

Optimal allocation and Neyman allocation assume univariate stratification, i.e., the stratified simple random sample is used to estimate the mean of a single study variable. If we have multiple study variables, optimal allocation becomes more complicated. In Bethel allocation, the total sampling costs, assuming a linear costs model (Equation (4.18)), are minimised given a constraint on the precision of the estimated mean for each study variable (Bethel, 1989), see Section 4.8. Bethel allocation can be computed with function bethel of package **SamplingStrata** (Barcaroli et al., 2020).

Exercises

1. Use function strata of package **sampling** to select a stratified simple random sample with replacement of size 40 from Voorst, using proportional allocation. Check that the sum of the stratum sample sizes is 40.
   - Estimate the population mean and the standard error of the estimator.
   - Compute the true standard error of the estimator. Hint: compute the population variances of the study variable z per stratum, and divide these by the stratum sample sizes.

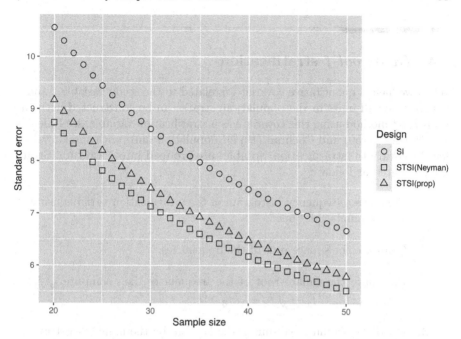

FIGURE 4.5: Standard error of the π estimator of the mean SOM concentration (g kg^{-1}) as a function of the total sample size, for simple random sampling (SI) and for stratified simple random sampling with proportional (STSI(prop)) and Neyman allocation (STSI(Neyman)) for Voorst.

- Compute a 95% confidence interval estimate of the population mean, using function confint of package **survey**.

2. Looking at Figure 4.4, which strata do you expect can be merged without losing much precision of the estimated population mean?

3. Use function fct_collapse of package **forcats** (Wickham, 2021) to merge the strata EA and PA.
   - Compute the true sampling variance of the estimator of the mean for this new stratification, for a total sample size of 40 and proportional allocation.
   - Compare this true sampling variance with the true sampling variance using the original five strata (same sample size, proportional allocation). What is your conclusion about the new stratification?

4. Proof that the sum of the inclusion probabilities over all population units with stratified simple random sampling equals the sample size n.

4.4   *Cum-root-f* stratification

When we have a quantitative covariate x related to the study variable z and x is known for all units in the population, strata can be constructed with the *cum-root-f* method using this covariate as a stratification variable, see Dalenius and Hodges (1959) and Cochran (1977). Population units with similar values for the covariate (stratification variable) are grouped into a stratum. Strata are computed as follows:

1. Compute a frequency histogram of the stratification variable using a large number of bins.

2. Compute the square root of the frequencies.

3. Cumulate the square root of the frequencies, i.e., compute $\sqrt{f_1}$, $\sqrt{f_1} + \sqrt{f_2}$, $\sqrt{f_1} + \sqrt{f_2} + \sqrt{f_3}$, etc.

4. Divide the cumulative sum of the last bin by the number of strata, multiply this value by $1, 2, \ldots, H - 1$, with H the number of strata, and select the boundaries of the histogram bins closest to these values.

In *cum-root-f* stratification, it is assumed that the covariate values are nearly perfect predictions of the study variable, so that the prediction errors do not affect the stratification. Under this assumption the stratification is optimal.

Cum-root-f stratification is illustrated with the data of Xuancheng in China. We wish to estimate the mean organic matter concentration in the topsoil (SOM, g kg^{-1}) of this area. Various covariates are available that are correlated with SOM, such as elevation, yearly average temperature, slope, and various other terrain attributes. Elevation, the name of this variable in the tibble is dem, is used as as a single stratification variable, see Figure 4.6. The correlation coefficient of SOM and elevation in a sample of 183 observations is 0.59. The positive correlation can be explained as follows. Temperature is decreasing with elevation, leading to a smaller decomposition rate of organic matter in the soil.

The strata can be constructed with the package **stratification** (Baillargeon and Rivest, 2011). Care should be taken that the data are sorted in ascending order by the variable used for stratification, see help of function strata.cumrootf. Argument n of this function is the total sample size, but this value has no effect on the stratification. Argument Ls is the number of strata. I arbitrarily chose to construct five strata. Argument nclass is the number of bins of the histogram. The output object of function strata.cumrootf is a list containing

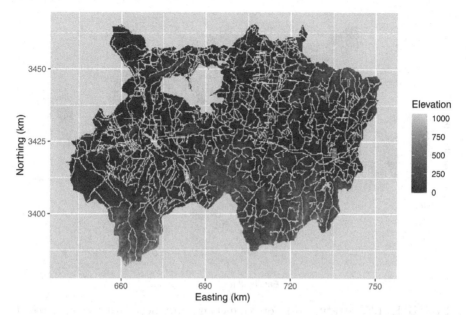

FIGURE 4.6: Elevation used as a stratification variable in *cum-root-f* stratification of Xuancheng.

amongst others a numeric vector with the stratum bounds (bh) and a factor with the stratum levels of the grid cells (stratumID). Finally, note that the values of the stratification variable must be positive. The minimum elevation is -5 m, so I added the absolute value of this minimum to elevation.

```
library(stratification)
grdXuancheng <- grdXuancheng %>%
  arrange(dem) %>%
  mutate(dem_new = dem + abs(min(dem)))
crfstrata <- strata.cumrootf(
  x = grdXuancheng$dem_new, n = 100, Ls = 5, nclass = 500)
bh <- crfstrata$bh
grdXuancheng$crfstrata <- crfstrata$stratumID
```

Stratum bounds are threshold values of the stratification variable elevation; these stratum bounds are equal to 46.7, 108.3, 214.5, 384.4. Note that the number of stratum bounds is one less than the number of strata. The resulting stratification is shown in Figure 4.7. Note that most strata are not single polygons, but are made up of many smaller polygons. This may be even more so if the stratification variable shows a noisy spatial pattern. This is not a problem at all, as a stratum is just a collection of population units (raster cells) and need not be spatially contiguous.

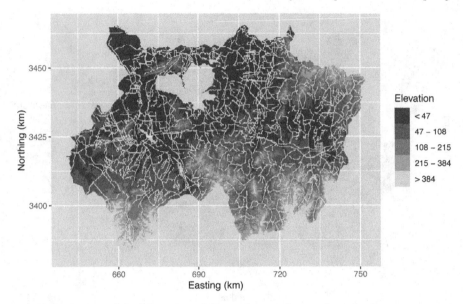

FIGURE 4.7: Stratification of Xuancheng obtained with the *cum-root-f* method, using elevation as a stratification variable.

Exercises

5. Write an **R** script to compute five *cum-root-f* strata for Eastern Amazonia (grdAmazonia in package **sswr**) to estimate the population mean of aboveground biomass (AGB), using log-transformed short-wave infrared radiation (SWIR2) as a stratification variable.

   - Compute ten *cum-root-f* strata, using function strata of package **sampling**. Sort the units first in ascending order on lnSWIR2. Use the stratum sample sizes as computed by function strata.cumrootf. What allocation is used for computing the stratum sample sizes?
   - Select a stratified simple random sample of 100 units. First, compute the stratum sample sizes for proportional allocation.
   - Estimate the population mean of AGB and its sampling variance.
   - Compute the true sampling variance of the estimator of the mean for this sampling design (see Exercise 1 for a hint).
   - Compute the stratification effect (gain in precision). Hint: compute the sampling variance for simple random sampling by computing the population variance of AGB, and divide this by the total sample size.

4.5 Stratification with multiple covariates

If we have multiple variables that are possibly related to the study variable, we may want to use them all or a subset of them as stratification variables. Using the quantitative variables one-by-one in *cum-root-f* stratification, followed by overlaying the maps with univariate strata, may lead to numerous cross-classification strata.

A simple solution is to construct homogeneous groups, referred to as clusters, of population units (raster cells). The units within a cluster are more similar to each other than to the units in other clusters. Various clustering techniques are available. Here, I use hard k-means.

This is illustrated again with the Xuancheng case study. Five quantitative covariates are used for constructing the strata. Besides elevation, which was used as a single stratification variable in the previous section, now also temperature, slope, topographic wetness index (twi), and profile curvature are used to construct clusters that are used as strata in stratified simple random sampling. To speed up the computations, a subgrid with a spacing of 0.4 km is selected, using function spsample of package **sp**, see Chapter 5 (Bivand et al., 2013).

```
library(sp)
gridded(grdXuancheng) <- ~ s1 + s2
subgrd <- spsample(
  grdXuancheng, type = "regular", cellsize = 400, offset = c(0.5, 0.5))
subgrd <- data.frame(coordinates(subgrd), over(subgrd, grdXuancheng))
```

Five clusters are computed with k-means using as clustering variables the five covariates mentioned above. The scale of these covariates is largely different, and for this reason they must be scaled before being used in clustering. The k-means algorithm is a deterministic algorithm, i.e., the same initial clustering will end in the same final, optimised clustering. This final clustering can be suboptimal, and therefore it is recommended to repeat the clustering as many times as feasible, with different initial clusterings. Argument nstart is the number of initial clusterings. The best clustering, i.e., the one with the smallest within-cluster sum-of-squares, is kept.

```
x <- c("dem", "temperature", "slope", "profile.curvature", "twi")
set.seed(314)
myClusters <- kmeans(
  scale(subgrd[, x]), centers = 5, iter.max = 1000, nstart = 100)
subgrd$cluster <- myClusters$cluster
```

Figure 4.8 shows the five clusters obtained by k-means clustering of the raster cells. These clusters can be used as strata in random sampling.

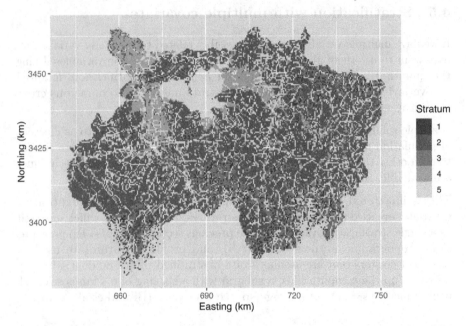

FIGURE 4.8: Five clusters obtained by k-means clustering of the raster cells of Xuancheng, using five scaled covariates in clustering.

The size of the clusters used as strata is largely different (Table 4.3). This table also shows means of the unscaled covariates used in clustering.

Categorical variables can be accommodated in clustering using the technique proposed by Huang (1998), implemented in package **clustMixType** (Szepannek, 2018).

In the situation that we already have some data of the study variable, an alternative solution is to calibrate a model for the study variable, for instance

TABLE 4.3: Size (Nh) and means of clustering variables of the five strata of Xuancheng obtained with k-means clustering of raster cells.

Stratum	Nh	Elevation	Temperature	Slope	Profilecurv	Twi
1	1,581	300	14.45	12.21	-0.00147	6.34
2	15,987	54	15.44	2.11	0.00001	9.24
3	4,255	181	14.64	11.11	0.00068	7.75
4	4,955	20	15.59	0.47	0.00006	17.08
5	1,625	416	13.70	21.21	0.00012	6.45

a multiple linear regression model, using the covariates as predictors, and to use the predictions of the study variable as a single stratification variable in *cum-root-f* stratification or in optimal spatial stratification, see Section 13.2.

4.6 Geographical stratification

When no covariate is available, we may still decide to apply a *geographical stratification*. For instance, a square study area can be divided into 4 × 4 equal-sized subsquares that are used as strata. When we select one or two points per subsquare, we avoid strong spatial clustering of the sampling points. Geographical stratification improves the *spatial coverage*. When the study variable is spatially structured, think for instance of a spatial trend, then geographical stratification will lead to more precisely estimated means (smaller sampling variances).

A simple method for constructing geographical strata is k-means clustering (Brus et al., 1999). See Section 17.2 for a simple illustrative example of how geographical strata are computed with k-means clustering. In this approach, the study area is discretised by a large number of grid cells. These grid cells are the objects that are clustered. The clustering variables are simply the spatial coordinates of the centres of the grid cells. This method leads to compact geographical strata, briefly referred to as geostrata. Geostrata can be computed with function kmeans, as shown in Section 4.5. The two clustering variables have the same scale, so they should not be scaled because this would lead to an arbitrary distortion of geographical distances. The geostrata generally will not have the same number of grid cells. Geostrata of equal size can be attractive, as then the sample becomes selfweighting, i.e., the sample mean is an unbiased estimator of the population mean.

Geostrata of the same size can be computed with function stratify of the package **spcosa** (Walvoort et al. (2020), Walvoort et al. (2010)), with argument equalArea = TRUE.

If the total number of grid cells divided by the number of strata is an integer, the stratum sizes are exactly equal; otherwise, the difference is one grid cell. Walvoort et al. (2010) describe the k-means algorithms implemented in this package in detail. Argument object of function stratify specifies a spatial object of the population units. In the **R** code below grdVoorst is converted to a SpatialPixelsDataFrame with function gridded of the package **sp**. The spatial object can also be of class SpatialPolygons. In that case, either argument nGridCells or argument cellsize must be set, so that the vector map in object can be discretised by a finite number of grid cells. Argument nTry specifies the number of initial stratifications in k-means clustering, and therefore is comparable with argument nstart of function kmeans. For more details on spatial stratification using k-means clustering, see Section 17.2. The k-means algorithm used with equalArea = TRUE takes much more computing time than the one used with equalArea = FALSE.

```
library(spcosa)
library(sp)
set.seed(314)
gridded(subgrd) <- ~ x1 + x2
mygeostrata <- stratify(
  object = subgrd, nStrata = 50, nTry = 1, equalArea = TRUE)
```

Function spsample of package **spcosa** is used to select from each geostratum a simple random sample of two points.

```
set.seed(314)
mysample <- spcosa::spsample(mygeostrata, n = 2)
```

Figure 4.9 shows fifty compact geostrata of equal size for Xuancheng with the selected sampling points. Note that the sampling points are reasonably well spread throughout the study area[1].

Once the observations are done, the population mean can be estimated with function estimate. For Xuancheng I simulated data from a normal distribution, just to illustrate estimation with function estimate. Various statistics can be estimated, among which the population mean (spatial mean), the standard error, and the CDF. The CDF is estimated by transforming the data into indicators (Subsection 3.1.2).

```
library(spcosa)
mysample <- spcosa::spsample(mygeostrata, n = 2)
mydata <- data.frame(z = rnorm(100, mean = 10, sd = 2))
mean <- estimate("spatial mean", mygeostrata, mysample, data = mydata)
se <- estimate("standard error", mygeostrata, mysample, data = mydata)
cdf <- estimate("scdf", mygeostrata, mysample, data = mydata)
```

The estimated population mean equals 9.8 with an estimated standard error of 0.2.

---

[1]The compact geostrata and the sample are plotted with package **ggplot2**. A simple alternative is to use method plot of **spcosa**: plot(mygeostrata, mysample).

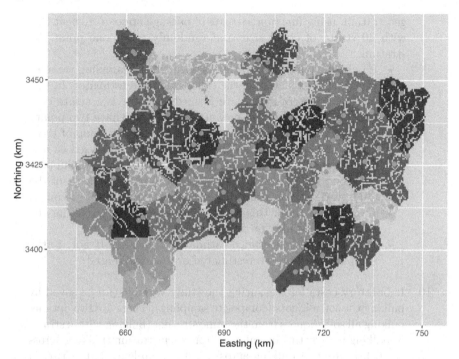

FIGURE 4.9: Compact geostrata of equal size for Xuancheng and stratified simple random sample of two points per stratum.

Exercises

6. Why is it attractive to select at least two points per geostratum?

7. The alternative to 50 geostrata and two points per geostratum is 100 geostrata and one point per geostratum. Which sampling strategy will be more precise?

8. The geostrata in Figure 4.9 have equal size (area), which can be enforced by argument equalArea = TRUE. Why are equal sizes attractive? Work out the estimator of the population mean for strata of equal size.

9. Write an **R** script to construct 20 compact geographical strata of equal size for agricultural field Leest. The geopackage file of this field can be read with **sf** function read_sf(system.file("extdata/leest.gpkg", package = "sswr")). Remove the projection attributes with st_set_crs(NA_crs_), and convert the simple feature object to a spatial object with method as_Spatial. Select two points per

geostratum, using function spsample of package **spcosa**. Repeat this with 40 strata of equal size, and randomly select one point per stratum.

- If only one point per stratum is selected, the sampling variance can be approximated by the collapsed strata estimator. In this method, pairs of strata are formed, and the two strata of a pair are joined. In each new stratum we now have two points. With an odd number of strata there will be one group of three strata and three points. The sample is then analysed as if it were a random sample from the new collapsed strata. Suppose we group the strata on the basis of the measurements of the study variable. Do you think this is a proper way of grouping?
- In case you think this is not a proper way of grouping the strata, how would you group the strata?
- Is the sampling variance estimator unbiased? If not, is the sampling variance overestimated or underestimated?

10. Laboratory costs for measuring the study variable can be saved by bulking the soil aliquots (composite sampling). There are two options: bulking all soil aliquots from the same stratum (bulking within strata) or bulking by selecting one aliquot from each stratum (bulking across strata). In **spcosa** bulking across strata is implemented. Write an **R** script to construct 20 compact geographical strata for study area Voorst. Use argument equalArea = TRUE. Select four points per stratum using argument type = "composite", and convert the resulting object to SpatialPoints. Extract the z-values in grdVoorst at the selected sampling points using function over. Add a variable to the resulting data frame indicating the composite (points 1 to 4 are from the first stratum, points 5 to 8 from the second stratum, etc.), and estimate the means for the four composites using function tapply. Finally, estimate the population mean and its standard error.

- Can the sampling variance of the estimator of the mean be estimated for bulking within the strata?
- The alternative to analysing the concentration of four composite samples obtained by bulking across strata is to analyse all 20 × 4 aliquots separately. The strata have equal size, so the inclusion probabilities are equal. As a consequence, the sample mean is an unbiased estimator of the population mean. Is the precision of this estimated population mean equal to that of the estimated population mean with composite sampling? If not, is it smaller or larger, and why?
- If you use argument equalArea = FALSE in combination with argument type = "composite", you get an error message. Why does this combination of arguments not work?

4.7 Multiway stratification

In Section 4.5 multiple continuous covariates are used to construct clusters of raster cells using k-means. These clusters are then used as strata. This section considers the case where we have multiple categorical and/or continuous variables that we would like to use as stratification variables. The continuous stratification variables are first used to compute strata based on that stratification variable, e.g., using the *cum-root-f* method. What could be done then is to compute the cross-classification of each unit and use these cross-classifications as strata in random sampling. However, this may lead to numerous strata, maybe even more than the intended sample size. To reduce the total number of strata, we may aggregate cross-classification strata with similar means of the study variable, based on our prior knowledge.

An alternative to aggregation of cross-classification strata is to use the separate strata, i.e., the strata based on an individual stratification variable, as *marginal* strata in random sampling. How this works is explained in Subsection 9.1.4.

4.8 Multivariate stratification

Another situation is where we have multiple study variables and would like to optimise the stratification and allocation for estimating the population means of all study variables. Optimal stratification for multiple study variables is only relevant if we would like to use different stratification variables for the study variables. In many cases, we do not have reliable prior information about the different study variables justifying the use of multiple stratification variables. We are already happy to have one stratification variable that may serve to increase the precision of the estimated means of all study variables.

However, in case we do have multiple stratification variables tailored to different study variables, the objective is to partition the population in strata, so that for a given allocation, the total sampling costs, assuming a linear costs model (Equation (4.18)), are minimised given a constraint on the precision of the estimated mean for each study variable.

Package **SamplingStrata** (Barcaroli et al., 2020) can be used to optimise multivariate strata. Barcaroli (2014) gives details about the objective function and the algorithm used for optimising the strata. Sampling units are allocated to the strata by Bethel allocation (Bethel, 1989). The required precision is specified in terms of a coefficient of variation, one per study variable.

Multivariate stratification is illustrated with the Meuse data set of package **gstat** (Pebesma, 2004). The prior data of heavy metal concentrations of Cd and Zn are used in spatial prediction to create maps of these two study variables.

The maps of natural logs of the two metal concentrations are created by kriging with an external drift, using the square root of the distance to the Meuse river as a predictor for the mean, see Section 21.3 for how this spatial prediction method works.

Figure 4.10 shows the map with the predicted log Cd and log Zn concentrations.

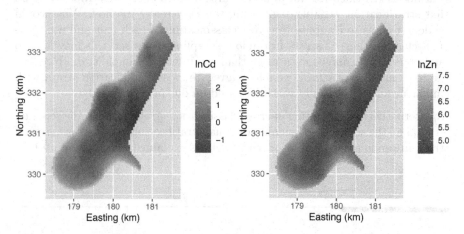

FIGURE 4.10: Kriging predictions of natural logs of Cd and Zn concentrations in the study area Meuse, used as stratification variables in bivariate stratification.

The predicted log concentrations of the two heavy metals are used as stratification variables in designing a new sample for design-based estimation of the population means of Cd and Zn. For the log of Cd, there are negative predicted concentrations (Figure 4.10). This leads to an error when running function optimStrata. The minimum predicted log Cd concentration is -1.7, so I added 2 to the predictions. A variable indicating the domains of interest is added to the data frame. The value of this variable is 1 for all grid cells, so that a sample is designed for estimating the mean of the entire population. As a first step, function buildFrameDF is used to create a data frame that can be handled by function optimStrata. Argument x specifies the stratification variables, and argument y the study variables. In our case, the stratification variables and the study variables are the same. This is typical for the situation where the stratification variables are obtained by mapping the study variables.

```
library(SamplingStrata)
df <- data.frame(cd = lcd_kriged$var1.pred + 2,
```

```
                    zn = lzn_kriged$var1.pred,
                    dom = 1,
                    id = seq_len(nrow(lcd_kriged)))
frame <- buildFrameDF(
    df = df, id = "id",
    X = c("cd", "zn"), Y = c("cd", "zn"),
    domainvalue = "dom")
```

Next, a data frame with the precision requirements for the estimated means is created. The precision requirement is given as a coefficient of variation, i.e., the standard error of the estimated population mean, divided by the estimated mean. The study variables as specified in Y are used to compute the estimated means and the standard errors for a given stratification and allocation.

```
cv <- as.data.frame(list(DOM = "DOM1", CV1 = 0.02, CV2 = 0.02, domainvalue = 1))
```

Finally, the multivariate stratification is optimised by searching for the optimal stratum bounds using a genetic algorithm (Gershenfeld, 1999).

```
set.seed(314)
res <- optimStrata(
    method = "continuous", errors = cv, framesamp = frame, nStrata = 5,
    iter = 50, pops = 20, showPlot = FALSE)
```

A summary of the strata can be obtained with function summaryStrata.

```
smrstrata <- summaryStrata(res$framenew, res$aggr_strata, progress = FALSE)
```

Stratum	Population	Allocation	Lower_X1	Upper_X1	Lower_X2	Upper_X2
1	1	717	7	0.266	1.421	4.502	5.576
2	2	694	5	1.421	2.090	4.950	6.010
3	3	597	3	2.091	2.630	5.163	6.358
4	4	704	6	2.630	3.476	5.472	6.802
5	5	391	5	3.480	4.781	6.234	7.527

Column Population contains the sizes of the strata, i.e., the number of grid cells. The total sample size equals 26. The sample size per stratum is computed with Bethel allocation, see Section 4.3. The last four columns contain the lower and upper bounds of the orthogonal intervals.

Figure 4.11 shows a 2D-plot of the bivariate strata. The strata can be plotted as a series of nested rectangles. All population units in the smallest rectangle belong to stratum 1; all units in the one-but-smallest rectangle that are not in the smallest rectangle belong to stratum 2, etc. If we have more than two stratification variables, the strata form a series of nested hyperrectangles or boxes. The strata are obtained as the Cartesian product of orthogonal intervals.

```
plt <- plotStrata2d(res$framenew, res$aggr_strata,
    domain = 1, vars = c("X1", "X2"), labels = c("Cd", "Zn"))
```

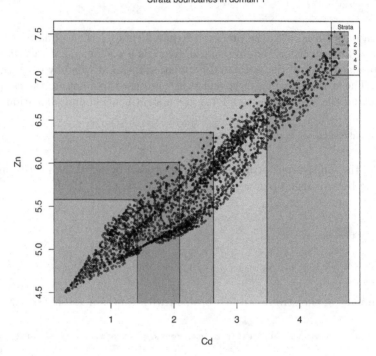

FIGURE 4.11: 2D-plot of optimised bivariate strata of the study area Meuse.

It may happen that after the optimisation of the stratum bounds in some resulting strata, no units are contained. If the stratification with a smaller number of strata requires fewer sampling units so that the sampling costs are lower (and still the precision requirement is met), then this is retained as the optimal stratification.

Figure 4.12 shows a map of the optimised strata.

The expected coefficient of variation can be extracted with function `expected_CV`.

```
expected_CV(res$aggr_strata)
```

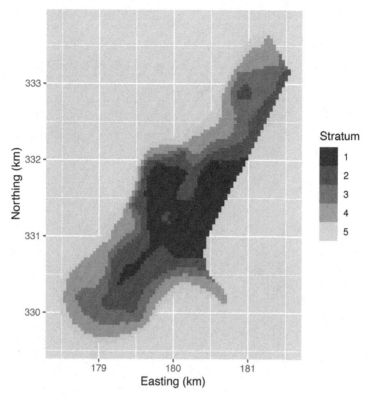

FIGURE 4.12: Map of optimised bivariate strata of the study area Meuse.

```
       cv(Y1)     cv(Y2)
DOM1    0.02 0.0087401
```

The coefficient of variation of Cd is indeed equal to the desired level of 0.02, for Zn it is smaller. So, in this case Cd is the study variable that determines the total sample size of 26 units.

Note that these coefficients of variation are computed from the stratification variables, which are predictions of the study variable. Errors in these predictions are not accounted for. It is well known that kriging is a smoother, so that the variance of the predicted values within a stratum is smaller than the variance of the true values. As a consequence, the coefficients of variation of the predictions underestimate the coefficients of variation of the study variables. See Section 13.2 for how prediction errors and spatial correlation of prediction errors can be accounted for in optimal stratification. An additional problem is that I added a value of 2 to the log Cd concentrations. This does not affect the standard error of the estimated mean, but does affect the estimated mean, so that also for this reason the coefficient of variation of the study variable Cd is underestimated.

5

Systematic random sampling

A simple way of drawing probability samples whose units are spread uniformly over the study area is systematic random sampling (SY), which from a two-dimensional spatial population entails the selection of a regular grid randomly placed on the area. A systematic sample can be selected with function `spsample` of package **sp** with argument `type = "regular"` (Bivand et al., 2013). Argument `offset` is not used, so that the grid is randomly placed on the study area. This is illustrated with Voorst. First, `data.frame grdVoorst` is converted to `SpatialPixelsDataFrame` with function `gridded`.

```
library(sp)
gridded(grdVoorst) <- ~ s1 + s2
n <- 40
set.seed(777)
mySYsample <- spsample(x = grdVoorst, n = n, type = "regular") %>%
  as("data.frame")
```

Figure 5.1 shows the randomly selected systematic sample. The shape of the grid is square, and the orientation is East-West (E-W), North-South (N-S). There is no strict need for random selection of the orientation of the grid. Random placement of the grid on the study area suffices for design-based estimation.

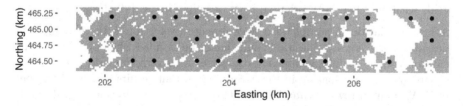

FIGURE 5.1: Systematic random sample (square grid) from Voorst.

Argument `n` in function `spsample` is used to set the sample size. Note that this is the *expected* sample size, i.e., on average over repeated sampling the sample size is 40. In Figure 5.1 the number of selected sampling points equals 38. Given the expected sample size, the spacing of the square grid can be computed with $\sqrt{A/n}$, with A the area of the study area. This area A can be computed by the total number of cells of the discretisation grid multiplied by the area of a grid cell. Note that the area of the study area is smaller than the number of grid cells in the horizontal direction multiplied by the number of grid cells in the vertical direction multiplied by the grid cell area, as we have non-availables (built-up areas, roads, etc.).

```
cell_size <- 25
A <- nrow(grdVoorst) * cell_size^2
(spacing <- sqrt(A / n))
```

[1] 342.965

Instead of argument n we may use argument cell_size to select a grid with a specified spacing. The expected sample size of a square grid can then be computed with $A/spacing^2$.

The spatial coverage with random grid sampling is better than that with stratified random sampling using compact geographical strata (Section 4.6), even with one sampling unit per geostratum. Consequently, in general systematic random sampling results in more precise estimates of the mean or total.

However, there are also two disadvantages of systematic random sampling compared to geographically stratified random sampling. First, for systematic random sampling, no design-unbiased estimator of the sampling variance exists. Second, the number of sampling units with random grid sampling is not fixed, but varies among randomly drawn samples. We may choose the grid spacing such that *on average* the number of sampling units equals the required (allowed) number of sampling units, but for the actually drawn sample, this number can be smaller or larger. In Voorst the variation of the sample size is quite large. The approximated sampling distribution, obtained by repeating the sampling 10,000 times, is bimodal (Figure 5.2). The smaller sample sizes are of square grids with only two E-W oriented rows of points instead of three rows.

A large variation in sample size over repeated selection with the sampling design under study is undesirable and should be avoided when possible. In the case of Voorst, a simple solution is to select a rectangular grid instead of a square grid, with a spacing in the N-S direction that results in a fixed number of E-W oriented rows of sampling points over repeated selection of grids. This is achieved with a N-S spacing equal to the dimension of the study area in N-S direction divided by an integer. The spacing in E-W direction is then adapted so that on average a given number of sampling points is selected. As the N-S dimension of Voorst is 1,000 m, a N-S spacing of 1,000/3 m is chosen, so that the number of E-W oriented rows of sampling points in the systematic sample equals three for any randomly selected rectangular grid.

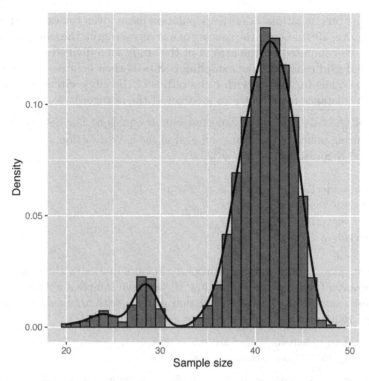

FIGURE 5.2: Approximated sampling distribution of the sample size of systematic random samples from Voorst. The expected sample size is 40.

```
dy <- 1000 / 3
dx <- A / (n * dy)
mySYsample_rect <- spsample(
  x = grdVoorst, cellsize = c(dx, dy), type = "regular")
```

The E-W spacing is somewhat larger than the N-S spacing: 352.875 m vs. 333.333 m. The variation in sample size with the random rectangular grid is much smaller than that of the square grid. The sample size now ranges from 33 to 46, whereas with the square grid the range varies from 20 to 48.

```
summary(sampleSizes)
```

```
  Min. 1st Qu.  Median    Mean 3rd Qu.    Max.
 33.00   38.00   40.00   39.99   42.00   46.00
```

An alternative shape for the sampling grid is triangular. Triangular grids can be selected with argument `type = "hexagonal"`. The centres of hexagonal sampling grid cells form a triangular grid. The triangular grid was shown to yield most precise estimates of the population mean given the expected sample size (Matérn, 1986). Given the spacing of a triangular grid, the expected sample size can be computed by the area A of the study area divided by the area of hexagonal grid cells with the sampling points at their centres. The area of a hexagon equals $6\sqrt{3}/4\ r^2$, with r the radius of the circle circumscribing the hexagon (distance from centre to a corner of the hexagon). So, by choosing a radius of $\sqrt{A/(6\sqrt{3}/4)}\ n$ the expected sample equals n. The distance between neighbouring points of the triangular grid in the E-W direction, dx, then equals $r\sqrt{3}$. The N-S distance equals $\sqrt{3}/2\ dx$.

```
cnst <- 6 * sqrt(3) / 4
r <- sqrt(A / (cnst * n))
dx <- r * sqrt(3)
dy <- sqrt(3) / 2 * dx
```

Function `spsample` does not work properly in combination with argument `type = "hexagonal"`. Over repeated sampling, the average sample size is not equal to the chosen sample size passed to function `spsample` with argument `n`. The same problem remains when using argument `cellsize`.

```
  Min. 1st Qu.  Median    Mean 3rd Qu.    Max.
 18.00   23.00   26.00   28.39   35.00   41.00
```

The following code can be used for random selection of triangular grids.

```
SY_triangular <- function(dx, grd) {
  dy <- sqrt(3) / 2 * dx
  #randomly select offset
  offset_x <- runif(1, min = 0, max = dx)
  offset_y <- runif(1, min = 0, max = dy)
  #compute x-coordinates of 1 row and y-coordinates of 1 column
  bbox <- bbox(grd)
  nx <- ceiling((bbox[1, 2] - bbox[1, 1]) / dx)
  ny <- ceiling((bbox[2, 2] - bbox[2, 1]) / dy)
  x <- (-1:nx) * dx + offset_x
  y <- (0:ny) * dy + offset_y
  #compute coordinates of rectangular grid
  xy <- expand.grid(x, y)
  names(xy) <- c("x", "y")
  #shift points of even rows in horizontal direction
  units <- which(xy$y %in% y[seq(from = 2, to = ny, by = 2)])
  xy$x[units] <- xy$x[units] + dx / 2
  #add coordinates of origin
  xy$x <- xy$x + bbox[1, 1]
  xy$y <- xy$y + bbox[2, 1]
```

```
#overlay with grid
coordinates(xy) <- ~ x + y
mysample <- data.frame(coordinates(xy), over(xy, grd))
#delete points with NA
mysample <- mysample[!is.na(mysample[, 3]), ]
}
set.seed(314)
mySYsample_tri <- SY_triangular(dx = dx, grd = grdVoorst)
```

Figure 5.3 shows a triangular grid, selected randomly from Voorst with an
expected sample size of 40. The selected triangular grid has 42 points.

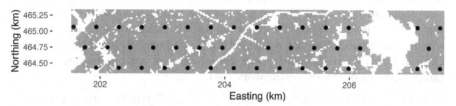

FIGURE 5.3: Systematic random sample (triangular grid) from Voorst.

5.1 Estimation of population parameters

With systematic random sampling, all units have the same inclusion probability, equal to $E[n]/N$, with $E[n]$ the expected sample size. Consequently, the
population total can be estimated by

$$\hat{t}(z) = \sum_{k \in \mathcal{S}} \frac{z_k}{\pi_k} = N \sum_{k \in \mathcal{S}} \frac{z_k}{E[n]} \ . \tag{5.1}$$

The population mean can be estimated by dividing this π estimator of the
population total by the population size:

$$\hat{\bar{z}} = \sum_{k \in \mathcal{S}} \frac{z_k}{E[n]} \ . \tag{5.2}$$

In this π estimator of the population mean the sample sum of the observations
is not divided by the number of selected units n, but by the expected number
of units $E[n]$.

An alternative estimator is obtained by dividing the π estimator of the population total by the π estimator of the population size:

$$\hat{N} = \sum_{k \in \mathcal{S}} \frac{1}{\pi_k} = n \frac{N}{E[n]} \; . \qquad (5.3)$$

This yields the ratio estimator of the population mean:

$$\hat{\bar{z}}_{\text{ratio}} = \frac{\hat{t}(z)}{\hat{N}} = \frac{1}{n} \sum_{k \in \mathcal{S}} z_k \; . \qquad (5.4)$$

So, the ratio estimator of the population total is equal to the unweighted sample mean. In general, the variance of this ratio estimator is smaller than that of the π estimator. On the other hand the π estimator is design-unbiased, whereas the ratio estimator is not, although its bias can be negligibly small. Only in the very special case where the sample size with systematic random sampling is fixed, the two estimators are equivalent.

Recall that for Voorst we have exhaustive knowledge of the study variable z: values of the soil organic matter (SOM) concentration were simulated for all grid cells. To determine the z-values at the selected sampling points, an overlay of the systematic random sample and the `SpatialPixelsDataFrame` is made, using function `over` of package **sp**.

```
res <- over(mySYsample, grdVoorst)
mySYsample <- as(mySYsample, "data.frame")
mySYsample$z <- res$z
mz_HT <- sum(mySYsample$z) / n
mz_ratio <- mean(mySYsample$z)
```

Using the systematic random sample of Figure 5.1, the π estimated mean SOM concentration equals 69.8 g kg^{-1}, the ratio estimate equals 73.5 g kg^{-1}. The ratio estimate is larger than the π estimate, because the size of the selected sample is two units smaller (38) than the expected sample size (40).

5.2   Approximating the sampling variance of the estimator of the mean

An unbiased estimator of the sampling variance of the estimator of the mean is not available. A simple, often applied procedure is to calculate the sampling variance as if the sample were a simple random sample (Equation (3.14) or

(3.15)). In general, this procedure overestimates the sampling variance, so that we are on the safe side.

```
av_SI_mz <- var(mySYsample$z) / nrow(mySYsample)
```

The approximated variance equals 50.3 $(g\ kg^{-1})^2$.

Alternatively, the sampling variance can be estimated by treating the systematic random sample as if it were a stratified simple random sample (Equation (4.4)). The sampling units are clustered on the basis of their spatial coordinates into $H = n/2$ clusters (n even) or $H = (n-1)/2$ clusters (n odd). In the next code chunk, a simple k-means function is defined to cluster the sampling units of the grid into equal-sized clusters. Arguments s1 and s2 are the spatial coordinates of the sampling units, k is the number of clusters. First, in this function the ids of equal-sized clusters are randomly assigned to the sampling units on the nodes of the sampling grid (initial clustering). Next, the centres of the clusters, i.e., the means of the spatial coordinates of the clusters (initial cluster centres), are computed. There are two for-loops. In the inner loop it is determined whether the cluster id of the unit selected in the outer loop should be swopped with the cluster id of the next unit. If both units have the same cluster id the next unit is selected, until a unit of a different cluster is found. The cluster ids of the two units are swopped when the sum of the squared distances of the two units to their corresponding cluster centres is reduced. When the cluster ids are swopped, the centres are recomputed. The two loops are repeated until no swops are made anymore.

```
.kmeans_equal_size <- function(s1, s2, k) {
  n <- length(s1)
  cluster_id <- rep(1:k, times = ceiling(n / k))
  cluster_id <- cluster_id[1:n]
  cluster_id <- cluster_id[sample(n, size = n)]
  s1_c <- tapply(s1, INDEX = cluster_id, FUN = mean)
  s2_c <- tapply(s2, INDEX = cluster_id, FUN = mean)
  repeat {
    n_swop <- 0
    for (i in 1:(n - 1)) {
      ci <- cluster_id[i]
      for (j in (i + 1):n) {
        cj <- cluster_id[j]
        if (ci == cj) {
          next
        }
        d1 <- (s1[i] - s1_c[ci])^2 + (s2[i] - s2_c[ci])^2 +
          (s1[j] - s1_c[cj])^2 + (s2[j] - s2_c[cj])^2
        d2 <- (s1[i] - s1_c[cj])^2 + (s2[i] - s2_c[cj])^2 +
```

```
            (s1[j] - s1_c[ci])^2 + (s2[j] - s2_c[ci])^2
        if (d1 > d2) {
            #swop cluster ids and recompute cluster centres
            cluster_id[i] <- cj; cluster_id[j] <- ci
            s1_c <- tapply(s1, cluster_id, mean)
            s2_c <- tapply(s2, cluster_id, mean)
            n_swop <- n_swop + 1
            break
        }
      }
    }
    if (n_swop == 0) {
      break
      }
  }
  D <- fields::rdist(x1 = cbind(s1_c, s2_c), x2 = cbind(s1, s2))
  dmin <- apply(D, MARGIN = 2, FUN = min)
  MSSD <- mean(dmin^2)
  list(clusters = cluster_id, MSSD = MSSD)
}
```

The clustering is repeated 100 times (ntry = 100). The clustering with the
smallest mean of the squared distances of the sampling units to their cluster
centres (mean squared shortest distance, MSSD) is selected.

```
kmeans_equal_size <- function(s1, s2, k, ntry) {
  res_opt <- NULL
  MSSD_min <- Inf
  for (i in 1:ntry) {
      res <- .kmeans_equal_size(s1, s2, k)
      if (res$MSSD < MSSD_min) {
        MSSD_min <- res$MSSD
        res_opt <- res
      }
  }
  res_opt
}
n <- nrow(mySYsample); k <- floor(n / 2)
set.seed(314)
res <- kmeans_equal_size(s1 = mySYsample$x1 / 1000, s2 = mySYsample$x2 / 1000,
    k = k, ntry = 100)
mySYsample$cluster <- res$clusters
```

Figure 5.4 shows the clustering of the systematic random sample of Figure 5.1. The two or three sampling units of a cluster are treated as a simple random sample from a stratum, and the variance estimator for stratified random sampling is used. The weights are computed by $w_h = n_h/n$. With n even the stratum weight is $1/H$ for all strata. For more details on variance estimation with stratified simple random sampling, refer to Section 4.1.

```
S2z_h <- tapply(mySYsample$z, INDEX = mySYsample$cluster, FUN = var)
nh <- tapply(mySYsample$z, INDEX = mySYsample$cluster, FUN = length)
v_mz_h <- S2z_h / nh
w_h <- nh / sum(nh)
av_STSI_mz <- sum(w_h^2 * v_mz_h)
```

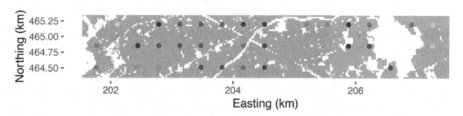

FIGURE 5.4: Clustering of grid points for approximating the variance of the ratio estimator of the mean SOM concentration in Voorst.

This method yields an approximated variance of 51.2 $(g\ kg^{-1})^2$, which is for the selected triangular grid slightly larger than the simple random sample approximation. Hereafter, we will see that on average the stratified simple random sample approximation of the variance is smaller than the simple random sample approximation. For an individual sample, the reverse can be true.

A similar approach for approximating the variance was proposed by Matérn (Matérn, 1947) a long time ago. In this approach the variance is approximated by computing the squared difference of two local means. A local mean is computed by linear interpolation of the observations at the two nodes on the diagonal of a square sampling grid cell. The four corners of a sampling grid cell serve as a group. Every sampling grid node belongs to four groups, and so the observation at a sampling grid node is used four times in computing a local mean. Near the edges of the study area, we have incomplete groups: one, two, or even three observations are missing. To compute a squared difference, these missing values are replaced by the sample mean. This results in as many squared differences as we have groups. Note that the number of groups is larger than the sample size. The squared differences are computed by

$$d_{r,s}^2 = \left(\frac{z_{r,s} + z_{r+1,s+1}}{2} - \frac{z_{r+1,s} + z_{r,s+1}}{2} \right)^2$$

$$= \frac{(z_{r,s} - z_{r+1,s} - z_{r,s+1} + z_{r+1,s+1})^2}{4}, \tag{5.5}$$

with $r = 0, 1, \ldots, R$ an index for the column number and $s = 0, 1, \ldots, S$ an index for the row number of the extended grid. The variance of the estimator of the mean (sample mean) is then approximated by the sum of the squared differences divided by the squared sample size:

$$\hat{V}(\bar{z}_\mathcal{S}) = \frac{\sum_{g=1}^{G} d_g^2}{n^2}, \tag{5.6}$$

with d_g^2 the squared difference of group unit g, and G the total number of groups.

To approximate the variance with Matérn's method, a function is defined.

```
matern <- function(s) {
  g_11 <- within(s, {gr <- i; gs <- j; z11 <- z})[, c("gr", "gs", "z11")]
  g_12 <- within(s, {gr <- i; gs <- j - 1; z12 <- z})[, c("gr", "gs", "z12")]
  g_21 <- within(s, {gr <- i - 1; gs <- j; z21 <- z})[, c("gr", "gs", "z21")]
  g_22 <- within(s, {gr <- i - 1; gs <- j - 1; z22 <- z})[, c("gr", "gs", "z22")]
  g <- Reduce(function(x, y) merge(x = x, y = y, by = c("gr", "gs"), all = TRUE),
              list(g_11, g_12, g_21, g_22))
  g[is.na(g)] <- mean(s$z)
  g <- within(g, T <- (z11 - z12 - z21 + z22)^2 / 4)
  sum(g$T) / ((nrow(s))^2)
}
```

Before using this function the data frame with the sample data must be extended with two variables: an index i for the column number and an index j for the row number of the square grid.

```
mySYsample <- mySYsample %>%
  mutate(
    i = round((x1 - min(x1)) / spacing),
    j = round((x2 - min(x2)) / spacing))
matern(mySYsample)
```

```
[1] 41.63163
```

Figure 5.5 shows the approximated sampling distributions of estimators of the mean SOM concentration for systematic random sampling, using a randomly placed square grid with fixed orientation and an expected sample size of 40, and for simple random sampling, obtained by repeating the random sampling with each design and estimation 10,000 times. To estimate the population mean from the systematic random samples, both the π estimator and the ratio estimator are used.

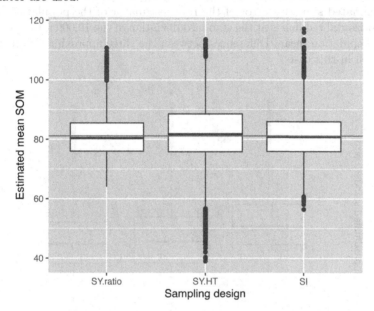

FIGURE 5.5: Approximated sampling distribution of estimators of the mean SOM concentration (g kg^{-1}) in Voorst, for systematic random sampling (square grid) and simple random sampling and an expected sample size of 40. With systematic random sampling, both the π estimator (SY.HT) and the ratio estimator (SY.ratio) are used in estimation.

The boxplots of the estimated means indicate that systematic random sampling in combination with the ratio estimator is more precise than simple random sampling. The variance of the 10,000 ratio estimates equals 49.0 (g kg^{-1})^2, whereas for simple random sampling this variance equals 55.4 (g kg^{-1})^2. Systematic random sampling in combination with the π estimator performs very poorly: the variance equals 142.6 (g kg^{-1})^2. This can be explained by the strong variation in sample size (Figure 5.2), which is not accounted for in the π estimator.

The mean of the 10,000 ratio estimates is 81.2 g kg^{-1}, which is about equal to the population mean 81.1 g kg^{-1}, showing that in this case the design-bias of the ratio estimator is negligibly small indeed.

The average of the 10,000 approximated variances treating the systematic sample as a simple random sample equals 56.4 (g kg^{-1})^2. This is larger than the variance of the ratio estimator (49.0 (g kg^{-1})^2). The stratified simple random sample approximation of the variance somewhat underestimates the variance: the mean of this variance approximation equals 47.1 (g kg^{-1})^2. Also with Matérn's method, the variance is underestimated in this case: the mean of the 10,000 variances equals 45.6 (g kg^{-1})^2. Figure 5.6 shows boxplots of the approximated standard error of the ratio estimator of the population mean. The horizontal red line is at the standard deviation of the 10,000 ratio estimates of the population mean. Differences between the three approximation methods are small in this case.

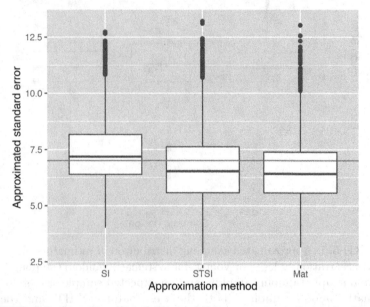

FIGURE 5.6: Sampling distribution of the approximated standard error of the ratio estimator of the mean SOM concentration (g kg^{-1}) in Voorst, with systematic random sampling (square grid) and an expected sample size of 40. Approximations are obtained by treating the systematic sample as a simple random sample (SI) or a stratified simple random sample (STSI), and with Matérn's method (Mat).

The variance of the 10,000 ratio estimates of the population mean with the triangular grid and an expected sample size of 40 equals 46.9 (g kg^{-1})^2. Treating the triangular grid as a simple random sample strongly overestimates the variance: the average approximated variance equals 60.1 (g kg^{-1})^2. The stratified simple random sample approximation performs much better in this case: the average of the 10,000 approximated variances equals 46.8 (g kg^{-1})^2. Matérn's method cannot be used to approximate the variance with a triangular grid.

The approximated variance for this clustering equals round(av_STSI_mz_SYtri,1).

Brus and Saby (2016) compared various variance approximations for systematic random sampling, among which model-based prediction of the variance, using a semivariogram that is estimated from the systematic sample, see Chapter 13.

Exercises

1. One solution to the problem of variance estimation with systematic random sampling is to select multiple systematic random samples independently from each other. So, for instance, instead of one systematic random sample with an expected sample size of 40, we may select two systematic random samples with an expected size of 20.

   - Write an **R** script to select two systematic random samples (random square grids) both with an expected size of 20 from Voorst.
   - Use each sample to estimate the population mean, so that you obtain two estimated means. Overlay the points of each sample with grdVoorst, using function over and extract the z-values.
   - Use the two estimated means to estimate the sampling variance of the estimator of the mean for systematic random sampling *with an expected sample size of 20.*
   - Use the two estimated means to compute a single, final estimate of the population mean, as estimated from *two systematic random samples, each with an expected sample size of 20.*
   - Estimate the sampling variance of the final estimate of the population mean.

2. Do you like this solution? What about the variance of the estimator of the mean, obtained by selecting two systematic random samples of half the expected size, as compared with the variance of the estimator of the mean, obtained with a single systematic random sample? Hint: plot the two random square grids. What do you think of the spatial coverage of the two samples?

6

Cluster random sampling

With stratified random sampling using geographical strata and systematic random sampling, the sampling units are well spread throughout the study area. In general, this leads to an increase of the precision of the estimated mean (total). This is because many spatial populations show spatial structure, so that the values of the study variable at two close units are more similar than those at two distant units. With large study areas the price to be paid for this is long travel times, so that fewer sampling units can be observed in a given survey time. In this situation, it can be more efficient to select *spatial clusters* of population units. In cluster random sampling, once a cluster is selected, *all* units in this cluster are observed. Therefore, this design is also referred to as *single-stage* cluster random sampling. The clusters are not subsampled as in two-stage cluster random sampling (see Chapter 7).

In spatial sampling, a popular cluster shape is a transect. This is because the individual sampling units of a transect can easily be located in the field, which was in particular an advantage in the pre-GPS era.

The implementation of cluster random sampling is not straightforward. Frequently this sampling design is improperly implemented. A proper selection technique is as follows (de Gruijter et al., 2006). In the first step, a starting unit is selected, for instance by simple random sampling. Then the remaining units of the cluster to which the starting unit belongs are identified by making use of the definition of the cluster. For instance, with clusters defined as E-W oriented transects with a spacing of 100 m between the units of a cluster, all units E and W of the starting unit at a distance of 100 m, 200 m, etc. that fall inside the study area are selected. These two steps are repeated until the required number of *clusters*, not the number of units, is selected.

A requirement of a valid selection method is that the same cluster is selected, regardless of which of its units is used as a starting unit. In the example above, this is the case: regardless of which of the units of the transect is selected first, the final set of units selected is the same because, as stated above, all units E and W of the starting unit are selected.

An example of an improper implementation of cluster random sampling is the following selection procedure. A cluster is defined as an E-W oriented transect of four units with a mutual spacing of 100 m. A cluster is selected by randomly selecting a starting unit. The remaining three units of the cluster are selected E of this starting unit. Units outside the study area are ignored. With this selection method, the set of selected units is *not* independent of the starting unit, and therefore this selection method is invalid.

Note that the size, i.e., the number of units, of a cluster need not be constant. With the proper selection method described above, the selection probability of a cluster is proportional to its size. With irregularly shaped study areas, the size of the clusters can vary strongly. The size of the clusters can be controlled by subdividing the study area into blocks, for instance, stripes perpendicular to the direction of the transects, or square blocks in case the clusters are grids. In this case, the remaining units are identified by extending the transect or grid to the boundary of the block. With irregularly shaped areas, blocking will not entirely eliminate the variation in cluster sizes.

Cluster random sampling is illustrated with the selection of E-W oriented transects in Voorst. In order to delimit the length of the transects, the study area is split into six 1 km × 1 km zones. In this case, the zones have an equal size, but this is not needed. Note that these zones do not serve as strata. When used as strata, from each zone, one or more clusters would be selected, see Section 6.4.

In the code chunk below, function findInterval of the **base** package is used to determine for all discretisation points in which zone they fall.

```
cell_size <- 25
w <- 1000 #width of zones
grdVoorst <- grdVoorst %>%
    mutate(zone = s1 %>% findInterval(min(s1) + 1:5 * w + 0.5 * cell_size))
```

As a first step in the **R** code below, variable cluster is added to grdVoorst indicating to which cluster a unit belongs. Note that each unit belongs exactly to one cluster. The operator %% computes the modulus of the s1-coordinate and the spacing of units within a transect (cluster). Function stringr of package **stringr** (Wickham, 2019) joins the resulting vector, the vector with the s2-coordinate, and the vector with the zone into a single character vector. The sizes of the clusters are computed with function tapply.

```
spacing <- 100
grdVoorst <- grdVoorst %>%
    mutate(
        cluster = str_c(
            (s1 - min(s1)) %% spacing,
            s2 - min(s2),
```

```
            zone, sep = "_"),
        unit = row_number())
M_cl <- tapply(grdVoorst$z, INDEX = grdVoorst$cluster, FUN = length)
```

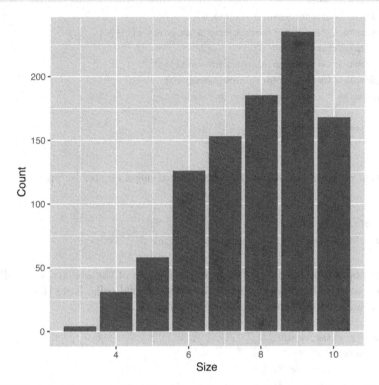

FIGURE 6.1: Frequency distribution of the size of clusters in Voorst. Clusters are E-W oriented transects within zones, with a spacing of 100 m between units.

In total, there are 960 clusters in the population. Figure 6.1 shows the frequency distribution of the size of the clusters.

Clusters are selected with probabilities proportional to their size and with replacement (ppswr). So, the sizes of all clusters must be known, which explains that all clusters must be enumerated. Selection of clusters by ppswr can be done by simple random sampling with replacement of elementary units (centres of grid cells) and identifying the clusters to which these units belong. Finally, all units of the selected clusters are included in the sample. In the code chunk below, a function is defined for selecting clusters by ppswr. Note variable cldraw, that has value 1 for all units selected in the first draw, value 2 for all units selected in the second draw, etc. This variable is needed in estimating the population mean, as explained in Section 6.1.

```
cl_ppswr <- function(sframe, n) {
  units <- sample(nrow(sframe), size = n, replace = TRUE)
  units_cl <- sframe$cluster[units]
  mysamples <- NULL
  for (i in seq_len(length(units_cl))) {
    mysample <- sframe[sframe$cluster %in% units_cl[i], ]
    mysample$start <- 0
    mysample$start[mysample$unit %in% units[i]] <- 1
    mysample$cldraw <- rep(i, nrow(mysample))
    mysamples <- rbind(mysamples, mysample)
  }
  mysamples
}
```

Function cl_ppswr is now used to select six times a cluster by ppswr.

```
n <- 6
set.seed(314)
mysample <- cl_ppswr(sframe = grdVoorst, n = n)
```

As our population actually is infinite, the centres of the selected grid cells are jittered to a random point within the selected grid cells. Note that the same noise is added to all units of a given cluster.

```
mysample <- mysample %>%
  group_by(cldraw) %>%
  mutate(s1 = s1 + runif(1, min = -12.5, max = 12.5),
         s2 = s2 + runif(1, min = -12.5, max = 12.5))
```

Figure 6.2 shows the selected sample. Note that in this case the second west-most zone has two transects (clusters), whereas one zone has none, showing that the zones are not used as strata. The total number of selected points equals 50. Similar to systematic random sampling, with cluster random sampling the total sample size is random, so that we do not have perfect control of the total sample size. This is because in this case the size, i.e., the number of points, of the clusters is not constant but varies.

The output data frame of function cl has a variable named start. This is an indicator with value 1 if this point of the cluster is selected first, and 0 otherwise. When in the field, it appears that the first selected point of a cluster does not belong to the target population, all other points of that cluster are also discarded. This is to keep the selection probabilities of the clusters exactly proportional to their size. Column cldraw is needed in estimation because clusters are selected with replacement. In case a cluster is selected more than once, multiple means of that cluster are used in estimation, see next section.

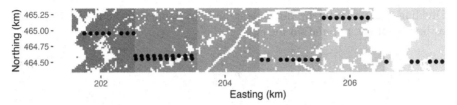

FIGURE 6.2: Cluster random sample from Voorst selected by ppswr.

6.1 Estimation of population parameters

With ppswr sampling of clusters, the population total can be estimated by the pwr estimator:

$$\hat{t}(z) = \frac{1}{n} \sum_{j \in \mathcal{S}} \frac{t_j(z)}{p_j} \,, \tag{6.1}$$

with n the number of cluster draws, p_j the draw-by-draw selection probability of cluster j, and $t_j(z)$ the total of cluster j:

$$t_j(z) = \sum_{k=1}^{M_j} z_{kj} \,, \tag{6.2}$$

with M_j the size (number of units) of cluster j and z_{kj} the study variable value of unit k in cluster j.

The draw-by-draw selection probability of a cluster equals

$$p_j = \frac{M_j}{M} \,, \tag{6.3}$$

with M the total number of population units (for Voorst M equals 7,528). Inserting this in Equation (6.1) yields

$$\hat{t}(z) = \frac{M}{n} \sum_{j \in \mathcal{S}} \frac{t_j(z)}{M_j} = \frac{M}{n} \sum_{j \in \mathcal{S}} \bar{z}_j \,, \tag{6.4}$$

with $\bar{z}_j$ the mean of cluster j. Note that if a cluster is selected more than once, multiple means of that cluster are used in the estimator.

Dividing this estimator by the total number of population units, M, yields the estimator of the population mean:

$$\hat{\bar{z}} = \frac{1}{n} \sum_{j \in \mathcal{S}} \bar{z}_j \; . \tag{6.5}$$

Note the two bars in $\hat{\bar{z}}$, indicating that the observations are averaged twice.

For an infinite population of points discretised by the centres of a finite number of grid cells, z_{kj} in Equation (6.2) is the study variable value at a randomly selected point within the grid cell multiplied by the area of the grid cell. The estimated population total thus obtained is equal to the estimated population mean (Equation (6.5)) multiplied by the area of the study area.

The sampling variance of the estimator of the mean with ppswr sampling of clusters is equal to (Cochran (1977), equation (9A.6))

$$V(\hat{\bar{z}}) = \frac{1}{n} \sum_{j=1}^{N} \frac{M_j}{M} (\bar{z}_j - \bar{z})^2 \; , \tag{6.6}$$

with N the total number of clusters (for Voorst, $N = 960$), $\bar{z}_j$ the mean of cluster j, and $\bar{z}$ the population mean. Note that M_j/M is the selection probability of cluster j.

This sampling variance can be estimated by (Cochran (1977), equation (9A.22))

$$\hat{V}\left(\hat{\bar{z}}\right) = \frac{\widehat{S^2}(\bar{z})}{n} \; , \tag{6.7}$$

where $\widehat{S^2}(\bar{z})$ is the estimated variance of cluster means (the between-cluster variance):

$$\widehat{S^2}(\bar{z}) = \frac{1}{n-1} \sum_{j \in \mathcal{S}} (\bar{z}_j - \hat{\bar{z}})^2 \; . \tag{6.8}$$

In **R** the population mean and the sampling variance of the estimator of the population means can be estimated as follows.

```
est <- mysample %>%
  group_by(cldraw) %>%
  summarise(mz_cl = mean(z)) %>%
  summarise(mz = mean(mz_cl),
            se_mz = sqrt(var(mz_cl) / n()))
```

The estimated mean equals 87.1 g kg^{-1}, and the estimated standard error equals 17.4 g kg^{-1}. Note that the size of the clusters does not appear in these formulas. This simplicity is due to the fact that the clusters are selected with probabilities proportional to size. The effect of the cluster size on the variance is implicitly accounted for. To understand this, consider that larger clusters result in smaller variance among their means.

The same estimates are obtained with functions svydesign and svymean of package **survey** (Lumley, 2021). Argument weights specifies the weights of the sampled clusters equal to $M/(M_j\ n)$ (Equation (6.4)).

```
library(survey)
M <- nrow(grdVoorst)
mysample$weights <- M / (M_cl[mysample$cluster] * n)
design_cluster <- svydesign(id = ~ cldraw, weights = ~ weights, data = mysample)
svymean(~ z, design_cluster, deff = "replace")
```

```
      mean     SE   DEff
z 87.077 17.428 4.0767
```

The design effect DEff as estimated from the selected cluster sample is considerably larger than 1. About 4 times more sampling points are needed with cluster random sampling compared to simple random sampling to estimate the population mean with the same precision.

A confidence interval estimate of the population mean can be computed with method confint. The number of degrees of freedom equals the number of cluster draws minus 1.

```
confint(svymean(~ z, design_cluster, df = degf(design_cluster), level = 0.95))
```

```
      2.5 %    97.5 %
z 52.91908 121.2347
```

Figure 6.3 shows the approximated sampling distribution of the pwr estimator of the mean soil organic matter (SOM) concentration with cluster random sampling and of the π estimator with simple random sampling, obtained by repeating the random sampling with each design and estimation 10,000 times. The size of the simple random samples is equal to the expected sample size of the cluster random sampling design (rounded to nearest integer).

The variance of the 10,000 estimated population means with cluster random sampling equals 126.2 (g kg^{-1})^2. This is considerably larger than with simple random sampling: 44.8 (g kg^{-1})^2. The large variance is caused by the strong spatial clustering of points. This may save travel time in large study areas, but in Voorst the saved travel time will be very limited, and therefore cluster random sampling in Voorst is not a good idea. The average of the estimated variances with cluster random sampling equals 125.9 (g kg^{-1})^2. The difference with the variance of the 10,000 estimated means is small because the estimator of the variance, Equation (6.7), is unbiased. Figure 6.4 shows the approximated

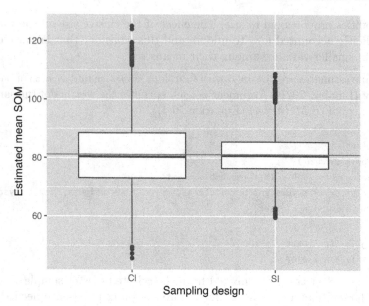

FIGURE 6.3: Approximated sampling distribution of the pwr estimator of the mean SOM concentration (g kg^{-1}) in Voorst with cluster random sampling (Cl) and of the π estimator with simple random sampling (SI). In Cl six clusters are selected by ppswr. The (expected) sample size is 49 units.

sampling distribution of the sample size. The expected sample size can be computed as follows:

```
p <- M_cl / sum(M_cl)
print(m_n <- n * sum(p * M_cl))
```

```
[1] 49.16844
```

So, the unequal draw-by-draw selection probabilities of the clusters are accounted for in computing the expected sample size.

Exercises

1. Write an **R** script to compute the true sampling variance of the estimator of the mean SOM concentration in Voorst for cluster random sampling and clusters selected with ppswr, $n = 6$, see Equation (6.6). Compare the sampling variance for cluster random sampling with the sampling variance for simple random sampling with a sample size equal to the expected sample size of cluster random sampling.

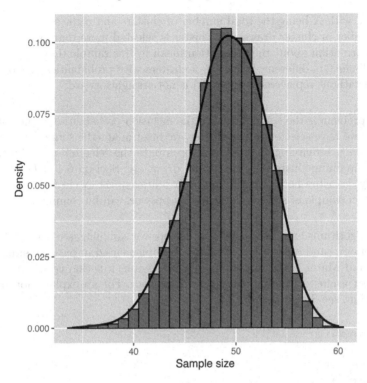

FIGURE 6.4: Approximated sampling distribution of the sample size with cluster random sampling from Voorst, for six clusters selected by ppswr.

2. As an alternative we may select three times a transect, using three 2 km × 1 km zones obtained by joining two neighbouring 1 km × 1 km zones of Figure 6.2. Do you expect that the sampling variance of the estimator of the population mean is equal to, larger or smaller than that of the sampling design with six transects of half the length?

6.2 Clusters selected with probabilities proportional to size, without replacement

In the previous section the clusters were selected with replacement (ppswr). The advantage of sampling with replacement is that this keeps the statistical inference simple, more specifically the estimation of the standard error of the estimator of the population mean. However, in sampling from finite populations, cluster sampling with replacement is less efficient than cluster sampling without replacement, especially with large sampling fractions of clusters, i.e., if $1 - n/N$

is small, with N being the total number of clusters and n the sample size, i.e., the number of cluster draws. If a cluster is selected more than once, there is less information about the population mean in this sample than in a sample with all clusters different. Selection of clusters with probabilities proportional to size without replacement (ppswor) is not straightforward.

The problem is the computation of the inclusion probabilities of the clusters. After we have selected a first cluster, we must adapt the sum of the sizes of the $N-1$ remaining clusters and recompute the selection probabilities of the remaining clusters in the second draw, etc. Section 6.4 of Lohr (1999) nicely describes how the inclusion probabilities of the N clusters in a cluster random sample of size two, selected by ppswor, can be computed.

Many algorithms have been developed for ppswor sampling, see Tillé (2006) for an overview, and quite a few of them are implemented in package **sampling** (Tillé and Matei, 2021). In the next code chunk, function UPpivotal is used to select a cluster random sample with ppswor. For an explanation of this algorithm, see Subsection 8.2.2.

```
library(sampling)
n <- 6
pi <- n * M_cl / M
set.seed(314)
eps <- 1e-6
sampleind <- UPpivotal(pik = pi, eps = eps)
clusters <- sort(unique(grdVoorst$cluster))
clusters_sampled <- clusters[sampleind == 1]
mysample <- grdVoorst[grdVoorst$cluster %in% clusters_sampled, ]
```

The population mean can be estimated by the π estimator by writing a few lines of **R** code yourself or by using function svymean of package **survey** as shown hereafter. Estimation of the sampling variance in pps sampling of clusters without replacement is difficult[1]. A simple solution is to treat the cluster sample as a ppswr sample and to estimate the variance with Equation (6.7). With small sampling fractions, this variance approximation is fine: the overestimation of the variance is negligible. For larger sampling fractions, various alternative variance approximations are developed, see Berger (2004) for details. One of the methods is Brewer's method, which is implemented in function svydesign.

```
mysample$pi <- n * M_cl[mysample$cluster] / M
design_clppswor <- svydesign(
```

---

[1]The problem is the computation of the joint inclusion probabilities of pairs of points.

```
 id = ~ cluster, data = mysample, pps = "brewer", fpc = ~ pi)
svymean(~ z, design_clppswor)
```

```
    mean    SE
z 96.83 13.454
```

Another variance estimator implemented in function svydesign is the Hartley-Rao estimator. The two estimated standard errors are nearly equal.

```
p2sum <- sum((n * M_cl[mysample$cluster] / M)^2) / n
design_hr <- svydesign(
  id = ~ cluster, data = mysample, pps = HR(p2sum), fpc = ~ pi)
svymean(~ z, design_hr)
```

```
    mean    SE
z 96.83 13.436
```

6.3 Simple random sampling of clusters

Suppose the clusters have unequal size, but we do not know the size of the clusters, so that we cannot select the clusters with probabilities proportional to their size. In this case, we may select the clusters by simple random sampling without replacement. The inclusion probability of a cluster equals n/N with n the number of selected clusters and N the total number of clusters in the population. This yields the following π estimator of the population total:

$$\hat{t}(z) = \frac{N}{n} \sum_{j \in \mathcal{S}} t_j(z) . \tag{6.9}$$

The population mean can be estimated by dividing this estimator of the population total by the total number of units in the population M:

$$\hat{\bar{z}}_\pi(z) = \frac{\hat{t}(z)}{M} . \tag{6.10}$$

Alternatively, we may estimate the population mean by dividing the estimate of the population total by the *estimated* population size:

$$\widehat{M} = \sum_{j \in \mathcal{S}} \frac{M_j}{\pi_j} = \frac{N}{n} \sum_{j \in \mathcal{S}} M_j . \tag{6.11}$$

This leads to the ratio estimator of the population mean:

$$\hat{\bar{z}}_{\text{ratio}}(z) = \frac{\hat{t}(z)}{\widehat{M}} \ . \tag{6.12}$$

The π estimator and the ratio estimator are equal when the clusters are selected with probabilities proportional to size. This is because the estimated population size is equal to the true population size.

```
print(M_HT <- sum(1 / mysample$pi))
```

```
[1] 7528
```

However, when clusters of different size are selected with equal probabilities, the two estimators are different. This is shown below. Six clusters are selected by simple random sampling without replacement.

```
set.seed(314)
clusters <- sort(unique(grdVoorst$cluster))
units_cl <- sample(length(clusters), size = n, replace = FALSE)
clusters_sampled <- clusters[units_cl]
mysample <- grdVoorst[grdVoorst$cluster %in% clusters_sampled, ]
```

The π estimate and the ratio estimate of the population mean are computed for the selected sample.

```
N <- length(clusters)
mysample$pi <- n / N
tz_HT <- sum(mysample$z / mysample$pi)
mz_HT <- tz_HT / M
M_HT <- sum(1 / mysample$pi)
mz_ratio <- tz_HT / M_HT
```

The π estimate equals 68.750 g kg^{-1}, and the ratio estimate equals 70.319 g kg^{-1}. The π estimate of the population mean can also be computed by first computing totals of clusters, see Equations (6.9) and (6.10).

```
tz_cluster <- tapply(mysample$z, INDEX = mysample$cluster, FUN = sum)
pi_cluster <- n / N
tz_HT <- sum(tz_cluster / pi_cluster)
print(mz_HT <- tz_HT / M)
```

```
[1] 68.74994
```

The variance of the π estimator of the population mean can be estimated by first estimating the variance of the estimator of the total:

$$\hat{V}(\hat{t}(z)) = N^2 \left(1 - \frac{n}{N}\right) \frac{\widehat{S^2}(t(z))}{n} \, , \tag{6.13}$$

and dividing this variance by the squared number of population units:

$$\hat{V}(\hat{\bar{z}}) = \frac{1}{M^2} \hat{V}(\hat{t}(z)) \, . \tag{6.14}$$

```
fpc <- 1 - n / N
v_tz <- N^2 * fpc * var(tz_cluster) / n
se_mz_HT <- sqrt(v_tz / M^2)
```

The estimated standard error equals 11.5 g kg^{-1}.

To compute the variance of the ratio estimator of the population mean, we first compute residuals of cluster totals:

$$e_j = t_j(z) - \hat{b}M_j \, , \tag{6.15}$$

with $\hat{b}$ the ratio of the estimated population mean of the cluster totals to the estimated population mean of the cluster sizes:

$$\hat{b} = \frac{\frac{1}{n} \sum_{j \in \mathcal{S}} t_j}{\frac{1}{n} \sum_{j \in \mathcal{S}} M_j} \, . \tag{6.16}$$

The variance of the ratio estimator of the population mean can be estimated by

$$\hat{V}(\hat{\bar{z}}_{\text{ratio}}) = \left(1 - \frac{n}{N}\right) \frac{1}{(\frac{1}{n} \sum_{j \in \mathcal{S}} M_j)^2} \frac{\widehat{S^2}_e}{n} \, , \tag{6.17}$$

with $\widehat{S^2}_e$ the estimated variance of the residuals.

```
m_M_cl <- mean(M_cl[unique(mysample$cluster)])
b <- mean(tz_cluster) / m_M_cl
e_cl <- tz_cluster - b * M_cl[sort(unique(mysample$cluster))]
S2e <- var(e_cl)
print(se_mz_ratio <- sqrt(fpc * 1 / m_M_cl^2 * S2e / n))
```

```
[1] 12.39371
```

The ratio estimate can also be computed with function svymean of package **survey**, which also provides an estimate of the standard error of the estimated mean.

```
design_SIC <- svydesign(
    id = ~ cluster, probs = ~ pi, fpc = ~ pi, data = mysample)
svymean(~ z, design_SIC)
```

```
      mean     SE
z 70.319 12.394
```

6.4   Stratified cluster random sampling

The basic sampling designs stratified random sampling (Chapter 4) and cluster random sampling can be combined into stratified cluster random sampling. So, instead of selecting simple random samples from the strata, within each stratum clusters are randomly selected. Figure 6.5 shows a stratified cluster random sample from Voorst. The strata consist of three 2 km × 1 km zones, obtained by joining two neighbouring 1 km × 1 km zones (Figure 6.2). The clusters are the same as before, i.e., E-W oriented transects within 1 km × 1 km zones, with an inter-unit spacing of 100 m. Within each stratum, two times a cluster is selected by ppswr. The stratification avoids the clustering of the selected transects in one part of the study area. Compared to (unstratified) cluster random sampling, the geographical spreading of the clusters is improved, which may lead to an increase of the precision of the estimated population mean. In Figure 6.5 and in the most western stratum, the two selected transects are in the same 1 km × 1 km zone. The alternative would be to use the six zones as strata, leading to an improved spreading of the clusters, but there is also a downside with this design, see Exercise 3. Note that the selection probabilities are now equal to

$$p_{jh} = M_j/M_h ,$$ (6.18)

with M_h the total number of population units of stratum h.

```
grdVoorst$zone_stratum <- as.factor(grdVoorst$zone)
levels(grdVoorst$zone_stratum) <- rep(c("a", "b", "c"), each = 2)
n_h <- c(2, 2, 2)
set.seed(324)
stratumlabels <- unique(grdVoorst$zone_stratum)
```

```
mysample <- NULL
for (i in 1:3) {
  grd_h <- grdVoorst[grdVoorst$zone_stratum == stratumlabels[i], ]
  mysample_h <- cl_ppswr(sframe = grd_h, n = n_h[i])
  mysample <- rbind(mysample, mysample_h)
}
```

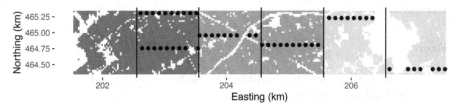

FIGURE 6.5: Stratified cluster random sample from Voorst, with three strata. From each stratum two times a cluster is selected by ppswr.

The population mean is estimated by first estimating the stratum means using Equation (6.5) at the level of the strata, followed by computing the weighted average of the estimated stratum means using Equation (4.3). The variance of the estimator of the population mean is estimated in the same way, by first estimating the variance of the estimator of the stratum means using Equations (6.7) and (6.8) at the level of the strata, followed by computing the weighted average of the estimated variances of the estimated stratum means (Equation (4.4)).

```
strata_size <- grdVoorst %>%
  group_by(zone_stratum) %>%
  summarise(M_h = n()) %>%
  mutate(w_h = M_h / sum(M_h))
est <- mysample %>%
  group_by(zone_stratum, cldraw) %>%
  summarise(mz_cl = mean(z), .groups = "drop_last") %>%
  summarise(mz_h = mean(mz_cl),
            v_mz_h = var(mz_cl) / n()) %>%
  left_join(strata_size, by = "zone_stratum") %>%
  summarise(mz = sum(w_h * mz_h),
            se_mz = sqrt(sum(w_h^2 * v_mz_h)))
```

The estimated mean equals 82.8 g kg^{-1}, and the estimated standard error equals 4.7 g kg^{-1}. The same estimates are obtained with function svymean. Weights for the clusters are computed as before, but now at the level of the strata. Note argument nest = TRUE, which means that the clusters are nested within the strata.

```
mysample$weights <- strata_size$M_h[mysample$zone_stratum] /
  (M_cl[mysample$cluster] * n_h[mysample$zone_stratum])
design_strcluster <- svydesign(id = ~ cldraw, strata = ~ zone_stratum,
  weights = ~ weights, data = mysample, nest = TRUE)
svymean(~ z, design_strcluster)
```

```
    mean     SE
z 82.796 4.6737
```

Exercises

3. Why is it attractive in stratified random cluster sampling to select at least two clusters per stratum?

7

Two-stage cluster random sampling

As opposed to cluster random sampling in which all population units of a cluster are observed (Chapter 6), in two-stage cluster random sampling not all units of the selected clusters are observed, but only some. In two-stage cluster random sampling the clusters will generally be contiguous groups of units, for instance all points in a map polygon (the polygons on the map are the clusters), whereas in single-stage cluster random sampling the clusters generally are non-contiguous. The units to be observed are selected by random subsampling of the randomly selected clusters. In two-stage cluster sampling, the clusters are commonly referred to as primary sampling units (PSUs) and the units selected in the second stage as the secondary sampling units (SSUs).

As with cluster random sampling, two-stage cluster random sampling may lead to a strong spatial clustering of the selected population units in the study area. This may save considerable time for fieldwork, and more population units can be observed for the same budget. However, due to the spatial clustering the estimates will generally be less precise compared to samples of the same size selected by a design that leads to a much better spreading of the sampling units throughout the study area, such as systematic random sampling.

In two-stage cluster random sampling, in principle any type of sampling design can be used at the two stages, leading to numerous combinations. An example is (SI,SI), in which both PSUs and SSUs are selected by simple random sampling.

Commonly, the PSUs have unequal size, i.e., the number of SSUs (finite population) or the area (infinite population) are not equal for all PSUs. Think for instance of the agricultural fields, forest stands, lakes, river sections, etc. in an area. If the PSUs are of unequal size, then PSUs can best be selected with probabilities proportional to their size (pps). Recall that in (one-stage) cluster random sampling, I also recommended to select the clusters with probabilities proportional to their size, see Chapter 6. If the total of the study variable of a PSU is proportional to its size, then pps sampling leads to more precise estimates compared to simple random sampling of PSUs. Also, with pps sampling of PSUs, the estimation of means or totals and of their sampling variances is much simpler compared to selection with equal probabilities. Implementation of selection with probabilities proportional to size is easiest when units are replaced (pps with replacement, ppswr). This implies that a PSU might be selected more than once, especially if the total number of PSUs in the population is small compared to the number of PSU draws (large sampling fraction in first stage).

Using a list as a sampling frame, the following algorithm can be used to select n times a PSU by ppswr from a total of N PSUs in the population:

1. Select randomly one SSU from the list with $M = \sum_{j=1}^{N} M_j$ SSUs (M_j is the number of SSUs of PSU j), and determine the PSU of the selected SSU.

2. Repeat step 1 until n selections have been made.

In the first stage, an SSU is selected in order to select a PSU. This may seem unnecessarily complicated. The reason for this is that this procedure automatically adjusts for the size of the PSUs (number of SSUs within a PSU), i.e., a PSU is selected with probability proportional to its size. In the second stage, a pre-determined number of SSUs, m_j, is selected every time PSU j is selected.

Note that the SSU selected in the first step of the two algorithms primarily serves to identify the PSU, but these SSUs can also be used as selected SSUs.

The selection of a two-stage cluster random sample is illustrated again with Voorst. Twenty-four 0.5 km squares are constructed that serve as PSUs.

> Due to built-up areas, roads, etc., the PSUs in Voorst have unequal size, i.e., the number of SSUs (points, in our case) within the PSUs varies among the PSUs.

```
cell_size <- 25
w <- 500 #width of zones
grdVoorst <- grdVoorst %>%
    mutate(zone_s1 = s1 %>% findInterval(min(s1) + 1:11 * w + 0.5 * cell_size),
           zone_s2 = s2 %>% findInterval(min(s2) + w + 0.5 * cell_size),
           psu = str_c(zone_s1, zone_s2, sep = "_"))
```

In the next code chunk, a function is defined to select a two-stage cluster random sample from an infinite population, discretised by a finite number of points, being the centres of grid cells.

```
twostage <- function(sframe, psu, n, m) {
  units <- sample(nrow(sframe), size = n, replace = TRUE)
  mypsusample <- sframe[units, psu]
```

```
ssunits <- NULL
for (psunit in mypsusample) {
  ssunit <- sample(
    x = which(sframe[, psu] == psunit), size = m, replace = TRUE)
  ssunits <- c(ssunits, ssunit)
}
psudraw <- rep(c(1:n), each = m)
mysample <- data.frame(ssunits, sframe[ssunits, ], psudraw)
mysample
}
```

Note that both the PSUs and the SSUs are selected with replacement. If a grid cell centre is selected, one point is selected fully randomly from that grid cell. This is done by shifting the centre of the grid cell to a random point within the selected grid cell with function jitter, see code chunk hereafter. In every grid cell, there is an infinite number of points, so we must select the grid cell centres with replacement. If a grid cell is selected more than once, more than one point is selected from the associated grid cell. Column psudraw in the output data frame of function twostage is needed in estimation because PSUs are selected with replacement. In case a PSU is selected more than once, multiple estimates of the mean of that PSU are used in estimation, see next section.

In the next code chunk, function twostage is used to select four times a PSU ($n = 4$), with probabilities proportional to size and with replacement (ppswr). The second stage sample size equals 10 for all PSUs ($m_j = 10$, $j = 1, ..., N$). These SSUs are selected by simple random sampling.

```
n <- 4
m <- 10
cell_size <- 25
set.seed(314)
mysample <- grdVoorst %>%
  twostage(psu = "psu", n = n, m = m) %>%
  mutate(s1 = s1 %>% jitter(amount = cell_size / 2),
         s2 = s2 %>% jitter(amount = cell_size / 2))
```

Figure 7.1 shows the selected sample.

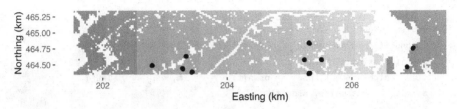

FIGURE 7.1: Two-stage cluster random sample from Voorst. PSUs are 0.5 km squares, built-up areas, roads, etc. excluded. Four times a PSU is selected by ppswr. Each time a PSU is selected, ten SSUs (points) are selected from that PSU by simple random sampling.

7.1 Estimation of population parameters

The population total can be estimated by substituting the estimated cluster (PSU) totals in Equation (6.4). This yields the following estimator for the population total:

$$\hat{t}(z) = \frac{M}{n} \sum_{j \in \mathcal{S}} \frac{\hat{t}_j(z)}{M_j} = \frac{M}{n} \sum_{j \in \mathcal{S}} \hat{\bar{z}}_j \ , \tag{7.1}$$

where n is the number of PSU selections and M_j is the total number of SSUs in PSU j. This shows that the mean of cluster j, $\bar{z}_j$, is replaced by the estimated mean of PSU j, $\hat{\bar{z}}_j$. Dividing this estimator by the total number of population units M gives the pwr estimator of the population mean:

$$\hat{\bar{z}} = \frac{1}{n} \sum_{j \in \mathcal{S}} \hat{\bar{z}}_j \ , \tag{7.2}$$

with $\hat{\bar{z}}_j$ the estimated mean of the PSU j. With simple random sampling of SSUs, this mean can be estimated by the sample mean of this PSU. Note the two bars in $\hat{\bar{z}}$, indicating that the population mean is estimated as the mean of estimated PSU means. When m_j is equal for all PSUs, the sampling design is self-weighting, i.e., the average of z over all selected SSUs is an unbiased estimator of the population mean.

For an infinite population of points, the population total is estimated by multiplying the estimated population mean (Equation (7.2)) by the area of the study area.

The sampling variance of the estimator of the mean with two-stage cluster random sampling, PSUs selected with probabilities proportional to size with replacement, SSUs selected by simple random sampling, with replacement in case of finite populations, and $m_j = m$, $j = 1, ..., N$, is equal to (Cochran (1977), equation (11.33)[1])

$$V(\hat{\bar{z}}) = \frac{S_{\mathrm{b}}^2}{n} + \frac{S_{\mathrm{w}}^2}{n\,m} , \qquad (7.3)$$

with

$$S_{\mathrm{b}}^2 = \sum_{j=1}^{N} p_j \left(\bar{z}_j - \bar{z}\right)^2 \qquad (7.4)$$

and

$$S_{\mathrm{w}}^2 = \sum_{j=1}^{N} p_j S_j^2 , \qquad (7.5)$$

with N the total number of PSUs in the population, $p_j = M_j/M$ the draw-by-draw selection probability of PSU j, $\bar{z}_j$ the mean of PSU j, $\bar{z}$ the population mean of z, and S_j^2 the variance of z within PSU j:

$$S_j^2 = \frac{1}{M_j} \sum_{k=1}^{M_j} (z_{kj} - \bar{z}_j)^2 . \qquad (7.6)$$

The first term of Equation (7.3) is equal to the variance of Equation (6.6). This variance component accounts for the variance of the true PSU means within the population. The second variance component quantifies our additional uncertainty about the population mean, as we do not observe all SSUs of the selected PSUs, but only a subset (sample) of these units.

The sampling variance of the estimator of the population mean can simply be estimated by

$$\hat{V}(\hat{\bar{z}}) = \frac{\widehat{S^2}(\hat{\bar{z}})}{n} , \qquad (7.7)$$

with $\widehat{S^2}(\hat{\bar{z}})$ the estimated variance of the *estimated* PSU means:

$$\widehat{S^2}(\hat{\bar{z}}) = \frac{1}{n-1} \sum_{j \in \mathcal{S}} (\hat{\bar{z}}_j - \hat{\bar{z}})^2 , \qquad (7.8)$$

---

[1]Equation (11.33) in Cochran (1977) is the variance estimator for the estimator of the population total. In Exercise 5 you are asked to derive the variance estimator for the estimator of the population mean from this variance estimator.

with $\hat{\bar{z}}_j$ the estimated mean of PSU j and $\hat{\bar{z}}$ the estimated population mean (Equation (7.2)).

> Neither the sizes of the PSUs, M_j, nor the secondary sample sizes m_j occur in Equations (7.7) and (7.8). This simplicity is due to the fact that the PSUs are selected with replacement and with probabilities proportional to their size. The effect of the secondary sample sizes on the variance is implicitly accounted for. To understand this, note that the larger m_j, the less variable $\hat{\bar{z}}_j$, and the smaller its contribution to the variance.

Let us assume a linear model for the total costs: $C = c_0 + c_1 n + c_2 nm$, with c_0 the fixed costs, c_1 the costs per PSU, and c_2 the costs per SSU. We want to minimise the total costs, under the constraint that the variance of the estimator of the population mean may not exceed V_{max}. The total costs can then be minimised by selecting (de Gruijter et al., 2006)

$$n = \frac{1}{V_{max}} \left(S_w S_b \sqrt{\frac{c_2}{c_1}} + S_b^2 \right) \tag{7.9}$$

PSUs and

$$m = \frac{S_w}{S_b} \sqrt{\frac{c_1}{c_2}} \tag{7.10}$$

SSUs per PSU.

Conversely, given a budget C_{max}, the optimal number of PSU selections can be computed with (de Gruijter et al., 2006)

$$n = \frac{C_{max} S_b}{S_w \sqrt{c_1 c_2} + S_b c_1}, \tag{7.11}$$

and m as above.

In **R** the population mean and the sampling variance of the estimator of the mean can be estimated as follows.

```
est <- mysample %>%
  group_by(psudraw) %>%
  summarise(mz_psu = mean(z)) %>%
  summarise(mz = mean(mz_psu),
            se_mz = sqrt(var(mz_psu) / n()))
```

The estimated mean equals 48.6 g kg^{-1}, and the estimated standard error equals 0.0 g kg^{-1}. The sampling design is self-weighting, and so the estimated mean is equal to the sample mean.

```
print(mean(mysample$z))
```

```
[1] 48.55792
```

The same estimate is obtained with functions svydesign and svymean of package **survey** (Lumley, 2021). The estimator of the population total can be written as a weighted sum of the observations with all weights equal to $M/(n\ m)$. These weights are passed to function svydesign with argument weight.

```
library(survey)
M <- nrow(grdVoorst)
mysample$weights <- M / (n * m)
design_2stage <- svydesign(
    id = ~ psudraw + ssunits, weight = ~ weights, data = mysample)
svymean(~ z, design_2stage, deff = "replace")
```

```
      mean     SE DEff
z 48.558  0.000    0
```

Similar to (one-stage) cluster random sampling, the estimated design effect is much larger than 1.

A confidence interval estimate of the population mean can be computed with method confint. The number of degrees of freedom equals the number of PSU draws minus 1.

```
confint(svymean(~ z, design_2stage, df = degf(design_2stage), level = 0.95))
```

```
      2.5 %    97.5 %
z 48.55792 48.55792
```

Figure 7.2 shows the approximated sampling distribution of the pwr estimator of the mean soil organic matter (SOM) concentration with two-stage cluster random sampling and of the π estimator with simple random sampling from Voorst, obtained by repeating the random sampling with each design and estimation 10,000 times. For simple random sampling the sample size is equal to $n \times m$.

The variance of the 10,000 means with two-stage cluster random sampling equals 179.6 (g kg^{-1})^2. This is considerably larger than with simple random

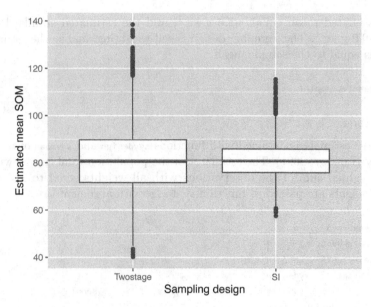

FIGURE 7.2: Approximated sampling distribution of the pwr estimator of the mean SOM concentration (g kg^{-1}) in Voorst with two-stage cluster random sampling (Twostage) and of the π estimator with simple random sampling (SI). The sample size with both sampling designs is 40. In two-stage sampling, four times a PSU is selected by ppswr and ten SSUs (points) are selected per PSU draw by simple random sampling.

sampling: 56.3 (g kg^{-1})^2. The average of the estimated variances with two-stage cluster random sampling equals 182.5 (g kg^{-1})^2.

Optimal sample sizes for two-stage cluster random sampling (ppswr in first stage, simple random sampling without replacement in second stage) can be computed with function clusOpt2 of **R** package **PracTools** (Valliant et al. (2021), Valliant et al. (2018)). This function requires as input various variance measures, which can be computed with function BW2stagePPS, in case the study variable is known for the whole population or estimated from a sample with function BW2stagePPSe. This is left as an exercise (Exercise 5).

Exercises

1. Write an **R** script to compute for Voorst the true sampling variance of the estimator of mean SOM concentration for two-stage cluster random sampling, PSUs selected by ppswr, $n = 4$, and $m = 10$, see Equation (7.3).

2. Do you expect that the standard error of the estimator of the population mean with ten PSU draws ($n = 10$) and four SSUs per PSU draw ($m = 4$) is larger or smaller than with four PSU draws ($n = 4$) and ten SSUs per PSU draw ($m = 10$)?

3. Compute the optimal sample sizes n and m for a maximum variance of the estimator of the mean SOM concentration of 1, $c_1 = 2$ monetary units, and $c_2 = 1$ monetary unit, see Equations (7.9) and (7.10).

4. Compute the optimal sample sizes n and m for a budget of 100 monetary units, $c_1 = 2$ monetary units, and $c_2 = 1$ monetary unit, see Equations (7.11) and (7.10).

5. Use function clusOpt2 of **R** package **PracTools** to compute optimal sample sizes given the precision requirement for the estimated population mean of Exercise 3 and given the budget of Exercise 4. Use function BW2stagePPS to compute the variance measures needed as input for function clusOpt2. Note that the precision requirement of function clusOpt2 is the coefficient of variation of the estimated population total, i.e., the standard deviation of the estimated population total divided by the population total. Compute this coefficient of variation from the maximum variance of the estimator of the population mean used in Exercise 3.

6. The variance of the estimator for the population total is (Cochran, 1977):

$$V(\hat{t}(z)) = \frac{1}{n} \sum_{j=1}^{N} p_j \left(\frac{t_j(z)}{p_j} - t(z) \right)^2 + \frac{1}{n} \sum_{j=1}^{N} \frac{M_j^2 (1 - f_{2j}) S_j^2}{m_j p_j} ,$$

(7.12)

with $\hat{t}(z)$ and $t(z)$ the estimated and the true population total of z, respectively, $t_j(z)$ the total of PSU j, and $p_j = M_j/M$. Use $m_j = m$, $j = 1, \ldots, N$, and $f_{2j} = 0$, i.e., sampling from infinite population, or sampling of SSUs within PSUs by simple random sampling *with* replacement from finite population. Derive the variance of the estimator for the population mean, Equation (7.3), from Equation (7.12).

7.2   Primary sampling units selected without replacement

Similar to cluster random sampling, we may prefer to select the PSUs without replacement. This leads to less strong spatial clustering of the sampling points, especially with large sampling fractions of PSUs. Sampling without replacement of PSUs can be done with function UPpivotal of package **sampling** (Tillé and Matei, 2021), see Subsection 8.2.2. The second stage sample of SSUs is selected with function strata of the same package, using the PSUs as strata.

```
library(sampling)
M_psu <- tapply(grdVoorst$z, INDEX = grdVoorst$psu, FUN = length)
n <- 6
pi <- n * M_psu / M
set.seed(314)
sampleind <- UPpivotal(pik = pi, eps = 1e-6)
psus <- sort(unique(grdVoorst$psu))
sampledpsus <- psus[sampleind == 1]
mysample_stage1 <- grdVoorst[grdVoorst$psu %in% sampledpsus, ]
units <- sampling::strata(mysample_stage1, stratanames = "psu",
    size = rep(m, n), method = "srswor")
mysample <- getdata(mysample_stage1, units)
mysample$ssunits <- units$ID_unit
mysample$pi <- n * m / M
print(mean_HT <- sum(mysample$z / mysample$pi) / M)
```

```
[1] 100.039
```

The population mean can be estimated with function svymean of package **survey**. To estimate the variance, a simple solution is to treat the two-stage cluster random sample as a pps sample *with replacement*, so that variance can be estimated with Equation (7.7). With small sampling fractions of PSUs, the overestimation of the variance is negligible. With larger sampling fractions, Brewer's method is recommended, see Berger (2004) (option 2).

```
mysample$fpc1 <- n * M_psu[mysample$psu] / M
mysample$fpc2 <- m / M_psu[mysample$psu]
design_2stageppswor <- svydesign(id = ~ psu + ssunits, data = mysample,
    pps = "brewer", fpc = ~ fpc1 + fpc2)
svymean(~ z, design_2stageppswor)
```

```
      mean     SE
z 100.04 19.883
```

7.3 Simple random sampling of primary sampling units

Suppose the PSUs are for some reason not selected with probabilities proportional to their size, but by simple random sampling without replacement. The inclusion probabilities of the PSUs then equal $\pi_j = n/N$, $j = 1, \dots, N$, and the population total can be estimated by (compare with Equation (6.9))

$$\hat{t}(z) = \sum_{j=1}^{n} \frac{\hat{t}_j(z)}{\pi_j} = \frac{N}{n} \sum_{j=1}^{n} \hat{t}_j(z), \qquad (7.13)$$

with $\hat{t}_j(z)$ an estimator of the total of PSU j. The population mean can be estimated by dividing this estimator by the population size M.

Alternatively, we may estimate the population mean by dividing the estimate of the population total by the *estimated* population size. The population size can be estimated by the π estimator, see Equation (6.11). The π estimator and the ratio estimator are equal when the PSUs are selected by ppswr, but not so when the PSUs of different size are selected with equal probabilities. This is shown below. First, a sample is selected by selecting both PSUs and SSUs by simple random sampling without replacement.

```
library(sampling)
set.seed(314)
psus <- sort(unique(grdVoorst$psu))
ids_psu <- sample(length(psus), size = n, replace = FALSE)
sampledpsus <- psus[ids_psu]
mysample_stage1 <- grdVoorst[grdVoorst$psu %in% sampledpsus, ]
units <- sampling::strata(mysample_stage1, stratanames = "psu",
    size = rep(m, n), method = "srswor")
mysample <- getdata(mysample_stage1, units)
mysample$ssunits <- units$ID_unit
```

The population mean is estimated by the π estimator and the ratio estimator.

```
N <- length(unique(grdVoorst$psu))
M_psu <- tapply(grdVoorst$z, INDEX = grdVoorst$psu, FUN = length)
pi_psu <- n / N
pi_ssu <- m / M_psu[mysample$psu]
est <- mysample %>%
  mutate(pi = pi_psu * pi_ssu,
         z_piexpanded = z / pi) %>%
  summarise(tz_HT = sum(z_piexpanded),
```

```
        mz_HT = tz_HT / M,
        M_HT = sum(1 / pi),
        mz_ratio = tz_HT / M_HT)
```

The π estimate equals 79.0 g kg^{-1}, and the ratio estimate equals 79.8 g kg^{-1}. The π estimate of the population mean can also be computed by first estimating totals of PSUs, see Equation (7.13).

```
tz_psu <- tapply(mysample$z / pi_ssu, INDEX = mysample$psu, FUN = sum)
tz_HT <- sum(tz_psu / pi_psu)
(mz_HT <- tz_HT / M)
```

[1] 78.99646

The variance of the π estimator of the population mean can be estimated by first estimating the variance of the estimator of the PSU totals:

$$\hat{V}(\hat{t}(z)) = N^2 \left(1 - \frac{n}{N}\right) \frac{\widehat{S^2}(\hat{t}_i(z))}{n} , \qquad (7.14)$$

and dividing this variance by the squared number of population units:

$$\hat{V}(\hat{\bar{z}}) = \frac{1}{M^2} \hat{V}(\hat{t}(z)) , \qquad (7.15)$$

as shown in the code chunk below (the final line computes the standard error).

```
fpc <- 1 - n / N
v_tz <- N^2 * fpc * var(tz_psu) / n
(se_mz_HT <- sqrt(v_tz / M^2))
```

[1] 9.467406

The ratio estimator of the population mean and its standard error can be computed with function svymean of package **survey**.

```
mysample$fpc1 <- N
mysample$fpc2 <- M_psu[mysample$psu]
design_2stage <- svydesign(
    id = ~ psu + ssunits, fpc = ~ fpc1 + fpc2, data = mysample)
svymean(~ z, design_2stage)
```

```
        mean      SE
z 79.845 7.7341
```

The estimated standard error of the ratio estimator is slightly smaller than the standard error of the π estimator.

7.4 Stratified two-stage cluster random sampling

The basic sampling designs stratified random sampling (Chapter 4) and two-stage cluster random sampling can be combined into stratified two-stage cluster random sampling. Figure 7.3 shows a stratified two-stage cluster random sample from Voorst. The strata are groups of eight PSUs within 2 km × 1 km blocks, as before in stratified cluster random sampling (Figure 6.2). The PSUs are 0.5 km squares (built-up areas, roads, etc. excluded), as before in (unstratified) two-stage cluster random sampling (Figure 7.1). Within each stratum two times a PSU is selected by ppswr, and every time a PSU is selected, six SSUs (points) are selected by simple random sampling. The stratification avoids the clustering of the selected PSUs in one part of the study area. Compared to (unstratified) two-stage cluster random sampling, the geographical spreading of the PSUs is somewhat improved, which may lead to an increase of the precision of the estimated population mean.

```
n_h <- rep(2, 3)
m <- 6
set.seed(314)
stratumlabels <- unique(grdVoorst$zone_stratum)
mysample <- NULL
for (i in 1:3) {
  grd_h <- grdVoorst[grdVoorst$zone_stratum == stratumlabels[i], ]
  mysample_h <- twostage(sframe = grd_h, psu = "psu", n = n_h[i], m = m)
  mysample <- rbind(mysample, mysample_h)
```

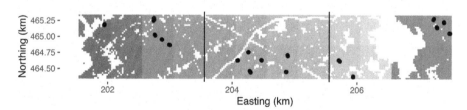

FIGURE 7.3: Stratified two-stage random sample from Voorst. Strata are groups of eight PSUs (0.5 km squares) within 2 km × 1 km blocks. From each stratum two times a PSU is selected by ppswr, and six SSUs (points) are selected per PSU draw by simple random sampling.

```
}
mysample$s1 <- jitter(mysample$s1, amount = cell_size / 2)
mysample$s2 <- jitter(mysample$s2, amount = cell_size / 2)
```

The population mean can be estimated in much the same way as with stratified cluster random sampling. With function svymean this is an easy task.

```
N_h <- tapply(grdVoorst$psu, INDEX = grdVoorst$zone_stratum,
  FUN = function(x) {
    length(unique(x))
    })
M_h <- tapply(grdVoorst$z, INDEX = grdVoorst$zone_stratum, FUN = length)
mysample$w1 <- N_h[mysample$zone_stratum]
mysample$w2 <- M_h[mysample$zone_stratum]
design_str2stage <- svydesign(id = ~ psudraw + ssunits, strata = ~ zone_stratum,
  weights = ~ w1 + w2, data = mysample, nest = TRUE)
svymean(~ z, design_str2stage)
```

```
    mean SE
z 73.654  0
```

8

Sampling with probabilities proportional to size

In simple random sampling, the inclusion probabilities are equal for all population units. The advantage of this is simple and straightforward statistical inference. With equal inclusion probabilities the unweighted sample mean is an unbiased estimator of the spatial mean, i.e., the sampling design is *self-weighting*. However, in some situations equal probability sampling is not very efficient, i.e., given the sample size the precision of the estimated mean or total will be relatively low. An example is the following. In order to estimate the total area of a given crop in a country, a raster of square cells of, for instance, 1 km × 1 km is constructed and projected on the country. The square cells are the population units, and these units serve as the sampling units. Note that near the country border cells cross the border. Some of them may contain only a few hectares of the target population, the country under study. We do not want to select many of these squares with only a few hectares of the study area, as intuitively it is clear that this will result in a low precision of the estimated crop area. In such situation it can be more efficient to select units with probabilities proportional to the area of the target population within the squares, so that small units near the border have a smaller probability of being selected than interior units. Actually, the sampling units are not the square cells, but the pieces of land obtained by overlaying the cells and the GIS map of the country under study. As a consequence, the sampling units have unequal size. The sampling units of unequal size are selected by probabilities proportional to their size (pps).

In Chapters 6 and 7 pps sampling was already used to select clusters (primary sampling units) of population units. In this chapter the *individual* population units (elementary sampling units) are selected with probabilities proportional to size.

If we have a GIS map of land use categories such as agriculture, built-up areas, water bodies, forests, etc., we may use this file to further adapt the selection probabilities. The crop will be grown in agricultural areas only, so we expect small crop areas in cells largely covered by non-agricultural land. As a size measure in computing the selection probabilities, we may use the agricultural area, as represented in the GIS map, in the country under study within the cells. Note that size now has a different meaning. It does not refer to the area of the sampling units anymore, but to an ancillary variable that we expect to be related to the study variable, i.e., the crop area. When the crop area per cell is proportional to the agricultural area per cell, then the precision of the estimated total area of the crop can be increased by selecting the cells with probabilities proportional to the agricultural area.

In this example the sampling units have an area. However, sampling with probabilities proportional to size is not restricted to areal sampling units, but can also be used for selecting points. If we have a map of an ancillary variable that is expected to be positively related to the study variable, this ancillary variable can be used as a size measure. For instance, in areas where soil organic matter shows a positive relation with elevation, it can be efficient to select sampling points with a selection probability proportional to this environmental variable. The ancillary variable must be strictly positive for all points.

Sampling units can be selected with probabilities proportional to their size (pps) *with* or *without* replacement. This distinction is immaterial for infinite populations, as in sampling points from an area. pps sampling with replacement (ppswr) is much easier to implement than pps sampling without replacement (ppswor). The problem with ppswor is that after each draw the selected unit is removed from the sampling frame, so that the sum of the size variable over all remaining units changes and as a result the draw-by-draw selection probabilities of the units.

pps sampling is illustrated with the simulated map of poppy area per 5 km square in the province of Kandahar (Figure 1.6). The first six rows of the data frame are shown below. Variable poppy is the study variable, variable agri is the agricultural area within the 5 km squares, used as a size variable.

```
grdKandahar
```

```
# A tibble: 965 x 4
        s1        s2     poppy     agri
     <dbl>     <dbl>     <dbl>    <dbl>
 1 809232. 3407627.   0.905     65.7
 2 814232. 3412627.   0.00453   15.6
 3 794232. 3417627.  11.3       17.6
 4 809232. 3417627.   0.110     14.0
 5 814232. 3417627.   0.0344    22.2
 6 819232. 3417627.   0.143     13.3
 7 794232. 3422627.   3.66      34.1
 8 799232. 3422627.   3.66       6.12
 9 809232. 3422627.   0.688     10.6
10 814232. 3422627.   4.79     130.
# ... with 955 more rows
```

8.1 Probability-proportional-to-size sampling with replacement

In the first draw, a sampling unit is selected with probability $p_k = x_k/t(x)$, with x_k the size variable for unit k and $t(x) = \sum_{k=1}^{N} x_k$ the population total of the size variable. The selected unit is then replaced, and these two steps are repeated n times. Note that with this sampling design population units can be selected more than once, especially with large sampling fractions n/N.

The population total can be estimated by the pwr estimator:

$$\hat{t}(z) = \frac{1}{n} \sum_{k \in \mathcal{S}} \frac{z_k}{p_k} \, , \qquad (8.1)$$

where n is the sample size (number of draws). The population mean can be estimated by the estimated population total divided by the population size N. With independent draws, the sampling variance of the estimator of the population total can be estimated by

$$\hat{V}(\hat{t}(z)) = \frac{1}{n(n-1)} \sum_{k \in \mathcal{S}} \left(\frac{z_k}{p_k} - \hat{t}(z) \right)^2 . \qquad (8.2)$$

The sampling variance of the estimator of the mean can be estimated by the variance of the estimator of the total divided by N^2.

As a first step, I check whether the size variable is strictly positive in our case study of Kandahar. The minimum equals 0.307 m^2, so this is the case. If there are values equal to or smaller than 0, these values must be replaced by a small number, so that all units have a positive probability of being selected. Then the draw-by-draw selection probabilities are computed, and the sample is selected using function sample.

```
grdKandahar$p <- grdKandahar$agri / sum(grdKandahar$agri)
N <- nrow(grdKandahar)
n <- 40
set.seed(314)
units <- sample(N, size = n, replace = TRUE, prob = grdKandahar$p)
mysample <- grdKandahar[units, ]
```

To select the units, computing the selection probabilities is not strictly needed. Exactly the same units are selected when the agricultural area within the units (variable agri in the data frame) is used in argument prob of sample.

Four units are selected twice.

```
table_frq <- table(units) %>% data.frame()
print(table_frq[table_frq$Freq > 1, ])
```

```
   units Freq
9    278    2
13   334    2
14   336    2
24   439    2
```

Figure 8.1 shows the selected sampling units, plotted on a map of the agricultural area within the units which is used as a size variable.

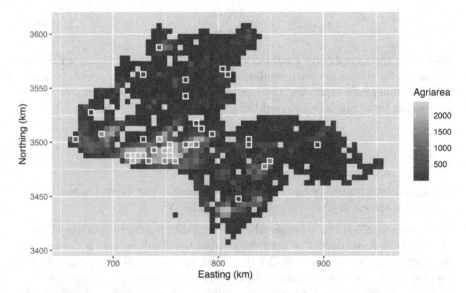

FIGURE 8.1: Sample of size 40 from Kandahar, selected with probabilities proportional to agricultural area with replacement. Four units are selected twice, so that the number of distinct units is 36.

The next code chunk shows how the population total of the poppy area can be estimated, using Equation (8.1), as well as the standard error of the estimator of the population total (square root of estimator of Equation (8.2)). As a first step, the observations are inflated, or expanded, through division of the observations by the selection probabilities of the corresponding units.

```
z_pexpanded <- mysample$poppy / mysample$p
tz <- mean(z_pexpanded)
se_tz <- sqrt(var(z_pexpanded) / n)
```

The estimated total equals 65,735 ha, with a standard error of 12,944 ha. The same estimates are obtained with package **survey** (Lumley, 2021).

```
library(survey)
mysample$weight <- 1 / (mysample$p * n)
design_ppswr <- svydesign(id = ~ 1, data = mysample, weights = ~ weight)
svytotal(~ poppy, design_ppswr)
```

```
        total    SE
poppy   65735 12944
```

In ppswr sampling, a sampling unit can be selected more than once, especially with large sampling fractions n/N. This may decrease the sampling efficiency. With large sampling fractions, the alternative is pps sampling without replacement (ppswor), see next section.

The estimators of Equations (8.1) and (8.2) can also be used for infinite populations. For infinite populations, the probability that a unit is selected more than once is zero.

Exercises

1. Write an **R** script to select a pps with replacement sample from Eastern Amazonia (grdAmazonia in package **sswr**) to estimate the population mean of aboveground biomass (AGB), using log-transformed short-wave infrared radiation (SWIR2) as a size variable.
   - The correlation of AGB and lnSWIR2 is negative. The first step is to compute an appropriate size variable, so that the larger the size variable, the larger the selection probability. Multiply the lnSWIR2 values by -1. Then add a small value, so that the size variable becomes strictly positive.
   - Select in a for-loop 1,000 times a ppswr sample of size 100 ($n = 100$), and estimate from each sample the population mean of AGB with the pwr estimator (Hansen-Hurwitz estimator) and its sampling variance. Compute the variance of the 1,000 estimated population means and the mean of the 1,000 estimated variances. Make a histogram of the 1,000 estimated means.
   - Compute the true sampling variance of the π estimator with simple random sampling with replacement and the same sample size.
   - Compute the gain in precision by the ratio of the variance of the estimator of the mean with simple random sampling to the variance with ppswr.

8.2 Probability-proportional-to-size sampling without replacement

The alternative to pps sampling with replacement (ppswr) is pps sampling without replacement (ppswor). In ppswor sampling the *inclusion* probabilities are proportional to a size variable, not the draw-by-draw selection probabilities as in ppswr. For this reason, ppswor sampling is referred to as πps sampling by Särndal et al. (1992). ppswor sampling starts with assigning target inclusion probabilities to all units in the population. With inclusion probabilities proportional to a size variable x the target inclusion probabilities are computed by $\pi_k = n \, x_k / \sum_{j=1}^{N} x_j, \ k = 1, \ldots, N$.

8.2.1 Systematic pps sampling without replacement

Many algorithms are available for ppswor sampling, see Tillé (2006) for an overview. A simple, straightforward method is systematic ppswor sampling. Two subtypes can be distinguished, systematic ppswor sampling with fixed frame order and systematic ppswor sampling with random frame order (Rosén, 1997). Given some order of the units, the cumulative sum of the inclusion probabilities is computed. Each population unit is then associated with an interval of cumulative inclusion probabilities. The larger the inclusion probability of a unit, the wider the interval. Then a random number from the uniform distribution is drawn, which serves as the start of a one-dimensional systematic sample of size n with an interval of 1. Finally, the units are determined for which the systematic random values are in the interval of cumulative inclusion probabilities, see Figure 8.2 for ten population units and a sample size of four. The units selected are 2, 5, 7, and 9. Note that the sum of the interval lengths equals the sample size. Further note that a unit cannot be selected more than once because the inclusion probabilities are < 1 and the sampling interval equals 1.

```
library(sampling)
set.seed(314)
N <- 10
n <- 4
x <- rnorm(N, mean = 20, sd = 5)
pi <- inclusionprobabilities(x, n)
print(data.frame(id = seq_len(N), x, pi))
```

```
   id        x        pi
1   1 13.55882 0.3027383
```

```
2    2 23.63731 0.5277684
3    3 15.83538 0.3535687
4    4 16.48162 0.3679978
5    5 20.63624 0.4607613
6    6 18.32529 0.4091630
7    7 16.50655 0.3685545
8    8 20.06336 0.4479702
9    9 22.94495 0.5123095
10  10 11.15957 0.2491684
```

```
cumsumpi <- c(0, cumsum(pi))
start <- runif(1, min = 0, max = 1)
sys <- 0:(n - 1) + start
print(units <- findInterval(sys, cumsumpi))
```

```
[1] 2 5 7 9
```

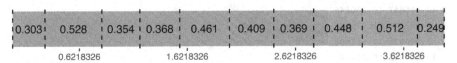

FIGURE 8.2: Systematic random sample along a line with unequal inclusion probabilities.

Sampling efficiency can be increased by ordering the units by the size variable (Figure 8.3). With this design, the third, fourth, fifth, and second units in the original frame are selected, with sizes 15.8, 16.5, 20.6, and 23.6, respectively. Ordering the units by size leads to a large within-sample and a small between-sample variance of the size variable x. If the study variable is proportional to the size variable, this results in a smaller sampling variance of the estimator of the mean of the study variable. A drawback of systematic ppswor sampling with fixed order is that no unbiased estimator of the sampling variance exists.

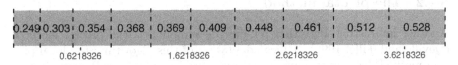

FIGURE 8.3: Systematic random sample along a line with unequal inclusion probabilities. Units are ordered by size.

A small simulation study is done next to see how much gain in precision can be achieved by ordering the units by size. A size variable x and a study variable z are simulated by drawing 1,000 values from a bivariate normal distribution with a correlation coefficient of 0.8. Function mvrnorm of package **MASS** (Venables and Ripley, 2002) is used for the simulation.

```
library(MASS)
rho <- 0.8
mu1 <- 10; sd1 <- 2
mu2 <- 15; sd2 <- 4
mu <- c(mu1, mu2)
sigma <- matrix(
    data = c(sd1^2, rep(sd1 * sd2 * rho, 2), sd2^2),
    nrow = 2, ncol = 2)
N <- 1000
set.seed(314)
dat <- as.data.frame(mvrnorm(N, mu = mu, Sigma = sigma))
names(dat) <- c("z", "x")
head(dat)
```

```
          z         x
1   9.462930  9.149784
2  12.605847 17.306046
3   7.892686 11.979986
4   7.945021 12.567608
5  11.004325 15.165744
6  10.369943 13.258177
```

Twenty units are selected by systematic ppswor sampling with random order and ordered by size. This is repeated 10,000 times.

The standard deviation of the 10,000 estimated means with systematic ppswor sampling with random order is 0.336, and when ordered by size 0.321. So, a small gain in precision is achieved through ordering the units by size. For comparison, I also computed the standard error for simple random sampling without replacement (SI) of the same size. The standard error with this basic sampling design is 0.424.

8.2.2   The pivotal method

Another interesting algorithm for ppswor sampling is the pivotal method (Deville and Tillé, 1998). A nice adaptation of this algorithm, the local pivotal method, leading to samples with improved (geographical) spreading, is described in Section 9.2. In the pivotal method, the N-vector with inclusion probabilities is successively updated to a vector with indicators. If the indicator value for sampling unit k becomes 1, then this sampling unit is selected, if it becomes 0, then it is not selected. The updating algorithm can be described as follows:

1. Select randomly two units k and l with $0 < \pi_k < 1$ and $0 < \pi_l < 1$.

2. If $\pi_k + \pi_l < 1$, then update the probabilities by

$$(\pi'_k, \pi'_l) = \begin{cases} (0, \pi_k + \pi_l) & \text{with probability} \frac{\pi_l}{\pi_k + \pi_l} \\ (\pi_k + \pi_l, 0) & \text{with probability} \frac{\pi_k}{\pi_k + \pi_l} \end{cases}, \qquad (8.3)$$

and if $\pi_k + \pi_l \geq 1$, update the probabilities by

$$(\pi'_k, \pi'_l) = \begin{cases} (1, \pi_k + \pi_l - 1) & \text{with probability} \frac{1-\pi_l}{2-(\pi_k+\pi_l)} \\ (\pi_k + \pi_l - 1, 1) & \text{with probability} \frac{1-\pi_k}{2-(\pi_k+\pi_l)} \end{cases}. \qquad (8.4)$$

3. Replace (π_k, π_l) by (π'_k, π'_l), and repeat the first two steps until each population unit is either selected (inclusion probability equals 1) or not selected (inclusion probability equals 0).

In words, when the sum of the inclusion probabilities is smaller than 1, the updated inclusion probability of one of the units will become 0, which means that this unit will not be sampled. The inclusion probability of the other unit will become the sum of the two inclusion probabilities, which means that the probability increases that this unit will be selected in one of the subsequent iterations. The probability of a unit of being excluded from the sample is proportional to the inclusion probability of the other unit, so that the larger the inclusion probability of the other unit, the larger the probability that it will not be selected.

When the sum of the inclusion probabilities of the two units is larger than or equal to 1, then one of the units is selected (updated inclusion probability is one), while the inclusion probability of the other unit is lowered by 1 minus the inclusion probability of the selected unit. The probability of being selected is proportional to the complement of the inclusion probability of the other unit. After the inclusion probability of a unit has been updated to either 0 or 1, this unit cannot be selected anymore in the next iteration.

With this ppswor design, the population total can be estimated by the π estimator, Equation (2.2). The π estimator of the mean is simply obtained by dividing the estimator for the total by the population size N.

The inclusion probabilities π_k used in the π estimator are not the final probabilities obtained with the local pivot method, which are either 0 or 1, but the initial inclusion probabilities.

An alternative estimator of the population mean is the ratio estimator, also known as the Hájek estimator:

$$\hat{\bar{z}}_{\text{Hajek}} = \frac{\sum_{k \in \mathcal{S}} w_k z_k}{\sum_{k \in \mathcal{S}} w_k} , \tag{8.5}$$

with $w_k = 1/\pi_k$. The denominator is an estimator of the population size N. The Hájek estimator of the population total is obtained by multiplying the Hájek estimator of the mean with the population size N. Recall that the ratio estimator of the population mean was presented before in the chapters on systematic random sampling (Equation (5.4)), cluster random sampling with simple random sampling of clusters (Equation (6.12)), and two-stage cluster random sampling with simple random sampling of PSUs. These sampling designs have in common that the sample size (for cluster random sampling, the number of SSUs) is random.

Various functions in package **sampling** (Tillé and Matei, 2021) can be used to select a ppswor sample. In the code chunk below, I use function UPrandompivotal. With this function, the order of the population units is randomised before function UPpivotal is used. Argument pi is a numeric with the inclusion probabilities. These are computed with function inclusionprobabilities. Recall that $\pi_k = n\, x_k/t(x)$. The sum of the inclusion probabilities should be equal to the sample size n. Function UPpivotal returns a numeric of length N with elements 1 and 0, 1 if the unit is selected, 0 if it is not selected.

```
library(sampling)
n <- 40
size <- ifelse(grdKandahar$agri < 1E-12, 0.1, grdKandahar$agri)
pi <- inclusionprobabilities(size, n)
set.seed(314)
sampleind <- UPrandompivotal(pik = pi)
mysample <- data.frame(grdKandahar[sampleind == 1, ], pi = pi[sampleind == 1])
nrow(mysample)
```

```
[1] 39
```

As can be seen, not 40 but only 39 units are selected. The reason is that function UPrandompivotal uses a very small number that can be set with argument eps. If the updated inclusion probability of a unit is larger than the complement of this small number eps, the unit is treated as being selected. The default value of eps is 10^{-6}. If we replace sampleind == 1 by sampleind > 1 - eps, 40 units are selected.

```
eps <- 1e-6
mysample <- data.frame(
```

```
  grdKandahar[sampleind > 1 - eps, ], pi = pi[sampleind > 1 - eps])
nrow(mysample)
```

```
[1] 40
```

The total poppy area can be estimated from the ppswor sample by

```
tz_HT <- sum(mysample$poppy / mysample$pi)
tz_Hajek <- N * sum(mysample$poppy / mysample$pi) / sum(1 / mysample$pi)
```

The total poppy area as estimated with the π estimator equals 88,501 ha. The Hájek estimator results in a much smaller estimated total: 62,169 ha.

The π estimate can also be computed with function svytotal of package **survey**, which also provides an approximate estimate of the standard error. Various methods are implemented in function svydesign for approximating the standard error. These methods differ in the way the pairwise inclusion probabilities are approximated from the unitwise inclusion probabilities. These approximated pairwise inclusion probabilities are then used in the π variance estimator or the Yates-Grundy variance estimator. In the next code chunks, Brewer's method is used, see option 2 of Brewer's method in Berger (2004), as well as Hartley-Rao's method for approximating the variance.

```
library(survey)
design_ppsworbrewer <- svydesign(
  id = ~ 1, data = mysample, pps = "brewer", fpc = ~ pi)
svytotal(~ poppy, design_ppsworbrewer)
```

```
        total    SE
poppy 88501 14046
```

```
p2sum <- sum(mysample$pi^2) / n
design_ppsworhr <- svydesign(
  id = ~ 1, data = mysample, pps = HR(p2sum), fpc = ~ pi)
svytotal(~ poppy, design_ppsworhr)
```

```
        total    SE
poppy 88501 14900
```

In package **samplingVarEst** (Escobar et al., 2019), also various functions are available for approximating the variance: VE.Hajek.Total.NHT, VE.HT.Total.NHT, and VE.SYG.Total.NHT. The first variance approximation is the Hájek-Rosén variance estimator, see equation (4.3) in Rosén (1997). The latter two functions require the pairwise inclusion probabilities, which can be estimated by function Pkl.Hajek.s.

```
library(samplingVarEst)
se_tz_Hajek <- sqrt(VE.Hajek.Total.NHT(mysample$poppy, mysample$pi))
pikl <- Pkl.Hajek.s(mysample$pi)
se_tz_HT <- sqrt(VE.HT.Total.NHT(mysample$poppy, mysample$pi, pikl))
se_tz_SYG <- sqrt(VE.SYG.Total.NHT(mysample$poppy, mysample$pi, pikl))
```

The three approximated standard errors are 14,045, 14,068, and 14,017 ha. The differences are small when related to the estimated total.

Figure 8.4 shows the approximated sampling distribution of estimators of the total poppy area with ppswor sampling and simple random sampling without replacement of size 40, obtained by repeating the random sampling with each design and estimation 10,000 times. With the ppswor samples, the total poppy area is estimated by the π estimator and the Hájek estimator. For each ppswor sample, the variance of the π estimator is approximated by the Hájek-Rosén variance estimator (using function VE.Hajek.Total.NHT of package **samplingVarEst**).

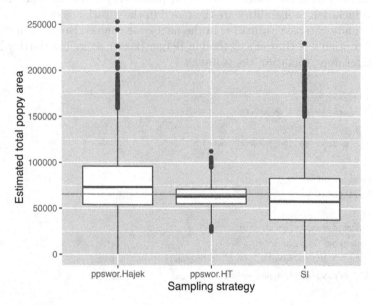

FIGURE 8.4: Approximated sampling distribution of the π estimator (ppswor.HT) and the Hájek estimator (ppswor.Hajek) of the total poppy area (ha) in Kandahar with ppswor sampling of size 40, and of the π estimator with simple random sampling without replacement (SI) of size 40.

Sampling design ppswor in combination with the π estimator is clearly much more precise than simple random sampling. The standard deviation of the 10,000 π estimates of the total poppy area with ppswor equals 11,684 ha. The average of the square root of the Hájek-Rosén approximated variances equals 12,332 ha.

Interestingly, with ppswor sampling the variance of the 10,000 Hájek estimates is much larger than that of the π estimates. The standard deviation of the 10,000 Hájek estimates with ppswor sampling is about equal to that of the π estimates with simple random sampling: 31,234 ha and 33,178 ha, respectively.

Exercises

2. A field with poppy was found outside Kandahar in a selected sampling unit crossing the boundary. Should this field be included in the sum of the poppy area of that sampling unit?

3. In another sampling unit, a poppy field was encountered in Kandahar but in the area represented as non-agricultural in the GIS map. Should this field be included in the sum of that sampling unit?

9

Balanced and well-spread sampling

In this chapter two related but fundamentally different sampling designs are described and illustrated. The similarity and difference are shortly outlined below, but hopefully will become clearer in following sections.

Roughly speaking, for a balanced sample the sample means of covariates are equal to the population means of these covariates. When the covariates are linearly related to the study variable, this may yield a more precise estimate of the population mean or total of the study variable.

A well-spread sample is a sample with a large range of values for the covariates, from small to large values, but also including intermediate values. In more technical terms: the sampling units are well-spread along the axes spanned by the covariates. If the spatial coordinates are used as covariates (spreading variables), this results in samples that are well-spread in geographical space. Such samples are commonly referred to as spatially balanced samples, which is somewhat confusing, as the geographical spreading is not implemented through balancing on the geographical coordinates. On the other hand, the averages of the spatial coordinates of a sample well-spread in geographical space will be close to the population means of the coordinates. Therefore, the sample will be approximately balanced on the spatial coordinates (Grafström and Schelin, 2014). The reverse is not true: with balanced sampling, the spreading of the sampling units in the space spanned by the balancing variables can be poor. A sample with all values of a covariate used in balancing near the population mean of that variable has a poor spreading along the covariate axis, but can still be perfectly balanced.

9.1 Balanced sampling

Balanced sampling is a sampling method that exploits one or more quantitative covariates that are related to the study variable. The idea behind balanced sampling is that, if we know the mean of the covariates, then the sampling efficiency can be increased by selecting a sample whose averages of the covariates must be equal to the population means of the covariates.

Let me illustrate balanced sampling with a small simulation study. The simulated population shown in Figure 9.1 shows a linear trend from West to East and besides a trend from South to North. Due to the West-East trend, the simulated study variable z is correlated with the covariate Easting and, due to the South-North trend, also with the covariate Northing. To estimate the population mean of the simulated study variable, intuitively it is attractive to select a sample with an average of the Easting coordinate that is equal to the population mean of Easting (which is 10). Figure 9.1 (subfigure on the left) shows such a sample of size four; we say that the sample is 'balanced' on the covariate Easting. The sample in the subfigure on the right is balanced on Easting as well as on Northing.

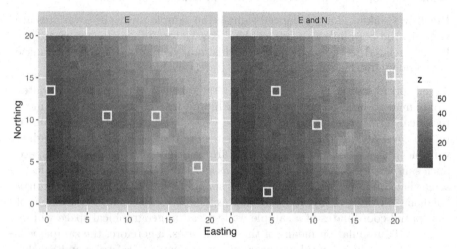

FIGURE 9.1: Sample balanced on Easting (E) and on Easting and Northing (E and N).

9.1.1 Balanced sample vs. balanced sampling design

We must distinguish a balanced *sample* from a balanced sampling *design*. A sampling design is balanced on a covariate x when *all possible* samples that can be generated by the design are balanced on x.

Simple random sampling is not a balanced sampling design, because for many simple random samples the sample mean of the balancing variable x is not equal to the population mean of x. Only the *expectation* of the sample mean of x, i.e., the mean of the sample means obtained by selecting an infinite number of simple random samples, equals the population mean of x.

Figure 9.2 shows for 1,000 simple random samples the squared error of the estimated population mean of the study variable z against the difference between the sample mean of balancing variable Easting and the population mean of Easting. Clearly, the larger the absolute value of the difference, the larger on average the squared error. So, to obtain a precise and accurate estimate of the population mean of z, we better select samples with a difference close to 0.

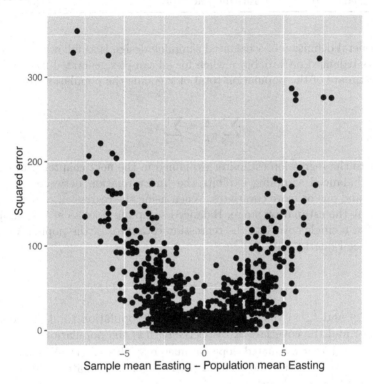

FIGURE 9.2: Squared error in the estimated population mean of z against the difference between the sample mean and the population mean of Easting, for 1,000 simple random samples of size four selected from the population shown in Figure 9.1.

Using only Easting as a balancing variable reduces the sampling variance of the estimator of the mean substantially. Using Easting and Northing as balancing variables further reduces the sampling variance. See Table 9.1.

9.1.2 Unequal inclusion probabilities

Until now we have assumed that the inclusion probabilities of the population units are equal, but this is not a requirement for balanced sampling designs. A

TABLE 9.1: Sampling variance of the π estimator of the mean for simple random sampling (SI) and balanced sampling of four units.

Sampling design	Balancing variables	Sampling variance
SI	-	39.70
Balanced	Easting	14.40
Balanced	Easting and Northing	9.77

more general definition of a balanced sampling design is as follows. A sampling design is balanced on variable x when for all samples generated by the design the π estimate of the population total of x equals the population total of x:

$$\sum_{k \in \mathcal{S}} \frac{x_k}{\pi_k} = \sum_{k=1}^{N} x_k \ . \tag{9.1}$$

Similar to the regression estimator explained in the next chapter (Subsection 10.1.1), balanced sampling exploits the linear relation between the study variable and one or more covariates. When using the regression estimator, this is done at the estimation stage. Balanced sampling does so at the sampling stage. For a single covariate the regression estimator of the population total equals (see Equation (10.10))

$$\hat{t}_{\text{regr}}(z) = \hat{t}_{\pi}(z) + \hat{b}\left(t(x) - \hat{t}_{\pi}(x)\right) \ , \tag{9.2}$$

with $\hat{t}_{\pi}(z)$ and $\hat{t}_{\pi}(x)$ the π estimators of the population total of the study variable z and the covariate x, respectively, $t(x)$ the population total of the covariate, and $\hat{b}$ the estimated slope parameter (see hereafter). With a perfectly balanced sample the second term in the regression estimator, which adjusts the π estimator, equals zero.

Balanced samples can be selected with the cube algorithm of Deville and Tillé (2004). The population total and mean can be estimated by the π estimator. The approximated variance of the π estimator of the population mean can be estimated by (Deville and Tillé (2005), Grafström and Tillé (2013))

$$\hat{V}(\hat{\bar{z}}) = \frac{1}{N^2} \frac{n}{n-p} \sum_{k \in \mathcal{S}} c_k \left(\frac{e_k}{\pi_k}\right)^2 \ , \tag{9.3}$$

with p the number of balancing variables, c_k a weight for unit k (see hereafter), and e_k the residual of unit k given by

$$e_k = z_k - \mathbf{x}_k^{\mathsf{T}} \hat{\mathbf{b}} \ , \tag{9.4}$$

with $\mathbf{x}_k$ a vector of length p with the balancing variables for unit k, and $\hat{\mathbf{b}}$ the estimated population regression coefficients, given by

$$\hat{\mathbf{b}} = \left(\sum_{k \in \mathcal{S}} c_k \frac{\mathbf{x}_k}{\pi_k} \frac{\mathbf{x}_k^{\mathrm{T}}}{\pi_k} \right)^{-1} \sum_{k \in \mathcal{S}} c_k \frac{\mathbf{x}_k}{\pi_k} \frac{z_k}{\pi_k} . \tag{9.5}$$

Working this out for balanced sampling without replacement with equal inclusion probabilities, $\pi_k = n/N, \ k = 1, \dots, N$, yields

$$\hat{V}(\hat{\bar{z}}) = \frac{1}{n(n-p)} \sum_{k \in \mathcal{S}} c_k e_k^2 . \tag{9.6}$$

Deville and Tillé (2005) give several formulas for computing the weights c_k, one of which is $c_k = (1 - \pi_k)$.

Balanced sampling is now illustrated with aboveground biomass (AGB) data of Eastern Amazonia, see Figure 1.8. Log-transformed short-wave infrared radiation (lnSWIR2) is used as a balancing variable. The `samplecube` function of the **sampling** package (Tillé and Matei, 2021) implements the cube algorithm. Argument x of this function specifies the matrix of ancillary variables on which the sample must be balanced. The first column of this matrix is filled with ones, so that the sample size is fixed. To speed up the computations, a 5 km × 5 km subgrid of `grdAmazonia` is used.

Recall that a sample is balanced on a covariate x if the π estimate of the population total of x is equal to the known true population total of x (Equation (9.1)). If we know the total number of units in a population, N, we can balance the sample on this known total using a constant with value 1 as a balancing variable. Only for samples of size n the π estimate of the total number of population units equals N: $\sum_{k \in \mathcal{S}} 1/\pi_k = N$ for $|\mathcal{S}| = n$.

Equal inclusion probabilities are used, i.e., for all population units the inclusion probability equals n/N.

```
grdAmazonia <- grdAmazonia %>%
  mutate(lnSWIR2 = log(SWIR2))
library(sampling)
N <- nrow(grdAmazonia)
n <- 100
X <- cbind(rep(1, times = N), grdAmazonia$lnSWIR2)
pi <- rep(n / N, times = N)
sample_ind <- samplecube(X = X, pik = pi, comment = FALSE, method = 1)
eps <- 1e-6
```

```
units <- which(sample_ind > (1 - eps))
mysample <- grdAmazonia[units, ]
```

The population mean can be estimated by the sample mean.

```
mz <- mean(mysample$AGB)
```

To estimate the variance, a function is defined for estimating the population regression coefficients.

```
estimate_b <- function(z, X, c) {
  cXX <- matrix(nrow = ncol(X), ncol = ncol(X), data = 0)
  cXz <- matrix(nrow = 1, ncol = ncol(X), data = 0)
  for (i in seq_len(length(z))) {
    x <- X[i, ]
    cXX_i <- c[i] * (x %*% t(x))
    cXX <- cXX + cXX_i
    cXz_i <- c[i] * t(x) * z[i]
    cXz <- cXz + cXz_i
  }
  b <- solve(cXX, t(cXz))
  return(b)
}
```

The next code chunk shows how the estimated variance of the π estimator of the population mean can be computed.

```
pi <- rep(n / N, n)
c <- (1 - pi)
b <- estimate_b(z = mysample$AGB / pi, X = X[units, ] / pi, c = c)
zpred <- X %*% b
e <- mysample$AGB - zpred[units]
v_tz <- n / (n - ncol(X)) * sum(c * (e / pi)^2)
v_mz <- v_tz / N^2
```

Figure 9.3 shows the selected balanced sample. Note the spatial clustering of some units. The estimated population mean (as estimated by the sample mean) of AGB equals 224.5 10^9 kg ha^{-1}. The population mean of AGB equals 225.3 10^9 kg ha^{-1}. The standard error of the estimated mean equals 6.1 10^9 kg ha^{-1}.

Figure 9.4 shows the approximated sampling distribution of the π estimator of the mean AGB with balanced sampling and simple random sampling, obtained

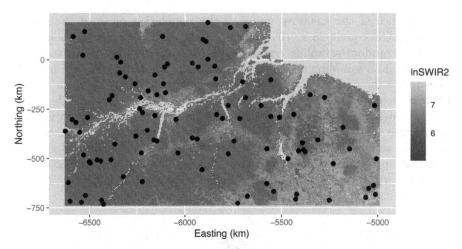

FIGURE 9.3: Sample balanced on lnSWIR2 from Eastern Amazonia.

by repeating the random sampling with both designs and estimation 1,000 times.

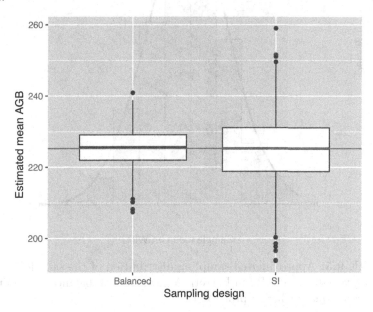

FIGURE 9.4: Approximated sampling distribution of the π estimator of the mean AGB (10^9 kg ha^{-1}) in Eastern Amazonia, with balanced sampling, balanced on lnSWIR2 and using equal inclusion probabilities, and simple random sampling without replacement (SI) of 100 units.

The variance of the 1,000 estimates of the population mean of the study variable AGB equals 28.8 $(10^9$ kg ha$^{-1})^2$. The gain in precision compared to simple random sampling equals 2.984 (design effect is 0.335), so with simple random sampling about three times more sampling units are needed to estimate the population mean with the same precision. The mean of the 1,000 estimated variances equals 26.4 $(10^9$ kg ha$^{-1})^2$, indicating that the approximated variance estimator somewhat underestimates the true variance in this case. The population mean of the balancing variable lnSWIR2 equals 6.414. The sample mean of lnSWIR2 varies a bit among the samples. Figure 9.5 shows the approximated sampling distribution of the sample mean of lnSWIR2. In other words, many samples are not perfectly balanced on lnSWIR2. This is not exceptional; in most cases perfect balance is impossible.

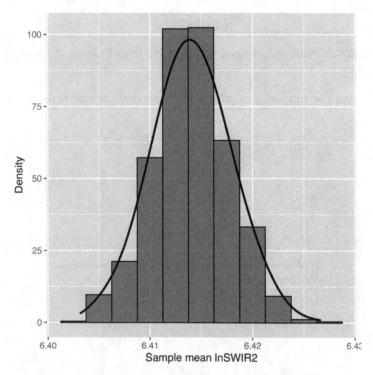

FIGURE 9.5: Approximated sampling distribution of the sample mean of balancing variable lnSWIR2 in Eastern Amazonia with balanced sampling of size 100 and equal inclusion probabilities.

Exercises

1. Select a sample of size 100 balanced on lnSWIR2 and Terra_PP from Eastern Amazonia, using equal inclusion probabilities for all units.

- First, select a subgrid of 5 km × 5 km using function spsample, see Chapter 5.
- Estimate the population mean.
- Estimate the standard error of the π estimator. First, estimate the regression coefficients, using function estimate_b defined above, then compute the residuals, and finally compute the variance.

2. Spatial clustering of sampling units is not avoided in balanced sampling. What effect do you expect of this spatial clustering on the precision of the estimated mean? Can you think of a situation where this effect does not occur?

9.1.3 Stratified random sampling

Much in the same way as we controlled in the previous subsection the sample size n by balancing the sample on the known total number of population units N, we can balance a sample on the known total number of units in subpopulations. A sample balanced on the sizes of subpopulations is a stratified random sample. Figure 9.6 shows four subpopulations or strata. These four strata can be used in balanced sampling by constructing the following design matrix $\mathbf{X}$ with as many columns as there are strata and as many rows as there are population units:

$$
\mathbf{X} = \begin{bmatrix} 1 & 0 & 0 & 0 \\ 1 & 0 & 0 & 0 \\ 1 & 0 & 0 & 0 \\ 1 & 0 & 0 & 0 \\ 0 & 1 & 0 & 0 \\ 0 & 1 & 0 & 0 \\ 0 & 0 & 1 & 0 \\ \vdots & \vdots & \vdots & \vdots \\ 0 & 0 & 0 & 1 \end{bmatrix} . \tag{9.7}
$$

The first four rows refer to the four leftmost bottom row population units in Figure 9.6. These units belong to class A, which explains that the first column for these units contain ones. The other three columns for these rows contain all zeroes. The fifth and sixth unit belong to stratum B, so that the second column for these rows contain ones, and so on. The final row is the upperright sampling unit in stratum D, so the first three columns contain zeroes, and the fourth column is filled with a one. The sum of the indicators in the columns is the total number of population units in the strata.

In the next code chunk, the inclusion probabilities are computed by $\pi_{hk} = n_h/N_h$, $k = 1, \ldots, N_h$, with $n_h = 5$ for all four strata. The stratum sample

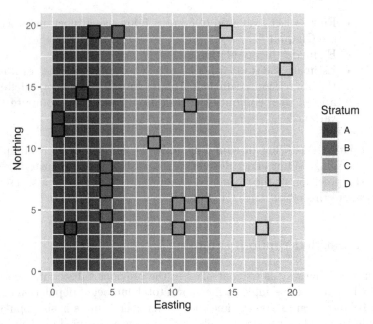

FIGURE 9.6: Sample balanced on a categorical variable with four classes.

sizes are equal, but the number of population units of a stratum differ among the strata, so the inclusion probabilities also differ among the strata.

```
N_h <- tapply(mypop$s1, INDEX = mypop$stratum, FUN = length)
n_h <- rep(5, times = 4)
n <- sum(n_h)
print(pi_h <- n_h / N_h)
```

```
         A          B          C          D
0.06250000 0.12500000 0.03125000 0.04166667
```

The inclusion probabilities are added to tibble `mypop` with the 400 population units, using a look-up table `lut` and function `left_join`. The ten leftmost units on the bottom row of Figure 9.6 are shown below. Variables s1 and s2 are the spatial coordinates of the centres of the units.

```
lut <- data.frame(stratum = sort(unique(mypop$stratum)), pi = n_h / N_h)
mypop <- mypop %>%
  as.tibble(mypop) %>%
  left_join(lut, by = "stratum") %>%
  arrange(s2, s1)
mypop
```

```
# A tibble: 400 x 4
     stratum    s1    s2      pi
     <fct>    <dbl> <dbl>   <dbl>
 1 A           0.5   0.5  0.0625
 2 A           1.5   0.5  0.0625
 3 A           2.5   0.5  0.0625
 4 A           3.5   0.5  0.0625
 5 B           4.5   0.5  0.125
 6 B           5.5   0.5  0.125
 7 C           6.5   0.5  0.0312
 8 C           7.5   0.5  0.0312
 9 C           8.5   0.5  0.0312
10 C           9.5   0.5  0.0312
# ... with 390 more rows
```

Next, the design matrix $\mathbf{X}$ is computed with function model.matrix, expanding the factor stratum to a set of dummy variables, see code chunk below. By adding - 1 to the formula, the usual first column with ones in the design matrix is omitted. The design matrix has four columns with dummy variables (indicators), indicating to which stratum a unit belongs.

The columns in the design matrix with dummy variables are multiplied by the vector with inclusion probabilities, using function sweep, resulting in the following design matrix:

$$\mathbf{X} = \begin{bmatrix} 0.0625 & 0 & 0 & 0 \\ 0.0625 & 0 & 0 & 0 \\ 0.0625 & 0 & 0 & 0 \\ 0.0625 & 0 & 0 & 0 \\ 0 & 0.125 & 0 & 0 \\ 0 & 0.125 & 0 & 0 \\ 0 & 0 & 0.03125 & 0 \\ \vdots & \vdots & \vdots & \vdots \\ 0 & 0 & 0 & 0.04167 \end{bmatrix} . \tag{9.8}$$

The multiplication by the inclusion probabilities is not strictly needed. Using the design matrix with dummy variables implies that we balance the sample on the known total number of population units in the strata, N_h. For samples with stratum sample sizes equal to n_h, the sample sums of the dummy variables used in balancing, divided by the inclusion probability, are equal to N_h.

Multiplication of the dummy variables by the vector with inclusion probabilities implies that we balance the sample on the population totals of the inclusion probabilities, which are equal to the targeted stratum sample sizes. For samples with stratum sample sizes n_h equal to these targeted sample sizes, the sample sums of the balancing variables, divided by the inclusion probability (having value $\pi_{hk}/\pi_{hk} = 1$ or 0), are equal to the targeted sample sizes.

```
X <- model.matrix(~ stratum - 1, data = mypop)
X <- sweep(X, MARGIN = 1, mypop$pi, `*`)
set.seed(314)
sample_ind <- samplecube(X = X, pik = mypop$pi, comment = FALSE, method = 1)
mysample <- mypop[sample_ind > (1 - eps), ]
```

In the above example all units in a stratum have the same inclusion probability, yielding a stratified simple random sample. We may also use variable inclusion probabilities, for instance proportional to a size measure of the units, yielding a stratified ppswor random sample (Section 8.2).

The advantage of selecting a stratified random sample by balancing the sample on a categorical variable becomes clear in case we have multiple classifications that we would like to use in stratification, and we cannot afford to use all cross-classifications as strata. This is the topic of the next subsection.

9.1.4 Multiway stratification

Falorsi and Righi (2008) describe how a multiway stratified sample can be selected as a balanced sample. Multiway stratification is of interest when one has multiple stratification variables, each stratification variable leading to several strata, so that the total number of cross-classification strata becomes so large that the stratum sample sizes are strongly disproportional to their size or even exceed the total sample size. For instance, suppose we have three maps with 4, 3, and 5 map units. Further, suppose that all combinations of map units are non-empty, so that we have $4 \times 3 \times 5 = 60$ combinations. We may not like to use all combinations (cross-classifications) as strata. The alternative is then to use the $4 + 3 + 5 = 12$ map units as strata.

The sample sizes of the marginal strata can be controlled using a design matrix with as many columns as there are strata. The units of an individual map used for stratification are referred to as marginal strata. Each row $k = 1, \ldots, N$ in the design matrix $\mathbf{X}$ has as many non-zero values as we have maps, in entries corresponding to the cross-classification map unit of population unit k, and zeroes in the remaining entries. The non-zero value is the inclusion probability of that unit. Each column of the design matrix has non-zero values in entries corresponding to the population units in that marginal stratum and zeroes in all other entries.

Two-way stratified random sampling is illustrated with a simulated population of 400 units (Figure 9.7). Figure 9.8 shows two classifications of the population units. Classification A consists of four classes (map units), classification B of three classes. Instead of using $4 \times 3 = 12$ cross-classifications as strata in random sampling, only $4 + 3 = 7$ marginal strata are used in two-way stratified random sampling.

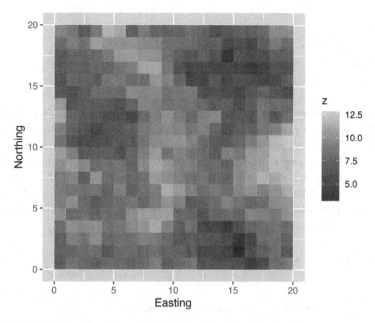

FIGURE 9.7: Simulated population used for illustration of two-way stratified random sampling.

As a first step, the inclusion probabilities are added to data.frame mypop with the spatial coordinates and simulated values. To keep it simple, I computed inclusion probabilities equal to 2 divided by the number of population units in a cross-classification stratum. Note that this does not imply that a sample is selected with two units per cross-classification stratum. As we will see later, it is possible that in some cross-classification strata no units are selected at all, while in other cross-classification strata more than two units are selected. In multiway stratified sampling, the marginal stratum sample sizes are controlled. The inclusion probabilities should result in six selected units for all four units of map A and eight selected units for all three units of map B.

```
mypop <- mypop %>%
    group_by(A, B) %>%
    summarise(N_h = n(), .groups = "drop") %>%
    mutate(pih = rep(2, 12) / N_h) %>%
    right_join(mypop, by = c("A", "B"))
```

The next step is to create the design matrix. Two submatrices are computed, one per stratification. The two submatrices are joined columnwise, using function cbind. The columns are multiplied by the vector with inclusion probabilities.

```
XA <- model.matrix(~ A - 1, mypop)
XB <- model.matrix(~ B - 1, mypop)
X <- cbind(XA, XB)
X <- sweep(X, MARGIN = 1, mypop$pih, '*')
```

Matrix **X** can be reduced by one column if in the first column the inclusion probabilities of *all* population units are inserted. This first column contains no zeroes. Balancing on this variable implies that the total sample size is controlled. Now there is no need anymore to control the sample sizes of all marginal strata. It is sufficient to control the sample sizes of three marginal strata of map A (A2, A3, and A4) and two marginal strata of map B (B2 and B3). Given the total sample size, the sample sizes of map units A1 and B1 then cannot be chosen freely anymore.

```
X <- model.matrix(~ A + B, mypop)
colnames(X)
```

```
[1] "(Intercept)" "AA2"          "AA3"          "AA4"          "BB2"
[6] "BB3"
```

```
X <- sweep(X, MARGIN = 1, mypop$pih, '*')
```

This reduced design matrix is not strictly needed for selecting a multiway stratified sample, but it must be used in estimation. If in estimation, as many balancing variables are used as we have marginal strata, the matrix with the sum of squares of the balancing variables (first sum in Equation (9.5)) cannot be inverted (the matrix is singular), and as a consequence the population regression coefficients cannot be estimated.

Finally, the two-way stratified random sample is selected with function samplecube of package **sampling**.

```
sample_ind <- samplecube(X = X, pik = mypop$pih, method = 1, comment = FALSE)
units <- which(sample_ind > (1 - eps))
mysample <- mypop[units, ]
```

Figure 9.8 shows the selected sample.

All marginal stratum sample sizes of map A are six and all marginal stratum sample sizes of map B are eight, as expected. The sample sizes of the cross-classification strata vary from zero to four.

```
addmargins(table(mysample$A, mysample$B))
```

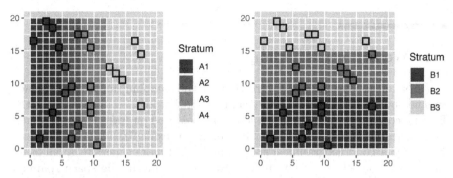

FIGURE 9.8: Two-way stratified sample.

	B1	B2	B3	Sum
A1	2	0	4	6
A2	2	3	1	6
A3	3	1	2	6
A4	1	4	1	6
Sum	8	8	8	24

The population mean can be estimated by the π estimator.

```
N <- nrow(mypop)
print(mean <- sum(mysample$z / mysample$pih) / N)
```

```
[1] 8.688435
```

The variance is estimated as before (Equation (9.3)).

```
c <- (1 - mysample$pih)
b <- estimate_b(
    z = mysample$z / mysample$pih, X = X[units, ] / mysample$pih, c = c)
zpred <- X %*% b
e <- mysample$z - zpred[units]
n <- nrow(mysample)
v_tz <- n / (n - ncol(X)) * sum(c * (e / mysample$pih)^2)
print(v_mz <- v_tz / N^2)
```

```
[1] 0.1723688
```

9.2   Well-spread sampling

With balanced sampling, the spreading of the sampling units in the space spanned by the balancing variables can be poor. For instance, in Figure 9.1 the Easting coordinates of all units of a sample balanced on Easting can be equal or close to the population mean of 10. So, in this example, balancing does not guarantee a good geographical spreading. Stated more generally, a balanced sample can be selected that shows strong clustering in the space spanned by the balancing variables. This clustering may inflate the standard error of the estimated population total and mean. The clustering in geographical or covariate space can be avoided by the local pivotal method (Grafström et al., 2012) and the spatially correlated Poisson sampling method (Grafström, 2012).

For spreading in *geographical* space various other designs are available. A simple design is stratified random sampling from compact geographical strata, see Section 4.6. Alternative designs are generalised random-tessellation stratified sampling (Stevens and Olson, 2004), see Subsection 9.2.2, and balanced acceptance sampling (Robertson et al., 2013).

9.2.1   Local pivotal method

The local pivotal method (LPM) is a modification of the pivotal method explained in Subsection 8.2.2. The only difference with the pivotal method is the selection of the pairs of units. In the pivotal method, at each step two units are selected, for instance, the first two units in the vector with inclusion probabilities after randomising the order of the units. In the local pivotal method, the first unit is selected fully randomly, and the nearest neighbour of this unit is used as its counterpart. Recall that when one unit of a pair is included in the sample, the inclusion probability of its counterpart is decreased. This leads to a better spreading of the sampling units in the space spanned by the spreading variables.

LPM can be used for arbitrary inclusion probabilities. The inclusion probabilities can be equal, but as with the pivotal method these probabilities may also differ among the population units.

Selecting samples with LPM can be done with functions lpm, lpm1, or lpm2 of package **BalancedSampling** (Grafström and Lisic, 2019). Functions lpm1 and lpm2 only differ in the selection of neighbours that are allowed to compete, for details see Grafström et al. (2012). For most populations, the two algorithms perform similarly. The algorithm implemented in function lpm is only recommended when the population size is too large for lpm1 or lpm2. It only uses a subset of the population in search for nearest neighbours and is thus not as good. Another function `lpm2_kdtree` of package **SamplingBigData** (Lisic and Grafström, 2018) is developed for big data sets.

Inclusion probabilities are computed with function `inclusionprobabilities` of package **sampling**. A matrix **X** must be defined with the values of the spreading variables of the population units. Figure 9.9 shows a ppswor sample of 40 units selected from the sampling frame of Kandahar, using the spatial coordinates of the population units as spreading variables. Inclusion probabilities are proportional to the agricultural area within the population units. The geographical spreading is improved compared with the sample shown in Figure 8.1.

```
library(BalancedSampling)
library(sampling)
n <- 40
pi <- inclusionprobabilities(grdKandahar$agri, n)
X <- cbind(grdKandahar$s1, grdKandahar$s2)
set.seed(314)
units <- lpm1(pi, X)
myLPMsample <- grdKandahar[units, ]
```

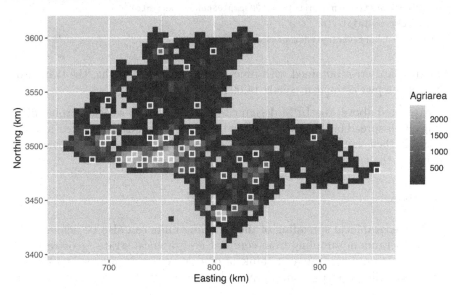

FIGURE 9.9: Spatial ppswor sample of size 40 from Kandahar, selected by the local pivotal method, using agricultural area as a size variable.

The total poppy area can be estimated with the π estimator (Equation (2.2)).

```
myLPMsample$pi <- pi[units]
tz_HT <- sum(myLPMsample$poppy / myLPMsample$pi)
```

The estimated total poppy area equals 62,232 ha. The sampling variance of the estimator of the population total with the local pivotal method can be estimated by (Grafström and Schelin, 2014)

$$\hat{V}(\hat{t}(z)) = \frac{1}{2} \sum_{k \in \mathcal{S}} \left(\frac{z_k}{\pi_k} - \frac{z_{k_j}}{\pi_{k_j}} \right)^2 , \tag{9.9}$$

with k_j the nearest neighbour of unit k in the sample. This variance estimator is for the case where we have only one nearest neighbour.

Function vsb of package **BalancedSampling** is an implementation of a more general variance estimator that accounts for more than one nearest neighbour (equation (6) in Grafström and Schelin (2014)). We expect a somewhat smaller variance compared to pps sampling, so we may use the variance of the pwr estimator (Equation (8.2)) as a conservative variance estimator.

```
Xsample <- X[units, ]
se_tz_HT <- sqrt(vsb(pi[units], myLPMsample$poppy, Xsample))
pk <- myLPMsample$pi / n
se_tz_pwr <- sqrt(var(myLPMsample$poppy / pk) / n)
```

The standard error obtained with function vsb equals 12,850 ha, the standard error of the pwr estimator equals 14,094 ha.

As explained above, the LPM design can also be used to select a probability sample well-spread in the space spanned by one or more quantitative covariates. Matrix **X** then should contain the values of the *scaled* (standardised) covariates instead of the spatial coordinates.

Exercises

    3. Geographical spreading of the sampling units can also be achieved by random sampling from compact geographical strata (geostrata) (Section 4.6). Can you think of one or more advantages of LPM sampling over random sampling from geostrata?

9.2.2 Generalised random-tessellation stratified sampling

Generalised random-tessellation stratified (GRTS) sampling is designed for sampling discrete objects scattered throughout space, think for instance of the lakes in Finland, segments of hedgerows in England, etc. Each object is represented by a point in 2D-space. It is a complicated design, and for sampling points from a continuous universe or raster cells from a finite population, I recommend more simple designs such as the local pivotal method (Subsection 9.2.1), balanced sampling with geographical spreading (Section 9.3), or sampling from compact geographical strata (Section 4.6). Let me try to explain the GRTS design with a simple example of a finite population of point objects in a circular study area (Figure 9.10). For a more detailed description of this design, refer to Hankin et al. (2019). As a first step, a square bounding box of the study area is constructed. This bounding box is recursively partitioned into square grid cells. First, 2 × 2 grid cells are constructed. These grid cells are numbered in a predefined order. In Figure 9.10 this numbering is from lower left, lower right, upper left to upper right. Each grid cell is then subdivided into four subcells; the subcells are numbered using the same order. This is repeated until at most one population unit occurs in each subcell. For our population only two iterations were needed, leading to 4 × 4 subcells. Note that two subcells are empty. Each address of a subcell consists of two digits: the first digit refers to the grid cell, the second digit to the subcell.

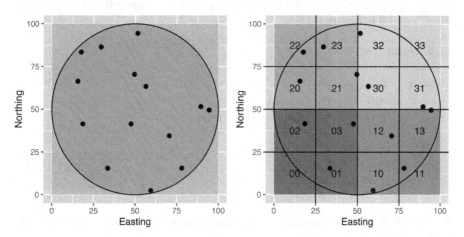

FIGURE 9.10: Numbering of grid cells and subcells for GRTS sampling.

The next step is to place the 16 subcells on a line in a random order. The randomisation is done hierarchically. First, the four grid cells at the highest level are randomised. In our example, the randomised order is 1, 2, 3, 0 (Figure 9.11). Next, within each grid cell, the order of the subcells is randomised. This is done independently for the grid cells. In our example, for grid cell 1 the randomised order of the subcells is 2, 1, 3, 0 (Figure 9.11). Note that the empty subcells (0,0) and (3,3) are removed from the line.

```
set.seed(314)
ord <- sample(4, 4)
myfinpop_rand <- NULL
for (i in ord) {
  units <- which(myfinpop$partit1 == i)
  units_rand <- sample(units, size = length(units))
  myfinpop_rand <- rbind(myfinpop_rand, myfinpop[units_rand, ])
}
```

After the subcells have been placed on a line, a one-dimensional systematic random sample is selected (Figure 9.11), see also Subsection 8.2.1. This can be done either with equal or unequal inclusion probabilities. With equal inclusion probabilities, the length of the intervals representing the population units is constant. With unequal inclusion probabilities, the interval lengths are proportional to a size variable. For a sample size of n, the total line is divided into n segments of equal length. A random point is selected in the first segment, and the other points of the systematic sample are determined. Finally, the population units corresponding to the selected systematic sample are identified. With equal probabilities, the five selected units are the units in subcells 11, 23, 22, 32, and 03 (Figure 9.11).

```
size <- rep(1, N)
n <- 5
interval <- sum(size) / n
start <- round(runif(1) * interval, 2)
mysys <- c(start, 1:(n - 1) * interval + start)
```

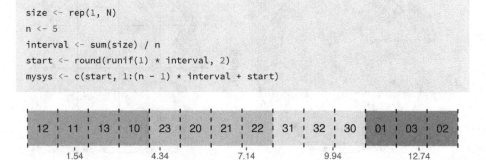

FIGURE 9.11: Systematic random sample along a line with equal inclusion probabilities.

Figure 9.12 shows a systematic random sample along a line with unequal inclusion probabilities. The inclusion probabilities are proportional to a size variable, with values 1, 2, 3, or 4. The selected population units are the units in subcells 10, 20, 31, 01, and 02.

GRTS samples can be selected with function grts of package **spsurvey** (Dumelle et al., 2021). The next code chunk shows the selection of a GRTS sample of 40 units from Kandahar. Tibble grdKandahar is first converted to an sf object with function st_as_sf of package **sf** (Pebesma, 2018). The data set is using a UTM projection (zone 41N) with WGS84 datum. This projection is

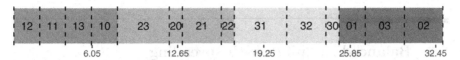

FIGURE 9.12: Systematic random sample along a line with inclusion probabilities proportional to size.

passed to function `st_as_df` with argument `crs` (`crs = 32641`). Argument `sframe` of function `grts` specifies the sampling frame. The sample size is passed to function `grts` with argument `n_base`. Argument `seltype` is set to `proportional` to select units with probabilities proportional to an ancillary variable which is passed to function `grts` with argument `aux_var`.

```
library(spsurvey)
library(sf)
sframe_sf <- st_as_sf(grdKandahar, coords = c("s1", "s2"), crs = 32641)
set.seed(314)
res <- grts(
    sframe = sframe_sf, n_base = 40, seltype = "proportional", aux_var = "agri")
myGRTSsample <- res$sites_base
```

Function `cont_analysis` computes the ratio estimator of the population mean and its standard error. The estimated mean is multiplied by the total number of population units to obtain a ratio estimate of the population total.

```
myGRTSsample$siteID <- paste0("siteID", seq_len(nrow(myGRTSsample)))
res <- cont_analysis(myGRTSsample,
        vars = "poppy", siteID = "siteID", weight = "wgt", statistics = "Mean")
tz_ratio <- res$Mean$Estimate * nrow(grdKandahar)
se_tz_ratio <- res$Mean$StdError * nrow(grdKandahar)
```

The estimated total poppy area is 109,809 ha, and the estimated standard error is 24,327 ha.

The alternative is to estimate the total poppy area by the π estimator. Function `vsb` of package **BalancedSampling** can be used to estimate the standard error of the π estimator.

```
tz_HT <- sum(myGRTSsample$poppy / myGRTSsample$ip)
Xsample <- st_coordinates(myGRTSsample)
se_tz_HT <- sqrt(vsb(myGRTSsample$ip, myGRTSsample$poppy, Xsample))
```

The estimated total is 71,634 ha, and the estimated standard error is 12,593 ha.

9.3   Balanced sampling with spreading

As mentioned in the introduction to this chapter, a sample balanced on a covariate still may have a poor spreading along the axis spanned by the covariate. Grafström and Tillé (2013) presented a method for selecting balanced samples that are also well-spread in the space spanned by the covariates, which they refer to as doubly balanced sampling. If we take one or more covariates as balancing variables and, besides, Easting and Northing as spreading variables, this leads to balanced samples with good *geographical* spreading. When the residuals of the regression model show spatial structure (are spatially correlated), the estimated population mean of the study variable becomes more precise thanks to the improved geographical spreading. Balanced samples with spreading can be selected with function lcube of package **BalancedSampling**. This is illustrated with Eastern Amazonia, using as before lnSWIR2 for balancing the sample.

```
library(BalancedSampling)
N <- nrow(grdAmazonia)
n <- 100
Xbal <- cbind(rep(1, times = N), grdAmazonia$lnSWIR2)
Xspread <- cbind(grdAmazonia$x1, grdAmazonia$x2)
pi <- rep(n / N, times = N)
set.seed(314)
units <- lcube(Xbal = Xbal, Xspread = Xspread, prob = pi)
mysample <- grdAmazonia[units, ]
```

The selected sample is shown in Figure 9.13. Comparing this sample with the balanced sample of Figure 9.3 shows that the geographical spreading of the sample is improved, although there still are some close points. I used equal inclusion probabilities, so the π estimate of the mean is equal to the sample mean, which is equal to $225.6 \ 10^9$ kg ha^{-1}.

The variance of the π estimator of the mean can be estimated by (equation (7) of Grafström and Tillé (2013))

$$\hat{V}(\hat{\bar{z}}) = \frac{n}{n-p}\frac{p}{p+1}\sum_{k\in\mathcal{S}}(1-\pi_k)\left(\frac{e_k}{\pi_k}-\bar{e}_k\right)^2, \qquad (9.10)$$

with p the number of balancing variables, e_k the regression model residual of unit k (Equation (9.4)), and $\bar{e}_k$ the local mean of the residuals of this unit, computed by

$$\bar{e}_k = \frac{\sum_{j=1}^{p+1}(1-\pi_j)\frac{e_j}{\pi_j}}{\sum_{j=1}^{p+1}(1-\pi_j)}. \qquad (9.11)$$

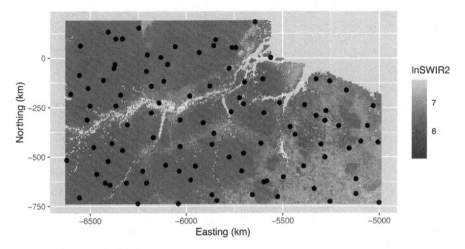

FIGURE 9.13: Sample balanced on lnSWIR2 with geographical spreading from Eastern Amazonia.

The variance estimator can be computed with functions `localmean_weight` and `localmean_var` of package **spsurvey** (Dumelle et al., 2021).

```
library(spsurvey)
pi <- rep(n / N, n)
c <- (1 - pi)
b <- estimate_b(z = mysample$AGB / pi, X = Xbal[units, ] / pi, c = c)
zpred <- Xbal %*% b
e <- mysample$AGB - zpred[units]
weights <- localmean_weight(x = mysample$x1, y = mysample$x2, prb = pi, nbh = 3)
v_mz <- localmean_var(z = e / pi, weight_1st = weights) / N^2
```

The estimated standard error is 2.8×10^9 kg ha^{-1}, which is considerably smaller than the estimated standard error of the balanced sample without geographical spreading.

10

Model-assisted estimation

In many cases ancillary information is available that could be useful to increase the accuracy of the estimated mean or total of the study variable. The ancillary variable(s) can be qualitative (i.e., classifications) or quantitative. As we have seen before, both types of ancillary variable can be used at the design stage, i.e., in selecting the sampling units, to improve the performance of the sampling strategy, for instance by stratification (Chapter 4), selecting sampling units with probabilities proportional to size (Chapter 8), or through balancing and/or spreading the sample on the covariates (Chapter 9). This chapter explains how these covariates can be used at the stage of *estimation*, once the data are collected.

In the design-based approach for sampling, various estimators are developed that exploit one or more covariates. These estimators are derived from different superpopulation models of the study variable. A superpopulation model is a statistical model that can be used to generate an infinite number of populations, a superpopulation, through simulation. An example is the simulation of spatial populations using a geostatistical model, see Chapter 13. A superpopulation is a construct, it does not exist in reality. We assume that the population of interest is one of the populations that can be generated with the chosen model. The combination of probability sampling and estimators that are built on a superpopulation model is referred to as the model-assisted approach. Also in the model-based approach a superpopulation model is used; however, its role is fundamentally different from that in the model-assisted approach, see Chapter 26. To stress the different use of the superpopulation model in the model-assisted approach, this model is referred to as the "working model", i.e., the superpopulation model that is used to derive a model-assisted estimator.

Breidt and Opsomer (2017) present an overview of model-assisted estimators derived from a general working model:

$$Z_k = \mu(\mathbf{x}_k) + \epsilon_k , \tag{10.1}$$

with $\mu(\mathbf{x}_k)$ the model-mean for population unit k which is a function of the covariate values of that unit collected in vector $\mathbf{x}_k = (1, x_{1,k}, \ldots, x_{J,k})^{\mathrm{T}}$ and ϵ_k a random variable with zero mean. Note that I use uppercase Z to distinguish the random variable Z_k of unit k from one realisation of this random variable for unit k in the population of interest, z_k. The model-mean $\mu(\mathbf{x}_k)$ can be a linear or a non-linear combination of the covariates. If the study variable and the covariate values were observed for all population units, all these data could be used to compute a so-called hypothetical population fit of the model parameters. These model parameters can then be used to compute *estimates* of the model-means $\mu(\mathbf{x}_k)$, denoted by $m(\mathbf{x}_k)$, for all population units. For instance, with a (multiple) regression model $m(\mathbf{x}_k) = \mathbf{x}_k^T \mathbf{b}$, with $\mathbf{b}$ the vector with regression coefficients estimated from observations of the study variable z and the covariates on *all* population units. In practice, we have a sample only, which is used to estimate $m(\mathbf{x}_k)$ by $\hat{m}(\mathbf{x}_k)$. For the multiple regression model $\hat{m}(\mathbf{x}_k) = \mathbf{x}_k^T \hat{\mathbf{b}}$, with $\hat{\mathbf{b}}$ the vector with regression coefficients estimated from the sample data. This leads to the generalised difference estimator (Wu and Sitter, 2001):

$$\hat{\bar{z}}_{\mathrm{dif}} = \frac{1}{N} \sum_{k=1}^{N} \hat{m}(\mathbf{x}_k) + \frac{1}{N} \sum_{k \in \mathcal{S}} \frac{z_k - \hat{m}(\mathbf{x}_k)}{\pi_k} \, , \tag{10.2}$$

with π_k the inclusion probability of unit k. The first term is the population mean of model predictions of the study variable, and the second term is the π estimator of the population mean of the residuals.

A wide variety of model-assisted estimators have been developed and tested over the past decades. They differ in the working model used to obtain the estimates $\hat{m}(\mathbf{x}_k)$ in Equation (10.2). The best known class of model-assisted estimators is the generalised regression estimator that uses a linear model in prediction (Särndal et al., 1992). Alternative model-assisted estimators are the estimators using machine learning techniques for prediction. In the era of big data with a vastly increasing number of exhaustive data sets and a rapid development of machine learning techniques, these estimators have great potentials for spatial sample survey.

10.1   Generalised regression estimator

The working model of the generalised regression estimator is the heteroscedastic multiple linear regression model:

$$Z_k = \mathbf{x}_k^T \boldsymbol{\beta} + \epsilon_k \, , \tag{10.3}$$

with ϵ_k uncorrelated residuals, with zero mean and variance $\sigma^2(\epsilon_k)$. Note that the variance of the residuals $\sigma^2(\epsilon_k)$ need not be constant but may differ among the population units. If $\{z_k, x_{1,k}, \dots, x_{J,k}\}$ were observed for all units

$k = 1, \dots, N$ in the population, the regression coefficients $\boldsymbol{\beta}$ would be estimated by

$$\mathbf{b} = \left(\sum_{k=1}^{N} \frac{\mathbf{x}_k \mathbf{x}_k^{\mathrm{T}}}{\sigma^2(\epsilon_k)} \right)^{-1} \sum_{k=1}^{N} \frac{\mathbf{x}_k z_k}{\sigma^2(\epsilon_k)} \,, \qquad (10.4)$$

with $\mathbf{x}_k$ the vector $(1, x_{1,k}, \dots, x_{J,k})^{\mathrm{T}}$ and $\sigma^2(\epsilon_k)$ the variance of the residual of unit k. Similar to the distinction between model-mean and population mean (see Chapter 26), here the model regression coefficients $\boldsymbol{\beta}$ are distinguished from the population regression coefficients $\mathbf{b}$. The means $m(\mathbf{x}_k)$ would then be computed by

$$m(\mathbf{x}_k) = \mathbf{x}_k^{\mathrm{T}} \mathbf{b} \,. \qquad (10.5)$$

If we have a probability sample from the population of interest, $\mathbf{b}$ is estimated by replacing the population totals in Equation (10.4) by their π estimators:

$$\hat{\mathbf{b}} = \left(\sum_{k \in \mathcal{S}} \frac{\mathbf{x}_k \mathbf{x}_k^{\mathrm{T}}}{\sigma^2(\epsilon_k) \pi_k} \right)^{-1} \sum_{k \in \mathcal{S}} \frac{\mathbf{x}_k z_k}{\sigma^2(\epsilon_k) \pi_k} \,. \qquad (10.6)$$

With unequal inclusion probabilities, the design-based estimators of the population regression coefficients differ from the usual ordinary least squares (OLS) estimators of the regression coefficients defined as model parameters. The values $\hat{b}_j$ are estimates of the *population parameters* b_j.

The mean values $m(\mathbf{x}_k)$ are now estimated by

$$\hat{m}(\mathbf{x}_k) = \mathbf{x}_k^{\mathrm{T}} \hat{\mathbf{b}} \,. \qquad (10.7)$$

Plugging Equation (10.7) into the generalised difference estimator, Equation (10.2), leads to the generalised regression estimator for the population mean:

$$\hat{\bar{z}}_{\mathrm{regr}} = \frac{1}{N} \sum_{k=1}^{N} \mathbf{x}_k^{\mathrm{T}} \hat{\mathbf{b}} + \frac{1}{N} \sum_{k \in \mathcal{S}} \frac{z_k - \mathbf{x}_k^{\mathrm{T}} \hat{\mathbf{b}}}{\pi_k} \,. \qquad (10.8)$$

This estimator can also be written as

$$\hat{\bar{z}}_{\mathrm{regr}} = \hat{\bar{z}}_\pi + \sum_{j=1}^{J} \hat{b}_j (\bar{x}_j - \hat{\bar{x}}_{j,\pi}) \,, \qquad (10.9)$$

with $\hat{\bar{z}}_\pi$ and $\hat{\bar{x}}_{j,\pi}$ the π estimator of the study variable and the jth covariate, respectively, $\bar{x}_j$ the population mean of the jth covariate, and $\hat{b}_j$ the estimated slope coefficient associated with the jth covariate. So, the generalised regression estimate is equal to the π estimate when the estimated means of the covariates are equal to the population means. This is the rationale of balanced sampling (Chapter 9).

The alternative formulation of the regression estimator (Equation (10.9)) shows that we do not need to know the covariate values for all population units. Knowledge of the population means of the covariates is sufficient. This is because a linear relation is assumed between the study variable and the covariates. On the contrary, for non-linear working models such as a random forest model, exhaustive knowledge of the covariates is needed so that the estimated mean $\hat{m}(\mathbf{x}_k)$ in Equation (10.2) can be computed for every unit in the population.

Särndal et al. (1992) worked out the generalised regression estimator for various superpopulation models, such as the simple and multiple linear regression model, the ratio model, and the analysis of variance (ANOVA) model.

10.1.1 Simple and multiple regression estimators

The working model of the simple and the multiple regression estimator is the homoscedastic linear regression model. The only difference with the heteroscedastic model is that the variance of the residuals is assumed constant: $\sigma^2(\epsilon_k) = \sigma^2(\epsilon), k = 1, \dots, N$.

In the simple linear regression model, the mean is a linear function of a single covariate, $\mu(x_k) = \alpha + \beta\, x_k$. The simple linear regression model leads to the simple regression estimator. With simple random sampling, this estimator for the population mean is

$$\hat{\bar{z}}_{\text{regr}} = \bar{z}_\mathcal{S} + \hat{b}\,(\bar{x} - \bar{x}_\mathcal{S})\ , \tag{10.10}$$

where $\bar{z}_\mathcal{S}$ and $\bar{x}_\mathcal{S}$ are the sample means of the study variable and the covariate, respectively, $\bar{x}$ is the population mean of the covariate, and $\hat{b}$ is the estimated slope coefficient:

$$\hat{b} = \frac{\sum_{k\in\mathcal{S}}(x_k - \bar{x}_\mathcal{S})(z_k - \bar{z}_\mathcal{S})}{\sum_{k\in\mathcal{S}}(x_k - \bar{x}_\mathcal{S})^2}\ . \tag{10.11}$$

The rationale of the regression estimator is that when the estimated mean of the covariate is, for instance, smaller than the population mean of the covariate, then with a positive correlation between study variable and covariate, also the estimated mean of the study variable is expected to be smaller than the population mean of the study variable. The difference between the population mean and the estimated mean of the covariate can be used to improve the π estimate of the mean of z (which is for simple random sampling equal to the sample mean $\bar{z}_\mathcal{S}$), by adding a term proportional to the difference between the estimated mean and the population mean of the covariate. As a scaling factor, the estimated slope of the fitted regression line is used.

The sampling variance of this regression estimator can be estimated by computing first the regression residuals $e_k = z_k - \hat{z}_k$, $k = 1, \dots, n$ at the sampling units, with $\hat{z}_k = \hat{a} + \hat{b}x_k$ the predicted value for unit k. Note that I use symbol ϵ (Equation (10.3)) for the residuals from the model with the model regression coefficients β, whereas for the residuals from the model with the estimated population regression coefficients $\hat{\mathbf{b}}$ I use symbol e. To compute the residuals e also an estimate of the intercept a is needed. With simple random sampling, this intercept can be estimated by

$$\hat{a} = \bar{z}_\mathcal{S} - \hat{b}\,\bar{x}_\mathcal{S} \, . \tag{10.12}$$

The sampling variance of the regression estimator of the population mean is *approximately* equal to the sampling variance of the π estimator of the mean of the model residuals:

$$\hat{V}\!\left(\hat{\bar{z}}_{\mathrm{regr}}\right) = \left(1 - \frac{n}{N}\right) \frac{\widehat{S^2}(e)}{n} \, , \tag{10.13}$$

with $\widehat{S^2}(e)$ the estimated population variance of the regression residuals:

$$\widehat{S^2}(e) = \frac{1}{n-1} \sum_{k \in \mathcal{S}} e_k^2 \, . \tag{10.14}$$

The variance estimator is an approximation because the regression coefficients are also estimated from the sample, which makes the regression estimator non-linear. The approximation of the variance is based on a Taylor linearisation of the regression estimator (Särndal et al. (1992), p. 235).

For simple random sampling with replacement from finite populations and simple random sampling of infinite populations, the finite population correction factor $1 - n/N$ must be dropped, see Chapter 3.

In the multiple linear regression model, the mean is a linear function of multiple covariates. This model leads to the multiple regression estimator. With simple random sampling, the population regression coefficients of this estimator can be estimated by

$$\hat{\mathbf{b}} = \left(\sum_{k \in \mathcal{S}} \mathbf{x}_k \mathbf{x}_k^{\mathrm{T}} \right)^{-1} \sum_{k \in \mathcal{S}} \mathbf{x}_k z_k \ . \tag{10.15}$$

Comparison with the general estimator of the population regression coefficients (Equation (10.6)) shows that the variance of the residuals, $\sigma^2(\epsilon_k)$, is missing as they are assumed constant. Besides, the inclusion probabilities π_k are missing because they are equal for all population units with simple random sampling.

The simple regression estimator is illustrated with Eastern Amazonia. The population mean of the aboveground biomass (AGB) is estimated by the simple regression estimator, using natural logs of MODIS short-wave infrared radiation (SWIR2) as a covariate.

A simple random sample without replacement of 100 units is selected using slice_sample of package **dplyr**, and the two population regression coefficients are estimated with Equation (10.15).

```
grdAmazonia <- grdAmazonia %>%
  mutate(lnSWIR2 = log(SWIR2))
set.seed(321)
n <- 100
mysample <- grdAmazonia %>%
  dplyr::select(AGB,lnSWIR2) %>%
  slice_sample(n = n)
X <- matrix(nrow = n, ncol = 2, data = 1)
X[, 2] <- mysample$lnSWIR2
XXinv <- solve(t(X) %*% X)
Xz <- t(X) %*% mysample$AGB
print(ab <- t(XXinv %*% Xz))
```

```
          [,1]       [,2]
[1,] 1751.636 -237.1379
```

The same estimates are obtained by ordinary least squares (OLS) fitting of the model with function lm.

```
lm_sample <- lm(AGB ~ lnSWIR2, data = mysample)
print(ab_mb <- coef(lm_sample))
```

```
(Intercept)     lnSWIR2
  1751.6363   -237.1379
```

As already stressed above, the design-based estimates of the population regression coefficients are only equal to the model-based OLS estimates of the regression coefficients for equal probability sampling designs. Also be aware that the variance of the design-based estimates of the population regression coefficients is not equal to the model-based variance of the model regression coefficients. See section (11.2.2.1) in Lohr (1999) for how to estimate the variance of the design-based estimates of the population regression coefficients.

Figure 10.1 shows the scatter plot for the simple random sample and the fitted simple linear regression model.

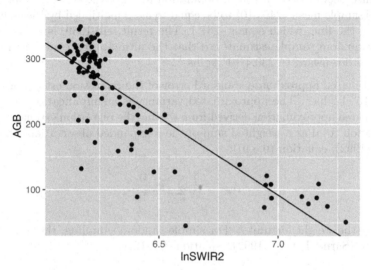

FIGURE 10.1: Scatter plot of AGB (10^9 kg ha^{-1}) against lnSWIR2 of a simple random sample of size 100 from Eastern Amazonia and the fitted simple linear regression model for AGB.

The simple random sample is used to estimate the population mean of the study variable AGB by the simple regression estimator and to approximate the sampling variance of the regression estimator. The residuals of the fitted model can be extracted with function residuals because in this case the OLS estimates of the regression coefficients are equal to the design-based estimates. With unequal inclusion probabilities, the residuals must be computed by predicting the study variable for the selected units, using the design-based estimates of the regression coefficients, and subtracting the observations of the study variable.

```
mx_pop <- mean(grdAmazonia$lnSWIR2)
mx_sam <- mean(mysample$lnSWIR2)
mz_sam <- mean(mysample$AGB)
mz_regr <- mz_sam + ab[2] * (mx_pop - mx_sam)
e <- residuals(lm_sample)
S2e <- var(e)
```

```
N <- nrow(grdAmazonia)
se_mz_regr <- sqrt((1 - n / N) * S2e / n)
```

The difference $\delta(x)$ between the population mean of the covariate lnSWIR2 (6.415) and its estimated mean (6.347) equals 0.068. We may expect the difference between the unknown population mean of the study variable AGB and its sample mean (246.510) to be equal to $\delta(x)$, multiplied by the estimated slope of the line, which equals -237.1. The result, -16.1039, is added to the simple random sample estimate, so that the ultimate regression estimate is adjusted downward to 230.4 10^9 kg ha^{-1}.

The estimated approximate standard error of the regression estimator equals 4.458 10^9 kg ha^{-1}. The approximated variance is a simplification of a more complicated approximation derived from writing the regression estimator of the population total as a weighted sum of the π-expanded observations (Särndal et al. (1992), equation (6.5.9)):

$$\hat{\bar{z}}_{\text{regr}} = \frac{1}{N} \sum_{k \in \mathcal{S}} g_k \frac{z_k}{\pi_k} , \qquad (10.16)$$

with g_k the weight for unit k. For simple random sampling, the weights are equal to (Särndal et al. (1992), equation (6.5.12))

$$g_k = 1 + \frac{(\bar{x} - \bar{x}_{\mathcal{S}})(x_k - \bar{x}_{\mathcal{S}})}{\widehat{S^2}(x)} . \qquad (10.17)$$

These weights are now computed.

```
S2x <- sum((mysample$lnSWIR2 - mean(mysample$lnSWIR2))^2) / n
g <- 1 + ((mx_pop - mx_sam) * (mysample$lnSWIR2 - mx_sam)) / S2x
```

The sample mean of the weights equals 1,

```
mean(g)
```

```
[1] 1
```

and the sample mean of the product of the weights and the covariate x equals the population mean of the covariate.

```
all.equal(mean(g * mysample$lnSWIR2), mean(grdAmazonia$lnSWIR2))
```

```
[1] TRUE
```

In other words, the sample is calibrated on the known population means. The variance of the regression estimator of the population mean can be approximated by (Särndal et al. (1992), section 6.6)

$$\hat{V}(\hat{\bar{z}}_{\text{regr}}) = \left(1 - \frac{n}{N}\right) \frac{\sum_{k \in \mathcal{S}} g_k^2 e_k^2}{n(n-1)} . \tag{10.18}$$

Comparing this with Equation (10.13) shows that in the first approximation we assumed that all weights are equal to 1.

The alternative approximate standard error is computed in the next code chunk.

```
S2ge <- sum(g^2 * e^2) / (n - 1)
print(se_mz_regr <- sqrt((1 - n / N) * S2ge / n))
```

```
[1] 4.546553
```

The regression estimator and its standard error can be computed with package **survey** (Lumley, 2021). After specifying the sampling design with function svydesign, function calibrate is used to calibrate the sample on the known population totals N and $t(x) = \sum_{k=1}^{N} x_k$, with x_k the value of covariate lnSWIR2 for unit k.

```
library(survey)
mysample$fpc <- N
design_si <- svydesign(id = ~ 1, data = mysample, fpc = ~ fpc)
populationtotals <- c(N, sum(grdAmazonia$lnSWIR2))
mysample_cal <- calibrate(design_si, formula = ~ lnSWIR2,
    population = populationtotals, calfun = "linear")
```

The calibrated weights can be extracted with function weights.

The calibrated weights are divided by the inclusion probabilities $\pi = n/N$, so that the sample sum of the weights equals N and not the sample size n (as in the code chunk above).

```
g <- weights(mysample_cal)
all.equal(sum(g), N)
```

```
[1] TRUE
```

The sample sum of the product of the weights and the covariate equals the population total of the covariate.

```
all.equal(sum(g * mysample$lnSWIR2), sum(grdAmazonia$lnSWIR2))
```

```
[1] TRUE
```

Finally, the population mean can be estimated with function svymean. This is simply the sample sum of the product of the weights and the study variable AGB, divided by N.

```
svymean(~ AGB, mysample_cal)
```

```
        mean      SE
AGB 230.41 4.5466
```

The standard error is computed with Equation (10.18). Figure 10.2 shows the sampling distribution of the simple regression estimator along with the distribution of the π estimator, obtained by repeating simple random sampling of 100 units and estimation 10,000 times.

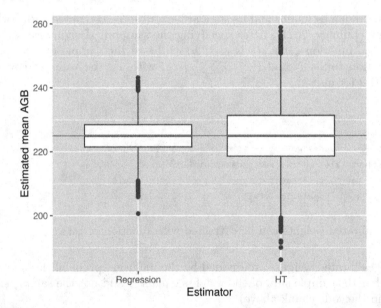

FIGURE 10.2: Approximated sampling distribution of the simple regression estimator (Regression) and the π estimator (HT) of the mean AGB (10^9 kg ha^{-1}) in Eastern Amazonia, for simple random sampling without replacement of size 100.

The average of the 10,000 regression estimates equals 224.9 10^9 kg ha^{-1}. The population mean of the study variable AGB equals 225.0 10^9 kg ha^{-1}, so the estimated bias of the regression estimator equals -0.1 10^9 kg ha^{-1}, which is negligibly small related to the estimated population mean. The variance of the 10,000 regression estimates equals 26.70 $(10^9$ kg ha$^{-1})^2$, and the average of the 10,000 estimated approximate variances using Equation (10.18) equals 26.86 $(10^9$ kg ha$^{-1})^2$. The gain in precision due to the regression estimator, quantified by the ratio of the variance of the π estimator to the variance of the regression estimator equals 3.192.

For simple random sampling, the ratio of the variances of the simple regression estimator and the π estimator is independent of the sample size and equals $1 - r^2$, with r the correlation coefficient of the study variable and the covariate (Särndal et al. (1992), p. 274).

Using multiple covariates in the regression estimator is straightforward with function calibrate of package **survey**. As a first step, the best model is selected with function regsubsets of package **leaps** (Lumley, 2020).

```
library(leaps)
n <- 100
set.seed(321)
mysample <- grdAmazonia %>%
  dplyr::select(AGB, lnSWIR2, Terra_PP, Prec_dm, Elevation, Clay) %>%
  slice_sample(n = n)
models <- regsubsets(AGB ~ ., data = mysample, nvmax = 4)
res_sum <- summary(models)
res_sum$outmat
```

	lnSWIR2	Terra_PP	Prec_dm	Elevation	Clay
1 (1)	"*"	" "	" "	" "	" "
2 (1)	"*"	"*"	" "	" "	" "
3 (1)	"*"	"*"	" "	"*"	" "
4 (1)	"*"	"*"	"*"	"*"	" "

The best model with one predictor is the model with lnSWIR2, the best model with two predictors is the one with lnSWIR2 and Terra_PP, etc. Of these models, the third model, i.e., the model with lnSWIR2, Terra_PP, and Elevation, is the best when using adjusted R^2 as a selection criterion.

```
which.max(res_sum$adjr2)
```

```
[1] 3
```

The standard error of the estimated mean AGB is somewhat reduced by adding the covariates Terra_PP and Elevation to the regression estimator.

```
mysample$fpc <- nrow(grdAmazonia)
design_si <- svydesign(id = ~ 1, data = mysample, fpc = ~ fpc)
totals <- c(nrow(grdAmazonia), sum(grdAmazonia$lnSWIR2),
```

```
    sum(grdAmazonia$Terra_PP), sum(grdAmazonia$Elevation))
mysample_cal <- calibrate(design_si, formula = ~ lnSWIR2 + Terra_PP + Elevation,
  population = totals, calfun = "linear")
svymean(~ AGB, mysample_cal)
```

```
        mean       SE
AGB 230.54 4.2224
```

Another interesting package for model-assisted estimation is package **mase** (McConville et al., 2021). The regression estimate can be computed with function greg.

```
library(mase)
covars <- c("lnSWIR2", "Terra_PP", "Elevation")
res <- greg(y = mysample$AGB, xsample = mysample[covars],
  xpop = grdAmazonia[covars], pi = rep(n / N, n),
  var_est = TRUE, var_method = "LinHTSRS", model = "linear")
res$pop_mean
```

```
[1] 230.5407
```

The multiple regression estimate is equal to the estimate obtained with function calibrate of package **survey**. The estimated standard error equals

```
sqrt(res$pop_mean_var)
```

```
        [,1]
[1,] 4.207809
```

which is slightly smaller than the standard error computed with package **survey**. The standard error obtained with function greg is computed by ignoring the g-weights (McConville et al., 2020). In an exercise, the two approximate standard errors are compared in a sampling experiment.

10.1.2   Penalised least squares estimation

In the previous subsection, I first selected a best subset of covariates before using these covariates in estimating the population regression coefficients. The alternative is to skip the selection of the best model and to estimate the population regression coefficients of *all* covariates by penalised least squares (PLS) estimation. In PLS estimation a penalty equal to the sum of the absolute or squared values of the population regression coefficients is added to the minimisation criterion, see McConville et al. (2020) for details. PLS estimation is implemented in function gregElasticNet of package **mase**.

```
covars <- c("lnSWIR2", "Terra_PP", "Prec_dm", "Elevation", "Clay")
res <- gregElasticNet(
  y = mysample$AGB, xsample = mysample[covars],
  xpop = grdAmazonia[covars], pi = rep(n / N, n),
  var_est = TRUE, var_method = "LinHTSRS", model = "linear",
  lambda = "lambda.min", cvfolds = 100)
signif(res$coefficients, 4)
```

```
(Intercept)    lnSWIR2    Terra_PP    Prec_dm   Elevation      Clay
  -71.07000   -2.83800     0.02204    0.52710    -0.03507   0.13630
```

All five covariates are used in prediction, but the coefficients associated with these predictors are small except for lnSWIR2.

As shown below, the estimated standard error is considerably larger than the standard error obtained with lnSWIR2, Terra_PP, and Elevation as predictors. In this case, the elastic net regression estimator does not work as well as the multiple regression estimator using the best subset of the covariates.

```
sqrt(res$pop_mean_var)
```

```
        s1
s1 6.207637
```

Exercises

1. Write an **R** script to select a simple random sample without replacement of size 50 from Eastern Amazonia. Compute the regression estimator of the population mean of AGB and its standard error "by hand", i.e., without using package **survey**, using lnSWIR2 as a covariate. Use Equation (10.13) to estimate the standard error.
   - Use the same sample to compute the regression estimator with functions calibrate and svymean of package **survey**. The regression estimate and its standard error can be extracted from the output object of svymean with methods coef and SE, respectively.
   - Repeat both estimation procedures 1,000 times (for-loop). Check that the 2 × 1,000 estimated population means obtained with both estimators are all equal (use function all.equal), and compute summary statistics of the two approximated standard errors. Which approximate standard error estimator has the largest mean value?

2. Write an **R** script to compute the sampling variance of the simple regression estimator of the mean AGB, using lnSWIR2 as a covariate, for simple random sampling and sample sizes 10, 25, and 100, assuming that the population regression coefficients are perfectly known. Hint: fit a simple linear regression model on all data, and compute the population variance of the residuals.

- Next, select 10,000 times a simple random sample with replacement of size 10 (for-loop). Use each sample to estimate the population mean of AGB with the simple regression estimator (using sample estimates of the population regression coefficients), and estimate the approximate variance of the estimator of the mean. Compute the variance of the 10,000 regression estimates and the average of the 10,000 approximate variance estimates. Repeat this for sample sizes 25 and 100.

- Compute for each sample size the difference between the experimental variance (variance of the 10,000 regression estimates) and the variance obtained with the population fit of the regression model as a proportion of the experimental variance. Explain what you see.

- Compute for each sample size the difference between the average of the 10,000 approximated variances and the experimental variance as a proportion of the experimental variance. Explain what you see.

10.1.3 Regression estimator with stratified simple random sampling

With stratified simple random sampling there are two regression estimators: *separate* and *combined*. In the first estimator, the regression estimator for simple random sampling is applied at the level of the strata. This implies that for each stratum separately a vector with population regression coefficients $\mathbf{b}_h$ is estimated. The regression estimates of the stratum means are then combined by computing the weighted average, using the relative sizes of the strata as weights:

$$\hat{\bar{z}}_{\text{sregr}} = \sum_{h=1}^{H} w_h \hat{\bar{z}}_{\text{regr},h} \,, \tag{10.19}$$

with, for the simple linear estimator

$$\hat{\bar{z}}_{\text{regr},h} = \bar{z}_{sh} + \hat{b}_h \left(\bar{x}_h - \bar{x}_{sh} \right) \,, \tag{10.20}$$

with $\bar{z}_{sh}$ and $\bar{x}_{sh}$ the stratum sample means of the study variable and the covariate, respectively, $\bar{x}_h$ the mean of the covariate in stratum h, and $\hat{b}_h$ the estimated slope coefficient for stratum h.

The variance of this separate regression estimator of the population mean can be estimated by first estimating the variances of the regression estimators of the stratum means using Equation (10.13), and then combining these variances using Equation (4.4).

The separate regression estimator is illustrated with Eastern Amazonia. Biomes are used as strata. There are four biomes, the levels of which are given short names using function levels.

```
grdAmazonia$Biome <- as.factor(grdAmazonia$Biome)
levels(grdAmazonia$Biome)
```

```
[1] "Mangroves"
[2] "Tropical & Subtropical Dry Broadleaf Forests"
[3] "Tropical & Subtropical Grasslands, Savannas & Shrublands"
[4] "Tropical & Subtropical Moist Broadleaf Forests"
```

```
biomes <- c("Mangrove", "Forest_dry", "Grassland", "Forest_moist")
levels(grdAmazonia$Biome) <- biomes
```

Moist forest is by far the largest stratum, it covers 92% of the area. Mangrove, Forest_dry, and Grassland cover 0.4, 2.3, and 5.5% of the area, respectively. A stratified simple random sample of size 100 is selected using function strata of package **sampling**, see Chapter 4. I chose five units as a minimum sample size. Note that the stratum sample sizes are not proportional to their size.

```
library(sampling)
N_h <-  table(grdAmazonia$Biome)
n_h <- c(5, 5, 5, 85)
set.seed(314)
units <- sampling::strata(grdAmazonia, stratanames = "Biome",
  size = n_h[unique(grdAmazonia$Biome)], method = "srswor")
mysample <- getdata(grdAmazonia, units)
```

As a first step in estimation, for each stratum the mean of the covariate over all units in a stratum (population mean per stratum) and the sample means of the study variable and the covariate are computed.

```
mx_h_pop <- tapply(grdAmazonia$lnSWIR2, INDEX = grdAmazonia$Biome, FUN = mean)
mzh_sam <- tapply(mysample$AGB, INDEX = mysample$Biome, FUN = mean)
mx_h_sam <- tapply(mysample$lnSWIR2, INDEX = mysample$Biome, FUN = mean)
```

The next step is to estimate the regression coefficients (intercept and slope) per stratum. This is done in a for-loop. The estimated slope coefficient is used to compute the regression estimator per stratum. The residuals are extracted to approximate the variance of the regression estimator per stratum.

```
b_h <- mz_h_regr <- v_mz_h_regr <- numeric(length = 4)
for (i in 1:4) {
  subsam <- subset(mysample, mysample$Biome == levels(grdAmazonia$Biome)[i])
  lm_sample <- lm(AGB ~ lnSWIR2, data = subsam)
  b_h[i] <- coef(lm_sample)[2]
  mz_h_regr[i] <- mzh_sam[i] + b_h[i] * (mx_h_pop[i] - mx_h_sam[i])
  e <- residuals(lm_sample)
  S2e_h <- var(e)
  v_mz_h_regr[i] <- (1 - n_h[i] / N_h[i]) * S2e_h / n_h[i]
}
```

Finally, the separate regression estimate is computed as a weighted average of the regression estimates per stratum.

```
w_h <- N_h / sum(N_h)
print(mz_sepreg <- sum(w_h * mz_h_regr))
```

```
[1] 223.9426
```

The standard error of the separate regression estimator is computed by the square root of the pooled variances of the regression estimator per stratum, using the squared relative sizes of the strata as weights.

```
sum(w_h^2 * v_mz_h_regr) %>% sqrt(.)
```

```
[1] 5.077558
```

The separate regression estimator can be computed with package **survey**. The computation of the population totals merits special attention. For the simple regression estimator using simple random sampling, these totals are the total number of population units and the population total of the covariate lnSWIR2. These are the population totals associated with the columns of the design matrix that is constructed with function lm to estimate the regression coefficients. The column with ones results in an estimated intercept, the column with lnSWIR2 values in an estimated slope.

The model that is fitted now is an analysis of covariance (ANCOVA) model with factor Biome and covariate lnSWIR2.

```
ancova <- lm(AGB ~ Biome * lnSWIR2, data = mysample)
```

R uses the so-called cornerstone representation of the ANCOVA model. The reference level is stratum Mangrove. The question is what population totals must be passed to function `calibrate` with this ANCOVA model. This can be determined by printing the design matrix that is used to fit the ANCOVA model. Only the first two rows are printed.

```
designmat <- model.matrix(ancova, mysample)
```

```
      (Intercept) BiomeForest_dry BiomeGrassland BiomeForest_moist  lnSWIR2
[1,]            1               0              0                 1 6.307024
[2,]            1               0              0                 1 6.236278
      BiomeForest_dry:lnSWIR2 BiomeGrassland:lnSWIR2 BiomeForest_moist:lnSWIR2
[1,]                        0                      0                  6.307024
[2,]                        0                      0                  6.236278
```

With this model formulation, the first population total is the total number of population units. The second, third, and fourth population totals are the number of population units in stratum levels 2, 3, and 4. The fifth population total is the population total of covariate lnSWIR2 and the sixth, seventh, and eighth population totals are the totals of covariate lnSWIR2 in stratum levels 2, 3, and 4.

```
N_h <- as.numeric(N_h)
lut <- data.frame(Biome = biomes, N_h)
mysample <- merge(x = mysample, y = lut)
design_stsi <- svydesign(
  id = ~ 1, strata = ~ factor(Biome), data = mysample, fpc = ~ N_h)
tx_pop <- sum(grdAmazonia$lnSWIR2)
tx_h_pop <- N_h * mx_h_pop
totals <- c(sum(N_h), N_h[c(2, 3, 4)], tx_pop, tx_h_pop[c(2, 3, 4)])
names(totals) <- names(coef(ancova))
mysample_cal <- calibrate(
  design_stsi, formula = ~ Biome * lnSWIR2,
  population = totals, calfun = "linear")
svymean(~ AGB, mysample_cal)
```

```
      mean     SE
AGB 223.94 5.8686
```

The line `names(totals) <- names(coef(ancova))` is not strictly needed. This is just to suppress a warning that the names of the numeric with the population totals does not match the names of the columns of the design matrix. As a consequence, we do not need to fit the ANCOVA model either.

Alternatively, we may use the following formula in function `lm`.

```
ancova2 <- lm(AGB ~ 0 + Biome / lnSWIR2, data = mysample)
designmat <- model.matrix(ancova, mysample)
```

```
     (Intercept) BiomeForest_dry BiomeGrassland BiomeForest_moist  lnSWIR2
[1,]           1               0              0                 1 6.307024
[2,]           1               0              0                 1 6.236278
     BiomeForest_dry:lnSWIR2 BiomeGrassland:lnSWIR2 BiomeForest_moist:lnSWIR2
[1,]                       0                      0                  6.307024
[2,]                       0                      0                  6.236278
```

With this formula, the population totals are the number of population units in stratum levels 1, 2, 3, and 4, as well as the population totals of covariate lnSWIR2 of the strata.

```
totals <- c(N_h, tx_h_pop)
names(totals) <- names(coef(ancova2))
mysample_cal <- calibrate(
  design_stsi, formula = ~ 0 + Biome / lnSWIR2, population = totals,
  calfun = "linear")
svymean(~ AGB, mysample_cal)
```

```
      mean     SE
AGB 223.94 5.8686
```

10.1.3.1   Combined regression estimator

The alternative to the separate simple regression estimator is the combined simple regression estimator:

$$\hat{\bar{z}}_{\text{cregr}} = \hat{\bar{z}}_\pi + \hat{b}\left(\bar{x} - \hat{\bar{x}}_\pi\right) , \tag{10.21}$$

with $\hat{b}$ the estimated slope coefficient, estimated by Equation (10.6), discarding the variance of the residuals $\sigma^2(\epsilon_k)$ as they are assumed constant, and using the appropriate inclusion probabilities which differ among the strata, and $\hat{\bar{z}}_\pi$ and $\hat{\bar{x}}_\pi$ the π estimators of the population mean of the study variable and the covariate for stratified simple random sampling, respectively. Working Equation (10.6) out for stratified simple random sampling yields

$$\hat{b} = \frac{w_h^2 \widehat{S^2}_h(z, x)}{w_h^2 \widehat{S^2}_h(x)} , \tag{10.22}$$

with $\widehat{S^2}_h(z, x)$ the estimated covariance of the study variable and the covariate in stratum h and $\widehat{S^2}_h(x)$ the estimated variance of the covariate.

In the combined simple regression estimator only one regression coefficient b is estimated, the slope coefficient for the entire population. This combined regression estimator is recommended when the stratum sample sizes are so small, as in our case, that the estimated regression coefficients per stratum, $\hat{b}_h$, become unreliable.

Estimator (10.22) is for infinite populations and for stratified simple random sampling with replacement of finite populations. For sampling without replacement from finite populations, finite population corrections $1 - n_h/N_h$ must be added to the numerator and denominator of $\hat{b}$ (Cochran (1977), p. 202).

The approximate variance of the combined regression estimator can be estimated as follows:

1. Compute residuals: $e_k = z_k - (\hat{a} + \hat{b}x_k)$, with $\hat{a}$ and $\hat{b}$ the estimated regression coefficients for the whole population.

2. Estimate for each stratum the variance of the estimator of the mean of the residuals: $\hat{V}(\hat{\bar{e}}_h) = \widehat{S^2}_h(e)/n_h$, with $\widehat{S^2}_h(e)$ the estimated variance of the residuals in stratum h.

3. Combine the estimated variances per stratum: $\hat{V}(\hat{\bar{z}}_{\text{cregr}}) = \sum_{h=1}^{H} w_h^2 \hat{V}(\hat{\bar{e}}_h)$.

The next code chunks show the estimation procedure. First, the population means of the study variable AGB and of the covariate lnSWIR2 are estimated by the π estimator, see Chapter 4.

```
mz_h_HT <- tapply(mysample$AGB, INDEX = mysample$Biome, FUN = mean)
mx_h_HT <- tapply(mysample$lnSWIR2, INDEX = mysample$Biome, FUN = mean)
mz_HT <- sum(w_h * mz_h_HT)
mx_HT <- sum(w_h * mx_h_HT)
```

The next step is to estimate the population regression coefficients, using Equation (10.6) in which the variances $\sigma^2(\epsilon_k)$ can be dropped, as these are assumed constant. The inclusion probabilities are in column Prob of mysample.

```
W <- diag(x = 1 / mysample$Prob, nrow = n, ncol = n)
X <- matrix(nrow = n, ncol = 2, data = 1)
X[, 2] <- mysample$lnSWIR2
XWX <- t(X) %*% W %*% X
```

```
XWz <- t(X) %*% W %*% mysample$AGB
print(ab <- t(solve(XWX, XWz)))
```

```
        [,1]      [,2]
[1,] 1678.268 -226.6772
```

Note that the same estimates are obtained by model-based estimation, using
weighted least squares, based on the assumption that the variances $\sigma^2(\epsilon_k)$ are
proportional to the inclusion probabilities (which is a weird assumption).

```
lm_wls <- lm(AGB ~ lnSWIR2, weights = 1 / Prob, data = mysample)
coef(lm_wls)
```

```
(Intercept)     lnSWIR2
  1678.2684   -226.6772
```

In model-based estimation, the weights differ among the units because of
assumed differences in the variance of the residuals, whereas in design-based
estimation we assign different weights to the observations because the units
have different inclusion probabilities (Lohr, 1999).

Finally, the combined regression estimate is computed.

```
print(mz_combreg <- mz_HT + ab[2] * (mx_pop - mx_HT))
```

```
[1] 224.1433
```

To approximate the variance of the combined regression estimator, first the
residuals are computed. Then these residuals are used to estimate the spatial
variance of the residuals within the strata, $\widehat{S^2}_h(e)$, and the variance of the
estimator of the mean of the residuals, $\hat{V}(\bar{\hat{e}}_h)$. Finally, by taking the square
root, the estimated standard error is obtained.

```
mysample$e <- mysample$AGB - (ab[1] + ab[2] * mysample$lnSWIR2)
v_me_h <- numeric(length = 4)
for (i in 1:4) {
  subsam <- subset(mysample, mysample$Biome == levels(grdAmazonia$Biome)[i])
  S2e_h <- var(subsam$e)
  v_me_h[i] <- (1 - n_h[i] / N_h[i]) * S2e_h / n_h[i]
}
print(se_mz_combreg <- sqrt(sum(w_h^2 * v_me_h)))
```

```
[1] 5.122518
```

Computing the combined regression estimator with package **survey** proceeds as follows.

```
design_stsi <- svydesign(
  id = ~ 1, strata = ~ factor(Biome), data = mysample, fpc = ~ N_h)
totals <- c(nrow(grdAmazonia), sum(grdAmazonia$lnSWIR2))
mysample_cal <- calibrate(
  design_stsi, formula = ~ lnSWIR2, population = totals,
  calfun = "linear")
svymean(~ AGB, mysample_cal)
```

```
        mean     SE
AGB 224.14 5.8707
```

Function `calibrate` computes the regression estimate and its standard error with the calibrated weights g_k (Särndal et al. (1992), equation (6.5.12)). This explains the difference between the two standard errors.

10.2 Ratio estimator

In some cases it is reasonable to assume that the fitted line passes through the origin. An example is the case study on poppy area in Kandahar (Chapter 8). The covariate is the agricultural area within the 5 km squares that serve as sampling units. It is reasonable to assume that when the covariate equals zero, also the poppy area is zero. So, if we have an estimate of the ratio of the total poppy area in the population to the total agricultural area in the population and besides know the total agricultural area in the population, the total poppy area in the population can be estimated by multiplying the estimated ratio with the known population total agricultural area:

$$\hat{t}_{\text{ratio}}(z) = \frac{\hat{t}_\pi(z)}{\hat{t}_\pi(x)} \, t(x) = \hat{b} \, t(x) \, , \qquad (10.23)$$

with $\hat{t}_\pi(z)$ and $\hat{t}_\pi(x)$ the π estimators of the total of the study variable (poppy area) and the ancillary variable (agricultural area), respectively, and $t(x)$ the total of the ancillary variable, which must be known.

The working model of the ratio estimator is a heteroscedastic model, i.e., a model with non-constant variance, without intercept (see Exercise 3 hereafter):

$$Z(x_k) = \beta\, x_k + \epsilon_k$$
$$\sigma^2(\epsilon_k) = \sigma^2 x_k \,, \tag{10.24}$$

with β the slope of the line and σ^2 a constant (variance of residual for $x_k = 1$). The residual variance is assumed proportional to the covariate x.

The ratio estimator was applied before to estimate the population mean or population total from a systematic random sample (Chapter 5), a one-stage and two-stage cluster random sample (Sections 6.3 and 7.3), and a ppswor sample (Section 8.2). By taking $x_k = 1$, $k = 1, \dots, N$, $\hat{t}_\pi(x)$ in Equation (10.23) is equal to $\hat{N}$, and $t(x)$ is equal to N. For (two-stage) cluster random sampling M is used for the total number of population units (N is the total number of clusters or primary sampling units in the population) and therefore $\hat{t}_\pi(x) = \hat{M}$ and $t(x) = M$. This yields the ratio estimators of the population total appropriate for these sampling designs.

Equation (10.23) is a general estimator that can be used for any probability sampling design, not only for simple random sampling. For simple random sampling, the coefficient b is estimated by the ratio of the sample means of z and x.

For simple random sampling, the sampling variance of the ratio estimator of the population total can be approximated by

$$\hat{V}(\hat{t}_{\mathrm{ratio}}(z)) = N^2 \frac{\widehat{S^2}(e)}{n} \,, \tag{10.25}$$

with $\widehat{S^2}(e)$ the estimated variance of the residuals $e_k = z_k - \hat{b} x_k$:

$$\widehat{S^2}(e) = \frac{1}{n-1} \sum_{k \in \mathcal{S}} e_k^2 \,. \tag{10.26}$$

For simple random sampling without replacement from finite populations, Equation (10.25) must be multiplied by $(1 - \frac{n}{N})$.

In **R** the ratio estimator for the total poppy area and the estimator of its variance for a simple random sample without replacement can be computed as follows.

```
n <- 50
N <- nrow(grdKandahar)
units <- sample(N, size = n, replace = FALSE)
```

```
mysample <- grdKandahar[units, ]
b <- mean(mysample$poppy) / mean(mysample$agri)
tx_pop <- sum(grdKandahar$agri)
print(tz_ratio <- b * tx_pop)
```

```
[1] 55009.69
```

```
e <- mysample$poppy - b * mysample$agri
print(se_tz_ratio <- sqrt(N^2 * (1 - (n / N)) * var(e) / n))
```

```
[1] 18847.31
```

An improved variance approximation is obtained with Equation (10.18). For the ratio model and simple random sampling, the calibrated weights are equal to (Särndal et al. (1992), p. 248)

$$g = \frac{t(x)}{\hat{t}_\pi(x)} \, , \tag{10.27}$$

with $t(x)$ the population total of the covariate and $\hat{t}_\pi(x)$ the π estimate of the population total of the covariate.

```
pi <- n / N
tx_HT <- sum(mysample$agri / pi)
g <- tx_pop / tx_HT
S2ge <- sum(g^2 * e^2) / (n - 1)
print(se_tz_ratio <- sqrt(N^2 * (1 - n / N) * S2ge / n))
```

```
[1] 17149.62
```

The ratio estimate and the estimated standard error of the ratio estimator can be computed with package **survey** as follows.

```
mysample$N <- N
design_si <- svydesign(id = ~ 1, data = mysample, fpc = ~ N)
b <- svyratio(~ poppy, ~ agri, design = design_si)
predict(b, total = tx_pop)
```

```
$total
          agri
poppy 55009.69

$se
          agri
poppy 17149.62
```

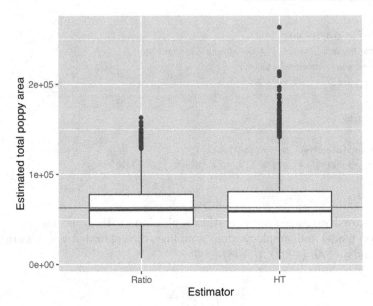

FIGURE 10.3: Approximated sampling distribution of the ratio estimator (Ratio) and the π estimator (HT) of the total poppy area (ha) in Kandahar with simple random sampling without replacement of size 50.

Figure 10.3 shows the sampling distribution of the ratio estimator and the π estimator, obtained by repeating simple random sampling of size 50 and estimation 10,000 times. The average of the 10,000 ratio estimates of the total poppy area equals 62,512 ha. The population total of poppy equals 63,038 ha, so the estimated bias of the ratio estimator equals -526 ha. The boxplots in Figure 10.3 show that the ratio estimator has less extreme outliers. The standard deviation of the 10,000 ratio estimates equals 24,177 ha. The gain in precision due to the ratio estimator, quantified by the ratio of the variance of the π estimator to the variance of the ratio estimator, equals 1.502.

Exercises

3. Write an **R** script to compute the ratio of the population total poppy area to the population total agricultural area $(t(z)/t(x))$. Then use all data to fit a linear model without intercept for the poppy area, using the agricultural area as a covariate, assuming that the variance of the residuals is proportional to the agricultural area (heteroscedastic model). Hint: use function `lm` with argument `formula = poppy ~ agri - 1` and argument `weights = 1 / agri`. Also fit a model without intercept, assuming a constant variance of the residuals (homoscedastic model). Compare the estimated slopes of

the two models with the ratio of the total poppy area to the total agricultural area.

10.2.1 Ratio estimators with stratified simple random sampling

With stratified simple random sampling, there are, similar to the regression estimator, two options for estimating a population parameter: either estimate the ratios separately for the strata or estimate a combined ratio. The separate ratio estimator of the population total is

$$\hat{t}_{\mathrm{sratio}}(z) = \sum_{h=1}^{H} \hat{t}_{\mathrm{ratio},h}(z) , \qquad (10.28)$$

with

$$\hat{t}_{\mathrm{ratio},h}(z) = \frac{\hat{t}_{\pi,h}(z)}{\hat{t}_{\pi,h}(x)} t_h(x) , \qquad (10.29)$$

in which $\hat{t}_{\pi,h}(z)$ and $\hat{t}_{\pi,h}(x)$ are the π estimators of the population total of the study variable and the covariate for stratum h, respectively.

The combined ratio estimator is

$$\hat{t}_{\mathrm{cratio}}(z) = \frac{\sum_{h=1}^{H} \hat{t}_{\pi,h}(z)}{\sum_{h=1}^{H} \hat{t}_{\pi,h}(x)} t(x) . \qquad (10.30)$$

The code chunks below show how the combined and separate regression estimate can be computed with package **survey**. First, two equal-sized strata are computed using the median of the covariate agri as a stratum bound. Stratum sample sizes are computed, and a stratified simple random sample without replacement is selected.

```
median_agri <- quantile(grdKandahar$agri, probs = 0.5)
grdKandahar$stratum <- findInterval(grdKandahar$agri, median_agri) + 1
N_h <-   table(grdKandahar$stratum)
n_h <- round(n * N_h / sum(N_h))
set.seed(314)
units <- sampling::strata(grdKandahar, stratanames = "stratum",
  size = n_h, method = "srswor")
mysample <- getdata(grdKandahar, units)
```

The stratum sizes N_h are added to mysample, function svydesign specifies the sampling design, function svyratio estimates the population ratio and its variance, and finally function predict estimates the population total.

```
lut <- data.frame(stratum = c(1, 2), N_h)
mysample <- merge(x = mysample, y = lut)
design_stsi <- svydesign(
    id = ~ 1, strata = ~ stratum, data = mysample, fpc = ~ Freq)
common <- svyratio(~ poppy, ~ agri, design_stsi, separate = FALSE)
predict(common, total = sum(grdKandahar$agri))
```

```
$total
         agri
poppy 28389.02

$se
         agri
poppy 8845.847
```

The same estimate is obtained with function calibrate.

```
mysample_cal <- calibrate(
    design_stsi, ~ agri - 1, population = tx_pop, variance = 1)
svytotal(~ poppy, mysample_cal)
```

```
      total     SE
poppy 28389 8845.8
```

Computing the separate ratio estimator goes along the same lines. Function svyratio with argument separate = TRUE estimates the ratio and its variance for each stratum separately. To predict the population total, the stratum totals of the covariate must be passed to function predict using argument total.

```
separate <- svyratio(~ poppy, ~ agri, design_stsi, separate = TRUE)
tx_h_pop <- tapply(grdKandahar$agri, INDEX = grdKandahar$stratum, FUN = sum)
predict(separate, total = tx_h_pop)
```

```
$total
         agri
poppy 28331.32

$se
         agri
poppy 8882.492
```

10.2.2 Poststratified estimator

In stratified random sampling (Chapter 4), the population is divided into several disjoint subpopulations and from each subpopulation a probability sample is selected. The subpopulations then serve as strata. The larger the difference in the stratum means and the smaller the variance within the strata, the larger the gain in precision compared to simple random sampling, see Subsection 4.1.2.

The alternative to using the subpopulations as strata at the stage of sampling is to use them as poststrata in estimating the population mean. For instance, if we have selected a simple random sample from a spatial population and we have a map of subpopulations possibly related to the study variable, then these subpopulations still can be used in the poststratified estimator. What needs to be done only is to classify the selected units. Hereafter, the subpopulations that serve as poststrata are referred to as groups.

For any probability sampling design, the population mean can be estimated by

$$\hat{\bar{z}}_{\text{pos}} = \sum_{g=1}^{G} w_g \frac{\hat{t}_g(z)}{\widehat{N}_g} = \sum_{g=1}^{G} w_g \frac{\sum_{k \in \mathcal{S}_g} \frac{z_k}{\pi_k}}{\sum_{k \in \mathcal{S}_g} \frac{1}{\pi_k}} ,$$ (10.31)

where $\mathcal{S}_g$ is the sample from group g, $w_g = N_g/N$ is the relative size of group g, $\hat{t}_g(z)$ is the estimated total of the study variable for group g, $\widehat{N}_g$ is the estimator of the size of group g, and π_k is the inclusion probability of unit k. The estimated group means are weighted by their relative sizes w_g, which are assumed to be known. In spite of this, the group means are estimated by dividing the estimated group totals by their *estimated* size, $\widehat{N}_g$, because this ratio estimator is more precise than the π estimator of the group mean.

The poststratified estimator is the natural estimator for the one-way ANOVA model,

$$\begin{aligned} Z_k &= \mu_g + \epsilon_k \\ \sigma_k^2 &= \sigma_g^2 , \end{aligned}$$ (10.32)

with μ_g the mean for group (subpopulation) $g = 1, \dots, G$ and σ_g^2 the variance of the study variable of group g.

For simple random sampling, the poststratified estimator reduces to

$$\hat{\bar{z}}_{\text{pos}} = \sum_{g=1}^{G} w_g \bar{z}_{\mathcal{S}_g} ,$$ (10.33)

where $\bar{z}_{\mathcal{S}_g}$ is the sample mean of group g. If for all groups we have at least two sampling units, $n_g \geq 2$, the variance of this poststratified estimator of the mean can be estimated by

$$\hat{V}\!\left(\hat{\bar{z}}_{\mathrm{pos}}|\mathbf{n}_g\right) = \sum_{g=1}^{G} w_g^2 \frac{\widehat{S_g^2}}{n_g} \;, \qquad (10.34)$$

where n_g is the number of sampling units in group g, and $\widehat{S_g^2}$ is the estimated spatial variance of z in group g, which for simple random sampling can be estimated by

$$\widehat{S_g^2} = \frac{1}{n_g - 1} \sum_{k \in \mathcal{S}_g} (z_k - \bar{z}_{\mathcal{S}_g})^2 \;. \qquad (10.35)$$

This is an estimator of the *conditional* sampling variance, i.e., the variance of the poststratified estimator over all simple random samples with group sample sizes, collected in the vector $\mathbf{n}_g$, equal to the group sample sizes in the sample actually selected. The poststratified estimator requires that the sizes (areas) of the strata are known. See Section 11.1 for a sampling strategy that does not require known stratum sizes.

The poststratified estimator is illustrated with study area Voorst. We consider the situation that we do not have the map with the five combinations of soil type and land use that served as strata in Chapter 4. The soil-land use classes (groups) used in the poststratified estimator are only observed at the selected sampling units. Only three poststrata are distinguished: the original strata BA, EA, and PA are merged into one stratum SA with function fct_collapse of package **forcats** (Wickham, 2021). The sizes of these poststrata must be known.

```
library(forcats)
grdVoorst$poststratum <- fct_collapse(
  grdVoorst$stratum, SA = c("BA", "EA", "PA"))
print(N_g <- tapply(grdVoorst$z, INDEX = grdVoorst$poststratum, FUN = length))
```

```
  SA   RA   XF
5523  659 1346
```

One hundred points are selected by simple random sampling with replacement. The expected sample sizes per group are proportional to the size of the groups, $E(n_g/n) = N_g/N$, but for a single sample the sample proportions may deviate considerably from the population proportions.

```
n <- 100
N <- nrow(grdVoorst)
set.seed(314)
units <- sample(N, size = n, replace = TRUE)
mysample <- grdVoorst[units, ]
n_g <- tapply(mysample$z, INDEX = mysample$poststratum, FUN = length)
print(n_g)
```

```
SA RA XF
71  6 23
```

The population mean is estimated by first computing the sample means per group, followed by computing the weighted average of the sample means, using the relative sizes of the groups as weights.

```
mz_g <- tapply(mysample$z, INDEX = mysample$poststratum, FUN = mean)
w_g <- N_g / N
print(mz_pst <- sum(w_g * mz_g))
```

```
[1] 85.11039
```

The variance of the estimator of the mean is estimated by computing the sample variances per group, dividing these by the sample sizes per group, and computing the weighted average, using as weights the squared relative group sizes. This estimated sampling variance is the variance of the estimator of the mean over all simple random samples with 71 units of group SA, 6 units of group RA, and 23 units of XF.

```
S2z_g <- tapply(mysample$z, INDEX = mysample$poststratum, FUN = var)
v_mz_g <- S2z_g / as.numeric(n_g)
print(condse_mz_pst <- sqrt(sum(w_g^2 * v_mz_g)))
```

```
[1] 4.49969
```

Note that this variance estimator can only be computed with at least two units per group. For this reason, I recommend using a limited number of groups, especially for small sample sizes.

Function postStratify of package **survey** can be used to compute the post-stratified estimator and its standard error.

```
mysample$weights <- N / n
design_si <- svydesign(id = ~ 1, weights = ~ weights, data = mysample)
pop <- data.frame(poststratum = c("SA", "RA", "XF"), Freq = N_g)
mysample_pst <- postStratify(
```

```
design_si, strata = ~ poststratum, population = pop)
svymean(~ z, mysample_pst)
```

```
  mean    SE
z 85.11 4.3942
```

 Lohr (1999) warns about data snooping. By defining groups after analysing the data, arbitrarily small sampling variances of the estimated mean can be obtained.

10.3 Model-assisted estimation using machine learning techniques

Breidt and Opsomer (2017) review model-assisted estimators based on machine learning techniques. Of special interest is the general approach proposed by Wu and Sitter (2001) for incorporating non-linear predictions in the model-assisted estimator. They show how non-linear predictions of the study variable, for instance obtained by a regression tree or random forest, can be used in the model-calibration estimator:

$$\hat{\bar{z}}_{\text{MC}} = \hat{\bar{z}}_\pi + \hat{a}\left(1 - \frac{1}{N}\sum_{k\in\mathcal{S}}\frac{1}{\pi_k}\right) + \hat{b}\left(\frac{1}{N}\sum_{k=1}^{N}\hat{m}(\mathbf{x}_k) - \frac{1}{N}\sum_{k\in\mathcal{S}}\frac{\hat{m}(\mathbf{x}_k)}{\pi_k}\right),$$

$$(10.36)$$

with $\hat{b}$ a slope coefficient estimated by

$$\hat{b} = \frac{\sum_{k\in\mathcal{S}} 1/\pi_k\{\hat{m}(\mathbf{x}_k) - \hat{\bar{m}}_\pi\}\{z_k - \hat{\bar{z}}_\pi\}}{\sum_{k\in\mathcal{S}} 1/\pi_k\{\hat{m}(\mathbf{x}_k) - \hat{\bar{m}}_\pi\}^2},$$

$$(10.37)$$

with $\hat{\bar{z}}_\pi$ the π estimator of the population mean of the study variable, $\hat{\bar{m}}_\pi$ the π estimator of the population mean of the predicted values, and $\hat{a}$ an intercept estimated by

$$\hat{a} = (1 - \hat{b})\left(\frac{1}{N}\sum_{k\in\mathcal{S}}\frac{z_k}{\pi_k}\right).$$

$$(10.38)$$

The second term in Equation (10.36) cancels for all sampling designs for which the sum of the design weights, i.e., the sum of the reciprocal of the inclusion probabilities, equals the population size: $\sum_{k \in \mathcal{S}} 1/\pi_k = N$. Only for some unequal probability sampling designs this may not be the case.

The alternative is to plug the fitted values $\hat{m}(\mathbf{x}_k)$ into the generalised difference estimator, Equation (10.2). If we drop the second term, the model-calibration estimator can be rewritten as

$$\hat{\bar{z}}_{\mathrm{MC}} = \frac{1}{N} \sum_{k=1}^{N} \hat{b}\, \hat{m}(\mathbf{x}_k) + \frac{1}{N} \sum_{k \in \mathcal{S}} \frac{z_k - \hat{b}\, \hat{m}(\mathbf{x}_k)}{\pi_k} . \qquad (10.39)$$

Comparison with the generalised difference estimator, Equation (10.2), shows that these two estimators are equivalent when $\hat{b} = 1$. For non-linear working models, generally $\hat{b} \neq 1$, so that these two estimators are not the same. Wu (2003) shows that the calibration estimator has a general optimality property.

In case you are confused by all these model-assisted estimators, let me clarify. The most general estimator is the model-calibration estimator. If we take for $\hat{b}$ the value 1, this estimator is equivalent to the generalised difference estimator (Equation (10.2)). The predictions $\hat{m}(\mathbf{x}_k)$ in these estimators can be computed either by a linear model or a non-linear model. If a linear model is used in the generalised difference estimator, this estimator is equal to the generalised regression estimator (Equation (10.8)). With linear models, $\hat{b}$ in Equation (10.36) equals 1, so that all three estimators are equal.

For simple random sampling, the inclusion probabilities of the units are the same for all units: $\pi_k = n/N$, reducing Equations (10.36) and (10.37) to

$$\hat{\bar{z}}_{\mathrm{MC}} = \frac{1}{n} \sum_{k \in \mathcal{S}} z_k + \hat{b}_{\mathrm{SI}} \left(\frac{1}{N} \sum_{k=1}^{N} \hat{m}(\mathbf{x}_k) - \frac{1}{n} \sum_{j \in \mathcal{S}} \hat{m}(\mathbf{x}_j) \right) , \qquad (10.40)$$

with $\hat{b}_{\mathrm{SI}}$ equal to

$$\hat{b}_{\mathrm{SI}} = \frac{\sum_{k \in \mathcal{S}} \{\hat{m}(\mathbf{x}_k) - \bar{m}_{\mathcal{S}}\}\{z_k - \bar{z}_{\mathcal{S}}\}}{\sum_{k \in \mathcal{S}} \{\hat{m}(\mathbf{x}_k) - \bar{m}_{\mathcal{S}}\}^2} , \qquad (10.41)$$

with $\bar{m}_{\mathcal{S}}$ the sample mean of the predicted values.

An estimator of the variance of the model-assisted calibration estimator is

$$\hat{V}(\hat{\bar{z}}_{\mathrm{MC}}) = \hat{V}(\hat{\bar{e}}_\pi) , \qquad (10.42)$$

with $\hat{\bar{e}}_\pi$ the π estimator of the population mean of the residuals e. For sampling designs with fixed sample size, these residuals are equal to $e_k = z_k - \hat{b}\, \hat{m}(\mathbf{x}_k)$. For simple random sampling with replacement from finite populations and simple random sampling from infinite populations, the variance estimator equals

$$\hat{V}(\hat{\bar{z}}_{\mathrm{MC}}) = \frac{\widehat{S^2}(e)}{n} \, , \tag{10.43}$$

with $\widehat{S^2}(e)$ the estimated population variance of the residuals.

An estimator of the variance of the generalised difference estimator is

$$\hat{V}(\hat{\bar{z}}_{\mathrm{dif}}) = \hat{V}(\hat{\bar{d}}_{\pi}) \, , \tag{10.44}$$

with $\hat{\bar{d}}_{\pi}$ the π estimator of the population mean of the differences $d_k = z_k - \hat{m}(\mathbf{x}_k)$.

The data of Eastern Amazonia are used to illustrate model-assisted estimation of AGB, using five environmental covariates in predicting AGB. First, a regression tree is used for prediction, after that a random forest is used for prediction. For an introduction to regression trees and random forest modelling, see this blog[1]. In this blog the study variable is a categorical variable, whereas in our example the study variable is quantitative and continuous. This is not essential. The only difference is the measure for quantifying how good a split is. With a quantitative study variable, this is quantified by the following sum of squares:

$$SS = \sum_{g=1}^{2} \sum_{k \in \mathcal{S}_g} (z_{gk} - \bar{z}_{\mathcal{S}_g})^2 \, , \tag{10.45}$$

with $\bar{z}_{\mathcal{S}_g}$ the sample mean of group g.

10.3.1   Predicting with a regression tree

A simple random sample without replacement of size 100 is selected.

```
N <- nrow(grdAmazonia)
n <- 100
set.seed(314)
units <- sample(N, size = n, replace = FALSE)
covs <- c("SWIR2", "Terra_PP", "Prec_dm", "Elevation", "Clay")
mysample <- grdAmazonia[units, c("AGB", covs)]
```

---

[1]https://victorzhou.com/blog/intro-to-random-forests/

Package **rpms** (Toth, 2021) is used to build a regression tree for AGB, using all five covariates as predictors. Note that I now use the original untransformed SWIR2 as a predictor. Transforming predictors so that the relation with the study variable becomes linear is not needed when fitting a non-linear model such as a regression tree. Figure 10.4 shows the fitted tree.

```
library(rpms)
tree <- rpms(
  rp_equ = AGB ~ SWIR2 + Terra_PP + Prec_dm + Elevation + Clay,
  data = as.data.frame(mysample), pval = 0.05)
```

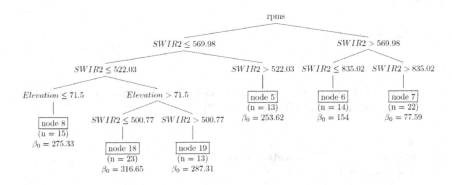

FIGURE 10.4: Regression tree for AGB (10^9 kg ha^{-1}) calibrated on a simple random sample of size 100 from Eastern Amazonia.

The regression tree is used to predict AGB for all population units.

```
AGBpred <- predict(tree, newdata = grdAmazonia)
```

The population mean is then estimated by the generalised difference estimator.

```
d <- grdAmazonia$AGB[units] - AGBpred[units]
mean(AGBpred) + mean(d)
```

```
[1] 226.7433
```

Its standard error is estimated by the square root of the variance of the estimator of the mean differences.

```
S2d <- var(d)
sqrt((1 - n / N) * S2d / n)
```

```
[1] 3.212222
```

This estimation procedure is implemented in function `gregTree` of package **mase** (McConville et al., 2021).

```
library(mase)
pi <- rep(n / N, n)
res <- gregTree(
  mysample$AGB, xsample = mysample[, covs],
  xpop = grdAmazonia[, covs], pi = pi,
  var_est = TRUE, var_method = "LinHTSRS")
res$pop_mean
```

```
[1] 226.7433
```

```
sqrt(res$pop_mean_var)
```

```
[1] 3.212222
```

The variance of the estimator of the mean can also be estimated by bootstrapping the sample (Lohr (1999), section 9.3.3).

```
res <- gregTree(
  mysample$AGB, xsample = mysample[, covs],
  xpop = grdAmazonia[, covs], pi = pi,
  var_est = TRUE, var_method = "bootstrapSRS", B = 100)
```

```
sqrt(res$pop_mean_var)
```

```
       [,1]
[1,] 4.076
```

The standard error obtained by the bootstrap is considerably larger than the previous standard error based on a Taylor linearisation of the estimator of the mean. As we will see hereafter, the Taylor linearisation seriously underestimates the true standard error.

The simple random sampling of 100 units and the model-assisted estimation are repeated 500 times, using a regression tree for prediction. The variance is estimated by Taylor linearisation (`var_method = LinHTSRS`) and by bootstrapping (`var_method = bootstrapSRS`) using 100 bootstrap samples.

The variance of the 500 estimated population means of AGB is 20.8 $(10^9$ kg ha$^{-1})^2$. Estimation of the variance through Taylor linearisation strongly underestimates the variance: the average of the 500 estimated variances equals 14.5 $(10^9$ kg ha$^{-1})^2$. On the contrary, the bootstrap variance estimator overestimates the variance: the average of the 500 estimated variances equals 23.4 $(10^9$ kg ha$^{-1})^2$. I prefer to overestimate my uncertainty about the mean, instead of being overoptimistic, and so I would recommend to report the bootstrap variance.

10.3.2 Predicting with a random forest

The package **ranger** (Wright and Ziegler, 2017) is used to fit a random forest (RF) model for AGB using the five environmental covariates as predictors and the simple random sample of size 100 selected in the previous subsection. Function importance shows how often the covariates are used in a binary splitting. All five covariates are used, SWIR2 by far most often.

```
library(ranger)
set.seed(314)
forest.sample <- ranger(
  AGB ~ ., data = mysample, num.trees = 1000, importance = "impurity")
importance(forest.sample)
```

```
    SWIR2   Terra_PP   Prec_dm  Elevation     Clay
466318.39 214716.35 136505.65   62429.66 34612.68
```

Out-of-bag predictions for the selected units are saved in element predictions of the output object of function ranger. The fitted model is also used to predict AGB at all units (raster cells), using function predict.

```
AGBpred_OOB <- forest.sample$predictions
res <- predict(forest.sample, data = grdAmazonia, type = "response")
AGBpred <- res$predictions
```

Finally, the model-calibration estimate and the generalised difference estimate are computed. Both estimators and their variances are computed in two ways. They differ in how the study variable AGB is predicted for the sampling units:

1. using all trees of the forest (the predictions obtained with function predict); or
2. using only the trees calibrated on bootstrap samples that do not include the sampling unit used as a prediction unit. These out-of-bag predictions are stored in element predictions of the output object of function ranger.

The next code chunk shows how the model-calibration estimate can be computed with the AGB data of the simple random sample and the RF predictions of AGB. First, all trees are used.

```
numer <- sum((AGBpred[units] - mean(AGBpred[units])) *
            (mysample$AGB - mean(mysample$AGB)))
denom <- sum((AGBpred[units] - mean(AGBpred[units]))^2)
b <- numer / denom
mz_MC <- mean(mysample$AGB) + b * (mean(AGBpred) - mean(AGBpred[units]))
u <- mysample$AGB - AGBpred[units] * b
v_mz_MC <- (1 - n / N) * var(u) / n
```

Next, the out-of-bag predictions are used.

```
numer <- sum((AGBpred_OOB - mean(AGBpred_OOB)) *
            (mysample$AGB - mean(mysample$AGB)))
denom <- sum((AGBpred_OOB - mean(AGBpred_OOB))^2)
b_OOB <- numer / denom
mz_MC_OOB <- mean(mysample$AGB) + b_OOB * (mean(AGBpred) - mean(AGBpred_OOB))
u_OOB <- mysample$AGB - AGBpred_OOB * b_OOB
v_mz_MC_OOB <- (1 - n / N) * var(u_OOB) / n
```

The two calibration estimates are about equal: 226.8 10^9 kg ha^{-1} using sample predictions obtained with function predict, and 227.3 10^9 kg ha^{-1} with the out-of-bag sample predictions. However, their estimated variances are largely different: 2.35 $(10^9$ kg ha$^{-1})^2$ and 12.46 $(10^9$ kg ha$^{-1})^2$, respectively.

In the next code chunk, the generalised difference estimate (Equation (10.2)) is computed. Similar to the model-calibration estimate, this difference estimate is computed from predictions based on all trees and from the out-of-bag predictions.

```
d <- mysample$AGB - AGBpred[units]
mz_MD <- mean(AGBpred) + mean(d)
v_mz_MD <- (1 - n / N) * var(d) / n
#using out-of-bag predictions
d_OOB <- mysample$AGB - AGBpred_OOB
mz_MD_OOB <- mean(AGBpred) + mean(d_OOB)
v_mz_MD_OOB <- (1 - n / N) * var(d_OOB) / n
```

For the difference estimator the results are very similar. The two difference estimates are 226.6 10^9 kg ha^{-1} and 227.0 10^9 kg ha^{-1}, and their estimated variances are 2.70 $(10^9$ kg ha$^{-1})^2$ and 12.80 $(10^9$ kg ha$^{-1})^2$, respectively. The model-calibration estimate and the generalised difference estimate are nearly equal.

The sampling and estimation are repeated: 1,000 simple random samples without replacement of size 100 are selected. Each sample is used to calibrate a RF, each forest consisting of 1,000 trees. This results in 2 × 1,000 model-calibration estimates and their estimated variances as well as $2 \times 1{,}000$ difference estimates and their estimated variances. To limit the computing time, a 5 km $\times$ 5 km subgrid of grdAmazonia is used for selecting the simple random samples and for predicting AGB with the RF.

For each estimator, the 1,000 estimated means are used to compute the relative bias:

$$bias = \frac{\frac{1}{1000} \sum_{i=1}^{1000} \hat{\bar{z}}_i - \bar{z}}{\bar{z}} . \tag{10.46}$$

Besides, for each estimator the variance of the 1,000 estimates is computed, which can be compared with the mean of the 1,000 estimated variances. The mean of the estimated variances is used to compute the variance to mean squared error ratio:

$$R = \frac{\frac{1}{1000} \sum_{i=1}^{1000} \hat{V}(\hat{\bar{z}}_i)}{MSE} , \tag{10.47}$$

with

$$MSE = \frac{1}{1000} \sum_{i=1}^{1000} (\hat{\bar{z}}_i - \bar{z})^2 . \tag{10.48}$$

Ideally, this ratio equals 1. If it is smaller than 1, the variance estimator underestimates the mean squared error.

Finally, the relative efficiency is computed as the ratio of the MSE of the π estimator and the MSE of a model-assisted estimator. The π estimator is unbiased, so the MSE equals the variance, which can be computed without error by the population variance divided by the sample size. If the relative efficiency is larger than 1, the model-assisted estimator is more accurate than the π estimator.

The variance of the 1,000 model-calibration estimates (experimental variance), using all trees to predict AGB for the sampled units, equals 15.0. This is 5.65 times larger than the average of the 1,000 estimated variances, which equals 2.66. When using the out-of-bag sample predictions, the experimental variance is about equal to the average of the 1,000 variance estimates: 15.5 vs. 15.0.

The reason of underestimation of the variance when predicting AGB at sample units with function predict is that all 1,000 trees are used in prediction, including the trees calibrated on bootstrap samples that contain the unit in the sample to be predicted. On the contrary, the out-of-bag predicted values are computed as the average of predictions from the trees calibrated on bootstrap samples that do not contain the sample unit to be predicted. The default sample fraction is 0.632, see argument sample.fraction of function ranger, so

TABLE 10.1: Summary statistics of 1,000 calibration estimates of the mean AGB (10^9 kg ha^{-1}) and their estimated variances in Eastern Amazonia, using out-of-bag sample predictions from a RF model with five covariates as a working model, for simple random sampling without replacement and sample sizes 50, 100, and 250.

	50	100	250
Relative bias	-0.0014	-0.0006	-0.0012
Experimental variance	33.9075	15.5255	5.6111
Mean variance estimates	36.1512	14.9750	5.0467
Variance to MSE ratio	1.0642	0.9642	0.8882
Relative efficiency	5.0066	5.4755	5.9866

with 1,000 trees these predictions are the average of, on average, 368 tree predictions. This explains why the out-of-bag prediction errors are larger than the prediction errors obtained with function `predict`. In other words, the variance of the out-of-bag differences d and of the out-of-bag residuals u are larger than those obtained with predicting using all trees.

Hereafter, I report the results obtained with the out-of-bag samples only.

The relative bias is negligibly small for all sample sizes (Table 10.1). For $n = 250$ and 100 the average of the 1,000 estimated variances is smaller than the variance of the 1,000 estimated means, whereas for $n = 50$ the average of the 1,000 variance estimates is larger than the experimental variance of the estimated means. The variance to MSE ratio is smaller than 1 for $n = 250$ and 100, but larger than 1 for $n = 50$. The model-calibration estimator is much more accurate than the π estimator for all three sample sizes, as shown by the high relative efficiencies. The relative efficiency increases with the sample size.

The summary statistics for the performance of the generalised difference estimator are very similar to those of the model-calibration estimator (Table 10.2).

10.4 Big data and volunteer data

Over the past decades numerous large data sets have become available, and this number will further increase in the future; think of data sets collected by satellites. These data sets may contain valuable information about study variables, so that they can be used in model-assisted estimation of global (this chapter) or local means and totals (Chapter 14) of these study variables.

TABLE 10.2: Summary statistics of 1,000 generalised difference estimates of the mean AGB (10^9 kg ha^{-1}) and their estimated variances in Eastern Amazonia, using out-of-bag sample predictions from a RF model with five covariates as a working model, for simple random sampling without replacement and and sample sizes 50, 100, and 250.

	50	100	250
Relative bias	-0.0008	-0.0006	-0.0013
Experimental variance	34.5188	16.2339	5.6891
Mean variance estimates	38.4629	15.4568	5.1125
Variance to MSE ratio	1.1144	0.9520	0.8867
Relative efficiency	4.9275	5.2379	5.8997

Another interesting source of information is the geographic data collected by volunteers. Although these data typically are from non-probability samples, they can nevertheless render valuable information about the global or local means of study variables.

When the volunteer data are supplemented by a probability sample with observations of the study variable, the volunteer data can be used at the design stage and/or at the estimation stage. As an example of the first approach, the volunteer data are used to predict the study variable at a fine discretisation grid. These predictions are then used to construct strata for supplemental sampling, for instance by the *cum-root-f* method (Section 4.4) or using the approach described in Section 13.2.

At the estimation stage, the volunteer data are used to predict the study variable at points of the supplemental probability sample and at the nodes of a discretisation grid. These predictions are then used in model-assisted estimation, using the generalised difference or regression estimator, as explained in this chapter. For more details and a simulation study, see Brus and de Gruijter (2003).

Stehman et al. (2018) compared the model-assisted estimation approach with a certainty stratum approach for estimating the area covered by land cover classes and the accuracy of land cover maps. The volunteer data are treated as the data of a stratum of which all units are observed. A probability sample is selected from the remaining units not observed by the volunteers. The total (area of a land cover class) of the certainty stratum is added to the estimated total of the subpopulation not observed by the volunteers.

The model-assisted approach requires a supplemental sample with observations of the study variable z. Kim and Wang (2019) described an approach in which the big data sample is combined with a probability sample with observations of one or more ancillary variables.

Kim and Wang (2019) also describe an alternative approach that does not require a probability sample at all. In this approach, the big data sample is subsampled to correct the selection bias in the big data sample. The subsample is selected by inverse sampling, using data on an ancillary variable x, either from a census or a probability sample. The subsample is selected with conditional inclusion probabilities equal to the subsample size multiplied by an importance weight (Kim and Wang (2019), equation 4).

11

Two-phase random sampling

The regression and ratio estimators of Chapter 10 require that the means of the ancillary variables are known. If these are unknown, but the ancillary variables can be measured cheaply, one may decide to estimate the population means of the ancillary variables from a large sample. The study variable is measured in a random subsample of this large sample only. This technique is known in the sampling literature as two-phase random sampling or double sampling. Another application of two-phase sampling is two-phase sampling for stratification. Stratified random sampling (Chapter 4) requires a map with the strata. The poststratified estimator of Subsection 10.2.2 requires that the sizes of the strata are known. With two-phase sampling for stratification, neither a map of the strata nor knowledge of the stratum sizes is required. Note that the term 'phase' does not refer to a period of time; all data can be collected in one sampling campaign. Let me also explain the difference with two-stage cluster sampling (Chapter 7). In two-stage cluster random sampling, we have two types of sampling units, clusters of population units and individual population units. In two-phase sampling, we have one type of sampling unit only, the objects of a discrete population or the elementary sampling units of a continuous population (Section 1.1).

In two-phase sampling for regression and two-phase sampling for stratification, the two phases have the same aim, i.e., to estimate the population mean of the study variable. The observations of the covariate(s) and/or strata in the first phase are merely done to increase the precision of the estimated mean of the study variable. Another application of two-phase sampling is subsampling an existing probability sample designed for a different aim. So, in this case the study variable observed in the second-phase sample may not be related to the variables observed in the first-phase sample.

An example is LUCAS-Topsoil (Ballabio et al., 2019) which is a subsample of approximately 22,000 units sampled from a much larger sample, the LUCAS sample, designed for estimating totals of land use and land cover classes across the European Union. It was not feasible to observe the soil properties at all sites of the LUCAS sample, and for this reason a subsample was selected. Regrettably, this subsample is not a probability sample from the LUCAS sample: the inclusion probabilities are either zero or unknown. Design-based or model-assisted estimation of means of soil properties for domains of interest is not feasible. The only option is model-based prediction.

In case the subsample is a probability subsample from the first-phase sample and no variable observed in the first-phase sample is of use for estimating the total or mean of the study variable observed in the subsample, the population total can be estimated by the π estimator:

$$\hat{t}(z) = \sum_{k \in \mathcal{S}_2} \frac{z_k}{\pi_{1k}\pi_{k|\mathcal{S}_1}} = \sum_{k \in \mathcal{S}_2} \frac{z_k}{\pi_k^*} , \tag{11.1}$$

with π_{1k} the probability that unit k is selected in the first phase, and $\pi_{k|\mathcal{S}_1}$ the probability that unit k is selected in the second phase, given the first-phase sample $\mathcal{S}_1$. This general π estimator for two-phase sampling, referred to as the π^* estimator by Särndal et al. (1992), can be used for any combination of probability sampling designs in the first and second phase.

To derive the variance, it is convenient to write the total estimation error as the sum of two errors:

$$\hat{t}(z) - t(z) = \left(\sum_{k \in \mathcal{S}_1} \frac{z_k}{\pi_{1k}} - t(z) \right) + \left(\sum_{k \in \mathcal{S}_2} \frac{z_k}{\pi_k^*} - \sum_{k \in \mathcal{S}_1} \frac{z_k}{\pi_{1k}} \right) \tag{11.2}$$
$$= e_1 + e_2 .$$

The first error e_1 is the error in the estimated population total, as estimated by the usual π estimator using the study variable values for the units in the first-phase sample. This estimator cannot be computed in practice, as the study variable values are only known for a subset of the units in the first-phase sample. The second error e_2 is the difference between the π^* estimator using the study variable values for the units in the subsample only, and the π estimator using the study variable values for all units in the first-phase sample.

The variance of the π^* estimator can be decomposed into the variance of these two errors as follows:

$$V_{p_1,p_2}(\hat{t}) = V_{p_1}E_{p_2}(\hat{t}|\mathcal{S}_1) + E_{p_1}V_{p_2}(\hat{t}|\mathcal{S}_1) = V_{p_1}(e_1) + E_{p_1}V_{p_2}(e_2|\mathcal{S}_1) , \tag{11.3}$$

with V_{p_1} and E_{p_1} the variance and expectation of the estimator for the population total over repeated sampling with the design of the first phase, respectively, and V_{p_2} and E_{p_2} the variance and expectation of the estimator for the population total over repeated sampling with the design of the second phase, respectively. The population mean can be estimated by the estimated total divided by the population size N.

11.1 Two-phase random sampling for stratification

In two-phase sampling for stratification, in the first phase a large sample is taken and the selected sampling units are all classified. The classes thus formed are then used as strata in the second sampling phase. A stratified subsample is selected, and the study variable is observed on the units in the subsample only.

This sampling design is applied, for instance, to monitor land use and land cover in the European Union by the LUCAS monitoring network mentioned above. In the first phase, a systematic random sample is selected, consisting of the nodes of a square sampling grid with a spacing of 2 km. Land use and land cover (LULC) are then determined at the selected grid nodes, using orthophotographs, satellite imagery, and fieldwork. The idea is that this procedure results in a more accurate classification of LULC at the selected units than by overlaying the grid nodes with an existing LULC map such as the Corine Land Cover map. The site-specific determinations of LULC classes are then used to select a stratified random subsample (second-phase sample). In 2018 the monitoring network was redesigned (Ballin et al., 2018).

Two-phase sampling for stratification is now illustrated with study area Voorst. A map with five combinations of soil type and land use is available of this study area. These combinations were used as strata in Chapter 4, and the stratum sizes were used in the poststratified estimator of Subsection 10.2.2. Here, we consider the situation that we do not have this map and that we do not know the sizes of these strata either. In the first phase, a simple random sample of size 100 is selected. In the field, the soil-land use combination is determined for the selected points, see Figure 11.1. This time we assume that the field determinations are equal to the classes as shown on the map.

```
n1 <- 100
set.seed(123)
N <- nrow(grdVoorst)
units <- sample(N, size = n1, replace = FALSE)
mysample <- grdVoorst[units, ]
```

The simple random sample is subsampled by stratified simple random sampling, using the soil-land use classes as strata. The total sample size of the second phase is set to 40. The number of points in the simple random sample per stratum is determined. Then the subsample size per stratum is computed for proportional allocation. Finally, function `strata` of package **sampling** (Tillé and Matei, 2021) is used to select a stratified simple random sample without replacement, see Chapter 4 for details. At the 40 points of the second-phase, the soil organic matter (SOM) concentration is measured.

```
library(sampling)
n2 <- 40
n1_h <- tapply(mysample$z, INDEX = mysample$stratum, FUN = length)
n2_h <- round(n1_h / n1 * n2, 0)
units <- sampling::strata(mysample, stratanames = "stratum",
  size = n2_h[unique(mysample$stratum)], method = "srswor")
mysubsample <- getdata(mysample, units)
table(mysubsample$stratum)
```

```
BA EA PA RA XF
15  8  6  4  7
```

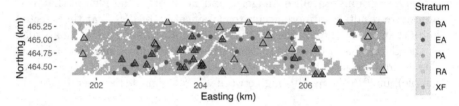

FIGURE 11.1: Two-phase random sample for stratification from Voorst. Coloured dots: first-phase sample of 100 points selected by simple random sampling, with observations of the soil-land use combination. Triangles: second-phase sample of 40 points selected by stratified simple random subsampling of the first-phase sample, using the soil-land use combinations as strata, with measurements of SOM.

With simple random sampling in the first phase and stratified simple random sampling in the second phase, the population mean can be estimated by

$$\hat{\bar{z}} = \sum_{h=1}^{H_{\mathcal{S}_1}} \frac{n_{1h}}{n_1} \, \bar{z}_{\mathcal{S}_{2h}} \,, \tag{11.4}$$

where $H_{\mathcal{S}_1}$ is the number of strata used for stratification of the first-phase sample, n_{1h} is the number of units in the first-phase sample that form stratum h in the second phase, n_1 is the total number of units of the first-phase sample, and $\bar{z}_{\mathcal{S}_{2h}}$ is the mean of the subsample from stratum h.

```
mz_h_subsam <- tapply(mysubsample$z, INDEX = mysubsample$stratum, FUN = mean)
mz <- sum(n1_h / n1 * mz_h_subsam, na.rm = TRUE)
```

The estimated population mean equals 85.6 g kg^{-1}. The sampling variance over repeated sampling with both designs can be approximated[1] by (Särndal et al. (1992), equation at bottom of p. 353)

$$\hat{V}(\hat{\bar{z}}) = \sum_{h=1}^{H_{s_1}} \left(\frac{n_{1h}}{n_1} \right)^2 \frac{\widehat{S^2}_{s_{2h}}}{n_{2h}} + \frac{1}{n_1} \sum_{h=1}^{H_{s_1}} \frac{n_{1h}}{n_1} \left(\bar{z}_{s_{2h}} - \hat{\bar{z}} \right)^2 , \qquad (11.5)$$

with $\widehat{S^2}_{s_{2h}}$ the variance of z in the subsample from stratum h.

```
S2z_h_subsam <- tapply(mysubsample$z, INDEX = mysubsample$stratum, FUN = var)
w1_h <- n1_h / n1
v_mz_1 <- sum(w1_h^2 * S2z_h_subsam / n2_h)
v_mz_2 <- 1 / n1 * sum(w1_h * (mz_h_subsam - mz)^2)
se_mz <- sqrt(v_mz_1 + v_mz_2)
```

The estimated standard error equals 7.1 g kg^{-1}.

The mean and its standard error can be estimated with functions twophase and svymean of package **survey** (Lumley, 2021). A data frame with the first-phase sample is passed to function twophase using argument data. A variable in this data frame, passed to function twophase with argument subset, is an indicator with value TRUE if this unit is selected in the second phase, and FALSE otherwise.

```
library(survey)
lut <- data.frame(stratum = sort(unique(mysample$stratum)), fpc2 = n1_h)
mysample <- mysample %>%
  mutate(ind = FALSE,
         fpc1 = N) %>%
  left_join(lut, by = "stratum")
mysample$ind[units$ID_unit] <- TRUE
design_2phase <- survey::twophase(
  id = list(~ 1, ~ 1), strata = list(NULL, ~ stratum),
  data = mysample, subset = ~ ind, fpc = list(~ fpc1, ~ fpc2))
svymean(~ z, design_2phase)
```

```
      mean    SE
z 85.606 7.033
```

As shown in the next code chunk, the standard error is computed with the original variance estimator, without approximation (Särndal et al. (1992), equation (9.4.14)).

---

[1]In the approximation, it is assumed that N is much larger than n_1, and $(n_{1h}-1)/(n_1-1)$ is replaced by n_{1h}/n_1.

```
v_mz_1 <- 1 / N^2 * N * (N - 1) *
  sum((((n1_h - 1) / (n1 - 1)) - ((n2_h - 1) / (N - 1)))
      * w1_h * S2z_h_subsam / n2_h)
v_mz_2 <- 1 / N^2 * (N * (N - n1)) / (n1 - 1) *
  sum(w1_h * (mz_h_subsam - mz)^2)
sqrt(v_mz_1 + v_mz_2)
```

```
[1] 7.032964
```

11.2   Two-phase random sampling for regression

The simple regression estimator of Equation (10.10) requires that the population mean of the ancillary variable x is known. This section, however, is about applying the regression estimator in situations where the mean of x is unknown. A possible application is estimating the soil organic carbon (SOC) stock in an area. To estimate this carbon stock, soil samples are collected and analysed in a laboratory. The laboratory measurements can be very accurate, but also expensive. Proximal sensors can be used to derive soil carbon concentrations from the spectra. Compared to laboratory measurements of soil the proximal sensor determinations are much cheaper, but also less accurate. If there is a relation between the laboratory and the proximal sensing determinations of SOC, then we expect that the regression estimator of the carbon stock will be more accurate than the π estimator which does not exploit the proximal sensing measurements. However, the population mean of the proximal sensing determinations is unknown. What we can do is estimate this mean from a large sample. Additionally, for a subsample of this large sample, SOC concentration is also measured in the laboratory. This is another example of two-phase sampling.

Intuitively, we understand that with two-phase sampling the variance of the regression estimator of the total carbon stock is larger than when the population mean of the proximal sensing determinations is known. There is a sampling error in the estimated population mean of the proximal sensing determinations, estimated from the large first-phase sample, and this error propagates to the error in the estimated total carbon stock.

Two-phase sampling for regression is now illustrated with Eastern Amazonia (Subsection 1.3.3). The study variable is the aboveground biomass (AGB), and lnSWIR2 is used here as a covariate. We do have a full coverage map of lnSWIR2, so two-phase sampling with a large first-phase sample to estimate the population mean of lnSWIR2 is not needed. Nevertheless, hereafter a two-phase sample is selected, and the population mean of lnSWIR2 is estimated from the first-phase sample. In doing so, the effect of ignorance of the population mean of the covariate on the variance of the regression estimator becomes apparent.

In the next code chunk, a first-phase sample of 250 units, the dots in the plot, is selected by simple random sampling without replacement. In the second phase a subsample of 100 units, the triangles in the plot, is selected from the 250 units by simple random sampling without replacement. At all 250 units of the first-phase sample the covariate lnSWIR2 is measured, whereas AGB is measured at the 100 subsample units only.

```
grdAmazonia <- grdAmazonia %>%
  mutate(lnSWIR2 = log(SWIR2))
n1 <- 250; n2 <- 100
set.seed(314)
units_1 <- sample(nrow(grdAmazonia), size = n1, replace = FALSE)
mysample <- grdAmazonia[units_1, ]
units_2 <- sample(n1, size = n2, replace =. FALSE)
mysubsample <- mysample[units_2, ]
```

Figure 11.2 shows the selected two-phase sample.

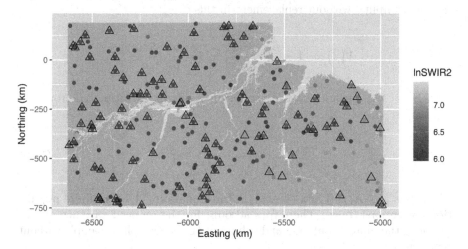

FIGURE 11.2: Two-phase random sample for the regression estimator of the mean AGB in Eastern Amazonia. Coloured dots: simple random sample without replacement of 250 units with measurements of covariate lnSWIR2 (first-phase sample). Triangles: simple random subsample without replacement of 100 units with measurements of AGB (second-phase sample).

Estimation of the population mean or total by the regression estimator from a two-phase sample is very similar to estimation when the covariate mean is known, as described in Subsection 10.1.1 (Equation (10.10)). The observations of the *subsample* can be used to estimate the regression coefficient b. The true population mean of the ancillary variable, $\bar{x}$ in Equation (10.10), is unknown now. This true mean is replaced by the mean as estimated from the relatively large first-phase sample, $\bar{x}_{\mathcal{S}_1}$. The estimated mean of the covariate, $\bar{x}_{\mathcal{S}}$ in Equation (10.10), is estimated from the subsample, $\bar{x}_{\mathcal{S}_2}$. This leads to the following estimator:

$$\hat{\bar{z}} = \bar{z}_{\mathcal{S}_2} + \hat{b}\left(\bar{x}_{\mathcal{S}_1} - \bar{x}_{\mathcal{S}_2}\right) , \tag{11.6}$$

where $\bar{z}_{\mathcal{S}_2}$ is the subsample mean of the study variable, and $\bar{x}_{\mathcal{S}_1}$ and $\bar{x}_{\mathcal{S}_2}$ are the means of the covariate in the first-phase sample and the subsample (i.e., the second-phase sample), respectively.

The sampling variance is larger than that of the regression estimator with known mean of x. The variance can be decomposed into two components. The first component is equal to the sampling variance of the π estimator of the mean of z with the sampling design of the first phase (in this case, simple random sampling without replacement), supposing that the study variable is observed on all units of the first-phase sample. The second component is equal to the sampling variance of the regression estimator of the mean of z in the first-phase sample, with the design of the second-phase sample (again simple random sampling without replacement in this case):

$$\hat{V}\left(\hat{\bar{z}}\right) = (1 - \frac{n_1}{N})\frac{\widehat{S^2}(z)}{n_1} + (1 - \frac{n_2}{n_1})\frac{\widehat{S^2}(e)}{n_2} , \tag{11.7}$$

with $\widehat{S^2}(e)$ the variance of the regression residuals as estimated from the subsample:

$$\widehat{S^2}(e) = \frac{1}{(n_2 - 1)} \sum_{k \in \mathcal{S}_2} e_k^2 . \tag{11.8}$$

The ratios $(1 - n_1/N)$ and $(1 - n_2/n_1)$ in Equation (11.7) are finite population corrections (fpcs). These fpcs account for the reduced variance due to sampling the finite population and subsampling the first-phase sample without replacement.

```
lm_subsample <- lm(AGB ~ lnSWIR2, data = mysubsample)
ab <- coef(lm_subsample)
mx_sam <- mean(mysample$lnSWIR2)
mx_subsam <- mean(mysubsample$lnSWIR2)
mz_subsam <- mean(mysubsample$AGB)
mz_reg2ph <- mz_subsam + ab[2] * (mx_sam - mx_subsam)
```

The estimated population mean equals 228.1 10^9 kg ha^{-1}. The standard error can be approximated as follows.

```
e <- residuals(lm_subsample)
S2e <- sum(e^2) / (n2 - 1)
S2z <- var(mysubsample$AGB)
N <- nrow(grdAmazonia)
se_mz_reg2ph <- sqrt((1 - n1 / N) * S2z / n1 + (1 - n2 / n1) * S2e / n2)
```

The estimated standard error equals 6.35 10^9 kg ha^{-1}.

The regression estimator for two-phase sampling and its standard error can also be computed with package **survey**, as shown below. The standard error differs from the standard error computed above because it is computed with the g-weights, see Subsection 10.1.1. Note argument fpc = list(~ N, NULL). There is no need to add the first-phase sample size as a second element of the list, because this sample size is simply the number of rows of the data frame. Setting the second element of the list to NULL does not mean that the standard error is computed for sampling with replacement in the second phase. Function twophase assumes that the second-phase units are always selected without replacement.

```
mysample <- mysample %>%
  mutate(id = row_number(),
         N = N,
         ind = id %in% units_2)
design_2phase <- survey::twophase(
  id = list(~ 1, ~ 1), data = mysample, subset = ~ ind, fpc = list(~ N, NULL))
mysample_cal <- calibrate(
  design_2phase, formula = ~ lnSWIR2, calfun = "linear", phase = 2)
svymean(~ AGB, mysample_cal)
```

```
        mean      SE
AGB  228.07  7.2638
```

Exercises

1. Write an **R** script to select a simple random sample without replacement of 250 units from Eastern Amazonia and a subsample of 100 units by simple random sampling without replacement. Repeat this 1,000 times in a for-loop.
   - Use each sample selected in the first phase (sample of 250 units) to estimate the population mean of AGB by the regression estimator (Equation (10.10) in Chapter 10). Assume that the AGB data are known for all units selected in the first phase. Use lnSWIR2 as a covariate.

- Compute the variance of the 10,000 regression estimates of the population mean of AGB.
- Use each two-phase sample to compute the regression estimator of AGB for two-phase sampling (Equation (11.6)). Now only use the AGB data of the subsample. Estimate the population mean of lnSWIR2 from the first-phase sample of 250 units. Approximate the variance of the regression estimator for two-phase sampling (Equation (11.7)).
- Compute the variance of the 10,000 regression estimates of the population mean of AGB for the two-phase sampling design.
- Compare the two variances and explain the difference.
- Compute the average of the 10,000 approximate variances and compare the result with the variance of the 10,000 estimated means, as estimated by the regression estimator for two-phase sampling.

12

Computing the required sample size

An important decision in designing sampling schemes is the number of units to select. In other words, what should the sample size be? If a certain budget is available for sampling, we can determine the affordable sample size from this budget. A costs model is then needed.

The alternative to deriving the affordable sample size from the budget is to start from a requirement on the quality of the survey result obtained by statistical inference. Two types of inference are distinguished, estimation and testing. The required sample size depends on the type of sampling design. With stratified random sampling, we expect that we need fewer sampling units compared to simple random sampling to estimate the population mean with the same precision, whereas with cluster random sampling and two-stage cluster random sampling in general we need more sampling units. To compute the sample size given some quality requirement, we may start with computing the required sample size for simple random sampling and then correct this sample size to account for the design effect. Therefore, I start with presenting formulas for computing the required sample size for simple random sampling. Section 12.4 describes how the required sample sizes for other types of sampling design can be derived.

Hereafter, formulas for computing the required sample size are presented for simple random sampling *with replacement* of finite populations and simple random sampling of infinite populations. For simple random sampling *without replacement* (SI) of finite populations, these sample sizes can be corrected by (Lohr, 1999)

$$n_{\mathrm{SI}} = \frac{n_{\mathrm{SIR}}}{1 + \frac{n_{\mathrm{SIR}}}{N}} \, , \tag{12.1}$$

with n_{SIR} the required sample size for simple random sampling with replacement.

12.1 Standard error

A first option is to set a limit on the variance of the π estimator of the population mean, see Equation (3.11), or on the square root of this variance, the standard error of the estimator. Given a chosen limit for the standard error se_{max}, the required sample size for simple random sampling with replacement can be computed by

$$n = \left(\frac{S^*(z)}{se_{max}} \right)^2 , \tag{12.2}$$

with $S^*(z)$ a prior estimate of the population standard deviation. The required sample size n should be rounded to the nearest integer greater than the right-hand side of Equation (12.2). This also applies to the following equations.

For the population proportion (areal fraction) as the parameter of interest, the required sample size can be computed by (see Equation (3.18))

$$n = \left(\frac{\sqrt{p^*(1-p^*)}}{se_{max}} \right)^2 + 1 , \tag{12.3}$$

with p^* a prior estimate of the population proportion.

> To determine the required sample size for estimating the population proportion, we need a prior estimate of the population parameter of interest itself, whereas for the population mean a prior estimate is needed of the population standard deviation. The parameter of which a prior estimate is needed for sample size determination is referred to as the design parameter.

Alternatively, we may require that the *relative* standard error, i.e., the standard error of the estimator divided by the population mean, may not exceed a given limit rse_{max}. In this case the required sample size can be computed by

$$n = \left(\frac{cv^*}{rse_{max}} \right)^2 , \tag{12.4}$$

with cv^* a prior estimate of the population coefficient of variation $S(z)/\bar{z}$. For a constraint on the relative standard error of the population proportion estimator, we obtain

$$n = \left(\frac{p^*(1-p^*)}{rse_{max}\, p^*} \right)^2 + 1 = \left(\frac{1-p^*}{rse_{max}} \right)^2 + 1 . \tag{12.5}$$

12.2   Length of confidence interval

Another option is to require that the length of the confidence interval of the population mean may not exceed a given limit l_{max}:

$$2\, t_{\alpha/2,n-1} \frac{S(z)}{\sqrt{n}} \leq l_{max} , \tag{12.6}$$

with $t_{\alpha/2,n-1}$ the $(1-\alpha/2)$ quantile of the t distribution with $n-1$ degrees of freedom, $S(z)$ the population standard deviation of the study variable, and n the sample size. The problem is that we do not know the degrees of freedom (we want to determine the sample size n). Therefore, $t_{\alpha/2,n-1}$ is replaced by $u_{\alpha/2}$, the $(1-\alpha/2)$ quantile of the standard normal distribution. Rearranging yields

$$n = \left(u_{\alpha/2} \frac{S^*(z)}{l_{max}/2} \right)^2 . \tag{12.7}$$

The requirement can also be formulated as

$$P(|\hat{\bar{z}} - \bar{z}| \leq d_{max}) \leq 1 - \alpha , \tag{12.8}$$

with d_{max} the margin of error: $d_{max} = l_{max}/2$.

An alternative is to require that with a large probability $1 - \alpha$ the absolute value of the *relative* error of the estimated mean may not exceed a given limit r_{max}. In formula:

$$P\left(\frac{|\hat{\bar{z}} - \bar{z}|}{\bar{z}} \leq r_{max} \right) \leq 1 - \alpha . \tag{12.9}$$

Noting that the absolute error equals $r_{max}\bar{z}$ and inserting this in Equation (12.7) gives

$$n = \left(u_{\alpha/2} \frac{cv^*}{r_{max}} \right)^2 . \tag{12.10}$$

As an example, the required sample size is computed for estimating the population mean of the soil organic matter concentration in Voorst. The requirement is that with a probability of 95% the absolute value of the *relative* error does not exceed 10%. A prior estimate of 0.5 for the population coefficient of variation is used.

```
cv <- 0.5
rmax <- 0.1
u <- qnorm(p = 1 - 0.05 / 2, mean = 0, sd = 1)
n <- ceiling((u * cv / rmax)^2)
```

The required sample size is 97. The same result is obtained with function nContMoe of package **PracTools** (Valliant et al. (2021), Valliant et al. (2018)).

```
library(PracTools)
print(ceiling(nContMoe(moe.sw = 2, e = rmax, alpha = 0.05, CVpop = cv)))
```

```
[1] 97
```

12.2.1   Length of confidence interval for a proportion

Each of the methods for computing a confidence interval of a proportion described in Subsection 3.3.1 can be used to compute the required sample size given a limit for the length of the confidence interval of a proportion. The most simple option is to base the required sample size on the Wald interval (Equation (3.21)), so that the required sample size can be computed by

$$n = \left(u_{\alpha/2} \frac{\sqrt{p^*(1-p^*)}}{l_{\max}/2} \right)^2 + 1 . \qquad (12.11)$$

The Wald interval approximates the discrete binomial distribution by a normal distribution. See the rule of thumb in Subsection 3.3.1 for when this approximation is reasonable.

Package **binomSamSize** (Höhle, 2017) has quite a few functions for computing the required sample size. Function ciss.wald uses the normal approximation. In the next code chunk, the required sample sizes are computed for a prior estimate of the population proportion p^* of 0.2.

 Argument d in the functions below is *half* the length of the confidence interval.

```
library(binomSamSize)
p_prior <- 0.2
n_prop_wald <- ciss.wald(p0 = p_prior, d = 0.1, alpha = 0.05)
n_prop_agrcll <- ciss.agresticoull(p0 = p_prior, d = 0.1, alpha = 0.05)
n_prop_wilson <- ciss.wilson(p0 = p_prior, d = 0.1, alpha = 0.05)
```

The required sample sizes are 62, 58, and 60, for the Wald, Agresti-Coull, and Wilson approximation of the binomial proportion confidence interval, respectively. The required sample size with function `ciss.wald` is one unit smaller than as computed with Equation (12.11), as shown in the code chunk below.

```
ceiling((qnorm(0.975) * sqrt(p_prior * (1 - p_prior)) / 0.1)^2 + 1)
```

```
[1] 63
```

12.3 Statistical testing of hypothesis

The required sample size for testing a population mean with a two-sided alternative hypothesis can be computed by (Ott and Longnecker, 2015)

$$n = \frac{S^2(z)}{\Delta^2} (u_{\alpha/2} + u_\beta)^2 , \qquad (12.12)$$

with Δ the smallest relevant difference of the population mean from the test value, α the tolerable probability of a type I error, i.e., the probability of rejecting the null hypothesis when the population mean is equal to the test value, β the tolerable probability of a type II error, i.e., the probability of not rejecting the null hypothesis when the population mean is not equal to the test value, $u_{\alpha/2}$ as before, and u_β the $(1-\beta)$ quantile of the standard normal distribution. The quantity $1 - \beta$ is the power of a test: the probability of correctly rejecting the null hypothesis. For a one-sided test, $u_{\alpha/2}$ must be replaced by u_α.

In the next code chunk, the sample size required for a given target power is computed with the standard normal distribution (Equation (12.12)), as well as with the t distribution using function `pwr.t.test` of package **pwr** (Champely, 2020)[1]. This requires some iterative algorithm, as the degrees of freedom of the t distribution are a function of the sample size. The required sample size is computed for a one-sample test and a one-sided alternative hypothesis.

```
library(pwr)
sd <- 4; delta <- 1; alpha <- 0.05; beta <- 0.2
n_norm <- (sd / delta)^2 * (qnorm(1 - alpha) + qnorm(1 - beta))^2
n_t <- pwr.t.test(
```

---

[1]The same result is obtained with function `power.t.test` of the **stats** package.

```
d = delta / sd, sig.level = alpha, power = (1 - beta),
type = "one.sample", alternative = "greater")
```

In this example, the required sample size computed with the t distribution is two units larger than that obtained with the standard normal distribution: 101 vs. 99. Package **pwr** has various functions for computing the power of a test given the sample size, or reversely, the sample size for a given power, such as for the two independent samples t test, binomial test (for one proportion), test for two proportions, etc.

12.3.1 Sample size for testing a proportion

For testing a proportion, a graph is computed with the power of a binomial test against the sample size. This is illustrated with a one-sided alternative $H_a : p > 0.20$ and a smallest relevant difference of 0.10.

```
p_test <- 0.20; alpha <- 0.10; delta <- 0.10
n <- 1:150
power <- k_min <- numeric(length = length(n))
for (i in seq_len(length(n))) {
  k_min[i] <- qbinom(p = 1 - alpha, size = n[i], prob = p_test)
  power[i] <- pbinom(
    q = k_min[i], size = n[i], prob = p_test + delta, lower.tail = FALSE)
}
```

As can be seen in the **R** code, as a first step for each total sample size the smallest number of successes k_{min} is computed at which the null hypothesis is rejected. Then the binomial probability is computed of $k_{min} + 1$ or more successes for a probability of success equal to $p_{test} + \Delta$. Note that there is no need to add 1 to k_min as with argument lower.tail = FALSE the value specified by argument q is not included.

Figure 12.1 shows that the power does not increase monotonically with the sample size. The graph shows a saw-toothed behaviour. This is caused by the stepwise increase of the critical number of successes (k_min) with the total sample size.

The required sample size can be computed in two ways. The first option is to compute the smallest sample size for which the power is larger than or equal to the required power $1 - \beta$. The alternative is to compute the smallest sample size for which the power is larger than or equal to $1 - \beta$ *for all sample sizes larger than this.*

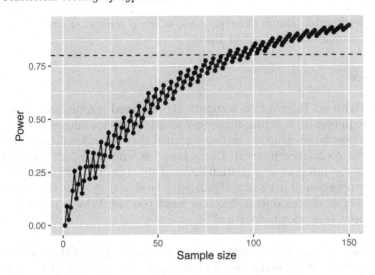

FIGURE 12.1: Power of right-tail binomial test (test proportion: 0.2; significance level: 0.10).

```
n1 <- min(n[which(power > 1 - beta)])
ind <- (power > 1 - beta)
for (i in seq_len(length(n))) {
  if (ind[length(n) - i] == FALSE)
    break
}
n2 <- n[length(n) - i + 1]
```

The smallest sample size at which the desired level of 0.8 is reached is 88. However, as can be seen in Figure 12.1, for sample sizes 89, 90, 93, 94, and 97, the power drops below the desired level of 0.80. The smallest sample size at which the power stays above the level of 0.8 is 98.

Alternatively, we may use function `pwr.p.test` of package **pwr**. This is an approximation, using an arcsine transformation of proportions. The first step is to compute Cohen's h, which is a measure of the distance between two proportions: $h = 2 \ arcsin(\sqrt{p_1}) - 2 \ arcsin(\sqrt{p_2})$. This can be done with function `ES.h`. The value of h must be positive, which is achieved when the proportion specified by argument `p1` is larger than the proportion specified by argument `p2`.

```
h <- ES.h(p1 = 0.30, p2 = 0.20)
n_approx <- pwr.p.test(
  h, power = (1 - beta), sig.level = alpha, alternative = "greater")
```

The approximated sample size equals 84, which is somewhat smaller than the required sample sizes computed above.

Exercises

1. Write an **R** script to compute the required sample size, given a requirement in terms of the half-length of the confidence interval of a population proportion. Use a normal approximation for computing the confidence interval. Use a range of values for half the length of the interval: $d = (0.01, 0.02, \dots, 0.49)$. Use a prior (anticipated) proportion of 0.1 and a significance level of 0.95. Plot the required sample size against d. Explain what you see. Why is it needed to provide a prior proportion?

2. Do the same for a single value for the half-length of the confidence interval of 0.2 and a range of values for the prior proportion $p^* = (0.01, 0.02, \dots, 0.49)$. Explain what you see. Why is it not needed to compute the required sample size for prior proportions > 0.5?

12.4   Accounting for design effect

The required sample sizes computed in the previous sections are all for simple random sampling in combination with the π estimator of the population mean. But what is the required sample size for other types of sampling design, such as stratified (simple) random sampling, systematic random sampling, two-stage cluster random sampling, and cluster random sampling? Broadly speaking, we expect that with stratified random sampling and systematic random sampling the sampling variance of the estimator of the mean will be smaller than with simple random sampling of the same number of units, whereas with two-stage cluster random sampling and cluster random sampling we expect larger sampling variances. Therefore, reversely, for the first two types of sampling design, we expect that the sample size required to achieve the same level of accuracy or confidence will be smaller than with simple random sampling, and for the latter two design types this sample size will be larger. The design effect is commonly quantified by the ratio of two sampling variances of the population mean estimator (Lohr, 1999):

$$de(p, \hat{\bar{z}}) = \frac{V_p(\hat{\bar{z}})}{V_{\mathrm{SI}}(\hat{\bar{z}}_\pi)} = \frac{V_p(\hat{\bar{z}})}{S^2(z)/n} \,, \tag{12.13}$$

with $V_p(\hat{\bar{z}})$ the sampling variance of an estimator (π estimator, regression estimator) of the population mean with sampling design p and $V_{SI}(\hat{\bar{z}}_\pi)$ the sampling variance of the π estimator of the population mean with simple random sampling. Given an estimate of this design effect, the required sample size for a more complex sampling strategy (combination of sampling design and estimator), given a constraint on the standard error or the half-length of a confidence interval, can be computed by

$$n(p, \hat{\bar{z}}) = \sqrt{de(p, \hat{\bar{z}})}\, n(SI, \pi) \,. \tag{12.14}$$

The design effect can also be quantified by the ratio of two standard errors. Then there is no need to take the square root of the design effect, as done in Equation (12.14), to compute the required sample size for a more complex design, given a constraint on the standard error or the half-length of a confidence interval.

12.5 Bayesian sample size determination

A serious drawback of the classical frequentist approach of computing the required sample size explained in the previous sections is that the required sample sizes are sensitive to the design parameters S^*, p^*, and cv^*. We are rather uncertain about these parameters, and therefore it is attractive to replace a single value for these parameters by a probability distribution. This leads to a different statistical approach of computing the required sample size, the Bayesian approach. This Bayesian approach also offers the possibility of accommodating existing information about the population mean or proportion. In this section I show how this approach can be used to compute the required sample size for estimating a population mean or proportion.

But before going into details, let me explain the basics of the Bayesian approach of statistical inference. In the previous sections, the statistical inference was from the frequentist perspective. How does the frequency distribution of the estimator of the population mean look like if we repeat the selection of a sample with a given sampling design? Is the mean of this frequency distribution, referred to as the sampling distribution, equal to the population mean, and what is the variance of this sampling distribution?

The Bayesian approach is fundamentally different. The frequency distribution of the frequentist approach is replaced by a probability distribution of the population mean reflecting our *belief* about the population mean. Note that expressing our belief in terms of a probability distribution implies that in the Bayesian approach, contrary to the frequentist approach, the population mean is a random variable. Where in the frequentist approach, it is incorrect to say that the probability that the population mean is inside the 95% confidence interval equals 95% (see Section 3.3), this is perfectly fine in the Bayesian approach. The term confidence interval is replaced by the term *credible interval* to underline the fundamental different meaning of the interval.

The first step in the Bayesian approach of statistical inference is to postulate a *prior distribution* for the population parameter of interest. This prior distribution expresses our belief and uncertainty about the parameter before the sample data are taken into account.

The next step is to formalise a theory about the data. This boils down to making an assumption about the type of distribution function of the data. Can we safely assume that the data follow a normal or a binomial distribution? Once the type of distribution has been specified, we can write an equation for the probability of the data *as a function of the parameter*. This function is referred to as the *likelihood function*.

The final step is to revise our prior belief about the population parameter of interest, using the data and our theory about the data as expressed in the likelihood function. This results in the *posterior distribution* of the parameter. Our revised or updated belief is computed with Bayes' rule:

$$f(\theta|\mathbf{z}) = \frac{f(\theta)f(\mathbf{z}|\theta)}{f(\mathbf{z})} \ , \tag{12.15}$$

with $f(\theta|\mathbf{z})$ the posterior distribution, i.e., the probability density[2] of the parameter given the sample data, $f(\theta)$ our prior belief in the parameters specified by a probability distribution (prior distribution), $f(\mathbf{z}|\theta)$ the likelihood of the data, and $f(\mathbf{z})$ the probability distribution of the data.

12.5.1 Bayesian criteria for sample size computation

Equation (12.15) shows that the posterior distribution of the population parameter of interest depends on the probability distribution of the new data $f(\mathbf{z})$. The problem is that these new data are not yet known. We are designing a sample, and the data yet are to be collected, so at first glance this might seem an unsolvable problem. However, what we could do is to simulate with the prior probability density function a large number of values of the population parameter(s), and with each parameter a large number of possible vectors with n data. Each data vector is then used to update the prior to the posterior, using Bayes' rule (Equation (12.15)). For each posterior either the length of the

---

[2] I assume here that the parameter of interest θ is a continuous random variable.

highest posterior density (HPD) interval with a coverage probability of $1 - \alpha$ is computed, or reversely, the coverage probability of the HPD interval of length $l_{\max}$. Finally, the average of the lengths of the HPD intervals or the average of the coverage probabilities is computed, and these averages are compared with our precision requirement. If the average length is larger than $l_{\max}$, or the coverage probability of intervals of length $l_{\max}$ is smaller than $1 - \alpha$, then we must increase n; if the average length is smaller than $l_{\max}$, or the coverage probability of intervals of length $l_{\max}$ is larger than $1 - \alpha$, then we must decrease n. This whole procedure is repeated until our precision requirement is met. Simulation is one option to compute the sample size, (partly) analytical approaches are also available.

More formally, the procedure is as follows. The prior probability density function on the population parameter(s) θ is used to compute for a given sample size n the *predictive* distribution of the data:

$$f(\mathbf{z}|n) = \int_{\Theta} f(\mathbf{z}|\theta, n) f(\theta) \mathrm{d}\theta \,, \tag{12.16}$$

with Θ the parameter space for θ containing all possible values of θ. This predictive distribution is also named the *preposterior* distribution, stressing that the data are not yet accounted for in the distribution.

Even if θ would be fixed, we do not have only one vector $\mathbf{z}$ with n data values but a probability distribution, from which we can simulate possible data vectors, referred to as the data space $\mathcal{Z}$. In case of a binomial probability and sample size n, the data space $\mathcal{Z}$ (in the form of the number of observed successes given sample size n) can be written as the set $\{0, 1, \ldots, n\}$, i.e., one vector of length n with all "failures", n vectors of length n with one success, $\binom{n}{2}$ vectors with two successes, etc. Each data vector is associated with a probability density (for continuous data) or probability mass (for discrete data). As a consequence, we do not have only one posterior distribution function $f(\theta|\mathbf{z})$, but as many as we have data vectors in the data space. For each posterior distribution function the coverage of the HPD interval of a given length can be computed, or reversely, the length of the HPD interval for a given coverage. This leads to various criteria for computing the required sample size, among which are the average length criterion (ALC), the average coverage criterion (ACC), and the worst outcome criterion (WOC) (Joseph et al. (1995), Joseph and Bélisle (1997)).

12.5.1.1 Average length criterion

For a fixed posterior HPD interval coverage of $100(1-\alpha)\%$, the smallest sample size n is determined such that

$$\int_{\mathcal{Z}} l(\mathbf{z}, n) f(\mathbf{z}|n) \mathrm{d}\mathbf{z} \leq l_{\max} \,, \tag{12.17}$$

where $f(\mathbf{z}|n)$ is the predictive distribution of the data (Equation (12.16)) and $l(\mathbf{z}, n)$ is the length of the $100(1 - \alpha)\%$ HPD interval for data $\mathbf{z}$ and sample size n, obtained by solving

$$\int_{v}^{v+l(\mathbf{z},n)} f(\theta|\mathbf{z}, n)\mathrm{d}\theta = 1 - \alpha , \tag{12.18}$$

for $l(\mathbf{z}, n)$, for each possible data set $\mathbf{z} \in \mathcal{Z}$. $f(\theta|\mathbf{z}, n)$ is the posterior density of the population parameter of interest given the data $\mathbf{z}$ and sample size n. ALC ensures that the average length of $100(1 - \alpha)\%$ posterior HPD intervals, weighted by $f(\mathbf{z}|n)$, is at most $l_{\max}$.

12.5.1.2   Average coverage criterion

For a fixed posterior HPD interval of length $l_{\max}$, the smallest sample size n is determined such that

$$\int_{\mathcal{Z}} \left\{ \int_{v}^{v+l_{\max}} f(\theta|\mathbf{z}, n)\mathrm{d}\theta \right\} f(\mathbf{z}|n)\mathrm{d}\mathbf{z} \geq 1 - \alpha . \tag{12.19}$$

ACC ensures that the average coverage of HPD intervals of length $l_{\max}$ is at least $1 - \alpha$. The integral inside the curly brackets is the integral of the posterior density of the population parameter of interest over the HPD interval $(v, v + l_{\max})$, given a data vector $\mathbf{z}$ of size n. The mean of this integrated posterior density of the parameter of interest θ is obtained by multiplying the integrated density with the predictive probability of the data and integrating over all possible data sets in $\mathcal{Z}$.

12.5.1.3   Worst outcome criterion

Neither ALC nor ACC guarantee that for a particular data set $\mathbf{z}$ the criterion is met, as both are defined as averages over all possible data sets in $\mathcal{Z}$. A more conservative sample size can be computed by requiring that for all data sets $\mathcal{Z}$ both criteria are met. Joseph and Bélisle (1997) modified this criterion by restricting the data sets to a subset $\mathcal{W}$ of most likely data sets. The criterion thus obtained is referred to as the modified worst outcome criterion, or for short, the worst outcome criterion (WOC). So, the criterion is

$$\inf_{\mathbf{z}\in\mathcal{W}} \left\{ \int_{v}^{v+l(\mathbf{z},n)} f(\theta|\mathbf{z}, n)\mathrm{d}\theta \right\} \geq 1 - \alpha . \tag{12.20}$$

The smallest sample size satisfying this condition is used as the sample size. For instance, if the 95% most likely data sets are chosen as subspace $\mathcal{W}$, WOC guarantees that there is 95% assurance that the length of the $100(1 - \alpha)\%$ posterior HPD intervals will be at most $l_{\max}$. The fraction of most likely data sets in subspace $\mathcal{W}$ is referred to as the worst level.

12.5.2 Mixed Bayesian-likelihood approach

Besides the fully Bayesian approach, Joseph and Bélisle (1997) describe a mixed Bayesian-likelihood approach for determining the sample size. In the mixed Bayesian-likelihood approach of sample size determination, the prior distribution of the parameter or parameters is only used to derive the predictive distribution of the data (Equation (12.16)), not the posterior distributions of the parameter of interest for each data vector. For analysis of the posterior distribution, an uninformative prior is therefore used. This mixed approach is of interest when, after the data have been collected, we prefer to estimate the population mean from these data only, using the frequentist approach described in previous sections.

An example of a situation where the mixed Bayesian-likelihood approach can be attractive is the following. Suppose some data of the study variable from the population of interest are already available, but we would like to collect more data so that we will be more confident about the (current) population mean once these new data are collected. The legacy data are used to construct a prior distribution. We have doubts about the quality of the legacy data because they were collected a long time ago and the study variable might have changed in the meantime. In that case, the mixed Bayesian-likelihood approach can be a good option – we are willing to use the legacy data to plan the sampling, but not to make statements about the current population.

No closed formula for computing the required sample size exists for this approach because the posterior density function $f(\theta|z, n)$ is not a well-defined distribution as before. However, the required sample size still can be approximated by simulation.

12.5.3 Estimation of population mean

The three criteria (ALC, ACC, and WOC) described above are now used to compute the required sample size for estimating the population mean, assuming that the data come from a normal distribution. As we are uncertain about the population standard deviation σ ($S^*(z)$ in Equation (12.7) is only a prior point estimate of σ), a prior distribution is assigned to this parameter. It is convenient to assign a gamma distribution as a prior distribution to the *reciprocal* of the population variance, referred to as the precision parameter $\lambda = 1/\sigma^2$. More precisely, a prior *bivariate* normal-gamma distribution is assigned to the population mean and the precision parameter[3]. With this prior distribution, the *posterior* distribution of the population mean is fully defined, i.e., both the type of distribution and its parameters are known. The prior distribution is so-called *conjugate* with the normal distribution.

The gamma distribution has two parameters: a and b. Figure 12.2 shows the gamma distribution for $a = 5$ and $b = 100$.

```
a <- 5; b <- 100
x <- seq(from = 0, to = 0.2, length = 1000)
dg <- dgamma(x = x, shape = a, scale = 1 / b)
plot(x = x, y = dg, type = "l", ylab = "Density", xlab = "Precision")
```

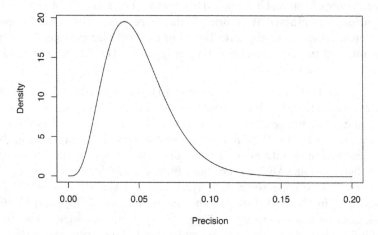

FIGURE 12.2: Prior gamma distribution for the precision parameter for a shape parameter $a = 5$ and a scale parameter $1/b = 1/100$.

The mean of the precision parameter λ is given by a/b and its standard deviation by $\sqrt{a/b^2}$.

The normal-gamma prior is used to compute the predictive distribution for the data. For ACC the required sample size can then be computed with (Adcock, 1988)

$$n = \frac{4b}{a\, l_{max}^2} t_{2a;\alpha/2}^2 - n_0 , \tag{12.21}$$

with $t_{2a;\alpha/2}^2$ the squared $(1 - \alpha/2)$ quantile of the (usual, i.e., neither shifted nor scaled) t distribution with $2a$ degrees of freedom and n_0 the number of prior points. The prior sample size n_0 is only relevant if we have prior

---

[3]This is equal to a normal-inverse gamma distribution to the population mean and population variance.

information about the population mean and an informative prior is used for this population mean. If we have no information about the population mean, a non-informative prior is used and n_0 equals 0. Note that as a/b is the prior mean of the inverse of the population variance, Equation (12.21) is similar to Equation (12.7). The only difference is that a quantile from the standard normal distribution is replaced by a quantile from a t distribution with $2a$ degrees of freedom.

No closed-form formula exists for computing the smallest n satisfying ALC, but the solution can be found by a bisectional search algorithm (Joseph and Bélisle, 1997).

Package **SampleSizeMeans** (Joseph and Bélisle, 2012) is used to compute Bayesian required sample sizes, using both criteria, ACC and ALC, for the fully Bayesian and the mixed Bayesian-likelihood approach. The gamma distribution plotted in Figure 12.2 is used as a prior distribution for the precision parameter λ. As a reference, also the frequentist required sample size is computed.

```
library(SampleSizeMeans)
lmax <- 2
n_freq <- mu.freq(len = lmax, lambda = a / b, level = 0.95)
n_alc <- mu.alc(len = lmax, alpha = a, beta = b, n0 = 0, level = 0.95)
n_alcmbl <- mu.mblalc(len = lmax, alpha = a, beta = b, level = 0.95)
n_acc <- mu.acc(len = lmax, alpha = a, beta = b, n0 = 0, level = 0.95)
n_accmbl <- mu.mblacc(len = lmax, alpha = a, beta = b, level = 0.95)
n_woc <- mu.modwoc(
  len = lmax, alpha = a, beta = b, n0 = 0, level = 0.95, worst.level = 0.95)
n_wocmbl <- mu.mblmodwoc(
  len = lmax, alpha = a, beta = b, level = 0.95, worst.level = 0.95)
```

Table 12.1 shows that all six required sample sizes are larger than the frequentist required sample size. This makes sense, as the frequentist approach does not account for uncertainty in the population variance parameter. The mixed approach leads to slightly larger required sample sizes than the fully Bayesian

TABLE 12.1: Required sample sizes for estimating a normal mean, computed with three criteria for the fully Bayesian and the mixed Bayesian-likelihood (MBL) approach.

Freq	ALC	ALC-MBL	ACC	ACC-MBL	WOC	WOC-MBL
77	92		93	100	102	194	201

Freq: required sample size computed with the frequentist approach; ALC: average length criterion; ACC: average coverage criterion; WOC: worst outcome criterion.

approach. This is because in the mixed approach the prior distribution of the precision parameter is not used. Apparently, we do not lose much information by ignoring this prior. With WOC the required sample sizes are about twice the sample sizes obtained with the other two criteria, but this depends of course on the size of the subspace $\mathcal{W}$. If, for instance the 80% most likely data sets are chosen as subspace $\mathcal{W}$, the required sample sizes are much smaller.

```
n_woc80 <- mu.modwoc(
  len = lmax, alpha = a, beta = b, n0 = 0, level = 0.95, worst.level = 0.80)
n_wocmbl80 <- mu.mblmodwoc(
  len = lmax, alpha = a, beta = b, level = 0.95, worst.level = 0.80)
```

The required sample sizes with this criterion are 124 and 128 using the fully Bayesian and the mixed Bayesian-likelihood approach, respectively.

12.5.4   Estimation of a population proportion

The same criteria can be used to estimate the proportion of a population or, in case of an infinite population, the areal fraction, satisfying some condition (Joseph et al., 1995). With simple random sampling, this boils down to estimating the probability-of-success parameter p of a binomial distribution. In this case the space of possible outcomes $\mathcal{Z}$ is the number of successes, which is discrete: $\mathcal{Z} = \{0, 1, ..., n\}$ with n the sample size.

The conjugate prior for the binomial likelihood is the beta distribution:

$$p \sim \frac{1}{B(c,d)} \pi^{c-1} (1-\pi)^{d-1} , \tag{12.22}$$

where $B(c,d)$ is the beta function. The two parameters c and d correspond to the number of 'successes' and 'failures' in the problem context. The larger these numbers, the more the prior information, and the more sharply defined the probability distribution. The plot below shows this distribution for $c = 0.6$ and $d = 2.4$.

```
c <- 0.6; d <- 2.4
x <- seq(from = 0, to = 1, length = 1000)
dbt <- dbeta(x = x, shape1 = c, shape2 = d)
plot(x = x, y = dbt, type = "l", ylab = "Density", xlab = "Proportion")
```

The mean of the binomial proportion equals $c/(c+d)$ and its standard deviation $\sqrt{cd/\{(c+d+1)(c+d)^2\}}$.

The preposterior marginal distribution of the data is the beta-binomial distribution:

$$f(z|n) = \binom{n}{z} \frac{B(z+c, n-z+d)}{B(c,d)} , \qquad (12.23)$$

and for a given number of successes z out of n trials the posterior distribution of p equals

$$f(p|z, n, c, d) = \frac{1}{B(z+c, n-z+d)} p^{z+c-1} (1-p)^{n-z+d-1} . \qquad (12.24)$$

For the binomial parameter, criterion ALC (Equation (12.17)) can be written as

$$\sum_{z=0}^{n} l(z,n) f(z,n) \leq l_{\max} . \qquad (12.25)$$

To compute the smallest n satisfying this condition, for each value of z and each n, $l(z,n)$ must be computed so that

$$\int_{v}^{v+l(z,n)} f(p|z, n, c, d) \mathrm{d}p = 1 - \alpha , \qquad (12.26)$$

with v the lower bound of the HPD credible set given the sample size and the observed number of successes z.

For the binomial parameter, criterion ACC (Equation (12.19)) can be written as

$$\sum_{z=0}^{n} \Pr\{p \in (v, v + l_{\max})\} f(z,n) \geq 1 - \alpha , \qquad (12.27)$$

with

$$\Pr\{p \in (v, v + l_{\max})\} \propto \int_{v}^{v+l_{\max}} p^{z} (1-p)^{n-z} f(p) \mathrm{d}p , \qquad (12.28)$$

with $f(p)$ the prior density of the binomial parameter.

For more details about ACC and ALC, and about how the required sample size can be computed with WOC in case of the binomial parameter p, refer to Joseph et al. (1995).

The required sample sizes for ALC, ACC, and WOC described in the previous subsection, using the fully Bayesian approach or the mixed Bayesian-likelihood approach, can be computed with package **SampleSizeBinomial**[4](Joseph

---

[4] http://www.medicine.mcgill.ca/epidemiology/Joseph/software/Bayesian-Sample-Size.html

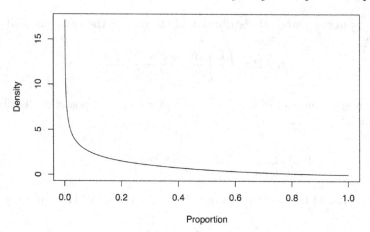

FIGURE 12.3: Prior beta distribution for the binomial proportion for a beta function $B(0.6, 2.4)$.

et al., 2018). This package is used to compute the required sample sizes using the beta distribution shown in Figure 12.3 as a prior for the population proportion. Note that argument `len` of the various functions of package **SampleSizeBinomial** specifies the total length of the confidence interval, not *half* the length as passed to function `ciss.wald` using argument `d`.

```
library(SampleSizeBinomial)
n_alc <- prop.alc(
   len = 0.2, alpha = c, beta = d, level = 0.95, exact = TRUE)$n
n_alcmbl <- prop.mblalc(
   len = 0.2, alpha = c, beta = d, level = 0.95, exact = TRUE)$n
n_acc <- prop.acc(
   len = 0.2, alpha = c, beta = d, level = 0.95, exact = TRUE)$n
n_accmbl <- prop.mblacc(
   len = 0.2, alpha = c, beta = d, level = 0.95, exact = TRUE)$n
n_woc <- prop.modwoc(
   len = 0.2, alpha = c, beta = d, level = 0.95, exact = TRUE,
   worst.level = 0.80)$n
n_wocmbl <- prop.mblmodwoc(
   len = 0.2, alpha = c, beta = d, level = 0.95, exact = TRUE,
   worst.level = 0.80)$n
library(binomSamSize)
n_freq <- ciss.wald(p0 = c / (c + d), d = 0.1, alpha = 0.05)
```

The required sample sizes are shown in Table 12.2.

TABLE 12.2: Required sample sizes for estimating a binomial proportion, computed with three criteria for the fully Bayesian and the mixed Bayesian-likelihood (MBL) approach.

Freq	ALC	ALC-MBL	ACC	ACC-MBL	WOC	WOC-MBL
62	33	38	50	53	80	81

Freq: required sample size computed with the frequentist approach; ALC: average length criterion; ACC: average coverage criterion; WOC: worst outcome criterion.

13

Model-based optimisation of probability sampling designs

Chapter 10 on model-assisted estimation explained how a linear regression model or a non-linear model obtained with a machine learning algorithm can be used to increase the precision of design-based estimates of the population mean or total using the data collected by a given probability sampling design. This chapter will explain how a model of the study variable can be used at an earlier stage to optimise probability sampling designs. It will show how a model can help in choosing between alternative sampling design types, for instance between systematic random sampling, spreading the sampling units throughout the study area, and two-stage cluster random sampling, resulting in spatial clusters of sampling units. Besides, the chapter will explain how to use a model to optimise the sample size of a given sampling design type, for instance, the number of primary and secondary sampling units with two-stage cluster random sampling. The final section of this chapter is about how a model can be used to optimise spatial strata for stratified simple random sampling.

The models used in this chapter are all geostatistical models of the spatial variation. Chapter 21 is an introduction to geostatistical modelling. Several geostatistical concepts explained in that chapter are needed here to predict the sampling variance.

A general geostatistical model of the spatial variation is

$$Z(\mathbf{s}) = \mu(\mathbf{s}) + \epsilon(\mathbf{s})$$
$$\epsilon(\mathbf{s}) \sim \mathcal{N}(0, \sigma^2) \qquad (13.1)$$
$$\mathrm{Cov}(\epsilon(\mathbf{s}), \epsilon(\mathbf{s}')) = C(\mathbf{h}) \,,$$

with $Z(\mathbf{s})$ the study variable at location $\mathbf{s}$, $\mu(\mathbf{s})$ the mean at location $\mathbf{s}$, $\epsilon(\mathbf{s})$ the residual at location $\mathbf{s}$, and $C(\mathbf{h})$ the covariance of the residuals at two locations separated by vector $\mathbf{h} = \mathbf{s} - \mathbf{s}'$. The residuals are assumed to have a normal distribution with zero mean and a constant variance σ^2 ($\mathcal{N}(0, \sigma^2)$).

The model of the spatial variation has several parameters. In case of a model in which the mean is a linear combination of covariates, these are the regression coefficients associated with the covariates and the parameters of a semivariogram describing the spatial dependence of the residuals. A semivariogram is

231

a model for half the expectation of the squared difference of the study variable or the residuals of a model at two locations, referred to as the semivariance, as a function of the length (and direction) of the vector separating the two locations (Chapter 21).

Using the model to predict the sampling variance of a design-based estimator of a population mean requires prior knowledge of the semivariogram. When data from the study area of interest are available, these data can be used to choose a semivariogram model and to estimate the parameters of the model. If no such data are available, we must make a best guess, based on data collected in other areas. In all cases I recommend keeping the model as simple as possible.

13.1   Model-based optimisation of sampling design type and sample size

Chapter 12 presented methods and formulas for computing the required sample size given various measures to quantify the quality of the survey result. These required sample sizes are for simple random sampling. For other types of sampling design, the required sample size can be approximated by multiplying the required sample size for simple random sampling with the design effect, see Section 12.4. An alternative is to use a model of the spatial variation to predict the sampling variance of the estimator of the mean for the type of sampling design under study and a range of sample sizes, plotting the predicted variance, or standard error, against the sample size, and using this plot inversely to derive the required sample size given a constraint on the sampling variance or standard error.

The computed required sample size applies to several given parameters of the sampling design. For instance, for stratified random sampling, the sample size is computed for a given stratification and sample size allocation scheme, for cluster random sampling for given clusters, and for two-stage cluster random sampling for given primary sampling units (PSUs) and the number of secondary sampling units (SSUs) selected per PSU draw. However, the model can also be used to optimise these sampling design parameters. For stratified random sampling, the optimal allocation can be computed by predicting the population standard deviations within strata and using these predicted standard deviations in Equation (4.17). Even the stratification can be optimised, see Section 13.2. If we have a costs model for two-stage cluster random sampling, the number of PSU draws and the number of SSUs per PSU draw can be optimised.

Model-based prediction of the sampling variance can also be useful to compare alternative types of sampling design at equal total costs or equal variance of the estimated population mean or total. For instance, to compare systematic random sampling, leading to good spatial coverage, and two-stage cluster random sampling, resulting in spatial clusters of observations.

Three approaches for model-based prediction of the sampling variance of a design-based estimator of the population mean, or total, are described: the analytical approach (Subsection 13.1.1), the geostatistical simulation approach (Subsection 13.1.2), and the Bayesian approach (Subsection 13.1.3). In the analytical approach we assume that the mean, $\mu(\mathbf{s})$ in Equation (13.1), is everywhere the same. This assumption is relaxed in the geostatistical simulation approach. This simulation approach can also accommodate models in which the mean is a linear combination of covariates and/or spatial coordinates to predict the sampling variance. Furthermore, this simulation approach can be used to predict the sampling variance of the estimator of the mean of a trans-Gaussian variable, i.e., a random variable that can be transformed to a Gaussian variable.

The predicted sampling variances of the estimated population mean obtained with the analytical and the geostatistical simulation approach are conditional on the model of the spatial variation. Uncertainty about this model is not accounted for. On the contrary, in the Bayesian approach, we do account for our uncertainty about the assumed model, and we analyse how this uncertainty propagates to the sampling variance of the estimator of the mean.

In some publications, the sampling variance as predicted with a statistical model is referred to as the anticipated variance (Särndal et al. (1992), p. 450).

13.1.1   Analytical approach

In the analytical approach, the sampling variance of the estimator of the mean is derived from mean semivariances within the study area and mean semivariances within the sample. Assuming isotropy, the mean semivariances are a function of the separation distance between pairs of points.

The sampling variance of the π estimator of the population mean can be predicted by (Domburg et al. (1994), de Gruijter et al. (2006))

$$E_\xi\{V_p(\hat{\bar{z}})\} = \bar{\gamma} - E_p(\boldsymbol{\lambda}^\mathrm{T}\boldsymbol{\Gamma}_s\boldsymbol{\lambda}) , \qquad (13.2)$$

where $E_\xi(\cdot)$ is the statistical expectation over realisations from the model ξ, $E_p(\cdot)$ is the statistical expectation over repeated sampling with sampling design p, $V_p(\hat{\bar{z}})$ is the variance of the π estimator of the population mean over repeated sampling with sampling design p, $\bar{\gamma}$ is the mean semivariance of the random variable at two randomly selected locations in the study area, $\boldsymbol{\lambda}$ is the vector of design-based weights of the units of a sample selected with design p, and $\boldsymbol{\Gamma}_s$ is the matrix of semivariances between the units of a sample $\mathcal{S}$ selected with design p.

The mean semivariance $\bar{\gamma}$ is a model-based prediction of the population variance, or spatial variance, i.e., the model-expectation of the population variance:

$$\bar{\gamma} = E_\xi\{\sigma^2(z)\} . \tag{13.3}$$

The mean semivariance $\bar{\gamma}$ can be calculated by discretising the study area by a fine square grid, computing the matrix with geographical distances between the discretisation nodes, transforming this into a semivariance matrix, and computing the average of all elements of the semivariance matrix. The second term $E_p(\boldsymbol{\lambda}^T\boldsymbol{\Gamma}_s\boldsymbol{\lambda})$ can be evaluated by Monte Carlo simulation, repeatedly selecting a sample according to design p, calculating $\boldsymbol{\lambda}^T\boldsymbol{\Gamma}_s\boldsymbol{\lambda}$, and averaging.

> The semivariance at zero distance (same location) is 0, so the diagonal of a semivariance matrix is filled with zeroes. If a semivariogram with nugget is assumed, the zeroes on the diagonal must be replaced by the nugget to compute $\bar{\gamma}$. The same holds for the diagonal zeroes in $\boldsymbol{\Gamma}_s$.

This generic procedure is still computationally demanding, but it is the only option for complex spatial sampling designs. For basic sampling designs, the general formula can be worked out. For simple random sampling, the sampling variance can be predicted by

$$E_\xi\{V_{\mathrm{SI}}(\hat{\bar{z}})\} = \bar{\gamma}/n , \tag{13.4}$$

and for stratified simple random sampling by

$$E_\xi\{V_{\mathrm{STSI}}(\hat{\bar{z}})\} = \sum_{h=1}^{H} w_h^2 \bar{\gamma}_h/n_h , \tag{13.5}$$

with H the number of strata, w_h the stratum weight (relative size), $\bar{\gamma}_h$ the mean semivariance of stratum h, and n_h the number of sampling units of stratum h.

> The model-based predictions of the variances within the strata, $\bar{\gamma}_h$, can also be used to compute the sample sizes for Neyman allocation, which are the optimal sample sizes when the mean costs per unit are equal for the strata. To compute these sample sizes, the standard deviations $S_h(z)$ in Equation (4.16) are replaced by $\sqrt{\bar{\gamma}_h}$.

For systematic random sampling, i.e., sampling on a randomly placed grid, the variance can be predicted by

$$E_\xi\{V_{\mathrm{SY}}(\hat{\bar{z}})\} = \bar{\gamma} - E_{\mathrm{SY}}(\bar{\gamma}_{\mathrm{SY}}) , \tag{13.6}$$

with $E_{SY}(\bar{\gamma}_{SY})$ the design-expectation, i.e., the expectation over repeated systematic sampling, of the mean semivariance within the grid. With systematic random sampling, the number of grid points within the study area can vary among samples, as well as the spatial pattern of the points (Chapter 5). Therefore, multiple systematic random samples must be selected, and the average of the mean semivariance within the systematic sample must be computed.

The analytical approach is illustrated with the data of agricultural field Leest (Hofman and Brus, 2021). Nitrate-N (NO_3-N) in kg ha^{-1} in the layer $0-90$ cm, using a standard soil density of 1,500 kg m^{-3}, is measured at 30 points. In the next code chunk, these data are used to compute a sample semivariogram using the method-of-moments with function variogram, see Chapter 21. A spherical model without nugget is fitted to the sample semivariogram using function fit.variogram. The numbers in this plot are the numbers of pairs of points used to compute the semivariances.

```
library(gstat)
coordinates(sampleLeest) <- ~ s1 + s2
vg <- variogram(N ~ 1, data = sampleLeest)
vgm_MoM <- fit.variogram(
  vg, model = vgm(model = "Sph", psill = 2000, range = 20))
```

The few data lead to a very noisy sample semivariogram. For the moment, I ignore my uncertainty about the semivariogram parameters; Subsection 13.1.3 will show how we can account for our uncertainty about the semivariogram parameters in model-based prediction of the sampling variance. A spherical semivariogram model without nugget is fitted to the sample semivariogram, i.e., the intercept is 0. The fitted range of the model is 45 m, and the fitted sill equals 966 (kg ha^{-1})^2. The fitted semivariogram is used to predict the sampling variance for three sampling designs: simple random sampling, stratified simple random sampling, and systematic random sampling. The costs for these three design types will be about equal, as the study area is small, so that the access time of the sampling points selected with the three designs is about equal. The sample size of the evaluated sampling designs is 25 points. As for systematic random sampling, the number of points varies among the samples, this sampling design has an *expected* sample size of 25 points.

Simple random sampling

For simple random sampling, we must compute the mean semivariance within the field (Equation (13.4)). As shown in the next code chunk, the mean semivariance is approximated by discretising the field by a square grid of 2,000 points, computing the 2,000 × 2,000 matrix with distances between all pairs of discretisation nodes, transforming this distance matrix into a semivariance matrix using function `variogramLine` of package **gstat** (Pebesma, 2004), and finally averaging the semivariances. Note that in this case we do not need to replace the zeroes on the diagonal of the semivariance matrix by the nugget, as a model without nugget is fitted. The geopackage file is read with function `read_sf` of package **sf** (Pebesma, 2018), resulting in a simple feature object. The projection attributes of this object are removed with function `st_set_crs`. The centres of square grid cells are selected with function `st_make_grid`. The centres inside the field are selected with `mygrid[field]`, and finally the coordinates are extracted with function `st_coordinates`.

```
field <- read_sf(system.file("extdata/leest.gpkg", package = "sswr")) %>%
  st_set_crs(NA_crs_)
mygrid <- st_make_grid(field, cellsize = 2, what = "centers")
mygrid <- mygrid[field] %>%
  st_coordinates(mygrid)
H <- as.matrix(dist(mygrid))
G <- variogramLine(vgm_MoM, dist_vector = H)
m_semivar_field <- mean(G)
n <- 25
Exi_V_SI <- m_semivar_field / n
```

The model-based prediction of the sampling variance of the estimator of the mean with this design equals 35.0.

Stratified simple random sampling

The strata of the stratified simple random sampling design are compact geographical strata of equal size (Section 4.6). The number of geostrata is equal to the sample size, 25 points, so that we have one point per stratum. With this design, the sampling points are reasonably well spread over the field, but not as good as with systematic random sampling. To predict the sampling variance, we must compute the mean semivariances within the geostrata, see Equation (13.5). Note that the stratum weights are constant as the strata have equal size, $w_h = 1/n$, and that $n_h = 1$. Therefore, Equation (13.5) reduces to

$$E_\xi\{V_{\mathrm{STSI}}(\hat{\bar{z}})\} = \frac{1}{n^2} \sum_{h=1}^{H} \bar{\gamma}_h \ . \tag{13.7}$$

The next code chunk shows the computation of the mean semivariance per stratum and the model-based prediction of the sampling variance of the estimator of the mean. The matrix with the coordinates is first converted to a tibble with function `as_tibble`.

```
library(spcosa)
mygrid <- mygrid %>%
  as_tibble() %>%
  setNames(c("x1", "x2"))
gridded(mygrid) <- ~ x1 + x2
mygeostrata <- stratify(mygrid, nStrata = n, equalArea = TRUE, nTry = 10) %>%
  as("data.frame")
m_semivar_geostrata <- numeric(length = n)
for (i in 1:n) {
 ids <- which(mygeostrata$stratumId == (i - 1))
 mysubgrd <- mygeostrata[ids, ]
 H_geostratum <- as.matrix(dist(mysubgrd[, c(2, 3)]))
 G_geostratum <- variogramLine(vgm_MoM, dist_vector = H_geostratum)
 m_semivar_geostrata[i] <- mean(G_geostratum)
}
Exi_V_STSI <- sum(m_semivar_geostrata) / n^2
```

The model-based prediction of the sampling variance with this design equals 13.5 (kg ha^{-1})^2, which is much smaller than with simple random sampling. The large stratification effect can be explained by the assumed strong spatial structure of NO$_3$-N in the agricultural field and the improved geographical spreading of the sampling points, see Figure 13.1.

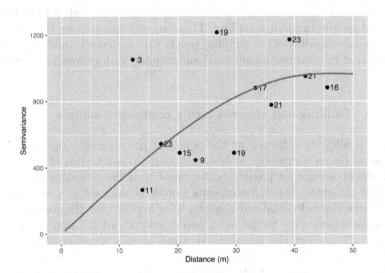

FIGURE 13.1: Sample semivariogram and fitted spherical model for NO$_3$-N in field Leest. The numbers refer to point-pairs used in computing semivariances.

Systematic random sampling

To predict the sampling variance for systematic random sampling with an expected sample size of 25 points, we must compute the design-expectation of the mean semivariance within the systematic sample (Equation (13.6)). As shown in the next code chunk, I approximated this expectation by selecting 100 systematic random samples, computing the mean semivariance for each sample, and averaging. Finally, the model-based prediction of the sampling variance is computed by subtracting the average of the mean semivariances within a systematic sample from the mean semivariance within the field computed above.

```
set.seed(314)
m_semivar_SY <- numeric(length = 100)
for (i in 1:100) {
  mySYsample <- spsample(x = mygrid, n = n, type = "regular") %>%
    as("data.frame")
  H_SY <- as.matrix(dist(mySYsample))
  G_SY <- variogramLine(vgm_MoM, dist_vector = H_SY)
  m_semivar_SY[i] <- mean(G_SY)
}
Exi_V_SY <- m_semivar_field - mean(m_semivar_SY)
```

The model-based prediction of the sampling variance of the estimator of the mean with this design equals 8.3 (kg ha^{-1})^2, which is smaller than that of stratified simple random sampling. This can be explained by the improved geographical spreading of the sampling points with systematic random sampling as compared to stratified simple random sampling with compact geographical strata.

13.1.1.1   Bulking soil aliquots into a composite sample

If the soil aliquots collected at the points of the stratified random sample are bulked into a composite, as is usually done in soil testing of agricultural fields, the procedure for predicting the variance of the estimator of the mean is slightly different. Only the composite sample is analysed in a laboratory on NO_3-N, not the individual soil aliquots. This implies that the contribution of the measurement error to the total uncertainty about the population mean is larger. To predict the sampling variance in this situation, we need the semivariogram of errorless measurements of NO_3-N, i.e., of the true NO_3-N contents of soil aliquots collected at points. The sill of this semivariogram will be smaller than the sill of the semivariogram of measured NO_3-N data. A simple option is to subtract an estimate of the measurement error variance from the semivariogram of measured NO_3-N data that contain a measurement error. So, the measurement error variance is subtracted from the nugget. This may lead to negative nuggets, which is not allowed (a variance cannot be negative). The preferable alternative is to add the measurement error variance to the diagonal of the covariance matrix of the data in fitting the model with maximum likelihood, see function ll in Subsection 13.1.3.

Exercises

1. Write an **R** script to predict the sampling variance of the estimator of the mean of NO_3-N of agricultural field Leest, for simple random sampling and a sample size of 25 points. Use in prediction a spherical semivariogram with a nugget of 483, a partial sill of 483, and a range of 44.6 m. The sum of the nugget and partial sill (966) is equal to the sill of the semivariogram used above in predicting sampling variances. Compare the predicted sampling variance with the predicted sampling variance for the same sampling design, obtained with the semivariogram without nugget. Explain the difference.

2. Write an **R** script to compute the required sample size for simple random sampling of agricultural field Leest, for a maximum length of a 95% confidence interval of 20. Use the semivariogram without nugget in predicting the sampling variance. See Section 12.2 (Equation (12.7)) for how to compute the required sample size given a prior estimate of the standard deviation of the study variable in the population.

3. Do the same for systematic random sampling. Note that for this sampling design, no such formula is available. Predict for a series of *expected* sample sizes, $n = 5, 6, \ldots, 40$, the sampling variance of the estimator of the mean, using Equation (13.6). Approximate $E_{SY}(\bar{\gamma}_{SY})$ from ten repeated selections. Compute the length of the confidence interval from the predicted sampling variances, and plot the interval length against the sample size. Finally, determine the required sample size for a maximum length of 20. What is the design effect for an expected sample size of 34 points (the required sample size for simple random sampling)? See Equation (12.13). Also compute the design effect for expected sample sizes of $5, 6, \ldots, 40$. Explain why the design effect is not constant.

13.1.2   Geostatistical simulation approach

The alternative to the analytical approach is to use a geostatistical simulation approach. It is computationally more demanding, but an advantage of this approach is its flexibility. It can also be used to predict the sampling variance of the estimator of the mean using a geostatistical model with a non-constant mean. And besides, this approach can also handle trans-Gaussian variables, i.e., variables whose distribution can be transformed into a normal distribution. In Subsection 13.1.3, geostatistical simulation is used to predict the variance of the estimator of the mean of a lognormal variable.

The geostatistical simulation approach for predicting the sampling variance of a design-based estimator of the population mean involves the following steps:

1. Select a large number S of random samples with sampling design p.

2. Use the model to simulate values of the study variable for all sampling points.

3. Estimate for each sample the population mean, using the design-based estimator of the population mean for sampling design p. This results in S estimated population means.

4. Compute the variance of the S estimated means.

5. Repeat steps 1 to 4 R times, and compute the mean of the R variances.

This approach is illustrated with the western part of the Amhara region in Ethiopia (hereafter referred to as West-Amhara) where a large sample is available with organic matter data in the topsoil (SOM) in decagram per kg dry soil (dag kg^{-1}; 1 decagram = 10 gram). The soil samples are collected along roads (see Figure 17.5). It is a convenience sample, not a probability sample, so these sample data cannot be used in design-based or model-assisted estimation of the mean or total soil carbon stock in the study area. However, the data can be used to model the spatial variation of the SOM concentration, and this geostatistical model can then be used to design a probability sample for design-based estimation of the total mass of SOM. Apart from the point data of the SOM concentration, maps of covariates are available, such as a digital elevation model and remote sensing reflectance data. In the next code chunk, four covariates are selected to model the mean of the SOM concentration: elevation (dem), average near infrared reflectance (rfl-NIR), average red reflectance (rfl-red), and average land surface temperature (lst). I assume a normal distribution for the residuals of the linear model. The model parameters are estimated by restricted maximum likelihood (REML), using package **geoR** (Ribeiro Jr et al., 2020), see Subsection 21.5.2 for details on REML estimation of a geostatistical model. As a first step, the projected coordinates of the sampling points are changed from m into km using function `mutate`. Using coordinates in m in function `likfit` could not find an optimal estimate for the range.

```
library(geoR)
sampleAmhara <- sampleAmhara %>%
  mutate(s1 = s1 / 1000, s2 = s2 / 1000)
dGeoR <- as.geodata(obj = sampleAmhara, header = TRUE,
  coords.col = c("s1", "s2"), data.col = "SOM",
  covar.col = c("dem", "rfl_NIR", "rfl_red", "lst"))
vgm_REML <- likfit(geodata = dGeoR,
  trend = ~ dem + rfl_NIR + rfl_red + lst,
  cov.model = "spherical", ini.cov.pars = c(1, 50), nugget = 0.2,
  lik.method = "REML", messages = FALSE)
```

The estimated parameters of the residual semivariogram of the SOM concentration are shown in Table 22.2. The estimated regression coefficients are 12.9 for the intercept, 0.922 for elevation (dem), 7.41 for NIR reflectance, -10.42 for red reflectance, and -0.039 for land surface temperature.

Package **gstat** is used for geostatistical simulation, and therefore first the REML estimates of the semivariogram parameters are passed to function vgm using arguments nugget, psill, and range of function vgm of this package.

```
vgm_REML_gstat <- vgm(model = "Sph", nugget = vgm_REML$tausq,
  psill = vgm_REML$sigmasq, range = vgm_REML$phi)
```

The fitted model of the spatial variation of the SOM concentration is used to compare systematic random sampling and two-stage cluster random sampling at equal variances of the estimator of the mean.

Systematic random sampling

One hundred systematic random samples ($S = 100$) with an expected sample size of 50 points ($E[n] = 50$) are selected. The four covariates at the selected sampling points are extracted by overlaying the SpatialPointsDataFrame mySYsamples and the SpatialPixelsDataFrame grdAmhara with function over of package **sp** (Pebesma and Bivand, 2005). Values at the sampling points are simulated by sequential Gaussian simulation (Goovaerts, 1997), using function krige with argument nsim = 1 of package **gstat**. Argument dummy is set to TRUE to enforce unconditional simulation.

The alternative is conditional simulation, using the data of the convenience sample as conditioning data. Conditional simulation is only recommended if the quality of these legacy data is sufficient, and we may trust that the study variable at the legacy points has not changed since these legacy data have been collected.

Note that by first drawing 100 samples, followed by simulating values of z at the selected sampling points, instead of first simulating values of z at the nodes of a discretisation grid, followed by selecting samples and overlaying with the simulated field, the simulated values of points in the same discretisation cell differ, so that we account for the infinite number of points in the population.

With systematic random sampling, the sample mean is an approximately unbiased estimator of the population mean (Chapter 5). Therefore, of each sample the mean of the simulated values is computed, using function `tapply`. Finally, the variance of the 100 sample means is computed. This is a conditional variance, conditional on the simulated values. In the code chunk below, the whole procedure is repeated 100 times ($R = 100$), leading to 100 conditional variances of sample means.

```r
grdAmhara <- grdAmhara %>%
  mutate(s1 = s1 / 1000, s2 = s2 / 1000)
gridded(grdAmhara) <- ~ s1 + s2
S <- R <- 100
v_mzsim_SY <- numeric(length = R)
set.seed(314)
for (i in 1:R) {
  mySYsamples <- NULL
  for (j in 1:S) {
    xy <- spsample(x = grdAmhara, n = 50, type = "regular")
    mySY <- data.frame(
      s1 = xy$x1, s2 = xy$x2, sample = rep(j, length(xy)))
    mySYsamples <- rbind(mySYsamples, mySY)
  }
  coordinates(mySYsamples) <- ~ s1 + s2
  res <- over(mySYsamples, grdAmhara)
  mySYs <- data.frame(mySYsamples, res[, c("dem", "rfl_NIR", "rfl_red", "lst")])
  coordinates(mySYs) <- ~ s1 + s2
  zsim <- krige(
    dummy ~ dem + rfl_NIR + rfl_red + lst,
    locations = mySYs, newdata = mySYs,
    model = vgm_REML_gstat, beta = vgm_REML$beta,
    nmax = 20, nsim = 1,
    dummy = TRUE,
    debug.level = 0) %>% as("data.frame")
  m_zsim <- tapply(zsim$sim1, INDEX = mySYs$sample, FUN = mean)
  v_mzsim_SY[i] <- var(m_zsim)
}
grdAmhara <- as_tibble(grdAmhara)
```

```
Exi_vmz_SY <- mean(v_mzsim_SY)
```

The mean of the 100 conditional variances equals 0.015 $(\text{dag kg}^{-1})^2$. This is a Monte Carlo approximation of the model-based prediction of the sampling variance of the ratio estimator of the mean for systematic random sampling with an expected sample size of 50.

Two-stage cluster random sampling

Due to the geographical spreading of the sampling points with systematic random sampling, the accuracy of the estimated mean is expected to be high compared to that of other sampling designs of the same size. However, with large areas, the time needed for travelling to the sampling points can become substantial, lowering the sampling efficiency. With large areas, sampling designs leading to spatial clusters of sampling points can be an attractive alternative. One option then is two-stage cluster random sampling, see Chapter 7. The question is whether this alternative design is more efficient than systematic random sampling.

In the next code chunk, 100 compact geostrata (see Section 4.6) are computed for West-Amhara. Here, these geostrata are not used as strata in stratified random sampling, but as PSUs in two-stage cluster random sampling. The difference is that in stratified random sampling from each geostratum at least one sampling unit is selected, whereas in two-stage cluster random sampling only a randomly selected subset of the geostrata is sampled. The compact geostrata, used as PSUs, are computed with function kmeans, and as a consequence the PSUs do not have equal size, see output of code chunk below. This is not needed in two-stage cluster random sampling, see Chapter 7. If PSUs of equal size are preferred, then these can be computed with function stratify of package **spcosa** with argument equalArea = TRUE, see Section 4.6.

```
set.seed(314)
res <- kmeans(
  grdAmhara[, c("s1", "s2")], iter.max = 1000, centers = 100, nstart = 100)
mypsus <- res$cluster
psusize <- as.numeric(table(mypsus))
summary(psusize)
```

```
   Min. 1st Qu.  Median    Mean 3rd Qu.    Max.
   79.0   103.8   109.0   108.4   113.0   131.0
```

In the next code chunks, I assume that the PSUs are selected with probabilities proportional to their size and with replacement (ppswr sampling), see Chapter 7. In Section 7.1 formulas are presented for computing the optimal number of PSU draws and SSU draws per PSU draw. The optimal sample sizes are a function of the pooled variance of PSU means, S_b^2, and the pooled variance of secondary units (points) within the PSUs, S_w^2. In the current subsection, these variance components are predicted with the geostatistical model.

As a first step, a large number of maps are simulated.

```
grdAmhara$psu <- mypsus
coordinates(grdAmhara) <- ~ s1 + s2
set.seed(314)
zsim <- krige(
  dummy ~ dem + rfl_NIR + rfl_red + lst,
  locations = grdAmhara, newdata = grdAmhara,
  model = vgm_REML_gstat, beta = vgm_REML$beta,
  nmax = 20, nsim = 1000,
  dummy = TRUE, debug.level = 0) %>% as("data.frame")
zsim <- zsim[, -c(1, 2)]
```

For each simulated field, the means of the PSUs and the variances of the simulated values within the PSUs are computed using function `tapply` in function `apply`.

```
m_zsim_psu <- apply(zsim, MARGIN = 2, FUN = function(x)
  tapply(x, INDEX = grdAmhara$psu, FUN = mean))
v_zsim_psu <- apply(zsim, MARGIN = 2, FUN = function(x)
  tapply(x, INDEX = grdAmhara$psu, FUN = var))
```

Next, for each simulated field, the pooled variance of PSU means and the pooled variance within PSUs are computed, and finally these pooled variances are averaged over all simulated fields. The averages are approximations of the model-expectations of the pooled between unit and within unit variances, $E_\xi[S_b^2]$ and $E_\xi[S_w^2]$.

```
p_psu <- psusize / sum(psusize)
S2b <- apply(m_zsim_psu, MARGIN = 2, FUN = function(x)
  sum(p_psu * (x - sum(p_psu * x))^2))
S2w <- apply(v_zsim_psu, MARGIN = 2, FUN = function(x)
  sum(p_psu * x))
Exi_S2b <- mean(S2b)
Exi_S2w <- mean(S2w)
```

The optimal sample sizes are computed for a simple linear costs model: $C = c_0 + c_1 n + c_2 nm$, with c_0 the fixed costs, c_1 the access costs per PSU, including the access costs of the SSUs (points) within a given PSU, and c_2 the observation costs per SSU. In the next code chunk, I use $c_1 = 2$ and $c_2 = 1$. For the optimal sample sizes only the ratio of c_1 and c_2 is important, not their absolute values.

Given values for c_1 and c_2, the optimal number of PSU draws n and the optimal number of SSU draws per PSU draw m are computed, required for a sampling variance of the estimator of the mean equal to the sampling variance with systematic random sampling of 50 points, see Equations (7.9) and (7.10).

```
c1 <- 2; c2 <- 1
nopt <- 1 / Exi_vmz_SY * (sqrt(Exi_S2w * Exi_S2b) * sqrt(c2 / c1) + Exi_S2b)
mopt <- sqrt(Exi_S2w / Exi_S2b) * sqrt(c1 / c2)
```

The optimal number of PSU draws is 26, and the optimal number of points per PSU draw equals 5. The total number of sampling points is $26 \times 5 = 130$. This is much larger than the sample size of 50 obtained with systematic random sampling. The total observation costs therefore are substantially larger. However, the access time can be substantially smaller due to the spatial clustering of sampling points. To answer the question of whether the costs saved by this reduced access time outweigh the extra costs of observation, the model for the access costs and observation costs must be further developed.

13.1.3   Bayesian approach

The model-based prediction of the variance of the design-based estimator of the population mean for a given sampling design is conditional on the model. If we change the model type or the model parameters, the predicted sampling variance also changes. In most situations we are quite uncertain about the model, even in situations where we have data that can be used to estimate the model parameters, as in the West-Amhara case study. Instead of using the best estimated model to predict the sampling variance as done in the previous sections, we may prefer to account for the uncertainty about the model parameters. This can be done through a Bayesian approach, in which the legacy data are used to update a prior distribution of the model parameters to a posterior distribution. For details about a Bayesian approach for estimating model parameters, see Section 22.5. A sample from the posterior distribution of the model parameters is used one-by-one to predict the sampling variance. This can be done either analytically, as described in Subsection 13.1.1, or through geostatistical simulation, as described in Subsection 13.1.2. Both approaches result in a *distribution* of sampling variances, reflecting our uncertainty about the sampling variance of the estimator of the population mean due to uncertainty about the model parameters. The mean or median of the distribution of sampling variances can be used as the predicted sampling variance.

The Bayesian approach is illustrated with a case study on predicting the sampling variance of NO_3-N in agricultural field Melle in Belgium (Hofman and Brus, 2021). As for field Leest used in Subsection 13.1.1, data of NO_3-N are available at 30 points. The sampling points are approximately on the nodes of a square grid with a spacing of about 4.5 m. As a first step, I check whether we can safely assume that the data come from a normal distribution.

```
ggplot(sampleMelle, aes(sample = N)) +
  geom_qq() +
  geom_qq_line()
```

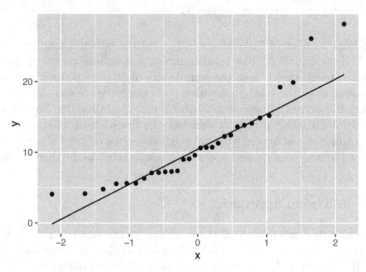

FIGURE 13.2: Q-Q plot of NO_3-N of field Melle.

```
pvalue <- shapiro.test(sampleMelle$N)$p.value
```

The Q-Q plot (Figure 13.2) shows that a normal distribution is not very likely: there are too many large values, i.e., the distribution is skewed to the right. Also the p-value of the Shapiro-Wilk test shows that we should reject the null hypothesis of a normal distribution for the data: $p = 0.0028$. I therefore proceed with the natural log of NO_3-N, in short lnN.

```
sampleMelle$lnN <- log(sampleMelle$N)
```

As a first step, the semivariogram of lnN is estimated by maximum likelihood (Subsection 21.4.2). An exponential semivariogram model is assumed, see Equation (21.13).

The parameters that are estimated are the reciprocal of the sill λ, the ratio of spatial dependence ξ, defined as the partial sill divided by the sill, and the distance parameter ϕ. This parameterisation of the semivariogram is chosen because hereafter in the Bayesian approach prior distributions are chosen for these parameters.

The likelihood function is defined, using a somewhat unusual parameterisation, tailored to the Markov chain Monte Carlo (MCMC) sampling from the posterior distribution of the semivariogram parameters. In MCMC a Markov chain of sampling units (vectors with semivariogram parameters) is generated using the previous sampling unit to randomly generate the next sampling unit (Gelman et al. (2013), chapter 11). In MCMC sampling, the probability of accepting a proposed sampling unit θ^* is a function of the ratio of the posterior density of the proposed sampling unit and that of the current sampling unit, $f(\theta^*|\mathbf{z})/f(\theta_{t-1}|\mathbf{z})$, so that the normalising constant, the denominator of Equation (12.15), cancels.

```
library(mvtnorm)
ll <- function(thetas) {
  sill <- 1 / thetas[1]
  psill <- thetas[2] * sill
  nugget <- sill - psill
  vgmodel <- vgm(
    model = model, psill = psill, range = thetas[3], nugget = nugget)
  C <- variogramLine(vgmodel, dist_vector = D, covariance = TRUE)
  XCX <- crossprod(X, solve(C, X))
  XCz <- crossprod(X, solve(C, z))
  betaGLS <- solve(XCX, XCz)
  mu <- as.numeric(X %*% betaGLS)
  logLik <- dmvnorm(x = z, mean = mu, sigma = C, log = TRUE)
  logLik
}
```

Next, initial estimates of the semivariogram parameters are computed by maximising the likelihood, using function optim.

```
lambda.ini <- 1 / var(sampleMelle$lnN)
xi.ini <- 0.5
phi.ini <- 20
pars <- c(lambda.ini, xi.ini, phi.ini)
D <- as.matrix(dist(sampleMelle[, c("s1", "s2")]))
X <- matrix(1, nrow(sampleMelle), 1)
z <- sampleMelle$lnN
model <- "Exp"
vgML <- optim(pars, ll, control = list(fnscale = -1),
  lower = c(1e-6, 0, 1e-6), upper = c(1000, 1, 150), method = "L-BFGS-B")
```

The maximum likelihood (ML) estimates of the semivariogram parameters are used as initial values in MCMC sampling. A uniform prior is used for the inverse of the sill parameter, $\lambda = 1/\sigma^2$, with a lower bound of 10^{-6} and an upper bound of 1. For the relative nugget, τ^2/σ^2, a uniform prior is assumed with a lower bound of 0 and an upper bound of 1. For the distance parameter ϕ of the exponential semivariogram a uniform prior is assumed, with a lower bound of 10^{-6} m and an upper bound of 150 m.

These priors can be defined by function `createUniformPrior` of package **BayesianTools** (Hartig et al., 2019). Function `createBayesianSetup` is then used to define the setup of the MCMC sampling, specifying the likelihood function, the prior, and the vector with best prior estimates of the model parameters, passed to function `createBayesianSetup` using argument `best`. Argument `sampler` of function `runMCMC` specifies the type of MCMC sampler. I used the differential evolution algorithm of ter Braak and Vrugt (2008). Argument `start` of function `getSample` specifies the burn-in period, i.e., the number of first samples that are discarded to diminish the influence of the initial semivariogram parameter values. Argument `numSamples` specifies the sample size, i.e., the number of saved vectors with semivariogram parameter values, drawn from the posterior distribution.

```
library(BayesianTools)
priors <- createUniformPrior(lower = c(1e-6, 0, 1e-6),
                             upper = c(1000, 1, 150))
bestML <- c(vgML$par[1], vgML$par[2], vgML$par[3])
setup <- createBayesianSetup(likelihood = ll, prior = priors,
  best = bestML, names = c("lambda", "xi", "phi"))
set.seed(314)
res <- runMCMC(setup, sampler = "DEzs")
MCMCsample <- getSample(res, start = 1000, numSamples = 1000) %>% data.frame()
```

Figure 13.3 shows several semivariograms, sampled by MCMC from the posterior distribution of the estimated semivariogram parameters.

The evaluated sampling design is the same as used in Subsection 13.1.1 for field Lecst: stratified simple random sampling, using compact geographical strata of equal size, a total sample size of 25 points, and one point per stratum.

The next step is to simulate with each of the sampled semivariograms a large number of maps of lnN. This is done by sequential Gaussian simulation, conditional on the available data. The simulated values are backtransformed. Each simulated map is then used to compute the variance of the simulated values within the geostrata S_h^2. These stratum variances are used to compute the sampling variance of the estimator of the mean. Plugging $w_h = 1/n$ (all strata have equal size) into Equation (4.4) and using $n_h = 1$ in Equation (4.5)

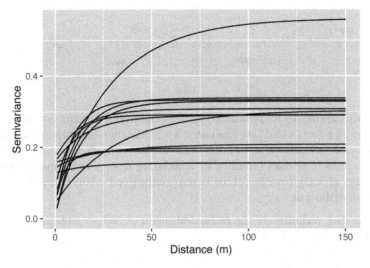

FIGURE 13.3: Semivariograms of the natural log of NO_3-N for field Melle obtained by MCMC sampling from posterior distribution of the estimated semivariogram parameters.

yield (compare with Equation (13.7))

$$V(\hat{\bar{z}}) = \frac{1}{n^2} \sum_{h=1}^{H} S_h^2 \ . \tag{13.8}$$

In the code chunk below, I use the first 100 sampled semivariograms to simulate with each semivariogram 100 maps.

```
V <- matrix(data = NA, nrow = 100, ncol = 100)
coordinates(sampleMelle) <- ~ s1 + s2
set.seed(314)
for (i in 1:100) {
  sill <- 1 / MCMCsample$lambda[i]
  psill <- MCMCsample$xi[i] * sill
  nug <- sill - psill
  range <- MCMCsample$phi[i]
  vgmdl <- vgm(model = "Exp", nugget = nug, psill = psill, range = range)
  ysim <- krige(
    lnN ~ 1, locations = sampleMelle, newdata = mygrid,
    model = vgmdl,
    nmax = 20, nsim = 100,
    debug.level = 0) %>% as("data.frame")
  zsim <- exp(ysim[, -c(1, 2)])
```

```
S2h <- apply(zsim, MARGIN = 2, FUN = function(x)
  tapply(x, INDEX = as.factor(mygeostrata$stratumId), FUN = var))
V[i, ] <- 1 / n^2 * apply(S2h, MARGIN = 2, FUN = sum)
}
```

Figure 13.4 shows 16 maps simulated with the first four semivariograms. The four maps in a row (a to d) are simulated with the same semivariogram. All maps show that the simulated data have positive skew, which is in agreement with the prior data. The data obtained by simulating from a lognormal distribution are always strictly positive. This is not guaranteed when simulating from a normal distribution.

The sampling variances of the estimated mean of NO_3-N obtained with these 16 maps are shown below.

```
      a     b     c     d
1 1.364 0.831 0.878 0.847
2 1.379 1.151 0.991 1.162
3 0.669 0.594 0.522 0.530
4 0.932 1.949 0.878 0.739
```

The sampling variance shows quite strong variation among the maps. The frequency distribution of Figure 13.5 shows our uncertainty about the sampling variance, due to uncertainty about the semivariogram, and about the spatial distribution of NO_3-N within the agricultural field given the semivariogram and the available data from that field.

As a model-based prediction of the sampling variance, we can take the mean or the median of the sampling variances over all 100×100 simulated maps, which are equal to 0.728 (dag kg^{-1}) and 0.666 (dag kg^{-1}), respectively. If we want to be more safe, we can take a high quantile, e.g., the P90 of this distribution as the predicted sampling variance, which is equal to 1.100 (dag kg^{-1}).

I used the 30 available NO_3-N data as conditioning data in geostatistical simulation. Unconditional simulation is recommended if we cannot rely on the quality of the legacy data, for instance due to a temporal change in lnN since the time the legacy data have been observed. For NO_3-N this might well be the case. I believe that, although the effect of 30 observations on the simulated fields and on the uncertainty distribution of the sampling variance will be very small, one still may prefer unconditional simulation. With unconditional simulation, we must assign the model-mean μ to argument beta of function krige. The estimated model-mean can be estimated by generalised least squares, see function ll above.

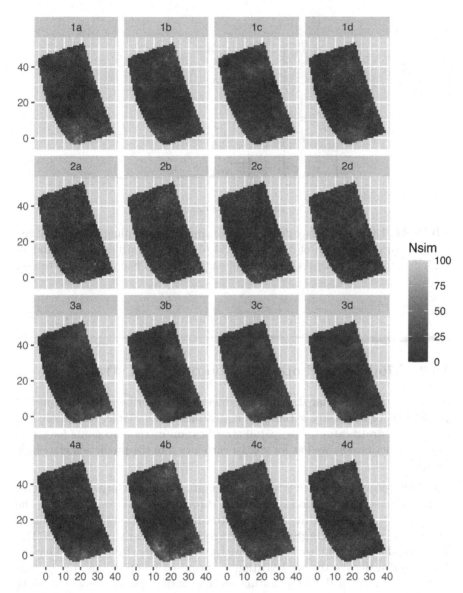

FIGURE 13.4: Maps of NO_3-N of field Melle simulated with four semivariograms (rows). Each semivariogram is used to simulate four maps (columns a-d).

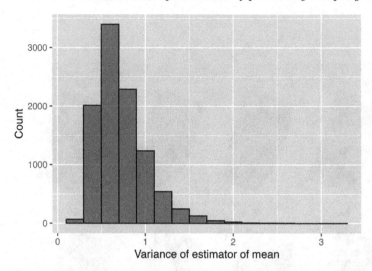

FIGURE 13.5: Frequency distribution of simulated sampling variances of the π estimator of the mean of NO_3-N of field Melle, for stratified simple random sampling, using 25 compact geostrata of equal size, and one point per stratum.

13.2   Model-based optimisation of spatial strata

In this section a spatial stratification method is described that uses model predictions of the study variable as a stratification variable. As opposed to *cum-root-f* stratification, this spatial stratification method accounts for errors in the predictions, as well as for spatial correlation of the prediction errors (de Gruijter et al., 2015).

The **Julia** package **Ospats** is an implementation of this stratification method. In **Ospats** the stratification is optimised through iterative reallocation of the raster cells to the strata. Recently, this stratification method was implemented in the package **SamplingStrata** (Barcaroli (2014), Barcaroli et al. (2020)). However, the algorithm used to optimise the strata differs from that in **Ospats**. In **SamplingStrata** the stratification is optimised by optimising the bounds (splitting points) on the stratification variable with a genetic algorithm. Optimisation of the strata through optimisation of the bounds on the stratification variable necessarily leads to non-overlapping strata, while with iterative reallocation the strata may overlap, i.e., when the strata are sorted on the mean of the stratification variable, the upper bound of a stratum can be larger than the lower bound of the next stratum. As argued by de Gruijter et al. (2015) optimisation of strata through optimisation of the stratum bounds can be suboptimal. On the other hand, optimisation of the stratum bounds needs fewer computations and therefore is quicker.

The situation considered in this section is that prior data are available, either from the study area itself or from another similar area, that can be used to fit a linear regression model for the study variable, using one or more quantitative covariates and/or factors as predictors. These predictors must be available in the study area so that the fitted model can be used to map the study variable in the study area. We wish to collect more data by stratified simple random sampling, to be used in design-based estimation of the population mean or total of the study variable. The central research question then is how to construct these strata.

Recall the variance estimator of the mean estimator for stratified simple random sampling (Equations (4.4) and (4.5)):

$$V(\hat{\bar{z}}) = \sum_{h=1}^{H} w_h^2 \frac{S_h^2(z)}{n_h} . \tag{13.9}$$

Plugging the stratum sample sizes under optimal allocation (Equation (4.17)) into Equation (13.9) yields

$$V(\hat{\bar{z}}) = \frac{1}{n} \left(\sum_{h=1}^{H} w_h S_h(z) \sqrt{c_h} \sum_{h=1}^{H} \frac{w_h S_h(z)}{\sqrt{c_h}} \right) . \tag{13.10}$$

So, given the total sample size n, the variance of the estimator of the mean is minimal when the criterion

$$O = \sum_{h=1}^{H} w_h S_h(z) \sqrt{c_h} \sum_{h=1}^{H} \frac{w_h S_h(z)}{\sqrt{c_h}} \tag{13.11}$$

is minimised.

Assuming that the costs are equal for all population units, so that the mean costs are the same for all strata, the minimisation criterion reduces to

$$O = \left(\sum_{h=1}^{H} w_h S_h(z) \right)^2 . \tag{13.12}$$

In practice, we do not know the values of the study variable z. de Gruijter et al. (2015) consider the situation where we have predictions of the study variable from a linear regression model: $\hat{z} = z + \epsilon$, with ϵ the prediction error. So, this implies that we do not know the population standard deviations within the strata, $S_h(z)$ of Equation (13.10). What we do have are the stratum standard deviations of the predictions of z: $S_h(\hat{z})$. With many statistical models, such as regression and kriging models, the standard deviation of the predictions is smaller than that of the study variable: $S_h(\hat{z}) < S_h(z)$. This is known as the smoothing or levelling effect.

The stratum standard deviations in the minimisation criterion are replaced by model-expectations of the stratum standard deviations, i.e., by model-based predictions of the stratum standard deviations, $E_\xi[S_h(z)]$. This leads to the following minimisation criterion:

$$E_\xi[O] = \left(\sum_{h=1}^{H} w_h E_\xi[S_h(z)] \right)^2 . \tag{13.13}$$

The stratum variances are predicted by

$$E_\xi[S_h^2(z)] = \frac{1}{N_h^2} \sum_{i=1}^{N_h-1} \sum_{j=i+1}^{N_h} E_\xi[d_{ij}^2] , \tag{13.14}$$

with $d_{ij}^2 = (z_i - z_j)^2$ the squared difference of the study variable values at two nodes of a discretisation grid. The model-expectation of the squared differences are equal to

$$E_\xi[d_{ij}^2] = (\hat{z}_i - \hat{z}_j)^2 + S^2(\epsilon_i) + S^2(\epsilon_j) - 2S^2(\epsilon_i, \epsilon_j) , \tag{13.15}$$

with $S^2(\epsilon_i)$ the variance of the prediction error at node i and $S^2(\epsilon_i, \epsilon_j)$ the covariance of the prediction errors at nodes i and j. The authors then argue that for smoothers, such as kriging and regression, the first term must be divided by the squared correlation coefficient R^2:

$$E_\xi[d_{ij}^2] = \frac{(\hat{z}_i - \hat{z}_j)^2}{R^2} + S^2(\epsilon_i) + S^2(\epsilon_j) - 2S^2(\epsilon_i, \epsilon_j) . \tag{13.16}$$

The predicted stratum standard deviations are approximated by the square root of Equation (13.16). Plugging these model-based predictions of the stratum standard deviations into the minimisation criterion, Equation (13.12), yields

$$E_\xi[O] = \frac{1}{N} \sum_{h=1}^{H} \left(\sum_{i=1}^{N_h-1} \sum_{j=i+1}^{N_h} \frac{(\hat{z}_i - \hat{z}_j)^2}{R^2} + S^2(\epsilon_i) + S^2(\epsilon_j) - 2S^2(\epsilon_i, \epsilon_j) \right)^{1/2} . \tag{13.17}$$

Optimal spatial stratification with package **SamplingStrata** is illustrated with a survey of the SOM concentration (g kg^{-1}) in the topsoil (A horizon) of Xuancheng (China). Three samples are available. These three samples are merged. The total number of sampling points is 183. This sample is used to fit a simple linear regression model for the SOM concentration, using the elevation of the surface (dem) as a predictor. Function lm of the **stats** package is used to fit the simple linear regression model.

```
lm_SOM <- lm(SOM_A_hori ~ dem, data = sampleXuancheng)
```

In fitting a linear regression model, we assume that the relation is linear, the residual variance is constant (independent of the fitted value), and the residuals have a normal distribution. These assumptions are checked with a scatter plot of the residuals against the fitted value and a Q-Q plot, respectively (Figure 13.6).

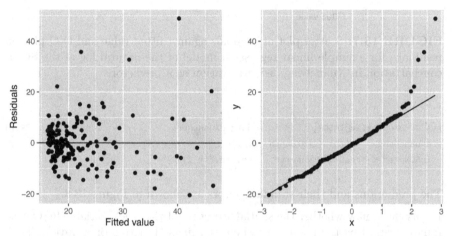

FIGURE 13.6: Scatter plot of residuals against fitted value and Q-Q plot of residuals, for a simple linear regression model of the SOM concentration in Xuancheng, using elevation as a predictor.

The scatter plot shows that the first assumption is realistic. No pattern can be seen: at all fitted values, the residuals are scattered around the horizontal line. However, the second and third assumptions are questionable: the residual variance clearly increases with the fitted value, and the distribution of the residuals has positive skew, i.e., it has a long upper tail. There clearly is some evidence that these two assumptions are violated. Possibly these problems can be solved by fitting a model for the natural log of the SOM concentration.

The variance of the residuals is more constant (Figure 13.7), and the Q-Q plot is improved, although we now have too many strong negative residuals for a normal distribution. I proceed with the model for natural-log transformed SOM (lnSOM). The fitted linear regression model is used to predict lnSOM at the nodes of a 200 m × 200 m discretisation grid.

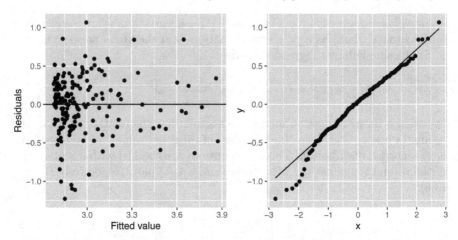

FIGURE 13.7: Scatter plot of residuals against fitted value and Q-Q plot of residuals, for a simple linear regression model of the natural log of the SOM concentration in Xuancheng, using elevation as a predictor.

```
res <- predict(lm_lnSOM, newdata = as(grdXuancheng, "data.frame"), se.fit = TRUE)
grdXuancheng <- within(grdXuancheng, {
  lnSOMpred <- res$fit; varpred <- res$se.fit^2})
```

The predictions and their standard errors are shown in Figure 13.8.

Let us check now whether the spatial structure of the study variable lnSOM is fully captured by the mean, modelled as a linear function of elevation. This can be checked by estimating the semivariogram of the model residuals. If the semivariogram of the residuals is pure nugget (the semivariance does not increase with distance), then we can assume that the prediction errors are independent. In that case, we do not need to account for a covariance of the prediction errors in optimisation of the spatial strata. However, if the semivariogram does show spatial structure, we must account for a covariance of the prediction errors. Figure 13.9 shows the sample semivariogram of the residuals computed with function variogram of package **gstat**.

```
library(gstat)
sampleXuancheng <- sampleXuancheng %>%
  mutate(s1 = s1 / 1000, s2 = s2 / 1000)
coordinates(sampleXuancheng) <- ~ s1 + s2
vg <- variogram(lnSOM ~ dem, data = sampleXuancheng)
```

The sample semivariogram does not show much spatial structure, but the first two points in the semivariogram have somewhat smaller values. This indicates

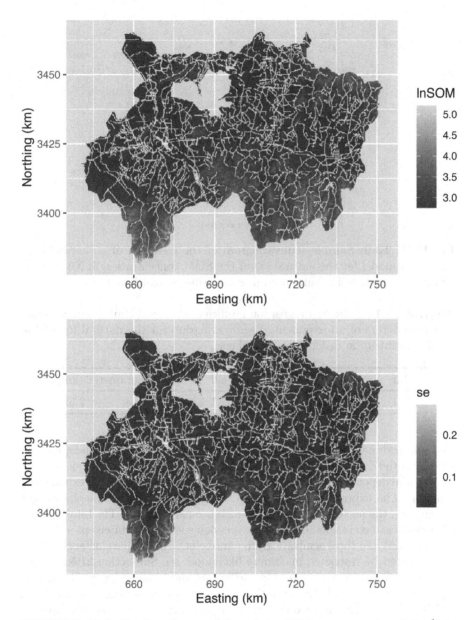

FIGURE 13.8: Predicted natural log of the SOM concentration (g kg⁻¹) in the topsoil of Xuancheng and the standard error (se) of the predictor, obtained with a linear regression model with elevation as a predictor.

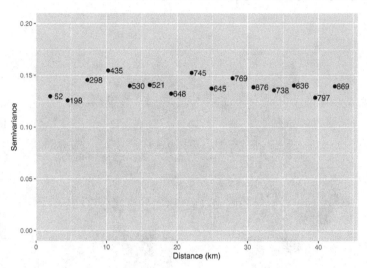

FIGURE 13.9: Sample semivariogram of the residuals of a simple linear regression model for the natural log of the SOM concentration in Xuancheng. Numbers refer to point-pairs used in computing semivariances.

TABLE 13.1: Estimated regression coefficients (intercept and slope for dem) and parameters of an exponential semivariogram for the natural log of the SOM concentration (g kg^{-1}) in Xuancheng.

Int	dem	Nugget	Partial sill	Distance parameter (km)
2.771	0.00222	0.085	0.061	2.588

that the residuals at two close points, say, $< \pm 5$ km, are not independent, whereas if the distance between the two points $> \pm 5$ km, they are independent. This spatial dependency of the residuals can be modelled, e.g., by an exponential function. The exponential semivariogram has three parameters, the nugget variance c_0, the partial sill c_1, and the distance parameter ϕ. The total number of model parameters now is five: two regression coefficients (intercept and slope for elevation) and three semivariogram parameters. All five parameters can best be estimated by restricted maximum likelihood, see Subsection 21.5.2. Table 13.1 shows the estimated regression coefficients and semivariogram parameters. Up to a distance of about three times the estimated distance parameter ϕ, which is about 8 km, the residuals are spatially correlated; beyond that distance, they are hardly correlated anymore.

We conclude that the errors in the regression model predictions are not independent, although the correlation will be weak in this case, and that we must account for this correlation in optimising the spatial strata.

The discretisation grid with predicted lnSOM consists of 115,526 nodes. These are too many for function optimStrata. The grid is therefore thinned to a grid with a spacing of 800 m × 800 m, resulting in 7,257 nodes.

The first step in optimisation of spatial strata with package **SamplingStrata** is to build the sampling frame with function buildFrameSpatial. Argument x specifies the stratification variables, and argument y specifies the study variables. In our case, we have only one stratification variable and one study variable, and these are the same variable. Argument variance specifies the variance of the prediction error of the study variable. Variable dom is an identifier of the domain of interest of which we want to estimate the mean or total. I assign the value 1 to all population units, see code chunk below, which implies that the stratification is optimised for the entire population. If we have multiple domains of interest, the stratification is optimised for each domain separately.

Finally, as a preparatory step we must specify how precise the estimated mean should be. This precision must be specified in terms of the coefficient of variation (cv), i.e., the standard error of the estimated mean divided by the mean. I use a cv of 0.005. In case of multiple domains of interest and multiple study variables, a cv must be specified per domain and per study variable. This precision requirement is used to compute the sample size for Neyman allocation (Equation (4.16))[1]. The optimal stratification is independent of the precision requirement.

```
library(SamplingStrata)
subgrd$id <- seq_len(nrow(subgrd))
subgrd$dom <- rep(1, nrow(subgrd))
frame <- buildFrameSpatial(df = subgrd, id = "id", X = c("lnSOMpred"),
  Y = c("lnSOMpred"), variance = c("varpred"), lon = "x1", lat = "x2",
  domainvalue = "dom")
cv <- as.data.frame(list(DOM = "DOM1", CV1 = 0.005, domainvalue = 1))
```

The optimal spatial stratification can be computed with function optimStrata, with argument method = "spatial". The R^2 value of the linear regression model, used in the minimisation criterion (Equation (13.17)), can be specified with argument fitting.

I am not sure that the correction factor R^2 in Equation (13.16) is really needed. I believe that the smoothing effect is already accounted for by the variances and covariances of the prediction errors. I used an R^2 value of 1.

Arguments range and kappa are parameters of an exponential semivariogram, needed for computing the covariance of the prediction errors. Function

---

[1]For multivariate stratification, i.e., stratification with multiple study variables, Bethel allocation is used to compute the required sample size.

optimStrata uses an extra parameter in the exponential semivariogram: $c_0 + c_1 \exp(-\kappa h/\phi)$. So, for the usual exponential semivariogram (Equation (21.13)) kappa equals 1.

```
res <- optimStrata(
    framesamp = frame, method = "spatial", errors = cv, nStrata = 5,
    fitting = 1, range = c(vgm_REML$phi), kappa = 1, showPlot = FALSE)
```

A summary of the optimised strata can be obtained with function summaryStrata.

```
print(smr_strata <- summaryStrata(
    res$framenew, res$aggr_strata, progress = FALSE))
```

	Domain	Stratum	Population	Allocation	SamplingRate	Lower_X1	Upper_X1
1	1	1	3090	12	0.004035	2.767950	2.862539
2	1	2	1931	10	0.005087	2.864846	2.991733
3	1	3	1133	10	0.008555	2.994040	3.215515
4	1	4	769	11	0.014398	3.217822	3.600789
5	1	5	334	11	0.033443	3.605403	5.098052

In the next code chunk, it is checked whether the coefficient of variation is indeed equal to the desired value of 0.005.

```
strata <- res$aggr_strata
framenew <- res$framenew
N_h <- strata$N
w_h <- N_h / sum(N_h)
se <- sqrt(sum(w_h^2 * strata$S1^2 / strata$SOLUZ))
se / mean(framenew$Y1)
```

```
[1] 0.005033349
```

The coefficient of variation can also be computed with function expected_CV.

```
expected_CV(strata)
```

```
        cv(Y1)
DOM1  0.005
```

Figure 13.10 shows the optimised strata. I used the stratum bounds in data.frame smr_strata, to compute the stratum for all raster cells of the original 200 m × 200 m grid.

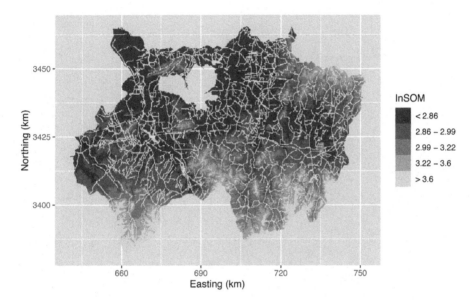

FIGURE 13.10: Model-based optimal strata for estimating the mean of the natural log of the SOM concentration in Xuancheng.

14

Sampling for estimating parameters of domains

This chapter is about probability sampling and estimation of means or totals of subpopulations (subareas, subregions). In the sampling literature, these subpopulations are referred to as domains of interest, or shortly domains. Ideally, at the stage of designing a sample, these domains are known, and of every population unit we know to which domain it belongs. In that situation it is most convenient to use these domains as strata in random sampling, so that we can control the sample size in each domain (Chapter 4).

If we have multiple maps with domains, think for instance of a soil class map, a map with land cover classes, and a map with countries, we can make an overlay of these maps to construct the cross-tabulation strata. However, this may result in numerous strata, in some cases even more than the sample size. In this situation, an attractive solution is multiway stratification (Subsection 9.1.4). With this design, the domains of interest are used as strata, not their cross-classification, and the sample sizes of these marginal strata are controlled.

Even with a multiway stratified sample, resulting in controlled sample sizes for each domain, the sample size of a domain can be too small for a reliable estimate of the mean or total when using just the data of this domain. In this case we may use model-assisted estimators (Chapter 10) to increase the precision. Not only the data collected from a given domain are used to estimate the mean or total, but also data outside the domain (Section 14.2) (Chaudhuri (1994), Rao (2003), Falorsi and Righi (2008)).

We may also wish to estimate the mean or total of domains that are not used as strata or marginal strata. The sample size in these domains is then not controlled and varies among samples selected with the sampling design. As before with multiway stratified sampling, the mean can either be estimated with the direct estimator, using the data from the domain only (Section 14.1), or a model-assisted estimator, also using data from outside the domain (Section 14.2).

14.1   Direct estimator for large domains

If the sample size of a domain d is considered large enough to obtain a reliable estimate of the mean and, besides, the size of the domain is known, the mean of that domain can be estimated by the direct estimator:

$$\hat{\bar{z}}_d = \frac{1}{N_d} \sum_{k \in \mathcal{S}_d} \frac{z_{dk}}{\pi_{dk}} \, , \qquad (14.1)$$

where N_d is the size of the domain, z_{dk} is the value for unit k of domain d, and π_{dk} is the inclusion probability of this point.

When the domain is not used as a (marginal) stratum, so that the sample size of the domain is random, the mean of the domain can be estimated best by the ratio estimator:

$$\hat{\bar{z}}_{\text{ratio},\,d} = \frac{\hat{t}_d(z)}{\widehat{N}_d} = \frac{\sum_{k \in \mathcal{S}_d} \frac{z_{dk}}{\pi_{dk}}}{\sum_{k \in \mathcal{S}_d} \frac{1}{\pi_{dk}}} \, . \qquad (14.2)$$

> The ratio estimator can also be used when the size of the domain is unknown. An example of this is estimating the mean of soil classes *as observed in the field*, not *as depicted on a soil map*. A soil map is impure, i.e., the map units contain patches with soil classes that differ from the soil class as indicated on the map. The area of a given true soil class is not known.

For simple random sampling without replacement, $\pi_{dk} = n/N$. Inserting this in Equation (14.2) gives

$$\hat{\bar{z}}_{\text{ratio},\,d} = \frac{1}{n_d} \sum_{k \in \mathcal{S}_d} z_{dk} \, . \qquad (14.3)$$

The mean of the domain is simply estimated by the mean of the z-values observed in the domain, i.e., the sample mean in domain d. The variance of this estimator can be estimated by

$$\widehat{V}\!\left(\hat{\bar{z}}_{\text{ratio},\,d}\right) = \frac{1}{\hat{a}_d^2} \cdot \frac{1}{n\,(n-1)} \sum_{k \in \mathcal{S}_d} (z_{dk} - \bar{z}_{\mathcal{S}_d})^2 \, , \qquad (14.4)$$

where $\bar{z}_{\mathcal{S}_d}$ is the sample mean in domain d, and $\hat{a}_d$ is the estimated relative size of domain d:

$$\hat{a}_d = \frac{n_d}{n} \, . \qquad (14.5)$$

Refer to section (8.2.2) in de Gruijter et al. (2006) for the ratio estimator and its standard error with stratified simple random sampling, in case the domains cut across the strata, and other sampling designs.

The ratio estimator and its standard error can be computed with function svyby of package **survey** (Lumley, 2021). This is illustrated with Eastern Amazonia. We wish to estimate the mean aboveground biomass (AGB) of the 16 ecoregions from a simple random sample of 200 units.

```
library(survey)
set.seed(314)
n <- 200
mysample <- grdAmazonia %>%
  mutate(N = n()) %>%
  slice_sample(n = n)
design_si <- svydesign(id = ~ 1, data = mysample, fpc = ~ N)
res <- svyby(~ AGB, by = ~ Ecoregion, design = design_si, FUN = svymean)
```

The ratio estimates of the mean AGB are shown in Table 14.1. Two ecoregions are missing in the table: no units are selected from these ecoregions so that a direct estimate is not available. There are three ecoregions with an estimated standard error of 0.0. These ecoregions have less than two sampling units only, so that the standard error cannot be estimated.

TABLE 14.1: Ratio estimates and estimated standard errors of the ratio estimator of the mean AGB (10^9 kg ha^{-1}) of ecoregions in Eastern Amazonia, with simple random sampling without replacement of size 200.

Ecoregion	AGB	se
Cerrado	99.7	15.6
Guianan highland moist forests	296.0	0.0
Guianan lowland moist forests	263.0	0.0
Gurupa varzea	80.0	0.0
Madeira-Tapajos moist forests	286.0	14.0
Marajo varzea	116.6	27.2
Maranhao Babassu forests	90.0	9.6
Mato Grosso tropical dry forests	177.0	90.7
Monte Alegre varzea	189.5	89.0
Purus-Madeira moist forests	145.5	47.1
Tapajos-Xingu moist forests	288.6	8.9
Tocantins/Pindare moist forests	176.3	17.9
Uatuma-Trombetas moist forests	274.7	6.7
Xingu-Tocantins-Araguaia moist forests	223.1	16.6

The estimated standard errors of 0.0 are non-availables.

TABLE 14.2: Standard deviations of 1,000 π estimates (HT) and 1,000 ratio estimates (Ratio) of the mean AGB (10^9 kg ha^{-1}) of ecoregions in Eastern Amazonia, with simple random sampling without replacement of size 200.

Ecoregion	HT	Ratio	n
Amazon-Orinoco-Southern Caribbean mangroves	136.9	36.9	0.87
Cerrado	38.6	18.2	8.16
Guianan highland moist forests	271.4	29.5	0.71
Guianan lowland moist forests	160.0	17.9	2.51
Guianan savanna	101.5	67.1	2.86
Gurupa varzea	103.7	57.8	0.99
Madeira-Tapajos moist forests	55.9	14.2	22.96
Marajo varzea	48.6	24.7	10.80
Maranhao Babassu forests	59.3	25.7	4.61
Mato Grosso tropical dry forests	72.7	41.1	2.98
Monte Alegre varzea	120.2	63.3	2.27
Purus-Madeira moist forests	288.0	55.5	0.45
Tapajos-Xingu moist forests	45.5	12.0	31.51
Tocantins/Pindare moist forests	31.5	15.3	28.39
Uatuma-Trombetas moist forests	33.4	8.1	52.37
Xingu-Tocantins-Araguaia moist forests	42.4	17.2	27.56

n: expected sample size.

The simple random sampling is repeated 1,000 times, and every sample is used to estimate the mean AGB of the ecoregions both with the π estimator and the ratio estimator. As can be seen in Table 14.2 the standard deviation of the ratio estimates is much smaller than that of the π estimates. The reason is that the number of sampling units in an ecoregion varies among samples, i.e., the sample size of an ecoregion is random. When many units are selected from an ecoregion, the estimated total of that ecoregion is large. The estimated mean as obtained with the π estimator then is large too, because the estimated total is divided by the fixed size (total number of population units, N_d) of the ecoregion. However, in the ratio estimator the size of an ecoregion is estimated from the same sample, although we know its size, see Equation (14.2). With many units selected from an ecoregion, the estimated size of that ecoregion, $\widehat{N}_d$, is also large. By dividing the large estimated total by the large estimated size, a more stable estimate of the mean of the domain is obtained. For quite a few ecoregions the standard deviations are very large, especially of the π estimator. These are the ecoregions with very small average sample sizes. With simple random sampling, the expected sample size can simply be computed by $E[n] = n\,N_d/N$. In the following section, alternative estimators are described for these ecoregions with small expected sample sizes. To speed up the computations, I used a 5 km × 5 km subgrid of grdAmazonia in this sampling experiment.

No covariates are used in the ratio estimator. If we wish to exploit covariates, the mean of a domain can be estimated best by the ratio of the regression estimate of the domain total and the estimated size of the domain:

$$\hat{\bar{z}}_{\text{ratio},d} = \frac{\hat{t}_{\text{regr},d}(z)}{\widehat{N}_d} \, . \tag{14.6}$$

For a large domain with a reasonable sample size, the regression estimate can be computed from the data of that domain (Chapter 10). For small domains, also the data from outside these domains can be used to estimate the population regression coefficients. This is explained in Subsection 14.2.1.

14.2 Model-assisted estimators for small domains

When the domains are not well represented in the sample, the direct estimators from the previous section lead to large standard errors. In this situation, we may try to increase the precision by also using observations from outside the domain. If we have covariates related to the study variable, we may exploit this ancillary information by fitting a regression model relating the study variable to the covariates and using the fitted model to predict the study variable for all population units (nodes of discretisation grid), see Chapter 10. However, for a small domain, we may have too few sampled units in that domain to fit a separate regression model. The alternative then is to use the entire sample to estimate the regression coefficients, and to use this global regression model to estimate the means of the domains. This introduces a systematic error, a design-bias, in the estimator. However, this extra error is potentially outweighed by the reduction of the random error due to the use of the globally estimated regression coefficients. If one or more units are selected from a domain, the observations of the study variable of these units can be used to correct for the bias. This leads to the regression estimator for small domains. In the absence of such data, the mean of the domain can still be estimated by the so-called synthetic estimator.

There are quite a few packages for model-assisted estimation of means of small areas, the **maSAE** package (Cullman, 2021), the **JoSAE** package (Breidenbach, 2018), the **rsae** package (Schoch, 2014), and the **forestinventory** package (Hill et al., 2021). I use package **forestinventory** for model-assisted estimation (Subsections 14.2.1 and 14.2.2) and package **JoSAE** for model-based prediction of the means of small areas (Section 14.3).

14.2.1   Regression estimator

In the regression estimator, the potential bias due to the globally estimated regression coefficients can be eliminated by adding the π estimator of the mean of the regression residuals to the mean of the predictions in the domain (compare with Equation (10.8)) (Mandallaz (2007), Mandallaz et al. (2013)):

$$\hat{\bar{z}}_{\mathrm{regr},d} = \frac{1}{N_d} \sum_{k=1}^{N_d} \mathbf{x}_{dk}^{\mathrm{T}} \hat{\mathbf{b}} + \frac{1}{N_d} \sum_{k \in \mathcal{S}_d} \frac{e_{dk}}{\pi_{dk}} = \bar{\mathbf{x}}_d^{\mathrm{T}} \hat{\mathbf{b}} + \frac{1}{N_d} \sum_{k \in \mathcal{S}_d} \frac{e_{dk}}{\pi_{dk}} , \qquad (14.7)$$

with $\mathbf{x}_{dk}$ the vector with covariate values for unit k in domain d, $\hat{\mathbf{b}}$ the vector with globally estimated regression coefficients, e_{dk} the residual for unit k in domain d, π_{dk} the inclusion probability of that unit, and $\bar{\mathbf{x}}_d$ the mean of the covariates in domain d. Alternatively, the mean of the residuals in a domain is estimated by the ratio estimator:

$$\hat{\bar{z}}_{\mathrm{regr},d} = \bar{\mathbf{x}}_d^{\mathrm{T}} \hat{\mathbf{b}} + \frac{1}{\widehat{N}_d} \sum_{k \in \mathcal{S}_d} \frac{e_{dk}}{\pi_{dk}} , \qquad (14.8)$$

with $\widehat{N}_d$ the estimated size of domain d, see Equation (14.2). The regression coefficients can be estimated by Equation (10.15). With simple random sampling, the second term in Equation (14.8) is equal to the sample mean of the residuals, so that the estimator reduces to

$$\hat{\bar{z}}_{\mathrm{regr},d} = \bar{\mathbf{x}}_d^{\mathrm{T}} \hat{\mathbf{b}} + \bar{e}_{\mathcal{S}_d} , \qquad (14.9)$$

with $\bar{e}_{\mathcal{S}_d}$ the sample mean of the residuals in domain d.

A regression estimate can only be computed if we have at least one observation of the study variable in the domain d. The variance of the regression estimator of the mean for a small domain can be estimated by (Hill et al., 2021)

$$\hat{V}\left(\hat{\bar{z}}_{\mathrm{regr},d}\right) = \bar{\mathbf{x}}_d^{\mathrm{T}} \widehat{\mathbf{C}}(\hat{\mathbf{b}}) \bar{\mathbf{x}}_d + \hat{V}\left(\hat{\bar{e}}_d\right) , \qquad (14.10)$$

with $\widehat{\mathbf{C}}(\hat{\mathbf{b}})$ the matrix with estimated sampling variances and covariances of the regression coefficients. The first variance component is the contribution due to uncertainty about the regression coefficients, the second component accounts for the uncertainty about the mean of the residuals in the domain. For simple random sampling, the sampling variance of the π estimator of the mean of the residuals in a domain can be estimated by the sample variance of the residuals in that domain divided by the sample size n_d. This variance estimator is presented in Hill et al. (2021). If the domain is not used as a stratum and the domain mean of the residuals is estimated by the ratio estimator, the second variance component can be estimated by

$$\hat{V}\left(\hat{\bar{e}}_{\text{ratio},d}\right) = \left(\frac{n}{n_d}\right)^2 \cdot \frac{1}{n\,(n-1)} \sum_{k \in \mathcal{S}_d} (e_{dk} - \bar{e}_{\mathcal{S}_d})^2 \,. \qquad (14.11)$$

With simple random sampling, the sampling variances and covariances of the estimated regression coefficients can be estimated by (equation 2 in Hill et al. (2021))

$$\widehat{\mathbf{C}}(\hat{\mathbf{b}}) = \frac{1}{n}\left(\sum_{k \in \mathcal{S}} \mathbf{x}_k \mathbf{x}_k^{\mathrm{T}}\right)^{-1}\left(\frac{1}{n^2}\sum_{k \in \mathcal{S}} e_k^2 \mathbf{x}_k \mathbf{x}_k^{\mathrm{T}}\right)\frac{1}{n}\left(\sum_{k \in \mathcal{S}}^{n} \mathbf{x}_k \mathbf{x}_k^{\mathrm{T}}\right)^{-1}. \quad (14.12)$$

The sampling variances and covariances of the estimators of the population regression coefficients are not equal to the model-variances and covariances as obtained with multiple linear regression, using functions lm and vcov, see Section 10.1 and Chapter 26.

Function twophase of package **forestinventory** (Hill et al., 2021) can be used to compute the regression estimate for small domains and its standard error.

> The function name 'twophase' is somewhat confusing. It suggests that we have a large sample which is subsampled in a second phase, as described in Chapter 11. This is not the case here. However, upon considering infinite populations, Hill et al. (2021) treat the grid that discretises the infinite population as the first-phase sample. The sampling error introduced by this discretisation grid can then be accounted for. I ignore this sampling error, which will be very small anyway, because the number of grid cells is very large.

By assigning the domain means of the covariates to argument exhaustive of function twophase the sampling error of the first phase is ignored. Function twophase assumes simple random sampling (unless optional argument cluster is used). Note that for the unobserved population units (not selected units) the AGB values are changed into non-availables. In package **survey** also a function twophase is defined, for this reason the name of the package is made explicit by forestinventory::twophase. With argument psmall = TRUE and element unbiased = TRUE in the list small_area the regression estimate is computed. Log-transformed SWIR2 is used as a covariate in the regression estimator of the mean AGB of the ecoregions.

```
library(forestinventory)
n <- 200
set.seed(314)
units <- sample(nrow(grdAmazonia), size = n, replace = FALSE)
grdAmazonia <- grdAmazonia %>%
  mutate(lnSWIR2 = log(SWIR2),
         id = row_number(),
         ind = as.integer(id %in% units))
grdAmazonia$AGB[grdAmazonia$ind == 0L] <- NA
mx_eco_pop <- tapply(
  grdAmazonia$lnSWIR2, INDEX = grdAmazonia$Ecoregion, FUN = mean)
mX_eco_pop <- data.frame(
  Intercept = rep(1, length(mx_eco_pop)), lnSWIR2 = mx_eco_pop)
ecos_in_sam <- unique(mysample$Ecoregion)
res <- forestinventory::twophase(AGB ~ lnSWIR2,
  data = as.data.frame(grdAmazonia),
  phase_id = list(phase.col = "ind", terrgrid.id = 1),
  small_area = list(sa.col = "Ecoregion",
                    areas = sort(ecos_in_sam),
                    unbiased = TRUE),
  psmall = TRUE, exhaustive = mX_eco_pop)
regr <- res$estimation
```

The alternative is to save the selected units (sample) in a data frame, passed to function twophase with argument data. The results are identical because the true means of the covariate x specified with argument exhaustive contains all required information at the population level.

For two ecoregions, no regression estimate of the mean AGB is obtained (Table 14.3). No units are selected from these domains. The estimated variance of the estimated domain mean is in the column g_var. In the estimated variance ext_var the first variance component of Equation (14.10) is ignored. Note that for the ecoregions with a sample size of one unit (the sample size per domain is in column n2G), no estimate of the variance is available, because the variance of the estimated mean of the residuals cannot be estimated from one unit.

Figure 14.1 shows the regression estimates plotted against the ratio estimates. The intercept of the line, fitted with ordinary least squares (OLS), is larger than 0, and the slope is smaller than 1. Using the regression model predictions in the estimation of the means leads to some smoothing.

I quantified the gain in precision of the estimated mean AGB due to the use of the regression model by the variance of the ratio estimator divided by the variance of the regression estimator (Table 14.4). For ratios larger than 1, there is a gain in precision. Both variances are estimated from 1,000 repeated ratio and regression estimates obtained with simple random sampling without

TABLE 14.3: Regression estimates of the mean AGB (10^9 kg ha^{-1}) of ecoregions in Eastern Amazonia, for simple random sample without replacement of size 200, using lnSWIR2 as a predictor.

Ecoregion	AGB	ext_var	g_var	n2G
Cerrado	105.5	51.6	82.6	12
Guianan highland moist forests	281.8	NA	NaN	1
Guianan lowland moist forests	280.3	NA	NaN	1
Gurupa varzea	57.8	NA	NaN	1
Madeira-Tapajos moist forests	296.1	91.2	107.3	19
Marajo varzea	163.1	535.2	546.0	10
Maranhao Babassu forests	114.2	157.1	178.1	7
Mato Grosso tropical dry forests	144.6	959.6	981.5	2
Monte Alegre varzea	209.1	4,105.7	4,117.3	2
Purus-Madeira moist forests	225.7	2,428.9	2,441.1	2
Tapajos-Xingu moist forests	277.8	23.4	36.9	38
Tocantins/Pindare moist forests	157.8	75.8	87.7	30
Uatuma-Trombetas moist forests	270.6	33.3	47.5	46
Xingu-Tocantins-Araguaia moist forests	223.6	51.1	61.6	29

For explanation of variances of regression estimator, see text. n2G: sample size of ecoregion; NA: not available; NaN: not a number.

replacement of size 200. For all but two small ecoregions, there is a gain. For quite a few ecoregions, the gain is quite large. These are the ecoregions where the globally fitted regression model explains a large part of the spatial variation of AGB.

14.2.2 Synthetic estimator

For small domains from which no units are selected, the mean can still be estimated by the synthetic estimator, also referred to as the synthetic regression estimator, by dropping the second term in Equation (14.7):

$$\hat{\bar{z}}_{\text{syn},d} = \bar{\mathbf{x}}_d^{\mathrm{T}} \hat{\mathbf{b}} . \tag{14.13}$$

The variance can be estimated by

$$\hat{V}\left(\hat{\bar{z}}_{\text{syn},d}\right) = \bar{\mathbf{x}}_d^{\mathrm{T}} \widehat{\mathbf{C}}(\hat{\mathbf{b}})\bar{\mathbf{x}}_d . \tag{14.14}$$

This is equal to the first variance component of Equation (14.10). The synthetic estimate can be computed with function twophase, with argument psmall = FALSE and element unbiased = FALSE in the list small_area.

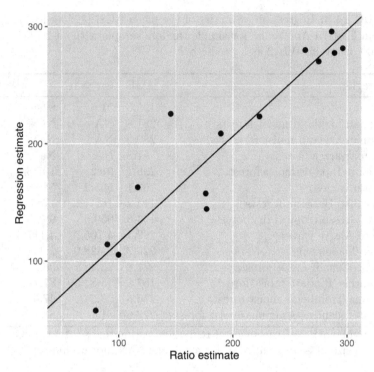

FIGURE 14.1: Scatter plot of the ratio and the regression estimates of the mean AGB (10^9 kg ha^{-1}) of ecoregions in Eastern Amazonia for simple random sample without replacement of size 200. In the regression estimate, lnSWIR2 is used as a predictor. The line is fitted by ordinary least squares.

```
res <- forestinventory::twophase(AGB ~ lnSWIR2,
  data = as.data.frame(grdAmazonia),
  phase_id = list(phase.col = "ind", terrgrid.id = 1),
  small_area = list(sa.col = "Ecoregion", areas = ecoregions, unbiased = FALSE),
  psmall = FALSE, exhaustive = mX_eco_pop)
synt <- res$estimation
```

For all ecoregions, also the unsampled ones, a synthetic estimate of the mean AGB is obtained (Table 14.5). For the sampled ecoregions, the synthetic estimate differs from the regression estimate. This difference can be quite large for ecoregions with a small sample size. Averaged over all sampled ecoregions, the difference, computed as synthetic estimate minus regression estimate, equals 14.9 10^9 kg ha^{-1}. The variance of the regression estimator is always much larger than the variance of the synthetic estimator. The difference is the variance of the estimator of the domain mean of the residuals. However, recall that the regression estimator is design-unbiased, whereas the synthetic

TABLE 14.4: Estimated gain in precision of the estimated mean AGB of ecoregions in Eastern Amazonia, as quantified by the ratio of the estimated variance of the ratio estimator (no covariate used) to the estimated variance of the regression estimator (using lnSWIR2 as a predictor), for simple random sampling without replacement of size 200.

Ecoregion	Gain
Amazon-Orinoco-Southern Caribbean mangroves	0.57
Cerrado	1.63
Guianan highland moist forests	1.01
Guianan lowland moist forests	1.26
Guianan savanna	6.70
Gurupa varzea	0.65
Madeira-Tapajos moist forests	1.44
Marajo varzea	1.87
Maranhao Babassu forests	1.70
Mato Grosso tropical dry forests	2.81
Monte Alegre varzea	1.21
Purus-Madeira moist forests	1.74
Tapajos-Xingu moist forests	2.73
Tocantins/Pindare moist forests	2.56
Uatuma-Trombetas moist forests	2.10
Xingu-Tocantins-Araguaia moist forests	4.06

estimator is not. A more fair comparison is on the basis of the root mean squared error (RMSE) (Table 14.6). For the regression estimator, the RMSE is equal to its standard error and therefore not shown in the table.

In the synthetic estimator and the regression estimator, both quantitative covariates and categorical variables can be used. If one or more categorical variables are included in the estimator, the variable names in the data frame with the true means of the ancillary variables per domain, specified with argument exhaustive, must correspond to the column names of the design matrix that is generated with function lm, see Subsection 10.1.3.

14.3 Model-based prediction

The alternative for design-based and model-assisted estimation of the means or totals of small domains is model-based prediction. The fundamental difference between model-assisted estimation and model-based prediction is explained

TABLE 14.5: Synthetic estimates of the mean AGB (10^9 kg ha^{-1}) of ecoregions in Eastern Amazonia, for simple random sample without replacement of size 200, using lnSWIR2 as a predictor.

Ecoregion	AGB	g_var	n2G
Amazon-Orinoco-Southern Caribbean mangroves	225.3	10.6	0
Cerrado	81.6	31.0	12
Guianan highland moist forests	278.6	16.0	1
Guianan lowland moist forests	277.3	15.8	1
Guianan savanna	171.8	12.2	0
Gurupa varzea	218.2	10.4	1
Madeira-Tapajos moist forests	279.2	16.1	19
Marajo varzea	230.6	10.8	10
Maranhao Babassu forests	118.3	20.9	7
Mato Grosso tropical dry forests	114.0	21.9	2
Monte Alegre varzea	242.6	11.6	2
Purus-Madeira moist forests	250.4	12.3	2
Tapajos-Xingu moist forests	261.1	13.4	38
Tocantins/Pindare moist forests	175.7	11.9	30
Uatuma-Trombetas moist forests	267.2	14.2	46
Xingu-Tocantins-Araguaia moist forests	221.9	10.5	29

n2G: sample size of ecoregion.

in Chapter 26. The models used in this section are linear mixed models. In a linear mixed model, the mean of the study variable is modelled as a linear combination of covariates, similar to a linear regression model. The difference with a linear regression model is that the residuals of the mean are not assumed independent. The dependency of the residuals is also modelled. Two types of linear mixed model are described: a random intercept model and a geostatistical model.

14.3.1   Random intercept model

A basic linear mixed model that can be used for model-based prediction of means of small domains is the random intercept model:

$$Z_{dk} = \mathbf{x}_{dk}^{\mathrm{T}}\boldsymbol{\beta} + v_d + \epsilon_{dk}$$
$$v_d \sim \mathcal{N}(0, \sigma_v^2) \tag{14.15}$$
$$\epsilon_{dk} \sim \mathcal{N}(0, \sigma_\epsilon^2) .$$

Two random variables are now involved, both with a normal distribution with mean zero: v_d, a random intercept at the domain level with variance σ_v^2, and the residuals ϵ_{dk} at the unit level with variance σ_ϵ^2. The variance σ_v^2 can

TABLE 14.6: Estimated standard error (se), bias, and root mean squared error (RMSE) of the regression estimator (reg) and the synthetic estimator (syn) of the mean AGB of ecoregions in Eastern Amazonia. The regression estimator is design-unbiased, so the RMSE of the regression estimator is equal to its standard error.

Ecoregion	RMSE reg	se syn	bias syn	RMSE syn
Amazon-Orinoco Carib. mangroves	48.8	3.7	96.2	96.3
Cerrado	14.2	7.1	-17.3	18.7
Guianan highland moist forests	29.4	4.9	-1.2	5.0
Guianan lowland moist forests	15.9	4.8	-7.2	8.7
Guianan savanna	25.9	4.1	12.3	13.0
Gurupa varzea	71.8	3.7	119.4	119.5
Madeira-Tapajos moist forests	11.8	4.9	-2.2	5.4
Marajo varzea	18.1	3.8	74.4	74.5
Maranhao Babassu forests	19.7	5.7	3.9	6.9
Mato Grosso tropical dry forests	24.5	5.8	3.4	6.7
Monte Alegre varzea	57.5	3.9	50.6	50.8
Purus-Madeira moist forests	42.1	4.2	32.9	33.1
Tapajos-Xingu moist forests	7.3	4.4	-18.5	19.0
Tocantins/Pindare moist forests	9.5	4.0	14.7	15.3
Uatuma-Trombetas moist forests	5.6	4.5	-14.2	14.9
Xingu-Toc.-Arag. moist forests	8.5	3.7	-2.5	4.4

be interpreted as a measure of the heterogeneity among the domains after accounting for the fixed effect (Breidenbach and Astrup, 2012). With this model, the mean of a domain can be predicted by

$$\hat{\bar{z}}_{\mathrm{mb},d} = \bar{\mathbf{x}}_d^{\mathrm{T}} \hat{\boldsymbol{\beta}} + \hat{v}_d \,, \qquad (14.16)$$

with $\hat{\boldsymbol{\beta}}$ the best linear unbiased estimates (BLUE) of the regression coefficients and $\hat{v}_d$ the best linear unbiased prediction (BLUP) of the intercept for domain d, v_d. The model-based predictor can also be written as

$$\hat{\bar{z}}_{\mathrm{mb},d} = \bar{\mathbf{x}}_d^{\mathrm{T}} \hat{\boldsymbol{\beta}} + \lambda_d \left(\frac{1}{n_d} \sum_{k \in \mathcal{S}_d} \epsilon_{dk} \right) \,, \qquad (14.17)$$

with λ_d a weight for the second term that corrects for the bias of the synthetic estimator. This weight is computed by

$$\lambda_d = \frac{\hat{\sigma}_v^2}{\hat{\sigma}_v^2 + \hat{\sigma}_\epsilon^2/n_d} \,. \qquad (14.18)$$

This equation shows that the larger the estimated residual variance $\hat{\sigma}_{\epsilon}^{2}$, the smaller the weight for the bias correction factor, and the larger the sample size n_{d}, the larger the weight. Comparing Equations (14.16) and (14.17) shows that the random intercept of a domain is predicted by the sample mean of the residuals of that domain, multiplied by a weight factor computed by Equation (14.18).

The means of the small domains can be computed with function `eblup.mse.f.wrap` of package **JoSAE** (Breidenbach, 2018). It requires as input a linear mixed model generated with function `lme` of package **nlme** (Pinheiro et al., 2021). The simple random sample of size 200 selected before is used to fit the linear mixed model, with lnSWIR2 as a fixed effect, i.e., the effect of lnSWIR2 on the mean AGB. The random effect is added by assigning another formula to argument `random`. The formula `~ 1 | Ecoregion` means that the intercept is treated as a random variable and that it varies among the ecoregions. This linear mixed model is referred to as a random intercept model: the intercepts are allowed to differ among the small domains, whereas the effects of the covariates, lnSWIR2 in our case, is equal for all domains.

Tibble `grdAmazonia` is converted to a `data.frame` to avoid problems with function `eblup.mse.f.wrap` hereafter. A simple random sample with replacement of size 200 is selected.

```
grdAmazonia <- grdAmazonia %>%
  as.data.frame() %>%
  mutate(x1 = x1 /1000,
         x2 = x2 / 1000)
set.seed(314)
mysample <- grdAmazonia %>%
  dplyr::select(x1, x2, AGB, lnSWIR2, Ecoregion) %>%
  slice_sample(n = n, replace = TRUE)
```

```
library(nlme)
library(JoSAE)
lmm_AGB <- lme(fixed = AGB ~ lnSWIR2, data = mysample, random = ~ 1 | Ecoregion)
```

The fixed effects of the linear mixed model can be extracted with function `fixed.effects`.

```
fixed_lmm <- fixed.effects(lmm_AGB)
```

The fixed effects of the linear mixed model differ somewhat from the fixed effects in the simple linear regression model (fixed_lm):

```
              fixed_lm fixed_lmm
(Intercept) 1778.1959 1667.9759
lnSWIR2      -241.1567 -225.6561
```

The random effect can be extracted with function `random.effects`.

```
random.effects(lmm_AGB)
```

	(Intercept)
Cerrado	21.439891
Guianan highland moist forests	6.397816
Guianan lowland moist forests	5.547995
Gurupa varzea	-52.985839
Madeira-Tapajos moist forests	27.479921
Marajo varzea	-50.587786
Maranhao Babassu forests	-1.702322
Mato Grosso tropical dry forests	18.812207
Monte Alegre varzea	-12.201148
Purus-Madeira moist forests	-9.320683
Tapajos-Xingu moist forests	28.760508
Tocantins/Pindare moist forests	-8.940962
Uatuma-Trombetas moist forests	16.165017
Xingu-Tocantins-Araguaia moist forests	11.135385

The random intercepts are added to the fixed intercept; the coefficient of lnSWIR2 is the same for all ecoregions:

```
coef(lmm_AGB)
```

	(Intercept)	lnSWIR2
Cerrado	1689.416	-225.6561
Guianan highland moist forests	1674.374	-225.6561
Guianan lowland moist forests	1673.524	-225.6561
Gurupa varzea	1614.990	-225.6561
Madeira-Tapajos moist forests	1695.456	-225.6561
Marajo varzea	1617.388	-225.6561
Maranhao Babassu forests	1666.274	-225.6561
Mato Grosso tropical dry forests	1686.788	-225.6561
Monte Alegre varzea	1655.775	-225.6561
Purus-Madeira moist forests	1658.655	-225.6561
Tapajos-Xingu moist forests	1696.736	-225.6561
Tocantins/Pindare moist forests	1659.035	-225.6561
Uatuma-Trombetas moist forests	1684.141	-225.6561
Xingu-Tocantins-Araguaia moist forests	1679.111	-225.6561

The fitted model can now be used to predict the means of the ecoregions as follows. As a first step, a data frame must be defined, with the size and the population mean of the covariate lnSWIR2 per domain. This data frame is passed to function eblup.mse.f.wrap with argument domain.data. This function computes the model-based prediction, as well as the regression estimator (Equation (14.7)) and the synthetic estimator (Equation (14.13)) and their variances. The model-based predictor is the variable EBLUP in the output data frame. For the model-based predictor, two standard errors are computed, see Breidenbach and Astrup (2012) for details.

```
N_eco <- tapply(grdAmazonia$AGB, INDEX = grdAmazonia$Ecoregion, FUN = length)
df_eco <- data.frame(Ecoregion = ecoregions, N = N_eco, lnSWIR2 = mx_eco_pop)
res <- eblup.mse.f.wrap(domain.data = df_eco, lme.obj = lmm_AGB)
df <- data.frame(Ecoregion = res$domain.ID, mb = res$EBLUP,
  se.1 = res$EBLUP.se.1, se.2 = res$EBLUP.se.2)
```

Table 14.7 shows the model-based predictions and the estimated standard errors of the mean AGB of the ecoregions, obtained with the random intercept model.

TABLE 14.7: Model-based predictions of the mean AGB (10^9 kg ha^{-1}) of ecoregions in Eastern Amazonia, for simple random sample without replacement of size 200, obtained with the random intercept model and lnSWIR2 as a predictor.

Ecoregion	AGB	se.1	se.2
Cerrado	101.9	11.4	11.5
Guianan highland moist forests	271.1	25.8	26.4
Guianan lowland moist forests	269.1	25.8	26.4
Gurupa varzea	155.3	36.0	31.8
Madeira-Tapajos moist forests	292.8	9.3	9.3
Marajo varzea	169.3	13.6	13.2
Maranhao Babassu forests	113.1	14.1	14.4
Mato Grosso tropical dry forests	129.6	22.9	23.1
Monte Alegre varzea	218.9	22.2	22.7
Purus-Madeira moist forests	229.0	22.2	22.7
Tapajos-Xingu moist forests	277.2	6.7	6.7
Tocantins/Pindare moist forests	159.6	7.4	7.5
Uatuma-Trombetas moist forests	270.2	6.0	6.0
Xingu-Tocantins-Araguaia moist forests	222.9	7.5	7.6

se.1 and se.2 are standard errors, for explanation see text.

Note that with this model no predictions of the mean AGB are obtained for the unsampled ecoregions. This is because the random intercept v_d cannot be predicted in the absence of data, see Equations (14.16) and (14.17).

14.3.2   Geostatistical model

In a geostatistical model, there is only one random variable, the residual of the model-mean, not two random variables as in the random intercept model. See Equation (21.2) for a geostatistical model with a constant mean and Equation (21.16) for a model with a mean that is a linear combination of covariates. In a geostatistical model, the covariance of the residuals of the mean at two locations is modelled as a function of the distance (and direction) of the points. Instead of the covariance, often the semivariance is modelled, i.e., half the variance of the difference of the residuals at two locations, see Chapter 21 for details.

The simple random sample of size 200 selected before is used to estimate the regression coefficients for the mean, an intercept, and a slope coefficient for lnSWIR2, and besides the parameters of a spherical semivariogram model for the residuals of the mean. The two regression coefficients and the three semivariogram parameters are estimated by restricted maximum likelihood (REML), see Subsection 21.5.2. This estimation procedure is also used in function lme to fit the random intercept model. Here, function likfit of package **geoR** (Ribeiro Jr et al., 2020) is used to estimate the model parameters. First, a geoR object must be generated with function as.geodata.

```
library(geoR)
dGeoR <- as.geodata(mysample, header = TRUE,
    coords.col = c("x1", "x2"), data.col = "AGB", covar.col = "lnSWIR2")
vgm_REML <- likfit(geodata = dGeoR, trend = ~ lnSWIR2,
    cov.model = "spherical",
    ini.cov.pars = c(600, 600), nugget = 1500,
    lik.method = "REML", messages = FALSE)
```

The estimated intercept and slope are 1,744 and -236.5, respectively. The estimated semivariogram parameters are 1,623 (10^9 kg ha^{-1})^2, 700 (10^9 kg ha^{-1})^2, and 652 km for the nugget, partial sill, and range, respectively. These model parameters are used to predict AGB for all units in the population, using function krige of package **gstat** (Pebesma, 2004). The REML estimates of the semivariogram parameters are passed to function vgm with arguments nugget, psill, and range. The coordinates of the sample are shifted to a random point within a 1 km × 1 km grid cell. This is done to avoid the coincidence of a sampling point and a prediction point, which leads to an error message when predicting AGB at the nodes of the grid.

```
library(gstat)
mysample$x1 <- jitter(mysample$x1, amount = 0.5)
mysample$x2 <- jitter(mysample$x2, amount = 0.5)
coordinates(mysample) <- ~ x1 + x2
vgm_REML_gstat <- vgm(model = "Sph",
  nugget = vgm_REML$nugget, psill = vgm_REML$sigmasq, range = vgm_REML$phi)
coordinates(grdAmazonia) <- ~ x1 + x2
predictions  <- krige(
  formula = AGB ~ lnSWIR2,
  locations = mysample,
  newdata = grdAmazonia,
  model = vgm_REML_gstat,
  debug.level = 0) %>% as("data.frame")
```

The first six rows of `predictions` are shown below.

```
        x1        x2 var1.pred var1.var
1 -6628.193 188.4642  295.8800 1987.472
2 -6627.193 188.4642  294.8188 1986.125
3 -6626.193 188.4642  287.2958 1984.268
4 -6625.193 188.4642  280.1586 1982.756
5 -6624.193 188.4642  290.3905 1982.185
6 -6623.193 188.4642  299.5091 1982.027
```

Besides a prediction (variable `var1.pred`), for every population unit the variance of the prediction error is computed (`var1.var`). The unitwise predictions can be averaged across all units of an ecoregion to obtain a model-based prediction of the mean of that ecoregion.

```
AGBpred_unit <- predictions$var1.pred
mz_eco_mb <- tapply(AGBpred_unit, INDEX = grdAmazonia$Ecoregion,
                    FUN = mean) %>% round(1)
```

A difficulty is the computation of the standard error of these model-based predictions of the ecoregion mean. We cannot simply sum the unitwise variances and divide the sum by the squared number of units, because the prediction errors of units with a mutual distance smaller than the estimated range of the spherical semivariogram are correlated. A straightforward approach to obtain the standard error of the predicted mean is geostatistical simulation. A large number of maps are simulated, conditional on the selected sample. For an infinite number of maps, the "average map", i.e., the map obtained by averaging for each unit all simulated values of that unit, is equal to the map with predicted AGB. For each simulated map, the average of the simulated values across all units of an ecoregion is computed. This results in as many averages as we have simulated maps. The variance of the averages of an ecoregion is an estimate of the variance of the predicted mean of that ecoregion. To reduce computing time, a 5 km × 5 km subgrid of grdAmazonia is used in the geostatistical simulation.

```
grdAmazonia <- read_rds(file = "results/grdAmazonia_5km.rds")
grdAmazonia <- grdAmazonia %>%
  mutate(lnSWIR2 = log(SWIR2))
nsim <- 1000
coordinates(grdAmazonia) <- ~ x1 + x2
simulations  <- krige(
  formula = AGB ~ lnSWIR2,
  locations = mysample,
  newdata = grdAmazonia,
  model = vgm_REML_gstat,
  nmax = 100, nsim = nsim,
  debug.level = 0) %>% as("data.frame")
grdAmazonia <- as_tibble(grdAmazonia)
AGBsim_eco <- matrix(nrow = length(ecoregions), ncol = nsim)
for (i in 1:nsim) {
  AGBsim_eco[, i] <- tapply(simulations[, i + 2],
    INDEX = grdAmazonia$Ecoregion, FUN = mean)
}
```

Similar to the synthetic estimator, for all ecoregions an estimate of the mean AGB is obtained, also for the unsampled ecoregions (Table 14.8). The model-based prediction is strongly correlated with the synthetic estimate (Figure 14.2).

The most striking difference is the standard error. The standard errors of the synthetic estimator range from 3.7 to 7.1 (Table 14.6), whereas the standard errors of the geostatistical predictions range from 6.2 to 28.1. However, these two standard errors are fundamentally different and should not be compared. The standard error of the synthetic estimator is a *sampling* standard error, i.e., it quantifies the variation of the estimated mean of an ecoregion over repeated random sampling with the sampling design, in this case simple random sampling of 200 units. The model-based standard error is not a sampling standard error but a model standard error, which expresses our uncertainty about the means of the domains due to our imperfect knowledge of the spatial variation of AGB. Given the observations of AGB at the selected sample, the map with the covariate lnSWIR2, and the estimated semivariogram model parameters, we are uncertain about the exact value of AGB at unsampled units. No samples are considered other than the one actually selected. For the fundamental difference between design-based, model-assisted, and model-based estimates of means, refer to Section 1.2 and Chapter 26.

TABLE 14.8: Model-based predictions of the mean AGB (10^9 kg ha^{-1}) of ecoregions in Eastern Amazonia, using a simple random sample without replacement of size 200, obtained with the geostatistical model and lnSWIR2 as a predictor for the mean.

Ecoregion	AGB	se
Amazon-Orinoco-Southern Caribbean mangroves	191.1	22.4
Cerrado	96.8	12.1
Guianan highland moist forests	299.1	28.1
Guianan lowland moist forests	279.3	16.4
Guianan savanna	166.1	10.2
Gurupa varzea	201.2	15.6
Madeira-Tapajos moist forests	287.0	8.6
Marajo varzea	194.6	11.3
Maranhao Babassu forests	121.6	12.0
Mato Grosso tropical dry forests	121.4	11.7
Monte Alegre varzea	241.4	10.8
Purus-Madeira moist forests	229.0	24.3
Tapajos-Xingu moist forests	273.8	8.2
Tocantins/Pindare moist forests	163.0	6.8
Uatuma-Trombetas moist forests	265.9	6.4
Xingu-Tocantins-Araguaia moist forests	220.0	6.2

se: standard error of predicted mean.

It makes more sense to compare the two model-based predictions, the random intercept model predictions and the geostatistical predictions, and their standard errors. Figure 14.3 shows that the two model-based predictions are very similar.

For four ecoregions, the standard errors of the geostatistical model predictions are much smaller than those of the random intercept model predictions (Figure 14.4). These are ecoregions with small sample sizes.

If a different semivariogram model were used, both the predicted means per ecoregion and the standard errors would be different. Especially the variance is sensitive to the semivariogram. For this reason, the model-based predictions are also referred to as model-dependent predictions, see Chapter 26.

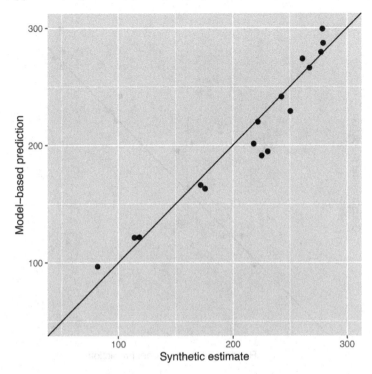

FIGURE 14.2: Scatter plot of the model-based prediction and the synthetic estimate of the mean AGB (10^9 kg ha^{-1}) of ecoregions in Eastern Amazonia. The solid line is the 1:1 line.

14.4 Supplemental probability sampling of small domains

The sample size in small domains of interest can be so small that no reliable statistical estimate of the mean or total of these domains can be obtained. In this case, we may decide to collect a supplemental sample from these domains. It is convenient to use these domains as strata in supplemental probability sampling, so that we can control the sample sizes in the strata. If we can safely assume that the study variable at the units of the first sample are not changed, there is no need to revisit these units; otherwise, we must revisit them to observe the current values.

There are two approaches for using the two probability samples to estimate the population mean or total of a small domain (Grafström et al., 2019). In the first approach, the two samples are combined, and then the merged sample

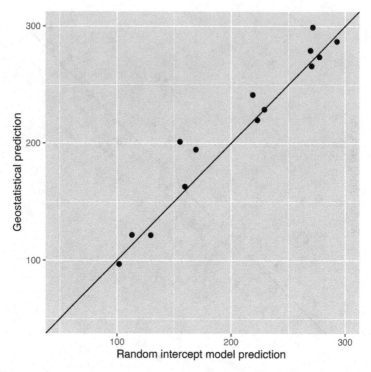

FIGURE 14.3: Scatter plot of model-based predictions of the mean AGB (10^9 kg ha^{-1}) of ecoregions in Eastern Amazonia, obtained with the random intercept model and the geostatistical model. The solid line is the 1:1 line.

is used to estimate the population mean or total. In the second approach, the samples are not combined, but the two estimates from the separate samples. In this section only the first approach is illustrated with a simple situation in which the two samples are easily combined. Refer to Grafström et al. (2019) for a more general approach of how multiple probability samples can be combined.

Suppose that the original sample is a simple random sample from the entire study area. A supplemental sample is selected from small domains, i.e., domains that have few selected units only. For a given small domain, the first sample is supplemented by selecting a simple random sample from the units not yet selected in the first sample. The size of the supplemental sample of a domain depends on the number of units of that domain in the first sample. The first sample is supplemented so that the total sample size of that domain is fixed. In this case, the combined sample of a domain is a simple random sample from that domain, so that the usual estimators for simple random sampling can be used to estimate the domain mean or total and its standard error.

This sampling strategy is illustrated with Eastern Amazonia. A simple random sample without replacement of 400 units is selected.

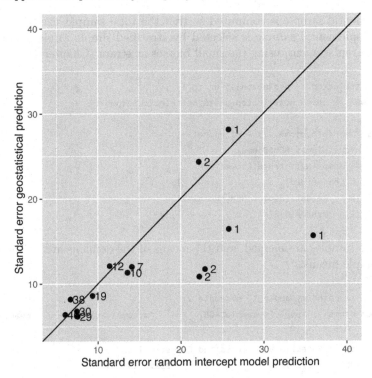

FIGURE 14.4: Scatter plot of the estimated standard error of model-based predictions of the mean AGB (10^9 kg ha^{-1}) of ecoregions obtained with the random intercept model and the geostatistical model, using a simple random sample without replacement of size 200 from Eastern Amazonia. The numbers refer to the number of sampling units in an ecoregion. The solid line is the 1:1 line.

```
grdAmazonia$Biome <- as.factor(grdAmazonia$Biome)
biomes <- c("Mangrove", "Forest_dry", "Grassland", "Forest_moist")
levels(grdAmazonia$Biome) <- biomes
n1 <- 400
set.seed(123)
units_1 <- sample(nrow(grdAmazonia), size = n1, replace = FALSE)
mysample_1 <- grdAmazonia[units_1, c("AGB", "Biome")]
print(n1_biome <- table(mysample_1$Biome))
```

```
  Mangrove   Forest_dry   Grassland Forest_moist
         2            9          26          363
```

The selected units are removed from the sampling frame. For each of the three small biomes, Mangrove, Forest_dry, and Grassland, the size of the supplemental sample is computed so that the total sample size becomes 40. The supplemental sample is selected by stratified simple random sampling without replacement, using the small biomes as strata (Chapter 4).

```
units_notselected <- grdAmazonia[-units_1, ]
Biomes_NFM <- units_notselected[units_notselected$Biome != "Forest_moist", ]
n_biome <- 40
n2_biome <- rep(n_biome, 3) - n1_biome[-4]
ord <- unique(Biomes_NFM$Biome)
units_2 <- sampling::strata(Biomes_NFM, stratanames = "Biome",
  size = n2_biome[ord], method = "srswor")
mysample_2 <- getdata(Biomes_NFM, units_2)
mysample_2 <- mysample_2[c("AGB", "Biome")]
```

The two samples are merged, and the means of the domains are estimated by the sample means.

```
mysample <- rbind(mysample_1, mysample_2)
print(mz_biome <- tapply(mysample$AGB, INDEX = mysample$Biome, FUN = mean))
```

```
  Mangrove    Forest_dry    Grassland Forest_moist
 112.8000      122.1750     123.6250     233.6749
```

Finally, the standard error is estimated, accounting for sampling without replacement from a finite population (Equation (3.15)).

```
N_biome <- table(grdAmazonia$Biome)
fpc <- (1 - n_biome / N_biome)
S2z_biome <- tapply(mysample$AGB, INDEX = mysample$Biome, FUN = var)
print(se_mz_biome <- sqrt(fpc * (S2z_biome / n_biome)))
```

```
  Mangrove    Forest_dry    Grassland Forest_moist
  5.227434      8.213407    11.709257    13.937597
```

This sampling approach and estimation are repeated 10,000 times, i.e., a simple random sample without replacement of size 400 is selected 10,000 times from Eastern Amazonia, and the samples from the three small domains are supplemented so that the total sample sizes in these domains become 40. In two out of the 10,000 samples, the size of the first sample in one of the domains exceeded 40 units. These two samples are discarded. Ideally, these samples are not discarded, but their sizes in the small domains are reduced to 40 units, which are then used to estimate the means of the domains.

For all three small domains, the average of the 10,000 estimated means of AGB is about equal to the true mean (Table 14.9). Also the mean of the 10,000 estimated standard errors is very close to the standard deviation of the 10,000

TABLE 14.9: Summary statistics of 10,000 estimated means of AGB (10^9 kg ha^{-1}) of small domains (biomes) in Eastern Amazonia, estimated by combining a simple random sample without replacement of size 400 from all units and a supplemental stratified simple random sample without replacement from the units in the small domains not included in the simple random sample. The total sample size per small domain is 40.

	Mangrove	Dry forest	Grassland
Average of estimated means	122.476	113.983	114.462
True means	122.494	113.931	114.390
Standard deviation of estimated means	6.186	7.563	10.986
Average of estimated standard errors	6.169	7.450	10.946
Coverage rate 95%	0.950	0.937	0.945
Coverage rate 90%	0.903	0.888	0.896
Coverage rate 80%	0.801	0.792	0.799

estimated means. The coverage rates of 95, 90, and 80% confidence intervals are about equal to the nominal coverage rates.

This simple approach is feasible because at the domain level the two merged samples are a simple random sample. This approach is also applicable when the first sample is a stratified simple random sample from the entire population, and the supplemental sample is a stratified simple random sample from a small domain using as strata the intersections of the strata used in the first phase and that domain.

15

Repeated sample surveys for monitoring population parameters

The previous chapters are all about sampling to estimate population parameters *at a given time*. The survey is done in a relatively short period of time, so that we can safely assume that the study variable has not changed during that period. This chapter is about repeating the sample survey two or more times, to estimate, for instance, a temporal change in a population parameter. Sampling locations are selected by probability sampling, by any design type. In most cases, sampling times are not selected randomly, but purposively. For instance, to monitor the carbon stock in the soil of a country, we may decide to repeat the survey after five years, in the same season of the year as the first survey.

15.1 Space-time designs

An overview of space-time designs is presented by de Gruijter et al. (2006). Five of these designs are schematically shown in Figure 15.1. With repeated sampling in two-dimensional space, there are three dimensions: two spatial dimensions and one time dimension. Sampling locations shown in Figure 15.1 are selected by simple random sampling, but this is not essential for the space-time designs.

In the static-synchronous (SS) design, referred to as a pure panel by Fuller (1999), all sampling locations selected in the first survey are revisited in all subsequent surveys. On the contrary, in an independent synchronous (IS) design, a probability sample is selected in each survey independently from the samples selected in the previous surveys. The serially alternating (SA) design is a compromise between an SS and an IS design. The sample selected in the first survey is revisited in the third survey. The sample of the second survey is selected independently from the sample of the first survey, and these locations are revisited in the fourth survey. In this case, the period of revisits is two, i.e., two sampling intervals between consecutive surveys, but this can also be increased. For instance, with a period of three, three samples are selected,

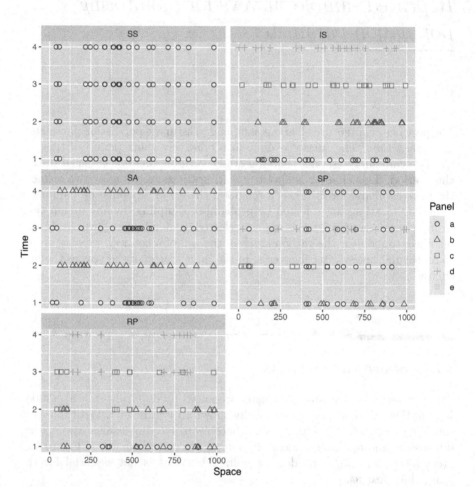

FIGURE 15.1: Space-time designs for monitoring population parameters. The sampling locations in 2D are plotted in one dimension, along the horizontal axis. A selected unit along this axis actually represents a sampling location in 2D. Twenty sampling locations are selected by simple random sampling. SS: static-synchronous design; IS: independent synchronous design; SA: serially alternating design; SP: supplemented panel design; RP: rotating panel design.

independently from each other, for the first three surveys, and these samples are revisited in subsequent surveys.

Two other compromise designs are a supplemented panel (SP) design and a rotating panel (RP) design. In an SP design only a subset of the sampling locations of the first survey is revisited in the subsequent surveys. These are the permanent sampling locations observed in all subsequent surveys. The permanent sampling locations are supplemented by samples that are selected independently from the samples in the previous surveys. In Figure 15.1, half of the sampling locations (ten locations) is permanent (panel a), i.e., revisited in all surveys, but the proportion of permanent sampling locations can be smaller or larger and, if prior information on the variation in space and time is available, even can be optimised for estimating the current mean. Also in an RP design, sampling units of the previous survey are partially replaced by new units. The difference with an SP design is that there are no permanent sampling units, i.e., no units observed in all surveys. All sampling units are sequentially rotated out and in again at the subsequent sampling times.

In Figure 15.1 the shape and colour of the symbols represent a panel. A panel is a group of sampling locations that is observed in the same surveys. In the SS design, there is only one panel. All locations are observed in all surveys, so all locations are in the same panel. In the IS design, there are as many panels as there are surveys. In the SA design with a period of two, the number of panels equals the number of surveys divided by two. In these three space-time designs (SS, IS, and SA), all sampling locations of a given survey are in the same panel. This is not the case in the SP and RP designs. In Figure 15.1 in each survey, two panels are observed. In the SP sample, there is one panel of permanent sampling locations (pure panel part of sample) and another panel of swarming sampling locations observed in one survey only. In the RP sample of Figure 15.1, the sampling locations are observed in two consecutive surveys; however, this number can be increased. For instance, in an 'in-for-three' rotational sample (McLaren and Steel, 2001) the sampling locations stay in the sample for three consecutive surveys. The number of panels per sampling time is then three. Also, similar to an SA design, in an IS, SP, and RP design we may decide after several surveys to stop selecting new sampling locations and to revisit existing locations. The concept of panels is needed hereafter in estimating space-time population parameters.

15.2 Space-time population parameters

The data of repeated surveys can be used to estimate various parameters of the space-time universe. I will focus on the mean as a parameter, but estimation of a total or proportion is straightforward, think for instance of the total amount of greenhouse gas emissions from the soil in a given study area during some period. This chapter shows how to estimate the current mean, i.e., the population mean (spatial mean) in the last survey, the change of the mean between two surveys, the temporal trend of the mean, and the space-time mean. The current mean need not be defined here as only one survey (one sampling time) is involved in this parameter, so that the definition in Subsection 1.1.1 is also relevant here.

The change of the mean is defined as the spatial mean at a given survey minus this mean at an earlier survey. For finite populations, the definition is

$$\bar{d}_{ab} = \frac{1}{N} \left(\sum_{k=1}^{N} z_k(t_b) - \sum_{k=1}^{N} z_k(t_a) \right) = \frac{1}{N} \sum_{k=1}^{N} d_{abk} , \qquad (15.1)$$

with d_{abk} the change of the study variable in the period between time t_a and t_b for unit k. For infinite populations, the sums are replaced by integrals:

$$\bar{d}_{ab} = \frac{1}{A} \left(\int_{s \in \mathcal{A}} z(s, t_b) \, ds - \int_{s \in \mathcal{A}} z(s, t_a) \, ds \right) = \frac{1}{A} \int_{s \in \mathcal{A}} d_{ab}(s) , \qquad (15.2)$$

with $d_{ab}(s)$ the change of the study variable in the period between time t_a and t_b at location s.

With more than two surveys, an interesting population parameter is the *average change per time unit* of the mean, referred to as the temporal trend of the spatial mean. It is defined as a linear combination of the spatial means at the sampling times (Breidt and Fuller, 1999):

$$b = \sum_{j=1}^{R} w_j \bar{z}_j , \qquad (15.3)$$

with R the number of sampling times, $\bar{z}_j$ the spatial mean at time t_j, and weights w_j equal to

$$w_j = \frac{t_j - \bar{t}}{\sum_{j=1}^{R} (t_j - \bar{t})^2} , \qquad (15.4)$$

with $\bar{t}$ the mean of the sampling times.

The temporal trend is defined as a parameter of a space-time population, not as a parameter of a time-series model.

A space-time mean can be defined as the average of the spatial means at the sampling times. In this definition, the temporal universe is discrete and restricted to the sampling times. The target universe consists of a finite set of spatial populations:

$$\bar{\bar{z}}_{\mathcal{U}} = \frac{1}{R} \sum_{j=1}^{R} \bar{z}_j \,. \qquad (15.5)$$

Alternatively, a space-time mean for a continuous temporal universe $\mathcal{T}$ is defined as

$$\bar{\bar{z}}_{\mathcal{U}} = \frac{1}{T} \int_{t \in \mathcal{T}} \bar{z}_t \,, \qquad (15.6)$$

with T the length of the monitoring period and $\bar{z}_t$ the spatial mean at time t.

15.3 Design-based generalised least squares estimation of spatial means

Rotational sampling has a long tradition in agronomy, forestry, and in social studies. Early papers on how sample data from previous times can be used to increase the precision of estimates of the current mean are Jessen (1942), Patterson (1950), Ware and Cunia (1962), and Woodruff (1963). Gurney and Daly (1965) developed general theory for these estimators, which I will present now.

In overlapping samples such as an SP and an RP sample, we may define one estimate of a spatial mean per 'panel'. These panel-specific estimates of the mean at a given sampling time, based on observations at that time only, are referred to as elementary estimates.

The essence of the estimation method described in this section is to estimate the spatial mean at a given time point as a weighted average of the elementary estimates *of all time points*, with the weights determined by the variances and covariances of the elementary estimates. Collecting all elementary estimates of the spatial means of the different sampling times in vector $\hat{\mathbf{z}}$, we can write

$$\hat{\mathbf{z}} = \mathbf{X}\mathbf{z} + \mathbf{e} \,, \qquad (15.7)$$

with $\mathbf{z}$ the vector of true spatial means $\bar{z}(t_1), \dots, \bar{z}(t_R)$ at the R sampling times, $\mathbf{X}$ the $(P \times R)$ design matrix with zeroes and ones that selects the appropriate elements from $\mathbf{z}$ (P is the total number of elementary estimates), and $\mathbf{e}$ the P-vector of sampling errors with variance-covariance matrix $\mathbf{C}$. With unbiased elementary estimators, the expectation of $\mathbf{e}$ is a vector with zeroes.

With an SS, IS, and SA design, the design matrix $\mathbf{X}$ is the identity matrix of size R, i.e., an $R \times R$ square matrix with ones on the diagonal and zeroes in all off-diagonal entries. For the SP design of Figure 15.1, the design matrix $\mathbf{X}$ is

$$\mathbf{X} = \begin{bmatrix} 1 & 0 & 0 & 0 \\ 0 & 1 & 0 & 0 \\ 0 & 0 & 1 & 0 \\ 0 & 0 & 0 & 1 \\ 1 & 0 & 0 & 0 \\ 0 & 1 & 0 & 0 \\ 0 & 0 & 1 & 0 \\ 0 & 0 & 0 & 1 \end{bmatrix} . \tag{15.8}$$

The first four rows of this matrix are associated with the elementary estimates of the spatial means at the four sampling times, estimated from panel a, the panel with permanent sampling locations. Hereafter, this panel is referred to as the static-synchronous subsample. The remaining rows correspond to the elementary estimates from the other four panels, the swarming locations, hereafter referred to as the independent-synchronous subsamples. For the RP design of Figure 15.1, the design matrix equals

$$\mathbf{X} = \begin{bmatrix} 1 & 0 & 0 & 0 \\ 1 & 0 & 0 & 0 \\ 0 & 1 & 0 & 0 \\ 0 & 1 & 0 & 0 \\ 0 & 0 & 1 & 0 \\ 0 & 0 & 1 & 0 \\ 0 & 0 & 0 & 1 \\ 0 & 0 & 0 & 1 \end{bmatrix} . \tag{15.9}$$

The first two rows correspond to the two elementary estimates of the mean at time t_1 from panels a and b, the third and fourth rows correspond to the elementary estimate at time t_2 from panels b and c, respectively, etc.

The minimum variance linear unbiased estimator (MVLUE) of the spatial means at the different times is the design-based generalised least squares (GLS) estimator (Binder and Hidiroglou, 1988):

$$\hat{\mathbf{z}}_{\mathrm{GLS}} = (\mathbf{X}^T \mathbf{C}^{-1} \mathbf{X})^{-1} \mathbf{X}^T \mathbf{C}^{-1} \hat{\mathbf{z}} . \tag{15.10}$$

To define matrix $\mathbf{C}$ for the SP design in Figure 15.1, let $\hat{\bar{z}}_{jp}$ denote the estimated mean at time $t_j, j = 1, 2, 3, 4$ in subsample $p, p \in (a, b, c, d, e)$, with panel a the permanent sampling locations (SS subsample) and panels b, c, d, e the swarming sampling locations (IS subsamples). If the eight elementary estimates in $\hat{\mathbf{z}}$ are ordered as $(\hat{\bar{z}}_{1a}, \hat{\bar{z}}_{2a}, \hat{\bar{z}}_{3a}, \hat{\bar{z}}_{4a}, \hat{\bar{z}}_{1b}, \hat{\bar{z}}_{2c}, \hat{\bar{z}}_{3d}, \hat{\bar{z}}_{4e})$, the variance-covariance matrix $\mathbf{C}$ equals

$$
\mathbf{C} = \begin{bmatrix}
V_{1a} & C_{1,2} & C_{1,3} & C_{1,4} & 0 & 0 & 0 & 0 \\
C_{2,1} & V_{2a} & C_{2,3} & C_{2,4} & 0 & 0 & 0 & 0 \\
C_{3,1} & C_{3,2} & V_{3a} & C_{3,4} & 0 & 0 & 0 & 0 \\
C_{4,1} & C_{4,2} & C_{4,3} & V_{4a} & 0 & 0 & 0 & 0 \\
0 & 0 & 0 & 0 & V_{1b} & 0 & 0 & 0 \\
0 & 0 & 0 & 0 & 0 & V_{2c} & 0 & 0 \\
0 & 0 & 0 & 0 & 0 & 0 & V_{3d} & 0 \\
0 & 0 & 0 & 0 & 0 & 0 & 0 & V_{4e}
\end{bmatrix}. \tag{15.11}
$$

The covariances of the elementary estimates of the IS subsamples are zero because these are estimated from independently selected samples (off-diagonal elements in lower right (4×4) submatrix). Also the covariances of the elementary estimates from the SS subsample and an IS subsample are zero for the same reason (upper right submatrix and lower left submatrix). The covariances of the four elementary estimates from the SS subsample are not zero because these are estimated from the same set of sampling locations.

Ordering the elementary estimates of the RP sample by the sampling times, the variance-covariance matrix equals

$$
\mathbf{C} = \begin{bmatrix}
V_{1a} & 0 & 0 & 0 & 0 & 0 & 0 & 0 \\
0 & V_{1b} & C_{1,2} & 0 & 0 & 0 & 0 & 0 \\
0 & C_{2,1} & V_{2b} & 0 & 0 & 0 & 0 & 0 \\
0 & 0 & 0 & V_{2c} & C_{2,3} & 0 & 0 & 0 \\
0 & 0 & 0 & C_{3,2} & V_{3c} & 0 & 0 & 0 \\
0 & 0 & 0 & 0 & 0 & V_{3d} & C_{3,4} & 0 \\
0 & 0 & 0 & 0 & 0 & C_{4,3} & V_{4d} & 0 \\
0 & 0 & 0 & 0 & 0 & 0 & 0 & V_{4e}
\end{bmatrix}. \tag{15.12}
$$

Only the elementary estimates of the same panel are correlated, for instance the elementary estimates of the spatial means at times t_1 and t_2, estimated from panel b.

For the SA design of Figure 15.1 the variance-covariance matrix equals (there is only one estimate per time)

$$
\mathbf{C} = \begin{bmatrix}
V_1 & 0 & C_{1,3} & 0 \\
0 & V_2 & 0 & C_{2,4} \\
C_{3,1} & 0 & V_3 & 0 \\
0 & C_{4,2} & 0 & V_4
\end{bmatrix}. \tag{15.13}
$$

In practice, matrix $\mathbf{C}$ in Equation (15.10) is unknown and is replaced by a matrix with design-based estimates of the variances and covariances of the elementary estimators. With simple random sampling with replacement from finite populations and simple random sampling of infinite populations, the variance of an elementary estimator of the spatial mean at a given time can be estimated by Equation (3.14). The covariance of the elementary estimators of the spatial means at two sampling times, using the data of the same panel, can be estimated by

$$\widehat{C}_{ab} = \frac{\widehat{S^2}_{ab}}{m} , \qquad (15.14)$$

with m the number of sampling locations in the panel and $\widehat{S^2}_{ab}$ the estimated covariance of the study variable at times t_a and t_b, estimated by

$$\widehat{S^2}_{ab} = \frac{1}{m-1} \sum_{k=1}^{m} (z_{apk} - \hat{\bar{z}}_{ap})(z_{bpk} - \hat{\bar{z}}_{bp}) , \qquad (15.15)$$

with z_{apk} the study variable of unit k in panel p at time t_a and $\hat{\bar{z}}_{ap}$ the spatial mean at time t_a as estimated from panel p.

The variances and covariances of the GLS estimators of the spatial means at the R sampling times can be estimated by

$$\mathrm{Cov}(\hat{\mathbf{z}}_{\mathrm{GLS}}) = (\mathbf{X}^\mathsf{T}\widehat{\mathbf{C}}^{-1}\mathbf{X})^{-1} . \qquad (15.16)$$

Given the design-based GLS estimates of the spatial means at the different times, it is an easy job to compute the estimated change of the mean between two surveys, the estimated temporal trend of the mean, and the estimated space-time mean.

15.3.1   Current mean

As explained above, with the SS, IS, and SA designs, the design matrix $\mathbf{X}$ is the identity matrix of size R. From this it follows that for these space-time designs $\hat{\mathbf{z}}_{\mathrm{GLS}} = \hat{\mathbf{z}}$, see Equation (15.10), and $\mathrm{Cov}(\hat{\mathbf{z}}_{\mathrm{GLS}}) = \mathrm{Cov}(\hat{\mathbf{z}}) = \mathbf{C}$. In words, the GLS estimator of the spatial mean at a given time equals the usual π estimator of the mean at that time, and the variance-covariance matrix of the GLS estimators of the spatial means equals the variance-covariance matrix of the π estimators.

With SP and RP sampling in space-time, there is partial overlap between the samples at the different times, and so the samples at the previous times can be used to increase the precision of the estimated mean at the last time (current mean). The estimated current mean is simply the last element in $\hat{\mathbf{z}}_{\text{GLS}}$. The estimated variance of the estimator of the current mean is the element in the final row and final column of the variance-covariance matrix of the estimated spatial means (Equation (15.16)). These two space-time designs with partial replacement of sampling locations may yield a more precise estimate of the current mean than the other three space-time designs.

15.3.2   Change of the spatial mean

The change of the spatial mean between two sampling times can simply be estimated by subtracting the estimated spatial means at these two times. With the SS, IS, and SA designs, these means are estimated by the π estimators. With the SP and RP designs, the two spatial means are estimated by the GLS estimators. The variance of the estimator of the change can be estimated by the sum of the estimated variances of the spatial mean estimators at the two sampling times, minus two times the estimated covariance of the two estimators. The covariance is maximal when all sampling locations are revisited, leading to the most precise estimate of the change of the spatial mean. With SP and RP sampling, the covariance of the two spatial mean estimators is smaller, and so the variance of the change estimator is larger.

15.3.3   Temporal trend of the spatial mean

The temporal trend of the mean is estimated by the weighted average of the (GLS) estimated means at $t_1, \ldots, t_R$, with weights equal to Equation (15.4):

$$\hat{b} = \sum_{j=1}^{R} w_j \hat{\bar{z}}_{\text{GLS},j} \, . \tag{15.17}$$

The variance of the estimator of the temporal trend can be estimated by

$$\widehat{V}(\hat{b}) = \mathbf{w}' \widehat{\mathbf{C}}(\hat{\mathbf{z}}_{\text{GLS}}) \mathbf{w} \, . \tag{15.18}$$

Brus and de Gruijter (2011) compared the space-time designs for estimating the temporal trend of the spatial means, under a first order autoregressive time-series model of the spatial means. The SS design performed best when the correlation is strong, say > 0.8. What is the best design depends amongst others on the strength of the correlation and the number of sampling times. A safe choice is an SA design. With strong positive correlation, say > 0.9, the SS design can be a good choice, but remarkably for weak positive correlation this design performed relatively poorly.

For an application of an SP design to estimate the temporal trend of the areal fractions of several vegetation types, see Brus et al. (2014). Sampling locations are selected by a design that spreads the locations evenly over the study area (systematic unaligned sampling, which is a modified version of systematic sampling).

15.3.4   Space-time mean

The space-time mean, as defined in Equation (15.5), can be estimated by the average of the (GLS) estimated spatial means at the R sampling times. The variance of this estimator can be estimated by Equation (15.18) using constant weights, equal to $1/R$, for the R estimators of the mean. An IS design yields the most precise estimate of the space-time mean compared to the other space-time designs when the correlation of collocated measurements of the study variable is positive (Cochran, 1977). With the other space-time designs, there is redundant information due to the revisits.

For design-based estimation of the space-time mean of a continuous temporal universe as defined in Equation (15.6), both the sampling locations and the sampling times must be selected by probability sampling. Figure 15.2 shows an SS sample and an IS sample of twenty locations and six times, where both locations and times are selected by simple random sampling.

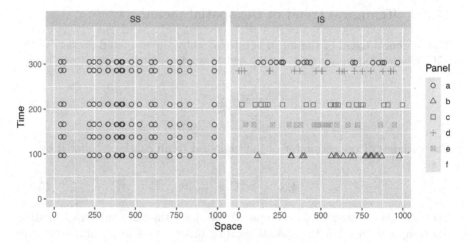

FIGURE 15.2: Space-time designs for estimating the space-time mean of a continuous temporal universe. Both locations and times are selected by simple random sampling. SS: static-synchronous design; IS: independent synchronous design.

An IS sample in which both locations and times are selected by probability sampling can be considered as a two-stage cluster random sample from a space-time universe (Chapter 7). The primary sampling units (PSUs) are the spatial sections of that universe (horizontal lines in Figure 15.2), the secondary sampling units (SSUs) are the sampling locations. The space-time mean can therefore be estimated by Equation (7.2), and its variance by Equation (7.7). For simple random sampling, both in space and in time, and a linear costs model $C = c_0 + c_1 n + c_2 nm$ Equations (7.9) and (7.10) can be used to optimise the number of sampling times (PSUs, n) and the number of sampling locations (SSUs, m) per time. The pooled within-unit variance, S_w^2, is in this case the time-averaged spatial variance of the study variable at a given time, and the between-unit variance, S_b^2, is the variance of the spatial means over time.

Estimation of the space-time mean from an SS sample in which both locations and times are selected by probability sampling is the same as for an IS sample. However, estimation of the variance of the space-time mean estimator is more complicated. For the variance of the estimator of the space-time mean with an SS space-time design and simple random sampling of both locations and times, see equation (15.8) in de Gruijter et al. (2006). Due to the two-fold alignment of the sampling units, no unbiased estimator of the variance is available. The variance estimator of two-stage cluster sampling can be used to approximate the variance, but this variance estimator does not account for a possible temporal correlation of the estimated spatial means, resulting in an underestimation of the variance.

For an application of an IS design, to estimate the space-time mean of nutrients (nitrogen and phosphorous) in surface waters, see Brus and Knotters (2008) and Knotters and Brus (2010). In both applications, sampling times are selected by stratified simple random sampling, with periods of two months as strata. In Brus and Knotters (2008), sampling locations are selected by stratified simple random sampling as well.

15.4 Case study: annual mean daily temperature in Iberia

The space-time designs are illustrated with the annual mean air temperature at two metres above the earth surface (TAS) in Iberia for 2004, 2009, 2014, and 2019 (Subsection 1.3.4).

Sampling locations are selected by simple random sampling. The sample size is 100 locations per survey; so with four surveys we have 400 observations in total, but not with all space-time designs at 400 different sampling locations. In the next sections, I will show how a space-time sample with a given space-time design can be selected, and how the population parameters described in Section 15.2 can be estimated.

15.4.1   Static-synchronous design

Selecting an SS space-time sample, using simple random sampling as a spatial design, is straightforward. We can simply select a single simple random sample of size $n = 100$. The locations of this sample are observed at all times (Figure 15.3).

```
grd <- grdIberia %>%
  mutate(x = x / 1000,
         y = y / 1000)
set.seed(314)
n <- 100
units <- sample(nrow(grd), size = n, replace = TRUE)
mysample_SS <- grd[units, ]
```

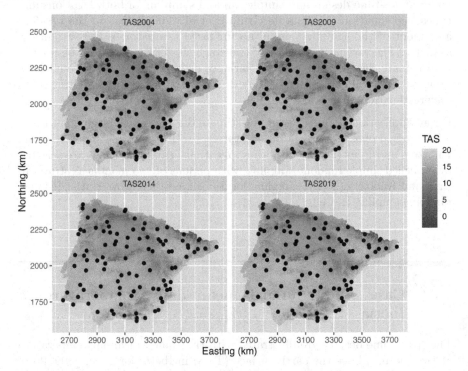

FIGURE 15.3: Static-synchronous space-time sample from Iberia. Locations are selected by simple random sampling.

The spatial means at the four times can be estimated by the sample means (Equation (3.2)), the variances of the mean estimators by Equation (3.14). The covariances of the estimators of the means at two different times can be estimated by Equation (15.14) with m equal to the sample size n. The estimated current mean (the spatial mean at the fourth survey) and the estimated standard error of the estimator of the current mean can be simply extracted from the vector with estimated means and from the matrix with estimated variances and covariances.

```
mz <- apply(mysample_SS[, -c(1, 2)], MARGIN = 2, FUN = mean)
C <- var(mysample_SS[, -c(1, 2)]) / n
#current mean
mz_cur_SS <- mz[4]
se_mz_cur_SS <- sqrt(C[4, 4])
```

The change of the spatial mean from the first to the fourth survey can simply be estimated by subtracting the estimated spatial mean of the first survey from the estimated mean of the fourth survey. The standard error of this estimator can be estimated by the sum of the estimated variances of the two spatial mean estimators, minus two times the estimated covariance of the two mean estimators, and finally taking the square root.

```
d_mz_SS <- mz[4] - mz[1]
se_d_mz_SS <- sqrt(C[4, 4] + C[1, 1] - 2 * C[1, 4])
```

The same estimates are obtained by defining a weight vector with values -1 and 1 for the first and last element, respectively, and 0 for the other two elements.

```
w <- c(-1, 0, 0, 1)
d_mz_SS <- t(w) %*% mz
se_d_mz_SS <- sqrt(t(w) %*% C %*% w)
```

The temporal trend of the spatial means can be estimated much in the same way, but using a different vector with weights (Equation (15.4)).

```
t <- seq(from = 2004, to = 2019, by = 5)
w <- (t - mean(t)) / sum((t - mean(t))^2)
mz_trend_SS <- t(w) %*% mz
se_mz_trend_SS <- sqrt(t(w) %*% C %*% w)
```

The estimated temporal trend equals $0.0403°C \ y^{-1}$, and the estimated standard error equals $0.0024794°C \ y^{-1}$. Using t = 1:4 yields the estimated average change in annual mean temperature *per five years*.

```
t <- 1:4
w <- (t - mean(t)) / sum((t - mean(t))^2)
print(mz_trend_SS <- t(w) %*% mz)
```

```
         [,1]
[1,] 0.2016378
```

Using a constant weight vector with values $1/4$ yields the estimated space-time mean and the standard error of the space-time mean estimator.

```
w <- rep(1 / 4, 4)
mz_st_SS <- t(w) %*% mz
se_mz_st_SS <- sqrt(t(w) %*% C %*% w)
```

15.4.2 Independent synchronous design

To select an IS space-time sample with four sampling times, we simply select $4n = 400$ sampling locations. Figure 15.4 shows the selected IS space-time sample. A variable identifying the panel of the selected sampling units is added to the data frame.

```
units <- sample(nrow(grd), size = 4 * n, replace = TRUE)
mysample_IS <- grd[units, ]
mysample_IS$panel <- rep(c("a", "b", "c", "d"), each = n)
```

The units of the finite population are selected by simple random sampling *with replacement*. As a consequence, there can be partial overlap between the samples at the different times, i.e., some units are observed at multiple times. However, this overlap is by chance; it is not coordinated as in an SP and RP design. By selecting the units with replacement, the estimators of the spatial means are independent (covariance of estimators equals zero). For infinite populations such as points in an area, there will be no overlap, so that the covariance of the estimators equals zero.

The spatial means are estimated with the π estimator as there is no partial overlap of the spatial samples. All covariances of the mean estimators are zero. Estimation of the space-time parameters is done as before with the SS space-time sample. Four data frames of n rows are first made with the data observed in a specific panel. The variables of these four data frames are joined into a single data frame. The spatial means at the four times are then estimated by the sample means, computed with function `apply`.

```
panel_a <- filter(mysample_IS, panel == "a")[, c("TAS2004")]
panel_b <- filter(mysample_IS, panel == "b")[, c("TAS2009")]
panel_c <- filter(mysample_IS, panel == "c")[, c("TAS2014")]
panel_d <- filter(mysample_IS, panel == "d")[, c("TAS2019")]
```

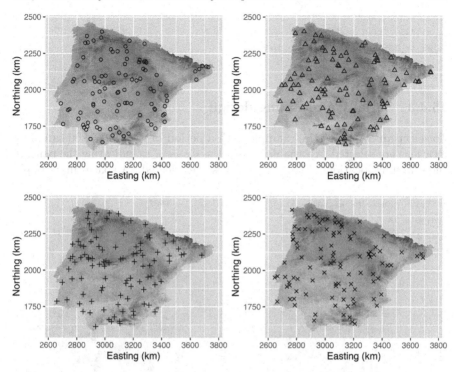

FIGURE 15.4: Independent synchronous space-time sample from Iberia. Locations are selected by simple random sampling.

```
panel_abcd <- cbind(panel_a, panel_b, panel_c, panel_d)
mz <- apply(panel_abcd, MARGIN = 2, FUN = mean)
C <- var(panel_abcd) / n
C[row(C) != col(C)] <- 0
#current mean
mz_cur_IS <- mz[4]
se_mz_cur_IS <- sqrt(C[4, 4])
#change of mean
w <- c(-1, 0, 0, 1)
d_mz_IS <- t(w) %*% mz
se_d_mz_IS <- sqrt(t(w) %*% C %*% w)
#trend of mean
w <- (t - mean(t)) / sum((t - mean(t))^2)
mz_trend_IS <- t(w) %*% mz
se_mz_trend_IS <- sqrt(t(w) %*% C %*% w)
#space-time mean
w <- rep(1 / 4, 4)
```

```
mz_st_IS <- t(w) %*% mz
se_mz_st_IS <- sqrt(t(w) %*% C %*% w)
```

15.4.3 Serially alternating design

To select an SA space-time sample with a period of two, $2n = 200$ sampling
locations are selected. A variable is added to mysample_SA indicating the panel of
the sampling locations. Figure 15.5 shows the selected SA space-time sample.

```
units <- sample(nrow(grd), size = 2 * n, replace = TRUE)
mysample_SA <- grd[units, ]
mysample_SA$panel <- rep(c("a", "b"), each = n)
```

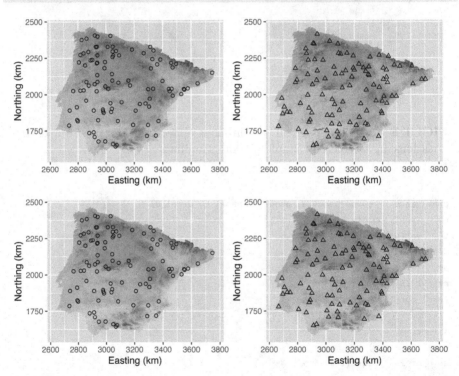

FIGURE 15.5: Serially alternating space-time sample from Iberia. Locations
are selected by simple random sampling.

In SA sampling there is no partial overlap of the spatial samples at different
times: there is either no coordinated overlap or full overlap. Spatial means
therefore can be estimated by the usual π estimator. Two data frames of n

rows are first made with the data observed in a specific panel. The variables of these two data frames are joined into a single data frame. The spatial means at the four times are then estimated by the sample means, computed with function `apply`.

```
panel_a <- filter(mysample_SA, panel == "a")[, c("TAS2004", "TAS2014")]
panel_b <- filter(mysample_SA, panel == "b")[, c("TAS2009", "TAS2019")]
panel_ab <- cbind(panel_a[1], panel_b[1], panel_a[2], panel_b[2])
mz <- apply(panel_ab, MARGIN = 2, FUN = mean)
```

To compute the matrix with estimated variances and covariances of the spatial mean estimators, first the full matrix is computed. Then the estimated covariances of spatial means of consecutive surveys are replaced by zeroes as the samples of these consecutive surveys are selected independently from each other, so that the two estimators are independent. Estimation of the space-time parameters is done as before with the SS space-time sample.

```
C <- var(panel_ab) / n
odd <- c(1, 3)
C[row(C) %in% odd & !(col(C) %in% odd)] <- 0
C[!(row(C) %in% odd) & col(C) %in% odd] <- 0

#current mean
mz_cur_SA <- mz[4]
se_mz_cur_SA <- sqrt(C[4, 4] / n)
#change of mean from time 1 to time 4
w <- c(-1, 0, 0, 1)
d_mz_SA <- t(w) %*% mz
se_d_mz_SA <- sqrt(t(w) %*% C %*% w)
#trend of mean
w <- (t - mean(t)) / sum((t - mean(t))^2)
mz_trend_SA <- t(w) %*% mz
se_mz_trend_SA <- sqrt(t(w) %*% C %*% w)
#space-time mean
mz_st_SA <- mean(mz)
w <- rep(1 / 4, 4)
se_mz_st_SA <- sqrt(t(w) %*% C %*% w)
```

15.4.4 Supplemented panel design

With SP sampling and four sampling times we have five panels: one panel with fixed sampling locations and four panels with swarming locations (Figure 15.1). Each panel consists of $n/2$ sampling locations, so in total $5n/2 = 250$

locations are selected. A variable indicating the panel is added to the data frame with the selected sampling locations. Figure 15.6 shows the selected SP sample.

```
units <- sample(nrow(grd), size = 5 * n / 2, replace = TRUE)
mysample_SP <- grd[units, ]
mysample_SP$panel <- rep(c("a", "b", "c", "d", "e"), each = n / 2)
```

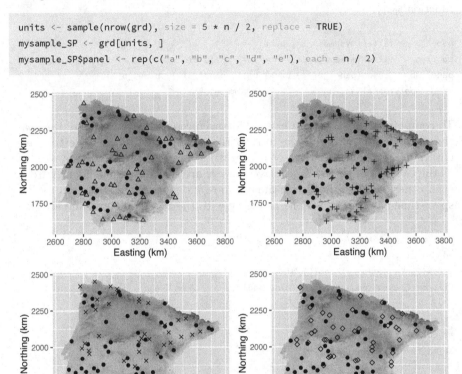

FIGURE 15.6: Supplemented panel space-time sample from Iberia. Locations are selected by simple random sampling. The permanent sampling locations are indicated by the filled dots, the swarming locations by the other symbols.

With SP sampling, the spatial means are estimated by the design-based GLS estimator (Equation (15.10)). As a first step, the eight elementary estimates (two per sampling time) are computed and collected in a vector. Note the order of the elementary estimates: first the estimated spatial means of 2004, 2009, 2014, and 2019, estimated from the panel with fixed sampling locations, then the spatial means estimated from the panels with swarming locations. The design matrix **X** corresponding to this order of elementary estimates is constructed.

Ordering the elementary estimates by sampling time is also fine, but then the design matrix **X** should be adapted to this order.

```
mz_1 <- tapply(
  mysample_SP$TAS2004, INDEX = mysample_SP$panel, FUN = mean)[c(1, 2)]
mz_2 <- tapply(
  mysample_SP$TAS2009, INDEX = mysample_SP$panel, FUN = mean)[c(1, 3)]
mz_3 <- tapply(
  mysample_SP$TAS2014, INDEX = mysample_SP$panel, FUN = mean)[c(1, 4)]
mz_4 <- tapply(
  mysample_SP$TAS2019, INDEX = mysample_SP$panel, FUN = mean)[c(1, 5)]
mz_el <- c(mz_1["a"], mz_2["a"], mz_3["a"], mz_4["a"],
           mz_1["b"], mz_2["c"], mz_3["d"], mz_4["e"])
X <- rbind(diag(4), diag(4))
```

The variances and covariances of the elementary estimates of the panel with fixed locations (SS subsample) are estimated, as well as the variances of the elementary estimates of the panels with swarming locations (IS subsample). The two variance-covariance matrices and a 4×4 submatrix with all zeroes are combined into a single matrix, see matrix (15.11).

```
mysubsample_SS <- mysample_SP[mysample_SP$panel == "a", ]
C_SS <- var(
  mysubsample_SS[, c("TAS2004", "TAS2009", "TAS2014", "TAS2019")]) / (n / 2)
mysubsample_IS <- cbind(mysample_SP$TAS2004[mysample_SP$panel == "b"],
                        mysample_SP$TAS2009[mysample_SP$panel == "c"],
                        mysample_SP$TAS2014[mysample_SP$panel == "d"],
                        mysample_SP$TAS2019[mysample_SP$panel == "e"])
C_IS <- var(mysubsample_IS) / (n / 2)
C_IS[row(C_IS) != col(C_IS)] <- 0
zeroes <- matrix(0, nrow = 4, ncol = 4)
C <- rbind(cbind(C_SS, zeroes), cbind(zeroes, C_IS))
```

The design-based GLS estimates of the spatial means can be computed as follows, see Equation (15.10).

```
XCXinv <- solve(crossprod(X, solve(C, X)))
XCz <- crossprod(X, solve(C, mz_el))
mz_GLS <- XCXinv %*% XCz
```

Computing the estimated space-time parameters from the design-based GLS estimated spatial means is straightforward.

```
#current mean
mz_cur_SP <- mz_GLS[4]
se_mz_cur_SP <- sqrt(XCXinv[4, 4])
#change of mean
w <- c(-1, 0, 0, 1)
d_mz_SP <- t(w) %*% mz_GLS
se_d_mz_SP <- sqrt(t(w) %*% XCXinv %*% w)
#trend of mean
w <- (t - mean(t)) / sum((t - mean(t))^2)
mz_trend_SP <- t(w) %*% mz_GLS
se_mz_trend_SP <- sqrt(t(w) %*% XCXinv %*% w)
#space-time mean
w <- rep(1 / 4, 4)
mz_st_SP <- t(w) %*% mz_GLS
se_mz_st_SP <- sqrt(t(w) %*% XCXinv %*% w)
```

15.4.5   Rotating panel design

Similar to the SP design, with an in-for-two RP design and four sampling times we have five panels, each consisting of $n/2$ sampling locations, so that in total $5n/2 = 250$ locations are selected. Figure 15.7 shows the selected space-time sample.

```
units <- sample(nrow(grd), size = 5 * n / 2, replace = TRUE)
mysample_RP <- grd[units, ]
mysample_RP$panel <- rep(c("a", "b", "c", "d", "e"), each = n / 2)
```

Two elementary estimates per sampling time are computed and collected in a vector. Note that now the elementary estimates are ordered by sampling time. The design matrix corresponding to this order is constructed.

```
mz_1 <- tapply(
  mysample_RP$TAS2004, INDEX = mysample_RP$panel, FUN = mean)[c(1, 2)]
mz_2 <- tapply(
  mysample_RP$TAS2009, INDEX = mysample_RP$panel, FUN = mean)[c(2, 3)]
mz_3 <- tapply(
  mysample_RP$TAS2014, INDEX = mysample_RP$panel, FUN = mean)[c(3, 4)]
mz_4 <- tapply(
  mysample_RP$TAS2019, INDEX = mysample_RP$panel, FUN = mean)[c(4, 5)]
mz_el <- c(mz_1, mz_2, mz_3, mz_4)
X <- matrix(c(rep(c(1, 0, 0, 0), 2),
              rep(c(0, 1, 0, 0), 2),
```

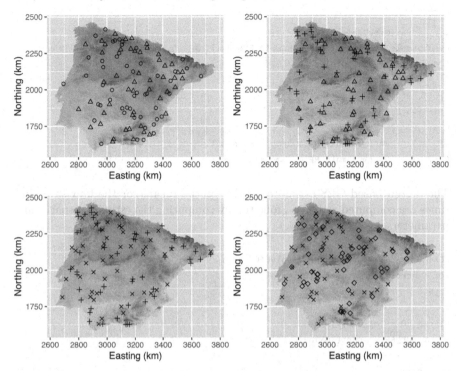

FIGURE 15.7: In-for-two rotating panel space-time sample from Iberia. Locations are selected by simple random sampling. Half of the sampling locations observed in a given year are also observed in the consecutive survey.

```
      rep(c(0, 0, 1, 0), 2),
      rep(c(0, 0, 0, 1), 2)), nrow = 8, ncol = 4, byrow = TRUE)
```

To construct the variance-covariance matrix of the eight elementary estimates, first the 2×2 matrices with estimated variances and covariances are computed for panels b, c, and d. These three panels are used to estimate the spatial means of two consecutive years: the locations of panel b are used to estimate the spatial means for 2004 and 2009, panel c for 2009 and 2014, and panel d for 2014 and 2019 (Figure 15.1). These three matrices are copied into the 8×8 matrix, see matrix (15.12). Finally, the estimated variances of the estimators of the spatial means in 2004 and 2019 are computed and copied to the upper left and lower right entry of the variance-covariance matrix, respectively.

```
mysubsample <- mysample_RP[mysample_RP$panel == "b", c("TAS2004", "TAS2009")]
C_b <- var(mysubsample) / (n / 2)
mysubsample <- mysample_RP[mysample_RP$panel == "c", c("TAS2009", "TAS2014")]
```

```
C_c <- var(mysubsample) / (n / 2)
mysubsample <- mysample_RP[mysample_RP$panel == "d", c("TAS2014", "TAS2019")]
C_d <- var(mysubsample) / (n / 2)
C <- matrix(data = 0, ncol = 8, nrow = 8)
C[2:3, 2:3] <- C_b
C[4:5, 4:5] <- C_c
C[6:7, 6:7] <- C_d
C[1, 1] <- var(mysample_RP[mysample_RP$panel == "a", "TAS2004"]) / (n / 2)
C[8, 8] <- var(mysample_RP[mysample_RP$panel == "e", "TAS2019"]) / (n / 2)
```

The design-based GLS estimates of the spatial means for the four sampling times are computed as before, followed by computing the estimated space-time parameters.

```
XCXinv <- solve(crossprod(X, solve(C, X)))
XCz <- crossprod(X, solve(C, mz_el))
mz_GLS <- XCXinv %*% XCz
#current mean
mz_cur_RP <- mz_GLS[4]
se_mz_cur_RP <- sqrt(XCXinv[4, 4])
#change of mean
w <- c(-1, 0, 0, 1)
d_mz_RP <- t(w) %*% mz_GLS
se_d_mz_RP <- sqrt(t(w) %*% XCXinv %*% w)
#trend of mean
w <- (t - mean(t)) / sum((t - mean(t))^2)
mz_trend_RP <- t(w) %*% mz_GLS
se_mz_trend_RP <- sqrt(t(w) %*% XCXinv %*% w)
#space-time mean
w <- rep(1 / 4, 4)
mz_st_RP <- t(w) %*% mz_GLS
se_mz_st_RP <- sqrt(t(w) %*% XCXinv %*% w)
```

15.4.6 Sampling experiment

The random sampling with the five space-time designs and estimation of the four space-time parameters is repeated 10,000 times. The standard deviations of the 10,000 estimates of a space-time parameter are shown in Table 15.1. Note that to determine the standard errors of the estimators of the space-time parameters for the SS, IS, and SA designs, a sampling experiment is not really needed. These can be computed without error because we have exhaustive knowledge of the study variable at all sampling times. However, for

TABLE 15.1: Standard deviations of 10,000 estimates of space-time parameters of annual mean temperature in Iberia, with static-synchronous (SS), independent synchronous (IS), serially alternating (SA), supplemented panel (SP), and rotating panel (RP) space-time sampling, and simple random sampling with replacement of 100 locations per sampling time.

	Current mean	Change of mean	Trend of mean	Space-time mean
SS	0.2709	0.0343	0.0123	0.2741
IS	0.2653	0.3873	0.1221	0.1354
SA	0.2676	0.3894	0.0787	0.1910
SP	0.1755	0.0481	0.0171	0.1770
RP	0.1769	0.0840	0.0299	0.1744

the SP and RP designs, a sampling experiment is needed to approximate the design-expectation of the standard error of the estimators of the space-time parameters. This is because the space-time parameters are derived from the GLS estimator of the spatial means, and the GLS estimator is a function of the *estimated* covariances of the elementary estimates (Equation (15.10)). Using the true covariance of the elementary estimates in the GLS estimator, instead of the estimated covariance, leads to an underestimation of the standard error. Computing the true standard errors of the estimators of the space-time parameters for the various space-time designs is left as an exercise.

As a reference for the standard deviations in Table 15.1: the current mean (spatial mean air temperature in 2019) equals 14.59°C, the change of the mean from 2004 to 2019 equals 0.611°C, the temporal trend equals 0.198°C *per five years*, and the space-time mean equals 14.44°C.

Estimates of the current mean with the SP and RP designs are much more precise than with the SS, IS, and SA designs. This is because with designs SP and RP there is partial overlap with the samples of the other years. If the study variable at different years is correlated, we can profit from the data of previous years. In our case, this correlation is very strong:

```
cor(grd[, -c(1, 2)])
```

```
          TAS2004   TAS2009   TAS2014   TAS2019
TAS2004 1.0000000 0.9950227 0.9878301 0.9927014
TAS2009 0.9950227 1.0000000 0.9875005 0.9960541
TAS2014 0.9878301 0.9875005 1.0000000 0.9938060
TAS2019 0.9927014 0.9960541 0.9938060 1.0000000
```

The differences in standard deviations of the estimated current means among the SS, IS, and SA designs are due to random variation: the true standard errors of the current mean estimator are equal for these three space-time designs.

The strong correlation also explains that the estimated change of the spatial mean from 2004 to 2019 with the SS design is much more precise than with the IS and SA designs. With the IS and SA designs, the sample of 2019 is selected independently from the sample of 2004, so that the covariance of the two spatial mean estimators is zero. With the SS design this covariance is subtracted two times from the sum of the variances of the spatial mean estimators. The standard error of the estimator of the change of the spatial mean from 2009 to 2019 with the SA design (not shown in Table 15.1) is much smaller than that of the change from 2004 to 2019, because the spatial means at these two times are estimated from the same sample, so that we profit from the strong positive correlation. The standard error of the change estimator with the SP design is slightly larger than the standard error with the SS design, because with this design there is only partial overlap, so that we profit less from the correlation. The standard error with the RP design is larger than that of the SP design, because with the RP design there is no overlap of the samples of 2004 and 2019 (Figure 15.1). Despite the absence of overlap, the standard error is still considerably smaller than those with the IS and SA designs because the spatial means of 2004 and 2019 are estimated by the GLS estimator that uses the data of all years, so that we still profit from the correlation.

Estimation of the temporal trend of the spatial mean is most precise with the SS design, closely followed by the SP design, and least precise with the IS design. This is in agreement with the results of Brus and de Gruijter (2011) and Brus and de Gruijter (2013). On the contrary, estimation of the space-time mean is most precise with the IS design and least precise with the SS design. With strong persistence of the spatial patterns, as in our case, it is not efficient to observe the same sampling locations at all times when interest is in the space-time mean. In our case with very strong correlation, the larger the total number of sampling locations over all sampling times, the smaller the standard error of the space-time mean estimator. The total number of sampling locations in this case study are n with SS, $4n$ with IS, $2n$ with SA, and $5n/2$ with SP and RP.

15.5   Space-time sampling with stratified random sampling in space

In real-world applications, one will often use more efficient sampling designs than simple random sampling for selecting spatial sampling units. For instance, in the case study of the previous section, stratified simple random sampling using climate zones is most likely more efficient than simple random sampling.

To select a space-time sample with stratified simple random sampling as a spatial design, the selection procedures described above for the five basic types of space-time design are applied at the level of the strata. Estimation of the space-time parameters goes along the same lines, using the π estimator of the spatial mean and the estimator of the standard error presented in Chapter 4. With the SP and RP designs, the covariance of the elementary estimators of the spatial means at two sampling times using the data of the same panel, can be estimated by

$$\widehat{C}_{ab} = \sum_{h=1}^{H} w_h^2 \frac{\widehat{S^2}_{abh}}{m_h} , \qquad (15.19)$$

with $\widehat{S^2}_{abh}$ the estimated covariance of the study variable at times t_a and t_b in stratum h, and m_h the number of sampling locations in the panel in stratum h.

Interesting new developments are presented by Wang and Zhu (2019) and Zhao and Grafström (2020).

Exercises

1. Compute for the annual mean temperature data of Iberia the true standard error of the estimator of (i) the spatial mean in 2019; (ii) the change of the spatial mean from 2004 to 2019; (iii) the temporal trend of the spatial mean (average change per five years in the period from 2004 to 2019); and (iv) the space-time mean, for all five space-time designs and simple random sampling with replacement of 100 units per time. Use for the designs SP and RP the true covariances of the elementary estimates in the GLS estimators of the spatial means.

   - Compare the standard errors with the standard deviations in Table 15.1. Explain why for the designs SP and RP the true standard errors of the estimators of all space-time parameters are slightly smaller than the standard deviations in Table 15.1.

2. With an SP and an RP design, the change of the mean can also be estimated by the difference of the π estimates of the spatial means at the two times, instead of the difference of the two GLS estimates. The variance of the difference of the π estimators of two simple random samples at different times with partial overlap equals

$$V(\bar{d}_{ab}) = \frac{S_a^2}{n} + \frac{S_b^2}{n} - 2\frac{m\, S_{ab}^2}{n^2} , \qquad (15.20)$$

with S_a^2 and S_b^2 the spatial variance at time t_a and t_b, respectively, S_{ab}^2 the spatial covariance of the study variable at times t_a and t_b, n the size of the simple random samples, and m the number of units observed at both times. Compute for Iberia the standard error of the estimator of the change of the mean with Equation (15.20), using the *true* spatial variances and covariances for 2004 and 2019, for simple random samples of size 100 ($n = 100$) and a matching proportion of 0.5 ($m = 50$). Compare with the true standard error of the estimator of the change of the mean using the GLS estimators computed in the previous exercise. Explain that the standard error of the π estimators is larger than the standard error with the GLS estimators.

Part II

Sampling for mapping

16

Introduction to sampling for mapping

16.1 When is probability sampling not required?

This second part of the book deals with sampling for mapping, i.e., for predicting the study variable at the nodes of a fine discretisation grid. For mapping, a model-based sampling approach is the most natural option. When a statistical model, i.e., a model containing an error term modelled by a probability distribution, is used to map the study variable from the sample data, selection of the sampling units by probability sampling is not strictly needed anymore in order to make statistical statements about the population, i.e., statements with quantified uncertainty, see Section 1.2. As a consequence, there is room for optimising the sampling units by searching for those units that lead to the most accurate map, for instance, the map with the smallest squared prediction error averaged over all locations in the mapped study area, see Chapter 25.

As an illustration, consider the following statistical model to be used for mapping: a simple linear regression model for the study variable to be mapped:

$$Z_k = \beta_0 + \beta_1 x_k + \epsilon_k , \qquad (16.1)$$

with Z_k the study variable of unit k, β_0 and β_1 regression coefficients, x_k a covariate for unit k used as a predictor, and ϵ_k the error (residual) at unit k, normally distributed with mean zero and a constant variance σ^2. The errors are assumed independent, so that $\mathrm{Cov}(\epsilon_k, \epsilon_j) = 0$ for all $k \neq j$. Figure 16.1 shows a simple random sample without replacement and the sample optimised for mapping with a simple linear regression model. Both samples are plotted on a map of the covariate x.

The optimal sample for mapping with a simple linear regression model contains the units with the smallest and the largest values of the covariate x. The optimal sample shows strong spatial clustering. Spatial clustering is not avoided because in a simple linear regression model we assume that the residuals are not spatially correlated. In Chapter 23 I will show that when the residuals are spatially correlated, spatial clustering of sampling units is avoided. The standard errors of both regression coefficients are considerably smaller for the

317

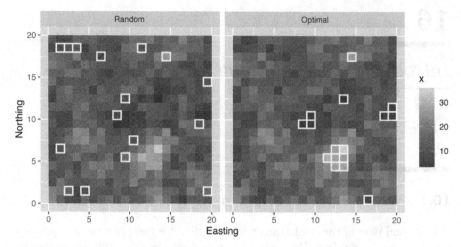

FIGURE 16.1: Simple random sample and optimal sample for mapping with a simple linear regression model, plotted on a map of the covariate.

TABLE 16.1: Standard errors and determinant of the variance-covariance matrix of estimators of the regression coefficients for the simple random sample (SI) and the optimal sample.

Sampling design	se intercept	se slope	Determinant
SI	1.70	0.118	0.003876
Optimal	1.06	0.050	0.000940

optimal sample (Table 16.1). The joint uncertainty about the two regression coefficients, quantified by the determinant of the variance-covariance matrix of the regression coefficient estimators, is also much smaller for the optimal sample. When we are less uncertain about the regression coefficients, we are also less uncertain about the regression model predictions of the study variable z at points where we have observations of the covariate x only. We can conclude that for mapping with a simple linear regression model, in this example simple random sampling is not a good option.

Of course, this simple example would only be applicable if we have evidence of a linear relation between study variable z and covariate x, and in addition if we are willing to rely on the assumption that the residuals are not spatially correlated.

16.2 Sampling for simultaneously mapping and estimating means

Although probability sampling is not strictly needed for mapping with a statistical model, in some situations, when feasible, it can still be advantageous to select a probability sample. If the aim of the survey is to map the study variable, as well as to estimate the mean or total for the entire study area or for several subareas, probability sampling can be a good option. Think, for instance, of sampling for the dual objectives of mapping and at the same time estimating soil carbon stocks. Although the statistical model used for mapping can also be used for model-based prediction of the total carbon stocks in the study area and subareas (Section 14.3), we may prefer to estimate these totals by design-based or model-assisted inference. The advantage of design-based and model-assisted estimation of these totals is their validity. Validity means that an objective assessment of the uncertainty of the estimated mean or total is warranted, and that the coverage of confidence intervals is (almost) correct, provided that the sample is large enough to assume an approximately normal distribution of the estimator and design-unbiasedness of the variance estimator, see Chapter 26. In design-based estimation, no model of the spatial variation is used. Therefore, discussions are avoided about how realistic modelling assumptions are. In model-assisted estimation, these discussions are irrelevant as well, because we do not rely on these assumptions. A poor model results in large variances of the estimated mean or total and, as a consequence, a wide confidence interval, so that the coverage of the confidence interval is in agreement with the nominal coverage, see Section 26.6 for more details.

The question then is: what is a suitable probability sampling design for both aims? First, I would recommend a sampling design with equal inclusion probabilities. This is because in standard model-based inference unequal inclusion probabilities are not accounted for, which may lead to systematic prediction errors when small or large values are overrepresented in the sample (Section 26.3).

Second, in case we have subareas of which we would like to estimate the mean or total (domains of interest), using these subareas as strata in stratified random sampling makes sense, unless there are too many. This requires that of all population units (nodes of discretisation grid) we must know to which subarea it belongs, so that this information can be added to the sampling frame.

Third, a sampling design spreading the sampling units in geographical space is attractive as well, for instance through compact geographical stratification (Section 4.6) or sampling with the local pivotal method (Subsection 9.2.1).

We may profit from this geographical spreading if some version of kriging is used for mapping (Chapter 21). In addition, the geographical spreading may enhance the coverage of the space spanned by covariates related to the study variable. Spreading in covariate space can also be explicitly accounted for using the covariates as spreading variables in the local pivotal method.

As an illustration, I selected a single sample of 500 units from Eastern Amazonia with the dual aim of mapping aboveground biomass (AGB) as well as estimating the means of AGB for four biomes. The biomes are used as strata in stratified random sampling. First, the stratum sample sizes are computed for proportional allocation, so that the inclusion probabilities are approximately equal for all population units.

```
grdAmazonia$Biome <- as.factor(grdAmazonia$Biome)
biomes <- c("Mangrove", "Forest_dry", "Grassland", "Forest_moist")
levels(grdAmazonia$Biome) <- biomes
N_h <- table(grdAmazonia$Biome)
n <- 500
n_h <- round(n * N_h / sum(N_h))
n_h[3] <- n_h[3] + 1
print(n_h)
```

```
    Mangrove   Forest_dry   Grassland  Forest_moist
           2           11          28           459
```

Biome Forest_moist is by far the largest biome with a sample size of 459 points.

In the next code chunk, a balanced sample is selected with equal inclusion probabilities, using both the categorical variable biome and the continuous variable lnSWIR2 as balancing variables (Subsection 9.1.3). The geographical coordinates are used as spreading variables.

```
library(BalancedSampling)
grdAmazonia$lnSWIR2 <- log(grdAmazonia$SWIR2)
pi <- n_h / N_h
stratalabels <- levels(grdAmazonia$Biome)
lut <- data.frame(Biome = stratalabels, pi = as.numeric(pi))
grdAmazonia <- merge(x = grdAmazonia, y = lut)
Xbal <- model.matrix(~ Biome - 1, data = grdAmazonia) %>%
  cbind(grdAmazonia$lnSWIR2)
Xspread <- cbind(grdAmazonia$x1, grdAmazonia$x2)
set.seed(314)
units <- lcube(Xbal = Xbal, Xspread = Xspread, prob = grdAmazonia$pi)
mysample <- grdAmazonia[units, ]
```

Figure 16.2 shows the selected sample.

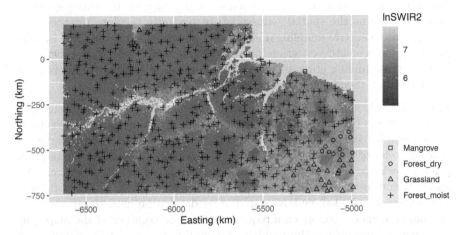

FIGURE 16.2: Balanced sample of size 500 from Eastern Amazonia, balanced on biome and lnSWIR2, with geographical spreading. Equal inclusion probabilities are used.

I think this is a suitable sample, both for mapping AGB across the entire study area, for instance by kriging with an external drift (Section 21.3), and for estimating the mean AGB of the four biomes. For biome Forest_moist, the population mean can be estimated from the data of this biome only, using the π estimator, as the sample size of this biome is very large (Section 9.3). For the other three biomes, we may prefer model-assisted estimation for small domains as described in Section 14.2.

In this example I used one quantitative covariate, lnSWIR2, for balancing the sample. If we have a legacy sample that can be used to fit a linear or non-linear model, for instance a random forest using multiple covariates and factors as predictors (Chapter 10), then this model can be used to predict the study variable for all population units, so that we can use the predictions of the study variable to balance the sample, see Section 10.3.

16.3 Broad overview of sampling designs for mapping

The non-probability sampling designs for mapping described in the following chapters can be grouped into three categories (Brus, 2019):

1. geometric sampling designs (Chapters 17 and 18);
2. adapted experimental designs (Chapters 19 and 20); and
3. model-based sampling designs (Chapters 22 and 23).

Square and triangular grids are examples of geometric sampling designs; the sampling units show a regular, geometric spatial pattern. In other geometric sampling designs the spatial pattern is not perfectly regular. Yet these are classified as geometric sampling designs when the samples are obtained by minimising some geometric criterion, i.e., a criterion defined in terms of distances between the sampling units and the nodes of a fine prediction grid discretising the study area (Section 17.2 and Chapter 18).

In model-based sampling designs, the samples are obtained by minimising a criterion that is defined in terms of variances of prediction errors. An example is the mean kriging variance criterion, i.e., the average of the kriging variances over all nodes of the prediction grid. Model-based sampling therefore requires prior knowledge of the model of spatial variation. Such a model must be specified and justified. Once this model is given, the sample can be optimised. In Chapter 22 I will show how a spatial model can be used to optimise the spacing of a square grid given a requirement on the accuracy of the map. The grid spacing determines the number of sampling units, so this optimisation boils down to determining the required sample size. In Chapter 23 I will show how a sample of a given size can be further optimised through optimisation of the spatial coordinates of the sampling units.

In Chapter 1 the design-based and model-based approaches for sampling and statistical inference were introduced. Note that a model-based approach does not necessarily imply model-based sampling. The adjective 'model-based' refers to the model-based inference, not to the selection of the units. In a model-based approach sampling units can be, but need not be, selected by model-based sampling. If they are, then both in selecting the units and in mapping a statistical model is used. In most cases, the two models differ: once the sample data are collected, these are used to update the postulated model used for designing the sample. The updated model is then used in mapping.

Besides geometric and model-based sampling designs for a spatial survey, a third category can be distinguished: sampling designs that are adaptations of experimental designs. An adaptation is necessary because in contrast to experiments, in observational studies one is not free to choose combinations of levels of different factors. For instance, when two covariates are strongly positively correlated, it may happen that there are no units with a relatively large value for one covariate and a relatively small value for the other covariate.

In a full factorial design, all combinations of factor levels are observed. For instance, suppose we have only two covariates, e.g., application rates for N and P in an agricultural experiment, and four levels for each covariate. To account for possible non-linear effects, a good option is to have multiple plots for all 4×4 combinations. This is referred to as a full factorial design. With k factors and l levels per factor the total number of observations is l^k. With numerous factors and/or numerous levels per factor, this becomes unfeasible in practice. Alternative designs have been developed that need fewer observations but still provide detailed information about how the study variable responds to changes in the factor levels. Examples are Latin hypercube samples and response surface designs. The survey sampling analogues of these experimental designs are described in Chapters 19 and 20.

17

Regular grid and spatial coverage sampling

This chapter describes and illustrates two sampling designs by which the sampling locations are evenly spread throughout the study area: regular grid sampling and spatial coverage sampling. In a final section, the spatial coverage sampling design is used to fill in the empty spaces of an existing sample.

17.1 Regular grid sampling

Sampling on a regular grid is an attractive option for mapping because of its simplicity. The data collected on the grid nodes are not used for design-based estimation of the population mean or total. For this reason, the grid need not be placed randomly on the study area as in systematic random sampling (Chapter 5). The grid can be located such that the grid nodes optimally cover the study area in the sense of the average distance of the nodes of a fine discretisation grid to the nearest node of the sampling grid. Commonly used grid configurations are square and triangular. If the grid data are used in kriging (Chapter 21), the optimal configuration depends, among others, on the semivariogram model. If the study variable shows moderate to strong spatial autocorrelation (see Section 21.1), triangular grids outperform square grids.

Besides the shape of the sampling grid cells, we must decide on the grid spacing. The grid spacing determines the number of sampling units in the study area, i.e., the sample size. There are two options to decide on this spacing, either starting from the available budget or from a requirement on the quality of the map. The latter is explained in Chapter 22, as this requires a model of the spatial variation, and as a consequence this is an example of model-based sampling. Starting from the available budget and an estimate of the costs per sampling unit, we first compute the affordable sample size. Then we may derive from this number the grid spacing. For square grids, the grid spacing in meters is calculated as $\sqrt{A/n}$, where A is the area in m^2 and n is the number of sampling units (sample size).

Grids can be selected with function spsample of package **sp** (Pebesma and Bivand, 2005). Argument offset is used to select a grid non-randomly. Either a sample size can be specified, using argument n, or a grid spacing, using argument cellsize. In the next code chunk, a square grid is selected with a spacing of 200 m.

```
library(sp)
gridded(grdVoorst) <- ~ s1 + s2
mysample <- spsample(
  x = grdVoorst, type = "regular", cellsize = c(200, 200),
  offset = c(0.5, 0.5)) %>% as("data.frame")
```

Figure 17.1 shows the selected square grid.

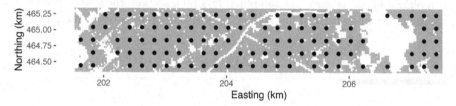

FIGURE 17.1: Non-random square grid sample with a grid spacing of 200 m from Voorst.

The number of grid points in this example equals 115. Nodes of the square grid in parts of the area not belonging to the population of interest, such as built-up areas and roads, are discarded by spsample (these nodes are not included in the sampling frame file grdVoorst). As a consequence, there are some undersampled areas, for instance in the middle of the study area where two roads cross. If we use the square grid in spatial interpolation, e.g., by ordinary kriging, we are more uncertain about the predictions in these undersampled areas than in areas where the grid is complete. The next section will show how this local undersampling can be avoided.

Exercises

1. Write an **R** script to select a square grid of size 100 from West-Amhara in Ethiopia. Use grdAmhara of package **sswr** as a sampling frame. Use a fixed starting point of the grid, i.e., do not select the grid randomly.
   - Compute the number of selected grid points. How comes it is not exactly equal to 100?
   - Select a square grid with a spacing of 10.2 km, and compute the sample size.
   - Write a for-loop to select 200 times a square grid of, on average, 100 points with random starting point. Set a seed so that the result can be reproduced. Determine for each randomly

    selected grid the number of selected grid points, and save this
in a numeric. Compute summary statistics of the sample size,
and plot a histogram.

- Select a square grid of exactly 100 points.

17.2 Spatial coverage sampling

Local undersampling with regular grids can be avoided by relaxing the constraint that the sampling units are restricted to the nodes of a regular grid. This is what is done in *spatial coverage sampling* or, in case of a sample that is added to an existing sample, in *spatial infill sampling*. Spatial coverage and infill samples cover the area or fill in the empty space as uniformly as possible. The sampling units are obtained by minimising a criterion that is defined in terms of the geographic distances between the nodes of a fine discretisation grid and the sampling units. Brus et al. (2007) proposed to minimise the mean of the squared distances of the grid nodes to their nearest sampling unit (mean squared shortest distance, MSSD):

$$ MSSD = \frac{1}{N} \sum_{k=1}^{N} \min_{j} \left(D_{kj}^2 \right) , \tag{17.1} $$

where N is the total number of nodes of the discretisation grid and D_{kj} is the distance between the kth grid node and the jth sampling point. This distance measure can be minimised by the k-means algorithm, which is a numerical, iterative procedure. Figure 17.2 illustrates the selection of a spatial coverage sample of four points from a square. In this simple example the optimal spatial coverage sample is known, being the centres of the four subsquares of equal size. A simple random sample of four points serves as the initial solution. Each raster cell is then assigned to the closest sampling point. This is the initial clustering. In the next iteration, the centres of the initial clusters are computed. Next, the raster cells are reassigned to the closest new centres. This continues until there is no change anymore. In this case only nine iterations are needed, where an iteration consists of computing the clusters by assigning the raster cells to the nearest centre (sampling unit), followed by computing the centres of these clusters. Figure 17.2 shows the first, second, and ninth iterations.

The same algorithm was used in Chapter 4 to construct compact geographical strata (briefly referred to as geostrata) for stratified random sampling. The clusters serve as strata. In stratified random sampling, one or more sampling units are selected randomly from each geostratum. However, for mapping purposes probability sampling is not required, so the random selection of a unit

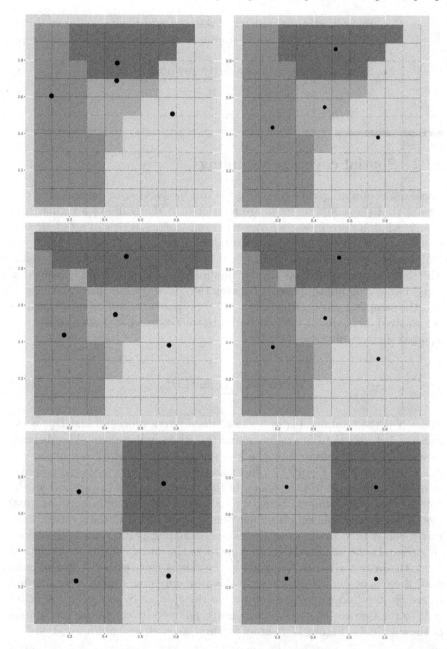

FIGURE 17.2: First, second, and ninth iterations of the k-means algorithm to select a spatial coverage sample of four points from a square. Iterations are in rows from top to bottom. In the left column of subfigures, the clusters are computed by assigning the raster cells to the nearest centre. In the right column of subfigures, the centres of the clusters are computed.

within each stratum is not needed. With random selection, the spatial coverage is suboptimal. Here, the centres of the final clusters (geostrata) are used as sampling points. This improves the spatial coverage compared to stratified *random* sampling.

In probability sampling, we may want to have strata of equal area (clusters of equal size) so that the sampling design becomes self-weighting. For mapping, equally sized clusters are not recommended, as this may lead to samples with suboptimal spatial coverage.

> In Figure 17.2 the clusters are of equal size, but this is an artefact. Equally sized clusters are not guaranteed by the illustrated k-means algorithm. Clustering the raster cells of a square into four clusters is a very special case. In other cases, the clusters computed with the k-means algorithm described above might have unequal sizes. In package **spcosa** also a different k-means algorithm is implemented, using swops, enforcing compact clusters of equal size.

Spatial coverage samples can be computed with package **spcosa** (Walvoort et al., 2010), using functions stratify and spsample, see code chunk below. Argument nTry of function stratify specifies the number of initial stratifications in k-means clustering. Note that function spsample of package **spcosa** without optional argument n selects non-randomly one point in each cluster, being the centre. Figure 17.3 shows a spatial coverage sample of the same size as the regular grid in study area Voorst (Figure 17.1). Note that the undersampled area in the centre of the study area is now covered by a sampling point.

```
library(spcosa)
n <- 115
set.seed(314)
gridded(grdVoorst) <- ~ s1 + s2
mystrata <- spcosa::stratify(
    grdVoorst, nStrata = n, equalArea = FALSE, nTry = 10)
mysample <- spsample(mystrata) %>% as("data.frame")
```

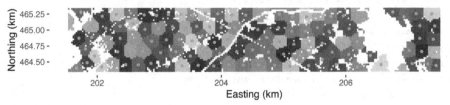

FIGURE 17.3: Spatial coverage sample from Voorst.

If the clusters need not be of equal size, we may also use function kmeans of the **stats** package, using the spatial coordinates as clustering variables. This requires less computing time, especially with large data sets.

```
grdVoorst <- as_tibble(grdVoorst)
mystrata_kmeans <- kmeans(
  grdVoorst[, c("s1", "s2")], centers = n, iter.max = 10000, nstart = 10)
mysample_kmeans <- mystrata_kmeans$centers %>% data.frame()
```

When function kmeans is used to compute the spatial coverage sample, there is no guarantee that the computed centres of the clusters, used as sampling points, are inside the study area. In Figure 17.4 there are eight such centres.

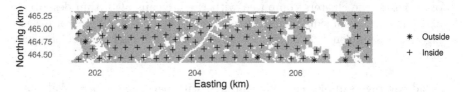

FIGURE 17.4: Centres of spatial clusters computed with function kmeans.

This problem can easily be solved by selecting points inside the study area closest to the centres that are outside the study area. Function rdist of package **fields** is used to compute a matrix with distances between the centres outside the study area and the nodes of the discretisation grid. Then function apply is used with argument FUN = which.min to compute the discretisation nodes closest to the centres outside the study area. A similar procedure is implemented in function spsample of package **spcosa** when the centres of the clusters are selected as sampling points (so, when argument n of function spsample is not used).

```
library(fields)
gridded(grdVoorst) <- ~ s1 + s2
coordinates(mysample_kmeans) <- ~ s1 + s2
res <- over(mysample_kmeans, grdVoorst)
inside <- as.factor(!is.na(res$z))
units_out <- which(inside == FALSE)
grdVoorst <- as_tibble(grdVoorst)
mysample_kmeans <- as_tibble(mysample_kmeans)
D <- fields::rdist(x1 = mysample_kmeans[units_out, ],
  x2 = grdVoorst[, c("s1", "s2")])
units_close <- apply(D, MARGIN = 1, FUN = which.min)
mysample_kmeans[units_out, ] <- grdVoorst[units_close, c("s1", "s2")]
```

Exercises

2. In forestry and vegetation surveys, square and circular plots are often used as sampling units, for instance, 2 m squares or circles with a diameter of 2 m. To study the relation between the vegetation and the soil, soil samples must be collected from the vegetation plots. Suppose we want to collect four soil samples from a square plot. Where would you locate the four sampling points, so that they optimally cover the plot?

3. Suppose we are also interested in the accuracy of the estimated plot means of the soil properties, not just the means. In that case, the soil samples should not be bulked into a composite sample, but analysed separately. How would you select the sampling points in this case?

4. For circular vegetation plots, it is less clear where the sampling points with smallest MSSD are (Equation (17.1)). Write an **R** script to compute a spatial coverage sample of five points from a circular plot discretised by the nodes of a fine square grid. Use argument equalArea = FALSE. Check the size (number of raster cells) of the strata. Repeat this for six sampling points.

5. Consider the case of six strata. The strata are not of equal size. If the soil samples are bulked into a composite sample, the measurement on this single sample is a biased estimator of the plot mean. How can this bias be avoided?

17.3 Spatial infill sampling

If georeferenced data are available that can be used for mapping the study variable, but we need more data for mapping, it is attractive to account for these existing sampling units when selecting the additional units. The aim now is to fill in the empty spaces, i.e., the parts of the study area not covered by the existing sampling units. This is referred to as *spatial infill sampling*. Existing sampling units can easily be accommodated in the k-means algorithm, using them as fixed cluster centres.

Figure 17.5 shows a spatial infill sample for West-Amhara. A large set of legacy data on soil organic matter (SOM) in mass percentage (dag kg⁻¹) is available, but these data come from strongly spatially clustered units along roads (prior points in Figure 17.5). This is a nice example of a convenience

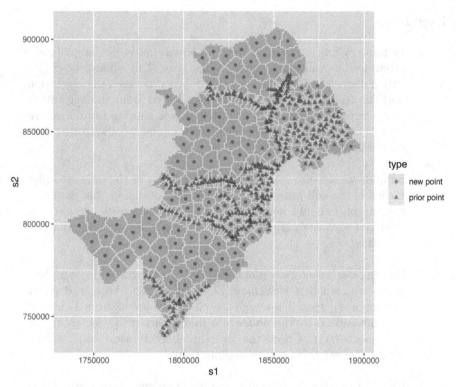

FIGURE 17.5: Spatial infill sample of 100 points from West-Amhara.

sample. The legacy data are not ideal for mapping the SOM concentration throughout West-Amhara. Clearly, it is desirable to collect additional data in the off-road parts of the study area, with the exception of the northeastern part where we have already quite a few data that are not near the main roads. The legacy data are passed to function stratify of package **spcosa** with argument priorPoints. The object assigned to this argument must be of class SpatialPoints or SpatialPointsDataFrame. This optional argument fixes these points as cluster centres. A spatial infill sample of 100 points is selected, taking into account these fixed points.

```
gridded(grdAmhara) <- ~ s1 + s2
n <- 100
ntot <- n + nrow(sampleAmhara)
coordinates(sampleAmhara) <- ~ s1 + s2
proj4string(sampleAmhara) <- NA_character_
set.seed(314)
mystrata <- spcosa::stratify(grdAmhara, nStrata = ntot,
    priorPoints = sampleAmhara, nTry = 10)
```

```
mysample <- spsample(mystrata)
plot(mystrata, mysample)
```

In the output object of spsample, both the prior and the new sampling points are included. The new points can be obtained as follows:

```
units <- which(mysample@isPriorPoint == FALSE)
mysample <- as(mysample, "data.frame")
mysample_new <- mysample[units, ]
```

Exercises

6. Write an **R** script to select a spatial infill sample of size 100 from study area Xuancheng in China. Use the iPSM sample in tibble sampleXuancheng of package **sswr** as a legacy sample. To map the SOM concentration, we want to measure the SOM concentration at 100 more sampling points.
   - Read the file data/Elevation_Xuancheng.rds with function rast of package **terra**, and use this file as a discretisation of the study area.
   - For computational reasons, there are far too many raster cells. That many cells are not needed to select a spatial infill sample. Subsample the raster file by selecting a square grid with a spacing of 900 m × 900 m. First, convert the SpatRaster object to a data.frame, and then change it to a SpatialPixelsDataFrame using function gridded. Then use function spsample with argument type = "regular".
   - Select a spatial infill sample using functions stratify and sample of package **spcosa**.

18

Covariate space coverage sampling

Regular grid sampling and spatial coverage sampling are pure spatial sampling designs. Covariates possibly related to the study variable are not accounted for in selecting sampling units. This can be suboptimal when the study variable is related to covariates of which maps are available, think for instance of remote sensing imagery or digital elevation models related to soil properties. Maps of these covariates can be used in mapping the study variable by, for instance, a multiple linear regression model or a random forest. This chapter describes a simple, straightforward method for selecting sampling units on the basis of the covariate values of the raster cells.

The simplest option for covariate space coverage (CSC) sampling is to cluster the raster cells by the k-means clustering algorithm in covariate space. Similar to spatial coverage sampling (Section 17.2) the mean squared shortest distance (MSSD) is minimised, but now the distance is not measured in geographical space but in a p-dimensional space spanned by the p covariates. Think of this space as a multidimensional scatter plot with the covariates along the axes. The covariates are centred and scaled so that their means become zero and standard deviations become one. This is needed because, contrary to the spatial coordinates used as clustering variables in spatial coverage sampling, the ranges of the covariates in the population can differ greatly. In the clustering of the raster cells, the mean squared shortest *scaled* distance (MSSSD) is minimised. The name 'scaled distance' can be confusing. The distances are not scaled, but rather they are computed in a space spanned by the scaled covariates.

In the next code chunk, a CSC sample of 20 units is selected from Eastern Amazonia. All five quantitative covariates, SWIR2, Terra_PP, Prec_dm, Elevation, and Clay, are used as covariates. To select 20 units, 20 clusters are constructed using function kmeans of the **stats** package (R Core Team, 2021). The number of clusters is passed to function kmeans with argument centers. Note that the number of clusters is not based, as would be usual in cluster analysis, on the assumed number of subregions with a high density of units in the multivariate distribution, but rather on the number of sampling units. The k-means clustering algorithm is a deterministic algorithm, i.e., the final optimised clustering is fully determined by the initial clustering. This final clustering can be suboptimal, i.e., the minimised MSSSD value is somewhat larger than the global minimum. Therefore, the clustering should be repeated many times, every time starting with a different random initial clustering.

The number of repeats is specified with argument nstart. The best solution is automatically kept. To speed up the computations, a 5 km × 5 km subgrid of grdAmazonia is used.

```
covs <-  c("SWIR2", "Terra_PP", "Prec_dm", "Elevation", "Clay")
n <- 20
set.seed(314)
myclusters <- kmeans(
  scale(grdAmazonia[, covs]), centers = n, iter.max = 10000, nstart = 100)
grdAmazonia$cluster <- myclusters$cluster
```

Raster cells with the shortest scaled Euclidean distance in covariate space to the centres of the clusters are selected as the sampling units. To this end, first a matrix with the distances of all the raster cells to the cluster centres is computed with function rdist of package **fields** (Nychka et al., 2021). The raster cells closest to the centres are computed with function apply, using argument FUN = which.min.

```
library(fields)
covs_s <- scale(grdAmazonia[, covs])
D <- rdist(x1 = myclusters$centers, x2 = covs_s)
units <- apply(D, MARGIN = 1, FUN = which.min)
myCSCsample <- grdAmazonia[units, ]
```

Figure 18.1 shows the clustering of the raster cells and the raster cells closest in covariate space to the centres that are used as the selected sample. In Figure 18.2 the selected sample is plotted in biplots of some pairs of covariates. In the biplots, some sampling units are clearly clustered. However, this is misleading, as actually we must look in five-dimensional space to see whether the units are clustered. Two units with a large separation distance in a five-dimensional space can look quite close when projected on a two-dimensional plane.

The next code chunk shows how the MSSSD of the selected sample can be computed.

```
D <- rdist(x1 = scale(
  myCSCsample[, covs], center = attr(covs_s, "scaled:center"),
  scale = attr(covs_s, "scaled:scale")), x2 = covs_s)
dmin <- apply(D, MARGIN = 2, min)
MSSSD <- mean(dmin^2)
```

Note that to centre and scale the covariate values in the CSC sample, the population means and the population standard deviations are used, as passed to function scale with arguments center and scale. If these means and standard deviations are unspecified, the *sample* means and the *sample* standard deviations are used, resulting in an incorrect value of the minimised MSSSD value. The MSSSD of the selected sample equals 1.004.

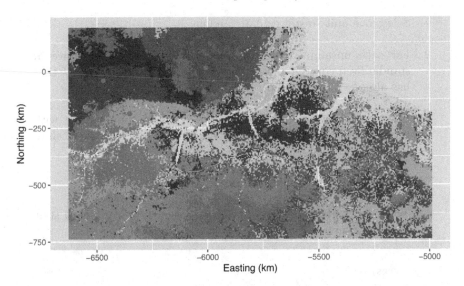

FIGURE 18.1: Covariate space coverage sample of 20 units from Eastern Amazonia, obtained with k-means clustering using five covariates, plotted on a map of the clusters.

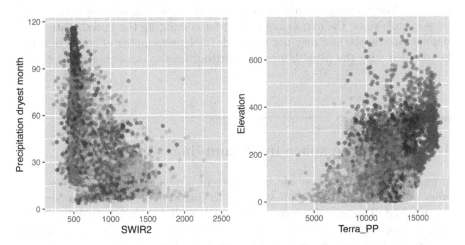

FIGURE 18.2: Covariate space coverage sample of Figure 18.1 plotted in biplots of covariates, coloured by cluster.

Instead of function kmeans we may use function kmeanspp of package **LICORS** (Goerg, 2013). This function is an implementation of the k-means++ algorithm (Arthur and Vassilvitskii, 2007). This algorithm consists of two parts, namely the selection of an optimised initial sample, followed by the standard k-means. The algorithm is as follows:

1. Select one unit (raster cell) at random.

2. For each unsampled unit j, compute d_{kj}, i.e., the distance in standardised covariate space between j and the nearest unit k that has already been selected.

3. Choose one new raster cell at random as a new sampling unit with probabilities proportional to d_{kj}^2 and add the selected raster cell to the set of selected cells.

4. Repeat steps 2 and 3 until n centres have been selected.

5. Now that the initial centres have been selected, proceed using standard k-means.

```
library(LICORS)
myclusters <- kmeanspp(
  scale(grdAmazonia[, covs]), k = n, iter.max = 10000, nstart = 30)
```

Due to the improved initial centres, the risk of ending in a local minimum is reduced. The k-means++ algorithm is of interest for small sample sizes. For large sample sizes, the extra time needed for computing the initial centres can become substantial and may not outweigh the larger number of starts that can be afforded with the usual k-means algorithm for the same computing time.

18.1   Covariate space infill sampling

If we have legacy data that can be used to fit a model for mapping, it is more efficient to select an infill sample, similar to spatial infill sampling explained in Section 17.3. The only difference with spatial infill sampling is that the legacy data are now plotted in the space spanned by the covariates. The empty regions we would like to fill in are now the undersampled regions in this covariate space. The legacy sample units serve as fixed cluster centres; they cannot move through the covariate space during the optimisation of the infill sample. In the next code chunk, a function is defined for covariate space infill sampling.

```
CSIS <- function(fixed, nsup, nstarts, mygrd) {
  n_fix <- nrow(fixed)
  p <- ncol(mygrd)
  units <- fixed$units
  mygrd_minfx <- mygrd[-units, ]
  MSSSD_cur <- NA
  for (s in 1:nstarts) {
    units <- sample(nrow(mygrd_minfx), nsup)
    centers_sup <- mygrd_minfx[units, ]
    centers <- rbind(fixed[, names(mygrd)], centers_sup)
    repeat {
      D <- rdist(x1 = centers, x2 = mygrd)
      clusters <- apply(X = D, MARGIN = 2, FUN = which.min) %>% as.factor(.)
      centers_cur <- centers
      for (i in 1:p) {
        centers[, i] <- tapply(mygrd[, i], INDEX = clusters, FUN = mean)
      }
      #restore fixed centers
      centers[1:n_fix, ] <- centers_cur[1:n_fix, ]
      #check convergence
      sumd <- diag(rdist(x1 = centers, x2 = centers_cur)) %>% sum(.)
      if (sumd < 1E-12) {
        D <- rdist(x1 = centers, x2 = mygrd)
        Dmin <- apply(X = D, MARGIN = 2, FUN = min)
        MSSSD <- mean(Dmin^2)
        if (s == 1 | MSSSD < MSSSD_cur) {
          centers_best <- centers
          clusters_best <- clusters
          MSSSD_cur <- MSSSD
        }
        break
      }
    }
  }
  list(centers = centers_best, clusters = clusters_best)
}
```

The function is used to select an infill sample of 15 units from Eastern Amazonia. A legacy sample of five units is randomly selected.

```
set.seed(314)
units <- sample(nrow(grdAmazonia), 5)
fixed <- data.frame(units, scale(grdAmazonia[, covs])[units, ])
```

```
mygrd <- data.frame(scale(grdAmazonia[, covs]))
res <- CSIS(fixed = fixed, nsup = 15, nstarts = 10, mygrd = mygrd)
```

Figures 18.3 and 18.4 show the selected sample plotted on a map of the clusters and in biplots of covariates, respectively.

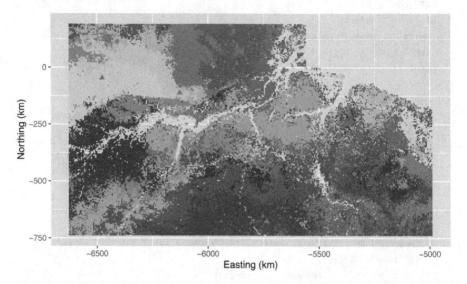

FIGURE 18.3: Covariate space infill sample of 15 units from Eastern Amazonia, obtained with k-means clustering and five fixed cluster centres, plotted on a map of the clusters. The dots represent the fixed centres (legacy sample), the triangles the infill sample.

18.2   Performance of covariate space coverage sampling in random forest prediction

CSC sampling can be a good candidate for a sampling design if we have multiple maps of covariates, and in addition if we do not want to rely on a linear relation between the study variable and the covariates. In this situation, we may consider mapping with machine learning algorithms such as neural networks and random forests (RF).

I used the Eastern Amazonia data set to evaluate CSC sampling for mapping the aboveground biomass (AGB). The five covariates are used as predictors in RF modelling. The calibrated models are used to predict AGB at the units of

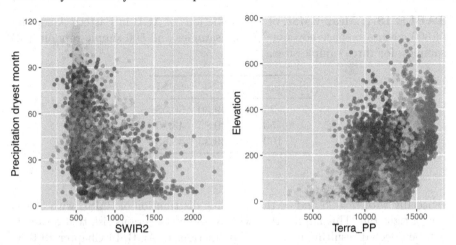

FIGURE 18.4: Covariate space infill sample of Figure 18.3 plotted in biplots of covariates, coloured by cluster. The dots represent the fixed centres (legacy sample), the triangles the infill sample.

a validation sample of size 25,000 selected by simple random sampling without replacement from the 1 km × 1 km grid, excluding the cells of the 10 km × 10 km grid from which the calibration samples are selected. The predicted AGB values at the validation units are compared with the true AGB values, and the prediction errors are computed. The sample mean of the squared prediction error is a design-unbiased estimator of the population mean squared error, i.e., the mean of the squared errors at all population units (excluding the units of the 10 km × 10 km grid), see Chapter 25.

Three sample sizes are used, $n = 25, 50, 100$. Of each sample size, 500 CSC samples are selected using the k-means algorithm, leading to 1,500 CSC samples in total. The numbers of starts are 500, 350, and 200 for $n = 25, 50$, and 100, respectively. With these numbers of starts, the computing time was about equal to conditioned Latin hypercube sampling, see next chapter. Each sample is used to calibrate a RF model. Simple random sampling (SI) is used as a reference sampling design that ignores the covariates.

In Figure 18.5 the root mean squared error (RMSE) of the RF predictions of AGB is plotted against the minimised MSSSD, both for the 3 × 500 CSC samples and for the 3 × 500 simple random samples. It is no surprise that for all three sample sizes the minimised MSSSD values of the CSC samples are substantially smaller than those of the SI samples. However, despite the substantial smaller MSSSD values, the RMSE values for the CSC samples are only a bit smaller than those of the SI samples. Only for $n = 50$ a moderately strong positive correlation can be seen: $r = 0.513$. For $n = 25$ the correlation is 0.264 only, and for $n = 100$ it is even negative: $r = -0.183$. On average in this case study, CSC and SI perform about equally (Table 18.1). However,

TABLE 18.1: Mean RMSE of RF predictions of AGB in Eastern Amazonia of 500 covariate space coverage (CSC) samples and 500 simple random (SI) samples, for three sample sizes.

Sample size	CSC	SI
25	49.30	50.58
50	40.85	43.16
100	39.33	38.83

especially with $n = 25$ and 50 the sampling distribution of RMSE with SI has a long right tail. This implies that with SI there is a serious risk that a sample will be selected resulting in poor RF predictions of AGB. In Chapter 19 CSC sampling is compared with conditioned Latin hypercube sampling.

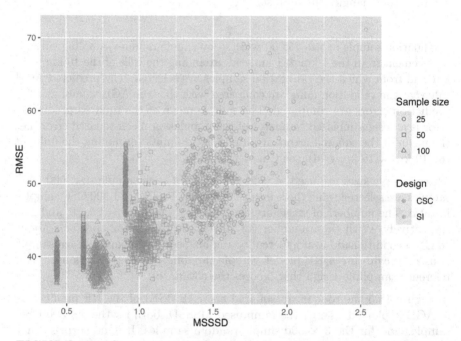

FIGURE 18.5: Scatter plot of the minimisation criterion MSSSD and the root mean squared error (RMSE) of RF predictions of AGB in Eastern Amazonia for covariate space coverage (CSC) sampling and simple random (SI) sampling, and three sample sizes.

Exercises

1. Write an **R** script to select a covariate space coverage sample of size
    20 from Hunter Valley (grdHunterValley of package **sswr**). Use the
    covariates cti (compound topographic index, which is the same as
    topographic wetness index), ndvi (normalised difference vegetation
    index), and elevation_m in k-means clustering of the raster cells.
    Plot the clusters and the sample on a map of cti and in a biplot of
    cti against ndvi.

19

Conditioned Latin hypercube sampling

This chapter and Chapter 20 on response surface sampling are about experimental designs that have been adapted for spatial surveys. Adaptation is necessary because, in contrast to experiments, in observational studies one is not free to choose any possible combination of levels of different factors. When two covariates are strongly positively correlated, it may happen that there are no population units with a relatively large value for one covariate and a relatively small value for the other covariate. By contrast, in experimental research it is possible to select any combination of factor levels.

In a full factorial design, all combinations of factor levels are observed. With k factors and l levels per factor, the total number of observations is l^k. With numerous factors and/or numerous levels per factor, observing l^k experimental units becomes unfeasible in practice. Alternative experimental designs have been developed that need fewer observations but still provide detailed information about how the study variable responds to changes in the factor levels. This chapter will describe and illustrate the survey sampling analogue of Latin hypercube sampling. Response surface sampling follows in the next chapter.

Latin hypercube sampling is used in designing industrial processes, agricultural experiments, and computer experiments, with numerous covariates and/or factors of which we want to study the effect on the output (McKay et al., 1979). A much cheaper alternative to a full factorial design is an experiment with, for all covariates, exactly one observation per level. So, in the agricultural experiment described in Chapter 16 with the application rates of N and P as factors and four levels for each factor, this would entail four observations only, distributed in a square in such way that we have in all rows and in all columns one observation, see Figure 19.1. This is referred to as a Latin square. The generalisation of a Latin square to a higher number of dimensions is a Latin hypercube (LH).

Minasny and McBratney (2006) adapted LH sampling for observational studies; this adaptation is referred to as conditioned Latin hypercube (cLH) sampling. For each covariate, a series of intervals (marginal strata) is defined. The number of marginal strata per covariate is equal to the sample size, so that the total number of marginal strata equals p^n, with p the number of covariates and n the sample size. The bounds of the marginal strata are chosen such that the numbers of raster cells in these marginal strata are equal. This is achieved by

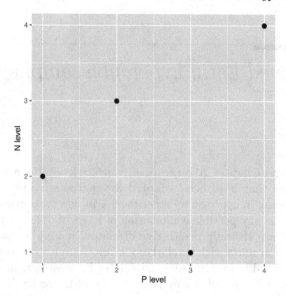

FIGURE 19.1: Latin square for agricultural experiment with four application rates of N and P.

using the quantiles corresponding to evenly spaced cumulative probabilities as stratum bounds. For instance, for five marginal strata we use the quantiles corresponding to the cumulative probabilities 0.2, 0.4, 0.6, and 0.8.

The minimisation criterion proposed by Minasny and McBratney (2006) is a weighted sum of three components:

1. O1: the sum over all marginal strata of the absolute deviations of the marginal stratum sample size from the targeted sample size (equal to 1);
2. O2: the sum over all classes of categorical covariates of the absolute deviations of the sample proportion of a given class from the population proportion of that class; and
3. O3: the sum over all entries of the correlation matrix of the absolute deviation of the correlation in the sample from the correlation in the population.

With cLH sampling, the marginal distributions of the covariates in the sample are close to these distributions in the population. This can be advantageous for mapping methods that do not rely on linear relations, for instance in machine learning techniques like classification and regression trees (CART), and random forests (RF). In addition, criterion O3 ensures that the correlations between predictors are respected in the sample set.

cLH samples can be selected with function `clhs` of package **clhs** (Roudier, 2021). With this package, the criterion is minimised by simulated annealing, see Section 23.1 for an explanation of this optimisation method. Arguments `iter`, `temp`, `tdecrease`, and `length.cycle` of function `clhs` are control parameters of the simulated annealing algorithm. In the next code chunk, I use default values for these arguments. With argument `weights`, the weights of the components of the minimisation criterion can be set. The default weights are equal to 1.

Argument `cost` is for cost-constrained cLH sampling (Roudier et al., 2012), and argument `eta` can be used to control the sampling intensities of the marginal strata (Minasny and McBratney, 2010). This argument is of interest if we would like to oversample the marginal strata near the edge of the multivariate distribution.

cLH sampling is illustrated with the five covariates of Eastern Amazonia that were used before in covariate space coverage sampling (Chapter 18).

```
library(clhs)
covs <- c("SWIR2", "Terra_PP", "Prec_dm", "Elevation", "Clay")
set.seed(314)
res <- clhs(
  grdAmazonia[, covs], size = 20, iter = 50000, temp = 1, tdecrease = 0.95,
  length.cycle = 10, progress = FALSE, simple = FALSE)
mysample_CLH <- grdAmazonia[res$index_samples, ]
```

Figure 19.2 shows the selected sample in a map of SWIR2. In Figure 19.3 the sample is plotted in a biplot of Prec_dm against SWIR2. Each black dot in the biplot represents one grid cell in the population. The vertical and horizontal lines in the biplot are at the bounds of the marginal strata of SWIR2 and Prec_dm, respectively. The number of grid cells between two consecutive vertical lines is constant, as well as the number of grid cells between two consecutive horizontal lines, i.e., the marginal strata have equal sizes. The intervals are the narrowest where the density of grid cells in the plot is highest. Ideally, in each column and row, there is exactly one sampling unit (red dot).

Figure 19.4 shows the sample sizes for all 100 marginal strata. The next code chunk shows how the marginal stratum sample sizes are computed.

```
probs <- seq(from = 0, to = 1, length.out = nrow(mysample_CLH) + 1)
bounds <- apply(grdAmazonia[, covs], MARGIN = 2,
  FUN = function(x) quantile(x, probs = probs))
mysample_CLH <- as.data.frame(mysample_CLH)
counts <- lapply(1:5, function(i)
  hist(mysample_CLH[, i + 3], bounds[, i], plot = FALSE)$counts)
```

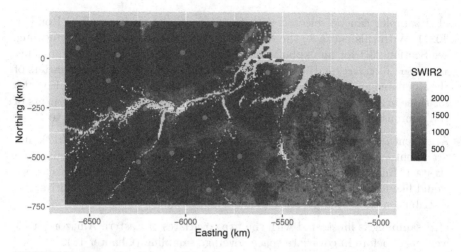

FIGURE 19.2: Conditioned Latin hypercube sample from Eastern Amazonia in a map of SWIR2.

For all marginal strata with one sampling unit, the contribution to component O1 of the minimisation criterion is 0. For marginal strata with zero or two sampling units, the contribution is 1, for marginal strata with three sampling units the contribution equals 2, etc. In Figure 19.4 there are four marginal strata with zero units and four marginal strata with two units. Component O1 therefore equals 8 in this case.

Figure 19.5 shows the trace of the objective function, i.e., the values of the minimisation criterion during the optimisation. The trace plot indicates that 50,000 iterations are sufficient. I do not expect that the criterion can be reduced anymore. The final value of the minimisation criterion is extracted with function `tail` using argument `n = 1`.

```
trace <- res$obj
tail(trace, n = 1)
```

```
[1] 9.51994
```

In the next code chunk, the minimised value of the criterion is computed "by hand".

```
O1 <- sum(abs(countslf$counts - 1))
rho <- cor(grdAmazonia[, covs])
r <- cor(mysample_CLH[, covs])
O3 <- sum(abs(rho - r))
print(O1 + O3)
```

```
[1] 9.51994
```

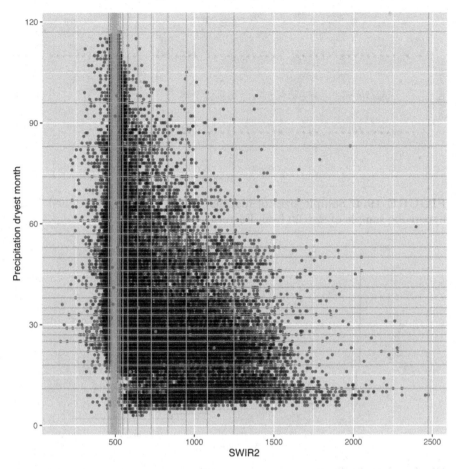

FIGURE 19.3: Conditioned Latin hypercube sample plotted in a biplot of precipitation in the dryest month against SWIR2. The vertical and horizontal lines are at the bounds of the marginal strata of the covariates SWIR2 and precipitation dryest month, respectively.

Exercises

1. Use the data of Hunter Valley (grdHunterValley of package **sswr**) to select a cLH sample of size 50, using elevation_m, slope_deg, cos_aspect, cti, and ndvi as covariates. Plot the selected sample in a map of covariate cti, and plot the selected sample in a biplot of cti against elevation_m. In which part of the biplot are most units selected, and which part is undersampled?

2. Load the simulated data of Figure 16.1 (results/SimulatedSquare.rda), and select a cLH sample of size 16, using the covariate x and the

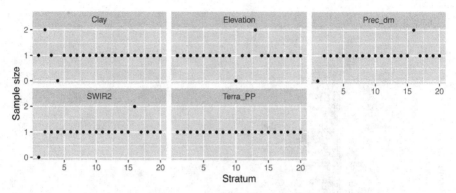

FIGURE 19.4: Sample sizes of marginal strata for the conditioned Latin hypercube sample of size 20 from Eastern Amazonia.

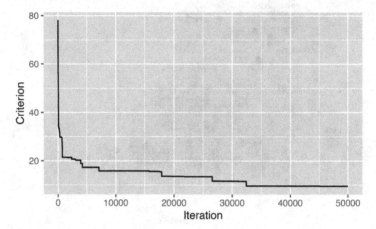

FIGURE 19.5: Trace of minimisation criterion during optimisation of conditioned Latin hypercube sampling from Eastern Amazonia.

spatial coordinates as stratification variables. Plot the selected sample in the square with simulated covariate values.

- What do you think of the geographical spreading of the sampling units? Is it optimal?
- Compute the number of sampling units in the marginal strata of $s1$, $s2$, and the covariate x. First, compute the bounds of these marginal strata. Are all marginal strata of $s1$ and $s2$ sampled? Suppose that all marginal strata of $s1$ and $s2$ are sampled (contain one sampling point), does this guarantee good spatial coverage?
- Plot the trace of the minimisation criterion, and retrieve the minimised value. Is this minimised value in agreement with the marginal stratum sample sizes?

19.1 Conditioned Latin hypercube infill sampling

Package **clhs** can also be used for selecting a conditioned Latin hypercube sample in addition to existing sampling units (legacy sample), as in spatial infill sampling (Section 17.2). The units of the legacy sample are assigned to argument must.include. Argument size must be set to the total sample size, i.e., the number of mandatory units (legacy sample units) plus the number of additional infill units.

To illustrate conditioned Latin hypercube *infill* sampling (cLHIS), in the next code chunk I select a simple random sample of ten units from Eastern Amazonia to serve as the legacy sample. Twenty new units are selected by cLHIS. The ten mandatory units (i.e., units which are already sampled and thus must be in the sample set computed by cLHIS) are at the end of the vector with the index of the selected raster cells.

```
set.seed(314)
units <- sample(nrow(grdAmazonia), 10, replace = FALSE)
res <- clhs(grdAmazonia[, covs], size = 30, must.include = units,
    tdecrease = 0.95, iter = 50000, progress = FALSE, simple = FALSE)
mysample_CLHI <- grdAmazonia[res$index_samples, ]
mysample_CLHI$free <- as.factor(rep(c(1, 0), c(20, 10)))
```

Figure 19.6 shows the selected cLHI sample in a map of SWIR2. In Figure 19.7 the sample is plotted in a biplot of SWIR2 against Prec_dm. The marginal strata already covered by the legacy sample are mostly avoided by the additional sample.

19.2 Performance of conditioned Latin hypercube sampling in random forest prediction

The performance of cLH sampling is studied in the same experiment as covariate space coverage sampling of the previous chapter. In total, 500 cLH samples of size 25 are selected and an equal number of samples of sizes 50 and 100. Each sample is used to calibrate a RF model for the aboveground biomass (AGB) using five covariates as predictors. The calibrated models are used to predict AGB at the 25,000 validation units selected by simple random sampling without replacement. Simple random (SI) sampling is added as a reference sampling design that ignores the covariates. The prediction errors

FIGURE 19.6: Conditioned Latin hypercube infill sample from Eastern Amazonia in a map of SWIR2. Legacy units have free-value 0; infill units have free-value 1.

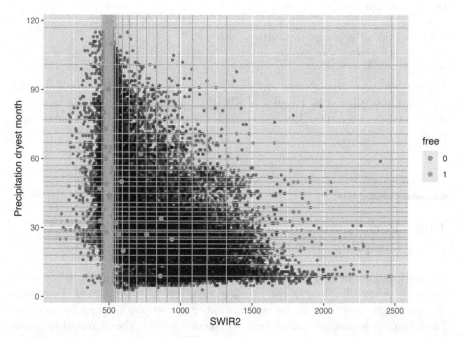

FIGURE 19.7: Conditioned Latin hypercube infill sample plotted in a biplot of SWIR2 against precipitation in the dryest month. Legacy units have free-value 0; infill units have free-value 1.

are used to estimate three map quality indices, the population mean error (ME), the population root mean squared error (RMSE), and the population Nash-Sutcliffe model efficiency coefficient (MEC), see Chapter 25.

Figure 19.8 shows the results as boxplots, each based on 500 estimates. For $n = 25$ and 100, cLH sampling performs best in terms of RMSE and MEC, whereas for $n = 50$ CSC sampling performs best. For $n = 25$ and 50, the boxplots of cLH and SI show quite a few outliers with large values of RMSE, resulting in small values of MEC. For CSC, these map quality indices are more stable. Remarkably, for $n = 100$ SI sampling performs about equally to CSC and cLH sampling.

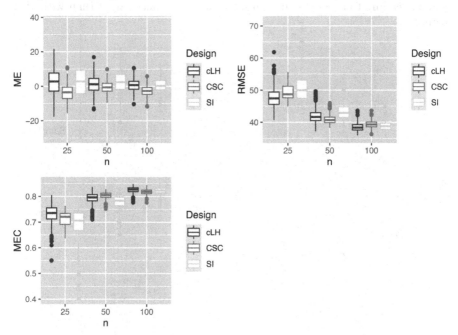

FIGURE 19.8: Boxplots of ME, RMSE, and MEC of predictions with RF models calibrated on conditioned Latin hypercube (cLH), covariate space coverage (CSC), and simple random (SI) samples from Eastern Amazonia, for sample sizes of 25, 50, and 100 units.

In Figure 19.9 the RMSE is plotted against the minimised criterion (O1 + O3) for the cLH and the SI samples. For all three sample sizes, there is a weak positive correlation of the minimisation criterion and the RMSE: for $n = 25$, 50, and 100 this correlation is 0.369, 0.290, and 0.140, respectively. On average, cLH performs slightly better than SI for $n = 25$ (Table 19.1). The gain in accuracy decreases with the sample size. For $n = 100$, the two designs perform about equally. Especially for $n = 25$ and 50, the distribution of RMSE with SI has a long right tail. For these small sample sizes, the risk of selecting an SI

TABLE 19.1: Mean RMSE of RF predictions of AGB in Eastern Amazonia of 500 conditioned Latin hypercube (cLH) samples and 500 simple random (SI) samples, and three sample sizes.

Sample size	cLH	SI
25	47.64	50.58
50	41.81	43.16
100	38.45	38.83

sample leading to a poor map with large RMSE is much larger than with cLH sampling.

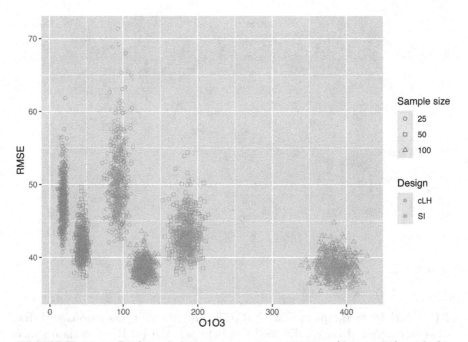

FIGURE 19.9: Biplot of the minimisation criterion (O1 + O3) and the RMSE of RF predictions of AGB in Eastern Amazonia for conditioned Latin hypercube (cLH) sampling and simple random (SI) sampling, and three sample sizes.

These results are somewhat different from the results of Wadoux et al. (2019) and Ma et al. (2020). In these case studies, cLH sampling appeared to be an inefficient design for selecting a calibration sample that is subsequently used for mapping. Wadoux et al. (2019) compared cLH, CSC, spatial coverage sampling (Section 17.2), and SI for mapping soil organic carbon in France with a RF model. The latter two sampling designs do not exploit the covariates in selecting the calibration units. Sample sizes were 100, 200, 500, and 1,000. cLH performed worse (larger RMSE) than CSC and not significantly better than SI for all sample sizes.

Ma et al. (2020) compared cLH, CSC, and SI for mapping soil classes by various models, among which a RF model, in a study area in Germany. Sample sizes were 20, 30, 40, 50, 75, and 100 points. They found no relation between the minimisation criterion of cLH and the overall accuracy of the map with predicted soil classes. Models calibrated on CSC samples performed better on average, i.e., on average the overall accuracy of the maps obtained by calibrating the models on these CSC samples was higher. cLH was hardly better than SI.

20

Spatial response surface sampling

As with conditioned Latin hypercube sampling, spatial response surface sampling is an experimental design adapted for spatial surveys. Experimental response surface designs aim at finding an optimum of the response within specified ranges of the factors. There are many types of response surface designs, see Myers et al. (2009). With response surface sampling one assumes that some type of low order regression model can be used to accurately approximate the relationship between the study variable and the covariates. A commonly used design is the central composite design. The data obtained with this design are used to fit a multiple linear regression model with quadratic terms, yielding a curved, quadratic surface of the response.

The response surface sampling approach is an adaptation of an experimental design, but at the same time it is an example of a model-based sampling design. Sampling units are selected to implicitly optimise the estimation of the quadratic regression model. However, this optimisation is done under one or more spatial constraints. Unconstrained optimisation of the sampling design under the linear regression model will not prevent the units from spatial clustering, see the optimal sample in Figure 16.1. The assumption of independent data might be violated when the sampling units are spatially clustered. For this reason, the response surface sampling design selects samples with good spatial coverage, so that the design becomes robust against violation of the independence assumption.

Lesch et al. (1995) adapted the response surface methodology for observational studies. Several problems needed to be tackled. First, when multiple covariates are used, the covariates must be decorrelated. Second, when sampling units are spatially clustered, the assumption in linear regression modelling of spatially uncorrelated model residuals can be violated. To address these two problems, Lesch et al. (1995) proposed the following procedure; see also Lesch (2005):

1. Transform the covariate matrix into a scaled, centred, decorrelated matrix by principal components analysis (PCA).

2. Choose the response surface design type.

3. Select candidate sampling units based on the distance from the design points in the space spanned by the principal components. Select multiple sampling units per design point.

4. Select the combination of candidate sampling units with the highest value for a criterion that quantifies how uniform the sample is spread across the study area.

This design has been applied, among others, for mapping soil salinity (ECe), using electromagnetic (EM) induction measurements and surface array conductivity measurements as predictors in multiple linear regression models. For applications, see Corwin and Lesch (2005), Lesch (2005), Fitzgerald et al. (2006), Corwin et al. (2010), and Fitzgerald (2010).

Spatial response surface sampling is illustrated with the EM measurements (mS m^{-1}) of the apparent electrical conductivity on the 80 ha Cotton Research Farm in Uzbekistan. The EM measurements in vertical dipole mode, with transmitter at 1 m and 0.5 m from the receiver, are on transects covering the Cotton Research Farm (Figure 20.1). As a first step, the natural log of the two EM measurements, denoted by lnEM, are interpolated by ordinary kriging to a fine grid (Figure 20.2). These ordinary kriging predictions of lnEM are used as covariates in response surface sampling. The two covariates are strongly correlated, $r = 0.73$, as expected since they are interpolations of measurements of the same variable but of different overlapping layers.

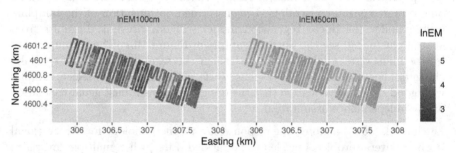

FIGURE 20.1: Natural log of EM measurements on the Cotton Research Farm (with transmitter at 1 m and 0.5 m from receiver).

Function `prcomp` of the **stats** package (R Core Team, 2021) is used to compute the principal component scores for all units in the population (grid cells). The two covariates are centred and scaled, i.e., standardised principal components are computed.

```
pc <- grdCRF %>%
  dplyr::select(lnEM100cm, lnEM50cm) %>%
  prcomp(center = TRUE, scale = TRUE)
```

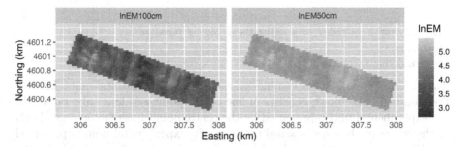

FIGURE 20.2: Interpolated surfaces of natural log of EM measurements on the Cotton Research Farm, used as covariates in spatial response surface sampling.

The means of the two principal component scores are 0; however, their standard deviations are not zero but 1.330 and 0.480. Therefore, the principal component scores are divided by these standard deviations. They then will have the same weight in the following steps.

```
grdCRF <- grdCRF %>%
  mutate(
    PC1 = pc$x[, 1] / pc$sdev[1],
    PC2 = pc$x[, 2] / pc$sdev[2])
```

Function ccd of package **rsm** (Lenth, 2009) is now used to generate a central composite response surface design (CCRSD). Argument basis specifies the number of factors, which is two in our case. Argument n0 is the number of centre points, and argument alpha determines the position of the star points (explained hereafter).

```
library(rsm)
set.seed(314)
print(ccdesign <- ccd(basis = 2, n0 = 1, alpha = "rotatable"))
```

```
   run.order std.order  x1.as.is   x2.as.is Block
1          1         4  1.000000   1.000000     1
2          2         5  0.000000   0.000000     1
3          3         2  1.000000  -1.000000     1
4          4         1 -1.000000  -1.000000     1
5          5         3 -1.000000   1.000000     1
6          1         5  0.000000   0.000000     2
7          2         3  0.000000  -1.414214     2
8          3         1 -1.414214   0.000000     2
9          4         4  0.000000   1.414214     2
10         5         2  1.414214   0.000000     2
```

```
Data are stored in coded form using these coding formulas ...
x1 ~ x1.as.is
x2 ~ x2.as.is
```

The experiment consists of two blocks, each of five experimental units. Block 1, the so-called cube block, consists of one centre point and four cube points. In the experimental unit represented by the centre point, both factors have levels in the centre of the experimental range. In the experimental units represented by the cube points, the levels of both factors is either -1 or +1 unit in the design space. Block 2, referred to as the star block, consists of one centre point and four star points. With `alpha = "rotatable"` the star points are on the circle circumscribing the square (Figure 20.3).

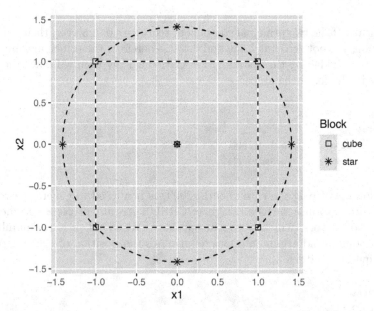

FIGURE 20.3: Rotatable central composite design for two factors.

To adapt this design for an observational study, we drop one of the centre points (0,0).

```
ccd_df <- data.frame(x1 = ccdesign$x1, x2 = ccdesign$x2)
ccd_df <- ccd_df[-6, ]
```

The coordinates of the CCRSD points are multiplied by a factor so that a large proportion p of the bivariate standardised principal component scores of the population units is covered by the circle that passes through the design points (Figure 20.3). The factor is computed as a sample quantile of the empirical distribution of the distances of the points in the scatter to the centre. For p, I chose 0.7.

```
d <- sqrt(grdCRF$PC1^2 + grdCRF$PC2^2)
fct <- quantile(d, p = 0.7)
print(fct)
```

```
     70%
1.472547
```

```
ccd_df <- ccd_df %>%
  mutate(x1 = x1 * fct, x2 = x2 * fct)
```

The next step is to select for each design point several candidate sampling points. For each of the nine design points, eight points are selected that are closest to that design point. This results in 9×8 candidate sampling points.

```
candi_all <- NULL
for (i in seq_len(nrow(ccd_df))) {
    d2dpnt <- sqrt((grdCRF$PC1 - ccd_df$x1[i])^2 +
      (grdCRF$PC2 - ccd_df$x2[i])^2)
    grdCRF <- grdCRF[order(d2dpnt), ]
    candi <- grdCRF[c(1:8), c("point_id", "x", "y", "PC1", "PC2")]
    candi$dpnt <- i
    candi_all <- rbind(candi_all, candi)
}
```

Figure 20.4 shows the nine clusters of candidate sampling points around the design points. Note that the location of the candidate sampling points associated with the design points with coordinates (0,-2.13), (1.51,-1.51), and (2.13,0) are all far inside the circle that passes through the design points. So, for the optimised sample, there will be three points with principal component scores that considerably differ from the ideal values according to the CCRSD design.

Figure 20.5 shows that in geographical space for most design points there are multiple spatial clusters of candidate units. For instance, for design point nine, there are three clusters of candidate sampling units. Therefore, there is scope to optimise the sample computationally.

As a first step, an initial subsample from the candidate sampling units is selected by stratified simple random sampling, using the levels of factor dpnt as strata. Function strata of package **sampling** is used for stratified random sampling (Tillé and Matei, 2021).

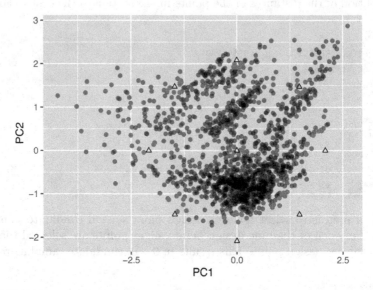

FIGURE 20.4: Clusters of points (red points) around the design points (triangles) of a CCRSD (two covariates), serving as candidate sampling points.

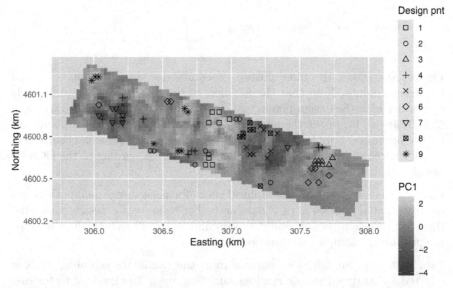

FIGURE 20.5: Candidate sampling points plotted on a map of the first standardised principal component (PC1).

```
library(sampling)
set.seed(314)
units_stsi <- sampling::strata(
  candi_all, stratanames = "dpnt", size = rep(1, 9))
mysample0 <- getdata(candi_all, units_stsi) %>%
  dplyr::select(-(ID_unit:Stratum))
```

The locations of the nine sampling units are now optimised by minimising a criterion that is a function of the distance between the nine sampling points. Two minimisation criteria are implemented, a geometric criterion and a model-based criterion.

In the geometric criterion (as proposed by Lesch (2005)) for each sampling point the log of the shortest distance to the other points is computed. The minimisation criterion is the negative of the sample mean of these distances.

The model-based minimisation criterion is the average correlation of the sampling points. This criterion requires as input the parameters of a residual correlogram (see Section 21.3). I assume an exponential correlogram without nugget, so that the only parameter to be chosen is the distance parameter ϕ (Equation (21.13)). Three times ϕ is referred to as the effective range of the exponential correlogram. The correlation of the random variables at two points separated by this distance is 0.05.

A penalty term is added to the geometric or the model-based minimisation criterion, equal to the average distance of the sampling points to the associated design points, multiplied by a weight. With weights > 0, sampling points close to the design points are preferred over more distant points.

In the next code chunk, a function is defined for computing the minimisation criterion. Given a chosen value for ϕ, the 9×9 distance matrix of the sampling points can be converted into a correlation matrix, using function variogramLine of package **gstat** (Pebesma, 2004). Argument weight is an optional argument with default value 0.

```
getCriterion <- function(mysample, dpnt, weight = 0, phi = NULL) {
  D2dpnt <- sqrt((mysample$PC1 - dpnt$x1)^2 + (mysample$PC2 - dpnt$x2)^2)
  D <- as.matrix(dist(mysample[, c("x", "y")]))
  if (is.null(phi)) {
    diag(D) <- NA
    logdmin <- apply(D, MARGIN = 1, FUN = min, na.rm = TRUE) %>% log
    criterion_cur <- mean(-logdmin) + mean(D2dpnt) * weight
  } else {
    vgmodel <- vgm(model = "Exp", psill = 1, range = phi)
    C <- variogramLine(vgmodel, dist_vector = D, covariance = TRUE)
    criterion_cur <- mean(C) + mean(D2dpnt) * weight
```

```
  }
  return(criterion_cur)
}
```

Function `getCriterion` is used to compute the geometric criterion for the initial sample.

```
criterion_geo <- getCriterion(mysample = mysample0, dpnt = ccd_df)
```

The initial value of the geometric criterion is -4.829. In the next code chunk, the initial value for the model-based criterion is computed for an effective range of 150 m.

It does not make sense to make the effective range smaller than the size of the grid cells, which is 25 m in our case. For smaller ranges, the correlation matrix is for any sample a matrix with zeroes. If the effective range is smaller than the smallest distance between two points in a cluster, the mean correlation is equal for all samples.

```
phi <- 50
criterion_mb <- getCriterion(mysample = mysample0, dpnt = ccd_df, phi = phi)
```

The initial value of the model-based criterion is 0.134.

The objective function defining the minimisation criterion is minimised with simulated annealing (Kirkpatrick et al. (1983), Aarts and Korst (1989)). One sampling point is randomly selected and replaced by another candidate sampling point from the same cluster. If the criterion of the new sample is smaller than that of the current sample, the new sample is accepted. If it is larger, it is accepted with a probability that is a function of the change in the criterion (the larger the increase, the smaller the acceptance probability) and of an annealing parameter named the temperature (the higher the temperature, the larger the probability of accepting a new, poorer sample, given an increase of the criterion). See Section 23.1 for a more detailed introduction to simulated annealing.

The sampling pattern can be optimised with function `anneal` of package **sswr**. The arguments of this function will be clear from the description of the sampling procedure above.

```
set.seed(314)
mySRSsample <- anneal(
  mysample = mysample0, candidates = candi_all, dpnt = ccd_df, phi = 50,
```

```
T_ini = 1, coolingRate = 0.9, maxPermuted = 25 * nrow(mysample0),
maxNoChange = 20, verbose = TRUE)
```

Figure 20.6 shows the optimised CCRSD samples plotted in the space spanned by the two principal components, obtained with the geometric and the model-based criterion, plotted together with the design points. The two optimised samples are very similar.

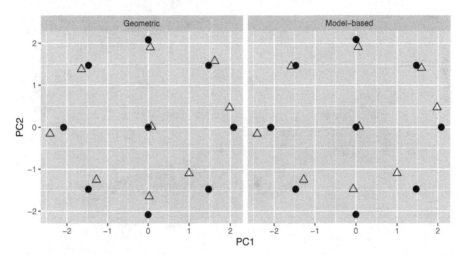

FIGURE 20.6: Principal component scores of the spatial CCRSD sample (triangles), optimised with the geometric and the model-based criterion. Dots: design points of CCRSD.

Figure 20.7 shows the two optimised CCRSD samples plotted in geographical space on the first standardised principal component scores.

20.1 Increasing the sample size

Nine points are rather few for fitting a polynomial regression model, especially for a second-order polynomial with interaction. Therefore, in experiments often multiple observations are done for each design point. Increasing the sample size of a response surface sample in observational studies is not straightforward. The challenge is to avoid spatial clustering of sampling points. A simple solution is to select multiple points from each subset of candidate sampling units. The success of this solution depends on how strong candidate sampling units are spatially clustered. For the Cotton Research Farm for most design points the

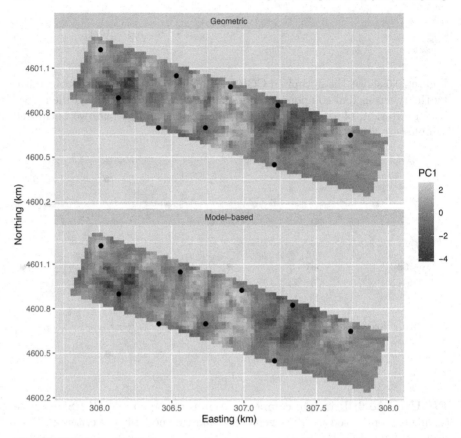

FIGURE 20.7: CCRSD sample from the Cotton Research Farm, optimised with the geometric and the model-based criterion, plotted on a map of the first standardised principal component (PC1).

candidate sampling units are not in one spatial cluster; so in this case, the solution may work properly. I increased the number of candidate sampling units per design point to 16, so that there is a larger choice in the optimisation of the sampling pattern.

```
candi_all <- NULL
for (i in seq_len(nrow(ccd_df))) {
    d2dpnt <- sqrt((grdCRF$PC1 - ccd_df$x1[i])^2 +
      (grdCRF$PC2 - ccd_df$x2[i])^2)
    grdCRF <- grdCRF[order(d2dpnt), ]
    candi <- grdCRF[c(1:16), c("point_id", "x", "y", "PC1", "PC2")]
    candi$dpnt <- i
```

```
        candi_all <- rbind(candi_all, candi)
}
```

A stratified simple random subsample of two points per stratum is selected, which serves as an initial sample.

```
set.seed(314)
units_stsi <- sampling::strata(
  candi_all, stratanames = "dpnt", size = rep(2, 9))
mysample0 <- getdata(candi_all, units_stsi) %>%
  dplyr::select(-(ID_unit:Stratum))
```

The data frame with the design points must be doubled. Note that the order of the design points must be equal to the order in the stratified subsample.

```
tmp <- data.frame(ccd_df, dpnt = 1:9)
ccd_df2 <- rbind(tmp, tmp)
ccd_df2 <- ccd_df2[order(ccd_df2$dpnt), ]
```

Figures 20.8 and 20.9 show the optimised CCRSD sample of 18 points in geographical and principal component space, respectively, obtained with the model-based criterion, an effective range of 150 m, and zero weight for the penalty term. Sampling points are not spatially clustered, so I do not expect violation of the assumption of independent residuals. In principal component space, all points are pretty close to the design points, except for the four design points in the lower right corner, where no candidate units near these design points are available.

20.2   Stratified spatial response surface sampling

The sample size can also be increased by stratified spatial response surface sampling. The strata are subareas of the study area. When the subsets of candidate sampling units for some design points are strongly spatially clustered, the final optimised sample obtained with the method of the previous section may also show strong spatial clustering. An alternative is then to split the study area into two or more subareas (strata) and to select from each stratum candidate sampling units. This guarantees that for each design point we have at least as many spatial clusters of candidate units as we have strata.

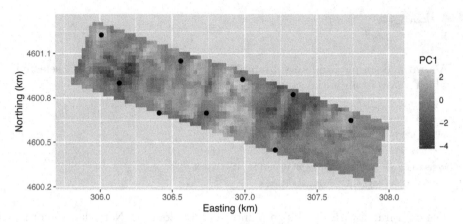

FIGURE 20.8: CCRSD sample with two points per design point, from the Cotton Research Farm, plotted on a map of the first standardised principal component (PC1).

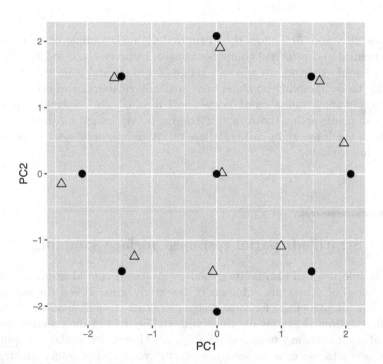

FIGURE 20.9: CCRSD sample (triangles) with two points per design point (dots), optimised with model-based criterion, plotted in the space spanned by the two standardised principal components.

The spatial strata are not used for fitting separate regression models. All data are used to fit one (second-order) polynomial regression model.

Figure 20.10 shows two subareas used as strata in stratified response surface sampling of the Cotton Research Farm.

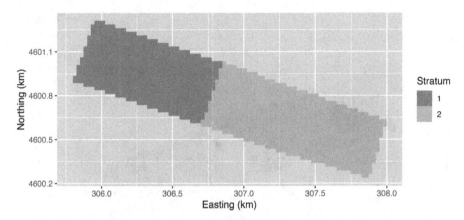

FIGURE 20.10: Two subareas of the Cotton Research Farm used as strata in stratified CCRSD sampling.

The candidate sampling units are selected in a double for-loop. The outer loop is over the strata, the inner loop over the design points. Note that variable dpnt continues to increase by 1 after the inner loop over the nine design points in subarea 1 is completed, so that variable dpnt (used as a stratification variable in subsampling the sample of candidate sampling points) now has values $1, 2, \ldots, 18$. An equal number of candidate sampling points per design point in both strata (eight points) is selected by sorting the points of a stratum by the distance to a design point using function order. Figure 20.11 shows the candidate sampling points for stratified CCRSD sampling.

```
candi_all <- NULL
for (h in c(1, 2)) {
  data_stratum <- grdCRF %>%
    filter(subarea == h)
  candi_stratum <- NULL
  for (i in seq_len(nrow(ccd_df))) {
    d2dpnt <- sqrt((data_stratum$PC1 - ccd_df$x1[i])^2 +
                   (data_stratum$PC2 - ccd_df$x2[i])^2)
    data_stratum <- data_stratum[order(d2dpnt), ]
    candi <- data_stratum[c(1:8),
        c("point_id", "x", "y", "PC1", "PC2", "subarea")]
```

```
      candi$dpnt <- i + (h - 1) * nrow(ccd_df)
      candi_stratum <- rbind(candi_stratum, candi)
  }
  candi_all <- rbind(candi_all, candi_stratum)
}
```

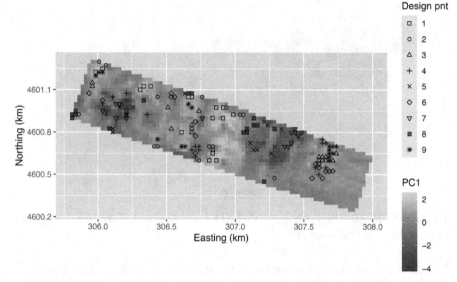

FIGURE 20.11: Candidate sampling points for stratified CCRSD sampling, plotted on a map of the first principal component (PC1).

As before, dpnt is used as a stratum identifier to subsample the candidate sampling units. Finally, the number of rows in data.frame ccd_df with the design points is doubled.

```
set.seed(314)
units_stsi <- sampling::strata(
  candi_all, stratanames = "dpnt", size = rep(1, 18))
mysample0 <- getdata(candi_all, units_stsi) %>%
  dplyr::select(-(ID_unit:Stratum))
ccd_df2 <- rbind(ccd_df, ccd_df)
```

Figures 20.12 and 20.13 show the optimised sample of 18 points in geographical and principal component space, obtained with the model-based criterion with an effective range of 150 m. The pattern in the principal component space is worse compared to the pattern in Figure 20.9. In stratum 1, the distance to the star point at the top and the upper left and upper right cube points is very large. In this stratum no population units are present that are close to these design points. By adding a penalty term to the minimisation criterion that is proportional to the distance to the design points, the distance is somewhat decreased, but not really for the three design points mentioned above (Figure 20.9). Also note the spatial cluster of three sampling units in Figure 20.12 obtained with a weight equal to 5.

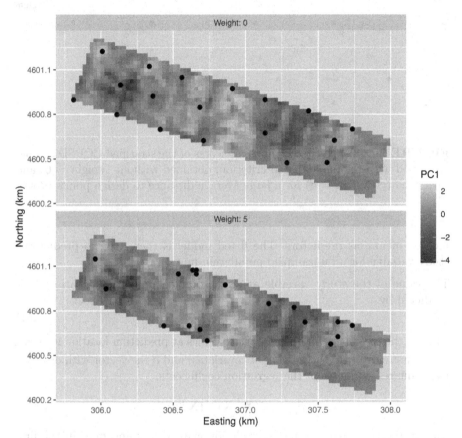

FIGURE 20.12: Stratified CCRSD samples from the Cotton Research Farm, optimised with the model-based criterion, obtained without (weight = 0) and with penalty (weight = 5) for a large average distance to design points.

20.3 Mapping

Once the data are collected, the study variable is mapped by fitting a multiple linear regression model using the two covariates, in our case the two EM

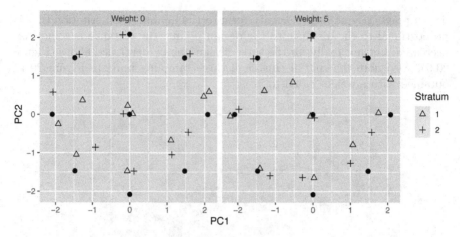

FIGURE 20.13: Principal component scores of the stratified CCRSD sample, optimised with the model-based criterion, obtained without (weight = 0) and with penalty (weight = 5) for a large average distance to design points (dots).

measurements, as predictors. The fitted model is then used to predict the study variable for all unsampled population units.

The value of the study variable at an unsampled prediction location $\mathbf{s}_0$ is predicted by

$$\widehat{Z}(\mathbf{s}_0) = \mathbf{x}_0 \hat{\boldsymbol{\beta}}_{\text{OLS}} \,, \tag{20.1}$$

with $\mathbf{x}_0$ the $(p+1)$-vector with covariate values at prediction location $\mathbf{s}_0$ and 1 in the first entry (p is the number of covariates) and $\hat{\boldsymbol{\beta}}$ the vector with ordinary least squares estimates of the regression coefficients:

$$\hat{\beta}_{\text{OLS}} = (\mathbf{X}^{\text{T}}\mathbf{X})^{-1}(\mathbf{X}^{\text{T}}\mathbf{z}) \,, \tag{20.2}$$

with $\mathbf{X}$ the $(n \times (p+1))$ matrix with covariate values and ones in the first column (n is the sample size, and p is the number of covariates) and $\mathbf{z}$ the n-vector with observations of the study variable.

Although the principal component scores are used to select the sampling locations, there is no need to use these scores as predictors in the linear regression model. When all principal components derived from the covariates are used as predictors, the predicted values and standard errors obtained with the model using the principal components as predictors are equal to those obtained with the model using the covariates as predictors.

The variance of the prediction error can be estimated by

$$\hat{V}(\hat{Z}(\mathbf{s}_0)) = \hat{\sigma}_\epsilon^2 (1 + \mathbf{x}_0^{\mathrm{T}}(\mathbf{X}^{\mathrm{T}}\mathbf{X})^{-1}\mathbf{x}_0) , \qquad (20.3)$$

with $\hat{\sigma}_\epsilon^2$ the estimated variance of the residuals.

In **R** the model can be calibrated with function lm, and the predictions can be obtained with function predict. The standard errors of the estimated means can be obtained with argument se.fit = TRUE. The variances of Equation (20.3) can be computed by squaring these standard errors and adding the squared value of the estimated residual variance, which can be extracted with sigma().

```
mdl <- lm(lnECe ~ lnEM100cm + lnEM50cm, data = mysample)
zpred <- predict(mdl, newdata = grdCRF, se.fit = TRUE)
v_zpred <- zpred$se.fit^2+sigma(mdl)^2
```

The assumption underlying Equations (20.2) and (20.3) is that the model residuals are independent. We assume that all the spatial structure of the study variable is explained by the covariates. Even the residuals at two locations close to each other are assumed to be uncorrelated. A drawback of the spatial response surface design is that it is hard or even impossible to check this assumption, as the sampling locations are spread throughout the study area. If the residuals are not independent, the covariance of the residuals can be accounted for by generalised least squares estimation of the regression coefficients (Equation (21.24)). The study variable can then be mapped by kriging with an external drift (Section 21.3). However, this requires an estimate of the semivariogram of the residuals (Section 21.5).

21

Introduction to kriging

In the following chapters a geostatistical model, i.e., a statistical model of the spatial variation of the study variable, is used to optimise the sample size and/or spatial pattern of the sampling locations. This chapter is a short introduction to geostatistical modelling.

In Chapter 13 we have already seen how a geostatistical model can be used to optimise probability sampling designs for estimating the population mean or total. In the following chapters, the focus is on mapping. A map of the study variable is obtained by predicting the study variable at the nodes of a fine discretisation grid. Spatial prediction using a geostatistical model is referred to as kriging (Webster and Oliver, 2007).

With this prediction method, besides a map of the kriging predictions, a map of the variance of the prediction error is obtained. I will show hereafter that the prediction error variance is not influenced by the values of the study variable at the sampling locations. For this reason, it is possible to search, before the start of the survey, for the sampling locations that lead to the minimum prediction error variance averaged over all nodes of a fine prediction grid, provided that the geostatistical model is known up to some extent.

21.1 Ordinary kriging

The kriging predictions and prediction error variances are derived from a statistical model of the spatial variation of the study variable. There are several versions of kriging, but most of them are special cases of the following generic model:

$$Z(\mathbf{s}) = \mu(\mathbf{s}) + \epsilon(\mathbf{s})$$
$$\epsilon(\mathbf{s}) \sim \mathcal{N}(0, \sigma^2) \qquad (21.1)$$
$$\mathrm{Cov}(\epsilon(\mathbf{s}), \epsilon(\mathbf{s}')) = C(\mathbf{h}),$$

with $Z(\mathbf{s})$ the study variable at location $\mathbf{s}$, $\mu(\mathbf{s})$ the mean at location $\mathbf{s}$, $\epsilon(\mathbf{s})$ the residual (difference between study variable z and mean $\mu(\mathbf{s})$) at location $\mathbf{s}$, and $C(\mathbf{h})$ the covariance of the residuals at two locations separated by vector $\mathbf{h} = \mathbf{s} - \mathbf{s}'$.

In *ordinary kriging* (OK) it is assumed that the mean of the study variable is constant, i.e., the same everywhere (Webster and Oliver, 2007):

$$Z(\mathbf{s}) = \mu + \epsilon(\mathbf{s}) , \qquad (21.2)$$

with μ the constant mean, independent of the location $\mathbf{s}$. Stated otherwise, in OK we assume *stationarity in the mean* over the area to be mapped.

$C(\cdot)$ is the covariance function, also referred to as the covariogram, and a scaled version of it, obtained by dividing $C(\cdot)$ by the variance $C(0)$, is the correlation function or correlogram.

If the data set is of substantial size, it is possible to define a neighbourhood: not all sample data are used to predict the study variable at a prediction location, but only the sample data in this neighbourhood. This implies that the stationarity assumption is relaxed to the often more realistic assumption of a constant mean within neighbourhoods.

In OK, the study variable at a prediction location $\mathbf{s}_0$, $\widehat{Z}(\mathbf{s}_0)$, is predicted as a weighted average of the observations at the sampling locations (within the neighbourhood):

$$\widehat{Z}_{\mathrm{OK}}(\mathbf{s}_0) = \sum_{i=1}^{n} \lambda_i \, Z(\mathbf{s}_i) , \qquad (21.3)$$

where $Z(\mathbf{s}_i)$ is the study variable at the ith sampling location and λ_i is the weight attached to this location. The weights should be related to the correlation of the study variable at the sampling location and the prediction location. Note that as the mean is assumed constant (Equation (21.2)), the correlation of the study variable Z is equal to the correlation of the residual ϵ. Roughly speaking, the stronger this correlation, the larger the weight must be. If we have a model for this correlation, then we can use this model to find the optimal weights. Further, if two sampling locations are very close, the weight attached to these two locations should not be twice the weight attached to a single, isolated sampling location at the same distance of the prediction location. This explains that in computing the kriging weights, besides the covariances of the n pairs of prediction location and sampling location, also the covariances of the $n(n-1)/2$ pairs that can be formed with the n sampling units are used, see Isaaks and Srivastava (1989) for a nice intuitive explanation. For OK, the optimal weights, i.e., the weights that lead to the model-unbiased[1]

---

[1]Model-unbiasedness is explained in Chapter 26.

predictor with minimum error variance (best linear unbiased predictor), can be found by solving the following $n + 1$ equations:

$$\begin{aligned}
\sum_{j=1}^{n} \lambda_j C(\mathbf{s}_1, \mathbf{s}_j) + \nu &= C(\mathbf{s}_1, \mathbf{s}_0) \\
\sum_{j=1}^{n} \lambda_j C(\mathbf{s}_2, \mathbf{s}_j) + \nu &= C(\mathbf{s}_2, \mathbf{s}_0) \\
&\vdots \\
\sum_{j=1}^{n} \lambda_j C(\mathbf{s}_n, \mathbf{s}_j) + \nu &= C(\mathbf{s}_n, \mathbf{s}_0) \\
\sum_{j=1}^{n} \lambda_j &= 1
\end{aligned} \tag{21.4}$$

where $C(\mathbf{s}_i, \mathbf{s}_j)$ is the covariance of the ith and jth sampling location, $C(\mathbf{s}_i, \mathbf{s}_0)$ is the covariance of the ith sampling location and the prediction location s_0, and ν is an extra parameter to be estimated, referred to as the Lagrange multiplier. This Lagrange multiplier must be included in the set of equations because the error variance is minimised under the constraint that the kriging weights sum to 1, see the final line in Equation (21.4). This constraint ensures that the OK-predictor is model-unbiased. It is convenient to write this system of equations in matrix form:

$$\begin{bmatrix}
C_{11} & C_{12} & \cdots & C_{1n} & 1 \\
C_{21} & C_{22} & \cdots & C_{2n} & 1 \\
\vdots & \vdots & \cdots & \vdots & \vdots \\
C_{n1} & C_{n2} & \cdots & C_{nn} & 1 \\
1 & 1 & \cdots & 1 & 0
\end{bmatrix}
\begin{bmatrix}
\lambda_1 \\
\lambda_2 \\
\vdots \\
\lambda_n \\
\nu
\end{bmatrix}
=
\begin{bmatrix}
C_{10} \\
C_{20} \\
\vdots \\
C_{n0} \\
1
\end{bmatrix}. \tag{21.5}$$

Replacing submatrices by single symbols results in the shorthand matrix equation:

$$\begin{bmatrix}
\mathbf{C} & \mathbf{1} \\
\mathbf{1}^{\mathrm{T}} & 0
\end{bmatrix}
\begin{bmatrix}
\boldsymbol{\lambda} \\
\nu
\end{bmatrix}
=
\begin{bmatrix}
\mathbf{c}_0 \\
1
\end{bmatrix}. \tag{21.6}$$

The kriging weights $\boldsymbol{\lambda}$ and the Lagrange multiplier ν can then be computed by premultiplying both sides of Equation (21.6) with the inverse of the first matrix of this equation:

$$\begin{bmatrix}
\boldsymbol{\lambda} \\
\nu
\end{bmatrix}
=
\begin{bmatrix}
\mathbf{C} & \mathbf{1} \\
\mathbf{1}^{\mathrm{T}} & 0
\end{bmatrix}^{-1}
\begin{bmatrix}
\mathbf{c}_0 \\
1
\end{bmatrix}. \tag{21.7}$$

The variance of the prediction error (ordinary kriging variance, OK variance) at a prediction location equals

$$V_{\mathrm{OK}}(\widehat{Z}(\mathbf{s}_0)) = \sigma^2 - \boldsymbol{\lambda}^{\mathrm{T}} \mathbf{c}_0 - \nu, \tag{21.8}$$

with σ^2 the a priori variance, see Equation (21.2). This equation shows that the OK variance is not a function of the data at the sampling locations. Given a covariance function, it is fully determined by the spatial pattern of the sampling locations and the prediction location. It is this property of kriging that makes it possible to optimise the grid spacing (Chapter 22) and, as we will see in Chapter 23, to optimise the spatial pattern of the sampling locations, given a requirement on the kriging variance. If the kriging variance were a function of the data at the sampling locations, optimisation would be much more complicated.

In general practice, the covariance function is not used in kriging, rather a semivariogram. A semivariogram $\gamma(\mathbf{h})$ is a model of the *dissimilarity* of the study variable at two locations, as a function of the vector $\mathbf{h}$ separating the two locations. The dissimilarity is quantified by half the variance of the difference of the study variable Z at two locations. Under the assumption that the expectation of Z is constant throughout the study area (stationarity in the mean), half the variance of the difference is equal to half the expectation of the squared difference:

$$\gamma(\mathbf{h}) = 0.5 V[Z(\mathbf{s}) - Z(\mathbf{s} + \mathbf{h})] = 0.5 E[\{Z(\mathbf{s}) - Z(\mathbf{s} + \mathbf{h})\}^2] . \qquad (21.9)$$

A covariance function and semivariogram are related by (see Figure 21.1)

$$\gamma(\mathbf{h}) = \sigma^2 - C(\mathbf{h}) . \qquad (21.10)$$

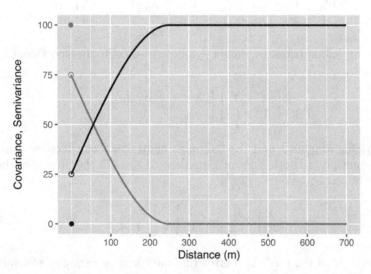

FIGURE 21.1: Spherical covariance function (red line and dot) and semivariogram (black line and dot).

Expressed in terms of the *semivariances* between the sampling locations and a prediction location, the OK variance is

$$V_{OK}(\widehat{Z}(\mathbf{s}_0)) = \lambda^T \gamma_0 + \nu, \tag{21.11}$$

with γ_0 the vector with semivariances between the sampling locations and a prediction location.

Computing the kriging predictor requires a model for the covariance (or semivariance) as a function of the vector separating two locations. Often, the covariance is modelled as a function of the length of the separation vector only, so as a function of the Euclidian distance between two locations. We then assume isotropy: given a separation distance between two locations, the covariance is the same in all directions. Only authorised functions are allowed for modelling the semivariance, ensuring that the variance of any linear combination of random variables, like the kriging predictor, is positive. Commonly used functions are an exponential and a spherical model.

The spherical semivariogram model has three parameters:

1. nugget (c_0): where the semivariogram touches the y-axis (in Figure 21.1: 25);
2. partial sill (c_1): the difference between the maximum semivariance and the nugget (in Figure 21.1: 75); and
3. range (ϕ): the distance at which the semivariance reaches its maximum (in Figure 21.1: 250 m).

The formula for the spherical semivariogram is

$$\gamma(h) = \begin{cases} 0 & \text{if } h = 0 \\ c_0 + c_1 \left[1 - \frac{3}{2}\left(\frac{h}{\phi}\right) + \frac{1}{2}\left(\frac{h}{\phi}\right)^3\right] & \text{if } 0 < h \leq \phi \\ c_0 + c_1 & \text{if } h > \phi \end{cases} \tag{21.12}$$

The sum of the nugget and the partial sill is referred to as the sill (or sill variance or a priori variance).

An exponential semivariogram model also has three parameters. Its formula is

$$\gamma(h) = \begin{cases} 0 & \text{if } h = 0 \\ c_0 + c_1 \exp(-h/\phi) & \text{if } h > 0 \end{cases} \tag{21.13}$$

In an exponential semivariogram, the semivariance goes asymptotically to a maximum; it never reaches it. In an exponential semivariogram, the range parameter is replaced by the distance parameter. In an exponential semivariogram without nugget, the semivariance at three times the distance parameter is at 95% of the sill. Three times the distance parameter is referred to as the *effective* or *practical* range.

In following chapters, I also use a correlogram, which is a scaled covariance function, such that the sill of the correlogram equals 1:

$$\rho(\mathbf{h}) = \frac{C(\mathbf{h})}{\sigma^2} \, . \tag{21.14}$$

To illustrate that the OK variance is independent of the values of the study variable at the sampling locations, I simulated a spatial population of 50 × 50 units. For each unit a value of the study variable is simulated, using the semivariogram of Figure 21.1. This is repeated ten times, resulting in ten maps of 2,500 units. Figure 21.2 shows two of the ten simulated maps. Note that the two maps clearly show spatial structure, i.e., there are patches of similar values.

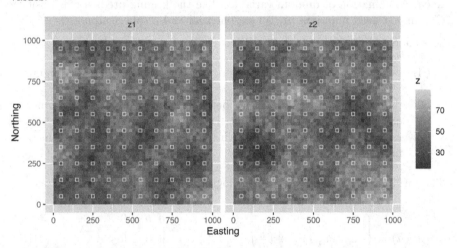

FIGURE 21.2: Two maps simulated with the spherical semivariogram of Figure 21.1, the centred square grid of sampling units, and the prediction unit (red cell with coordinates (590,670)).

The simulated maps are sampled on a centred square grid with a spacing of 100 distance units, resulting in a sample of 100 units. Each sample is used one-by-one to predict the study variable at one prediction location (see Figure 21.2), using again the semivariogram of Figure 21.1. The semivariogram is passed to function vgm of package **gstat** (Pebesma, 2004). Usually, this semivariogram is estimated from a sample, see Chapter 24, but here we assume that it is known. Function krige of package **gstat** is used for kriging. Argument formula specifies the dependent (study variable) and independent variables (covariates). The formula z ~ 1 means that we do not have covariates (we assume that the model-mean is a constant) and that predictions are done by OK (or simple kriging, see Section 21.3). Argument `locations` is a `SpatialPointsDataFrame` with the spatial coordinates and observations. Argument `newdata` is a `SpatialPoints` object with the locations we want to predict. Argument `nmax` can be used to specify the neighbourhood in terms of the number of nearest observations to be used in kriging (not used in the code chunk below, so that all 100 observations are used).

```
library(sp)
library(gstat)
vgmodel <- vgm(model = "Sph", nugget = 25, psill = 75, range = 250)
gridded(mypop) <- ~ s1 + s2
mysample <- spsample(x = mypop, type = "regular", cellsize = c(100, 100),
    offset = c(0.5, 0.5))
zsim_sample <- over(mysample, mypop)
coordinates(s_0) <- ~ s1 + s2
zpred_OK <- v_zpred_OK <- NULL
for (i in seq_len(ncol(Z))) {
  mysample$z <- zsim_sample[, i]
  predictions <- krige(
    formula = z ~ 1,
    locations = mysample,
    newdata = s_0,
    model = vgmodel,
    debug.level = 0)
  zpred_OK[i] <- predictions$var1.pred
  v_zpred_OK[i] <- predictions$var1.var
}
```

As can be seen in Table 21.1, unlike the predicted value, the OK variance produced from the different simulations is constant.

21.2 Block-kriging

In the previous section, the support of the prediction units is equal to that of the sampling units. So, if the observations are done at points (point support), the support of the predictions are also points, and if means of small blocks are observed, the predictions are predicted means of blocks of the same size and shape. There is no change of support. In some cases we may prefer predictions at a larger support than that of the observations. For instance, we may prefer predictions of the average concentration of some soil property of blocks of 5 m × 5 m, instead of predictions at points, simply because of practical relevance.

TABLE 21.1: Ordinary kriging predictions and kriging variance at a fixed prediction location for ten data sets with simulated values at a square sampling grid.

Kriging prediction	Kriging variance
51.44286	55.30602
57.29272	55.30602
52.44407	55.30602
51.40719	55.30602
63.09248	55.30602
40.57517	55.30602
54.48507	55.30602
47.42828	55.30602
43.65313	55.30602
44.52740	55.30602

If the observations are at points, there is a change of support, from points to blocks. Kriging with a prediction support that is larger than the support of the sample data is referred to as block-kriging. Kriging without change of support so that sample support and prediction support are equal, is referred to as point-kriging. Note that point-kriging does not necessarily imply that the support is a point; it can be, for instance, a small block.

In block-kriging the mean of a prediction block $\mathcal{B}_0$ is predicted as a weighted average of the observations at the sampling units. The kriging weights are derived much in the same way as in point-kriging (Equations (21.4) to (21.7)). In block-kriging the covariance between a sampling point i and a prediction point, $C(\mathbf{s}_i, \mathbf{s}_0)$, is replaced by the *mean* covariance between the sampling point and a prediction block $\overline{C}(\mathbf{s}_i, \mathcal{B}_0)$ (Equation (21.4)). This mean covariance can be approximated by discretising the prediction block by a fine grid, computing the covariance between a sampling point i and each of the discretisation points, and averaging.

The variance of the prediction error of the block-mean (block-kriging variance) equals

$$V_{\mathrm{OBK}}(\widehat{\overline{Z}}(\mathcal{B}_0)) = \lambda^{\mathrm{T}} \bar{\gamma}(\mathcal{B}_0) + \nu - \bar{\gamma}(\mathcal{B}_0, \mathcal{B}_0) , \qquad (21.15)$$

with $\bar{\gamma}(\mathcal{B}_0)$ the vector with mean semivariances between the sampling points and a prediction block and $\bar{\gamma}(\mathcal{B}_0, \mathcal{B}_0)$ the mean semivariance within the prediction block. Comparing this with Equation (21.11) shows that the block-kriging variance is smaller than the point-kriging variance by an amount approximately equal to the mean semivariance within a prediction block. Recall from Chapter 13 that the mean semivariance within a block is a model-based prediction of the variance within a block (Equation (13.3)).

21.3 Kriging with an external drift

In kriging with an external drift (KED), the spatial variation of the study variable is modelled as the sum of a linear combination of covariates and a spatially correlated residual:

$$Z(\mathbf{s}) = \sum_{k=0}^{p} \beta_k x_k(\mathbf{s}) + \epsilon(\mathbf{s})$$
$$\epsilon(\mathbf{s}) \sim \mathcal{N}(0, \sigma^2) \tag{21.16}$$
$$\mathrm{Cov}(\epsilon(\mathbf{s}), \epsilon(\mathbf{s}')) = C(\mathbf{h}) \,,$$

with $x_k(\mathbf{s})$ the value of the kth covariate at location $\mathbf{s}$ ($x_0 = 1$ for all locations), p the number of covariates, and $C(\mathbf{h})$ the covariance of the residuals at two locations separated by vector $\mathbf{h} = \mathbf{s} - \mathbf{s}'$. The constant mean μ in Equation (21.2) is replaced by a linear combination of covariates and, as a consequence, the mean is not constant anymore but varies in space.

With KED, the study variable at a prediction location $\mathbf{s}_0$ is predicted by

$$\hat{Z}_{\mathrm{KED}}(\mathbf{s}_0) = \sum_{k=0}^{p} \hat{\beta}_k x_k(\mathbf{s}_0) + \sum_{i=1}^{n} \lambda_i \left\{ Z(\mathbf{s}_i) - \sum_{k=0}^{p} \hat{\beta}_k x_k(\mathbf{s}_i) \right\}, \tag{21.17}$$

with $\hat{\beta}_k$ the estimated regression coefficient associated with covariate x_k. The first component of this predictor is the estimated model-mean at the new location based on the covariate values at this location and the estimated regression coefficients. The second component is a weighted sum of the residuals at the sampling locations.

The optimal kriging weights λ_i, $i = 1, \ldots, n$ are obtained in a similar way as in OK. The difference is that additional constraints on the weights are needed, to ensure unbiased predictions. Not only the weights must sum to 1, but also for all p covariates the weighted sum of the covariate values at the sampling locations must equal the covariate value at the prediction location: $\sum_{i=1}^{n} \lambda_i x_k(\mathbf{s}_i) = x_k(\mathbf{s}_0)$ for all $k = 1, \ldots, p$. This leads to a system of $n + p + 1$ simultaneous equations that must be solved. In matrix notation, this system is

$$\begin{bmatrix} \mathbf{C} & \mathbf{X} \\ \mathbf{X}^{\mathrm{T}} & \mathbf{0} \end{bmatrix} \begin{bmatrix} \lambda \\ \nu \end{bmatrix} = \begin{bmatrix} \mathbf{c}_0 \\ \mathbf{x}_0 \end{bmatrix}, \tag{21.18}$$

with

$$\mathbf{X} = \begin{bmatrix} 1 & x_{11} & x_{12} & \cdots & x_{1p} \\ 1 & x_{21} & x_{22} & \cdots & x_{2p} \\ \vdots & \vdots & \vdots & \cdots & \vdots \\ 1 & x_{n1} & x_{n2} & \cdots & x_{np} \end{bmatrix} . \tag{21.19}$$

The submatrix $\mathbf{0}$ is a $((p+1) \times (p+1))$ matrix with zeroes, ν a $(p+1)$ vector with Lagrange multipliers, and $\mathbf{x}_0$ a $(p+1)$ vector with covariate values at the prediction location (including a 1 as the first entry).

The kriging variance with KED equals

$$V_{\text{KED}}(\widehat{Z}(\mathbf{s}_0)) = \sigma^2 - \lambda^{\text{T}}\mathbf{c}_0 - \nu^{\text{T}}\mathbf{x}_0 . \tag{21.20}$$

The prediction error variance with KED can also be written as the sum of the variance of the predictor of the mean and the variance of the error in the interpolated residuals (Christensen, 1991):

$$\begin{aligned} V_{\text{KED}}(\widehat{Z}(\mathbf{s}_0)) = \sigma^2 - \mathbf{c}_0^{\text{T}}\mathbf{C}^{-1}\mathbf{c}_0 + \\ (\mathbf{x}_0 - \mathbf{X}^{\text{T}}\mathbf{C}^{-1}\mathbf{c}_0)^{\text{T}}(\mathbf{X}^{\text{T}}\mathbf{C}^{-1}\mathbf{X})^{-1}(\mathbf{x}_0 - \mathbf{X}^{\text{T}}\mathbf{C}^{-1}\mathbf{c}_0) . \end{aligned} \tag{21.21}$$

The first two terms constitute the interpolation error variance, the third term the variance of the predictor of the mean.

To illustrate that the kriging variance with KED depends on the values of the covariate at the sampling locations and the prediction location, values of a covariate x and of a correlated study variable z are simulated for the 50×50 units of a spatial population (Figure 21.3). First, a field with covariate values is simulated with a model-mean of 10. Next, a field with residuals is simulated. The field of the study variable is then obtained by multiplying the simulated field with covariate values by two ($\beta_1 = 2$), adding a constant of 10 ($\beta_0 = 10$), and finally adding the simulated field with residuals.

```
#simulate covariate values
vgm_x <- vgm(model = "Sph", psill = 10, range = 200, nugget = 0)
C <- variogramLine(vgm_x, dist_vector = H, covariance = TRUE)
Upper <- chol(C)
set.seed(314)
N <- rnorm(n = nrow(mypop), 0, 1)
mypop$x <- crossprod(Upper, N) + 10
#simulate values for residuals
vgm_resi <- vgm(model = "Sph", psill = 5, range = 100, nugget = 0)
C <- variogramLine(vgm_resi, dist_vector = H, covariance = TRUE)
```

```
Upper <- chol(C)
set.seed(314)
N <- rnorm(n = nrow(mypop), 0, 1)
e <- crossprod(Upper, N)
#compute mean of study variable
betas <- c(10, 2)
mu <- betas[1] + betas[2] * mypop$x
#compute study variable z
mypop$z <- mu  + e
```

As before, a centred square grid with a spacing of 100 distance units is selected. The simulated values of the study variable z and covariate x are used to predict z at a prediction location s_0 by kriging with an external drift (red cell in Figure 21.3). Although at the prediction location we have only one simulated value of covariate x, a series of covariate values is used to predict z at that location: $x_0 = 0, 2, 4, \dots, 20$. In practice, we have of course only one value of the covariate at a fixed location, but this is for illustration purposes only. Note that we have only one data set with 'observations' of x and z at the sampling locations (square grid).

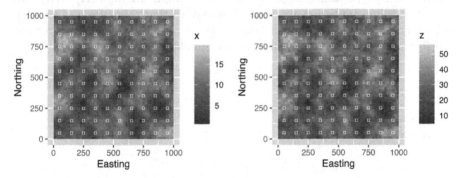

FIGURE 21.3: Maps with simulated values of covariate x and study variable z, the centred square grid of sampling units, and the prediction unit (red cell with coordinates (590,670)).

```
zxsim_sample <- over(mysample, mypop)
mysample$z <- zxsim_sample$z
mysample$x <- zxsim_sample$x
x0 <- seq(from = 0, to = 20, by = 2)
v_zpred_KED <- NULL
for (i in seq_len(length(x0))) {
  s_0$x <- x0[i]
  predictions  <- krige(
```

```
    formula = z ~ x,
    locations = mysample,
    newdata = s_0,
    model = vgm_resi,
    debug.level = 0)
  v_zpred_KED[i] <- predictions$var1.var
}
```

Note the formula z ~ x in the code chunk above, indicating that there is now
an independent variable (covariate). The covariate values are attached to the
file with the prediction location one-by-one in a for-loop. Also note that for
KED we need the semivariogram of the residuals, not of the study variable
itself. The residual semivariogram used in prediction is the same as the one
used in simulating the fields: a spherical model without nugget, with a sill of
5, and a range of 100 distance units.

To assess the contribution of the uncertainty about the model-mean $\mu(\mathbf{s})$, I also
predict the values assuming that the model-mean is known. In other words, I
assume that the two regression coefficients β_0 (intercept) and β_1 (slope) are
known. This type of kriging is referred to as simple kriging (SK). With SK,
the constraints explained above are removed, so that there are no Lagrange
multipliers involved. Argument beta is used to specify the known regression
coefficients. I use the same values used in simulation.

```
v_zpred_SK <- NULL
for (i in seq_len(length(x0))) {
  s_0$x <- x0[i]
  prediction <- krige(
    formula = z ~ x,
    locations = mysample,
    newdata = s_0,
    model = vgm_resi,
    beta = betas,
    debug.level = 0)
  v_zpred_SK[i] <- prediction$var1.var
}
```

Figure 21.4 shows that, contrary to the SK variance, the kriging variance with
KED is not constant but depends on the covariate value at the prediction
location. It is smallest near the mean of the covariate values at the sampling
locations, which is 10.0. The more extreme the covariate value at the prediction
location, the larger the kriging variance with KED. This is analogous to the
variance of predictions with a linear regression model.

The variance with SK is constant. This is because with SK we assume that the regression coefficients are known, so that we know the model-mean at a prediction location. What remains is the error in the interpolation of the residuals (first two terms in Equation (21.21)). This interpolation error is independent of the value of x at the prediction location. In Figure 21.4 the difference between the variances with KED and SK is the variance of the predictor of the model-mean, due to uncertainty about the regression coefficients. In real-world applications these regression coefficients are unknown and must be *estimated* from the sample data. This variance is smallest for a covariate value about equal to the sample mean of the covariate, and increases with the absolute difference of the covariate value and this sample mean.

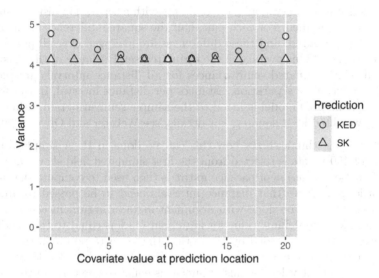

FIGURE 21.4: Variance of the prediction error as a function of the covariate value at a fixed prediction location, obtained with kriging with an external drift (KED) and simple kriging (SK).

21.4 Estimating the semivariogram

Kriging requires a semivariogram or covariance function as input for computing the covariance matrix of the study variable at the sampling locations, and the vector of covariance of the study variable at the sampling locations and the prediction location. In most cases the semivariogram model is unknown and must be estimated from sample data. The estimated parameters of the semivariogram model are plugged into the kriging equations. There are two different approaches for estimating the semivariogram parameters from sample data: the *method-of-moments* and *maximum likelihood estimation* (Lark, 2000).

21.4.1   Method-of-moments

With the method-of-moments (MoM) approach, the semivariogram is estimated in two steps. In the first step, a sample semivariogram, also referred to as an experimental semivariogram, is estimated. This is done by choosing a series of distance intervals. If a semivariogram in different directions is required, we must also choose direction intervals.

For each distance interval, all pairs of points with a separation distance in that interval are identified. For each pair, half the squared difference of the study variable is computed, and these differences are averaged over all point-pairs of that interval. This average is the estimated semivariance of that distance interval. The estimated semivariances for all distance intervals are plotted against the average separation distances per distance interval. In the second step, a permissible model is fitted to the sample semivariogram, using some form of weighted least squares. For details, see Webster and Oliver (2007).

The next code chunk shows how this can be done in **R**. A simple random sample of 150 points is selected from the first simulated field shown in Figure 21.2. Function variogram of package **gstat** is then used to compute the sample semivariogram. Note that distance intervals need to be passed to function variogram. This can be done with argument width or argument boundaries. In their absence, the default value for argument width is equal to the maximum separation distance divided by 15, so that there are 15 points in the sample semivariogram. The maximum separation distance can be set with argument cutoff. The default value for this argument is equal to one-third of the longest diagonal of the bounding box of the point set. The output is a data frame, with the number of point-pairs, average separation distance, and estimated semivariance in the first three columns.

```
set.seed(123)
units <- sample(nrow(mypop), size = 150)
mysample <- mypop[units, ]
coordinates(mysample) <- ~ s1 + s2
vg <- variogram(z ~ 1, data = mysample)
head(vg[, c(1, 2, 3)])
```

```
   np     dist    gamma
1  35  24.02379 38.73456
2  74  49.02384 42.57199
3 179  78.62401 62.13025
4 213 110.05088 72.41387
```

```
5 239 139.20163 82.21432
6 323 170.55712 88.38168
```

The next step is to fit a model. This can be done with function `fit.variogram` of the **gstat** package. Many models can be fitted with this function (type `vgm()` to see all models). I chose a spherical model. Function `fit.variogram` requires initial values of the semivariogram parameters. From the sample semivariogram, my eyeball estimates are 25 for the nugget, 250 for the range, and 75 for the partial sill. These are passed to function `vgm`. Figure 21.5 shows the sample semivariogram along with the fitted spherical model[2].

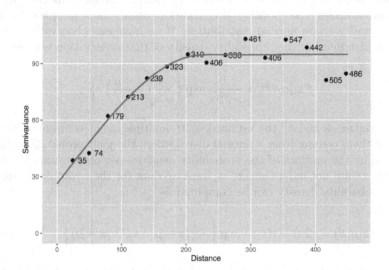

FIGURE 21.5: Sample semivariogram and fitted spherical model estimated from a simple random sample of 150 units selected from the first simulated field shown in Figure 21.2. Numbers refer to point-pairs used in computing semivariances.

```
print(vgm_MoM)
```

```
  model     psill     range
1   Nug  26.32048    0.0000
2   Sph  68.36364  227.7999
```

Function `fit.variogram` has several options for weighted least squares optimisation, see `?fit.variogram` for details. Also note that this non-linear fit may not converge to a solution, especially if the starting values passed to `vgm` are not near their optimal values.

---

[2]The figure is plotted with package **ggplot2**. The sample semivariogram and the fitted model can also be plotted with `plot(vg, vgm_MoM, plot.numbers = TRUE)`.

Further, this method depends on the choice of cutoff and distance intervals. We hope that modifying these does not change the fitted model too much, but this is not always the case, especially with smaller data sets.

21.4.2 Maximum likelihood

In contrast to the MoM, with the maximum likelihood (ML) method the data are not paired into couples and binned into a sample semivariogram. Instead, the semivariogram model is estimated in one step. To apply this method, one typically assumes that (possibly after transformation) the n sample data come from a multivariate normal distribution. If we have one observation from a normal distribution, the probability density of that observation is given by

$$f(z|\mu, \sigma^2) = \frac{1}{\sigma\sqrt{2\pi}} \exp\left\{-\frac{1}{2}\left(\frac{z-\mu}{\sigma}\right)^2\right\}, \tag{21.22}$$

with μ the mean and σ^2 the variance. With multiple independent observations, each of them coming from a normal distribution, the joint probability density is given by the product of the probability densities per observation. However, if the data are not independent, we must account for the covariances and the joint probability density can be computed by

$$f(\mathbf{z}|\boldsymbol{\mu}, \boldsymbol{\theta}) = (2\pi)^{-\frac{n}{2}} |\mathbf{C}|^{-\frac{1}{2}} \exp\left\{-\frac{1}{2}(\mathbf{z}-\boldsymbol{\mu})^{\mathrm{T}} \mathbf{C}^{-1} (\mathbf{z}-\boldsymbol{\mu})\right\}, \tag{21.23}$$

where $\mathbf{z}$ is the vector with the n sample data, $\boldsymbol{\mu}$ is the vector with means, $\boldsymbol{\theta}$ is the vector with parameters of the covariance function, and $\mathbf{C}$ is the $n \times n$ matrix with variances and covariances of the sample data. If the probability density of Equation (21.23) is regarded as a function of $\boldsymbol{\mu}$ and $\boldsymbol{\theta}$ with the data $\mathbf{z}$ fixed, this equation defines the likelihood.

ML estimates of the semivariogram can be obtained with function `likfit` of package **geoR** (Ribeiro Jr et al., 2020). First, a geoR object must be made specifying which columns of the data frame contain the spatial coordinates and the study variable.

```
library(geoR)
mysample <- as(mysample, "data.frame")
dGeoR <- as.geodata(obj = mysample, header = TRUE,
    coords.col = c("s1", "s2"), data.col = "z")
```

The model parameters can then be estimated with function `likfit`. Argument `trend = "cte"` means that we assume that the mean is constant throughout the study area.

TABLE 21.2: Estimated parameters of a spherical semivariogram obtained with method-of-moments (MoM) and maximum likelihood (ML) estimation.

Parameter	MoM	ML
nugget	26.3	19.5
partial sill	68.4	83.8
range	227.8	217.8

```
vgm_ML <- likfit(geodata = dGeoR, trend = "cte",
  cov.model = "spherical", ini.cov.pars = c(80, 200),
  nugget = 20, lik.method = "ML", messages = FALSE)
```

Table 21.2 shows the ML estimates together with the MoM estimates. As can be seen, the estimates are substantially different, especially the division of the a priori variance (sill) into partial sill and nugget. In general, I prefer the ML estimates because the arbitrary choice of distance intervals to compute a sample semivariogram is avoided. Also ML estimates of the parameters are more precise, given a sample size. On the other hand, in ML estimation we need to assume that the data are normally distributed.

21.5 Estimating the residual semivariogram

For KED, estimates of the regression coefficients and of the parameters of the residual semivariogram are needed. Estimation of these model parameters is not a trivial problem, as the estimated regression coefficients and the estimated residual semivariogram parameters are not independent. The residuals depend on the estimated regression coefficients and, as a consequence, also the parameters of the residual semivariogram depend on the estimated coefficients. Conversely, the estimated regression coefficients depend on the spatial correlation of the residuals, and so on the estimated residual semivariogram parameters. This is a classic "which came first, the chicken or the egg?" problem.

Estimation of the model parameters is illustrated with the simulated field of Figure 21.3. A simple random sample of size 150 is selected to estimate the model parameters.

21.5.1   Iterative method-of-moments

A simple option is iterative estimation of the regression coefficients followed by
MoM estimation of the sample semivariogram and fitting of a semivariogram
model. In the first iteration, the regression coefficients are estimated by ordinary
least squares (OLS). This implies that the data are assumed independent, i.e.,
we assume a pure nugget residual semivariogram. The sample semivariogram of
the OLS residuals is then computed by the MoM, followed by fitting a model
to this sample semivariogram. With package **gstat** this can be done with one
line of **R** code, using a formula specifying the study variable and the predictors
as the first argument of function `variogram`.

```
set.seed(314)
units <- sample(nrow(mypop), size = 150)
mysample <- mypop[units, ]
vg_resi <- variogram(z ~ x, data = mysample)
model_eye <- vgm(model = "Sph", psill = 10, range = 150, nugget = 0)
vgmresi_MoM <- fit.variogram(vg_resi, model = model_eye)
```

Given these estimates of the semivariogram parameters, the regression coefficients are reestimated by accounting for spatial dependency of the residuals.
This can be done by generalised least squares (GLS):

$$\hat{\beta}_{\mathrm{GLS}} = (\mathbf{X}^{\mathrm{T}}\mathbf{C}^{-1}\mathbf{X})^{-1}(\mathbf{X}^{\mathrm{T}}\mathbf{C}^{-1}\mathbf{z}) \,. \qquad (21.24)$$

The next code chunk shows how the GLS estimates of the regression coefficients
can be computed. Function `spDists` of package **sp** is used to compute the matrix
with distances between the sampling locations, and function `variogramLine` of
package **gstat** is used to transform the distance matrix into a covariance
matrix.

```
X <- matrix(data = 1, nrow = nrow(as(mysample, "data.frame")), ncol = 2)
X[, 2] <- mysample$x
z <- mysample$z
D <- spDists(mysample)
C <- variogramLine(vgmresi_MoM, dist_vector = D, covariance = TRUE)
Cinv <- solve(C)
XCXinv <- solve(crossprod(X, Cinv) %*% X)
XCz <- crossprod(X, Cinv) %*% z
betaGLS <- XCXinv %*% XCz
```

The inversion of the covariance matrix $\mathbf{C}$ can be avoided as follows:

```
XCX <- crossprod(X, solve(C, X))
XCz <- crossprod(X, solve(C, z))
betaGLS <- solve(XCX, XCz)
```

This coding is to be preferred as the inversion of a matrix can be numerically unstable.

The GLS estimates of the regression coefficients can then be used to re-compute the residuals of the mean, and so on, until the changes in the model parameters are negligible.

```
repeat {
  betaGLS.cur <- betaGLS
  mu <- X %*% betaGLS
  mysample$e <- z - mu
  vg_resi <- variogram(e ~ 1, data = mysample)
  vgmresi_MoM <- fit.variogram(vg_resi, model = model_eye)
  C <- variogramLine(vgmresi_MoM, dist_vector = D, covariance = TRUE)
  XCX <- crossprod(X, solve(C, X))
  XCz <- crossprod(X, solve(C, z))
  betaGLS <- solve(XCX, XCz)
  if (sum(abs(betaGLS - betaGLS.cur)) < 0.0001) {
    break
  }
}
```

Table 21.3 shows the estimates of the residual semivariogram parameters and regression coefficients, together with the estimates obtained by restricted maximum likelihood, which is explained in the next subsection.

TABLE 21.3: Estimated parameters of a spherical semivariogram for the residuals and estimated regression coefficients, obtained with iterative method-of-moments (iMoM) and restricted maximum likelihood (REML) estimation.

Parameter	iMoM	REML
nugget	0.000	0.000
partial sill	2.137	1.909
range	129.147	141.491
intercept	3.255	3.083
x	2.712	2.732

21.5.2   Restricted maximum likelihood

The estimates of the residual semivariogram parameters obtained by the iterative MoM procedure are not unbiased. When the mean is not constant but is a linear combination of one or more covariates, also ML estimation results in biased estimates of the residual semivariogram parameters. Unbiased estimates of the regression coefficients and residual semivariogram parameters can be obtained by restricted maximum likelihood (REML), also referred to as residual maximum likelihood. In REML the vector with the data is premultiplied by a so-called projection matrix $\mathbf{P}$ (Kitanidis, 1983). This projection matrix has the property that a vector with zeroes is obtained when the matrix $\mathbf{X}$ with the covariate values at the sampling locations (and ones in the first column) is premultiplied with $\mathbf{P}$:

$$\mathbf{PX} = \mathbf{0} \ . \tag{21.25}$$

Premultiplying both sides of the KED model (Equation (21.16)) with $\mathbf{P}$ gives (Webster and Oliver, 2007)

$$\mathbf{Pz}(\mathbf{s}) = \mathbf{y}(\mathbf{s}) = \mathbf{PX}\beta + \mathbf{P}\epsilon(\mathbf{s}) = \mathbf{P}\epsilon(\mathbf{s}) \ . \tag{21.26}$$

In words, by premultiplying variable $\mathbf{z}$ with matrix $\mathbf{P}$, a new variable $\mathbf{y}$ is obtained that has a constant mean. So, the trend is filtered out, whatever the regression coefficients are. The semivariogram parameters of this new variable can be estimated by ML. The projection matrix $\mathbf{P}$ can be computed by

$$\mathbf{P} = \mathbf{I} - \mathbf{X}(\mathbf{X}^{\mathrm{T}}\mathbf{X})^{-1}\mathbf{X}^{\mathrm{T}} \ , \tag{21.27}$$

with $\mathbf{I}$ the $n \times n$ identity matrix (matrix with ones on the diagonal and zeroes in all off-diagonal elements). The natural log of the residual likelihood can be computed by (Lark and Webster, 2006)

$$\ell(\boldsymbol{\theta}|\mathbf{z}) = \text{constant} - 0.5(\ln|\mathbf{C}| + |\mathbf{X}^{\mathrm{T}}\mathbf{C}^{-1}\mathbf{X}| + \mathbf{y}^{\mathbf{T}}\mathbf{C}^{-1}(\mathbf{I} - \mathbf{Q})\mathbf{z})) \ , \tag{21.28}$$

with $\mathbf{Q} = \mathbf{X}(\mathbf{X}^{\mathrm{T}}\mathbf{C}^{-1}\mathbf{X})^{-1}\mathbf{X}^{\mathrm{T}}\mathbf{C}^{-1}$

REML estimates of the semivariogram can be obtained with function likfit of package **geoR**, used above in ML estimation of the variogram (Ribeiro Jr et al., 2020).

```
vgm_REML <- likfit(geodata = dGeoR, trend = ~ x,
    cov.model = "spherical", ini.cov.pars = c(2, 100),
    nugget = 0, lik.method = "REML", messages = FALSE)
```

Table 21.3 shows that REML yields a smaller estimated (partial) sill and a larger estimated range than iterative MoM. Of the two regression coefficients, especially the estimated intercept differs considerably among the two estimation methods.

Realising that this is a rather short introduction to kriging, refer to Isaaks and Srivastava (1989) for an introduction to geostatistics, to Goovaerts (1997) for an exposé of the many versions of kriging, and to Webster and Oliver (2007) for an elaborate explanation of kriging. A nice educational tool for getting a feeling for ordinary kriging is E{Z}-Kriging[3].

---

[3] https://wiki.52north.org/AI_GEOSTATS/SWEZKriging

22

Model-based optimisation of the grid spacing

This is the first chapter on model-based sampling[1]. In Section 17.2 and Chapter 18 a geometric criterion is minimised, i.e., a criterion defined in terms of distances, either in geographic space (Section 17.2) or in covariate space (Chapter 18). In model-based sampling, the minimisation criterion is a function of the variance of the prediction errors.

This chapter on model-based sampling is about optimisation of the spacing of a square grid, i.e., the distance between neighbouring points in the grid. The grid spacing is derived from a requirement on the accuracy of the map. Here and in following chapters, I assume that the map is constructed by kriging; see Chapter 21 for an introduction. As we have seen in Chapter 21, a kriging prediction of the study variable at an unobserved location is accompanied by a variance of the prediction error, referred to as the kriging variance. The map accuracy requirement is a population parameter of this kriging variance, e.g., the population mean of the kriging variance.

22.1 Optimal grid spacing for ordinary kriging

Suppose that we require the population mean of the kriging variance not to exceed a given threshold. The question then is what the tolerable or maximum possible grid spacing is, given this requirement. For finding the tolerable grid spacing we must have prior knowledge of the spatial variation. I first consider the situation in which it is reasonable to assume that the model-mean of the study variable is constant throughout the study area, but is unknown. When the model-mean is unknown, ordinary kriging (OK) is used for mapping. Furthermore, we need a semivariogram of the study variable. In practice, we often do not have a reliable estimate of the semivariogram. In the best case scenario, we have some existing data, of sufficient quantity and suitable spatial distribution, that can be used to estimate the semivariogram. In other cases,

---

[1]Spatial response surface sampling can also be considered as model-based sampling, especially when a model-based criterion is used, see Chapter 20.

such data are lacking and a best guess of the semivariogram must be made, for instance using data for the same study variable from other, similar areas.

There is no simple equation that relates the grid spacing to the kriging variance. What can be done is calculate the mean OK variance for a range of grid spacings, plot the mean ordinary kriging variances against the grid spacings, and use this plot inversely to determine the tolerable grid spacing, given a constraint on the mean OK variance.

In the next code chunks, this procedure is used to compute the tolerable spacing of a square grid for mapping soil organic matter (SOM) in West-Amhara. The legacy data of the SOM concentration (dag kg^{-1}), used before to design a spatial infill sample (Section 17.3), are used here to estimate a semivariogram. A sample semivariogram is estimated by the method-of-moments (MoM), and a spherical model is fitted using functions of package **gstat** (Pebesma, 2004). The values for the partial sill, range, and nugget, passed to function fit.variogram with argument model, are guesses from an eyeball examination of the sample semivariogram obtained with function variogram, see Figure 22.1. The ultimate estimates of the semivariogram parameters differ from these eyeball estimates. First, the projected coordinates of the sampling points are changed from m into km using function mutate[2].

```
library(gstat)
grdAmhara <- grdAmhara %>%
  mutate(s1 = s1 / 1000, s2 = s2 / 1000)
sampleAmhara <- sampleAmhara %>%
  mutate(s1 = s1 / 1000, s2 = s2 / 1000)
coordinates(sampleAmhara) <- ~ s1 + s2
vg <- variogram(SOM ~ 1, data = sampleAmhara)
model_eye <- vgm(model = "Sph", psill = 0.6, range = 40, nugget = 0.6)
vgm_MoM <- fit.variogram(vg, model = model_eye)
```

The semivariogram of SOM can also be estimated by maximum likelihood (ML) using function likfit of package **geoR** (Ribeiro Jr et al., 2020), see Section 21.4.

```
library(geoR)
sampleAmhara <- as_tibble(sampleAmhara)
dGeoR <- as.geodata(
  obj = sampleAmhara, header = TRUE, coords.col = c("s1", "s2"),
  data.col = "SOM")
vgm_ML <- likfit(geodata = dGeoR, trend = "cte",
```

---

[2]This is mainly done to avoid problems in (restricted) maximum likelihood estimation of the (residual) semivariogram with function likfit of package **geoR**.

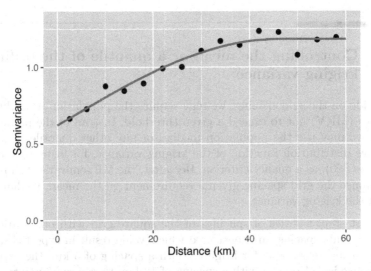

FIGURE 22.1: Sample semivariogram and fitted spherical model of the SOM concentration in West-Amhara, estimated from the legacy data.

TABLE 22.1: Method-of-moments (MoM) and maximum likelihood (ML) estimates of the parameters of a spherical semivariogram of the SOM concentration in West-Amhara.

Parameter	MoM	ML
nugget	0.62	0.56
partial sill	0.56	0.68
range	45.40	36.90

```
cov.model = "spherical", ini.cov.pars = c(0.6, 40),
nugget = 0.6, lik.method = "ML", messages = FALSE)
```

Table 22.1 shows the ML estimates of the parameters of the spherical semivariogram, together with the MoM estimates. Either could be used in the following steps.

22.2   Controlling the mean or a quantile of the ordinary kriging variance

To decide on the grid spacing, we may require the population mean kriging variance (MKV) not to exceed a given threshold. Instead of the population mean, we may use the population median or any other quantile of the cumulative distribution function of the kriging variance, for instance the 0.90 quantile (P90), as a quality criterion. Hereafter, the ML semivariogram is used to optimise the grid spacing given a requirement on the mean, median, and P90 of the kriging variance.

As a first step, a series of spacings of the square grid with observations is specified. Only spacings are considered which would result in expected sample sizes that are reasonable for kriging. With a spacing of 5 km, the expected sample size is 434 points; with a spacing of 12 km, these are 75 points.

```
spacing <- 5:12
```

The next step is to select a simple random sample of evaluation points. It is important to select a large sample, so that the precision of the estimated population mean or quantile of the kriging variance will be high.

To check whether the size of the simple random sample of evaluation points is sufficiently large, we may estimate the standard error of the estimator of the MKV, see Chapter 3, substituting the kriging variances at the evaluation points for the study variable values.

```
set.seed(314)
mysample <- grdAmhara %>%
  slice_sample(n = 5000, replace = TRUE) %>%
  mutate(s1 = s1 %>% jitter(amount = 0.5),
         s2 = s2 %>% jitter(amount = 0.5))
```

The **R** code below shows the next steps. Given a spacing, a square grid with a fixed starting point is selected with function spsample, using argument offset. A dummy variable is added to the data frame, having value 1 at all grid points, but any other value is also fine. The predicted value at all evaluation points equals 1. However, we are not interested in the predicted value but in the kriging variance only, and we have seen in Chapter 21 that the kriging variance is independent of the observations of the study variable. The ML estimates of the semivariogram are used in function vgm to define a semivariogram model of class variogramModel that can be handled by function krige. For each grid spacing the population mean, median, and P90 of the kriging variance are estimated from the evaluation sample. The estimated median and P90 can be computed with function `quantile`.

```
coordinates(mysample) <- ~ s1 + s2
gridded(grdAmhara) <- ~ s1 + s2
MKV_OK <- P50KV_OK <- P90KV_OK <- samplesize <-
  numeric(length = length(spacing))
vgm_ML_gstat <- vgm(model = "Sph", nugget = vgm_ML$nugget,
  psill = vgm_ML$sigmasq, range = vgm_ML$phi)
for (i in seq_len(length(spacing))) {
  mygrid <- spsample(x = grdAmhara, cellsize = spacing[i],
    type = "regular", offset = c(0.5, 0.5))
  mygrid$dummy <- rep(1, length(mygrid))
  samplesize[i] <- nrow(mygrid)
  predictions  <- krige(
    formula = dummy ~ 1,
    locations = mygrid,
    newdata = mysample,
    model = vgm_ML_gstat,
    nmax = 100,
    debug.level = 0)
  MKV_OK[i] <- mean(predictions$var1.var)
  P50KV_OK[i] <- quantile(predictions$var1.var, probs = 0.5)
  P90KV_OK[i] <- quantile(predictions$var1.var, probs = 0.9)
}
dfKV_OK <- data.frame(spacing, samplesize, MKV_OK, P50KV_OK, P90KV_OK)
```

The estimated mean and quantiles of the kriging variance are plotted against the grid spacing (Figure 22.2).

The tolerable grid spacing for the three quality indices can be computed with function `approx` of the **base** package, as shown below for the median kriging variance.

```
spacing_tol_P50 <- approx(x = dfKV_OK$P50, y = dfKV_OK$spacing, xout = 0.8)$y
```

For a mean kriging variance of 0.8 $(\text{dag kg}^{-1})^2$ the tolerable grid spacing is 8.6 km. For the median kriging variance this is 9.2 km, which is somewhat larger leading to a smaller sample size. The smaller grid spacing for the mean can be explained by the right-skewed distribution of the kriging variance, so that the mean kriging variance is larger than the median kriging variance. For the P90 of the kriging variance, the tolerable grid spacing is much smaller, 6.8 km, leading to a much larger sample size.

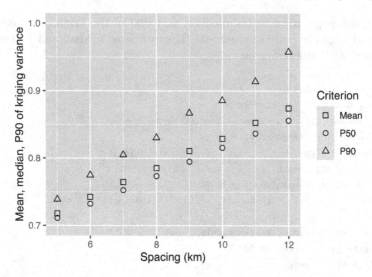

FIGURE 22.2: Mean, median (P50), and 0.90 quantile (P90) of the ordinary kriging variance of predictions of the SOM concentration in West-Amhara, as a function of the spacing of a square grid.

Exercises

1. Write an **R** script to determine the tolerable grid spacing so that the 0.50, 0.80, and 0.95 quantiles of the variance of OK predictions of SOM in West-Amhara do not exceed 0.85. Estimate the semivariogram by MoM.

2. In practice, we are uncertain about the semivariogram. For this reason, it can be wise to explore the sensitivity of the tolerable grid spacing for the semivariogram parameters.
   - Increase the nugget parameter of the MoM semivariogram by 5%, and change the partial sill parameter so that the sill (nugget + partial sill) is unchanged. Compute the tolerable grid spacing and the corresponding required sample size for a mean kriging variance of 0.85 $(dag\ kg^{-1})^2$. Explain the difference.
   - Reduce the range of the MoM semivariogram by 5%. Reset the nugget and the partial sill to their original values. Compute the tolerable grid spacing and the corresponding required sample size for a mean kriging variance of 0.85 $(dag\ kg^{-1})^2$. Explain the difference.

22.3 Optimal grid spacing for block-kriging

In the previous section, the tolerable grid spacing is derived from a constraint on the mean or quantile of the prediction error variances at points. The alternative is to put a constraint on the mean or quantile of the error variances of the predicted means of blocks. These means can be predicted with block-kriging (Section 21.2). Block-kriging predictions can be obtained with function krige of package **gstat** using argument block. In the code chunk below, the means of 100 m × 100 m blocks are predicted by ordinary block-kriging.

```
MKV_OBK <- P50KV_OBK <- P90KV_OBK <- numeric(length = length(spacing))
for (i in seq_len(length(spacing))) {
  mygrid <- spsample(x = grdAmhara, cellsize = spacing[i],
    type = "regular", offset = c(0.5, 0.5))
  mygrid$dummy <- rep(1, length(mygrid))
  samplesize[i] <- nrow(mygrid)
  predictions  <- krige(
    formula = dummy ~ 1,
    locations = mygrid,
    newdata = mysample,
    model = vgm_ML_gstat,
    block = c(0.1, 0.1),
    nmax = 100,
    debug.level = 0)
  MKV_OBK[i] <- mean(predictions$var1.var)
  P50KV_OBK[i] <- quantile(predictions$var1.var, probs = 0.5)
  P90KV_OBK[i] <- quantile(predictions$var1.var, probs = 0.9)
}
dfKV_OBK <- data.frame(spacing, MKV_OBK, P50KV_OBK, P90KV_OBK)
```

Figure 22.3 shows that the mean, P50, and P90 of the block-kriging predictions are substantially smaller than those of the point-kriging predictions (Figure 22.2). This can be explained by the large nugget of the semivariogram (Table 22.1). The side length of a prediction block (100 m) is much smaller than the range of the semivariogram (36.9 km), so that in this case the mean semivariance within a prediction block is about equal to the nugget. Roughly speaking, for a given grid spacing the mean point-kriging variance is reduced by an amount about equal to this mean semivariance to yield the mean block-kriging variance for this spacing (Section 21.2). Recall that the mean semivariance within a block is a model-based prediction of the variance within a block (Subsection 13.1.1, Equation (13.3)).

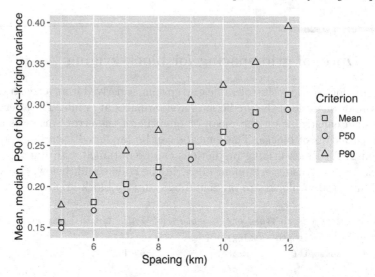

FIGURE 22.3: Mean, median (P50), and 0.90 quantile (P90) of the ordinary block-kriging variance of predictions of the mean SOM concentration of blocks of 100 m × 100 m, in West-Amhara, as a function of the spacing of a square grid.

22.4 Optimal grid spacing for kriging with an external drift

In the previous sections I assumed a constant model-mean for the study variable. I now consider the case where covariates that are related to the study variable are available. A model is calibrated that is the sum of a linear combination of the covariates (spatial trend) and a spatially structured residual, see Equation (21.16). Predictions at the nodes of a fine grid are obtained by kriging with an external drift (KED).

The SOM concentration data of West-Amhara are used to estimate the parameters (regression coefficients and residual semivariogram parameters) of the model by restricted maximum likelihood (REML), see Subsection 21.5.2.

```
library(geoR)
dGeoR <- as.geodata(obj = sampleAmhara, header = TRUE,
    coords.col = c("s1", "s2"), data.col = "SOM",
    covar.col = c("dem", "rfl_NIR", "rfl_red", "lst"))
vgm_REML <- likfit(geodata = dGeoR, trend = ~ dem + rfl_NIR + rfl_red + lst,
```

TABLE 22.2: Maximum likelihood (ML) estimates of the parameters of a spherical semivariogram for the SOM concentration and restricted maximum likelihood (REML) estimates of the parameters of a spherical semivariogram for the residuals of a multiple linear regression model, for West-Amhara.

Parameter	ML	REML
nugget	0.56	0.36
partial sill	0.68	0.44
range (km)	36.91	5.24

```
cov.model = "spherical", ini.cov.pars = c(1, 5),
  nugget = 0.2, lik.method = "REML", messages = FALSE)
```

The total sill (partial sill + nugget) of the residual semivariogram, estimated by REML, equals 0.80, which is considerably smaller than that of the ML semivariogram of SOM (Table 22.2). A considerable part of the variance of SOM is explained by the covariates. Besides, note the much smaller range of the residual semivariogram. The smaller sill and range of the residual semivariogram show that the spatial structure of SOM is largely captured by the covariates. The residuals of the model-mean, which is a linear combination of the covariates, no longer show much spatial structure.

The mean kriging variance as obtained with KED is used as the evaluation criterion. With KED, the kriging variance is also a function of the values of the covariates at the sampling locations and the prediction location (Section 21.3). Compared with the procedure above for OK, in the code chunk below, a slightly different procedure is used. The square grid of a given spacing is randomly placed on the area (option `offset` in function `spsample` is not used), and this is repeated ten times.

```
R <- 10
MKV_KED <- matrix(nrow = length(spacing), ncol = R)
vgm_REML_gstat <- vgm(model = "Sph", nugget = vgm_REML$nugget,
  psill = vgm_REML$sigmasq, range = vgm_REML$phi)
set.seed(314)
for (i in seq_len(length(spacing))) {
  for (j in 1:R) {
    mygrid <- spsample(x = grdAmhara, cellsize = spacing[i], type = "regular")
    mygrid$dummy <- rep(1, length(mygrid))
    mygrd <- data.frame(over(mygrid, grdAmhara), mygrid)
    coordinates(mygrd) <- ~ x1 + x2
    predictions <- krige(
      formula = dummy ~ dem + rfl_NIR + rfl_red + lst,
```

```
        locations = mygrd,
        newdata = mysample,
        model = vgm_REML_gstat,
        nmax = 100,
        debug.level = 0)
      MKV_KED[i, j] <- mean(predictions$var1.var)
    }
  }
}
dfKV_KED <- data.frame(spacing, MKV_KED)
```

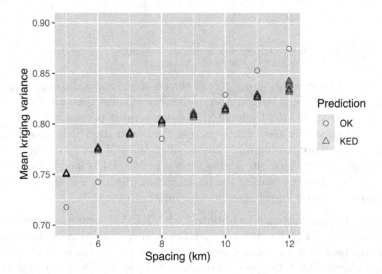

FIGURE 22.4: Mean kriging variance of OK and KED predictions of the
SOM concentration in West-Amhara, as a function of the spacing of a square
grid. With KED for each spacing, ten MKV values are shown obtained by
selecting ten randomly placed grids of that spacing.

Figure 22.4 shows the mean kriging variances, obtained with OK and KED,
as a function of the grid spacing. Interestingly, for grid spacings smaller than
about 9 km, the mean kriging variance with KED is larger than with OK. In
this case only for larger grid spacings KED outperforms OK in terms of the
mean kriging variance. Only for mean kriging variances larger than about 0.82
$(\mathrm{dag\ kg^{-1}})^2$ we can afford with KED a larger grid spacing (smaller sample size)
than with OK. Only with large spacings (small sample sizes) we profit from
modelling the mean as a linear function of covariates.

```
MMKV_KED <- apply(dfKV_KED[, -1], MARGIN = 1, FUN = mean)
spacing_tol_KED <- approx(x = MMKV_KED, y = dfKV_KED$spacing, xout = 0.8)$y
```

The tolerable grid spacing for a mean kriging variance of 0.8 (dag kg^{-1})^2, using KED, equals 7.9 km.

Exercises

3. Given a grid spacing, the mean kriging variance varies among randomly selected grids, especially for large spacings. Explain why.

4. Write an **R** script to compute the tolerable grid spacing for KED of natural logs of the electrical conductivity of the soil across the Cotton Research Farm of Uzbekistan, using natural logs of the electromagnetic induction (EM) measurements (lnEM100cm) as a covariate. Use a nugget of 0.126, a partial sill of 0.083, and a range of 230 m for an exponential semivariogram of the residuals (Table 23.1). Select a simple random sample of size 1,000 of evaluation points from the discretisation grid with interpolated lnEM100cm values to compute the mean kriging variance. Do this by selecting 1,000 grid cells by simple random sampling with replacement and jittering the centres of the selected grid cells by an amount equal to half the size of the grid cell. Use as grid spacings $70, 75, \dots, 100$ m. With a spacing of 100 m the number of grid points is about 100 (the farm has an area of about 97 ha). What is the tolerable grid spacing for a mean kriging variance of 0.165?

22.5 Bayesian approach

In practice, we do not know the semivariogram. In the best case we have prior data that can be used to estimate the semivariogram. However, even in this case we are uncertain about the semivariogram model (spherical, exponential, etc.) and the semivariogram parameters. Lark et al. (2017) showed how in a Bayesian approach we can account for uncertainty about the semivariogram parameters when we must decide on the grid spacing. In this approach a prior distribution of the semivariogram parameters is updated with the sample data to a posterior distribution (Gelman et al., 2013):

$$f(\boldsymbol{\theta}|\mathbf{z}) = \frac{f(\boldsymbol{\theta})f(\mathbf{z}|\boldsymbol{\theta})}{f(\mathbf{z})} , \qquad (22.1)$$

with $f(\boldsymbol{\theta}|\mathbf{z})$ the posterior distribution function, i.e., the probability density function of the semivariogram parameters given the sample data, $f(\boldsymbol{\theta})$ our prior belief in the parameters specified by a probability density function, $f(\mathbf{z}|\boldsymbol{\theta})$ the likelihood of the data, and $f(\mathbf{z})$ the probability density function of the data. This probability density function $f(\mathbf{z})$ is hard to obtain.

Problems with analytical derivation of the posterior distribution are avoided by selecting a large sample of units (vectors with semivariogram parameters) from the posterior distribution through Markov chain Monte Carlo (MCMC) sampling, see Subsection 13.1.3.

In a Bayesian approach, we must define the likelihood function of the data, see Subsection 13.1.3. I assume that the SOM concentration data in West-Amhara have a multivariate normal distribution, and that the spatial covariance of the data can be modelled by a spherical model, see Subsection 21.4.2. The likelihood is a function of the semivariogram parameters. Given a vector of semivariogram parameters, the variance-covariance matrix of the data is computed from the matrix with geographic distances between the sampling points. Inputs of the loglikelihood function ll are the matrix with distances between the sampling points, the design matrix x, and the vector with observations of the study variable z, see Subsection 13.1.3.

```
D <- as.matrix(dist(sampleAmhara[,c("s1","s2")]))
X <- matrix(1, nrow(sampleAmhara), 1)
z <- sampleAmhara$SOM
```

Besides the likelihood function, in a Bayesian approach we must define prior distributions for the semivariogram parameters. Here, we combine the partial sill and nugget into the *ratio of spatial dependence*, i.e., the proportion of the sill attributable to the partial sill. For the ratio of spatial dependence ξ and the distance parameter ϕ, I use uniform distributions as priors, with a lower bound of 0 and an upper bound of 1 for the ratio of spatial dependence, and a lower bound of 10^{-6} km and an upper bound of 100 km for the range. A uniform distribution for the sill is not recommended (Gelman et al., 2013). Instead, I assume a uniform distribution for the *inverse* of the sill, with a lower bound of 10^{-6} and an upper bound of 2.

These priors can be defined by function createUniformPrior of package **BayesianTools** (Hartig et al., 2019). There are also functions to define a beta density function (commonly used as a prior for proportions) and a truncated normal distribution as a prior. Function createBayesianSetup is then used to define the setup of the MCMC sampling, specifying the likelihood function, the prior, and the vector with best prior estimates of the model parameters, specified with argument best. The ML estimates computed in Section 22.1 are used as starting values for the inverse of the sill parameter, the ratio of spatial dependence, and the range.

```
library(BayesianTools)
priors <- createUniformPrior(
```

```
    lower = c(1E-6, 0, 1E-6), upper = c(2, 1, 100))
sill_ML <- vgm_ML$nugget + vgm_ML$sigmasq
thetas_ML <- c(1 / sill_ML, vgm_ML$sigmasq / sill_ML, vgm_ML$phi)
model <- "Sph"
setup <- createBayesianSetup(likelihood = ll, prior = priors,
    best = thetas_ML, names = c("lambda", "xi", "range"))
```

A sample from the posterior distribution of the semivariogram parameters is then obtained with function runMCMC. Various sampling algorithms are implemented in package **BayesianTools**. I used the default sampler DEzs, which is based on the differential evolution Markov chain (ter Braak and Vrugt, 2008). This algorithm is passed to function runMCMC with argument sampler. It is common not to use all sampled units, but to discard the units of the burn-in period that are possibly influenced by the initial arbitrary settings, and to thin the series of units after this period. The extraction of the ultimate sample is done with function getSample. Argument start specifies the unit where the extraction starts, and argument numSamples specifies how many units are selected through systematic sampling of the full MCMC sample. The alternative is to use argument thin which defines the thinning interval.

```
set.seed(314)
res <- runMCMC(setup, sampler = "DEzs")
mcmcsample <- getSample(res, start = 1000, numSamples = 1000) %>%
  data.frame()
```

Table 22.3 shows the first ten units of the MCMC sample from the posterior distribution of the semivariogram parameters.

The units of the MCMC sample (vectors with semivariogram parameters) are used one-by-one to compute the average of the kriging variances at the simple random sample of evaluation points.

For each unit in the MCMC sample, the tolerable grid spacing is computed for a target MKV of 0.8. Figure 22.5 shows that for most sampled semivariograms (MCMC sample units) the tolerable grid spacing equals 8 km, which roughly corresponds with the tolerable grid spacing derived above for OK. For 165 sampled semivariograms, the tolerable grid spacing exceeds 12 km. However, this grid spacing leads to a sample size that is too small for estimating the semivariogram and kriging.

Finally, for each grid spacing, the proportion of MCMC samples with a MKV smaller than or equal to the target MKV of 0.8 is computed. Figure 22.6 shows, for instance, that if the MKV is required not to exceed a target MKV of 0.8 with a probability of 80%, the tolerable grid spacing is 6.6 km. With a grid spacing of 8.6 km, as determined before, the probability that the MKV exceeds 0.8 is 54%.

TABLE 22.3: First ten units of a MCMC sample from the posterior distribution of the parameters of a spherical semivariogram for the SOM concentration in West-Amhara.

Inverse of sill	Ratio of spatial dependence	Range (km)
0.624	0.655	55.0
0.828	0.588	33.3
0.769	0.480	51.9
0.624	0.655	55.0
0.872	0.538	47.2
0.559	0.643	60.6
0.605	0.690	66.8
0.764	0.585	42.7
0.793	0.608	44.8
0.480	0.741	87.1

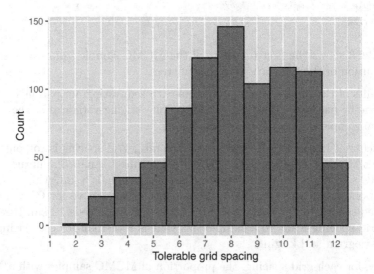

FIGURE 22.5: Frequency distribution of tolerable grid spacings for a target MKV of 0.8.

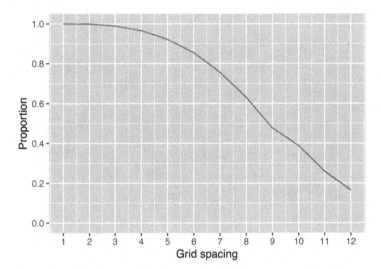

FIGURE 22.6: Proportion of sampled semivariograms with a MKV smaller than or equal to a target MKV of 0.8.

23

Model-based optimisation of the sampling pattern

In Chapter 22 a model of the spatial variation is used to optimise the spacing of a regular grid. The grid spacing determines the number of grid points within the study area, so optimisation of the grid spacing is equivalent to optimisation of the sample size of a square grid.

This chapter is about optimisation of the spatial coordinates of the sampling units *given the sample size*. So, we are searching for the optimal spatial sampling pattern of a fixed number of sampling units. The constraint of sampling on a regular grid is dropped. In general, the optimal spatial sampling pattern is irregular. Similar to spatial coverage sampling (Section 17.2), we search for the optimal sampling pattern through minimisation of an explicit criterion. In spatial coverage sampling, the minimisation criterion is the mean squared shortest distance (MSSD) which is minimised by k-means. In this chapter the minimisation criterion is the mean kriging variance (MKV) or a quantile of the kriging variance. Algorithm k-means cannot be used for minimising this criterion, as it uses (standardised) distances between cluster centres (the sampling locations) and the nodes of a discretisation grid, and the kriging variance is not a simple linear function of these distances. A different optimisation algorithm is needed. Here, spatial simulated annealing is used which is explained in the next subsection. Non-spatial simulated annealing was used before in conditioned Latin hypercube sampling using package **clhs** (Chapter 19).

23.1   Spatial simulated annealing

Inspired by the potentials of optimisation through simulated annealing (Kirkpatrick et al., 1983), van Groenigen and Stein (1998) proposed to optimise the sampling pattern by spatial simulated annealing (SSA), see also van Groenigen et al. (1999) and van Groenigen et al. (2000). This is an iterative, random search procedure, in which a sequence of samples is generated. A newly proposed sample is obtained by slightly modifying the current sample. One sampling location of the current sample is randomly selected, and this location is shifted to a random location within the neighbourhood of the selected location.

The minimisation criterion is computed for the proposed sample and compared with that of the current sample. If the criterion of the proposed sample is smaller, the sample is accepted. If the criterion is larger, the sample is accepted with a probability equal to

$$P = e^{\frac{-\Delta}{T}} , \qquad (23.1)$$

with Δ the increase of the criterion and T the "temperature".

The name of this parameter shows the link with annealing in metallurgy. Annealing is a heat treatment of a material above its recrystallisation temperature. Simulated annealing mimics the gradual cooling of metal alloys, resulting in an optimum or near-optimum structure of the atoms in the alloy.

The larger the value of T, the larger the probability that a proposed sample with a given increase of the criterion is accepted (Figure 23.1). The temperature T is stepwise decreased during the optimisation: $T_{k+1} = \alpha T_k$. In Figure 23.1 α equals 0.9. The effect of decreasing the temperature is that the acceptance probability of worse samples decreases during the optimisation and approaches 0 towards the end of the optimisation. Note that the temperature remains constant during a number of iterations, referred to as the chain length. In Figure 23.1 this chain length equals 100 iterations. Finally, a stopping criterion is required. Various stopping criteria are possible; one option is to set the maximum numbers of chains with no improvement. T, α, the chain length, and

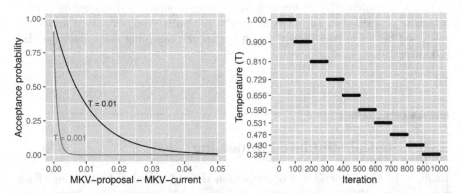

FIGURE 23.1: Acceptance probability as a function of the change in the mean kriging variance (MKV) used as a minimisation criterion, and cooling schedule in spatial simulated annealing. For negative changes (MKV of proposed sample smaller than of current sample) the acceptance probability equals 1.

the stopping criterion are annealing schedule parameters that must be chosen by the user.

23.2   Optimising the sampling pattern for ordinary kriging

In ordinary kriging (OK), we assume a constant model-mean. No covariates are available that are related to the study variable. Optimisation of the sampling pattern for OK is illustrated with the Cotton Research Farm in Uzbekistan which was used before to illustrate spatial response surface sampling (Chapter 20). The spatial coordinates of 50 sampling locations are optimised for mapping of the soil salinity (as measured by the electrical conductivity, ECe, of the soil) by OK. In this section, the coordinates of the sampling points are optimised for OK. In Section 23.3 this is done for kriging with an external drift. In that section, a map of interpolated electromagnetic (EM) induction measurements is used to further optimise the coordinates of the sampling points.

Model-based optimisation of the sampling pattern for OK requires as input a semivariogram of the study variable. For the Cotton Research Farm, I used the ECe (dS m^{-1}) data collected in eight surveys in the period from 2008 to 2011 at 142 points to estimate this semivariogram (Akramkhanov et al., 2014). The ECe data are natural-log transformed. The sample semivariogram is shown in Figure 23.2. The **R** code below shows how I fitted the semivariogram model with function nls ("non-linear least squares") of the **stat** package. I did not use function fit.variogram of the **gstat** package (Pebesma, 2004), because this function requires the output of function variogram as input, whereas the sample semivariogram is here computed in a different way.

> The sample semivariogram is computed by first estimating sample semivariograms for each of the eight surveys separately, followed by computing weighted averages of semivariances and distances per lag, using the numbers of pairs as weights (**R** code not shown).

The semivariogram parameters as estimated by nls are then used to define a semivariogram model of class variogramModel of package **gstat**, using function vgm. This is done because function optimMKV requires a semivariogram model of this class, see hereafter. As already mentioned in Chapter 22, in practice we often do not have legacy data from which we can estimate the semivariogram, and a best guess of the semivariogram then must be made.

```
library(gstat)
res_nls <- nls(semivar ~ nugget + psill * (1 - exp(-h / range)),
   start = list(nugget = 0.1, psill = 0.4, range = 200), weights = somnp)
vgm_lnECe <- vgm(model = "Exp", nugget = coef(res_nls)[1],
   psill = coef(res_nls)[2], range = coef(res_nls)[3])
```

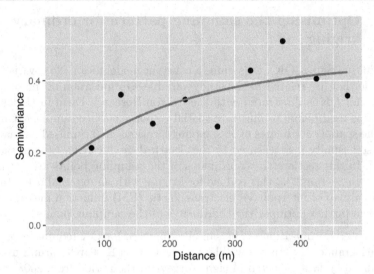

FIGURE 23.2: Sample semivariogram and fitted exponential model of lnECe at the Cotton Research Farm.

The estimated semivariogram parameters are shown in Table 23.1. The nugget-to-sill ratio is about 1/4, and the effective range is about 575 m (three times the distance parameter of an exponential model).

The coordinates of the sampling points are optimised with function optimMKV of package **spsann** (Samuel-Rosa, 2019)[1]. First, the candidate sampling points are specified by the nodes of a grid discretising the population. As explained hereafter, this does not necessarily imply that the population is treated as a finite population. Next, the parameters of the annealing schedule are set. Note that both the initial acceptance rate and the initial temperature are set, which may seem weird as the acceptance rate is a function of the temperature, see Equation (23.1). The optimisation stops when an initial temperature is chosen leading to an acceptance rate outside the interval specified with argument initial.acceptance. If the acceptance rate is smaller than the lower bound of the interval, a larger value for the initial temperature must be chosen; if the rate is larger than the upper bound, a smaller initial temperature must be chosen.

---

[1]At the moment of writing this book, package **spsann** is not available on CRAN. You can install **spsann** and its dependency **pedometrics** with remotes::install_github("samuel-rosa/spsann") and remotes::install_github("samuel-rosa/pedometrics").

TABLE 23.1: Estimated parameters of an exponential semivariogram for lnECe (estimated by method-of-moments) and for the residuals of a linear regression model for lnECe using lnEM100cm as a predictor (estimated by REML).

Variable	Nugget	Partial sill	Distance parameter (m)
lnECe	0.116	0.336	192
residuals	0.126	0.083	230

Arguments `chain.length` and `stopping` of function `scheduleSPSANN` are multipliers. So, for a chain length of five, the number of iterations equals $5n$, with n the sample size.

During the optimisation, a sample is perturbed by replacing one randomly selected point of the current sample by a new point. This selection of the new point is done in two steps. In the first step, one node of the discretisation grid (specified with argument `candi`) is randomly selected. Only the nodes within a neighbourhood defined by `x.min`, `x.max`, `y.min`, and `y.max` can be selected. The nodes within this neighbourhood have equal probability of being selected. In the second step, one point is selected within a grid cell with the selected node at its centre and a side length specified with argument `cellsize`. So, it is natural to set `cellsize` to the spacing of the discretisation grid. With `cellsize = 0`, the sampling points are restricted to the nodes of the discretisation grid.

```
library(spsann)
candi <- grdCRF[, c("x", "y")]
schedule <- scheduleSPSANN(
  initial.acceptance = c(0.8,0.95),
  initial.temperature = 0.004, temperature.decrease = 0.95,
  chains = 500, chain.length = 2, stopping = 10, cellsize = 25)
```

The **R** code for optimising the sampling pattern is as follows.

```
set.seed(314)
res <- optimMKV(
  points = 50, candi = candi,
  vgm = vgm_lnECe, eqn = z ~ 1,
  schedule = schedule, nmax = 20,
  plotit = FALSE, track = TRUE)
mysample <- res$points
trace <- res$objective$energy
```

The spatial pattern of the sample in Figure 23.3 and the trace of the MKV in Figure 23.4 suggest that we are close to the global optimum.

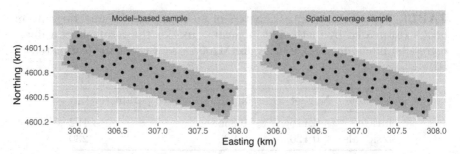

FIGURE 23.3: Optimised sampling pattern for the mean variance of OK predictions of lnECe (model-based sample) and spatial coverage sample of the Cotton Research Farm.

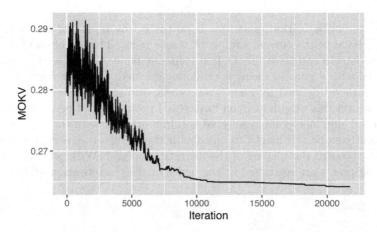

FIGURE 23.4: Trace of the mean ordinary kriging variance (MOKV).

For comparison I also computed a spatial coverage sample of the same size. The spatial patterns of the two samples are quite similar (Figure 23.3). The MKV of the spatial coverage sample equals 0.2633 (dS m⁻¹)², whereas for the model-based sample the MKV equals 0.2642 $(dS\ m^{-1})^2$. So, no gain in precision is achieved by the model-based optimisation of the sampling pattern compared to spatial coverage sampling. With `cellsize = 0` the minimised MKV is slightly smaller: 0.2578 $(dS\ m^{-1})^2$. This outcome is in agreement with the results reported by Brus et al. (2007).

Instead of the mean OK variance (MOKV), we may prefer to use some quantile of the cumulative distribution function of the OK variance as a minimisation criterion. For instance, if we use the 0.90 quantile as a criterion, we are searching for the sampling locations so that the 90th percentile (P90) of the OK variance is minimal. This can be done with function `optimUSER` of package

spsann. The objective function to be minimised can be passed to this function with argument `fun`. In this case the objective function is as follows.

```
QOKV <- function(points, esample, model, nmax, prob) {
  points <- as.data.frame(points)
  coordinates(points) <- ~ x + y
  points$dum <- 1
  res <- krige(
    formula = dum ~ 1,
    locations = points,
    newdata = esample,
    model = model,
    nmax = nmax,
    debug.level = 0)
  quantile(res$var1.var, probs = prob)
}
```

The next code chunk shows how this objective function can be minimised.

```
mysample_eval <- candi
coordinates(mysample_eval) <- ~ x + y
set.seed(314)
res <- optimUSER(
  points = 50, candi = candi,
  fun = QOKV,
  esample = mysample_eval,
  model = vgm_lnECe,
  nmax = 20, prob = 0.9,
  schedule = schedule)
```

Argument `esample` specifies a `SpatialPoints` object with the evaluation points, i.e., the points at which the kriging variance is computed. Above I used all candidate sampling points as evaluation points. Computing time can be reduced by selecting a coarser square grid with evaluation points. The number of points used in kriging is specified with argument `nmax`, and the probability of the cumulative distribution function of the kriging variance is specified with argument `prob`. Optimisation of the sampling pattern for a quantile of the OK variance is left as an exercise.

Exercises

1. Write an **R** script to optimise the spatial coordinates of 16 points in a square for OK. First, create a discretisation grid of 20 × 20 nodes. Use an exponential semivariogram without nugget, with a

sill of 2, and a distance parameter of four times the spacing of the discretisation grid. Optimise the sampling pattern with SSA (using functions scheduleSPSANN and optimMKV of package **spsann**).

- Check whether the optimisation has converged by plotting the trace of the optimisation criterion MKV.
- Based on the coordinates of the sampling points, do you think the sample is the global optimum, i.e., the sample with the smallest possible MKV?

2. Write an **R** script to optimise the sampling pattern of 50 points, using the P90 of the variance of OK predictions of lnECe on the Cotton Research Farm as a minimisation criterion. Use the semivariogram parameters of Table 23.1. Compare the optimised sample with the sample optimised with the mean OK variance (shown in Figure 23.3).

23.3   Optimising the sampling pattern for kriging with an external drift

If we have one or more covariates that are linearly related to the study variable, the study variable can be mapped by kriging with an external drift (KED). A requirement is that we have maps of the covariates so that, once we have estimated the parameters of the model for KED from the data collected at the optimised sample, these covariate maps can be used to map the study variable (see Equation (21.21)).

Optimisation of the sampling pattern for KED requires as input the semivariogram of the residuals. Besides, we must decide on the covariates for the model-mean. Note that we do not need estimates of the regression coefficients associated with the covariates as input, but just which combination of covariates we want to use for modelling the model-mean of the study variable.

Optimisation of the sampling pattern for KED is illustrated with the Cotton Research Farm. The interpolated natural log of the EM data (with transmitter at 1 m) is used as a covariate, see Figure 20.1. The data for fitting the model are in data file sampleCRF. The parameters of the residual semivariogram are estimated by restricted maximum likelihood (REML), see Subsection 21.5.2.

At several points, multiple pairs of observations of the study variable ECe and the covariate EM have been made. These calibration data have exactly the same spatial coordinates. This leads to problems with REML estimation. The covariance matrix is not positive definite, so that it cannot be inverted. To solve this problem, I jittered the coordinates of the sampling points by a small amount.

```
library(geoR)
sampleCRF$lnEM100 <- log(sampleCRF$EMv1m)
sampleCRF$x <- jitter(sampleCRF$x, amount = 0.001)
sampleCRF$y <- jitter(sampleCRF$y, amount = 0.001)
dGeoR <- as.geodata(obj = sampleCRF, header = TRUE,
    coords.col = c("x", "y"), data.col = "lnECe", covar.col = "lnEM100")
vgm_REML <- likfit(geodata = dGeoR, trend = ~ lnEM100,
    cov.model = "exponential", ini.cov.pars = c(0.1, 200),
    nugget = 0.1, lik.method = "REML", messages = FALSE)
```

The REML estimates of the parameters of the residual semivariogram are shown in Table 23.1. The estimated sill (sum of nugget and partial sill) of the residual semivariogram is substantially smaller than that of lnECe, showing that the linear model for the model-mean explains a considerable part of the spatial variation of lnECe.

To optimise the sampling pattern for KED, using the mean KED variance as a minimisation criterion, a data frame with the covariates at the candidate sampling points must be specified with argument covars. The formula for the model-mean is specified with argument eqn.

```
set.seed(314)
res <- optimMKV(
    points = 50, candi = candi, covars = grdCRF,
    vgm = vgm_REML_gstat, eqn = z ~ lnEM100cm,
    schedule = schedule, nmax = 20,
    plotit = FALSE, track = FALSE)
```

Figure 23.5 shows the optimised locations of a sample of 50 points. This clearly shows the irregular spatial pattern of the sampling points induced by the covariate lnEM100cm. Computing time was substantial: 35.06 minutes (processor AMD Ryzen 5, 16 GB RAM).

Comparing the population and sample histograms of the covariate clearly shows that locations with small and large values for the covariate are preferentially selected (Figure 23.6). The optimised sampling pattern is a compromise between spreading in geographic space and covariate space, see also Heuvelink et al. (2007) and Brus and Heuvelink (2007). More precisely, locations are selected by spreading them throughout the study area, while accounting for the values of the covariates at the selected locations, in a way that locations with covariate values near the minimum and maximum are preferred. This can be explained by

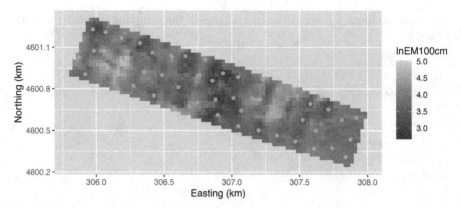

FIGURE 23.5: Optimised sampling pattern for KED of lnECe at the Cotton Research Farm, using lnEM100cm as a covariate.

noting that the variance of the KED prediction error can be decomposed into two components: the variance of the interpolated residuals and the variance of the estimator of the model-mean, see Section 21.3. The contribution of the first variance component is minimised through geographical spreading, that of the second component by selecting locations with covariate values near the minimum and maximum.

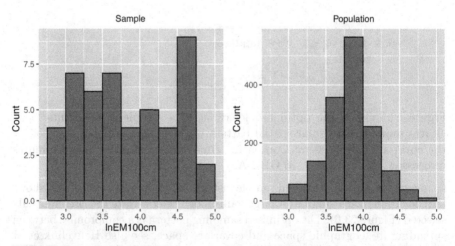

FIGURE 23.6: Sample frequency distribution and population frequency distribution of lnEM100cm used as covariate in model-based optimisation of the sampling pattern for mapping with KED.

A sample with covariate values close to the minimum and maximum only is not desirable if we do not want to rely on the assumption of a linear relation between the study variable and the covariates. To identify a non-linear relation, locations with intermediate covariate values are needed. Optimisation using a semivariogram with clear spatial structure leads to geographical spreading of the sampling units, so that most likely also locations with intermediate covariate values are selected.

When one or more covariates are used in optimisation of the sampling pattern but not used in KED once the data are collected, the sample is suboptimal for the model used in prediction. Inversely, ignoring a covariate in optimisation of the sampling pattern while using this covariate as a predictor also leads to suboptimal samples. The selection of covariates to be used in sampling design therefore should be done with care. Besides, as we will see in the next exercise, the nugget of the residual semivariogram has a strong effect on the optimised sampling pattern, stressing the importance of a reliable prior estimate of this semivariogram parameter.

Exercises

3. Write an **R** script to optimise the sampling pattern of 16 points in a square for KED. Use the x-coordinate as a covariate. First, create a discretisation grid of 20×20 nodes. Use an exponential residual semivariogram without nugget, with a sill of 2, and a distance parameter of four times the spacing of the discretisation grid. Optimise the sampling pattern with SSA (using functions scheduleSPSANN and optimMKV of package **spsann**).
   - What do you think of the spatial coverage of the optimised sample? Compare the sample with the optimised sample for OK, see exercise of Section 23.2.
   - Repeat the optimisation using a residual semivariogram with a nugget of 1.5 and a partial sill of 0.5. Note that the sill is again 2, as before.
   - Compare the optimised sample with the previous sample. What is the most striking difference?
   - How will the optimised sample look with a pure nugget semivariogram? Check your assumption using such semivariogram in SSA.

23.4   Model-based infill sampling for ordinary kriging

Similar to spatial infill sampling using MSSD as a minimisation criterion (Section 17.3), we may design a model-based infill sample. Package **spsann** can be used for this, using argument points of function optimMKV.

In Section 22.1 the legacy data of West-Amhara were used to estimate the parameters of a spherical semivariogram for the SOM concentration. The estimated parameters are shown in Table 22.1. The maximum likelihood estimates are used in this section to optimise the spatial coordinates of the infill sample.

In the next code chunk, a list is created containing a data frame with the coordinates of the fixed points (specified with subargument fixed) and an integer of the number of additional points to be selected (specified with subargument free). The list is passed to function optimMKV with argument points. For kriging, I reduced the number of legacy points by keeping one point only per grid cell of 1 km × 1 km. This is done with function remove.duplicates of package **sp**.

```
library(sp)
coordinates(sampleAmhara) <- ~ s1 + s2
legacy <- remove.duplicates(sampleAmhara, zero = 1, remove.second = TRUE)
pnts <- list(fixed = coordinates(legacy), free = 100)
candi <- grdAmhara[, c("s1", "s2")]
names(candi) <- c("x", "y")
```

The number of points used in kriging can be passed to function optimMKV with argument nmax.

```
set.seed(314)
vgm_ML_gstat <- vgm(model = "Sph", psill = vgm_ML$sigmasq,
  range = vgm_ML$phi, nugget = vgm_ML$nugget)
res <- optimMKV(
  points = pnts, candi = candi,
  vgm = vgm_ML_gstat, eqn = z ~ 1,
  nmax = 20, schedule = schedule, track = FALSE)
infillSample <- res$points %>%
  filter(free == 1)
```

Figure 23.7 shows a model-based infill sample of 100 points for OK of the soil organic matter (SOM) concentration (dag kg^{-1}) throughout West-Amhara. Comparison of the model-based infill sample with the spatial infill sample of Figure 17.5 shows that in a wider zone on both sides of the roads no new sampling points are selected. This can be explained by the large range, 36.9 km, of the semivariogram.

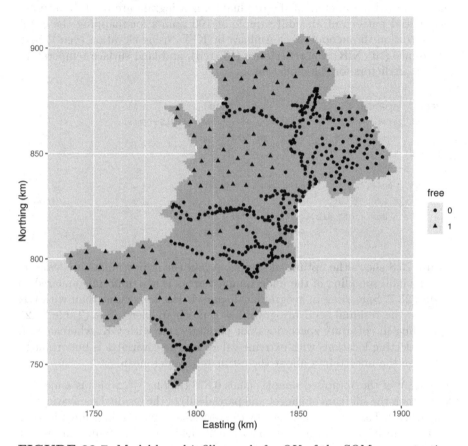

FIGURE 23.7: Model-based infill sample for OK of the SOM concentration throughout West-Amhara. Legacy units have free-value 0; infill units have free-value 1.

23.5 Model-based infill sampling for kriging with an external drift

For West-Amhara, maps of covariates are available that can be used in KED, see Section 22.4. The prediction error variance with KED is partly determined by the covariate values (see Section 23.3), and therefore, when filling in the undersampled areas, locations with extreme values for the covariates are preferably selected. In Section 22.4 the legacy data were used to estimate the residual semivariogram by REML, see Table 22.2. In the next code chunk, the estimated parameters of the residual semivariogram are used to optimise the spatial pattern of an infill sample of 100 points for mapping the SOM concentration throughout West-Amhara by KED, using elevation (dem), NIR-reflectance (rfl_NIR), red-reflectance (rfl_red), and land surface temperature (lst) as predictors for the model-mean.

```
covars <- grdAmhara[, c("dem", "rfl_NIR", "rfl_red", "lst")]
vgm_REML_gstat <- vgm(model = "Sph", psill = vgm_REML$sigmasq,
  range = vgm_REML$phi, nugget = vgm_REML$nugget)
set.seed(314)
res <- optimMKV(
  points = pnts, candi = candi, covars = covars,
  vgm = vgm_REML_gstat,
  eqn = z ~ dem + rfl_NIR + rfl_red + lst,
  nmax = 20, schedule = schedule, track = TRUE)
```

Figure 23.8 shows the optimised sample. Again the legacy points are avoided, but the infill sampling of the undersampled areas is less uniform compared to Figure 23.7. Spreading in geographical space is less important than with OK because the residual semivariogram has a much smaller range (Table 22.2). Spreading in covariate space does not play any role with OK, whereas with KED selecting locations with extreme values for the covariates is important to minimise the uncertainty about the estimated model-mean.

The MKV of the optimised sample equals 0.878 (dag kg^{-1})^2, which is somewhat larger than the sill (sum of nugget and partial sill) of the residual semivariogram (Table 22.2). This can be explained by the very small range of the semivariogram, so that ignoring the uncertainty about the model-mean, the kriging variance at nearly all locations in the study area equals the sill. Besides, we are uncertain about the model-mean, explaining that the MKV can be larger than the sill.

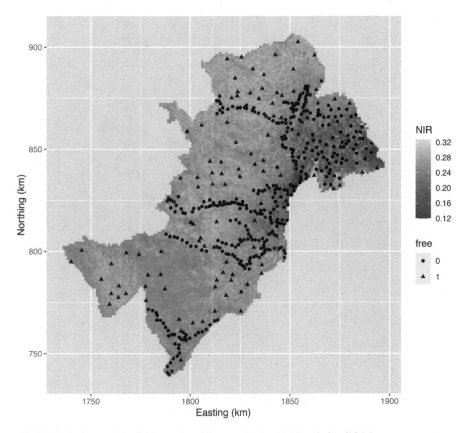

FIGURE 23.8: Model-based infill sample for KED of the SOM concentration throughout West-Amhara, plotted on a map of one of the covariates. Legacy units have free-value 0; infill units have free-value 1.

24

Sampling for estimating the semivariogram

For model-based sampling as described in Chapters 22 and 23, we must specify the (residual) semivariogram. In case we do not have a reasonable prior estimate of the semivariogram, we may decide to first collect data with the specific aim of estimating the semivariogram. This semivariogram is subsequently used to design a model-based sample for mapping. This chapter is about how to design a reconnaissance sample survey for estimating the semivariogram.

The first question is how many observations we need for this. Webster and Oliver (1992) gave as a rule of thumb that 150 to 225 points are needed to obtain a reliable semivariogram when estimated by the method-of-moments (MoM). Lark (2000) showed that with maximum likelihood (ML) estimation two-thirds to only half of the observations are needed to achieve equal precision of the estimated semivariogram parameters.

Once we have decided on the sample size, we must select the locations of the sampling units. Two random sampling designs for semivariogram estimation are described, nested sampling (Section 24.1) and independent sampling of pairs of points (Section 24.2). Section 24.3 is devoted to model-based optimisation of the sampling pattern for semivariogram estimation. Section 24.4 is about how to design a single sample that can be used both for estimation of the semivariogram and prediction (mapping). In a final section, a practical solution is described for the problem of how to design a sample for semivariogram estimation and prediction.

24.1 Nested sampling

Nested sampling can be used to estimate the semivariance at a limited number of separation distances, see Oliver and Webster (1986) and Webster et al. (2006). First, we must decide on these separation distances. We need point-pairs at various separation distances, especially for small separation distances, so that we get reliable estimates of this part of the semivariogram which has a strong effect on the kriging weights. Usually, separation distances are chosen in a geometric progression, for instance 2, 8, 32, 128, and 512 m. The multiplier, which is four in this example, should not be too small; as a rule of thumb, use three or larger.

There are two versions of nested sampling. In the first stage of the first version, several main stations are selected in a way that they cover the study area well, for instance by spatial coverage sampling. In the second stage, each of the main stations is used as a starting point to select one point at a distance equal to the largest chosen separation distance (512 m in the example) in a random direction from the main station. This doubles the sample size. In the third stage, all points selected in the previous stages (main stations of stage 1 plus the points of stage 2) are used as starting points to select one point at a distance equal to the second largest separation distance (128 m), and so on. All points selected in the various stages are included in the nested sample. The code chunk below shows the function for random selection of one point at distance h from a starting point. Note the while loop which continues until a point is found that is inside the area. This is checked with function over of package **sp**.

```
SelectPoint <- function(start, h, area) {
  dxy <- numeric(length = 2)
  inArea <- NA
  while (is.na(inArea)) {
    angle <- runif(n = 1, min = 0, max = 2 * pi)
    dxy[1] <- h * sin(angle); dxy[2] <- h * cos(angle)
    xypnt <- start + dxy
    coordinates(xypnt) <- ~ s1 + s2
    inArea <- as.numeric(over(x = xypnt, y = area))[1]
  }
  xypoint <- as.data.frame(xypnt)
  xypoint
}
```

The first stage of the second version is equal to that of the first version. However, in the second stage each of the main stations serves as a starting point for randomly selecting a *pair of points* with a separation distance equal to the largest chosen separation distance. The main station is halfway the selected pair of points. In the third stage, each of the substations is used to select in the same way a pair of points separated by the second largest chosen distance, and so on. Only the points selected in the final stage are used as sampling points. The **R** code below shows the function for random selection of two points separated by h distance units with a starting point halfway the pair of points. The while loop continues until both points of a pair are inside the area.

```
SelectPair <- function(start, h, area) {
  dxy <- numeric(length = 2)
```

```
  xypoints <- NULL
  inArea1 <- inArea2 <- NA
  while (is.na(inArea1) | is.na(inArea2)) {
    angle <- runif(n = 1, min = 0, max = 2 * pi)
    dxy[1] <- h * sin(angle) / 2; dxy[2] <- h * cos(angle) / 2
    xypnt1 <- start + dxy
    coordinates(xypnt1) <- ~ s1 + s2
    inArea1 <- as.numeric(over(x = xypnt1, y = area))[1]
    dxy[1] <- -dxy[1]; dxy[2] <- -dxy[2]
    xypnt2 <- start + dxy
    coordinates(xypnt2) <- ~ s1 + s2
    inArea2 <- as.numeric(over(x = xypnt2, y = area))[1]
  }
  xypoints <- rbind(as.data.frame(xypnt1), as.data.frame(xypnt2))
  xypoints
}
```

The **R** code below shows the selection of a nested sample from Hunter Valley using both versions. Only one main station is selected. In total 16 points are selected in four stages. The separation distances are 2,000, 1,000, 500, and 250 m. Sixteen points is not enough for estimating the semivariogram and a multiplier of two is rather small, but this example is for illustrative purposes only.

Note that the separation distances are in descending order. The largest separation distance should not be chosen too large, because then, when the main station is somewhere in the middle of the study area, it may happen that using the first version, no pair can be found with that separation distance. A similar problem may occur with the second version when in subsequent stages a station is selected near the border of the study area. A copy of grdHunterValley is made because both the original data frame is needed, as well as a gridded version of this data frame.

```
library(sp)
grid <- grdHunterValley
gridded(grdHunterValley) <- ~ s1 + s2
lags <- c(2000, 1000, 500, 250)
```

The next code chunk is an implementation of the first version of nested sampling.

```
set.seed(614)
unit <- sample(nrow(grid), 1)
mainstation <- grid[unit, c("s1", "s2")]
```

```
newpnt <- SelectPoint(start = mainstation, h = lags[1], area = grdHunterValley)
mysample_nested <- rbind(mainstation, newpnt)
for (j in 2:length(lags)) {
  newpnts <- NULL
  for (i in seq_len(nrow(mysample_nested))) {
    pnts <- SelectPoint(
      start = mysample_nested[i, ], h = lags[j], area = grdHunterValley)
    newpnts <- rbind(newpnts, pnts)
  }
  mysample_nested <- rbind(mysample_nested, newpnts)
}
```

The **R** code for the second version is presented in the next code chunk.

```
unit <- sample(nrow(grid), 1)
mainstation <- grid[unit, c("s1", "s2")]
pnt <- SelectPoint(start = mainstation, h = lags[1], area = grdHunterValley)
stations <- rbind(mainstation, pnt)
allstations <-  rbind(mainstation, pnt)
for (j in 2:length(lags)) {
  newstations <- NULL
  for (i in seq_len(nrow(stations))) {
    pnts <- SelectPair(
      start = stations[i, ], h = lags[j], area = grdHunterValley)
    newstations <- rbind(newstations, pnts)
    allstations <- rbind(allstations, pnts)
  }
  stations <- newstations
}
mysample_nested_2 <- as_tibble(stations)
```

Figure 24.1 shows the two selected nested samples. For the sample selected with the second version, also the stations that served as starting points for the selection of the point-pairs are plotted.

The samples of Figure 24.1 are examples of *balanced* nested samples. The number of point-pairs separated by a given distance doubles with every stage. As a consequence, the estimated semivariances for the smallest separation distance are much more precise than for the largest distance. We are most uncertain about the estimated semivariances for the largest separation distances. If in the first stage only one point-pair separated by the largest distance is selected, then we have only one degree of freedom for estimating the variance component associated with this stage. It is more efficient to select more than one main station, say about ten, and to select fewer points in the final stages. For instance, with the second version we may decide to select a point-pair at

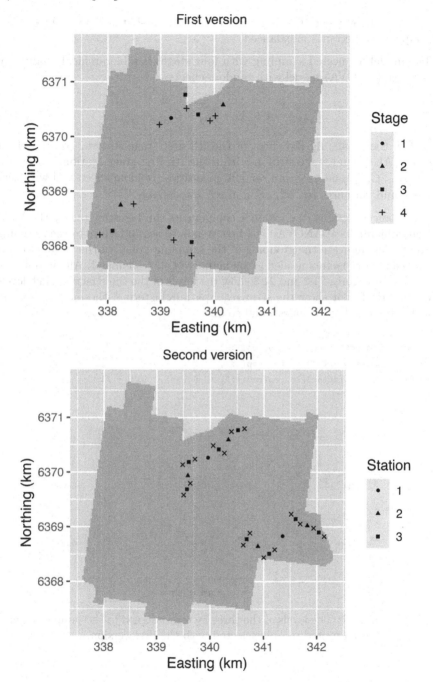

FIGURE 24.1: Balanced nested samples from Hunter Valley, selected with the two versions of nested sampling. In the subfigure of the second version the selected sampling points (symbol x) are plotted together with the selected stations (halfway the two points of a pair).

only half the number of stations selected in the one-but-last stage. The nested sample then becomes unbalanced.

The model for nested sampling with four stages is a hierarchical analysis of variance (ANOVA) model with random effects:

$$Z_{ijkl} = \mu + A_i + B_{ij} + C_{ijk} + \epsilon_{ijkl} , \qquad (24.1)$$

with μ the mean, A_i the effect of the ith first stage station, B_{ij} the effect of the jth second stage station within the ith first stage station, and so on. A_i, B_{ij}, C_{ijk}, and ϵ_{ijkl} are random quantities (random effects) all with zero mean and variances σ_1^2, σ_2^2, σ_3^2, and σ_4^2, respectively.

For balanced designs, the variance components can be estimated by the MoM from a hierarchical ANOVA. The first step is to assign factors to the sampling points that indicate the grouping of the sampling points in the various stages. The number of factors needed is the number of stages minus 1. All factors have two levels. Figures 24.2 and 24.3 show the levels of the three factors. The levels of the first factor show the strongest spatial clustering, those of the second factor the one-but-strongest, and so on.

```
mysample_nested$factor1 <- rep(rep(1:2), times = 8)
mysample_nested$factor2 <- rep(rep(1:2, each = 2), times = 4)
mysample_nested$factor3 <- rep(rep(1:2, each = 4), times = 2)
```

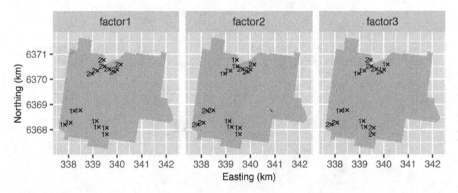

FIGURE 24.2: The levels of the three factors assigned to the sampling points of the balanced nested sample selected with the first version.

The **R** code below shows the construction of the three factors for the second version of nested sampling.

```
mysample_nested_2$factor1 <- rep(1:2, each = 8)
mysample_nested_2$factor2 <- rep(rep(1:2, each = 4), times = 2)
mysample_nested_2$factor3 <- rep(rep(1:2, each = 2), times = 4)
```

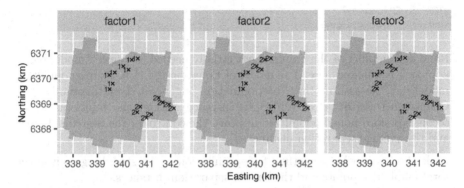

FIGURE 24.3: The levels of the three factors assigned to the sampling points of the balanced nested sample selected with the second version.

For unbalanced nested designs, the variance components can be estimated by restricted maximum likelihood (REML) (Webster et al., 2006). REML estimation is also recommended if in Equation (24.1) instead of a constant mean μ the mean is a linear combination of one or more covariates (fixed effects). The semivariances at the chosen separation distances are obtained by cumulating the estimated variance components.

The **R** code below shows how the variance components and the semivariances can be estimated with function lme of the package **nlme** (Pinheiro et al., 2021), once the data are collected and added to the data frame. This function fits linear mixed-effects models and allows for nested random effects. It can be used both for balanced and unbalanced nested samples, and for a constant mean or a mean that is a linear combination of covariates. Argument fixed is a formula describing the fixed effects with the response variable on the left-hand side of the $\sim$ operator and the covariates for the mean on the right-hand side. If a constant mean is assumed, as in our example, this is indicated by the 1 on the right-hand side of the $\sim$ operator. Argument random is a one-sided formula (no response variable is on the left-hand side of the $\sim$ operator). On the right-hand side of the | separator, the nested structure of the data is specified using the factors of Figure 24.2. The 1 on the left-hand side of the | separator means that we assume that all regression coefficients associated with the covariates are fixed (non-random) quantities.

```
library(nlme)
lmodel <- lme(
```

```
  fixed = z ~ 1, data = mysample_nested,
    random = ~ 1 | factor1 / factor2 / factor3)
res <- as.matrix(VarCorr(lmodel))
sigmas <- as.numeric(res[c(2, 4, 6, 7), 1])
sigma <- rev(sigmas)
semivar <- cumsum(sigmas)
```

Random sampling of the points is not strictly needed, because a model-based approach is followed here. The model of Equation (24.1) is a superpopulation model, i.e., we assume that the population is generated by this model (see Chapter 26). Papritz et al. (2011), for instance, selected the points (using the second version) non-randomly to improve the control of the nested subareas and the average separation distances.

Lark (2011) describes a method for optimisation of a nested design, given the total number of points and the chosen separation distances.

Exercises

1. Write an **R** script to select with the first version a balanced nested sample from Hunter Valley. Use as separation distances 1,000, 500, 200, 100, and 50 m.
   - Add the factors that are needed for estimating the variance components to the data frame with the selected sampling points.
   - Overlay the sampling points with the SpatialPixelsDataFrame, and estimate the semivariances for the attribute compound topographic index (cti).

24.2   Independent sampling of pairs of points

With the nested design, the estimated semivariances for the different separation distances are not independent. Independent estimated semivariances can be obtained by independent random selection of pairs of points (IPP sampling). Independence here means design-independence, see Section 26.2. Similar to a regression model, a semivariogram can be defined as a superpopulation model or as a population model. Only in the current section a semivariogram is defined at the population level. Such a semivariogram is referred to as a non-ergodic semivariogram or local semivariogram (Brus and de Gruijter, 1994).

IPP sampling is straightforward for simple random sampling. For each separation distance a point-pair is selected by first selecting fully randomly one point from the study area. Then the second point is randomly selected from the circle with the first point at its centre and a radius equal to the chosen separation distance. If this second point is outside the study area, both points are discarded. This is repeated until we have the required point-pairs for this separation distance. The next code chunk is an implementation of this selection procedure.

```
SIpairs <- function(h, n, area) {
  topo <- as(getGridTopology(area), "data.frame")
  cell_size <- topo$cellsize[1]
  xy <- coordinates(area)
  dxy <- numeric(length = 2)
  xypnts1 <- xypnts2 <- NULL
  i <- 1
  while (i <= n) {
    unit1 <- sample(length(area), size = 1)
    xypnt1 <- xy[unit1, ]
    xypnt1[1] <- jitter(xypnt1[1], amount = cell_size / 2)
    xypnt1[2] <- jitter(xypnt1[2], amount = cell_size / 2)
    angle <- runif(n = 1, min = 0, max = 2 * pi)
    dxy[1] <- h * sin(angle); dxy[2] <- h * cos(angle)
    xypnt2 <- as.data.frame(t(xypnt1 + dxy))
    coordinates(xypnt2) <- ~ s1 + s2
    inArea <- as.numeric(over(x = xypnt2, y = area))[1]
    if (!is.na(inArea)) {
      xypnts1 <- rbind(xypnts1, xypnt1)
      xypnts2 <- rbind(xypnts2, as.data.frame(xypnt2))
      i <- i + 1
    }
    rm(xypnt1, xypnt2)
  }
  cbind(xypnts1, xypnts2)
}
```

IPP sampling is illustrated with the compound topographic index (cti, which is the same as topographic wetness index) data of Hunter Valley. Five separation distances are chosen, collected in numeric h, and for each distance $n = 100$ point-pairs are selected by simple random sampling.

```
library(sp)
h <- c(50, 100, 200, 500, 1000)
n <- 100
set.seed(123)
allpairs <- NULL
```

```
for (i in seq_len(length(h))) {
  pairs <- SIpairs(h = h[i], n = n, area = grdHunterValley)
  allpairs <- rbind(allpairs, pairs, make.row.names = FALSE)
}
```

The data.frame allpairs has four variables: the spatial coordinates of the first and of the second point of a pair. An overlay is made of the selected points with the SpatialPixelsDataFrame, and the cti values are extracted.

```
pnt1 <- allpairs[, c(1, 2)]
coordinates(pnt1) <- ~ s1 + s2
z1 <- over(x = pnt1, y = grdHunterValley)["cti"]
pnt2 <- allpairs[, c(3, 4)]
coordinates(pnt2) <- ~ s1 + s2
z2 <- over(x = pnt2, y = grdHunterValley)["cti"]
mysample <- data.frame(h = rep(h, each = n), z1, z2)
names(mysample)[c(2, 3)] <- c("z1", "z2")
```

The semivariances for the chosen separation distances are estimated as well as the variance of these estimated semivariances.

```
gammah <- vgammah <- numeric(length = length(h))
for (i in seq_len(length(h))) {
  units <- which(mysample$h == h[i])
  pairsh <- mysample[units, ]
  gammah[i] <- mean((pairsh$z1 - pairsh$z2)^2, na.rm = TRUE) / 2
  vgammah[i] <- var((pairsh$z1 - pairsh$z2)^2, na.rm = TRUE) / (n * 4)
}
```

A spherical model with nugget is fitted to the sample semivariogram, using function nls, with weights equal to the reciprocal of the estimated variances of the estimated semivariances.

```
sample_vg <- data.frame(h, gammah, vgammah)
SphNug <- function(h, range, psill, nugget) {
  h <- h / range
  nugget + psill * ifelse(h < 1, (1.5 * h - 0.5 * h^3), 1)
}
fit.var <- nls(gammah ~ SphNug(h, range, psill, nugget),
  data = sample_vg, start = list(psill = 4, range = 200, nugget = 1),
  weights = 1 / vgammah, algorithm = "port", lower = c(0, 0, 0))
print(pars <- signif(coef(fit.var), 3))
```

```
psill   range nugget
 3.29 188.00   1.21
```

Figure 24.4 shows the sample semivariogram and the fitted model.

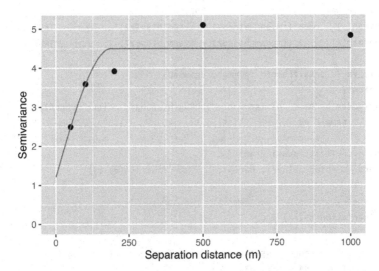

FIGURE 24.4: Sample semivariogram, obtained by independent sampling of pairs of points, and fitted spherical model of compount topographic index in Hunter Valley.

The covariances of the estimated semivariances at different separation distances are zero, as the point-pairs are selected independently. This keeps estimation of the variances and covariances of the estimated semivariogram parameters simple. In the next code chunk, this is done by bootstrapping.

In bootstrapping, for each separation distance a simple random sample *with replacement* of point-pairs is selected from the original sample of point-pairs. A point-pair can be selected more than once. The sample size (number of draws) is equal to the total number of point-pairs per separation distance in the original sample.

Every run of the bootstrap results in as many bootstrap samples as there are separation distances. The bootstrap samples are used to fit a semivariogram model. The whole procedure is repeated 500 times, resulting in 500 vectors with model parameters. These vectors can be used to estimate the variances and covariances of the estimators of the three semivariogram parameters.

```
allpars <- NULL
R <- 500
for (j in 1:R) {
  gammah <- vgammah <- numeric(length = length(h))
```

```
for (i in seq_len(length(h))) {
  units <- which(mysample$h == h[i])
  mysam_btsp <- mysample[units, ] %>%
    slice_sample(n = n, replace = TRUE)
  gammah[i] <- mean((mysam_btsp$z1 - mysam_btsp$z2)^2, na.rm = TRUE) / 2
  vgammah[i] <- var((mysam_btsp$z1 - mysam_btsp$z2)^2, na.rm = TRUE) / (n * 4)
}
sample_vg <- data.frame(h, gammah, vgammah)
tryCatch({
  fittedvariogram <- nls(gammah ~ SphNug(h, range, psill, nugget),
    data = sample_vg, start = list(psill = 4, range = 200, nugget = 1),
    weights = 1 / vgammah, algorithm = "port", lower = c(0, 0, 0))
  pars <- coef(fittedvariogram)
  allpars <- rbind(allpars, pars)}, error = function(e) {})
}
#compute variance-covariance matrix
signif(var(allpars), 3)
```

```
          psill    range   nugget
psill     1.160    -44.6   -0.803
range   -44.600  66700.0  172.000
nugget   -0.803    172.0    1.070
```

Note the large variance for the range parameter (the standard deviation is 258 m) as well as the negative covariance of the nugget and the partial sill parameter (the Pearson correlation coefficient is -0.72). Histograms of the three estimated semivariogram parameters are shown in Figure 24.5.

Marcelli et al. (2019) show how a probability sample of *points* (instead of pairs of points) can be used in design-based estimation of the semivariogram. From the n randomly selected points all $n(n-1)/2$ point-pairs are constructed. The *second-order inclusion probabilities* of these point-pairs are used to estimate the mean semivariance for separation distance classes. This sampling strategy makes better use of the data and is therefore potentially more efficient than IPP sampling.

Exercises

2. Write an **R** script to select simple random samples of pairs of points for estimating the semivariogram of cti in Hunter Valley. Use as separation distances 25, 50, 100, 200, and 400 m. Note that these separation distances are smaller than those used above. Select 100 pairs per separation distance.

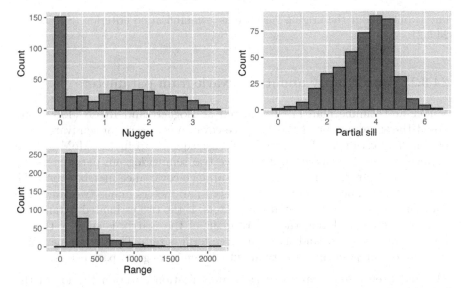

FIGURE 24.5: Frequency distributions of estimated parameters of a spherical semivariogram of compound topographic index in Hunter Valley.

- Compute the sample semivariogram, and estimate a spherical model with nugget using function nls.
- Compare the estimated semivariogram parameters with the estimates obtained with the larger separation distances.
- Estimate the variance-covariance matrix of the estimated semivariogram parameters by bootstrapping.
- Compare the variances of the estimated semivariogram parameters with the variances obtained with the larger separation distances. Which variance is changed most?

24.3 Optimisation of sampling pattern for semivariogram estimation

There is rich literature on model-based optimisation of the sampling locations for semivariogram estimation. Several design criteria (minimisation criteria) have been proposed for optimising the sampling pattern. Various authors have proposed a measure of the uncertainty about the semivariogram parameters as a minimisation criterion. These criteria are described and illustrated in the next subsection. The kriging variance is sensitive to errors in the estimated semivariogram. Therefore, Lark (2002) proposed to use a measure of the uncertainty about the kriging variance as a minimisation criterion (Subsection 24.3.2).

24.3.1   Uncertainty about semivariogram parameters

Müller and Zimmerman (1999) as well as Bogaert and Russo (1999) proposed the determinant of the variance-covariance matrix of semivariogram parameters, estimated by generalised least squares to fit the MoM sample semivariogram. For instance, if we have two semivariogram parameters, θ_1 and θ_2, the determinant of the 2×2 variance-covariance matrix equals the sum of the variances of the two estimated parameters minus two times the covariance of the two estimated parameters. If the two estimated parameters are positively correlated, the determinant of the matrix is smaller than if they are uncorrelated, and the covariance term is zero. The determinant is a measure of our *joint* uncertainty about the semivariogram parameters.

Zhu and Stein (2005) proposed as a minimisation criterion the log of the determinant of the inverse Fisher information matrix in ML estimation of the semivariogram, hereafter shortly denoted by logdet. The Fisher information about a semivariogram parameter is a function of the likelihood of the semivariogram parameter; the likelihood of a semivariogram parameter is the probability of the data as a function of the semivariogram parameter. The log of this likelihood can be plotted against values of the parameter. The flatter the log-likelihood surface, the less information is in the data about the parameter. The flatness of the surface can be measured by the first derivative of the log-likelihood to the semivariogram parameter. Strong negative or positive derivative values indicate a steep surface. The Fisher information for a model parameter is defined as the expectation of the *square* of the first derivative of the log-likelihood to that semivariogram parameter, see Ly et al. (2017) for a nice tutorial on this subject. The more information we have about a semivariogram, the less uncertain we are about that parameter. This explains why the inverse of the Fisher information can be used as a measure of uncertainty. The inverse Fisher information matrix contains the variances and covariances of the estimated semivariogram parameters.

The code chunks hereafter show how logdet can be computed. It makes use of the result of Kitanidis (1987) who showed that each element of the Fisher information matrix $\mathbf{I}(\theta)$ can be obtained with (see also Lark (2002))

$$[\mathbf{I}(\theta)]_{ij} = \frac{1}{2} \text{Tr} \left[\mathbf{A}^{-1} \frac{\partial \mathbf{A}}{\partial \theta_i} \mathbf{A}^{-1} \frac{\partial \mathbf{A}}{\partial \theta_j} \right], \tag{24.2}$$

with $\mathbf{A}$ the correlation matrix of the sampling points, $\frac{\partial \mathbf{A}}{\partial \theta_i}$ the partial derivative of the correlation matrix to the ith semivariogram parameter, and $\text{Tr}[\cdot]$ the trace of a matrix.

As an illustration, I selected a simple random sample of 50 points from Hunter Valley. A matrix with distances between the points of a sample is computed. Preliminary values for the semivariogram parameters ξ (ratio of spatial dependence) and ϕ (distance parameter) are obtained by visual inspection of the sample semivariogram, and the **gstat** (Pebesma, 2004) function variogramLine is used to compute the correlation matrix.

```
library(sp)
library(gstat)
set.seed(314)
mysample0 <- grdHunterValley %>%
  slice_sample(n = 50)
coordinates(mysample0) <- ~ s1 + s2
D <- spDists(mysample0)
xi <- 0.8; phi <- 200
thetas <- c(xi, phi)
vgmodel <- vgm(model = "Exp", psill = thetas[1],
  range = thetas[2], nugget = 1 - thetas[1])
A <- variogramLine(vgmodel, dist_vector = D, covariance = TRUE)
```

In the next step, the semivariogram parameters are slightly changed one-by-one. The changes, referred to as perturbations, are a small fraction of the preliminary semivariogram parameter values. The perturbed semivariogram parameters are used to compute the perturbed correlation matrices (pA) and the partial derivatives of the correlation matrix (dA) for each perturbation.

```
perturbation <- 0.01
pA <- dA <- list()
for (i in seq_len(length(thetas))) {
  thetas_pert <- thetas
  thetas_pert[i] <- (1 + perturbation) * thetas[i]
  vgmodel_pert <- vgm(model = "Exp", psill = thetas_pert[1],
    range = thetas_pert[2], nugget = 1 - thetas_pert[1])
  pA[[i]] <- variogramLine(vgmodel_pert, dist_vector = D, covariance = TRUE)
  dA[[i]] <- (pA[[i]] - A) / (thetas[i] * perturbation)
}
```

Finally, the Fisher information matrix is computed using Equation (24.2). We do not need to compute the inverse of the Fisher information matrix, because the determinant of the inverse of a matrix is equal to the inverse of the determinant of the (not inverted) matrix. The determinant is computed with function determinant.

```
I <- matrix(0, length(thetas), length(thetas))
for (i in seq_len(length(thetas))) {
  m_i <- solve(A, dA[[i]])
  for (j in i:length(thetas)) {
    m_j <- solve(A, dA[[j]])
    I[i, j] <- I[j, i] <- 0.5 * sum(diag(m_i %*% m_j))
  }
}
logdet0 <- -determinant(I, logarithm = TRUE)$modulus
```

The joint uncertainty about the semivariogram parameters, as quantified by the log of the determinant of the inverse of the information matrix, equals 8.198. Hereafter, we will see how much this joint uncertainty can be reduced by optimising the spatial pattern of the sample used for semivariogram estimation, compared to the simple random sample used in the above calculation. Note that a preliminary semivariogram is needed to compute an optimised sampling pattern for semivariogram estimation.

Function optimUSER of package **spsann** can be used to search for the sampling locations with the minimum value of logdet. This function has been used before in Section 23.2. Package **spsann** cannot deal with the 22,124 candidate grid nodes of Hunter Valley; these are too many. I therefore selected a subgrid of 50 m × 50 m.

The size of the sample for estimation of the semivariogram is passed to function optimUSER with argument points. The objective function to be minimised is passed to function optimUSER with argument fun. The objective function logdet is defined in package **sswr**. Argument model specifies the model *type*, using the characters for model types of package **gstat**. Argument thetas specifies the preliminary semivariogram parameter values. Argument perturbation specifies how much the semivariogram parameters are changed to compute the perturbed correlation matrices (pA) and the partial derivatives of the correlation matrix (dA).

```
gridded(grdHunterValley) <- ~ s1 + s2
candi <- spsample(grdHunterValley, type = "regular",
                  cellsize = c(50, 50), offset = c(0.5, 0.5))
candi <- as.data.frame(candi)
names(candi) <- c("x", "y")
schedule <- scheduleSPSANN(
  initial.acceptance = c(0.8, 0.95),
  initial.temperature = 0.15, temperature.decrease = 0.9,
  chains = 300, chain.length = 10, stopping = 10,
  x.min = 0, y.min = 0, cellsize = 50)
set.seed(314)
```

```
res <- optimUSER(
    points = 50, candi = candi,
    fun = logdet,
    model = "Exp", thetas = thetas, perturbation = 0.01,
    schedule = schedule, track = TRUE)
```

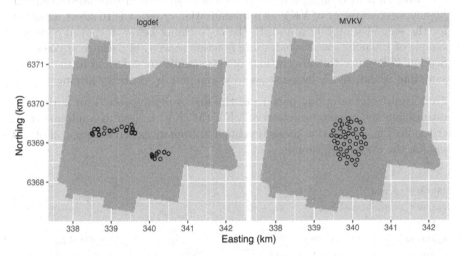

FIGURE 24.6: Optimised sampling pattern of 100 points for semivariogram estimation, using the log of the determinant of the inverse Fisher information matrix of the semivariogram parameters (logdet) and the mean estimation variance of the kriging variance (MVKV) as a minimisation criterion.

Figure 24.6 shows the optimised sampling pattern of 50 points. The logdet of the optimised sample equals 3.548, which is 43% of the value of the simple random sample used above to illustrate the computations. The optimised sample consists of two clusters. There are quite a few point-pairs with nearly coinciding points.

24.3.2 Uncertainty about the kriging variance

Lark (2002) proposed as a minimisation criterion the estimation variance of the kriging variance (VKV) due to uncertainty in the ML estimates of the semivariogram parameters. This variance is approximated by a first order Taylor series, requiring the partial derivatives of the kriging variance with respect to the semivariogram parameters:

$$VKV(\mathbf{s}_0) = \sum_{i=1}^{p} \sum_{j=1}^{p} \text{Cov}(\theta_i, \theta_j) \frac{\partial V_{\text{OK}}(\mathbf{s}_0)}{\partial \theta_i} \frac{\partial V_{\text{OK}}(\mathbf{s}_0)}{\partial \theta_j} , \qquad (24.3)$$

with p the number of semivariogram parameters, $\mathrm{Cov}(\theta_i, \theta_j)$ the covariances of the semivariogram parameters θ_i and θ_j (elements of the inverse of the Fisher information matrix $\mathbf{I}^{-1}(\boldsymbol{\theta})$, Equation (24.2)), and $\frac{\partial V_{\mathrm{OK}}(\mathbf{s}_0)}{\partial \theta_i}$ the partial derivative of the kriging variance to the ith semivariogram parameter at prediction location $\mathbf{s}_0$.

The first step in designing a sample for semivariogram estimation using a population parameter of VKV as a minimisation criterion is to select a sample for the second sampling round. In the code chunk below, a spatial coverage sample of 100 points is selected, using function `stratify` of package **spcosa**, see Section 17.2. Once the observations of this sample are collected in the second sampling round, these data are used for mapping by ordinary kriging.

To optimise the sampling pattern of the first sampling round for variogram estimation, the population mean of VKV (MVKV) is used as a minimisation criterion. This population mean is estimated from a centred square grid of 200 points, the evaluation sample.

```
library(spcosa)
gridded(grdHunterValley) <- ~ s1 + s2
set.seed(314)
mystrata <- stratify(grdHunterValley, nStrata = 100, equalArea = FALSE, nTry = 10)
mysample_SC <- as(spsample(mystrata), "SpatialPoints")
mysample_eval <- spsample(
  x = grdHunterValley, n = 200, type = "regular", offset = c(0.5, 0.5))
```

The following code chunks show how VKV at the evaluation point is computed. First, the correlation matrix of the spatial coverage sample (A) is computed as well as the correlation matrix of the spatial coverage sample and the evaluation points (A0). Correlation matrix A is extended with a column and a row with ones, see Equation (21.5).

```
D <- spDists(mysample_SC)
vgmodel <- vgm(model = "Exp", psill = thetas[1], range = thetas[2],
  nugget = 1 - thetas[1])
A <- variogramLine(vgmodel, dist_vector = D, covariance = TRUE)
nobs <- length(mysample_SC)
B <- matrix(data = 1, nrow = nobs + 1, ncol = nobs + 1)
B[1:nobs, 1:nobs] <- A
B[nobs + 1, nobs + 1] <- 0
D0 <- spDists(x = mysample_eval, y = mysample_SC)
A0 <- variogramLine(vgmodel, dist_vector = D0, covariance = TRUE)
b <- cbind(A0, 1)
```

Next, the semivariogram parameters are perturbed one-by-one, and the perturbed correlation matrices pA and pA0 are computed.

```
pA  <- pA0 <- list()
for (i in seq_len(length(thetas))) {
  thetas_pert <- thetas
  thetas_pert[i] <- (1 + perturbation) * thetas[i]
  vgmodel_pert <- vgm(model = "Exp", psill = thetas_pert[1],
    range = thetas_pert[2], nugget = 1 - thetas_pert[1])
  pA[[i]] <- variogramLine(vgmodel_pert, dist_vector = D, covariance = TRUE)
  pA0[[i]] <- variogramLine(vgmodel_pert, dist_vector = D0, covariance = TRUE)
}
pB <- pb <- list()
for (i in seq_len(length(thetas))) {
  pB[[i]] <- B
  pB[[i]][1:nobs, 1:nobs] <- pA[[i]]
  pb[[i]] <- cbind(pA0[[i]], 1)
}
```

Next, the kriging variance and the perturbed kriging variances are computed, and the partial derivatives of the kriging variance with respect to the semivariogram parameters are approximated. See Equations (21.7) and (21.8) for how the kriging weights l and the kriging variance var are computed.

```
var <- numeric(length = length(mysample_eval))
pvar <- matrix(nrow = length(mysample_eval), ncol = length(thetas))
for (i in seq_len(length(mysample_eval))) {
  #compute kriging weights and Lagrange multiplier
  l <- solve(B, b[i,])
  var[i] <- 1 - l[1:nobs] %*% A0[i, ] - l[nobs + 1]
  for (j in seq_len(length(thetas))) {
    pl <- solve(pB[[j]], pb[[j]][i, ])
    pvar[i, j] <- 1 - pl[1:nobs] %*% pA0[[j]][i, ] - pl[nobs + 1]
  }
}
dvar <- list()
for (i in seq_len(length(thetas))) {
  dvar[[i]] <- (pvar[, i] - var) / (thetas[i] * perturbation)
}
```

Finally, the partial derivatives of the kriging variance are used to approximate VKV at the 200 evaluation points (Equation (24.3)). For this, the variances and covariances of the estimated semivariogram parameters are needed, estimated by the inverse of the Fisher information matrix. The Fisher information matrix computed in Subsection 24.3.1 for the simple random sample of 50 points is also used here.

Note that the variance-covariance matrix of estimated semivariogram parameters is computed from the sample for semivariogram estimation only. The spatial coverage sample of the second sampling round is not used for estimating the semivariogram, but for prediction only. Section 24.4 is about designing one sample, instead of two samples, that is used both for estimation of the model parameters and for prediction.

```
invI <- solve(I)
VKV <- numeric(length = length(var))
for (i in seq_len(length(thetas))) {
  for (j in seq_len(length(thetas))) {
    VKVij <- invI[i, j] * dvar[[i]] * dvar[[j]]
    VKV <- VKV + VKVij
  }
}
MVKV0 <- mean(VKV)
```

For the simple random sample, the square root of MVKV equals 0.223. The mean kriging variance (MKV) at these points equals 0.787, so the uncertainty about the kriging variance is substantial. Hereafter, we will see how much MVKV can be reduced by optimising the sampling pattern with spatial simulated annealing.

As for logdet, the sample with minimum value for MVKV can be searched for using **spsann** function optimUSER. The objective function MVKV is defined in package **sswr**. Argument points specifies the size of the sample for semivariogram estimation. Argument psample is to specify the sample used for prediction at the evaluation points (after the second round of sampling). Argument esample is to specify the sample with evaluation points for estimating MVKV. The optimisation requires substantial computing time. With 200 evaluation points and the annealing schedule specified below the computing time was 46.25 minutes (processor AMD Ryzen 5, 16 GB RAM).

```
schedule <- scheduleSPSANN(
  initial.acceptance = c(0.8, 0.95),
  initial.temperature = 0.002, temperature.decrease = 0.8,
  chains = 300, chain.length = 2, stopping = 10,
  x.min = 0, y.min = 0, cellsize = 50)
set.seed(314)
res <- optimUSER(
  points = 50, candi = candi,
  fun = MVKV,
```

```
psample = mysample_SC, esample = mysample_eval,
model = "Exp", thetas = thetas, perturbation = 0.01,
schedule = schedule, track = TRUE)
```

Figure 24.6 shows the optimised sample. The minimised value of MVKV is 29% of the value of the simple random sample used to illustrate the computations. The optimised sample points are clustered in an ellipse.

Both minimisation criteria, logdet and MVKV, are a function of the semivariogram parameters $\boldsymbol{\theta}$, showing that the problem is circular. Using a preliminary estimate of the semivariogram parameters, $\hat{\boldsymbol{\theta}}$, leads to a locally optimal design at $\hat{\boldsymbol{\theta}}$. For this reason, Bogaert and Russo (1999) and Zhu and Stein (2005) proposed a Bayesian approach, in which a multivariate prior distribution for the semivariogram parameters is postulated. The expected value over this distribution of the criterion is minimised. Lark (2002) computed the average of VKV over a number of semivariograms.

Both methods for sample optimisation rely, amongst others, on the assumption that the mean and the variance are constant throughout the area. Under this assumption, it is no problem that the sampling units are spatially clustered. So, we assume that the semivariogram estimated from the data collected in a small portion of the study area is representative for the whole study area. If we do not feel comfortable with this assumption, spreading the sampling units throughout the study area by the sampling methods described in the next two sections can be a good option.

Exercises

3. Write an **R** script to design a model-based sample of 50 points for Hunter Valley, to estimate the semivariogram for a study variable. Use logdet as a minimisation criterion. Use as a prior estimate of the semivariogram an exponential model with a distance parameter of 200 m and a ratio of spatial dependence of 0.5. Compare the sample with the optimised sample in Figure 24.6, which was obtained with the same value for the distance parameter and a spatial dependence ratio of 0.8.

4. Repeat this for MVKV as a minimisation criterion. Use a spatial coverage sample of 100 points for prediction and a square grid of 200 points for evaluation.

24.4 Optimisation of sampling pattern for semivariogram estimation and mapping

In practice, a reconnaissance survey for semivariogram estimation often is not feasible. A single sample must be designed that is suitable both for estimating the semivariogram parameters and mapping, i.e., prediction with the estimated semivariogram parameters at the nodes of a fine discretisation grid. Another reason is that in a reconnaissance survey we can seldom afford a sample size large enough to obtain reliable estimates of the semivariogram parameters. Papritz et al. (2011) found that for a sample size of 192 points the estimated variance components with balanced and unbalanced nested designs were highly uncertain. For this reason, it is attractive to use also the sampling points designed for spatial prediction (mapping) for estimating the semivariogram. Designing two samples, one for estimation of the semivariogram and one for spatial prediction, is suboptimal. Designing one sample that can be used both for estimation of the semivariogram parameters and for prediction potentially is more efficient.

Finally, with nested sampling and IPP sampling, we aim at estimating the semivariogram of the residuals of a constant mean (see Equation (24.1)). In other words, with these designs we aim at estimating the parameters of a semivariogram model used in ordinary kriging. In situations where we have covariates that can partly explain the spatial variation of the study variable, kriging with an external drift is more appropriate. In these situations, the reconnaissance survey should be tailored to estimating both the regression coefficients associated with the covariates and the parameters of the residual semivariogram.

Model-based methods for designing a single sample for estimation of the model parameters and for prediction with the estimated model parameters are proposed, amongst others, by Zimmerman (2006), Zhu and Stein (2006), Zhu and Zhang (2006), and Marchant and Lark (2007). The methods use a different minimisation criterion. Zimmerman (2006) proposed to minimise the kriging variance (at the centre of a square grid cell) that is augmented by an amount that accounts for the additional uncertainty in the kriging predictions due to uncertainty in the estimated semivariogram parameters, hereafter referred to as the augmented kriging variance (AKV):

$$AKV(\mathbf{s}_0) = V_{\mathrm{OK}}(\mathbf{s}_0) + \mathrm{E}[\tau^2(\mathbf{s}_0)] \,, \qquad (24.4)$$

with $V_{\mathrm{OK}}(\mathbf{s}_0)$ the ordinary kriging variance, see Equation (21.8), and $\mathrm{E}[\tau^2(\mathbf{s}_0)]$ the expectation of the additional variance component due to uncertainty about the semivariogram parameters estimated by ML. The additional variance component is approximated by a first order Taylor series:

$$E[\tau^2(\mathbf{s}_0)] = \sum_{i=1}^{p} \sum_{j=1}^{p} \mathrm{Cov}(\theta_i, \theta_j) \frac{\partial \boldsymbol{\lambda}^{\mathrm{T}}}{\partial \theta_i} \mathbf{A} \frac{\partial \boldsymbol{\lambda}}{\partial \theta_j} , \tag{24.5}$$

with $\frac{\partial \boldsymbol{\lambda}}{\partial \theta_j}$ the vector of partial derivatives of the kriging weights with respect to the jth semivariogram parameter. Comparing Equations (24.5) and (24.3) shows that the two variances differ. VKV quantifies our uncertainty about the estimated kriging variance, whereas $E[\tau^2]$ quantifies our uncertainty about the kriging prediction due to uncertainty about the semivariogram parameters. I use the mean of the AKV over the nodes of a prediction grid (evaluation grid) as a minimisation criterion (MAKV). The same criterion can also be used in situations where we have maps of covariates that we want to use in prediction. In that case, the aim is to design a single sample that is used both for estimation of the *residual* semivariogram and for prediction by kriging with an external drift. The ordinary kriging variance $V_{\mathrm{OK}}(\mathbf{s}_0)$ in Equation (24.4) is then replaced by the prediction error variance with kriging with an external drift $V_{\mathrm{KED}}(\mathbf{s}_0)$, see Equation (21.20).

Zhu and Stein (2006) proposed as a minimisation criterion a linear combination of AKV (Equation (24.4)) and VKV (Equation (24.3)), referred to as the estimation adjusted criterion (EAC):

$$EAC(\mathbf{s}_0) = AKV(\mathbf{s}_0) + \frac{1}{2V_{\mathrm{OK}}(\mathbf{s}_0)} VKV(\mathbf{s}_0) . \tag{24.6}$$

Again, the mean of the EAC values (MEAC) over the nodes of a prediction grid (evaluation) is used as a minimisation criterion.

Computing time for optimisation of the coordinates of a large sample, say, > 50 points, can become prohibitively long. To reduce computing time, Zhu and Stein (2006) proposed a two-step approach. In the first step, for a fixed proportion $p \in (0, 1)$ the locations of $(1 - p)\,n$ points are optimised for prediction with given parameters, for instance by minimising MKV. This 'prediction sample' is supplemented with $p\,n$ points, so that the two combined samples of size n minimise logdet or MVKV. This is repeated for different values of p. In the second step, MEAC is computed for the combined samples of size n, and the proportion and the associated sample with minimum MEAC are selected.

A simplification of this two-step approach is to select in the first step a square grid or a spatial coverage sample (Section 17.2), and to supplement this sample by a fixed number of points whose coordinates are optimised by spatial simulated annealing (SSA), using either MAKV or MEAC computed from both samples (grid sample or spatial coverage sample plus supplemental sample) as a minimisation criterion. In SSA the grid or spatial coverage sample is fixed, i.e., the locations are not further optimised. Lark and Marchant (2018)

recommended as a rule of thumb to add about 10% of the fixed sample as
short distance points.

The following code chunks show how the AKV and EAC can be computed.
First, a spatial coverage sample of 90 points is selected using function stratify
of package **spcosa**, see Section 17.2. In addition, a simple random sample of
10 points is selected. This sample is the initial supplemental sample, whose
locations are optimised. As before, a square grid of 200 points is used as an
evaluation sample.

```
library(spcosa)
set.seed(314)
mystrata <- stratify(grdHunterValley, nStrata = 90, equalArea = FALSE, nTry = 10)
mysample_SC <- as(spsample(mystrata), "SpatialPoints")
nsup <- 10
units <- sample(nrow(grdHunterValley), nsup)
mysample_sup0 <- as(grdHunterValley[units, ], "SpatialPoints")
mysample_eval <- spsample(
  x = grdHunterValley, n = 200, type = "regular", offset = c(0.5, 0.5))
```

The next step is to compute the inverse of the Fisher information matrix, given
a preliminary semivariogram model, which is used as the variance-covariance
matrix of the estimated semivariogram parameters. Contrary to Section 24.3
now *all* sampling locations are used to compute this matrix. The locations of
the spatial coverage sample and the supplemental sample are merged into one
SpatialPoints object.

```
mysample <- rbind(mysample_sup0, mysample_SC)
```

To learn how the Fisher information matrix is computed, refer to the code
chunks in Section 24.3. The inverse of this matrix can be computed with
function solve.

In the next code chunk, for each evaluation point the kriging weights (L), the
kriging variance (var), the perturbed kriging weights (pL), and the perturbed
kriging variances (pvar) are computed. In the final lines, the partial derivatives
of the kriging weights (dL) and the kriging variances (dvar) with respect to
the semivariogram parameters are computed. The partial derivatives of the
kriging variances with respect to the semivariogram parameters are needed for
computing VKV, see Equation (24.3), which in turn is needed for computing
criterion EAC, see Equation (24.6).

```
L <- matrix(nrow = length(mysample_eval), ncol = nobs)
pL <- array(
  dim = c(length(mysample_eval), length(mysample), length(thetas)))
```

```
var <- numeric(length = length(mysample_eval))
pvar <- matrix(nrow = length(mysample_eval), ncol = length(thetas))
for (i in seq_len(length(mysample_eval))) {
  b <- c(A0[i, ], 1)
  l <- solve(B, b)
  L[i, ] <- l[1:nobs]
  var[i] <- 1 - l[1:nobs] %*% A0[i, ] - l[-(1:nobs)]
  for (j in seq_len(length(thetas))) {
    pl <- solve(pB[[j]], pb[[j]][i, ])
    pL[i, , j] <- pl[1:nobs]
    pvar[i, j] <- 1 - pl[1:nobs] %*% pA0[[j]][i, ] - pl[-(1:nobs)]
  }
}
dL <- dvar <- list()
for (i in seq_len(length(thetas))) {
  dL[[i]] <- (pL[, , i] - L) / (thetas[i] * perturbation)
  dvar[[i]] <- (pvar[, i] - var) / (thetas[i] * perturbation)
}
```

In the next code chunk, the expected variance due to uncertainty about the semivariogram parameters (Equation (24.5)) is computed.

```
tausq <- numeric(length = length(mysample_eval))
tausqk <- 0
for (k in seq_len(length(mysample_eval))) {
  for (i in seq_len(length(dL))) {
    for (j in seq_len(length(dL))) {
      tausqijk <- invI[i, j] * t(dL[[i]][k, ]) %*% A %*% dL[[j]][k, ]
      tausqk <- tausqk + tausqijk
    }
  }
  tausq[k] <- tausqk
  tausqk <- 0
}
```

The AKVs are computed by adding the kriging variances and the extra variances due to semivariogram uncertainty (Equation (24.4)). The VKV values and the EAC values are computed. Both the AKV and the EAC differ among the evaluation points. As a summary, the mean of the two variables is computed.

```
augmentedvar <- var + tausq
MAKV0 <- mean(augmentedvar)
VKV <- numeric(length = length(var))
```

```
for (i in seq_len(length(dvar))) {
  for (j in seq_len(length(dvar))) {
    VKVij <- invI[i, j] * dvar[[i]] * dvar[[j]]
    VKV <- VKV + VKVij
  }
}
EAC <- augmentedvar + (VKV / (2 * var))
MEAC0 <- mean(EAC)
```

For the spatial coverage sample of 90 points supplemented by a simple random sample of 10 points, MAKV equals 0.849 and MEAC equals 0.890.

The sample can be optimised with **spsann** function `optimUSER`. Argument `points` is a list containing a data frame, or matrix, with the coordinates of the fixed points (assigned to subargument `fixed`) and an integer of the number of supplemental points of which the locations are optimised (assigned to subargument `free`). As already stressed above, an important difference with Section 24.3 is that the free and the fixed sample are merged and used together both for estimation of the semivariogram and for prediction. The objective functions MAKV and MEAC are defined in package **sswr**. Computing time for minimisation of MAKV was 28.16 minutes and of MEAC 28.88 minutes.

```
candi <- spsample(grdHunterValley, type = "regular",
                  cellsize = c(50, 50), offset = c(0.5, 0.5))
candi <- as.data.frame(candi)
names(candi) <- c("x", "y")
schedule <- scheduleSPSANN(
  initial.acceptance = c(0.8, 0.95),
  initial.temperature = 0.008, temperature.decrease = 0.8,
  chains = 300, chain.length = 10, stopping = 10,
  x.min = 0, y.min = 0, cellsize = 50)
fixed <- coordinates(mysample_SC)
names(fixed) <- c("x", "y")
pnts <- list(fixed = fixed, free = nsup)
set.seed(314)
res <- optimUSER(
  points = pnts, candi = candi,
  fun = MAKV,
  esample = mysample_eval,
  model = "Exp", thetas = thetas, perturbation = 0.01,
  schedule = schedule, track = TRUE)
```

Figure 24.7 shows for Hunter Valley a spatial coverage sample of 90 points, supplemented by 10 points optimised by SSA, using MAKV and MEAC as a minimisation criterion.

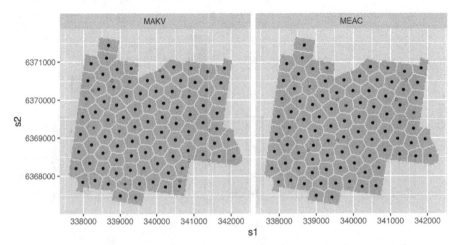

FIGURE 24.7: Optimised sampling pattern of 10 points supplemented to spatial coverage sample of 90 points, for semivariogram estimation and prediction, using the mean augmented kriging variance (MAKV) and the mean estimation adjusted criterion (MEAC) as a minimisation criterion. The prior semivariogram used in optimising the sampling pattern of the supplemental sample is an exponential semivariogram with a range of 200 m and a ratio of spatial dependence of 0.5.

The frequency distribution of the shortest distance to the spatial coverage sample is shown in Figure 24.8. With both criteria there are several supplemental points at very short distance of a point of the spatial coverage sample. The remaining points are at large distances of spatial coverage sample points. The average distance between neighbouring spatial coverage sampling points equals 381 m.

MAKV of the optimised sample equals 0.795 which is 94% of MAKV of the initial sample. MEAC of the optimised sample equals 0.808 which is 91% of MEAC of the initial sample. The reduction of these two criteria through the optimisation is much smaller than for logdet and MVKV in Section 24.3. This can be explained by the small number of sampling units that is optimised: only the locations of 10 points are optimised, 90 are fixed. In Section 24.3 all 100 locations were optimised.

Exercises

5. Write an **R** script to select from Hunter Valley a spatial coverage sample of 80 points supplemented by 20 points. Use MEAC as a minimisation criterion, an exponential semivariogram with a distance parameter of 200 m and a ratio of spatial dependence of 0.8. Compare

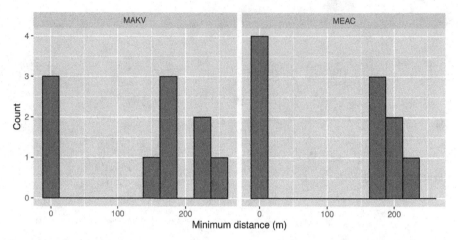

FIGURE 24.8: Frequency distributions of the shortest distance to the spatial coverage sample of the supplemental sample, optimised with the mean augmented kriging variance (MAKV) and the mean estimation adjusted criterion (MEAC).

the minimised MEAC with MEAC reported above, obtained by supplementing a spatial coverage sample of 90 points by 10 points.

24.5   A practical solution

Based on the optimised samples shown above, a straightforward, simple sampling design for estimation of the model parameters and for prediction is a spatial coverage sample supplemented with randomly selected points between the points of the spatial coverage sample at some chosen fixed distances. Figure 24.9 shows an example. A simple random subsample without replacement of size 10 is selected from the 90 points of the spatial coverage sample. These points are used as starting points to select a point at a distance of 20 m in a random direction.

```
h <- 20
m <- 10
set.seed(314)
units <- sample(nrow(mysample_SC), m, replace = FALSE)
mySCsubsample <- mysample_SC[units, ]
dxy <- matrix(nrow = m, ncol = 2)
```

```
angle <- runif(n = m, min = 0, max = 2 * pi)
dxy[, 1] <- h * sin(angle); dxy[, 2] <- h * cos(angle)
mysupsample <- mySCsubsample + dxy
```

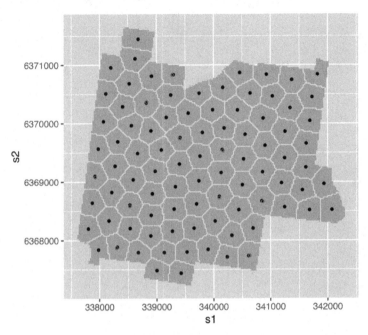

FIGURE 24.9: Spatial coverage sample of 90 points supplemented by 10 points at short distance (20 m) from randomly selected spatial coverage points.

MAKV of this sample equals 0.808, and MEAC equals 0.816. For MAKV, 25% of the maximal reduction is realised by this practical solution; for MEAC, this is 10%.

25

Sampling for validation of maps

In the previous chapters of Part II, various methods are described for selecting sampling units with the aim to map the study variable. Once the map has been made, we would like to know how good it is. It should come as no surprise that the value of the study variable at a randomly selected location as shown on the map differs from the value at that location in reality. This difference is a prediction error. The question is how large this error is on average, and how variable it is. This chapter describes and illustrates with a real-world case study how to select sampling units at which we will confront the predictions with the true values, and how to estimate map quality indices from the prediction errors of these sampling units.

If the map has been made with a statistical model, then the predictors are typically model-unbiased and the variance of the prediction errors can be computed from the model. Think, for instance, of kriging which also yields a map of the kriging variance. In Chapters 22 and 23 I showed how this kriging variance can be used to optimise the grid spacing (sample size) and the sampling pattern for mapping, respectively. So, if we have a map of these variances, why do we still need to collect new data for estimating the map quality?

The problem is that the kriging variances rely on the validity of the assumptions made in modelling the spatial variation of the study variable. Do we assume a constant mean, or a mean that is a linear combination of some covariates? In the latter case, which covariates are assumed to be related to the study variable? Or should we model the mean with a non-linear function as in a random forest model? How certain are we about the semivariogram model type (spherical, exponential, etc.), and how good are our estimates of the semivariogram parameters? If one or more of the modelling assumptions are violated, the variances of the prediction errors as computed with the model may become biased. For this reason, the quality of the map is preferably determined through independent validation, i.e., by comparing predictions with observations not used in mapping, followed by design-based estimation of the map quality indices. This process is often referred to as validation, perhaps better statistical validation, a subset of the more comprehensive term map quality evaluation, which includes the concept of fitness-for-use.

Statistical validation of maps is often done through data splitting or cross-validation. In data splitting the data are split into two subsets, one for calibrating the model and mapping and one for validation. In cross-validation the data set is split into a number of disjoint subsets of equal size. Each subset is used one-by-one for calibration and prediction. The remaining subsets are used for validation. Leave-one-out cross-validation (LOOCV) is a special case of this, in which each sampling unit is left out one-by-one, and all other units are used for calibration and prediction of the study variable of the unit that is left out. The problem with data splitting and cross-validation is that the data used for mapping typically are from non-probability samples. This makes design-based estimation of the map quality indices unfeasible (Brus et al., 2011). Designing a sampling scheme starts with a comprehensive description of the aim of the sampling project (de Gruijter et al., 2006). Mapping and validation are different aims which ask for different sampling approaches. For validation probability sampling is the best option because then a statistical model of the spatial variation of the prediction errors is not needed. Map quality indices, defined as population parameters, can be estimated model-free, by design-based inference (see also Section 1.2).

In statistical learning using large data sets a common approach is to randomly partition the data set in three subsets: a training subset, a validation subset, and a test subset (Hastie et al. (2009), chapter 7). The training subset is used for fitting the models, the validation subset is used to estimate prediction error for model selection and hyperparameter tuning, while the test subset is used for assessing the accuracy of the final model. The term validation as used in this chapter is therefore the equivalent of testing as used in statistical learning.

All probability sampling designs described in Part I are in principle appropriate for validation. Stehman (1999) evaluated five basic probability sampling designs and concluded that in general stratified random sampling is a good choice. For validation of categorical maps, natural strata are the map units, i.e., the groups of polygons or grid cells assigned to each class. Systematic random sampling is less suitable, as no unbiased estimator of the sampling variance of the estimator of a population mean exists for this design (see Chapter 5). For validation of maps of extensive areas, think of whole continents, travel time between sampling locations can become substantial. In this case, sampling designs that lead to spatial clustering of validation locations can become efficient, for instance cluster random sampling (Chapter 6) or two-stage cluster random sampling (Chapter 7).

25.1   Map quality indices

In validation we want to assess the accuracy of the map as a whole. We are not interested in the accuracy at a sample of population units only. For instance, we would like to know the population mean of the prediction error, i.e., the average of the errors over all population units, and not merely the average prediction error at a sample of units. Map quality indices are therefore defined as population parameters. We cannot afford to determine the prediction error for each unit of the mapping area to calculate the population means. If we could do that, there would be no need for a mapping model. Therefore, we have to take a sample of units at which the predictions of the study variable are confronted with the observations. This sample is then used to *estimate* population parameters of the prediction error and our uncertainty about these population parameters, as quantified, for instance, by their standard errors or confidence interval.

For quantitative maps, i.e., maps depicting a quantitative study variable, popular map quality indices are (i) the population mean error (ME); (ii) the population mean absolute error (MAE); and (iii) the population mean squared error (MSE), defined as

$$ME = \frac{1}{N} \sum_{k=1}^{N} (\hat{z}_k - z_k) \tag{25.1}$$

$$MAE = \frac{1}{N} \sum_{k=1}^{N} (|\hat{z}_k - z_k|) \tag{25.2}$$

$$MSE = \frac{1}{N} \sum_{k=1}^{N} (\hat{z}_k - z_k)^2 \, , \tag{25.3}$$

with N the total number of units (e.g., raster cells) in the population, $\hat{z}_k$ the predicted value for unit k, z_k the true value of that unit, and $|\cdot|$ the absolute value operator. For infinite populations, the sum must be replaced by an integral over all locations in the mapped area and divided by the size of the area. The ME quantifies the systematic error and ideally equals 0. It can be positive (in case of overprediction) and negative (in case of underprediction). Positive and negative errors cancel out and, as a consequence, the ME does not quantify the magnitude of the prediction errors. The MAE and MSE do quantify the magnitude of the errors, they are non-negative. Often, the square root of MSE is taken, denoted by RMSE, which is in the same units as the study variable and is therefore more intelligible. The RMSE is strongly affected by outliers, i.e., large prediction errors, due to the squaring of the errors, and for this reason I recommend estimating both MAE and RMSE.

Two other important map quality indices are the population coefficient of determination (R^2) and the Nash-Sutcliffe model efficiency coefficient (MEC). R^2 is defined as the square of the Pearson correlation coefficient r of the study variable and the predictions of the study variable, given by

$$r = \frac{\sum_{k=1}^{N}(z_k - \bar{z})(\hat{z}_k - \bar{\hat{z}})}{\sqrt{\sum_{k=1}^{N}(z_k - \bar{z})^2}\sqrt{(\hat{z}_k - \bar{\hat{z}})^2}} = \frac{S^2(z, \hat{z})}{S(z)S(\hat{z})} \, , \qquad (25.4)$$

with $\bar{z}$ the population mean of the study variable, $\bar{\hat{z}}$ the population mean of the predictions, $S^2(z, \hat{z})$ the population covariance of the study variable and the predictions of z, $S(z)$ the population standard deviation of the study variable, and $S(\hat{z})$ the population standard deviation of the predictions. Note that R^2 is unaffected by bias and therefore should not be used in isolation, but should always be accompanied by ME.

MEC is defined as (Janssen and Heuberger, 1995)

$$MEC = 1 - \frac{\sum_{k=1}^{N}(\hat{z}_k - z_k)^2}{\sum_{k=1}^{N}(z_k - \bar{z})^2} = 1 - \frac{MSE}{S^2(z)} \, , \qquad (25.5)$$

with $S^2(z)$ the population variance of the study variable. MEC quantifies the improvement made by the model over using the mean of the observations as a predictor. An MEC value of 1 indicates a perfect match between the observed and the predicted values of the study variable, whereas a value of 0 indicates that the mean of the observations is as good a predictor as the model. A negative value occurs when the mean of the observations is a better predictor than the model, i.e., when the residual variance is larger than the variance of the measurements.

For categorical maps, a commonly used map quality index is the overall purity, which is defined as the proportion of units that is correctly classified (mapped):

$$P = \frac{1}{N}\sum_{k=1}^{N} y_k \, , \qquad (25.6)$$

with y_k an indicator for unit k, having value 1 if the predicted class equals the true class, and 0 otherwise:

$$y_k = \begin{cases} 1 & \text{if } \hat{c}_k = c_k \\ 0 & \text{otherwise} \, , \end{cases} \qquad (25.7)$$

with c_k and $\hat{c}_k$ the true and the predicted class of unit k, respectively. For infinite populations the purity is the fraction of the area that is correctly classified (mapped).

The population ME, MSE, R^2, MEC, and purity can also be defined for subpopulations. For categorical maps, natural subpopulations are the classes depicted in the map, the map units. In that case, for infinite populations the purity of map unit u is defined as the fraction of the area of map unit u that is correctly mapped as u.

A different subpopulation is the part of the population that is *in reality* class u (but possibly not mapped as u). We are interested in the fraction of the area covered by this subpopulation that is correctly mapped as u. This is referred to as the class representation of class u, for which I use hereafter the symbol R_u.

25.1.1 Estimation of map quality indices

The map quality indices are defined as population or subpopulation means. To estimate these (sub)population means, a design-based sampling approach is the most appropriate. Sampling units are selected by probability sampling, and the map quality indices are estimated by design-based inference. For instance, the ME of a finite population can be estimated by the π estimator (see Equation (2.4)):

$$\widehat{ME} = \frac{1}{N} \sum_{k \in \mathcal{S}} \frac{1}{\pi_k} e_k \, , \qquad (25.8)$$

with $e_k = \hat{z}_k - z_k$ the prediction error for unit k. By taking the absolute value of the prediction errors e_k in Equation (25.8) or by squaring them, the π estimators for the MAE and MSE are obtained, respectively. By replacing e_k by the indicator y_k of Equation (25.7), the π estimator for the overall purity is obtained.

With simple random sampling, the square of the sample correlation coefficient, i.e., the correlation of the study variable and the predictions of the study variable in the sample, is an unbiased estimator of R^2. See Särndal et al. (1992) (p. $486 - 491$) for how to estimate R^2 for other sampling designs.

The population MEC can be estimated by

$$\widehat{MEC} = 1 - \frac{\widehat{MSE}}{\widehat{S^2}(z)} \, . \qquad (25.9)$$

For simple random sampling the sample variance, i.e., the variance of the observations of z in the sample, is an unbiased estimator of the population variance $S^2(z)$. For other sampling designs, this population variance can be estimated by Equation (4.9).

Estimation of the class representations is slightly more difficult, because the sizes of the classes (number of raster cells or area where in reality class u is present) are unknown and must therefore also be estimated. This leads to the ratio estimator:

$$\hat{R}_u = \frac{\sum_{k \in \mathcal{S}} \frac{y_k}{\pi_k}}{\sum_{k \in \mathcal{S}} \frac{x_k}{\pi_k}}, \qquad (25.10)$$

where y_k denotes an indicator defined as

$$y_k = \begin{cases} 1 & \text{if } \hat{c}_k = c_k = u \\ 0 & \text{otherwise}, \end{cases} \qquad (25.11)$$

and x_k denotes an indicator defined as

$$x_k = \begin{cases} 1 & \text{if } c_k = u \\ 0 & \text{otherwise}. \end{cases} \qquad (25.12)$$

This estimator is also recommended for estimating other map quality indices from a sample with a sample size that is not fixed but varies among samples selected with the sampling design. This is the case, for instance, when estimating the mean (absolute or squared) error or the purity of a given map unit from a simple random sample. The number of selected sampling units within the map unit is uncontrolled and varies among the simple random samples. In this case, we can estimate the mean error or the purity of a map unit u by dividing the estimated population total by either the *known* size (number of raster cells, area) of map unit u or by the *estimated* size. Interestingly, in general using the estimated size in the denominator, instead of the known size, yields a more precise estimator (Särndal et al., 1992). See also Section 14.1.

25.2   Real-world case study

As an illustration, two soil maps of three northern counties of Xuancheng (China), both depicting soil organic matter (SOM) concentration (g kg^{-1}) in the topsoil, are evaluated. In Section 13.2 the data of three samples, including the stratified random sample, were merged to estimate the parameters of a spatial model for the natural log of the SOM concentration. Here, only the data of the two non-random samples, the grid sample and the iPSM sample, are used to map the SOM concentration. The stratified simple random sample is used for validation.

Two methods are used in mapping, kriging with an external drift (KED) and random forest prediction (RF). For mapping with RF, seven covariates are used: planar curvature, profile curvature, slope, temperature, precipitation, topographic wetness index, and elevation. For mapping with KED only the two most important covariates in the RF model are used: precipitation and elevation.

The two maps that are to be validated are shown in Figure 25.1. Note that non-soil areas (built-up, water, roads) are not predicted. The maps are quite similar. The most striking difference between the maps is the smaller range of the RF predictions: they range from 9.8 to 61.5, whereas the KED predictions range from 5.3 to 90.5.

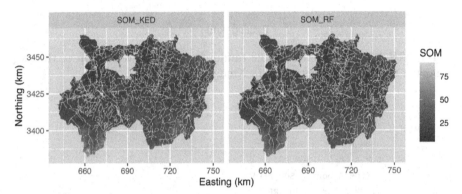

FIGURE 25.1: Map of the SOM concentration (g kg^{-1}) in the topsoil of Xuancheng, obtained by kriging with an external drift (KED) and random forest (RF).

The two maps are evaluated by statistical validation with a stratified simple random sample of 62 units (points). The strata are the eight units of a geological map (Figure 25.2).

25.2.1 Estimation of the population mean error and mean squared error

To estimate the population MSE of the two maps, first the squared prediction errors are computed. The name of the measured study variable at the validation sample in data.frame sample_test is SOM_A_hori. Four new variables are added to sample_test using function mutate, by computing the prediction errors for KED and RF and squaring these errors.

```
sample_test <- read.csv(file = "results/STSI_Xuancheng_SOMpred.csv")
sample_test <- sample_test %>%
```

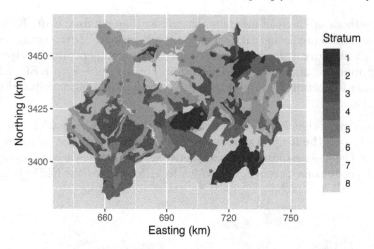

FIGURE 25.2: Stratified simple random sample for validation of the two maps of the SOM concentration in Xuancheng.

```
mutate(
    eKED = SOM_A_hori - SOM_KED,
    eRF = SOM_A_hori - SOM_RF,
    e2KED = (SOM_A_hori - SOM_KED)^2,
    e2RF = (SOM_A_hori - SOM_RF)^2)
```

These four new variables now are our study variables of which we would like to estimate the population means. The population means can be estimated as explained in Chapter 4. First, the stratum sizes and stratum weights are computed, i.e., the number and relative number of raster cells per stratum (Figure 25.2).

```
rmap <- rast(x = system.file("extdata/Geo_Xuancheng.tif", package = "sswr"))
strata_Xuancheng <- as.data.frame(rmap, xy = TRUE, na.rm = TRUE) %>%
  rename(stratum = Geo_Xuancheng) %>%
  filter(stratum != 99) %>%
  group_by(stratum) %>%
  summarise(N_h = n()) %>%
  mutate(w_h = N_h / sum(N_h))
```

Next, the stratum means of the prediction errors, obtained with KED and RF, are estimated by the sample means, and the population mean of the errors are estimated by the weighted mean of the estimated stratum means.

```
me <- sample_test %>%
    group_by(stratum) %>%
    summarise(
        meKED_h = mean(eKED),
        meRF_h = mean(eRF)) %>%
    left_join(strata_Xuancheng, by = "stratum") %>%
    summarise(
        meKED = sum(w_h * meKED_h),
        meRF = sum(w_h * meRF_h))
```

This is repeated for the squared prediction errors.

```
mse <- sample_test %>%
    group_by(stratum) %>%
    summarise(
        mseKED_h = mean(e2KED),
        mseRF_h = mean(e2RF)) %>%
    left_join(strata_Xuancheng, by = "stratum") %>%
    summarise(
        mseKED = sum(w_h * mseKED_h),
        mseRF = sum(w_h * mseRF_h))
```

The estimated MSE of the KED map equals 89.3 $(g\ kg^{-1})^2$, that of the RF map 93.8 $(g\ kg^{-1})^2$.

Exercises

1. Are you certain that the population MSE of the KED map is smaller than the population MSE of the RF map?

25.2.2 Estimation of the standard error of the estimator of the population mean error and mean squared error

We are uncertain about both population MSEs, as we measured the squared errors at 62 sampling points only. So, we would like to know how uncertain we are. This uncertainty is quantified by the standard error of the estimator of the population MSE. A problem is that in the second stratum we have only one sampling point. So, for this stratum we cannot compute the variance of the squared errors. To compute the variance, we need at least two sampling points.

```
n_strata <- sample_test %>%
    group_by(stratum) %>%
    summarise(n = n())
n_strata
```

```
# A tibble: 8 x 2
  stratum      n
    <int> <int>
1       1     5
2       2     1
3       3     8
4       4    10
5       5     2
6       6    23
7       7     9
8       8     4
```

A solution is to merge stratum 2 with stratum 1, which is a similar geological map unit (we know this from the domain expert). This is referred to as collapsing the strata. An identifier for the collapsed strata is added to n_strata. This table is subsequently used to add the collapsed stratum identifiers to sample_test and strata_Xuancheng.

```
n_strata <- n_strata %>%
    mutate(stratum_clp = c(1, 1:7))
sample_test <- sample_test %>%
    left_join(n_strata, by = "stratum")
strata_Xuancheng <- strata_Xuancheng %>%
    left_join(n_strata, by = "stratum")
```

The collapsed strata can be used to estimate the standard errors of the estimators of the population MSEs. As a first step, the weights and the sample sizes of the collapsed strata are computed.

```
strata_clp_Xuancheng <- strata_Xuancheng %>%
    group_by(stratum_clp) %>%
    summarise(N_hc = sum(N_h)) %>%
    mutate(w_hc = N_hc / sum(N_hc)) %>%
    left_join(
      sample_test %>%
        group_by(stratum_clp) %>%
        summarise(n_hc = n()),
      by = "stratum_clp")
```

TABLE 25.1: Estimated population mean error (ME) and population mean squared error (MSE) of KED and RF map, and their standard errors.

	KED	seKED	RF	seRF
ME	0.83	1.2	0.4	1.29
MSE	89.30	25.5	93.8	25.80

The sampling variance of the estimator of the mean of the (squared) prediction error can be estimated by Equation (4.4). The estimated ME and MSE and their estimated standard errors are shown in Table 25.1.

```
se <- sample_test %>%
    group_by(stratum_clp) %>%
    summarise(
        s2e_KED_hc = var(eKED),
        s2e2_KED_hc = var(e2KED),
        s2e_RF_hc = var(eRF),
        s2e2_RF_hc = var(e2RF)) %>%
    left_join(strata_clp_Xuancheng, by = "stratum_clp") %>%
    summarise(
        se_me_KED = sqrt(sum(w_hc^2 * s2e_KED_hc / n_hc)),
        se_mse_KED = sqrt(sum(w_hc^2 * s2e2_KED_hc / n_hc)),
        se_me_RF = sqrt(sum(w_hc^2 * s2e_RF_hc / n_hc)),
        se_mse_RF = sqrt(sum(w_hc^2 * s2e2_RF_hc / n_hc)))
```

Exercises

2. Do you think there is a systematic error in the KED and the RF predictions?

3. Do you think the difference between the two estimated population MSEs is statistically significant?

25.2.3 Estimation of model efficiency coefficient

To estimate the MEC, we must first estimate the population variance of the study variable from the stratified simple random sample (the denominator in Equation (25.9)). First, the sizes and the sample sizes of the collapsed strata must be added to sample_test. Then the population variance is estimated with function s2 of package **surveyplanning** (Subsection 4.1.2).

```
library(surveyplanning)
s2z <- sample_test %>%
  left_join(strata_clp_Xuancheng, by = "stratum_clp") %>%
  summarise(s2z = s2(SOM_A_hori, w = N_hc / n_hc)) %>%
  flatten_dbl
```

Now the MECs for KED and RF can be estimated.

```
mec <- 1 - mse / s2z
```

The estimated MEC for KED equals 0.016 and for RF -0.034, showing that the two models used in mapping are no better than the estimated mean SOM concentration used as a predictor. This is quite a disappointing result.

25.2.4 Statistical testing of hypothesis about population ME and MSE

The hypothesis that the population ME equals 0 can be tested by a one-sample t-test. The alternative hypothesis is that ME is unequal to 0 (two-sided alternative). The number of degrees of freedom of the t distribution is approximated by the total sample size minus the number of strata (Section 4.2). Note that we have a two-sided alternative hypothesis, so we must compute a two-sided p-value.

```
t_KED <- me$meKED / se$se_me_KED
df <- nrow(sample_test) - length(unique(sample_test$stratum_clp))
p_KED <- 2 * pt(t_KED, df = df, lower.tail = t_KED < 0)
```

The outcomes of the test statistics are 0.690 and 0.309 for KED and RF, respectively, with p-values 0.493 and 0.759. So, we clearly have not enough evidence for systematic errors, neither with KED nor with RF mapping.

Now we test whether the two population MSEs differ significantly. This can be done by a paired t-test. The first step in a paired t-test is to compute pairwise differences of squared prediction errors, and then we can proceed as in a one-sample t-test.

```
m_de2 <- sample_test %>%
  mutate(de2 = e2KED - e2RF) %>%
  group_by(stratum) %>%
  summarise(m_de2_h = mean(de2)) %>%
  left_join(strata_Xuancheng, by = "stratum") %>%
  summarise(m_de2 = sum(w_h * m_de2_h)) %>%
```

```
  flatten_dbl

se_m_de2 <- sample_test %>%
  mutate(de2 = e2KED - e2RF) %>%
  group_by(stratum_clp) %>%
  summarise(s2_de2_hc = var(de2)) %>%
  left_join(strata_clp_Xuancheng, by = "stratum_clp") %>%
  summarise(se_m_de2 = sqrt(sum(w_hc^2 * s2_de2_hc / n_hc))) %>%
  flatten_dbl

t <- m_de2 / se_m_de2
p <- 2 * pt(t, df = df, lower.tail = t < 0)
```

The outcome of the test statistic is -0.438, with a *p*-value of 0.663, so we clearly do not have enough evidence that the population MSEs obtained with the two mapping methods are different.

26

Design-based, model-based, and
model-assisted approach for sampling and
inference

Section 1.2 already mentioned the design-based and the model-based approach
for sampling and statistical inference. In this chapter, the fundamental differences between these two approaches are explained in more detail. Several
misconceptions about the design-based approach for sampling and statistical
inference, based on classical sampling theory, seem to be quite persistent.
These misconceptions are the result of confusion about basic statistical concepts such as independence, expectation, and bias and variance of estimators
or predictors. These concepts have a different meaning in the design-based
and the model-based approach. Besides, a population mean is still often confused with a model-mean, and a population variance with a model-variance,
leading to invalid formulas for the sampling variance of an estimator of the
population mean. The fundamental differences between these two approaches
are illustrated with simulations, so that hopefully a better understanding
of this subject is obtained. Besides, the difference between model-dependent
inference (as used in the model-based approach) and model-assisted inference
is explained. This chapter has been published as part of a journal paper, see
Brus (2021).

26.1 Two sources of randomness

In my classes about spatial sampling, I ask the participants the following
question. Suppose we have measurements of a soil property, for instance soil
organic carbon content, at two locations separated by 20 cm. Do you think
these two measurements are correlated? I ask them to vote for one of three
answers:

1. yes, they are (>80% confident);
2. no, they are not (>80% confident); or
3. I do not know.

Most students vote for answer 1, the other students vote for answer 3, nearly no one votes for answer 2. Then I explain that you cannot say which answer is correct, simply because for correlation we need two series of data, not just two numbers. The question then is how to generate two series of data. We need some random process for this. This random process differs between the design-based and the model-based approach.

In the design-based approach, the random process is the random selection of sampling units, whereas in the model-based approach randomness is introduced via the statistical model of the spatial variation (Table 1.1). So, the design-based approach requires probability sampling, i.e., random sampling, using a random number generator, in such way that all population units have a positive probability of being included in the sample and that these inclusion probabilities are known for at least the selected population units (Särndal et al., 1992). A probability sampling design can be used to generate an infinite number of samples in theory, although in practical applications only one is selected.

The spatial variation model used in the model-based approach contains two terms, one for the mean (deterministic part) and one for the error with a specified probability distribution. For instance, Equation (21.2) in Chapter 21 describes the model used in ordinary kriging. This model can be used to simulate an infinite number of spatial populations. All these populations together are referred to as a superpopulation (Särndal et al. (1992), Lohr (1999)). Depending on the model of spatial variation, the simulated populations may show spatial structure because the mean is a function of covariates, as in kriging with an external drift, and/or because the errors are spatially autocorrelated. A superpopulation is a construct, the populations do not exist in the real world. The populations are similar, but not identical. For instance, the mean differs among the populations. The expectation of the population mean, i.e., the average over all possible simulated populations, equals the superpopulation mean, commonly referred to as the model-mean, parameter μ in Equation (21.2). The variance also differs among the populations. Contrary to the mean, the average of the population variance over all populations generally is not equal to the model-variance, parameter σ^2 in Equation (21.2), but smaller. I will come back to this later. The differences between the simulated spatial populations illustrate our uncertainty about the spatial variation of the study variable in the population that is sampled or will be sampled.

In the design-based approach, only one population is considered, the one sampled, but the statistical inference is based on all samples that can be generated by a probability sampling. The top row of Figure 26.1 shows five simple random samples of size ten. The population is the same in all plots. Proponents of the design-based approach do not like to consider other populations than the one sampled. Their challenge is to characterise this one population from a probability sample.

On the contrary, in the model-based approach only one sample is considered, but the statistical inference is based on all populations that can be generated with the spatial variation model. Proponents of the model-based approach do not like to consider other samples than the one selected. Their challenge is to get the most out of the sample that is selected. The bottom row of Figure 26.1 shows a spatial coverage sample, superimposed on five different populations simulated with an ordinary kriging model, using a spherical semivariogram with a nugget of 0.1, partial sill of 0.6, and a range of 75 m. Note that in the model-based approach there is no need to select a probability sample (see Table 1.1); there are no requirements on how the units are selected.

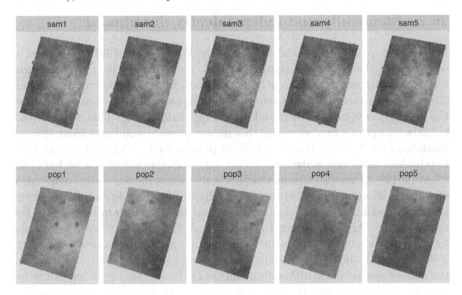

FIGURE 26.1: Random process considered in the design-based (top row) and the model-based approach (bottom row). The design-based approach considers only the sampled population, but all samples that can be generated by the sampling design. The model-based approach considers only the selected sample, but all populations that can be generated by the model.

As stressed by de Gruijter and ter Braak (1990) and Brus and de Gruijter (1997), both approaches have their strengths and weaknesses. Broadly speaking, the design-based approach is the most appropriate if interest is in the population mean (total, proportion) or the population means (totals, proportions) of a restricted number of subpopulations (subareas). The model-based approach is the most appropriate if our aim is to map the study variable. Further, the strength of the design-based approach is the strict validity of the estimates. Validity means that an objective assessment of the uncertainty of the estimator is warranted and that the coverage of confidence intervals is (almost) correct, provided that the sample is large enough to assume an approximately normal distribution of the estimator and design-unbiasedness of the variance estimator

(Särndal et al., 1992). The strength of the model-based approach is efficiency, i.e., more precise estimates of the (sub)population mean given the sample size, provided that a reasonably good model is used. So, if validity is more important than efficiency, the design-based approach is the best choice; in the reverse case, the model-based approach is preferable. For further reading, I recommend Cassel et al. (1977) and Hansen et al. (1983).

26.2   Identically and independently distributed

In a review paper on spatial sampling by Wang et al. (2012), there is a section with the caption 'Sampling of i.i.d. populations'. Here, i.i.d. stands for "identically and independently distributed". In this section of Wang et al. (2012) we can read: "In SRS (simple random sampling) it is assumed that the population is independent and identically distributed". This is one of the old misconceptions revitalised by this review paper. I will make clear that in statistics i.i.d. is not a characteristic of populations, so the concept of i.i.d. populations does not make sense. The same misconception can be found in Plant (2012): "There is considerable literature on sample size estimation, much of which is discussed by Cochran (1977, chapter 4). This literature, however, is valid for samples of independent data but may not retain its validity for spatial data". Also according to Wang et al. (2010), the classical formula for the variance of the estimator of the mean with simple random sampling, $V = \sigma^2/n$, only holds when data are independent. They say: "However in the case of spatial data, although members of the sample are independent by construction, data values that are near to one another in space, are unlikely to be independent because of a fundamental property of attributes in space, which is that they show spatial structure or continuity (spatial autocorrelation)". According to Wang et al. (2010), the variance should be approximated by

$$V(\hat{\bar{z}}) = \frac{\sigma^2 - \overline{\text{Cov}(z_i, z_j)}}{n} , \qquad (26.1)$$

with $V(\hat{\bar{z}})$ the variance of the estimator of the regional mean (mean of spatial population), σ^2 the population variance, n the sample size, and $\overline{\text{Cov}(z_i, z_j)}$ the average autocovariance between all pairs of individuals (i, j) in the population (sampled and unsampled). So, according to this formula, ignoring the mean covariance within the population leads to an overestimation of the variance of the estimator of the mean. In Section 26.4 I will make clear that this formula is incorrect and that the classical formula is still valid, also for populations showing spatial structure or continuity.

Remarkably, in other publications we can read that the classical formula for the variance of the estimator of the population mean with simple random sampling *underestimates* the true variance for populations showing spatial structure, see for instance Griffith (2005) and Plant (2012). The reasoning is that due to the spatial structure, there is less information in the sample data about the population mean. In Section 26.4 I explain that this is also a misconception. Do not get confused by these publications and stick to the classical formulas which you can find in standard textbooks on sampling theory, such as Cochran (1977) and Lohr (1999), as well as in Chapter 3 of this book.

The concept of independence of random variables is illustrated with a simulation. The top row of Figure 26.2 shows five simple random samples of size two. The two points are repeatedly selected from the same population (showing clear spatial structure), so this top row represents the design-based approach. The bottom row shows two points, not selected randomly and independently, but at a fixed distance of 10 m. These two points are placed on different populations generated by the model described above, so the bottom row represents the model-based approach.

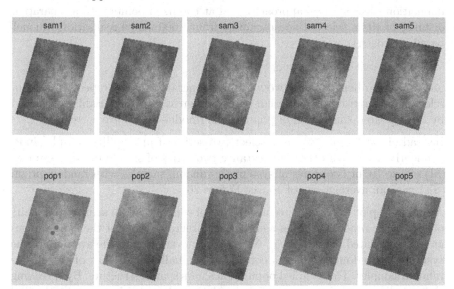

FIGURE 26.2: Illustration of independence in design-based and model-based approach. The top row shows five samples of two points selected randomly and independently from each other from one population (design-based approach). The bottom row shows two points not selected randomly, at a distance of 10 m from each other, from five model realisations (model-based approach).

The values measured at the two points are plotted against each other in a scatter plot, not for just five simple random samples or five populations, but for 1,000 samples and 1,000 populations (Figure 26.3). As we can see there is

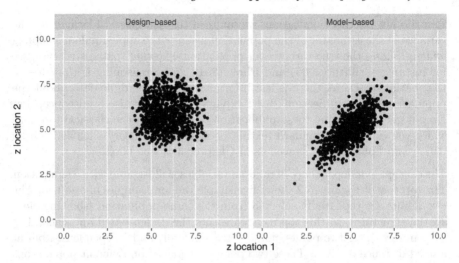

FIGURE 26.3: Scatter plots of the values of a study variable z at two randomly and independently selected points, 1,000 times selected from one population (design-based approach), and at two fixed points with a separation distance of 10 m, selected non-randomly from 1,000 model realisations (model-based approach).

no correlation between the two variables generated by the repeated random selection of the two points (design-based), whereas the two variables generated by the repeated simulation of populations (model-based) are correlated.

Instead of two points, we may select two series of probability samples independently from each other, for instance two series of simple random samples (SI) of size 10, or two series of systematic random samples with random origin (SY) with an average size of 10, see Figure 26.4.

Again, if we plot the sample means of pairs of simple random samples and pairs of systematic random samples against each other, we see that the two averages are not correlated (Figure 26.5). Note that the variation of the averages of the systematic random samples is considerably smaller than that of the simple random samples. The sampled population shows spatial structure. By spreading the sampling units over the spatial population, the precision of the estimated population mean is increased, see Chapter 5.

This sampling experiment shows that independence is not a characteristic of a population, as stated by Wang et al. (2012), but of random variables generated by a random process (in the experiment the values at points or the sample means). As the random process differs between the design-based and the model-based approach, independence has a different meaning in these two approaches. For this reason, it is imperative to be more specific when using

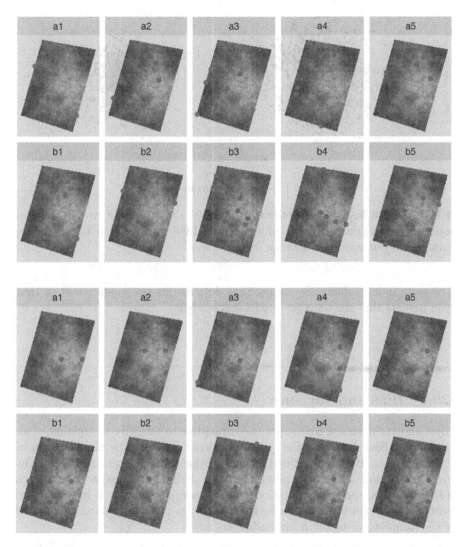

FIGURE 26.4: Two series (a and b) of simple random samples of ten points (top) and two series (a and b) of systematic random samples of, on average, ten points (bottom). The samples of series a and b are selected independently from each other.

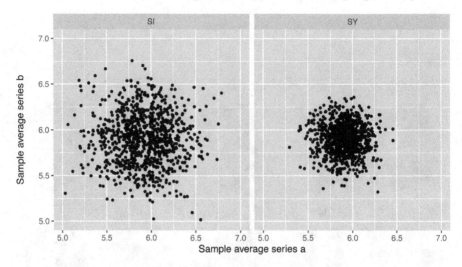

FIGURE 26.5: Scatter plots of averages of 1,000 pairs of simple random samples of ten points (SI) and of averages of 1,000 pairs of systematic random samples of ten points on average (SY).

the term independence, by saying that data are *design-independent* or that you *assume* that the data are *model-independent*.

26.3   Bias and variance

Bias and variance are commonly used statistics to quantify the quality of an estimator. Bias quantifies the systematic error, variance the random error of the estimator. Both are defined as expectations. But are these expectations over realisations of a probability sampling design (samples) or realisations of a statistical model (populations)? Like independence, it is important to distinguish *design-bias* from *model-bias* and *design-variance* (commonly referred to as sampling variance) from *model-variance*.

The concept of model-unbiasedness deserves more attention. Figure 26.6 shows a preferential sample from a population simulated by sequential Gaussian simulation with a constant mean of 10 and an exponential semivariogram without nugget, a sill of 5, and a distance parameter of 20. The points are selected by sampling with draw-by-draw selection probabilities proportional to size (pps sampling, Chapter 8), using the square of the simulated values as a size variable. We may have a similar sample that is collected for delineating soil contamination or detecting hot spots of soil bacteria, etc. Many samples are selected at locations with a large value, few points at locations with a small value. The sample data are used in ordinary kriging (Figure 26.6). The prediction errors are computed by subtracting the kriged map from the simulated population.

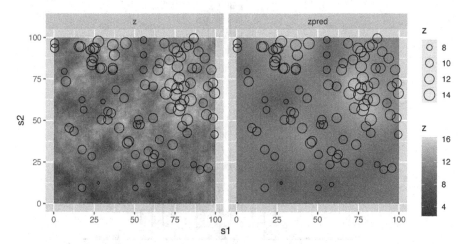

FIGURE 26.6: Preferential sample (size of open dots is proportional to value of study variable) from a simulated field (z) and map of ordinary kriging predictions (zpred).

```
error <- preds$zpred - sim$z
```

Figure 26.7 shows a histogram of the prediction errors. The population mean error equals 0.482, not 0. You may have expected a positive systematic error because of the overrepresentation of locations with large values, but on the other hand, kriging predictions are best linear unbiased predictions (BLUP), so from that point of view, this systematic error might be unexpected. BLUP means that at individual locations the ordinary kriging predictions are unbiased. However, apparently this does not guarantee that the average of the prediction errors, averaged over all population units, equals 0. The reason is that unbiasedness is defined here over all realisations (populations) of the statistical model of spatial variation. So, the U in BLUP stands for model-unbiasedness. For other model realisations, sampled at the same points, we may have much smaller values, leading to a negative mean error of that population. On average, over all populations, the error at any point will be 0 and consequently also the average over all populations of the mean error.

This experiment shows that model-unbiasedness does not protect us against selection bias, i.e., bias due to preferential sampling.

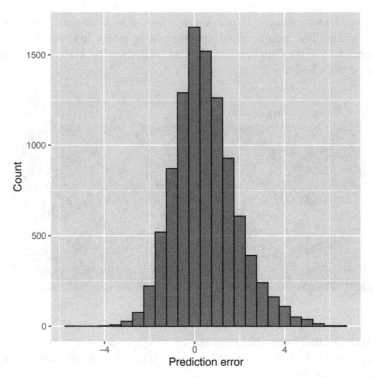

FIGURE 26.7: Frequency distribution of the errors of ordinary kriging predictions from a preferential sample.

26.4   Effective sample size

Another persistent misconception is that when estimating the variance of the estimator of the mean of a spatial population or the correlation of two variables of a population, we must account for autocorrelation of the sample data. This misconception occurs, for instance, in Griffith (2005) and in various sections (for instance, sections 3.5, 10.1, and 11.2) of Plant (2012). The reasoning is that, due to the spatial autocorrelation in the sample data, there is less information in the data about the parameter of interest, and so the effective sample size is smaller than the actual sample size. An early example of this misconception is Barnes' publication on the required sample size for estimating nonparametric tolerance intervals (Barnes, 1988). de Gruijter and ter Braak (1992) showed that a basic probability sampling design like simple random sampling requires fewer sampling points than the model-based sampling design proposed by Barnes.

The misconception is caused by confusing population parameters with model parameters. Recall that the population mean and the model-mean are not the same; the model-mean μ of Equation (21.2) is the expectation of the population means over all populations that can be simulated with the model. The same holds for the variance of a variable as well as for the covariance and the Pearson correlation coefficient of two variables. All these parameters can be defined as parameters of a finite or infinite population or of random variables generated by a superpopulation model. Using an effective sample size to quantify the variance of an estimator is perfectly correct for model parameters, but not so for population parameters. For instance, when the correlation coefficient is defined as a population parameter and sampling units are selected by simple random sampling, there is no need to apply the method proposed by Clifford et al. (1989) to correct the p-value in a significance test for the presence of spatial autocorrelation.

I elaborate on this for the mean as the parameter of interest. Suppose a sample is selected in some way (need not be random) and the sample mean is used as an estimator of the model-mean. Note that for a model with a constant mean as in Equation (21.2), the sample mean is a model-unbiased estimator of the model-mean, but in general not the best linear unbiased estimator (BLUE) of the model-mean. If the random variables are model-independent, the variance of the sample mean, used as an estimator of the model-mean, can be computed by

$$V(\hat{\mu}) = \frac{\sigma^2}{n} \, , \tag{26.2}$$

with σ^2 the model-variance of the random variable (see Equation (21.2)). The variance presented in Equation (26.2) necessarily is a model-variance as it quantifies our uncertainty about the model-mean, which only exists in the model-based approach. If the random variables are not model-independent, the model-variance of the sample mean can be computed by (de Gruijter et al., 2006)

$$V(\hat{\mu}) = \frac{\sigma^2}{n}\{1 + (n-1)\bar{\rho}\} \, , \tag{26.3}$$

with $\bar{\rho}$ the mean correlation within the sample (the average of the correlation of all pairs of sampling points). The term inside the curly brackets is larger than 1, unless $\bar{\rho}$ equals 0. So, the variance of the estimator of the model-mean with dependent data is larger than when data are independent. The number of independent observations that is equivalent to a spatially autocorrelated data set's sample size n, referred to as the effective sample size, can be computed by (de Gruijter et al., 2006)

$$n_{\text{eff}} = \frac{n}{\{1 + (n-1)\bar{\rho}\}} \, . \tag{26.4}$$

So, if we substitute n_{eff} for n in Equation (26.2), we obtain the variance presented in Equation (26.3). Equation (26.4) is equivalent to equation (2) in Griffith (2005). Figure 26.8 shows that the effective sample size decreases sharply with the mean correlation. With a mean correlation of 0, the effective sample size equals the actual sample size; with a mean correlation of 1, the effective sample size equals 1.

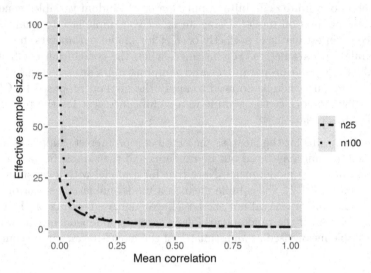

FIGURE 26.8: Effective sample sizes as a function of the mean correlation within the sample, for samples of size 25 and 100.

To illustrate the difference between the model-variance and the design-variance of a sample mean, I simulated a finite population of 100 units, located at the nodes of a square grid, with a model-mean of 10, an exponential semivariogram without nugget, an effective range of three times the distance between adjacent population units, and a sill of 1 (Figure 26.9). The model-variance of the average of a simple random sample *without replacement* of size n is computed using Equation (26.3), and the design-variance of the sample mean, used as an estimate of the population mean, is computed by (see Equation (3.15))

$$V(\hat{\bar{z}}) = \left(1 - \frac{n}{N}\right) \frac{S^2}{n}, \tag{26.5}$$

with N the total number of population units ($N = 100$). This is done for a range of sample sizes: $n = 10, 11, \ldots, 100$. Note that for $n < 100$ the model-variance of the sample mean for a given n, differs between samples. For samples showing strong spatial clustering, the mean correlation is relatively large, and consequently the model-variance is relatively large (see Equation (26.3)). There is less information in these samples about the model-mean than in samples without spatial clustering of the points. Therefore, to estimate the expectation of the model-variance over repeated simple random sampling for a given n, I selected 200 simple random samples of that size n, and I averaged the 200 model-variances. Figure 26.10 shows the result. Both the model-variance and the design-variance of the sample mean decrease with the sample size. For all sample sizes, the model-variance is larger than the design-variance. The design-variance goes to 0 for $n = 100$ (see Equation (26.5)), whereas the model-variance for $n = 100$ equals 0.0509. This can be explained as follows. Although with $n = 100$ we know the population mean without error, this population mean is only an estimate of the model-mean. Recall that the model-mean is the expectation of the population mean over all realisations of the model.

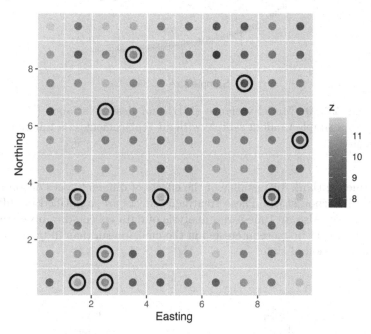

FIGURE 26.9: Simple random sample without replacement of ten points from a finite population simulated with a model with a model-mean of 10, a model-variance of 1, and an exponential semivariogram (without nugget) with a distance parameter equal to the distance between neighbours (effective range is three times this distance). The mean correlation within the sample equals 0.135, and the model-variance of the estimator of the model-mean equals 0.222.

In Figure 26.11 we can see that the population mean shows considerable variation. The variance of 10,000 simulated population means equals 0.0513, which is nearly equal to the value of 0.0509 for the model-variance computed with Equation (26.3).

In observational research, I cannot think of situations in which interest is in estimation of the mean of a superpopulation model. This in contrast to experimental research. In experimental research, we are interested in the effects

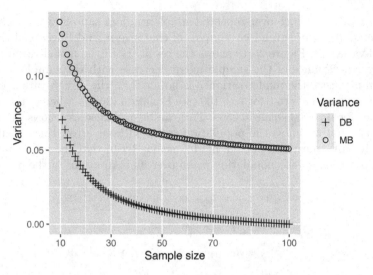

FIGURE 26.10: Model-variance (MB) and design-variance (DB) of the average of a simple random sample without replacement as a function of the sample size.

of treatments; think for instance of the effects of different types of soil tillage on the soil carbon stock. These treatment effects are quantified by different model-means. Also, in time-series analysis of data collected in observational studies, we might be more interested in the model-mean than in the mean over a bounded period of time.

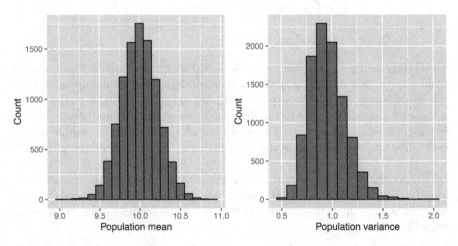

FIGURE 26.11: Frequency distributions of means and variances of 10,000 simulated populations.

Now let us return to Equation (26.1). What is wrong with this variance estimator? Where Griffith (2005) confused the population mean and the model-mean, Wang et al. (2010) confused the population variance with the sill (a priori variance) of the random process that has generated the population (Webster and Oliver, 2007). The parameter σ^2 in their formula is defined as the population variance. In doing so, the variance estimator is clearly wrong. However, if we define σ^2 in this formula as the sill, the formula makes more sense, but even then, the equation is not fully correct. The variance computed with this equation is not the design-variance of the average of a simple random sample selected from the sampled population, but the *expectation* of this design-variance over all realisations of the model. So, it is a model-based prediction of the design-variance of the estimator of the population mean, estimated from a simple random sample, see Chapter 13. For the population actually sampled, the design-variance is either smaller or larger than this expectation. Figure 26.11 shows that there is considerable variation in the population variance among the 10,000 populations simulated with the model. Consequently, for an individual population, the variance of the estimator of the population mean, estimated from a simple random sample, can largely differ from the model-expectation of this variance. Do not use Equation (26.1) for estimating the design-variance of the estimator of the population mean, but simply use Equation (26.5) (for simple random sampling with replacement and simple random sampling of infinite populations the term $(1 - n/N)$ can be dropped). Equation (26.1) is only relevant for comparing simple random sampling under a variety of models of spatial variation (Ripley (1981), Domburg et al. (1994)).

26.5 Exploiting spatial structure in design-based approach

A further misconception is that, in the design-based approach, the possibilities of exploiting our knowledge about the spatial structure of the study variable are limited, because the sampling units are selected randomly. This would indeed be a very serious drawback, but happily enough, this is not true. There are various ways of utilising this knowledge. Our knowledge about the spatial structure can be used either at the stage of designing the sample and/or at the stage of the statistical inference once the data are collected (Table 26.1).

I distinguish the situation in which maps of covariates are available from the situation in which such maps are lacking. In the first situation, the covariate maps can be used, for instance, to stratify the population (Chapter 4). With a quantitative covariate, optimal stratification methods are available. Other options are, for instance, pps sampling (Chapter 8), and balanced sampling and well-spread sampling in covariate space with the local pivotal method

TABLE 26.1: Strategies in the design-based approach for exploiting knowledge about the spatial structure of the study variable.

Stage	Covariates available	No covariates
Sampling	Stratified random sampling	Systematic random sampling
	pps sampling	Compact geographical stratification
	Balanced sampling	Geographical spreading with LPM
	Covariate space spreading with LPM	GRTS sampling
Inference	Model-assisted: regression model	Model-assisted: spatial regression model

LPM: local pivotal method.

(Chapter 9). At the inference stage, the covariate maps can be used in a model-assisted approach, using, for instance, a linear regression model to increase the precision of the design-based estimator (Chapter 10, Section 26.6).

If no covariate maps are available, we may anticipate the presence of spatial structure by spreading the sampling units throughout the study area. This spreading can be done in many ways, for instance by systematic random sampling (Chapter 5), compact geographical stratification (Section 4.6), well-spread sampling in geographical space with the local pivotal method (LPM) (Subsection 9.2.1), and generalised random-tessellation stratified (GRTS) sampling (Subsection 9.2.2). At the inference stage, again a model-assisted approach can be advantageous, using the spatial coordinates in a regression model.

26.6 Model-assisted vs. model-dependent

In this section the difference between the model-assisted approach and the model-based approach is explained. The model-assisted approach is a hybrid approach in between the design-based and the model-based approach. It tries to build the strength of the model-based approach, a potential increase of the accuracy of estimates, into the design-based approach. As in the design-based approach, sampling units are selected by probability sampling, and consequently bias and variance are defined as design-bias and design-variance (Table 26.2). As in the model-based approach, a superpopulation model is used. However, the role of this model in the two approaches is fundamentally different. In both approaches we assume that the population of interest is a realisation of the superpopulation model. However, as explained above, in the model-based approach, the statistical properties of the estimators (predictors), such as bias and variance, are defined over all possible realisations of the model (Table 26.2). So, unbiasedness and minimum variance of an estimator (predictor) means *model*-unbiasedness and minimum *model*-variance. On the contrary, in

TABLE 26.2: Three statistical approaches for sampling and inference.

Approach	Sampling	Inference	Regression coefficients	Quality criteria
Design-based	Prob. sampling	Design-based	No model	Design-bias, Design-variance
Model-assisted	Prob. sampling	Model-assisted	Population par.	Design-bias, Design-variance
Model-based	No requirement	Model-depend.	Superpop. par.	Model-bias, Model-variance

the model-assisted approach, the model is used to derive an efficient estimator (Chapter 10). To stress its different role in the model-assisted approach, the model is referred to as a working model.

An important property of model-assisted estimators is that, if a poor working model is used (our assumptions about how our population is generated are incorrect), then for moderate sample sizes the results are still valid, i.e., the empirical coverage rate of a model-assisted estimate of the confidence interval of the population mean still is approximately equal to the nominal coverage rate. This is because the mismatch of the superpopulation model and the applied model-assisted estimator results in a large design-variance of the estimator of the population mean. This is illustrated with a simulation study, in which I compare the effect of using a correct vs. an incorrect model in estimation.

A population is simulated with a simple linear regression model with an intercept of 15 ($\beta_0 = 15$), a slope coefficient of 0.5 ($\beta_1 = 0.5$), and a constant residual standard deviation of 2 ($\sigma_\epsilon = 2$). This is done by first simulating a population with covariate values with a model-mean of 20 ($\mu(x) = 20$), using an exponential semivariogram without nugget, a sill variance of 25, and a distance parameter of 20 distance units. This field with covariate values is then linearly transformed using the above-mentioned regression coefficients. Finally, 'white noise' is added by drawing independently for each population unit a random number from a normal distribution with zero mean and a standard deviation of 2 (Figure 26.12).

The population mean of the study variable equals 25.052, which is pretty close to the known model-mean $\mu(z)$: $\beta_0 + \beta_1 \mu(x) = 15 + 0.5 \cdot 20$.

Figure 26.13 shows a scatter plot for all population units. The Pearson correlation coefficient equals 0.745. Two models are fitted to the exhaustive scatter plot: a simple linear regression model and a ratio model. The ratio model assumes that the intercept β_0 equals 0 and that the residual variance is proportional to the covariate values: $\sigma_\epsilon^2 \propto x$. The population fits of the coefficients of the simple linear regression model are 14.9989 and 0.4997, which are very close to the model regression coefficients. The fitted ratio model is clearly very poor. The residual standard deviation of the population fit of the ratio model equals 3.887, which is much larger than 2.001 of the simple linear regression model.

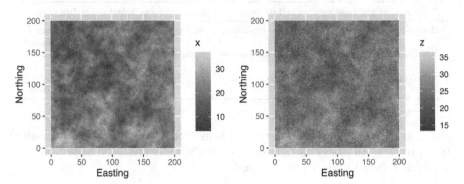

FIGURE 26.12: Realisation of simple linear regression model. x is the covariate, z is the study variable.

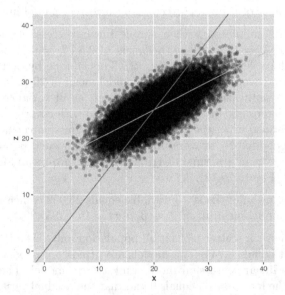

FIGURE 26.13: Exhaustive scatter plot of the simulated population, with population fit of a simple linear regression model (green line), and of a ratio model fitted with weights inversely proportional to the covariate (red line).

The population mean of the study variable is estimated by selecting 5,000 times a simple random sample of 25 units. Each sample is used to estimate the population mean by two model-assisted estimators: the simple regression estimator and the ratio estimator (Chapter 10). The first estimator correctly assumes that the population is a realisation of a simple linear regression model, whereas the latter incorrectly assumes that it is a realisation of a ratio model. For each sample, the standard error of the two estimators are estimated as well, which is used to compute a 95% confidence interval of the population mean. Then the empirical coverage rate is computed, i.e., the proportion of samples for which the population mean is inside the 95% confidence interval. Ideally, this empirical coverage rate is equal to the nominal coverage rate of 0.95.

The coverage rates of the simple regression estimator and the ratio estimator equal 0.931 and 0.948, respectively. Both coverage rates are very close to the nominal coverage rate of 0.95. So, despite the fact that the ratio estimator assumes an improper superpopulation model, the estimated confidence interval is still valid. The price we pay for the invalid model assumption is not an overestimated coverage rate of a confidence interval, but an increased standard error of the estimated population mean. The average over the 5,000 samples of the estimated standard error of the regression estimator equals 0.387, whereas that of the ratio estimator equals 0.772. The larger standard error of the ratio estimator leads to wider confidence intervals, which explains that the coverage rate is still correct.

This sampling experiment is now repeated for samples sizes $n = 10, 25, 50, 100$ and for confidence levels $1 - \alpha = 0.01, 0.02, \dots, 0.99$.

Figures 26.14 and 26.15 show that the empirical coverage rates are close to the nominal coverage rate, for all four sample sizes, both estimators, and all confidence levels. For the regression estimator and $n = 10$, the empirical coverage rate is somewhat too small. This is because the standard error of the regression estimator is slightly underestimated at this sample size. The average of the estimated standard errors (square root of estimated variance of regression estimator) equals 0.609, which is somewhat smaller than the standard deviation of the 5,000 regression estimates of 0.678. For all sample sizes, the standard deviation of the 5,000 ratio estimates is considerably larger than that of the 5,000 regression estimates (Table 26.3). For $n = 10$ also the standard error of the ratio estimator is underestimated (the average of the 5,000 estimated standard errors is smaller than the standard deviation of the 5,000 ratio estimates), but as a percentage of the standard deviation of the 5,000 ratio estimates, this underestimation is smaller than for the regression estimator.

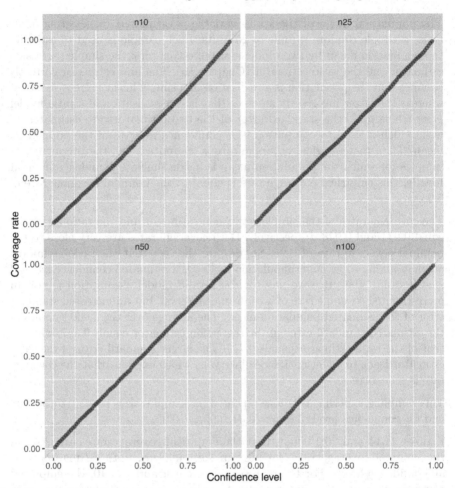

FIGURE 26.14: Empirical vs. nominal coverage rates of confidence intervals for the population mean, estimated by the simple regression estimator, for sample sizes 10, 25, 50, and 100.

The relative bias, computed by

$$bias = \frac{\frac{1}{5000}\sum_{s=1}^{5000}(\hat{\bar{z}}_s - \bar{z})}{\bar{z}} \ , \tag{26.6}$$

is about 0 for both estimators and all four sample sizes.

Contrarily, if in the model-based approach a poor superpopulation model is used, the predictions and the prediction error variances still are model-unbiased. However, for the sampled population, we may have serious systematic error in the estimated population mean and the variance of local predictions may be

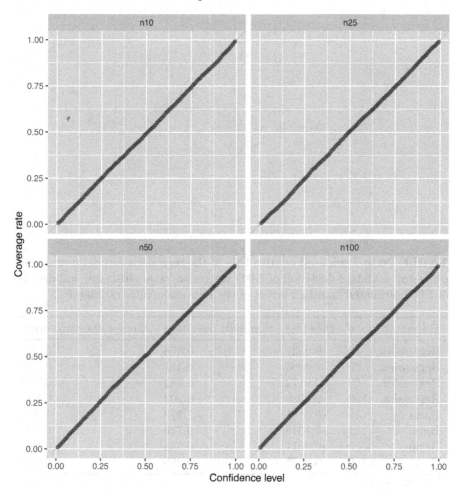

FIGURE 26.15: Empirical versus nominal coverage rates of confidence intervals for the population mean, estimated by the ratio estimator, for sample sizes 10, 25, 50, and 100.

seriously over- or underestimated. For this reason, model-based inference is also referred to as *model-dependent* inference, stressing that we fully rely on the model and that the validity of the estimates and predictions depends on the quality of the model (Hansen et al., 1983).

TABLE 26.3: Estimated relative bias of the regression estimator and ratio estimator, standard deviation of 5,000 regression/ratio estimates, and average of 5,000 estimated standard errors of the regression/ratio estimator.

Estimator	n	Bias (%)	Standard deviation	Average standard error
Regression	10	0.0037	0.678	0.609
Regression	25	0.0086	0.411	0.397
Regression	50	0.0172	0.282	0.282
Regression	100	0.0058	0.202	0.200
Ratio	10	-0.3191	1.273	1.206
Ratio	25	-0.1318	0.776	0.769
Ratio	50	-0.0611	0.548	0.549
Ratio	100	0.0175	0.390	0.388

n: sample size.

A

Answers to exercises

R scripts of the answers to the exercises are available in the Exercises folder at the github repository of this book.

Introduction to probability sampling

1. No, this is not a probability sample because, with this implementation, the probabilities of selection of the units are unknown.

2. For simple random sampling without replacement, the inclusion probability is 0.5 ($\pi_k = n/N = 2/4$). For simple random sampling with replacement, the inclusion probability is 0.4375 ($\pi_k = 1 - (1 - 1/N)^n = 1 - 0.75^2$).

Simple random sampling

1. The most remarkable difference is the much smaller range of values in the sampling distribution of the estimator of the population mean (Figure 3.2). This can be explained by the smaller variance of the average of n randomly selected values compared to the variance of an individual randomly selected value. A second difference is that the sampling distribution is more symmetric, less skewed to the right. This is an illustration of the central limit theorem.

2. The variance (and so the standard deviation) becomes smaller.

3. Then the difference between the average of the estimated population means and the true population mean will be very close to 0, showing that the estimator is unbiased.

4. For simple random sampling without replacement (from a finite population), the sampling variance will be smaller. When units are selected with replacement, a unit can be selected more than once. This is inefficient, as there is no extra information in the unit that has been selected before.

5. The larger the population size N, the smaller the difference between the sampling variances of the estimator of the mean for simple random sampling with replacement and simple random sampling without replacement (given a sample size n).

6. The true sampling variance of the estimator of the mean for simple random sampling from an infinite population can be computed with the population variance divided by the sample size: $V(\hat{\bar{z}}) = S^2(z)/n$.

7. In reality, we cannot compute the true sampling variance, because we do not know the values of z for all units in the population, so that we do not know the population variance $S^2(z)$.

8. See SI.R[1]. The 90% confidence interval is less wide than the 95% interval, because a larger proportion of samples is allowed not to cover the population mean. The estimated standard error of the estimated total underestimates the true standard error, because a constant bulk density is used. In reality this bulk density also varies.

Stratified simple random sampling

1. See STSI1.R[2].

2. Strata EA and PA can be merged without losing much precision: their means are about equal.

3. See STSI2.R[3]. The true sampling variance of the π estimator of the mean SOM obtained by collapsing strata EA and PA equals 42.89, whereas the sampling variance with the original stratification equals 42.53. So, the new stratification with four strata is only slightly worse.

---

[1] https://github.com/DickBrus/SpatialSamplingwithR/tree/master/Exercises/SI.R

[2] https://github.com/DickBrus/SpatialSamplingwithR/tree/master/Exercises/STSI1.R

[3] https://github.com/DickBrus/SpatialSamplingwithR/tree/master/Exercises/STSI2.R

4. The proof is as follows: $\sum_N \pi_k = \sum_H \sum_{N_h} \pi_{hk} = \sum_H \sum_{N_h} n_h/N_h = \sum_H n_h = n$.

5. See STSIcumrootf.R[4]. The default allocation is Neyman allocation, see help of function strata.cumrootf. The true sampling variance of the estimator of the mean equals 20.0. The stratification effect equals 4.26.

6. With at least two points per geostratum, the variance of the estimator of the stratum mean can be estimated without bias by the estimated stratum variance divided by the number of points in that stratum.

7. On average, the sampling variance of the estimator of the mean with 100×1 point is smaller than with 50×2 points, because the geographical spreading will be somewhat better (less spatial clustering).

8. With geostrata of equal size and equal number of sampling points per geostratum, the sampling intensity is equal for all strata, so that the sample mean is an unbiased estimator of the population mean. In formula: $\hat{\bar{z}} = \sum_{h=1}^{H} w_h \, \bar{z}_{Sh} = \frac{1}{H} \sum_{h=1}^{H} \bar{z}_{Sh} = \bar{z}_{S}$, with $\bar{z}_{Sh}$ the average of the sample from stratum h and $\bar{z}_{S}$ the average of all sampling points.

9. See STSIgeostrata.R[5].
   - Collapsing the geostrata on the basis of the measurements of the study variable is not a proper way, as it will lead to a biased estimator of the sampling variance of the estimator of the mean. The estimated stratum variances $\hat{S}^2(z)$ will be small, and so the estimated sampling variance will underestimate the true sampling variance.
   - I propose to group neighbouring geostrata, i.e., geostrata that are close to each other.
   - The sampling variance estimator is not unbiased. The sampling variance is slightly overestimated, because we assume that the two (or three) points within a collapsed stratum are selected by simple random sampling, whereas they are selected by stratified random sampling (a collapsed stratum consists of two or three geostrata), and so there is less spatial clustering compared to simple random sampling.

---

[4] https://github.com/DickBrus/SpatialSamplingwithR/tree/master/Exercises/STSIcumrootf.R

[5] https://github.com/DickBrus/SpatialSamplingwithR/tree/master/Exercises/STSIgeostrata.R

10. See `STSIgeostrata_composite.R`[6].

   - No, with bulking within strata the sampling variance cannot be estimated, because then we cannot estimate the sampling variances of the estimated stratum means, which are needed for estimating the sampling variance of the estimator of the population mean.
   - If all aliquots are analysed separately, the estimated population mean is more precise than with composite sampling (variance of the estimator of the mean is smaller), because the contribution of the measurement error to the total variance of the estimator of the mean is smaller.
   - This combination of arguments of function `stratify` does not work, because with geostrata of unequal area the mean of a composite sample is a biased estimator of the population mean. All aliquots bulked into a composite get equal weight, but they should get different weights, because they do not represent equal fractions of the population.

Systematic random sampling

1. See `SY.R`[7].

2. As can be seen in the plot, the spatial coverage of the study area by the two systematic random samples can be quite poor. So, I expect that the variance of the estimator of the mean using the data of two systematic random samples of half the expected size is larger than the variance of the estimator of the mean based on the data of a single systematic random sample.

Cluster random sampling

1. See `Cluster.R`[8].

---

[6] https://github.com/DickBrus/SpatialSamplingwithR/tree/master/Exercises/STSIgeostrata_composite.R

[7] https://github.com/DickBrus/SpatialSamplingwithR/tree/master/Exercises/SY.R

[8] https://github.com/DickBrus/SpatialSamplingwithR/tree/master/Exercises/Cluster.R

2. I expect that the sampling variance with three transects is larger than with six transects of half the length, as the sampling points are more spatially clustered.

3. With two independently selected clusters per stratum, the sampling variance of the estimator of the mean can be estimated without bias, as the variance of cluster means within the strata can be estimated from the two cluster means.

Two-stage cluster random sampling

1. See `TwoStage.R`[9].

2. With ten PSU draws and four SSUs per PSU draw (10×4), the expected standard error of the estimator of the population mean is smaller than with four PSU draws and ten SSUs per PSU draw (4×10), because spatial clustering of the sampling points is less strong.

3. See `TwoStage.R`[10].

4. See `TwoStage.R`[11].

5. See `TwoStage.R`[12].

6. For the first variance component:

$$
\frac{1}{n} \sum_{j=1}^{N} p_j \left(\frac{t_j(z)}{p_j} - t(z) \right)^2 = \frac{1}{n} \sum_{j=1}^{N} p_j \left(M \frac{t_j(z)}{M_j} - M\bar{z} \right)^2
$$
$$
= \frac{1}{n} \sum_{j=1}^{N} p_j \left(M(\bar{z}_j - \bar{z}) \right)^2 = \frac{M^2}{n} \sum_{j=1}^{N} p_j \left(\bar{z}_j - \bar{z} \right)^2 .
$$
(A.1)

[9] https://github.com/DickBrus/SpatialSamplingwithR/tree/master/Exercises/TwoStage.R
[10] https://github.com/DickBrus/SpatialSamplingwithR/tree/master/Exercises/TwoStage.R
[11] https://github.com/DickBrus/SpatialSamplingwithR/tree/master/Exercises/TwoStage.R
[12] https://github.com/DickBrus/SpatialSamplingwithR/tree/master/Exercises/TwoStage.R

For the second variance component:

$$\frac{1}{n}\sum_{j=1}^{N}\frac{M_j^2 S_j^2}{m_j p_j} = \frac{1}{nm}\sum_{j=1}^{N}\frac{M_j^2 S_j^2}{p_j} = \frac{1}{nm}\sum_{j=1}^{N}MM_j S_j^2$$
$$= \frac{1}{nm}\sum_{j=1}^{N}M^2\frac{M_j}{M}S_j^2 = \frac{M^2}{nm}\sum_{j=1}^{N}p_j S_j^2 . \tag{A.2}$$

Division of both variance components by M^2 yields the variance of the estimator of the population mean, see Equations (7.3), (7.4), and (7.5).

Sampling with probabilities proportional to size

1. See pps.R[13].

2. No, this field should not be included in the poppy area of that sampling unit, because it is located outside the target area.

3. Yes, this field must be included in the poppy area of that sampling unit, as it is located inside the target area. The target area is the territory of Kandahar, regardless of how an area inside this territory is depicted on the map, as agricultural land or otherwise.

Balanced and well-spread sampling

1. See Balanced.R[14].

2. Spatial clustering of sampling units with balanced sampling may lead to a less precise estimate of the population mean. This will be the case when the residuals of the regression model are spatially correlated (show spatial structure). The residuals will be correlated when the spatial variation of the study variable is also determined by covariates or factors that are not used in balancing the sample. If the residuals are not spatially correlated (white noise), spatial clustering does no harm.

---

[13] https://github.com/DickBrus/SpatialSamplingwithR/tree/master/Exercises/pps.R
[14] https://github.com/DickBrus/SpatialSamplingwithR/tree/master/Exercises/Balanced.R

3. One advantage is that unequal inclusion probabilities can be used in the LPM design. If the sampling units have unequal size (as in the poppy survey of Kandahar), or if a covariate is available that is linearly related to the study variable (as in the AGB survey of Eastern Amazonia), the sampling efficiency can be increased by sampling with (inclusion) probabilities proportional to size. The only option for random sampling from geostrata is then to select the units *within geostrata* by pps sampling.

Model-assisted estimation

1. See `RegressionEstimator.R`[15]. The approximate standard error estimator that uses the g-weights (computed with functions `calibrate` and `svymean` of package **survey**) has a larger mean (7.194) than the approximated standard error (7.130) computed with Equation (10.13).

2. See `VarianceRegressionEstimator.R`[16]. In reality, we do not have a population fit of the regression coefficients, but these coefficients must be estimated from a sample. The estimated coefficients vary among the samples, which explains that the experimental variance, i.e., the variance of the 10,000 regression estimates obtained by estimating the coefficients from the sample (Sample in Figure A.1), is larger than the variance as computed with the population fit of the regression coefficients (Exhaust in Figure A.1).

   The difference between the experimental variance (variance of regression estimator with sample fit of coefficients) and the variance obtained with the population fit, as a proportion of the experimental variance, decreases with the sample size. The same holds for the difference between the approximated variance and the experimental variance as a proportion of the experimental variance. Both findings can be explained by the smaller contribution of the variance of the estimated regression coefficients to the variance of the regression estimator with the large sample size. The approximated variance does not account for the uncertainty about the regression coefficients, so that for all three sample sizes this approximated variance is about

---

[15] https://github.com/DickBrus/SpatialSamplingwithR/tree/master/Exercises/RegressionEstimator.R

[16] https://github.com/DickBrus/SpatialSamplingwithR/tree/master/Exercises/VarianceRegressionEstimator.R

equal to the variance of the regression estimator as computed with the population fit of the regression coefficients.

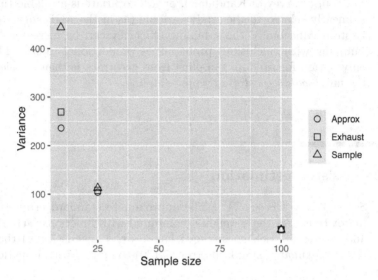

FIGURE A.1: Variance of the regression estimator of the mean AGB in Eastern Amazonia with population fit of regression coefficients (Exhaust), with sample fit of regression coefficients (Sample), and approximated variance of regression estimator (Approx).

3. See `RatioEstimator.R`[17]. The population fit of the slope coefficient of the homoscedastic model differs from the ratio of the population total poppy area to the population total agricultural area. For the heteroscedastic model, these are equal.

Two-phase random sampling

1. See `RegressionEstimator_Twophase.R`[18]. Figure A.2 shows the approximated sampling distribution of the simple regression estimator of the mean AGB in Eastern Amazonia when lnSWIR2 is observed for all sampling units (one-phase), and when AGB is observed for

---

[17] https://github.com/DickBrus/SpatialSamplingwithR/tree/master/Exercises/RatioEstimator.R
[18] https://github.com/DickBrus/SpatialSamplingwithR/tree/master/Exercises/RegressionEstimator_Twophase.R

the subsample only (two-phase). The variance of the regression estimator with two-phase sampling is considerably larger. Without subsampling, the regression estimator exploits our knowledge of the population mean of the covariate lnSWIR2, whereas in two-phase sampling, this population mean must be estimated from the first-phase sample, introducing additional uncertainty.

The average of the 10,000 approximated variances equals 40.5 $(10^9$ kg ha$^{-1})^2$, which is considerably smaller than the variance of the 10,000 regression estimates for two-phase sampling, which is equal to 51.2 $(10^9$ kg ha$^{-1})^2$.

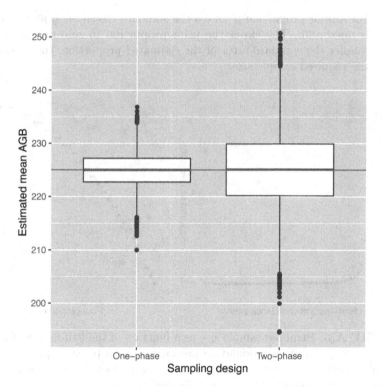

FIGURE A.2: Approximated sampling distribution of the simple regression estimator of the mean AGB $(10^9$ kg ha$^{-1})$ in Eastern Amazonia in the case that the covariate is observed for all sampling units (one-phase) and for the subsample only (two-phase).

Computing the required sample size

1. See `RequiredSampleSize_CIprop.R`[19]. Figure A.3 shows that the required sample size decreases sharply with the length of the confidence interval and increases with the prior (anticipated) proportion.

   A prior for the proportion is needed because the standard error of the estimated proportion is a function of the estimated proportion $\hat{p}$ itself: $se(\hat{p}) = \frac{\sqrt{\hat{p}(1-\hat{p})}}{\sqrt{n}}$, so that the length of the confidence interval, computed with the normal approximation, is also a function of $\hat{p}$, see Equation (12.11).

   For a prior proportion p^* of 0.5 the standard deviation $\sqrt{p^*(1-p^*)}$ is maximum. The closer the prior proportion to zero or one, the smaller the standard error of the estimated proportion, the smaller the required sample size.

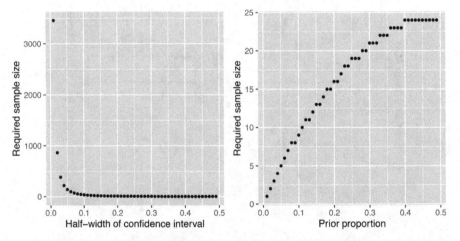

FIGURE A.3: Required sample size as a function of the half-length of a 95% confidence interval of the population proportion, for a prior proportion of 0.1 (left subfigure), and as a function of the prior proportion for a half-length of a 95% confidence interval of 0.2 (right subfigure).

2. See `RequiredSampleSize_CIprop.R`[20]. There is no need to compute the required sample size for prior proportions > 0.5, as this required

---

[19] https://github.com/DickBrus/SpatialSamplingwithR/tree/master/Exercises/RequiredSampleSize_CIprop.R

[20] https://github.com/DickBrus/SpatialSamplingwithR/tree/master/Exercises/RequiredSampleSize_CIprop.R

sample size is symmetric. For instance, the required sample size for $p^* = 0.7$ is equal to the required sample size for $p^* = 0.3$.

Model-based optimisation of probability sampling designs

1. See `MBSamplingVarSI_VariogramwithNugget.R`[21]. The predicted sampling variance is slightly larger compared to the predicted sampling variance obtained with the semivariogram without nugget (and the same sill and range), because 50% of the spatial variation is not spatially structured, so that the model-expectation of the population variance (the predicted population variance) is larger.

2. See first part of `MBRequiredSampleSize_SIandSY.R`[22].

3. See second part of `MBRequiredSampleSize_SIandSY.R`. The model-based prediction of the required sample size for simple random sampling is 34 and for systematic random sampling 13. The design effect at a sample size of 34 equals 0.185. The design effect decreases with the sample size, i.e., the ratio of the variance with systematic random sampling to the variance with simple random sampling becomes smaller. This is because the larger the sample size, the more we profit from the spatial correlation.

Repeated sample surveys for monitoring population parameters

1. See `SE_STparameters.R`[23]. For the designs SP and RP, the true standard errors of all space-time parameters are slightly smaller than the standard deviations in Table 15.1, because in the sampling experiment the *estimated* covariances of the elementary estimates are used in the GLS estimator of the spatial means, whereas in this exercise the true covariances are used. The estimated covariances

---

[21] https://github.com/DickBrus/SpatialSamplingwithR/tree/master/Exercises/MBSamplingVarSI_VariogramwithNugget.R

[22] https://github.com/DickBrus/SpatialSamplingwithR/tree/master/Exercises/MBRequiredSampleSize_SIandSY.R

[23] https://github.com/DickBrus/SpatialSamplingwithR/tree/master/Exercises/SE_STparameters.R

vary among the space-time samples. This variation propagates to
the GLS estimates of the spatial means and so to the estimated
space-time parameters.

2. See SE_ChangeofMean_HT.R[24]. The standard error of the change with
the GLS estimators of the two spatial means is much smaller than
the standard error of the change with the π estimators, because the
GLS estimators use the data of all four years to estimate the spatial
means of 2004 and 2019, whereas with the π estimators only the
data of 2004 and 2019 are used.

Regular grid and spatial coverage sampling

1. See SquareGrid.R[25]. The number of grid points specified with
argument n is the expected number of grid points over repeated
selection of square grids with a random start. With a fixed start
(using argument offset), the number of grid points can differ from
the expected sample size.

2. The optimal spatial coverage sample, optimal in terms of MSSD,
consists of the four points in the centre of the four subsquares of
equal size.

3. If we are also interested in the accuracy of the estimated plot means,
the sampling units can best be selected by probability sampling,
for instance by simple random sampling, from the subsquares, or
strata. Preferably at least two points should then be selected from
the strata, see Section 4.6.

4. See SpatialCoverageCircularPlot.R[26]. See Figure A.4.

5. Bias can be avoided by constructing strata of equal size. Note that
in this case we cannot use function spsample to select the centres of
these geostrata. These centres must be computed by hand.

6. See SpatialInfill.R[27].

---

[24] https://github.com/DickBrus/SpatialSamplingwithR/tree/master/Exercises/SE_ChangeofMean_HT.R

[25] https://github.com/DickBrus/SpatialSamplingwithR/tree/master/Exercises/SquareGrid.R

[26] https://github.com/DickBrus/SpatialSamplingwithR/tree/master/Exercises/
SpatialCoverageCircularPlot.R

[27] https://github.com/DickBrus/SpatialSamplingwithR/tree/master/Exercises/SpatialInfill.R

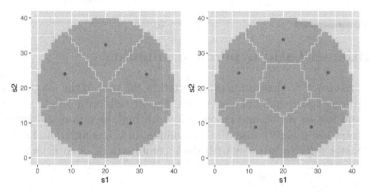

FIGURE A.4: Spatial coverage samples of five and six points in a circular plot.

Covariate space coverage sampling

1. See `CovariateSpaceCoverageSample.R`[28]. See Figure A.5.

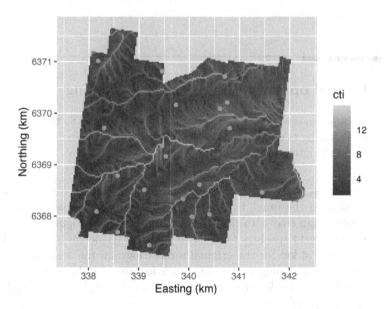

FIGURE A.5: Covariate space coverage sample from Hunter Valley, using cti, ndvi, and elevation as clustering variables, plotted on a map of cti.

---

[28]https://github.com/DickBrus/SpatialSamplingwithR/tree/master/Exercises/
CovariateSpaceCoverageSample.R

Conditioned Latin hypercube sampling

1. See cLHS.R[29]. Most units are selected in the part of the diagram with
    the highest density of raster cells. Raster cells with a large cti value
    and low elevation and raster cells with high elevation and small cti
    value are (nearly) absent in the sample. In the population, not many
    raster cells are present with these combinations of covariate values.

2. See cLHS_Square.R[30].
    *   Spatial coverage is improved by using the spatial coordinates
        as covariates, but it is not optimal in terms of MSSD.
    *   It may happen that not all marginal strata of $s1$ and $s2$ are
        sampled. Even when all these marginal strata are sampled, this
        does not guarantee a perfect spatial coverage.
    *   With set.seed(314) and default values for the arguments of
        function clhs, there is one unsampled marginal stratum and one
        marginal stratum with two sampling locations. So, component
        O1 equals 2. The minimised value (2.62) is slightly larger due
        to the contribution of O3 to the criterion.

Model-based optimisation of the grid spacing

1. See MBGridspacing_QOKV.Rmd[31]. For P50 not to exceed 0.85 the tolerable
    grid spacing is about 11.7 km, for P80 it is 9.4 km, and for P95 it is
    7.1 km (Figure A.6).

2. See MBGridspacing_Sensitivity.Rmd[32]. Increasing the nugget by 5% and
    decreasing the range by 5% yields a tolerable grid spacing that is
    smaller than that with the original semivariogram (Figure A.7). The
    tolerable grid spacings for a mean kriging variance of 0.85 are 10.6,
    8.9, and 7.4 km for the original semivariogram, the semivariogram
    with increased nugget, and the semivariogram with the smaller range,
    respectively, leading to a required expected sample size of 97, 137,
    and 200 points.

---

[29] https://github.com/DickBrus/SpatialSamplingwithR/tree/master/Exercises/cLHS.R

[30] https://github.com/DickBrus/SpatialSamplingwithR/tree/master/Exercises/cLHS_Square.R

[31] https://github.com/DickBrus/SpatialSamplingwithR/tree/master/Exercises/MBGridspacing_QOKV.Rmd

[32] https://github.com/DickBrus/SpatialSamplingwithR/tree/master/Exercises/MBGridspacing_
Sensitivity.Rmd

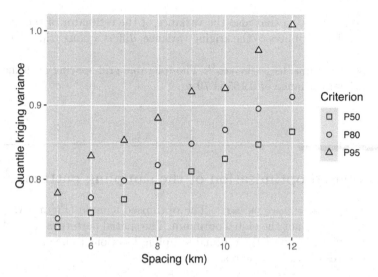

FIGURE A.6: Three quantiles of the ordinary kriging variance of predicted SOM concentrations in West-Amhara, as a function of the grid spacing.

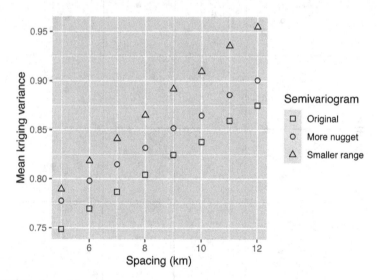

FIGURE A.7: Mean ordinary kriging variance of predicted SOM concentrations in West-Amhara, as a function of grid spacing for three semivariograms.

3. The variation in MKV for a given grid spacing can be explained by the random sample size: for a given spacing, the number of points of a randomly selected grid inside the study area is not fixed but varies. Besides, the covariate values at the grid

points vary, so that also the variance of the estimator of the mean, which contributes to the kriging variance, differs among grid samples.

4. See `MBGridspacing_MKEDV.Rmd`[33]. The tolerable grid spacing for a mean kriging variance of 0.165 is 79 m.

Model-based optimisation of the sampling pattern

1. See `MBSampleSquare_OK.Rmd`[34]. The optimised sample (Figure A.8) is most likely not the global optimum. The spatial pattern is somewhat irregular. I expect the optimal sampling locations to be close to the centres of the subsquares.

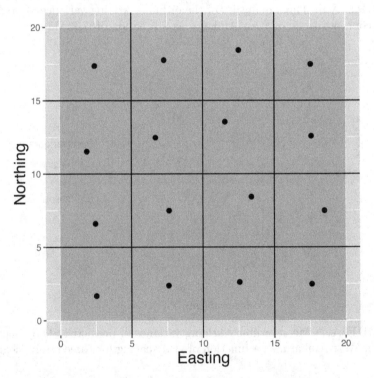

FIGURE A.8: Optimised sampling pattern of 16 points in a square for ordinary kriging.

---

[33] https://github.com/DickBrus/SpatialSamplingwithR/tree/master/Exercises/MBGridspacing_MKEDV.Rmd
[34] https://github.com/DickBrus/SpatialSamplingwithR/tree/master/Exercises/MBSampleSquare_OK.Rmd

2. See `MBSample_QOKV.Rmd`[35]. Figure A.9 shows the optimised sampling pattern. Compared with the optimised sampling pattern using the *mean* ordinary kriging variance (MOKV) as a minimisation criterion (Figure 23.3), the sampling locations are pushed more to the border of the study area. This is because with a sample optimised for MOKV (and a spatial coverage sample) near the border the kriging variances are the largest. By pushing sampling locations towards the border, the kriging variances in this border zone are strongly reduced.

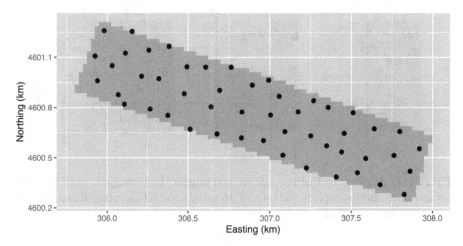

FIGURE A.9: Optimised sampling pattern of 50 points on the Cotton Research Farm, using the P90 of ordinary kriging predictions of lnECe as a minimisation criterion.

3. See `MBSampleSquare_KED.Rmd`[36]. Figure A.10 shows the optimised sampling patterns with the three semivariograms.
   - With zero nugget and a (partial) sill of 2, the sampling points are well spread throughout the area (subfigure on the left).
   - With a nugget of 1.5 and a partial sill of 0.5, the sampling points are pushed towards the left and right side of the square. With this residual semivariogram, the contribution of the variance of the predictor of the mean (as a proportion) to the total kriging variance is larger than with the previous semivariogram. By shifting the sampling points towards the left and right side of the square this contribution becomes smaller. At the same time the variance of the interpolation error increases as the spatial coverage becomes worse. The optimised sample is the right

[35] https://github.com/DickBrus/SpatialSamplingwithR/tree/master/Exercises/MBSample_QOKV.Rmd

[36] https://github.com/DickBrus/SpatialSamplingwithR/tree/master/Exercises/MBSampleSquare_KED.Rmd

balance of these two variance components (subfigure in the middle).

- With a pure nugget semivariogram, all sampling points are at the left and right side of the square. This is because with a pure nugget semivariogram, the variance of the interpolation error is independent of the locations (the variance equals the nugget variance everywhere), while the variance of the predictor of the mean is minimal for this sample (subfigure on the right).

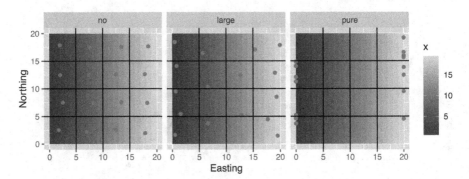

FIGURE A.10: Effect of the nugget (no nugget, large nugget, pure nugget) on the optimised sampling pattern of 16 points for KED, using Easting as a covariate for the mean.

Sampling for estimating the semivariogram

1. See NestedSampling_v1.R[37].

2. See SI_PointPairs.R[38]. With the seed I used (314), the variance of the estimator of the range parameter with the smaller separation distances is much smaller compared to that obtained with the larger separation distances (the estimated standard error is 115 m).

3. See MBSample_SSA_logdet.R[39]. Figure A.11 shows the optimised sampling pattern. The smaller ratio of spatial dependence of 0.5 (larger nugget) results in one cluster of sampling points and many point-pairs with nearly coinciding points.

[37]https://github.com/DickBrus/SpatialSamplingwithR/tree/master/Exercises/NestedSampling_v1.R

[38]https://github.com/DickBrus/SpatialSamplingwithR/tree/master/Exercises/SI_PointPairs.R

[39]https://github.com/DickBrus/SpatialSamplingwithR/tree/master/Exercises/MBSample_SSA_logdet.R

4. See `MBSample_SSA_MVKV.R`[40]. Figure A.11 shows the optimised sampling pattern. The circular cluster of sampling points covers a larger area than the cluster obtained with a ratio of spatial dependence of 0.8.

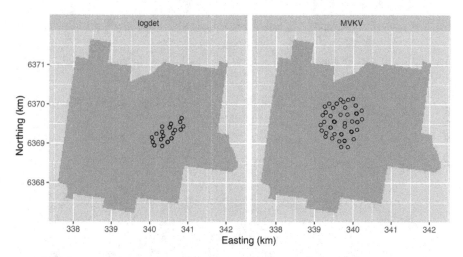

FIGURE A.11: Model-based sample for estimating the semivariogram, using the log of the determinant of the inverse Fisher information matrix (logdet) and the mean variance of the kriging variance (MVKV) as a minimisation criterion. The sampling pattern is optimised with an exponential semivariogram with a range of 200 m and a ratio of spatial dependence of 0.5.

5. See `MBSample_SSA_MEAC.R`[41]. Figure A.12 shows the optimised sampling pattern of the 20 sampling points together with the 80 spatial coverage sampling points. The minimised MEAC value equals 0.801, which is slightly smaller than that for the spatial coverage sample of 90 points supplemented by 10 points (0.808).

Sampling for validation of maps

1. I am not certain about that, because the computed MSEs are estimates of the population MSEs only and I am uncertain about both population MSEs.

---

[40] https://github.com/DickBrus/SpatialSamplingwithR/tree/master/Exercises/MBSample_SSA_MVKV.R

[41] https://github.com/DickBrus/SpatialSamplingwithR/tree/master/Exercises/MBSample_SSA_MEAC.R

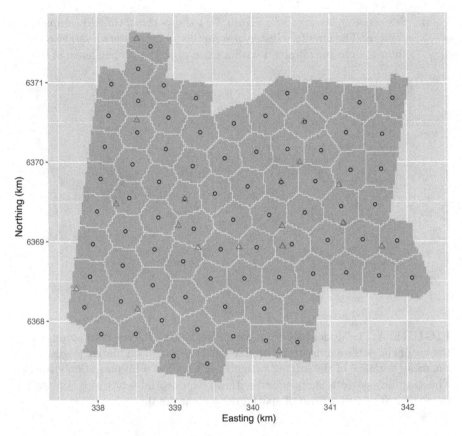

FIGURE A.12: Optimised sample of 20 points supplemented to a spatial coverage sample of 80 points, using MEAC as a minimisation criterion. The sampling pattern of the supplemental sample is optimised with an exponential semivariogram with a range of 200 m and a ratio of spatial dependence of 0.8.

2. The standard errors of the estimated MEs are large when related to the estimated MEs, so my guess is that we do not have enough evidence against the hypothesis that there is no systematic error.

3. Both standard errors are large compared to the difference in MSEs, so maybe there is no significant difference. However, we must be careful, because the variance of the difference in MSEs cannot be computed as the sum of the variances of estimated MSEs. This is because the two prediction errors at the same location are correlated, so the covariance must be subtracted from the sum of the variances to obtain the variance of the estimator of the difference in MSEs.

Bibliography

Aarts, E. and Korst, J. (1989). *Simulated Annealing and Boltzmann Machines: A Stochastic Approach to Combinatorial Optimization and Neural Computing.* John Wiley & Sons, Chichester.

Adcock, C. J. (1988). A Bayesian approach to calculating sample sizes. *Statistician*, 37:433–439.

Akramkhanov, A., Brus, D. J., and Walvoort, D. J. J. (2014). Geostatistical monitoring of soil salinity in Uzbekistan by repeated EMI surveys. *Geoderma*, 213:600–607.

Anonymous (2014). Afghanistan opium survey 2014. Technical report, United Nations Office on Drugs and Crime, Islamic Republic of Afghanistan, Ministry of Counter Narcotics.

Arthur, D. and Vassilvitskii, S. (2007). k-means++: The advantages of careful seeding. *Proceedings of the Annual ACM-SIAM Symposium on Discrete Algorithms*, 07-09-January-2007:1027–1035.

Baccini, A., Goetz, S. J., Walker, W. S., Laporte, N. T., Sun, M., Sulla-Menashe, D., Hackler, J., Beck, P. S. A., Dubayah, R., Friedl, M. A., Samanta, S., and Houghton, R. A. (2012). Estimated carbon dioxide emissions from tropical deforestation improved by carbon-density maps. *Nature Climate Change*, 2(3):182–185.

Bache, S. M. and Wickham, H. (2020). *magrittr: A Forward-Pipe Operator for R.* R package version 2.0.1.

Baillargeon, S. and Rivest, L.-P. (2011). The construction of stratified designs in R with the package stratification. *Survey Methodology*, 37(1):53–65.

Ballabio, C., Lugato, E., Fernández-Ugalde, O., Orgiazzi, A., Jones, A., Borrelli, P., Montanarella, L., and Panagos, P. (2019). Mapping LUCAS topsoil chemical properties at European scale using Gaussian process regression. *Geoderma*, 355:113912.

Ballin, M., Barcaroli, G., Masselli, M., and Scarnó, M. (2018). Redesign sample for Land Use/Cover Area frame Survey (LUCAS) 2018. Technical report, Eurostat.

Barcaroli, G. (2014). SamplingStrata: An R Package for the Optimization of Stratified Sampling. *Journal of Statistical Software*, 61(4):1–24.

Barcaroli, G., Ballin, M., Odendaal, H., Pagliuca, D., Willighagen, E., and Zardetto, D. (2020). *SamplingStrata: Optimal Stratification of Sampling Frames for Multipurpose Sampling Surveys*. R package version 1.5-1.

Barnes, R. J. (1988). Bounding the required sample size for geologic site characterization. *Mathematical Geology*, 20:477–490.

Berger, Y. G. (2004). A simple variance estimator for unequal probability sampling without replacement. *Canadian Journal of Applied Statistics*, 31(3):305–315.

Bethel, J. (1989). Sample allocation in multivariate surveys. *Survey Methodology*, 15(1):47–57.

Binder, D. A. and Hidiroglou, M. A. (1988). Sampling in time. In Krishnaiah, P. R. and Rao, C. R., editors, *Handbook of Statistics*, volume 6, pages 187–211. North-Holland, Amsterdam.

Bivand, R. S., Pebesma, E., and Gómez-Rubio, V. (2013). *Applied Spatial Data Analysis with R*. Springer, New York, second edition.

Bogaert, P. and Russo, D. (1999). Optimal spatial sampling design for the estimation of the variogram based on a least squares approach. *Water Resources Research*, 35(4):1275–1289.

Breidaks, J., Liberts, M., and Jukams, J. (2020). *surveyplanning: Survey planning tools*. R package version 4.0.

Breidenbach, J. (2018). *JoSAE: Unit-Level and Area-Level Small Area Estimation*. R package version 0.3.0.

Breidenbach, J. and Astrup, R. (2012). Small area estimation of forest attributes in the Norwegian National Forest Inventory. *European Journal of Forest Research*, 131:1255–1267.

Breidt, F. J. and Fuller, W. A. (1999). Design of supplemented panel surveys with application to the National Resources Inventory. *Journal of Agricultural, Biological, and Environmental Statistics*, 4(4):391–403.

Breidt, F. J. and Opsomer, J. D. (2017). Model-assisted survey estimation with modern prediction techniques. *Statistical Science*, 32(2):190–205.

Brown, L. D., Cai, T. T., and DasGupta, A. (2001). Interval estimation for a binomial proportion - Comment - Rejoinder. *Statistical Science*, 16(2):101–133.

Brus, D. J. (2019). Sampling for digital soil mapping: A tutorial supported by R scripts. *Geoderma*, 338:464–480.

Brus, D. J. (2021). Statistical approaches for spatial sample survey: Persistent misconceptions and new developments. *European Journal of Soil Science*, 72(2):686–703.

Brus, D. J. and de Gruijter, J. J. (1994). Estimation of non-ergodic variograms and their sampling variance by design-based sampling strategies. *Mathematical Geology*, 26:437–454.

Brus, D. J. and de Gruijter, J. J. (1997). Random sampling or geostatistical modelling? Choosing between design-based and model-based sampling strategies for soil (with Discussion). *Geoderma*, 80(1–2):1–59.

Brus, D. J. and de Gruijter, J. J. (2003). A method to combine non-probability sample data with probability sample data in estimating spatial means of environmental variables. *Environmental Monitoring and Assessment*, 83(3):303–317.

Brus, D. J. and de Gruijter, J. J. (2011). Design-based Generalized Least Squares estimation of status and trend of soil properties from monitoring data. *Geoderma*, 164(3–4):172–180.

Brus, D. J. and de Gruijter, J. J. (2013). Effects of spatial pattern persistence on the performance of sampling designs for regional trend monitoring analyzed by simulation of space-time fields. *Computers & Geosciences*, 61:175–183.

Brus, D. J., de Gruijter, J. J., and van Groenigen, J. W. (2007). Designing Spatial Coverage Samples Using the k-means Clustering Algorithm. In Lagacherie, P., McBratney, A. B., and Voltz, M., editors, *Digital Soil Mapping. An Introductory Perspective*, pages 183–192. Elsevier.

Brus, D. J. and Heuvelink, G. B. M. (2007). Optimization of sample patterns for universal kriging of environmental variables. *Geoderma*, 138(1–2):86–95.

Brus, D. J., Kempen, B., and Heuvelink, G. B. M. (2011). Sampling for validation of digital soil maps. *European Journal of Soil Science*, 62(3):394–407.

Brus, D. J. and Knotters, M. (2008). Sampling design for compliance monitoring of surface water quality: A case study in a Polder area. *Water Resources Research*, 44:W11410.

Brus, D. J. and Saby, N. P. A. (2016). Approximating the variance of estimated means for systematic random sampling, illustrated with data of the French Soil Monitoring Network. *Geoderma*, 279:77–86.

Brus, D. J., Slim, P. A., Heidema, A. H., and van Dobben, H. F. (2014). Trend monitoring of the areal extent of habitats in a subsiding coastal area by spatial probability sampling. *Ecological Indicators*, 45:313–319.

Brus, D. J., Spätjens, L. E. E. M., and de Gruijter, J. J. (1999). A sampling scheme for estimating the mean extractable phosphorus concentration of fields for environmental regulation. *Geoderma*, 89(1–2):129–148.

Cassel, C. M., Särndal, C. E., and Wretman, J. H. (1977). *Foundations of Inference in Survey Sampling*. Wiley, New York.

Champely, S. (2020). *pwr: Basic Functions for Power Analysis*. R package version 1.3-0.

Chaudhuri, A. (1994). Small domain statistics: a review. *Statistica Neerlandica*, 48(3):215–236.

Christensen, R. (1991). *Linear Models for Multivariate, Time Series, and Spatial Data*. Springer, New York.

Clifford, P., Richardson, S., and Hémon, D. (1989). Assessing the significance of the correlation between two spatial processes. *Biometrics*, 45:123–134.

Cochran, W. G. (1977). *Sampling Techniques*. Wiley, New York.

Corwin, D. L. and Lesch, S. M. (2005). Characterizing soil spatial variability with apparent soil electrical conductivity: Part II. Case study. *Computers and Electronics in Agriculture*, 46(1–3):135–152.

Corwin, D. L., Lesch, S. M., Segal, E., Skaggs, T. H., and Bradford, S. A. (2010). Comparison of sampling strategies for characterizing spatial variability with apparent soil electrical conductivity directed soil sampling. *Journal of Environmental and Engineering Geophysics*, 15(3):147–162.

Csárdi, G., Hester, J., Wickham, H., Chang, W., Morgan, M., and Tenenbaum, D. (2021). *remotes: R Package Installation from Remote Repositories, Including 'GitHub'*. R package version 2.4.2.

Cullman, A. D. (2021). *maSAE: Mandallaz' Model-Assisted Small Area Estimators*. R package version 2.0.3.

Dalenius, T. and Hodges, J. L. (1959). Minimum variance stratification. *Journal of the American Statistical Association*, 54(285):88–101.

de Gruijter, J. J., Brus, D. J., Bierkens, M. F. P., and Knotters, M. (2006). *Sampling for Natural Resource Monitoring*. Springer, Berlin.

de Gruijter, J. J., Minasny, B., and McBratney, A. B. (2015). Optimizing stratification and allocation for design-based estimation of spatial means using predictions with error. *Journal of Survey Statistics and Methodology*, 3(1):19–42.

de Gruijter, J. J. and ter Braak, C. J. F. (1990). Model-free estimation from spatial samples: a reappraisal of classical sampling theory. *Mathematical Geology*, 22(4):407–415.

de Gruijter, J. J. and ter Braak, C. J. F. (1992). Design-based versus model-based sampling strategies: Comment on R.J. Barnes' 'Bounding the required sample size for geologic site characterization'. *Mathematical Geology*, 24(7):859–864.

De Vries, P. G. (1986). *Sampling Theory for Forest Inventory: A Teach-Yourself Course*. Springer-Verlag, New York.

Deville, J. C. and Tillé, Y. (1998). Unequal probability sampling without replacement through a splitting method. *Biometrika*, 85(1):89–101.

Deville, J. C. and Tillé, Y. (2004). Efficient balanced sampling: The cube method. *Biometrika*, 91(4):893–912.

Deville, J. C. and Tillé, Y. (2005). Variance approximation under balanced sampling. *Journal of Statistical Planning and Inference*, 128(2):569–591.

Domburg, P., de Gruijter, J. J., and Brus, D. J. (1994). A structured approach to designing soil survey schemes with prediction of sampling error from variograms. *Geoderma*, 62:151–164.

Dumelle, M., Kincaid, T. M., Olsen, A. R., and Weber, M. H. (2021). *spsurvey: Spatial Sampling Design and Analysis*. R package version 5.0.1.

Escobar, E. L., Zamudio, E. B., and Munoz Rosas, J. F. (2019). *samplingVarEst: Sampling Variance Estimation*. R package version 1.4.

Falorsi, P. D. and Righi, P. (2008). A balanced sampling approach for multi-way stratification designs for small area estimation. *Survey Methodology*, 34(2):223–234.

Fitzgerald, G. J. (2010). Response surface sampling of remotely sensed imagery for precision agriculture. In Viscarra Rossel, R. A., McBratney, A. B., and Minasny, B., editors, *Proximal Soil Sensing*, pages 121–129. Springer, Dordrecht.

Fitzgerald, G. J., Lesch, S. M., Barnes, E. M., and Luckett, W. E. (2006). Directed sampling using remote sensing with a response surface sampling design for site-specific agriculture. *Computers and Electronics in Agriculture*, 53(2):98–112.

Fuller, W. A. (1999). Environmental surveys over time. *Journal of Agricultural, Biological, and Environmental Statistics*, 4(4):331–345.

Gelman, A., Carlin, J. B., Stern, H. S., Dunson, D. B., Vehtari, A., and Rubin, D. B. (2013). *Bayesian Data Analysis*. Chapman & Hall/CRC, Boca Raton, third edition.

Gershenfeld, N. (1999). *The Nature of Mathematical Modeling*. Cambridge University Press, Cambridge.

Goerg, G. M. (2013). *LICORS: Light Cone Reconstruction of States - Predictive State Estimation From Spatio-Temporal Data*. R package version 0.2.0.

Goovaerts, P. (1997). *Geostatistics for Natural Resources Evaluation*. Oxford University Press, New York.

Grafström, A. (2012). Spatially correlated Poisson sampling. *Journal of Statistical Planning and Inference*, 142(1):139–147.

Grafström, A., Ekström, M., Jonsson, B. G., Esseen, P.-A., and Ståhl, G. (2019). On combining independent probability samples. *Survey Methodology*, 45(2):349–364.

Grafström, A. and Lisic, J. (2019). *BalancedSampling: Balanced and Spatially Balanced Sampling*. R package version 1.5.5.

Grafström, A., Lundström, N. L. P., and Schelin, L. (2012). Spatially balanced sampling through the pivotal method. *Biometrics*, 68(2):514–520.

Grafström, A. and Schelin, L. (2014). How to select representative samples. *Scandinavian Journal of Statistics*, 41(2):277–290.

Grafström, A. and Tillé, Y. (2013). Doubly balanced spatial sampling with spreading and restitution of auxiliary totals. *Environmetrics*, 24(2):120–131.

Griffith, D. A. (2005). Effective geographic sample size in the presence of spatial autocorrelation. *Annals of the Association of American Geographers*, 95(4):740–760.

Gurney, M. and Daly, J. F. (1965). A multivariate approach to estimation in periodic sample surveys. In *Proceedings of the American Statistical Association, Section on Social Statistics*, pages 242–257.

Hankin, D. G., Mohr, M. S., and Newman, K. B. (2019). *Sampling Theory: For the Ecological and Natural Resource Sciences*. Oxford University Press, United Kingdom.

Hansen, M. H., Madow, W. G., and Tepping, B. J. (1983). An evaluation of model-dependent and probability sampling inferences in sample surveys. *Journal of the American Statistical Association*, 78(384):776–793.

Hartig, F., Minunno, F., and Paul, S. (2019). *BayesianTools: General-Purpose MCMC and SMC Samplers and Tools for Bayesian Statistics*. R package version 0.1.7.

Hastie, T., Tibshirani, R., and Friedman, J. (2009). *The Elements of Statistical Learning. Data Mining, Inference, and Prediction*. Springer, New York, second edition.

Heuvelink, G. B. M., Brus, D. J., and de Gruijter, J. J. (2007). Optimization of sample configurations for digital mapping of soil properties with universal kriging. In Lagacherie, P., McBratney, A. B., and Voltz, M., editors, *Digital Soil Mapping. An Introductory Perspective*, pages 137–151. Elsevier.

Hill, A., Massey, A., and Mandallaz, D. (2021). The R package forestinventory: Design-based global and small area estimations for multiphase forest inventories. *Journal of Statistical Software*, 97(4):1–40.

Hofman, S. C. K. and Brus, D. J. (2021). How many sampling points are needed to estimate the mean nitrate-N content of agricultural fields? A geostatistical simulation approach with uncertain variograms. *Geoderma*, 385:114816.

Höhle, M. (2017). *binomSamSize: Confidence Intervals and Sample Size Determination for a Binomial Proportion under Simple Random Sampling and Pooled Sampling*. R package version 0.1-5.

Huang, Z. (1998). Extensions to the k-means algorithm for clustering large data sets with categorical values. *Data Mining and Knowledge Discovery*, 2:283–304.

Hutson, A. D. (1999). Calculating nonparametric confidence intervals for quantiles using fractional order statistics. *Journal of Applied Statistics*, 26(3):343–353.

Hutson, N., Hutson, A., and Yan, L. (2019). *QuantileNPCI: Nonparametric Confidence Intervals for Quantiles*. R package version 0.9.0.

Hyndman, R. J. and Fan, Y. (1996). Sample quantiles in statistical packages. *American Statistician*, 50(4):361–365.

Isaaks, E. H. and Srivastava, R. M. (1989). *An Introduction to Applied Geostatistics*. Oxford University Press, New York.

Janssen, P. H. M. and Heuberger, P. S. C. (1995). Calibration of process-oriented models. *Ecological Modelling*, 83(1–2):55–66.

Jessen, R. J. (1942). Statistical investigation of a sample survey for obtaining farm facts. *Research Bulletin (Iowa Agriculture and Home Economics Experiment Station)*, 26(304):54–59.

Joseph, L. and Bélisle, P. (1997). Bayesian sample size determination for normal means and differences between normal means. *Journal of the Royal Statistical Society. Series D (The Statistician)*, 46(2):209–226.

Joseph, L. and Bélisle, P. (2012). *SampleSizeMeans: Sample size calculations for normal means*. R package version 1.1.

Joseph, L., Wolfson, D. B., and du Berger, R. (1995). Sample size calculations for binomial proportions via highest posterior density intervals. *Journal of the Royal Statistical Society. Series D (The Statistician)*, 44(2):143–154.

Joseph, L., Wolfson, D. B., du Berger, R., and Bélisle, P. (2018). *SampleSizeBinomial: Bayesian sample size determination for a single binomial proportion*. R package version 1.1.

Karger, D. N., Conrad, O., Böhner, J., Kawohl, T., Kreft, H., Soria-Auza, R. W., Zimmermann, N. E., Linder, H. P., and Kessler, M. (2017). Climatologies at high resolution for the earth's land surface areas. *Scientific Data*, 4:170122.

Kim, J. and Wang, Z. (2019). Sampling techniques for big data analysis. *International Statistical Review*, 87(S1):S177–S191.

Kirkpatrick, S., Gelatt, C. D., and Vecchi, M. P. (1983). Optimization by simulated annealing. *Science*, 220(4598):671–680.

Kitanidis, P. K. (1983). Statistical estimation of polynomial generalized covariance functions and hydrologic applications. *Water Resources Research*, 19(4):909–921.

Kitanidis, P. K. (1987). Parametric estimation of covariances of regionalized variables. *Water Resources Bulletin*, 23(4):557–567.

Knotters, M. and Brus, D. J. (2010). Estimating space-time mean concentrations of nutrients in surface waters of variable depth. *Water Resources Research*, 46:W08502.

Lark, R. M. (2000). Estimating variograms of soil properties by the method-of-moments and maximum likelihood. *European Journal of Soil Science*, 51(4):717–728.

Lark, R. M. (2002). Optimized spatial sampling of soil for estimation of the variogram by maximum likelihood. *Geoderma*, 105(1):49–80.

Lark, R. M. (2011). Spatially nested sampling schemes for spatial variance components: Scope for their optimization. *Computers & Geosciences*, 37(10):1633–1641.

Lark, R. M., Hamilton, E. M., Kaninga, B., Maseka, K. K., Mutondo, M., Sakala, G. M., and Watts, M. J. (2017). Planning spatial sampling of the soil from an uncertain reconnaissance variogram. *SOIL*, 3(4):235–244.

Lark, R. M. and Marchant, B. P. (2018). How should a spatial-coverage sample design for a geostatistical soil survey be supplemented to support estimation of spatial covariance parameters? *Geoderma*, 319:89–99.

Lark, R. M. and Webster, R. (2006). Geostatistical mapping of geomorphic variables in the presence of trend. *Earth Surface Processes and Landforms*, 31(7):862–874.

Lenth, R. V. (2009). Response-Surface Methods in R, Using rsm. *Journal of Statistical Software*, 32(7):1–17.

Lesch, S. M. (2005). Sensor-directed response surface sampling designs for characterizing spatial variation in soil properties. *Computers and Electronics in Agriculture*, 46(1–3):153–179.

Lesch, S. M., Strauss, D. J., and Rhoades, J. D. (1995). Spatial prediction of soil salinity using electromagnetic induction techniques, 2. An efficient spatial sampling algorithm suitable for multiple linear regression model identification and estimation. *Water Resources Research*, 31(2):387–398.

Lisic, J. and Grafström, A. (2018). *SamplingBigData: Sampling Methods for Big Data*. R package version 1.0.0.

Lohr, S. L. (1999). *Sampling: Design and Analysis*. Duxbury Press, Pacific Grove.

Lumley, T. (2020). *leaps: Regression Subset Selection*. R package version 3.1.

Lumley, T. (2021). *survey: Analysis of Complex Survey Samples*. R package version 4.1-1.

Ly, A., Marsman, M., Verhagen, J., Grasman, R. P. P. P., and Wagenmakers, E. J. (2017). A tutorial on Fisher information. *Journal of Mathematical Psychology*, 80:40–55.

Ma, T., Brus, D. J., Zhu, A.-X., Zhang, L., and Scholten, T. (2020). Comparison of conditioned Latin hypercube and feature space coverage sampling for predicting soil classes using simulation from soil maps. *Geoderma*, 370:114366.

Mandallaz, D. (2007). *Sampling Techniques for Forest Inventories*. Chapman & Hall/CRC, Boca Raton.

Mandallaz, D., Breschan, J., and Hill, A. (2013). New regression estimators in forest inventories with two-phase sampling and partially exhaustive information: A design-based Monte Carlo approach with applications to small-area estimation. *Canadian Journal of Forest Research*, 43(11):1023–1031.

Marcelli, A., Corona, P., and Fattorini, L. (2019). Design-based estimation of mark variograms in forest ecosystem surveys. *Spatial Statistics*, 30:27–38.

Marchant, B. P. and Lark, R. M. (2007). Optimized sample schemes for geostatistical surveys. *Mathematical Geology*, 39(1):113–134.

Matérn, B. (1947). Methods of estimating the accuracy of line and sample plot surveys. *Meddelanden från Statens Skogsforskningsinstitut*, 36(1).

Matérn, B. (1986). *Spatial Variation*, volume 36 of *Lecture Notes in Statistics*. Springer-Verlag, Berlin, second edition.

McConville, K., Tang, B., Zhu, G., Li, S., Chueng, S., and Toth, D. (2021). *mase: Model-Assisted Survey Estimation*. R package version 0.1.3.

McConville, K. S., Moisen, G. G., and Frescino, T. S. (2020). A tutorial on model-assisted estimation with application to forest inventory. *Forests*, 11(2):244.

McKay, M. D., Beckman, R. J., and Conover, W. J. (1979). A comparison of three methods for selecting values of input variables in the analysis of output from a computer code. *Technometrics*, 21(2):239–245.

McLaren, C. H. and Steel, D. G. (2001). Rotation patterns and trend estimation for repeated surveys using rotation group estimates. *Statistica Neerlandica*, 55(2):221–238.

Minasny, B. and McBratney, A. B. (2006). A conditioned Latin hypercube method for sampling in the presence of ancillary information. *Computers & Geosciences*, 32(9):1378–1388.

Minasny, B. and McBratney, A. B. (2010). Conditioned Latin hypercube sampling for calibrating soil sensor data to soil properties. In Viscarra Rossel, R. A., McBratney, A. B., and Minasny, B., editors, *Proximal Soil Sensing*, pages 111–119. Springer, Dordrecht.

Müller, W. G. and Zimmerman, D. L. (1999). Optimal designs for variogram estimation. *Environmetrics*, 10(1):23–37.

Myers, R. H., Montgomery, D. C., and Anderson-Cook, C. M. (2009). *Response Surface Methodology: Process and Product Optimization Using Designed Experiments*. John Wiley & Sons, Hoboken, third edition.

Müller, K. and Wickham, H. (2021). *tibble: Simple Data Frames*. R package version 3.1.6.

Nanthakumar, A. and Selvavel, K. (2004). Estimation of proportion of success from a stratified population: a comparative study. *Communications in Statistics*, 33(9):2245–2257.

Nychka, D., Furrer, R., Paige, J., Sain, S., Gerber, F., and Iverson, M. (2021). *fields: Tools for Spatial Data*. University Corporation for Atmospheric Research, Boulder, CO, USA. R package version 13.3.

Oliver, M. A. and Webster, R. (1986). Combining nested and linear sampling for determining the scale and form of spatial variation of regionalized variables. *Geographical Analysis*, 18(3):227–242.

Ott, R. L. and Longnecker, M. (2015). *An Introduction to Statistical Methods and Data Analysis*. Cengage Learning, Boston, seventh edition.

Papritz, A. J., Dümig, A., Zimmermann, C., Gerke, H. H., Felderer, B., Kögel-Knabner, I., Schaaf, W., and Schulin, R. (2011). Uncertainty of variance component estimates in nested sampling: a case study on the field-scale spatial variability of a restored soil. *European Journal of Soil Science*, 62(3):479–495.

Patterson, H. D. (1950). Sampling on successive occasions with partial replacement of units. *Journal of the Royal Statistical Society. Series B (Methodological)*, 12(2):241–255.

Pebesma, E. (2018). Simple features for R: Standardized support for spatial vector data. *The R Journal*, 10(1):439–446.

Pebesma, E. J. (2004). Multivariable geostatistics in S: the gstat package. *Computers & Geosciences*, 30(7):683–691.

Pebesma, E. J. and Bivand, R. S. (2005). Classes and methods for spatial data in R. *R News*, 5(2):9–13.

Pinheiro, J., Bates, D., DebRoy, S., Sarkar, D., and R Core Team (2021). *nlme: Linear and Nonlinear Mixed Effects Models*. R package version 3.1-152.

Plant, R. E. (2012). *Spatial Data Analysis in Ecology and Agriculture Using R*. CRC Press, Boca Raton.

R Core Team (2021). *R: A language and environment for statistical computing*. R Foundation for Statistical Computing, Vienna, Austria.

Rao, J. N. K. (2003). *Small Area Estimation*. John Wiley & Sons, Hoboken.

Ribeiro Jr, P. J., Diggle, P. J., Schlather, M., Bivand, R., and Ripley, B. (2020). *geoR: Analysis of Geostatistical Data*. R package version 1.8-1.

Ripley, B. D. (1981). *Spatial Statistics*. John Wiley & Sons, New York.

Robertson, B. L., Brown, J. A., McDonald, T., and Jaksons, P. (2013). BAS: Balanced Acceptance Sampling of Natural Resources. *Biometrics*, 69(3):776–784.

Rosén, B. (1997). On sampling with probability proportional to size. *Journal of Statistical Planning and Inference*, 62(2):159–191.

Roudier, P. (2021). *clhs: a R package for conditioned Latin hypercube sampling*. R package version 0.9.0.

Roudier, P., Hewitt, A. E., and Beaudette, D. E. (2012). A conditioned Latin hypercube sampling algorithm incorporating operational constraints. In Minasny, B., Malone, B. P., and McBratney, A. B., editors, *Digital Soil Assessments and Beyond. Proceedings of the 5th Global Workshop on Digital Soil Mapping*, pages 227–232. CRC Press/Balkema, Leiden.

Samuel-Rosa, A. (2019). *spsann: Optimization of Sample Configurations using Spatial Simulated Annealing*. R package version 2.2.0.

Särndal, C. E., Swensson, B., and Wretman, J. (1992). *Model Assisted Survey Sampling*. Springer, New York.

Schloerke, B., Cook, D., Larmarange, J., Briatte, F., Marbach, M., Thoen, E., Elberg, A., and Crowley, J. (2021). *GGally: Extension to 'ggplot2'*. R package version 2.1.2.

Schoch, T. (2014). *rsae: Robust Small Area Estimation*. R package version 0.1-5.

Signorell, A. (2021). *DescTools: Tools for Descriptive Statistics*. R package version 0.99.43.

Stehman, S. V. (1999). Basic probability sampling designs for thematic map accuracy assessment. *International Journal of Remote Sensing*, 20(12):2423–2441.

Stehman, S. V., Fonte, C. C., Foody, G. M., and See, L. (2018). Using volunteered geographic information (VGI) in design-based statistical inference for area estimation and accuracy assessment of land cover. *Remote Sensing of Environment*, 212:47–59.

Stevens, D. L. and Olson, A. R. (2004). Spatially balanced sampling of natural resources. *Journal of the American Statistical Association*, 99(465):262–278.

Szepannek, G. (2018). clustMixType: User-friendly clustering of mixed-type data in R. *The R Journal*, 10(2):200–208.

ter Braak, C. J. F. and Vrugt, J. A. (2008). Differential Evolution Markov Chain with snooker updater and fewer chains. *Statistics and Computing*, 18(4):435–446.

Tillé, Y. (2006). *Sampling Algorithms*. Springer, New York.

Tillé, Y. and Matei, A. (2021). *sampling: Survey Sampling*. R package version 2.9.

Toth, D. (2021). *rpms: Recursive Partitioning for Modeling Survey Data*. R package version 0.5.1.

Valliant, R., Dever, J. A., and Kreuter, F. (2018). *Practical Tools for Designing and Weighting Survey Samples*. Springer, New York, second edition.

Valliant, R., Dever, J. A., and Kreuter, F. (2021). *PracTools: Tools for Designing and Weighting Survey Samples*. R package version 1.2.3.

van Groenigen, J. W., Pieters, G., and Stein, A. (2000). Optimizing spatial sampling for multivariate contamination in urban areas. *Environmetrics*, 11(2):227–244.

van Groenigen, J. W., Siderius, W., and Stein, A. (1999). Constrained optimisation of soil sampling for minimisation of the kriging variance. *Geoderma*, 87(3):239–259.

van Groenigen, J. W. and Stein, A. (1998). Constrained optimization of spatial sampling using continuous simulated annealing. *Journal of Environmental Quality*, 27(5):1078–1086.

Venables, W. N. and Ripley, B. D. (2002). *Modern Applied Statistics with S*. Springer, New York, fourth edition.

Wadoux, A. M. J.-C., Brus, D. J., and Heuvelink, G. B. M. (2019). Sampling design optimization for soil mapping with random forest. *Geoderma*, 355:113913.

Walvoort, D., Brus, D., and de Gruijter, J. (2020). *Spatial Coverage Sampling and Random Sampling from Compact Geographical Strata*. R package version 0.3-9.

Walvoort, D. J. J., Brus, D. J., and de Gruijter, J. J. (2010). An R package for spatial coverage sampling and random sampling from compact geographical strata by k-means. *Computers & Geosciences*, 36(10):1261–1267.

Wang, J., Haining, R., and Cao, Z. (2010). Sample surveying to estimate the mean of a heterogeneous surface: reducing the error variance through zoning. *International Journal of Geographical Information Science*, 24(4):523–543.

Wang, J., Stein, A., Gao, B., and Ge, Y. (2012). A review of spatial sampling. *Spatial Statistics*, 2(1):1–14.

Wang, Z. and Zhu, Z. (2019). Spatiotemporal balanced sampling design for longitudinal area surveys. *Journal of Agricultural, Biological, and Environmental Statistics*, 24(2):245–263.

Ware, K. D. W. and Cunia, T. (1962). Continuous forest inventory with partial replacement of samples. *Forest Science Monographs*, 3:1–40.

Webster, R. and Oliver, M. A. (1992). Sample adequately to estimate variograms of soil properties. *Journal of Soil Science*, 43(1):177–192.

Webster, R. and Oliver, M. A. (2007). *Geostatistics for Environmental Scientists*. Wiley, Chichester, second edition.

Webster, R., Welham, S. J., Potts, J. M., and Oliver, M. A. (2006). Estimating the spatial scales of regionalized variables by nested sampling, hierarchical analysis of variance and residual maximum likelihood. *Computers & Geosciences*, 32(9):1320–1333.

Wickham, H. (2019). *stringr: Simple, Consistent Wrappers for Common String Operations*. R package version 1.4.0.

Wickham, H. (2021). *forcats: Tools for Working with Categorical Variables (Factors)*. R package version 0.5.1.

Wickham, H., Averick, M., Bryan, J., Chang, W., McGowan, L. D., François, R., Grolemund, G., Hayes, A., Henry, L., Hester, J., Kuhn, M., Pedersen, T. L., Miller, E., Bache, S. M., Müller, K., Ooms, J., Robinson, D., Seidel, D. P., Spinu, V., Takahashi, K., Vaughan, D., Wilke, C., Woo, K., and Yutani, H. (2019). Welcome to the tidyverse. *Journal of Open Source Software*, 4(43):1686.

Wickham, H., François, R., Henry, L., and Müller, K. (2021). *dplyr: A Grammar of Data Manipulation*. R package version 1.0.7.

Wickham, H. and Grolemund, G. (2017). *R for Data Science. Import, Tidy, Transform, Visualize, and Model Data*. O'Reilly Media, Sebastopol.

Woodruff, R. S. (1963). The use of rotating samples in the Census Bureau's monthly surveys. *Journal of the American Statistical Association*, 58(302):454–467.

Wright, M. N. and Ziegler, A. (2017). ranger: A Fast Implementation of Random Forests for High Dimensional Data in C++ and R. *Journal of Statistical Software*, 77(1):1–17.

Wu, C. (2003). Optimal calibration estimators in survey sampling. *Biometrika*, 90(4):937–951.

Wu, C. and Sitter, R. R. (2001). A model-calibration approach to using complete auxiliary information from survey data. *Journal of the American Statistical Association*, 96(453):185–193.

Xie, Y., Dervieux, C., and Riederer, E. (2020). *R Markdown Cookbook*. Chapman & Hall/CRC, Boca Raton, first edition.

Zhao, X. and Grafström, A. (2020). A sample coordination method to monitor totals of environmental variables. *Environmetrics*, 31(6).

Zhu, Z. and Stein, M. L. (2005). Spatial sampling design for parameter estimation of the covariance function. *Journal of Statistical Planning and Inference*, 134(2):583–603.

Zhu, Z. and Stein, M. L. (2006). Spatial sampling design for prediction with estimated parameters. *Journal of Agricultural, Biological, and Environmental Statistics*, 11(1):24–44.

Zhu, Z. and Zhang, H. (2006). Spatial sampling under the infill asymptotic framework. *Environmetrics*, 17:323–337.

Zimmerman, D. L. (2006). Optimal network design for spatial prediction, covariance parameter estimation, and empirical prediction. *Environmetrics*, 17(6):635–652.

Index

Printed in the United States
by Baker & Taylor Publisher Services